EUROPEAN FEMINISMS, 1700–1950

European Feminisms
1700-1950

A Political History

Karen Offen

STANFORD UNIVERSITY PRESS
STANFORD, CALIFORNIA

Stanford University Press
Stanford, California
© 2000 by the Board of Trustees of the
Leland Stanford Junior University
Printed in the United States of America
CIP data appear at the end of the book

Library of Congress Cataloging-in-Publication Data

Offen, Karen M.
  European feminisms, 1700–1950 : a political history / Karen Offen.
    p. cm.
  Includes bibliographical references and index.
  ISBN 0-8047-3419-4 (cloth) — ISBN 0-8047-3420-8 (paper : alk. paper)
    1. Feminism—Europe—History. 2. Feminism—Political aspects—
Europe. 3. Nationalism and feminism—Europe—History. 4. Europe—
Politics and government. 5. Europe—Social policy. I. Title.

HQ1586.O33   2000
305.42'094—dc21   99-044067

This book is printed on acid-free, archival-quality paper.

Original printing 2000

Last figure below indicates year of this printing:
09 08 07 06 05 04 03 02 01 00

Typeset by John Feneron in 9.5/12.5 Trump Mediaeval

Acknowledgments

At the top of the acknowledgments list must come Susan Groag Bell, with whom I fashioned *Women, the Family, and Freedom: The Debate in Documents*, published in 1983. Thanks, too, to Renate Bridenthal, Claudia Koonz, and Susan Mosher Stuard for inviting me to contribute an essay on the comparative history of nineteenth-century European feminisms to the second edition of *Becoming Visible: Women in European History* (1987), and to Merry Wiesner, with whom I worked on the severely truncated version that appeared in the third edition (1998). I owe a particular debt to the academic colleagues whose disagreements about what feminism is—or was historically—provoked my ruminations on "Defining Feminism" (1988). I am also grateful to Michael S. Roth, without whose initial invitation I would never have undertaken this book, which displaced so many other unfinished projects from the tall stack on my desk.

Deep thanks are also due to my colleagues and faithful friends Marilyn J. Boxer, Edith B. Gelles, Sondra Herman, Mary Lynn Stewart, Ann Taylor Allen, and Whitney Walton, who provided rich and sustaining doses of moral and intellectual support at critical moments in the course of this lengthy project. This is not to neglect the continuing enthusiasm of the Scholars' Group and staff at the Institute for Research on Women and Gender, without whose cheering section I could never have completed this work. Many other generous colleagues assisted by writing supporting letters for grants, reading individual chapters or clusters, providing expertise on short notice, and saving me from embarrassing mistakes; they will receive here a silent thanks—lest there be no one left to serve as a reviewer of the completed book. Although I have immensely appreciated their input, I have not always taken their advice and remain wholly responsible for the published text. Finally, I wish to thank Gerda Lerner for skipping over this period of continental European feminism in *The Creation of Feminist Consciousness* (1993) and leaving me a clear coast. I also thank Joan Wallach Scott for inadvertently helping me to clarify my approach; in response to her treatment of French feminisms, in particular, I discovered what kind of book about European feminisms really needed to be written.

My colleagues at the Green Library of Stanford University have been particularly helpful, from Mary Jane Parrine, curator for French and Italian, to Sonia H. Moss, impresario of the Interlibrary Borrowing Service, to the reference librarians, the circulation personnel, the microfilm and current periodicals staff, and staff members at the Auxiliary Library, where much of Stanford's raw material for doing "real history" is now housed. I also thank the dedicated staff members at the Hoover Institution Library, especially Agnes F. Peterson (now emerita), and Helen Solanum, curators of the Western European Collection, and staff members Annette Bender, Mollie Molloy, Maria Quinoñes, and Linda Wheeler for their interest and assistance with special items. Research for this book has taken me to virtually every library on the Stanford campus—Law, Medicine, Biology, Philosophy, and even Business—in addition to the general collections and the Hoover. I have also drawn heavily on the library resources of the University of California, Berkeley, whose European materials so nicely complement those at Stanford.

But this study could never have been adequately documented without the help of numerous libraries and colleagues in Europe. My deep appreciation goes to staff members at the Fawcett Library, London; the Bibliothèque Marguerite Durand and the Bibliothèque Nationale, Paris; the Internationaal Informatiecentrum en Archief voor de Vrouwenbeweging (IIAV), Amsterdam; the Kvindehistorisk Samling at the Statsbibliotheket, Aarhus; the Women's History Archive at the University of Göteborg; and the Gosteli Stiftung, Worflauben (near Bern). Special thanks go to European colleagues on whom I have drawn for consultation and assistance at various points in the research, some of whom have also organized conferences or events bearing on the history of feminisms in which I was invited to participate: Tjitske Akkerman, Ida Blom, Gisela Bock, Ginevra Conti Odorisio, Anne Cova, Linda Edmondson, Ute Gerhard, Francisca de Haan, Karen Hagemann, Gabriella Hauch, Karin Hausen, Yvonne Hirdman, Yvonne Knibiehler, Jitka Maleckova, Mary Nash, Marie Neudorfl, Sylvia Paletschek, Andrea Petö, Bianka Pietrow-Ennker, Jane Rendall, Michèle Riot-Sarcey, Florence Rochefort, Brigitte Studer, Siep Stuurman, Françoise Thébaud, Eleni Varikas, and Ulla Wischermann.

I wish to acknowledge the financial support of various foundations whose staffs may not have recognized that as they were subsidizing my project on the woman question in France, they were also assisting the formulation of questions that resulted in this book: the National Endowment for the Humanities, the Rockefeller Foundation, and the John Simon Guggenheim Memorial Foundation. Grants from the Marilyn Yalom Fund at the Institute for Research on Women and Gender at Stanford funded some of the translations used here (and translators are acknowledged individually in the endnotes). I am particularly grateful to participants in my four NEH Summer Seminars for College Teachers on "The Woman Question" (held at Stanford between 1984 and 1992) for contributing their expertise, curiosity, invaluable insights, and sources to the project that became this book; they will recognize some of the points we discussed together in these pages.

I would particularly like to acknowledge the long-term support and enthusiasm for my work of the staff at Stanford University Press, especially Norris Pope, now director of the press, and John Feneron, who transformed my antiquated WordStar 6.0 files into the latest high-tech typesetting format.

Finally, my deepest thanks to my family—especially to my husband, George, a sincere and committed male feminist, and to our daughters, Catherine and Stephanie—for being supportive of my obsession with European feminisms, especially when the research materials overflowed my home office (both of them) and oozed down the hallways into family spaces. I thank them too for the opportunity and the time to merge my personal and professional concerns, to inquire into these long-forgotten efforts to address issues that, in one form or another, still confront many women. Neither of my daughters took to women's studies at their respective universities; perhaps they had been overexposed at home. I know that they, too, are feminists, although they might like to deny it.

I do hope, though, that as adult readers they will ponder the story embedded in this book and perhaps acknowledge the long-term significance of this historic struggle by European feminists (and that of their American counterparts) for making possible the opportunities they now have to pursue their own respective destinies. To Cath and Steph—and to our new granddaughter, Emma Elly—who will weather the joys and sorrows of womanhood in the twenty-first century, and who will keep would-be patriarchs at bay, this book is dedicated.

K.O

Woodside, Calif.
October 1998 and January 2000

Contents

Preface

This book will explore challenges to male hegemony from 1700 to 1950 in the larger nations of continental Europe and will offer increasing comparative attention to developments in the smaller nations, aspiring nation-states, and national cultures as the twentieth century approaches. It has multiple objectives. For general readers and those interested primarily in history, it seeks both to provide a comprehensive, comparative account of feminist developments in European societies, as well as a re-reading of European history not only from a woman's perspective but from a feminist perspective. By placing gender, or relations between women and men, at the center of European politics (where it surely belongs, but from which it has long been marginalized), the book intends reconfigure our understanding of Europe's history and to render visible a long but hidden tradition of feminist thought and politics.

On another level, the book addresses issues under discussion by contemporary feminist theorists, seeking to disentangle some misperceptions and to demystify some confusing debates (about the Enlightenment, about "reason" and "nature," public vs. private, about the conundrum "equality vs. difference," among others) by providing a broad and accurate historical background. Historical feminism offers us far more than paradoxes and contradictions; it is about politics, not philosophy. Feminism's victories are not, strictly speaking, about getting the argument right. Gender is not merely "a useful category of analysis"; it lies at the heart of human thought and politics. Working through history has convinced me that we must, paraphrasing John F. Kennedy, ask not what feminist theory can do for history, but what history can do for feminist theory.

By the terms "Europe" and "European," I am referring not merely to Western Europe but to a variety of nations, states, and cultures of the Eurasian continent situated on the territorial land mass west of the Ural Mountains, plus certain of the contiguous islands, and to cultures that have developed within in the Judeo-Christian tradition, primarily on the Roman Catholic/Protestant side. I am exploring debate about the relations between the sexes in the territorial nation-states that we refer to (in English) as France, Germany, Italy, Spain, Portugal, the Netherlands, Belgium, Switzerland, Austria, Hungary, Poland, the current Czech state (comprising Bohemia and Moravia), the Scandinavian states of Norway, Sweden, Denmark, and Finland, and in Russia and Greece, where Orthodox Christianity long prevailed. I have not included modern Turkey or other dominantly Islamic southern European cultures in this study, as they are rooted in a very different set of cultural presuppositions. Nor have I included very small states such as Andorra, Luxembourg, or San Marino, on which there seems to be little secondary literature concerning historical feminist developments. Unfortunately, our ignorance is still great as concerns feminist developments before 1945 in many parts of northeastern and southern Europe such as Latvia and Estonia, or Slovakia and Croatia; scholarship on the early stages of feminist activity in these countries is just beginning.

As for the islands contiguous to the European land mass, of course, one cannot neglect the British Isles. English (and American) feminisms are the best-known to scholars in the English-speaking world, but they have only rarely been treated in comparative perspective, as will be done here. Great Britain's historic relationship to Europe has been close, yet troubled; each of the island societies of the United Kingdom has developed cultural features that are distinctive. England, in particular, has defined its approach to relations between the sexes in a constant oppositional dialogue with the continental societies, especially France, and English feminism mirrors this pattern. Irish feminism figures in this study in dialogue with that of England and of France. Developments located in the far-flung British Empire or other European colonial empires do not figure in this study.

Until recently our knowledge of feminisms (in the plural) on the European continent remained very limited. New research by feminist scholars in many languages, plus easier access to long-neglected published source materials in Western and Central Europe, now permits us to explore this history in considerable detail. Europe has spawned many feminisms, but comparative analysis suggests that they are all cousins, addressing a set of issues and dilemmas that have been framed with regard to shared cultural developments, earlier in the more westerly seaboard societies, relatively later in the incipient states of the Eastern empires. They do offer a common denominator, which allows us to arrive at a historically grounded definition of the phenomenon we call, in the singular, feminism. I will have more to say about issues of definition in Chapter 1.

European cultures and societies have been neither more nor less "patriarchal" or prone to subordinate women than other societies throughout the world. Instead, what seems significant historically is that European cultures became more permeable, and at an earlier date, to feminist complaint and criticism than those elsewhere. In the twentieth century, some of these societies—I am thinking here of the small, relatively homogeneous societies of Denmark, Norway, Sweden, Finland, and Iceland—effectively conceded the argument and set in place models of egalitarian relations between the sexes that, in spite of their shortcomings, are widely admired. Other historically more authoritarian, more militaristic societies such as Imperial Germany, following unification in 1871, engendered severe and sustained antifeminist responses; feminist impulses expressed themselves through the "women's movement" or through social democracy. In all European societies, however, feminist demands forced opponents to state and defend what Gerda Lerner has called their "set of unstated assumptions about gender," and the ensuing debates are rich and informative.

Despite the variety of linguistic cultures in Europe, criticisms of the subordination of women all had common roots, roots plunged into the fertile loam in which Roman Catholic Christianity had implanted itself. These cultures shared a secular intellectual tradition of Humanism informed by recovered debates in Greek and Latin from manuscripts of the ancient Mediterranean world. Adding to this mix were the controversies of the Protestant Reformation, and subsequently the emergence of a critical secular vocabulary of political and sociocultural reform during the seventeenth and eighteenth centuries that would come to be known as the Enlightenment. As European societies engaged in the separation of secular concerns from those of religiously dominated societies, they became porous, increasingly receptive to feminist challenges to male hegemony, and to the possibility of questioning the politics of the family, the configuration of relationships between men and women, and the relation of both to the state.

But it was ultimately the development of print culture, the rise of literacy and the growth of a broad reading public in the early modern period that made subsequent political action feasible. To say this is not to claim that there was a single determining trajectory—far from it—but it is to claim that feminisms and feminists found possibilities of expression and avenues for action in European print culture that would manifest themselves only decades or even centuries later in other parts of the world. Dissenters who are forcibly silenced cannot easily mobilize support behind their complaints or calls for change.

Indeed, the trajectory of the history of feminist challenge in Europe (and subsequently throughout the world) can be seen as an integral, developmental part of what Habermassians refer to as "public space" (*Offentlichkeit*) or the "public sphere"—what we know through the history of the press, of the book and the printed text, of journalism, of reading and imaginative literature. It is also part of the history of association, and of regional, national, and global communications, and of the history of transportation. It is part, as well, of the history of education, of organized religion and secular ideologies, of economic life, and of paid labor and the workers' movement. Finally, and most significantly, the history of feminism is integral to Europe's internal political history—the history of statebuilding, of armed conquest and defeat, and of challenges to the authority of kings and military elites. Hence, my subtitle—*A Political History*.

Although *European Feminisms* aspires to be comprehensive, it is by no means exhaustive. It will pay particular attention to France. Why should France play such a seemingly disproportionate role in this study? The answer bears highlighting for the benefit of readers who may know little about the history of Europe. Throughout the late seventeenth and eighteenth centuries, France was indisputably the dominant power of continental Europe and a constant rival of England for global maritime and colonial power. Around 1700, when this book begins, the French kingdom was wealthy and powerful, with one-fourth of the entire European population. Its writers and thinkers and its cultural and artistic models exercised enormous influence beyond France's borders, not least in the enlightened monarchies of Russia, Austria, and Prussia. French was not only the language of diplomacy but had replaced Latin as the common intellectual currency among the educated. French scholars pioneered in developing the biomedical and human sciences, especially sociology and anthropology, and they also played a central role in the elaboration of historiography. Indeed, the European Enlightenment had a very strong French component, which is all too often neglected today; the debate on the "woman question" was central to its concerns.

The pan-European impact of the French Revolution and its century-long aftermath (including the imposition of Napoleon's Civil Code) did much to stimulate further feminist initiatives far beyond France's borders. These initiatives were closely associated with the development of national political cultures and the strategic plans of incipient nation-states. Indeed, proposals that reconfigured the role of women as the quasi-public educated mothers of citizens, the promulgators of a national mother-tongue, were deemed by nineteenth-century progressives of both sexes to be the *sine qua non* for nation-building and key to the construction of successful self-governing societies. At the same time, feminist initiatives sprang from a plethora of experiments in societal reorganization, even as others became greatly concerned by issues of social order and control. In another book, I explore in greater depth the specific characteristics of the French debate on the so-called "woman question," but here I will simply underscore the point that throughout the eighteenth and nineteenth centuries, French sociopolitical critics made fundamental contributions to elaborating the feminist challenge that had pan-European repercussions, well beyond the geopolitical territory of the kingdom of France, the Empire, and the successive French republics.

Thus, until well into the twentieth century, most other societies in Europe—including England and the German states—defined themselves with reference to, or in opposition to, developments in France. The politics of sexual relations and issues regarding the relationship between the family and the state became touchstones for such comparisons. Newly emerging nations even developed gendered identities of their own with reference to—and sometimes against—French culture and society.

Feminist claims are primarily political claims, not philosophical claims. They never arise in—or respond to—a sociopolitical vacuum. They are put forward in concrete settings, and they pose explicit political demands for change. Thus, I am arguing in this book that the history of feminisms in Europe must be understood as intrinsically part of a broadly reconceived political history, which in my view encompasses concerns that have often been cordoned off into intellectual, social, economic, demographic, and cultural histories. The concerns of feminism, however, are intrinsically interdisciplinary: they call for the redressment and reconfiguration of the sexual balance of power in virtually every area of human life. My approach reflects my own historical interest and training in political and intellectual history, enriched by my focus on sexual politics, my interest in demographic issues, and a holistic perspective on the past.

HOW TO READ THIS BOOK

The book is organized in three chronological parts, each beginning with a contextual introduction. The Prologue further situates the book, while Chapter 1 provides my general definition of feminism and raises some questions about approach that can be skipped by readers who are not interested by methodological issues and want to get on with the story. The introductions to each part provide general historical background, along with brief summaries of the chapter contents. They are intended solely to orient readers.

I have attempted to write this book in a manner that suggests the range of possibilities for feminist challenge and retains an element of suspense. I try not to give away the ending, or the "what comes next"—say, by speaking of an "interwar" period. I talk a lot about "post-" but not about "pre-." I try to avoid retrospective claims—as for example, that feminism was in some way historically insignificant because it was never a "mass" movement, or that it lacked total independence as a movement, whatever that means, or that ending the subordination of women was not a freestanding goal. In my view, all movements for sociopolitical change are deeply embedded in and responsive to their surrounding cultures; they have to be judged on their own terms as well as in our retrospective ones. What is clear is that even in Western Europe, where the opportunities for challenging male domination were greatest, feminists nowhere occupied a sufficiently powerful position to realize their claims without reference to other, often competing sociopolitical claims and movements. This does not make feminism a failure. Indeed, in some societies, European feminisms have been stunningly successful, not least when their advocates have forced the upholders of patriarchal arrangements, whether religious or secular, to defend their views, to make their arguments explicit, and to launch repeated (and never wholly effective) counteroffensives. Backlashes against feminist challenges are not unique to the late twentieth century; they recur repeatedly throughout the period under discussion here.

The book embodies a rigorous practice of the historian's craft, with careful attention to chronological developments, and to debates and efforts at political mobilization as they unfolded and were experienced by contemporaries. My approach deliberately avoids the projection of current (and often distorting) theoretical preoccupations upon the past. It is particularly attentive to the historical contexts in which feminist criticism and political realities have intersected, and to the wording and argumentation that were used at the time: that is, to the intricate relationship between text and context. The entire work is based on primary published sources. If a work written in the 1780s, say, was never published until half a century later, I will not invoke it to prove anything about public arguments in the 1780s. Manuscripts do not count in this study. It is about public debate.

The book is, irreparably, a survey, one that provides something of a bird's-eye (or satellite) view, as seen from a point high above Europe. Due to the chronological and geographic sweep of the project, the book is regrettably short on biographical detail, even though many individuals are included by name. Individual contributions are discussed in connection with patterns of debate and political movements. Despite this, I do want to insist that individuals do make irreplaceable contributions to the history of feminisms and that neither individual thought nor individual activity can be dismissed as negligible relative to the play of "historic forces" or "discursive practices."

Although my book draws on a tremendous range of scholarship by others (not all of which could be incorporated in the bibliographical endnotes and suggested reading: my full bibliography is well over 100 pages—single-spaced), all my sources are deliberately cited in the endnotes from the original published sources in various languages. During the past two decades, I have made every effort to consult the original published sources; only when photocopies of the primary texts could not be located or previous citations verified do I resort to citing them through attributions provided in the secondary literature. I greatly dislike this latter practice because it perpetuates so many errors. A significant number of the continental sources are newly acquired and come from countries not included in (or less well covered in) *Women, the Family, and Freedom: The Debate in Documents*, the two-volume 1983 interpretative documentary history edited by Susan Groag Bell and myself. These include sources from Spain, Italy, Greece, the Austro-Hungarian Empire, Denmark, Switzerland, the Netherlands, Belgium, and so on. In a number of cases, I have commissioned expert English-language translations of documents from languages I do not read, or do not read well enough to feel secure. Where possible, my interpretations are grounded in available published scholarship, but in some cases I have had to rely directly on a smattering of sources or to rely heavily on still unpublished work made available by generous colleagues. My access to scholarly work and resources in many European societies has been greatly facilitated by new networks developed during the last ten years in conjunction with my organizational activities in the International Federation for Research in Women's History.

Chronology

A Framework for the Study of
European Feminisms

Founding of *Le Journal des dames* by Madame de Beaumer

From Sweden Charlotta Nordenflycht replies to Rousseau

1763 England defeats France in the Seven Years War

1772 *Essai sur le caractère, les mœurs, et l'esprit des femmes* by Antoine-Léonard Thomas

1770 Essay competitions concerning women's education in the French academies; polemics on the woman question by the *philosophes*; tracts by physicians on women's specific physiology and health issues

1776 American Declaration of Independence

1777 *Les Gynographes* by Restif de La Bretonne, an antifeminist tract proposing that women should not even be taught to read or write

1782 *Sarah Burgerhart*, novel by Betje Wolff and Aagje Deken

1787 Condorcet's *Lettres d'un bourgeois de New Haven à un citoyen de Virginie* advocates women's vote

Mémoire pour le sexe féminin contre le sexe masculin by Madame de Coicy

1789 Beginning of the French Revolution; publication of women's *cahiers*; women's march on Versailles (5–6 Oct.)

1790 Publication of Condorcet's *Sur l'Admission des femmes au droit de cité*

Josefa Amar y Borbón, *Discurso sobre la educación física y moral de las mugeres*

1791 Promulgation of the first French Constitution

Publication of Olympe de Gouges's *Déclaration des droits de la femme*; Talleyrand's report on public instruction

Enactment of equal inheritance for daughters; full civil (property) rights for unmarried French women

1792 Publication of Mary Wollstonecraft's *Vindication of the Rights of Woman* and Theodor Gottlieb von Hippel's *Über die bürgerliche Verbesserung der Weiber*; in Paris, Pauline Léon demands the right for women to bear arms

1793 The National Assembly votes for the execution of the French king; Prudhomme clashes with the presidents of the provincial women's clubs; Pierre Guyomar defends political equality between individuals, expressly including women; the Parisian Society of Revolutionary Republican Women campaigns for strict economic controls; Charlotte Corday assassinates Marat; the Committee of Public Safety shuts down the women's clubs; Olympe de Gouges, Manon Roland, Queen Marie Antoinette all guillotined

1794 French army under Napoleon "liberates" Italian states; petitions
–98 for women's rights in the new Italian republics; Dutch tracts on women's rights; Fichte publishes *The Science of Rights*; German scholars debate the difference between the sexes; English politicians ridicule demands for women's political rights

1800   Napoleon becomes First Consul, then Emperor; promulgation of the
–1804   French Civil Code; introduction of state-regulated prostitution
1807   Germaine de Staël publishes *Corinne*; Napoleon establishes schools
       for daughters of the Legion of Honor
1805   French military campaigns throughout Europe; women in the Ger-
–15   man states organize patriotic societies to resist the French
1808   *Théorie des quatre mouvements* by Charles Fourier
1815   Congress of Vienna; abolition of slave trade; restoration of monar-
       chies
1820s Severe restrictions on freedom of the press and association through-
       out Europe; publication of many tracts on women's education;
       Greek Revolution
1825   Publication of *Appeal of One Half the Human Race Against the Pre-
       tensions of the Other Half—Men—to Retain Them in Political
       and Thence in Civil and Domestic Slavery* by William
       Thompson and Anna Doyle Wheeler
1830   New Revolution in Paris; independence for Belgium; Polish Revolu-
       tion
1831   The Saint-Simonians launch their appeal, advocating rehabilitation
       of the flesh
1832   *La Femme libre* published by Suzanne Voilquin et al.
       Publication of George Sand's novel *Indiana*
       British Reform Act explicitly excludes women from suffrage
1833   Eugénie Niboyet founds the *Conseiller des femmes* (Lyon)
1834   Publication of Louis-Aimé Martin's *De l'éducation des mères de
       famille*; controversy over women's work and labor reform in *The
       Pioneer*; massacre of workers in Lyon
1836   *La Gazette des femmes* published by Madeleine Poutret de
       Mauchamps
       Publication of Parent-Duchâtelet's *De la Prostitution à Paris*
1837   Campaign to reform the position of women in Judaism
–1840s
1838   Publication of Caroline Norton's protest on custody of infants
1839   Publication of Carl Almqvist's novel *Det Går An* (in English, Sara
       Videbeck)
1841   *Voyage en Icarie* by Étienne Cabet (communist community as a
       paradise for women, where everyone will marry)
1843   Publication of Marion Reid's *A Plea for Women* (Edinburgh)
       Publication of Flora Tristan's *L'Union ouvrière*
1846   Proudhon gives women two choices, "Housewife or Harlot"
1847   Publication of *Jane Eyre: An Autobiography* by Charlotte Brontë
       under a male pseudonym; Tennyson's *The Princess*
1848   Revolutions in Paris, Berlin, Vienna, etc. (March)
       The French Provisional Government establishes universal manhood
       suffrage, abolishes black slavery in the colonies, sponsors Le-
       gouvé's lectures on women's history at the Collège de France

1861   Publication of Maine's *Ancient Law* and Bachofen's *Das Mutter-recht*
       Unification of Italy; codification of laws begins
       Julie-Victoire Daubié becomes the first woman to earn the French baccalaureate
       Jules Simon denounces the "working woman" in *L'Ouvrière*
1862   Swedish women taxpayers granted the municipal vote
1864   The University of Zurich opens its medical school to women auditors
1865   Founding of the Allgemeiner Deutscher Frauenverein (Association of German Women) by Louise Otto
       Founding of the American Ladies' Club in Prague by V. Fingerhut-Náperstek
1866   Massive women's suffrage petition in England
       Publication of Julie-Victoire Daubié's *La Femme pauvre*
1866   Debates on women's work in the International Working Men's
–67   Association (Geneva, Lausanne)
       Passage of Contagious Disease Acts (1866, 1867) in England
1867   The British House of Commons debates John Stuart Mill's woman suffrage amendment to Second Reform Act
       University of Zurich grants first medical degree to a woman
       Constitution of the Austrian-Hungarian "Dual Monarchy"
1867   Secularists and Catholics battle over lecture courses for girls in
–69   Paris
1868   Emily Davies argues that English girls must pass the same university entrance examinations as boys do
       Paule Mink and others defend women's right to work in Paris
       Marie Goegg founds the Association Internationale des Femmes
       Empress Eugénie opens the Paris Faculty of Medicine to women
1869   Publication of John Stuart Mill's *The Subjection of Women*
       Single women granted municipal vote in England
1869   Debates over women's physical and mental suitability for higher
–75   education
       Founding of Girton College and Newnham College at Cambridge; Sophia Jex-Blake and friends obtain permission to study medicine at Edinburgh University
1870   Franco-Prussian War; Paris Commune; unification of Germany;
–71   French establish Provisional Government that leads (1875) to the Third Republic; reestablishment of the Association Internationale des Femmes
1871   Founding of Dansk Kvindesamfund (Danish Women's Association)
       The German Constitution of 1871 establishes universal manhood suffrage for election of Reichstag delegates; abortion criminalized in the German Penal Code
1872   Russia establishes medical courses exclusively for women, in St. Petersburg (closed again in 1887)

Founding of *Solidarité* in Switzerland

1874 Josephine Butler and associates launch crusade against regulated prostitution on the Continent, especially against the French system

1876 British Parliament amends the Medical Act, removing restrictions based on sexual difference

1877 Founding of the British and Continental Federation for the Abolition of Prostitution, Geneva

1878 First International Congress on Women's Rights, Paris

Hubertine Auclert challenges the omission of woman suffrage from the International Congress agenda

Russia opens first women's university; Université de Neufchatel opened to women

1879 Publication of August Bebel's *Die Frau in der Vergangenheit, Gegenwart und Zukunft*

Hubertine Auclert challenges the French worker's congress to support women's rights

1880 First production in Copenhagen of Henrik Ibsen's play *Et Dukkehjem* (A Doll's House, published 1879)

France establishes free and obligatory primary education for both sexes, and separate state secondary schools for girls

1881 Founding in Milan of the Liga Promotrice degli Interessi Femminile by Anna Maria Mozzoni

1883 Repeal of the British Contagious Disease Acts

Publication of Olive Schreiner's *The Story of an African Farm*

1884 Publication of Theodore Stanton's *The Woman Question in Europe*

Publication of Friedrich Engels's *Der Ursprung der Familie, des Privateigenthums und des Staats*

Founding of Finsk Kvinnoförening, Norsk Kvindesagsforening, Fredrike-Bremer Førbundet (Sweden)

Transfer of regulation of prostitution from Paris municipal officials to French Ministry of the Interior

1887 Publication in Paris of Marie Bashkirtseff's *Journal*

1888 Founding of the International Council of Women (ICW) by the NWSA, in Washington, D.C.

1889 Centennial of the French Revolution; international expositions in Paris; two international women's congresses held in Paris

Founding of Second International Working Men's Association

Bertha von Suttner publishes *Die Waffen nieder* (Lay Down Your Arms)

1890 International congress on limitation of women's employment convened by the German government

Viennese women lose their municipal vote

1891 Founding of the Fédération Abolitionniste Internationale

1891 Papal encyclical *Rerum Novarum*

1892 First self-proclaimed "feminist" women's congress in Paris (May)

1893   Founding of the Allgemeiner Österreichischer Frauenverein
        (General Austrian Women's Association)
1894   Founding of the Bund Deutscher Frauenvereine
1895   German Social Democratic women denounce "bourgeois feminism"
1896   Ellen Key asserts importance of motherhood, rather than paid labor,
        and calls for state subsidies for mothers; second feminist congress
        in Paris; Marie Maugeret founds Christian feminism, Paris; inter-
        national congress in Berlin; feminists launch protests against new
        German Civil Code
1897   First congress of "Czechoslavic" women, Prague; founding of
        Ústřední Spolek Českýchžen (Central Association of Czech
        Women); international feminist congress in Belgium; founding of
        La Fronde, Paris; founding of the National Union of Women's
        Suffrage Societies (NUWSS), England; women admitted to study
        at the University of Vienna
1899   Women's petition (a million signatures) addressed to the Hague
        Peace Conference
1899   Huge ICW Congress in London; two international feminist con-
-1900   gresses in Paris
1900   Marie Maugeret founds Fédération Jeanne d'Arc (Catholic feminists)
1901   Norwegian women taxpayers obtain municipal vote and right of
        election; first suffrage proposal introduced in French Chamber of
        Deputies
1902   Belgian Workers Party betrays its support for woman suffrage
        International Woman Suffrage Alliance (IWSA) founded in Washing-
        ton, D.C.
1903   Founding of the Women's Social and Political Union (WSPU) in
        Manchester
1904   Founding of the IWSA conference in Berlin
        International agreement on the suppression of white slave trade
        Bertha Pappenheim founds the Jüdischer Frauenbund
        Ellen Key publishes the first volume of her Lifslinjer (Lifelines)
        Feminist protests in Paris and Vienna against the Civil Codes of
        France and Austria
1905   Founding of Soiuz Ravnopravnosti Zhenshchin (Union for Equal
        Rights for Women), Moscow
        Rosa Mayreder publishes Zur Kritik der Weiblichkeit
1906   Women (and men) accorded the national vote in Finland
        Russian Duma debates woman suffrage
        Sibilla Aleramo publishes Una donna
1907   Women's Section of the Second International Workingmen's Asso-
        ciation endorses unrestricted woman suffrage as a socialist goal
1908   All-Russian Congress of Women, St. Petersburg
        Prohibitions lifted on German women's participation in public life
1909   Kollontai publishes Sotsial'nye osnory zhenskogo voprosa (The So-
        cial Basis of the Woman Question)

Founding of the Union Française pour le Suffrage des Femmes
1910 Socialist women endorse International Women's Day
      International convention to end the white slave trade
      Founding of the Liga Republicana das Mulheres Portuguesas
        (Republican League of Portuguese Women)
1911 Norwegians elect a woman to the Storting (Parliament)
1912 Parliamentary defeat of the Third Conciliation Bill (electoral re-
        form), Great Britain
      Czechs elect a woman to the Bohemian Diet
1913 Norwegian women obtain full parliamentary suffrage
      IWSA meets in Budapest; abolitionist meetings in Paris & London;
        "Cat and Mouse" Act; English suffragette throws herself in front
        of the kings horse (June 4)
1914 Publication of Abraham Flexner's *Prostitution in Europe*
      Suffrage campaign peaks in France (spring & early summer)
      ICW meets in Rome; IWSA sponsors massive suffrage rally in Rome
        (May)
      Serbian conspirator assassinates the heir to the Austro-Hungarian
        throne in Sarajevo
1914 World War I (August 1914–November 1918)
–18
1914 IWSA Manifesto, calling for arbitration
1915 International Congress of Women at The Hague; International
        Women's League for Peace founded (becomes WILPF in 1919);
        Danish women enfranchised
1916 Easter Uprising, Dublin
1917 Outbreak of the Russian Revolution (Feb.)
      Bolsheviks seize power and confirm women's equality (Oct.)
1918 British women above age 30 granted the vote, along with all remain-
        ing unenfranchised men
      All-Russian Congress of Women (Nov.)
      Maternity and Child Welfare Act, Great Britain
      Founding of National Association of Spanish Women (ANME)
1917 Women granted the vote (in various forms) in the Netherlands, Rus-
–19   sia, United Kingdom, Germany, Austria, Czechoslovakia, Poland,
        but not in France, Italy, Spain, Greece, Romania, or Bulgaria
1919 Pro-suffrage Allied women meet in Paris to influence Treaty of Ver-
        sailles
      Founding of the League of Nations and the International Labour Or-
        ganization (ILO)
      Founding of Women's International League for Peace and Freedom
        (WILPF), Zurich
      ILO Conference on Women's Work, Washington, D.C.
      First International Congress of Working Women
1920 Russian revolutionary government legalizes abortion (Nov.)
      French pro-natalists proclaim the Rights of the Family

1922   Mussolini and Fascists come to power in Italy
1924   Publication of Eleanor Rathbone's *The Disinherited Family*
        ICW Conference on the Prevention of the Causes of War
1925   Sigmund Freud addresses the woman question; Karen Horney re-
–26   sponds
1926   The Soviet Code on Marriage and Divorce
        IWSA Congress in Paris: schism over protective legislation for
           women; IWSA becomes International Alliance of Women (IAW)
1927   *Report of the Special Body of Experts on Traffic in Women and
           Children* published by the League of Nations
        Oxford University restricts the number of women students admitted
1928   Kellogg-Briand Pact on the outlawry of war
        Radclyffe Hall publishes *The Well of Loneliness*
1929   Crash of the stock market; beginning of the Great Depression; as-
           saults begin on women's employment and feminist campaigners
           mobilize in its defense
        États-Généraux du Féminisme, Paris
1930   Papal encyclical *Casti Connubi*
1931   Spanish Republic; women get the vote in Spain
        ILO endorses Convention on Equal Pay for Equal Work
        Liaison Committee of Women's International Organizations estab-
           lished
1932   Women's massive petition for peace presented to the League of Na-
           tions Disarmament Conference in Geneva
1933   Hitler comes to power in Germany, Nazis order dissolution of or-
           ganizations; the Bund Deutscher Frauenvereine dissolves itself in
           protest
1934   Manifesto of the World Congress of Women against War and Fascism
        Winifred Holtby publishes *Women and a Changing Civilization*
1935   Mussolini invades Abyssinia (Ethiopia; Oct.)
1936   French Popular Front government appoints three women ministers
        Civil War breaks out in Spain; founding of Mujeres Libres
1936   Swedish pro-population reforms; Gunnar and Alva Myrdal reconfig-
–38   ure women as workers who have the right to children
1937   Congress of Women's World Committee against War and Fascism,
           Paris
        League of Nations authorizes formation of Committee on the Status
           of Women
        Constitution of the Irish Republic qualifies women's rights
1938   Publication of Virginia Woolf's *Three Guineas*
1938   Nazi Germany invades and annexes Austria, then Czechoslovakia
1939   Nazi-Soviet Pact; Nazi Germany invades Poland; outbreak of World
           War II; Nazi Germany defeats France
        IAW meets in Copenhagen
        Publication of *The Law and Women's Work* by the League of Na-
           tions

EUROPEAN FEMINISMS, 1700–1950

Prologue

History, Memory, and Empowerment

The campaign to end women's subordination to men that we call feminism is an ongoing, recurring, enduring political project, with deep roots in the European past. Feminisms, in the plural, can be documented in many European societies, past and present; in some societies they become a central and recurrent feature of political cultures, of European thought and politics. Feminist thought and action do not stand outside—or on the periphery of—the so-called Western tradition; they are integral to it.[1]

That these claims should have to be forcefully stated, that they have not been long acknowledged, reflects the obliteration of an extraordinary struggle, one of continuing importance to women and men today, whether they reside in Europe or far beyond Europe's boundaries. When the history of feminisms is incorporated into the history of European thought and politics, our understanding of the European past—and of its pertinence for our own present and future—is radically altered. Why, then, do we know so little about it? How did this knowledge become lost? Or might it be that we have been denied knowledge of the feminist tradition?

One answer lies in the account we have been handed of "Western thought" and politics, and what and how we have been taught to think Western thought (and politics) *is*. When reconsidered critically, from the perspective of feminist concerns, and with a whole new archive of recovered knowledge, the past looks different. No longer do we see a long, linear sequence of dynasties, wars, conquests, revolutions, or grand, overarching trends, such as the rise of the bourgeoisie, of capitalism, of the nation-state. No longer do we encounter a seamless history of great ideas generated by the grand old men of Western philosophy. What we encounter is far more intriguing—a long, irregular, but significant series of controversies, of debates, of competing factions, of advances, setbacks, defeats, and occasional victories, and not only of the conventionally accepted kind. Relations between women and men, that is, between the sexes, are not merely a lens through which to reread the past; they lie at the storm center of controversy.

This book, then, concerns a series of political challenges and responses to male dominance or hegemony in Europe, primarily on the European continent, that span the centuries from 1700 to 1950. This sequence of challenges embraces critical thought and political action launched both by women and by sympathetic male allies. It concerns issues of authority and the making of rules—about marriage, education, allocation of property, resources, and labor, political participation, family structures, indeed, even the organization of knowledge itself. Feminist efforts to emancipate women as well as the organized resistance to these efforts are, as the title and content of my book argue, central to our historical understanding of politics in European societies. They also bear on our historical understanding of societies that lie far away from Europe, but that have been deeply touched by Europe, and that continue to carry (or resist) the impress of European cultures. I will not be speaking of these societies here, but the connection must be pointed out.

The history of feminisms in Europe encompasses virtually every "field" of historical inquiry—political, intellectual, social, economic, cultural, religious, and so forth. In spite of its range and scope, historical memory of this multifaceted challenge has remained minimal, to the point that its very existence seemed questionable. The evidence lay, like buried treasure, below the surface of conventional historical accounts, an "unauthorized" aspect of the past.

How wrongheaded this "unauthorization" is! Listen to these voices from the early twentieth century. "The forward march of feminism," wrote the French activist Madame Avril de Sainte-Croix in 1907, "is a fact that no one can deny, a movement that no force can henceforth bring to a halt. Woman . . . has become a factor to be reckoned with."[2] "The women's movement," remarked the British suffragist Millicent Garrett Fawcett in 1913, "is one of the biggest things that has ever taken place in the history of the world":[3]

> Other movements towards freedom have aimed at raising the status of a comparatively small group or class. But the women's movement aims at nothing less than raising the status of an entire sex—half the human race—to lift it up to the freedom and value of womanhood. It affects more people than any former reform movement, for it spreads over the whole world. It is more deep-seated, for it enters into the home and modifies the personal character.

Or, consider this 1904 assertion by the Swedish writer and mother's advocate Ellen Key: "The struggle that woman is now carrying on is far more far-reaching than any other; and if no diversion occurs, it will finally surpass in fanaticism any war of religion or race."[4] Contemporary readers of this dramatic claim must have sat up and taken notice. We should too.

Despite such attestations as these, despite the vigor and momentum of successive feminist attempts to contest and dismantle male hegemony from the eighteenth century into the early twentieth century, neither the history of feminism—nor for that matter even the history of women, which is a broader, though related project of which the history of feminism is a part—seemed to develop any staying power. "Women," asserted Simone de Beauvoir in her introduction to *The Second Sex* (1949), "lack concrete means for organizing themselves into a unit which can stand face to face with the correlative unit. They have no past, no history, no religion of their own; and they have no such solidarity of work and interest as that of the proletariat."[5] Even in 1949 this was a seriously misleading claim.

OVERCOMING AMNESIA

By the early 1970s, a new generation of feminists in Europe thought, in good conscience, that they were beginning from "Year Zero." One has to ask how the memory of such a significant movement, such efforts, such challenges in thought and action could be so obliterated and forgotten. How could women and men not know? How could the history of feminism fail to have been treated seriously by professional historians or taught to the young women and men who swarmed into colleges and universities throughout Europe and America during the 1950s and 1960s? Why is it so rarely taught now? Knowledge—as everyone knows—can often be empowering; partial knowledge, or lack of knowledge, can disempower. Indeed, for decades knowledge of feminism's history has been poorly served by both national and international communities of historians, not to mention schoolteachers, and even today it remains an unwelcome intruder.

Not only the long-term, but even more recent developments in the history of feminism were effectively buried, erased, or, indeed, even suppressed, as Dale Spender eloquently pointed out in the 1980s with respect to the continuing feminist activities in 1920s England. "Does it really make any difference to our lives," she asked, "to know that . . .

there was a vigorous and varied women's movement which addressed similar issues and conducted comparable campaigns to those which we have engaged in over the last decade?" Spender's answer was an emphatic "Yes": "To believe that we are on our own, that we have started a protest for which there is no precedent, is to be plagued by doubts, to be vulnerable, to be without models, experience or guidance. . . . Great strength and great joy can be derived from the knowledge that . . . many women felt much the same about male power as many women do today."[6]

The growth of women's history in national contexts and the emergence of feminist scholarship since the 1970s have done much to remedy Dale Spender's discomfort, and even as this work goes to press, scholars and publishers in many countries collaborate to enrich our knowledge of women's history and the history of feminisms at the national level in ways that Beauvoir and her contemporaries could scarcely have imagined. Comparative, cross-national work on Europe, on the other hand, has remained relatively underdeveloped, with the exception of two important early works by Richard J. Evans and Jane Rendall.[7]

Within the field of interdisciplinary women's studies, at least in colleges and universities in North America, students can sometimes study the histories of feminisms in the United States, Britain, or Canada. At the secondary level, such offerings are still exceptional. But even women's studies programs at the university level have tended to shortchange the teaching of the history of feminisms in other parts of the world. Scholars and teachers whose expertise is located in other disciplines rarely feel an obligation to ground themselves in knowledge of women's history, much less the history of feminism, even though they expect their colleagues in history to speak across disciplinary boundaries, and even across cultures and continents. Feminist knowledge, to many today, seems to mean only "feminist theory" or feminist practice since the 1970s; although what "counts" as "knowledge" or as "theory" is continually questioned, the place of history in these matters remains greatly undervalued.[8]

In Europe the situation has been far more difficult; not only has a women's-studies curriculum been difficult to introduce, much less institutionalize, but even women's history—not to speak of the history of feminisms—has encountered serious and sustained resistance from educational authorities in many major state-controlled systems, who smugly defend "general" knowledge from the intrusion of what they see as "separatist" or compartmentalized knowledge.[9] It seems hard to convince such authorities that women's history is not that of a tiny minority, that indeed women constitute over half the population—and young women in some cultures now comprise a majority of university students—and that feminism is a politics bearing on the most salient relationship in human societies: that between women and men. That students should not be at least exposed to the history of this politics, whose successes and failures have so affected their own lives, seems scandalous!

When, in the early 1970s, I first began to investigate the history of feminisms in Europe, the few available English-language documentaries concerned mostly the debate on the woman question in the United States, sprinkled with a few additional texts from Virginia Woolf, Friedrich Engels, and August Bebel; other collections featured a far larger number of sensationalist antifeminist males, from Aristotle to Nietzsche.[10] One day in 1972, while seeking materials for a course I would co-teach on "Women in Western History," I was prowling in the deepest recesses of the Stanford library stacks, scanning old books on the shelves under the Dewey Decimal category 396—"Women." There I discovered two treasures. The first was Theodore Stanton's compendium *The Woman Question in Europe* (1884), of which more in Chapter 6. The second was *La Femme et le féminisme*, edited by H. J. Mehler, the catalog of the Gerritsen Collection in Women's History, published in 1900. What a revelation! The latter contained vast listings of works on European women's history, feminist periodicals, a treasure trove of references in a variety of European languages, all dating from before 1900. I subsequently learned that early in the twentieth century this magnificent collection of printed materials, constituted by the Dutch physician and suffrage activist Aletta Jacobs, had been acquired by the John Crerar Library in Chicago. The Crerar later sold the collection to the University of Kansas, where it remains today. Its extensive collection of books and periodicals in many European languages has since been microfilmed and is now available to researchers worldwide.

I was originally interested in French materials, but as an aspiring comparativist, I began to take notes on books, articles, and periodicals in other languages as well. I soon suspected that there must be much more unexcavated material, but when I began collecting and photocopying such texts, I had no idea how extensive would be the yield, how easily it could be located and consulted—or, how exciting it would be to read. My quest led me well beyond the Gerritsen Collection to libraries and archives of all sizes and descriptions throughout Europe and the United States.[11] Hundreds, then thousands of published texts emerged.

What I discovered in American libraries and archives was that—much like women's history—the history of feminisms has never been accorded a place in existing taxonomies of knowledge. In libraries, for instance, whether under the older Dewey Decimal System or the now hegemonic Library of Congress classification system, there is still no separate classification for feminism, as there has long been for male-dominated sociopolitical movements—socialism, anarchism, communism, and so on.[12] Socialism, for example, is classified under the category "J," for political science, while "women" are lumped together as "HQ," under "H" for social sciences. One can locate books about feminism and other, parallel women's movements scrambled together with a wide range of other studies under the "social science" category "Women," but they also can be found, somewhat randomly, under many and varied rubrics among the humanities (including literature, music, and the arts) and social sciences (sociology, anthropology, psychology), as well as in specialized libraries on law, medicine, biology, business, economics, education, or on war and peace. In short, materials concerning men's sociopolitical movements and issues have been far more deliberately and carefully classified. The same problem characterizes the situation in bookstores, where works about feminism are lumped into women's studies sections, when these exist, or under sociology, rather than under social movements or politics. In some respects, this practice makes it easier for today's interested buyers to locate such books, but all the more difficult for them to integrate their contents and concerns into prevailing compartments of knowledge. However artificial, these compartments continue to shape our understanding of the human sciences, even as women's studies raises complex and important questions about what truly "interdisciplinary" knowledge might mean.

RECOVERING THE PAST

Earlier generations of European feminists understood well that "remembrance of things past" is important for plotting the future. "Study, study our history, Spanish ladies and gentlemen, before accusing a feminist of being foreign," advised María Lejárraga Martínez Sierra in 1917, under the cover of her celebrated dramatist husband's name.[13] Indeed, in the twentieth century, the act of recording and remembering feminism's history and passing it along on behalf of the future has become an increasingly compelling concern to feminists throughout Europe. There is some truth in the sardonic yet extravagant observation made recently by a Czech historian, in response to a tiny glimmer of interest in Czech women's history: "The future is not enough for the feminists; they want to get hold of the past as well and reinterpret it from a women's point of view."[14] When women ask the questions, the past assumes new shapes. And not only from a woman's point of view, but from a feminist point of view, which encompasses more than efforts to write and teach the history of feminisms and to get women included in "standard accounts." Feminist scholars are also formulating a critique of how and why history has been written and taught by academic professionals, both in Europe and in North America.[15] For feminists, history has important implications, and setting the record straight is only part of the task. In the early 1930s the Polish historian Lucie Charewiczowa argued the case for writing women's history before the International Congress of Historical Sciences, noting that "the feminist movement . . . grows from day to day" and that knowledge of women's and feminist history could serve to overturn "every prejudice and antifeminist superstition that is still rooted in public opinion."[16]

Already in the early twentieth century feminists in Europe recognized the need for "a history of their own," and they began to organize initiatives to establish archives for the women's movement. One of the first initiatives was that of Eliska Vincent, in Paris, who already by the 1890s had accumulated a vast archive (estimated to include some 600,000 documents). Unfortunately, her legacy of these materials to the Musée Social was refused in 1919, despite the best efforts of her testamentary executors, Marguerite Durand and Maria Vérone, and the materials were lost.[17] This disaster did not go unnoticed by Durand and by Marie-Louise Bouglé, both of whom subsequently assembled collections that have found more secure institutional homes in Paris at the Bibliothèque Marguerite Durand and in the Bouglé collection at the Bibliothèque Historique de la Ville de Paris. By the mid-1980s the Durand library, established fifty years earlier as an auxiliary to the Paris Municipal Library in the fifth arrondissement—facing the Pantheon (where famous Frenchmen are buried)—had grown to the point where it had to relocate in a larger facility located in the thirteenth arrondissement. Recently there has been talk of merging the Durand and Bouglé collections.

In England, the materials that provided the core of what later became the Fawcett Library were deposited in 1926 at the library of the London Society for Women's Service. After a series of difficult skirmishes to relocate and maintain it, the library found a home in a basement at London Guildhall University (formerly the City of London Polytechnic). In 1998 plans for a new National Library for Women, funded by a £4.2 million grant from the British National Lottery, were announced to house and secure the collection, which contains the Josephine Butler Society collection as well as many papers and publications of the several women's suffrage societies, the Six Point Group, and St. Joan's International Alliance, among others.

In Germany, following the dissolution of the Bund Deutscher Frauenvereine in face of Nazi threats to take it over in 1933, the papers of the German women's movement and a number of its affiliated organizations were subsequently deposited (in 1935) in the Helene Lange Stiftung, in Berlin-Wilmersdorf. In 1934, the last president of the BDF, Agnes von Zahn–Harnack copublished (with Hans Sveistrup) an 800-page annotated bibliography, compiled between 1927 and 1932, on "The Woman Question in Germany," as a muted parting salvo against the Nazi regime, which had decreed the dissolution of all non–Nazi affiliated societies and organizations.[18] This work became a fundamental reference source for subsequent scholars of the German feminist movement. Since that time archives of the women's movement and of women's history have been established in several locations, including Kassel, home of the Archiv der deutschen Frauenbewegung (Archive of the German Women's Movement).[19]

In the Netherlands, the ambitious Internationaal Archief voor de Vrouwenbeweging (International Archive for the Women's Movement, or IAV) was established in 1935 by a small group of Dutch feminists, including Rosa Manus and Willemijn Hendrika Posthumus–van der Goot. Only barely begun when the Nazis occupied the Netherlands, the entire archive was seized and hauled away by the Nazi invaders. In 1948, as the Dutch throne passed from Queen Wilhelmina to her daughter Juliana, and in spite of the archival disaster, Posthumus–van der Goot and her associates researched and published *Van Moeder op Dochter* (From Mother to Daughter: History of the Women of Holland from 1798 till 1948) to commemorate their history. In the interim the archive organizers attempted to rebuild the collections of the IAV, operating until the late 1980s in the shadow of the International Archive for Social History in Amsterdam. One part of the original IAV archives, long believed destroyed, has recently resurfaced, intact by some miracle, in Moscow, presumably taken there by the Red Army, which had in turn captured the materials from the Nazis. The post-1989 Russian government has proved unwilling to release the materials to the reconstituted IAV, although it has allowed some microfilming of the papers.[20]

Other earlier collectors were less successful in their attempts to establish an independent archival existence. The ambitious project to establish a World Center for Women's Archives, initiated in the United States in late 1935 by the Hungarian suffragist Rozsika Schwimmer and promoted by the American historian and feminist Mary Beard, had to be aborted in 1940, in the shadow of the war, when adequate funding could not be obtained. The massive Schwimmer papers are now lodged in several collections, one at the New York Public Library and another at Swarthmore College. An extensive selection of European materials can also be found in the Sophia Smith College Collection at Smith College, in Massachusetts. Meanwhile, the archives of the International Council of Women (ICW) were seized by the Nazis when they occupied Brussels in 1940, and only in the 1960s, in conjunction with the publication of their own history, *Women in a Changing World*, did the ICW make efforts to reconstitute copies of the missing materials in a variety of locations. In 1955 the International Alliance of Women (IAW), whose archives had survived, published its own history, *Journey Toward Freedom*. Its publications, along with the Colorado-based papers and publications of the Women's International League for Peace and Freedom (WILPF), are now available on microfilm.[21]

More archives were founded following World War II. Swedish scholars established a women's-history archive at the University of Göteborg in the 1950s. Other archives came into being subsequently, such as the Women's History Collection at Aarhus, whose holdings include precious papers from the early Danish women's-rights movement. Records of the Swiss women's movement are preserved at the Gosteli Foundation Archive near Bern, thanks to the efforts and financial commitment of the women's-rights activist Marthe Gosteli.[22]

Lest one fetishize the development of archives for unpublished materials, however, I want to insist here on the riches of the published record, much of which is also preserved in these archives as well as in major library collections. Historians of European feminisms can glean extraordinary material, as I have done for this book, from the abundance of society publications, congress proceedings, newsletters, pamphlets, and other printed sources produced by feminists and feminist organizations—and by their opponents—during the last two centuries. Many such publications have been acquired and preserved, often quite incidentally, by American libraries, and many have been subsequently microfilmed, not only in the Gerritsen Collection but also in the complementary research collection microfilmed during the 1970s by the Connecticut-based Research Publications, Inc. (now known as Primary Source Media). Others can be traced through the magnificent National Union Pre-1956 Imprints Catalog and acquired through interlibrary loan.

"When a woman learned to read," wrote the celebrated Austrian writer Marie von Ebner–Eschenbach in 1880, "the woman question arose in the world."[23] And indeed, feminism has developed a historical record as much by a published political record as by a private one. The account readers will find in this book is derived primarily from this recuperated print material.

The history of feminisms in Europe is not a new undertaking, peculiar to academically trained historians. As the remarks by Lejárraga and Charewiczowa, cited above, attest, many publications by feminist activists strongly underscored their continuing concern about combatting rampant misinformation among the general public; others worried about the prospect of memory loss among their potential successors, particularly after feminists had achieved major goals such as the vote in representative or parliamentary governments. This issue was certainly on the mind of Eleanor Rathbone in 1934: "Do the young women of to-day who can say 'but we are free-born' often remember or even know their debt to these pioneers?"[24] Already in 1928, the year political citizenship became a reality for all English women, commemorative efforts began. One important example is Millicent Garrett Fawcett's tribute *Josephine Butler: Her Work and Principles, and Their Meaning for the Twentieth Century* (1927) honoring the centennial birthday of the great organizer of the pan-European campaign against state-regulated prostitution. As one reviewer put it, Butler's work and principles "wrought a change in social ethics, not only in her own country, but in the whole world greater perhaps than that effected by any other single person in recent times."[25] Fawcett's book was accompanied by Ray Strachey's *The Cause: A Short History of the Women's Movement in Great Britain* (1928). Again, a reviewer pointed to its significance:[26]

> Those of us who read with enough knowledge of the old order to realise what opposition women met with, and who perhaps from that deep realisation are sometimes tempted to groan in spirit at the opposition they know is still arrayed against "equal status," cannot but take heart at this chart of the track of a miraculous comet. What! has this bright thing moved so far and so fast?

In 1953 Vera Brittain's *Lady into Woman: A History of Women from Victoria to Elizabeth II* celebrated—and underscored for the benefit of posterity—the monumental changes that had taken place in English women's status in the fifty years since Queen Victoria's death in 1901.

ENCOUNTERING OBSTRUCTIONS

What happened to this history on the European continent? One thing seems certain: in virtually every political culture, it encountered strong opposition not only, as one might expect, on the Right, but also on the Left. The opposition of the political Right, still composed primarily of authoritarian, religiously affiliated, male-dominated groups, comes as no surprise. Opposition on the political Left seems more problematic. Already by 1900 the Marxist-socialists of the Second International Workingmen's Association viewed feminism as a rival enterprise and attempted to counter its attractiveness by smear and counterclaim, by allegations that feminism was irremediably "bourgeois," that capitalism was the bigger problem, that class conflict was the motor of history, and that only socialism could resolve the "woman question"—but only after the victory of the proletariat. Socialist women's intransigent and enduring refusal to cooperate with feminists has been amply documented since the 1970s.

Following the Russian Revolution and the advent of communist single-party states, first in the Soviet Union and later in Eastern Europe, socialist and communist antagonism to feminism continued. Communist claims to have found the unique solution to the "woman question" were convincingly and repeatedly restated well into the 1950s, when the leadership of the communist-dominated Women's International Democratic Federation (WIDF) and its member national organizations effectively coopted the feminist program, while repudiating its name and effacing its memory. From a feminist perspective, organized socialism in Europe—and, more broadly, the social-democratic left—has a lot to answer for, not only in terms of stigmatizing and trivializing feminism, or portraying feminists as a "special interest group," but also in terms of actively suppressing feminist activists and impulses and, given the opportunity, appropriating selected aspects of feminist history as well.[27] Indeed, it is tempting to suggest that what Heidi Hartmann once called the "unhappy marriage of marxism and feminism" was never a marriage, and certainly never a relationship made in heaven, even at the outset; "fatal attraction" might be a more appropriate term.[28] And the apparent fatality of the Party line was feminism.

Despite this lethal relationship, in France and Italy particularly, important scholarly initiatives and historical contributions concerning historical feminism have emerged from Communist Party commemorations, which, however politically motivated at the outset, inadvertently provided a forum for incipient feminist scholarship. The centennial of the revolutions of 1848 (and subsequently women's activism in the Paris Commune, 1871) furnished one postwar springboard for such work, particularly in studies by the historian Edith Thomas, *Les Femmes de 1848* (1948), *Pauline Roland: Socialisme et féminisme au XIXe siècle* (1956), and subsequently her *Les Pétroleuses* (1963; in English as *The Women Incendiaries* [1966]) and *Louise Michel, ou La Velléda de l'anarchie* (1971).[29] But socialism stood in a tense relationship with feminism in most of these histories, in accordance with the political priorities of the postwar period. If Beauvoir claimed that women "had no past, no history," and "no solidarity," Olga Wormser's *Les Femmes dans l'histoire* (1952) raised the question as to whether women constituted a "feminine class," and whether the historical action of women might have a special character. Other non–Communist affiliated scholar-activists, such as Evelyne Sullerot, became particularly fascinated by the long history of the French women's press, including the extraordinary run of short-lived early feminist periodicals.[30]

Italian inquiries began not long after, and not surprisingly histories of feminism in Italy began to percolate to the surface in conjunction with the centennial commemoration of Italian unification in 1861. In 1962 the Humanitarian Society (Società Umanitaria) published its landmark collection *L'Emancipazione femminile in Italia: Un Secolo di discussioni, 1861–1961* following a conference sponsored by a number of reactivated feminist organizations. The subsequent studies by Franca Pieroni Bortolotti, beginning with *Alle origini del movimento femminile in Italia, 1848–1892* (1963), helped to unearth a buried Italian feminist past.[31] Two journals devoted to feminist scholarship, *Memoria* and *DonnaWomanFemme*, published pathbreaking articles on the history of Italian feminism.

Commemorative events have since released a torrent of publications on the history of feminisms throughout Europe. The bicentennial of the French Revolution in 1989 provided exemplary proof of the way in which feminist historians and historians of feminism could seize an occasion and make it their own.[32] Commemorations of the revolutions of 1848 confirm the point.[33] Studies of women in the antifascist Resistance at the thirty- and fifty-year turning points have similarly turned attention toward the analysis of European women's activism and resurgent feminist questioning in specific sociocultural settings.

There is demonstrably material for many histories of European feminisms, or—more concretely—of the many varieties of feminisms that have manifested themselves in particular societies at particular moments across the centuries. This book is concerned with reconstructing and interpreting the feminisms that developed in Europe during the 250 years 1700–1950. It is far from exhaustive, though I have tried to be as comprehensive as extant materials and my own energy and language skills would permit; it does attempt to lay out a chronology and se-

quence, and to reconstruct long-forgotten debates and controversies that
have profoundly shaped the history of women and men in European
states and nations. It attempts to raise important issues for consideration by readers, particularly concerning the integral character of feminist
demands to European history, the character of the antifeminist opposi-
tions, and the relationship of feminism to socialism and to a broad as-
sortment of nation-building efforts and nationalisms.

This book will tell a story of feminisms, not as a "recurring critical
operation" in theory but as a story of political struggle, of setbacks and
some successes. I am less interested than many earlier historians in providing a "winner's account." To the extent that feminists in Europe
"won" anything between 1700 and 1950, they did so in rather unconventional ways, and through convincing others, mostly men in positions of
authority, that their cause was just and that dramatic changes would
have to be made in the laws, institutions, and practices that governed relations between the sexes. With only a few significant exceptions—
violence against property during the British suffragette campaigns for the
vote—feminists foreswore physically violent means of achieving their
ends; throughout the period we are examining reason and persuasive
eloquence, not muscle and mechanized weaponry, were their primary
tools. The fact is that in Europe, as elsewhere in the Western world,
feminists managed to achieve many of their pre-1950 objectives, despite
severe antifeminist opposition in some quarters, and despite sustained
attempts to co-opt, subordinate, and absorb their programs in others.
The difficulties feminists faced in realizing their goals in European societies cannot be overestimated. And yet, in spite of male fear that women
would end up "in charge," in spite of repeated waves of antifeminist
backlash, sometimes feminists succeeded brilliantly. Because of the
feminists, much changed for the better in the situation of women in
European societies between 1700 and 1950. Much more has changed
since then. Yet significant challenges remain, and once again today there
is much for feminists to accomplish and to monitor in the emerging new
Europe.

Unlike other political movements, feminism never aspired to authority in its own right. Its adherents sought a redress of grievances, but not
to take power; instead they wished to share power, and to change their
societies for the better by exercising what political theorist Kathleen
Jones has since termed "compassionate authority."[34] Perhaps this is why
feminism has never found its rightful classification among political
movements.

CELEBRATING THE FEMINIST PAST

But there is more. Those who seek more information about my personal itinerary into history and feminism will be able to find it elsewhere.[35] But here, perhaps, is the place for my confession of personal enthusiasm for my topic and my subjects. I am weary of historical accounts that treat persons as "sites of analysis," that skewer individual lives and group efforts on pins so they can be subjected, writhing, wriggling, and resistant, to "scientific" analysis through distorting theoretical lenses of various thicknesses and opacities and from various critical distances. I think this practice is dehumanizing and not to be tolerated. People's lives and their efforts to change the conditions under which they live, within particular political and cultural contexts, have an integrity that should be respected, especially by feminist scholars.

I consider myself a feminist, and my form of activism, in addition to raising two daughters, running a household, supporting women's rights organizations (I was a founding member of NOW and a charter subscriber to *MS Magazine* as well as to *Signs*), and pressing for women's history and women's space in the historical profession, both in the United States and around the world, is to write about women's history and the comparative history of feminism. But with all due respect to the dreams of utopians or other naive idealists who ardently yearn for a "gender-free" world, I do not see that happening or even as necessarily desirable. With the French I say, "Vive la différence!" As long as there are two sexes, with differing bodies and roles in reproduction, and differing degrees of physical strength, it seems to me that there will be sexual politics, though the forms they take may vary. As long as women are the ones who menstruate, who conceive, who bear children and who nurse them (either potentially or in fact), their lives will be differently structured than those of men, who occupy a different physiological, psychic, and sociopolitical space. This commonality is not, I think, reductive; charges of "essentialism" have to do with philosophical arguments about a common "nature" of "woman," not with the physiological realities that I am discussing here. "Biology" may not be destiny, and indeed, it may also be socially constructed, but physicality does pose constraints as well as opportunities. Difference does not, of necessity, imply dominance—or subordination.

Gender is not only about performance, as Judith Butler would have it, although performance is by no means a negligible factor. Because of women's differences from men, both physiological and socially constructed, achieving justice for women in societies where men seek dominance is a complex, difficult matter, and neither freedom nor equality can ever be satisfactorily constructed without due acknowledgment of these differences. This is where our European counterparts have been cleverer than we Americans, who sometimes mistake "equality" for "sameness" and advocate a freedom beyond gender "to be you and me." The differing vision that most Europeans share is undoubtedly more complex, more "relational" and less legalistic; it is also, in my view, more realistic.

In short, I do not think that feminist concerns about structures of male dominance are going to evaporate. Sexual politics is embedded in the human condition, and the struggles that it engenders will probably have to be refought with each generation. Patriarchy, as Judith Bennett and others keep reminding us, is a remarkably resilient thing. So let us learn from history, if nothing else, to be realistic in our expectations, even as we continue the struggle. Like Albert Camus's Sisyphus, we will need to keep pushing that boulder uphill and finding our pleasure in the act of pushing. Sharing our knowledge of the struggle will perhaps make that onerous task more tolerable, and maybe a bit easier, even as it enhances our happiness.

This book is a work of scholarship. It is also—unashamedly—an act of affirmation, a work born of engagement and passion, and executed with the intention of transmitting a once-lost legacy. Susan Stanford Friedman expresses my idea exactly when she says: "The loss of collective memories, of myriad stories about the past, has contributed greatly to the ongoing subordination of women. The unending, cumulative building of broadly-defined histories of women, including histories of feminism, is a critical component of resistance and change."[36]

As I have worked during the last twenty-five years at gathering the documentation for what has become this account of European feminisms, I have been profoundly moved by the immensity of the task of rediscovery and remembrance, but also by the compelling power of the project and of the women and men I have met, however vicariously, through this historical work. I have laughed at their cleverness and frowned at the indignities inflicted on them; I have drawn strength from their strength and courage from their courage, and have tried to learn from their weaknesses. I can be critical of them when the occasion demands, and from the perspective of the late twentieth century, I can acknowledge that they were not always perfect on every issue that some might think they should have attended to. I do not for one moment believe either that, *pace* Joan Scott, they were entangled in paradoxes, or that, *pace* other claimants, feminism is—or should be—"a movement that challenges all injustices."[37] It is, instead, a theory and a practice that challenges *one* injustice; it is first and foremost about challenging male hegemony, about obtaining justice for women, whatever their other descriptors or concerns—nationality, religion, class, ethnicity, and so on. It is not about making women the same as men, but rather about empowering women to realize their full potential as women without encumbrance. Feminism joins hands with other causes, to the degree that women are also disadvantaged by other causes, but I think it cannot be blended into other causes, confused with, merged into, or subordinated to other causes, irrespective of their merit. Feminism addresses a central issue that has implications for all the others, a point I will elaborate on when I offer a historically based definition of feminism in Chapter 1.

I confess to finding the feminist cause—as I now understand it historically—not only fascinating but inspiring, wholly worthy of a lifetime of work. The historical feminisms of Europe have been a revelation, and the individual speakers—both women and men—are so articulate, so brave, so splendid. The cautious feminists usually had good reasons for speaking cautiously, and the brave ones are simply magnificent! They state the case for women's emancipation so eloquently that it is difficult not to quote them at great length (a temptation I have not always resisted, though my publisher continues to remind me that *this* book, unlike its predecessors, is not a documentary). It does not bother me to find that some of these feminists were occasionally less than "politically correct" on all the issues now dear to late twentieth-century liberationists. That is asking too much.

I feel proud to have encountered these earlier feminists, both female and male. I have been deeply moved by their struggles. Like Margaret Camester and Jo Vellacott, I still weep to find that "so many fine things were said so long ago; it is shocking that they disappeared for so many years."[38] So many excellent ideas were expressed and so many brave acts performed by these European feminists, in the period from 1700 to 1950, as they tried in myriad ways to topple the structures of male domination in European societies. In many respects they did succeed, to the benefit of us all. They deserve not only to be recognized and remembered, but to be applauded and celebrated. Their ideas and initiatives should be claimed by feminists today and tomorrow, both as a precious heritage and as a well-stocked toolshed. Although Audre Lorde has asserted, in a much-quoted line, that "the master's tools will never dismantle the master's house," it seems important to qualify her statement in several respects. Not only is language—words and ideas—supple and available to all users, but the tools and methods of sound historical research, analysis, and synthesis can also serve varied ends. These days, neither language nor the tools and methods of research can be restricted to the master's use.[39]

Feminists from 1700 to 1950—even in France—did not need a new way of writing and thinking (*écriture féminine*, in Hélène Cixous's phrase) to make an incisive case for political change in sexual relations. They spoke very clearly about what they wanted, in whatever European language they used. They did not see linguistic phallocentrism as a problem, nor did their arguments require elaborate deconstruction. Indeed, aided by rising literacy and education, feminists throughout Europe assembled an impressive arsenal of ideological weaponry (to choose a very fitting military metaphor) of their own, the proof of which is this contextual account of a long-buried record of feminist thought and action. Amnesia, not lack of history, is feminism's worst enemy today. Let us then refresh our memory.

1

Thinking About Feminism in
European History

The words "feminism" and "feminist" are used today throughout the Western world and beyond to connote the ideas that advocate the emancipation of women, the movements that have attempted to realize it, and the individuals who support this goal. Few people in the English-speaking world realize, however, that the origin of these terms can be traced to late nineteenth-century French political discourse. *Féminisme* was then commonly used as a synonym for women's emancipation. French dictionaries (and many earlier historians) have erroneously attributed the invention of the word *féminisme* to Charles Fourier in the 1830s, but in fact its origins remain uncertain. No traces of the word have yet been identified prior to the 1870s.[1]

The first self-proclaimed *féministe* was the French women's suffrage advocate Hubertine Auclert, who beginning in 1882 used the term in her periodical, *La Citoyenne* (The Woman Citizen), to describe herself and her associates. The words gained currency following discussion in the French press of the first "feminist" congress in Paris, sponsored in May 1892 by Eugénie Potonié-Pierre and her colleagues from the women's group Solidarité, who shortly thereafter juxtaposed *féminisme* with *masculinisme*, by which they meant something analogous to what we now call male chauvinism.

By 1894–95 the terms "feminism" and "feminist" had crossed the Channel to Great Britain, and before 1900 they were appearing in Belgian, French, Spanish, Italian, German, Greek, and Russian publications. By the late 1890s the words had jumped the Atlantic to Argentina, Cuba, and the United States, though they were not commonly used in the United States much before 1910. During the twentieth century, the words also entered non-Western languages, including Arabic and Japanese.

Feminism is a term that we often treat as self-explanatory; yet it can have differing cultural meanings and connotations from one society to another. Like other "-isms" feminism has become a term that evokes strong emotions and often engenders fear of change, as well as embodying the promise of change; it has often been used pejoratively, prompting the response, "I'm not a feminist but . . . " In European settings it has taken on distinctive historical characteristics, featuring in particular a positive revaluation of the "feminine" in relation to the "masculine."[2] Since the mid-nineteenth century, its history is intertwined in complex ways with that of liberalism, nationalism, and socialism, as well as other innovative sociopolitical currents such as utopianism or anarchism. It is also closely associated with the emergence of nation-states, political parties, philanthropic causes, and workers' associations. Yet feminist claims have always traced distinctive—and often dissenting—paths within each of these arenas.

In order to address the history of feminism, it is first necessary to establish the field of inquiry. The question arises: Can one write a history of feminism that precedes the invention of these words? Can we appropriate this term anachronistically to speak about women's emancipation more broadly, that is, well before the 1890s? The answer to this question must, I believe, be "yes," but a careful definition of terms, grounded in historical evidence, is a required precondition for such a response.[3] What, then, do I mean by "feminism" for the purposes of such a study?

My own definition, distilled from historical evidence ranging over many centuries of European history, and on which this book is based, is briefly this: Feminism is the name given to a comprehensive critical response to the deliberate and systematic subordination of women as a group by men as a group within a given cultural setting. Note that I deliberately use the word "subordination," not the word "oppression"; subordination can be identified historically by examining laws, institutions, customs, and practices, whereas oppression connotes a highly subjective psychological response.[4] One can point to many instances of women who do not feel oppressed but who are unquestionably subordinated in the laws, institutions, and customs of their cultures.

Put another way, the concept of feminism (viewed historically and comparatively) can be said to encompass both a system of ideas and a movement for sociopolitical change based on a refusal of male privilege and women's subordination within any given society.[5] It addresses imbalances of power between the sexes that disadvantage women and attempts to renegotiate them. Feminism posits the notion of gender, or the differential sociocultural construction of the relationship and behaviors of the sexes, based on observed physiological differences, as its central analytical concern. By so doing, feminism raises issues concerning personal autonomy or individual freedom—but always in relation to basic issues of societal organization. In Western societies since 1700, these issues have centered on the long-standing debate over the family and its relationship to the state, and underlying this debate, on the historically inequitable distribution of political, social, and economic power between the sexes. Feminists oppose women's subordination to men in the family and society, along with men's claims to define what is best for women without consulting them; they squarely challenge patriarchal thought, sociopolitical organization, and control mechanisms. They seek to destroy masculinist hierarchy but not sexual dualism as such.

It follows that feminism is necessarily pro-woman. However, it does not follow that feminism must be anti-man. Neither are all women feminists nor are all feminists women. Surprising as it may seem, well into the twentieth century some of the most important advocates of women's emancipation have been men (though they have constituted a small minority).[6] Feminism makes claims for a rebalancing between women and men of the social, economic, and political power within a given society, on behalf of both sexes in the name of their common humanity, but with respect for their differences. The challenge is fundamentally a humanistic one, raising basic issues concerning individual freedom and responsibility as well as the collective responsibility of individuals to others in society and modes of dealing with others. Even so, feminism has been, and remains today, a political challenge to male authority and hierarchy in a profoundly transformational sense. As a historical movement in the Western world, feminism's fortunes have varied widely from one society to another, depending on the possibilities available within a given society for the expression of dissent through word or deed. Once these possibilities are in place, however, the messages are clearly transmitted; the deconstructive techniques so dear to postmodern literary theorists today are not needed in order to grasp the meaning.

Two broad yet distinct lines of argument, which I have called *relational* and *individualistic*, can be identified in the history of feminist thinking in European societies. Arguments in the relational feminist mode have proposed a gender-based but egalitarian vision of sociosexual organization. They feature the primacy of a companionate, nonhierarchical, male-female couple as the basic unit of society, whereas individualist arguments posit the individual, irrespective of sex or gender, as the basic unit.

Relational feminists emphasize women's rights *as women* (defined principally by their childbearing and/or nurturing capacities) in relation to men. They insist on *women's* distinctive contributions in these roles to the broader society and make claims on the commonwealth on the basis of these contributions. They insist on and value, in other words, "the feminine," or "womanliness," however these terms may be culturally configured.[7] They call for women's autonomy as individuals but always for autonomy as embodied, female individuals.

By contrast, the individualist feminist tradition of argumentation emphasizes more abstract concepts of individual human rights and celebrates the quest for personal independence (or autonomy) in all aspects of life, while downplaying, deprecating, or dismissing as insignificant all socially defined roles and minimizing discussion of sex-linked qualities or contributions, including childbearing and its attendant responsibilities. The emphasis in this tradition is on an individual who, in some sense, transcends sexual identification, who is effectively disembodied, beyond gender.

These two modes of argument, however, are not always as analytically distinct as this portrayal suggests. The ways in which they intertwine and interplay in specific historical situations are complex and require further analysis. Suffice it to say that in earlier centuries evidence of both these modes can often be located in the utterances of a single individual, such as Mary Wollstonecraft, or among members of a particular group. Any comprehensive discussion of feminism must therefore encompass both these argumentative traditions, account for the ways in which they point to very different societal outcomes, and examine the tensions between them in particular contexts.

Feminism can be viewed historically as a rapidly developing critical system of thought in its own right. As such, feminism incorporates a broad spectrum of ideas and possesses an international scope, a scope whose developmental stages have historically been dependent on and in tension with male-centered political and intellectual discourse but whose more recent manifestations transcend the latter. Feminism must be viewed as not intrinsically a subset of any other Western religious or secular ideology, whether Catholic or Protestant Christian, Judaic, liberal, socialist, humanist, or Marxist (although historically a feminist critique has emerged within each of these traditions by initially posing the question: "And what about women?"). In order to fully comprehend the historical range and possibilities of feminism, however, the origins and growth of its critique must be located within a variety of cultural and ideological traditions. It would not be appropriate to postulate a hegemonic model for their development on the experience of any single national, cultural, or sociolinguistic tradition, unless evidence can be shown to demonstrate the influence of that model beyond the borders of the initiating culture. Historically speaking, there can be—and have been—a multitude of feminisms, some of which have had more staying power and long-range influence than others.

FEMINISMS IN EUROPEAN SETTINGS

In the history of Europe, the primary claim made by feminists has been expressed as a broad, comprehensive demand for the *equality* of the sexes. But by equality, most Europeans did not mean "sameness" but rather equal treatment of women's difference, first in moral and intellectual terms, and then in terms of equality of opportunity.[8] The specific claims that have been made by feminists encompass arguments for an end to the maligning of women in print, for educational opportunity, for access to and participation in the formation of formal knowledge, for changes in man-made laws governing marriage that disadvantage women, for control of property and one's own person, and for valuation of women's unpaid labor along with opportunities for economic self-reliance and creative self-expression. In more recent times they include demands for admission to the liberal professions, for participation in lucrative industries, for readjustment of inequitable sexual mores and the abolition of prostitution and other forms of sexual exploitation, for control over women's health, reproductive, birthing, and childrearing practices, for state financial aid to mothers, for the revaluation of housework, and for representation and unrestricted participation in political and religious organizations (symbolized in democratizing Western societies not only by the vote but also by access to positions of authority, especially appointed and elective office).

Such claims can be seen as culturally specific subsets of a broader challenge to male pretensions to monopolize societal authority, that is, to patriarchy or male rule, which in European history was institutionally well entrenched, well defended, yet continually in need of reinforcement.[9] At the same time, each of these claims addresses a structural issue, a problematic practice with political dimensions, which transcends the boundaries of the Western world and has applicability to the experience of women in other societies. Statements of goals that are particular to specific cultural settings, such as an insistence on "*rights equal to those granted men*" and gaining the vote for women, or short-range issues of strategy and tactics, such as combatting state-sanctioned prostitution or gaining access for all women into the workforce (or, in non-Western cultures, opposing the practices of *sati*, footbinding, or clitoridectomy), should not be seen as coterminous with the phenomenon of feminism understood as a historical whole, whether in Europe or elsewhere.

The historical phenomenon I choose here to call feminism is larger than any single issue or any culturally driven choice of strategies or tactics. It is an encompassing program of sociopolitical critique and remediation, with gender issues at its very core. These issues may intersect with other more localized concerns—class, race, age, religion, etc.—in complex fashion, producing specific and differently situated expressions of feminism. But this in no way diminishes the centrality of gender, of relations between the sexes (women and men), as the fundamental point of concern. To be a feminist is not merely a matter of being woman-centered, or of cultivating one's own personal subjectivity or empowerment; it is not a matter either of adopting an emancipated (some might say "transgressive") personal lifestyle or of dedicating oneself wholeheartedly to a religious or revolutionary cause. To be a feminist is necessarily, specifically, and primarily to challenge male domination in culture and society, in whatever geographical location or situation in historical time, or in whatever combination with other issues.

In view of such a broad cross-cultural understanding of feminism, feminists can be identified as any persons, female or male, whose ideas and actions (insofar as they can be documented) show them to meet three criteria: (1) they recognize the validity of women's own interpretations of their lived experience and needs and acknowledge the values women claim publicly as their own (as distinct from an aesthetic ideal of womanhood invented by men) in assessing their status in society relative to men; (2) they exhibit consciousness of, discomfort at, or even anger over institutionalized injustice (or inequity) toward women as a group by men as a group in a given society; and (3) they advocate the elimination of that injustice by challenging, through efforts to alter prevailing ideas and/or sociopolitical institutions and practices, the coercive power, force, or authority that upholds male prerogatives in that particular culture.

MOVEMENTS AND METAPHORS

"The exploration of feminist history is severely limited," Rosalind Delmar has argued, "if the appearance of the social movement is assumed to be feminism's apotheosis and privileged form."[10] The formation of an organized feminist movement is a very significant political response to the critique of male domination of women, but it is not the whole of feminism as viewed historically, whether in Europe or elsewhere. As this book will suggest, an expanding body of feminist criticism in print precedes by centuries the development of the women's groups which do begin to form, from 1789 on, often in conjunction with various male-headed reform efforts, whether liberal, democratic, or socialist in persuasion. Without the development of women's literacy, writing, and access to print culture, however, no movement for women's emancipation could have emerged in the nineteenth and twentieth centuries. Feminism cannot be said to begin only in the 1890s, or in the 1830s, or in 1789, as others have claimed.[11] This book will demonstrate why.

Feminism has often been depicted by a metaphor of "waves," with the first wave beginning with the organized sociopolitical movements of the nineteenth century, and the second wave characterizing the activist campaigns of our own time (1970s–1990s; Gloria Steinem is currently calling for a "Third Wave"). Not only is this two-wave approach inaccurate, in the long view, but it is simply inadequate to describe the overall phenomenon, which, as I have suggested, predates the organized movements by several centuries. Colleagues in the Netherlands have postulated a six-wave model for feminism, beginning in late medieval times, but even this expansion of the earlier two-wave framework seems to understate the dimensions of the phenomenon.[12]

In this study, I suggest another image for thinking about feminism historically—by introducing a geologic metaphor, derived from study of volcanic phenomena, and accented by the notion of unstable terrain. As one who grew up in southern Idaho within a stone's throw of lava flows, hot springs, and ancient volcanic cones, and who now lives in California on the edge of the volatile San Andreas fault, I am comfortable with the notion of unstable earth. I will therefore speak about feminism in terms of eruptions, flows, fissures, molten lava (magma), looking at feminism as a threatening and rather fluid form of discontent that repeatedly presses against (and, when the pressure is sufficiently intense, bursts through) weak spots in the sedimented layers of a patriarchal crust, the institutional veneer of organized societies. Thus, in part, the historian's task in writing about feminism's past is, like that of a good geologist, to map and measure the terrain, to locate the fissures, to analyze the context in which they open, to gauge the pressure and magnitude of flows and eruptions of steam, liquefied rock, and minerals that surge forth, and to evaluate the shifting patterns of activity over time. It is also to examine antifeminist attempts to stanch the flow, to dam the fissures on the part of those who would, for one or another reason, keep women subordinate to male authority and control.

This geologic metaphor would not, I think, have surprised Europeans who lived in the period 1700–1950. The spectacular eruptions and flows of Mount Vesuvius, near Naples, were well known, both from Roman history (Pompeii and Herculaneum) and from repeated eruptions in the eighteenth century. Earthquakes flattened Lisbon in the early 1700s. To me, it seems even more descriptive, when one also considers that in the early stages of feminist challenge there are no book-length "founding texts." Instead, feminism's demands must be measured in terms of cumulative abundance, a groundswell and outpouring of multiple published contributions, taking shape through dialogues or debates, and involving many participants (usually town- or city-based) in many different European cultures over the course of these two hundred fifty years. Initially, these texts may seem—by late twentieth-century standards at least—to amount to no more than a trickle; by the mid-eighteenth century, however, they virtually bubble to the surface, gushing forth in increasing quantities, and in multiple locations, and at times, threatening to engulf and melt down the deceptively solid crust of male-dominated societies by challenging increasingly defensive claims of the necessity for or the desirability of patriarchal authority and control.

PART I

The Eighteenth Century

The feminist critique of women's subordinate status in Europe did not begin, as many recent interpreters have claimed, with the French Revolution or the Industrial Revolution. Its traces can be located in earlier centuries, not only in the French literary dispute known as the *querelle des femmes*, but well before. In the late seventeenth century, it received a great boost when François Poullain de la Barre turned the tools of Cartesian reason on the "woman question," and mixed-sex sociability evolved into a distinguishing feature of French courtly culture, which was swiftly imitated and further elaborated by urban elites. From that time forth women's "complaints" (emerging in an already simmering stew of discourse characterized by complaints about women) erupted into a full-scale critique of male domination and, by extension, male-dominated institutions. From a trickle, this critique began to gush forth in France and England, then in Holland, the German principalities, the Italian city-states, spreading eventually to the larger and smaller kingdoms of Central Europe.[1]

The chapters in Part I confront and attempt to revise several decades of historical writing about European feminisms during the eighteenth century. In Chapter 2, I step outside the conventional approach to the Enlightenment, which in the French context has focused so heavily on the male *philosophes*, the Encyclopedia project, and on political and economic theorists, and in the German context on the philosopher Immanuel Kant and his influential 1785 essay "What Is Enlightenment?"[2] Instead, I will survey an abundant but understudied cache of published materials that openly critiqued the subordinate status of women.[3] By thus decentering the leading male *philosophes*, I insist instead on the multiplicity of publishing voices in which European women and men expressed what we would now call feminist concerns, and on the broader context in which Enlightenment thought on the woman question developed and to which its thinkers responded.

Eighteenth-century writers confronted a variety of issues, centering on male authority in families and the legal and moral relationships of in-

dividuals and families to the state. In particular, they engaged the differential (and for women disadvantageous) construction of gender roles—
and some even used the terms *genre* (gender), *genre masculin*, and *genre
féminin* to refer explicitly to these roles. They raised questions about the
transmission of landed and other forms of property from one generation
to the next, about love, luxury, and sexual liberty as well as about the relationship between slavery and political liberty. They insisted on the
importance of education, both domestic and formal instruction, in the
formation of citizens for the state. They engaged, too, in the politics of
knowledge, which they called "science," and they witnessed the birth of
what I will call here the "knowledge wars" over questions of gender and
sociopolitical organization.[4] Throughout my reading, I have been constantly impressed by how these texts manifest far more a concrete level
of sociopolitical criticism than they do an abstract rationalism, much
less a concern with elaborating "women's nature" or the sex of "virtue"—all issues that have preoccupied feminist scholars of the Enlightenment in recent years.[5] The texts I have drawn on are quarrelsome,
heavily relational, engaging and confronting the concrete realities of
women's subordinate existence, and countering threats to women's independent existence. Indeed, their authors concerned themselves far less
with discussions of "virtue," "women's nature," or "the social contract"
than with denouncing women's slavery in marriage, often drawing an
analogy between the status of wives in the home countries and that of
enslaved blacks in the overseas colonies of England and France.

In particular, I attempt to shrink the long shadow of Jean-Jacques
Rousseau, which retrospectively has loomed so heavily over so many interpretations of the Enlightenment. Instead, I treat him as one among
many contributors—though clearly a very influential one—to the developing antifeminist resistance. There is no question that Rousseau's abstraction of an autonomous (male) individual, along with his insistence
on eliminating women from "public" life by confining them to "private"
or "domestic" roles, was important, particularly regarding the development of subsequent political theory. What I would argue, however, is
that the import of his ideas must be contextually evaluated, treated over
time and in reference to specific debates, rather than assumed (as has
long been the custom) as a foregone conclusion.[6]

Centered in France, Enlightenment criticism—perhaps precisely because of its secular character—facilitated the questioning of many of the
institutions and customs that structured existing societies, notably but
not exclusively those embodied by or controlled by organized religious
authorities such as the Roman Catholic Church. But this was not all.

Questions of male-female relations, embodied in marriage law, restricted educational opportunity and economic participation, and issues of
who should exercise authority rose to the forefront of public debate—
precisely because they had become issues contested in everyday life. In
consequence of the remarkable evidence that has emerged in the course
of revisiting eighteenth-century public discussion, and arguing against
those who have indicted the Enlightenment "universalism" envisioned
by Rousseau and by Kant, whom Rousseau so influenced, and seemingly
embodied in the 1789 Declaration of the Rights of Man, I propose that
we can—and must—reclaim the Enlightenment for feminism.

With the advent of the French Revolution, eruptions of feminist challenges proliferated, developing an astounding frequency and momentum
over several years' time. Claims to full citizenship for women arose almost immediately as the question of representation in the Estates-
General came to the fore. In contrast to the claims of other historians,
who have insisted on the ways in which the male-dominated Revolution
quickly foreclosed on women, or who (like Lynn Hunt) have attempted
to disengage a psychoanalytically driven script grounded in masculine
discourse, my argument in Chapter 3 is that between 1789 and 1793—a
period of some five years—feminists succeeded in posing frontal challenges to patriarchal institutions and control, confronting even the most
radical revolutionaries (some of whom were indeed followers of Rousseau) with the necessity of spelling out the gendered consequences of
their ideas and actions, and thereby forcing the systematic articulation
of resistance.[7] In contrast to other scholars, I argue that the revolutionary
notion of mother educators provided an innovative, quasi-public role for
women, one that not only could and did serve as a springboard for promoting women's formal education but that feminists used to pave the
way for a broadening of women's access to public roles.[8] By building on
contrasts between slavery and freedom, by insisting on the importance
of patriotic motherhood, on revisions of marriage institutions to emphasize partnership rather than male authority, and by applying notions of
public utility to justify women's interventions in public life, feminist
thinkers frontally challenged male domination and claimed parity for
women in the new society. This was no mean feat.

These challenges were raised not only in Paris, but throughout France
and around the Continent—as the ongoing recovery of long-forgotten
published texts underscores. Indeed, the emerging evidence (and we are
discovering more all the time) suggests that the critique of women's
subordination acquired far more champions—even as it disturbed far
more opponents—than many historians have been willing to acknowl-

edge. It suggests also that the subsequent backlash against claims for women's emancipation may be a central, yet to date wholly unappreciated characteristic of the better-known opposition to the French Revolution, a counterrevolutionary current that deeply marked the politics and cultural development of Europe in the nineteenth century. In particular, the evidence underscores that revolutionary men's attempts to assert claims on behalf of the abstract individual, and to invoke the Rights of Man even while attempting to disqualify women—on grounds of public utility—from their full application may be understood as *deliberate responses* to the ardent claims feminists were making for women's full equality, both on grounds of absolute right and by insisting on their sexual difference and complementarity.[9]

It is in this context that we may reevaluate what Elizabeth A. Williams has called the disaggregation of the French medical "science of man" into the distinctive fields of anthropology, physiology, and philosophical medicine, as well as the attempts by physicians to elaborate "scientific" arguments with the aim of insisting not only on the physical incommensurability of the sexes, as Thomas Laqueur has suggested, but, more important, on rejustifying women's physical, intellectual, and moral "inferiority" to men.[10] Learned men in other countries, in particular the German philosophers Kant and Hegel, may well have written women out of the realm of reason and public responsibility, but fortunately, apart from Rousseau's acolytes, sociopolitical critics in France (and in many other parts of Europe affected by French occupation and cultural hegemony) were far from supporting this position unilaterally. The controversies between feminists and antifeminists during the French Revolution would not end quickly or quietly; instead they would be exported throughout Europe, where they would simmer, bubble up, and erupt with increasing frequency and velocity throughout the entire nineteenth century.

2

Reclaiming the Enlightenment for Feminism

The European Enlightenment, a time of "social and intellectual flowering," in Francis Steegmuller's felicitous phrase,[1] was a privileged time for debate on the "woman question," as the controversy over relations between the sexes became known. Enlightenment inquiry was "feminocentric" in the sense that male writers focused intensively on "woman" and "woman's nature," and subsequent interpretation has typically discussed the views expressed by its leading male figures—Montesquieu, Voltaire, Diderot, Rousseau, Condorcet, and Kant. If one examines the broader spectrum of Enlightenment debate by decentering these leading male *philosophes*, however, it becomes evident that this time of "flowering" offered women and their male allies an arena to develop in print an impressive arsenal of concepts, vocabulary, and arguments capable of challenging what some feminist critics would denounce in 1789 as an "aristocracy of sex."[2]

THE CRITIQUE THAT HAD NO NAME

Enlightenment debate can thus be seen as a spawning ground, not simply for positioning "woman," as some have complained, but for asserting women's equality to men, for criticizing male privilege and domination, for analyzing historically the causes and constructions of women's subordination, and for devising eloquent arguments for the emancipation of women from male control. These were all defining features of that critical tradition we now call feminism, but which at the time remained a critique that had no name.

Throughout the eighteenth century, women and men wrote tracts that spoke explicitly to the emancipation and equality of women; what is particularly interesting, however, is the extent to which these issues permeated works whose main subjects ostensibly concerned other topics. In debating the woman question, imaginative fiction, plays, and poetry complemented polemical pamphlets, essays on political economy and aesthetics, and book-length treatises on law, philosophy, physiology, and animal taxonomy.[3]

The issues of choice in this debate were not restricted to topics in formal philosophy; they addressed fundamental aspects of societal organization. In the efforts of learned men (*savants*) and philosophers (*philosophes*) to understand what we know and how we know it, they posed many important questions about the world in which they lived. Their attempts to distinguish, through comparisons, what was "human" from what was "animal," what was "social" or "cultural" from what was "natural," to probe the difference between "laws" and "morals," quickly confronted them with the distinctions their own societies prescribed between men and women, and the rationales offered to support these distinctions. Critiques of women's subordinate status provoked an awareness that the relations between the sexes were neither God-given nor determined exclusively by "Nature," but socially constructed; in other words, they understood the concept that we today call "gender." Replying to a much-discussed exchange between two *philosophes*, Antoine-Léonard Thomas and Denis Diderot, Madame d'Épinay in 1776 used the terms *genre masculin* and *genre féminin*, insisting that she was speaking not only about grammar but about socialization.[4] Such criticism led quickly to disagreements about how relationships between the sexes should be structured and stimulated visions of alternative arrangements. Assertive claims for sexual hierarchies and male dominance, invoked in the name of "tradition," were countered by equally vehement claims for sexual equality and the emancipation of women from male control.

Eighteenth-century feminists claimed a "natural" equality of the sexes prior to all social and political organization, and demanded, accordingly, full equality of the sexes in organized society. They highlighted women's disadvantaged legal and economic situation in institutionalized marriage and called for an acknowledgment of women's rights *as women*. They criticized women's inadequate education and lack of economic alternatives to marriage, and—despite these disadvantages—the importance of their influence and societal role. Such arguments led in several directions. First, they pointed to the necessity of women's full spiritual/moral and intellectual development as individuals, a goal embedded in a discourse of "rights." Second, they led directly to a reassertion of so-called women's values, the claims of the heart and of the emotions—of sentiment, in short, as the complement to "masculine" rationality—even as women claimed reason for themselves. Third, they precipitated a rethinking, in the name of "public utility," of women's strategic societal importance as mothers and asserted their centrality as child nurturers and partners with men in the project of "civilization." To emphasize only one of these facets without insisting as well upon the others is to miss the complexity of Enlightenment feminism.

This debate did not begin with the Enlightenment; indeed, its roots lie much further back in European history. Feminist scholars have assembled abundant evidence to document vociferous debate in Italy, France, and England from the fifteenth century on.[5] Yet by the mid-eighteenth century the number of participants had expanded and the audience had grown dramatically. By this time educated Europeans were experiencing, along with great prosperity, a veritable explosion of printed criticism of the existing gender order. Books, periodicals, tracts, broadsides poured forth from the presses. Growing literacy among women as well as men of the privileged classes in urban settings guaranteed a sizable audience for these works. In France alone, according to Roger Chartier, the literacy rate for both women and men had nearly doubled (for women, from 14 to 27 percent) in the course of the eighteenth century, and many more people owned books; indeed, hundreds of French women were publishing their works, as Carla Hesse has discovered.[6] The rise of the novel itself, with its "heroine's text," was closely intertwined with what became a lively debate over sexual politics; literary historian Nancy K. Miller reminds us that "in the eighteenth century women writers were not the marginal figures they have become in the annals of literary history. They were active participants in the production and dissemination of the novel; . . . they wrote best sellers."[7] And not only in France. In the Netherlands, Betje Wolff and Aagje Deken pioneered the Dutch novel by publishing *Sarah Burgerhart* in 1782. This novel, which told the story of a spunky young Dutch girl's life in epistolary form, espoused Enlightenment values of reason, knowledge, and tolerance, and advocated women's access to life as free and independent persons.[8] It is still read by Dutch schoolgirls today.

Controversy over the asymmetrical relationship of the sexes occupied a prominent place in this print explosion. Defenders of the status quo sought new justifications for their strongly held views, and reformers eloquently articulated dissenting perspectives. Both drew not only on their sometimes spotty knowledge of Greek and Roman classics (interests inherited from Renaissance culture), but also on an ever broader range of "new" knowledge about human bodies and human societies, published in the major European languages. They gleaned this knowledge variously from the recent findings of the so-called "natural" scientists (primarily anatomists and physicians) as well as from the accounts of missionaries, ethnologists, and travelers to other parts of the world. Both sides increasingly invoked "natural" law and "natural" rights, distinguishing the "natural" from the "social" and "cultural," and they developed historical, sociological, or scientific, rather than theological or philosophical, arguments to support their proposals for change.

INFERIORITY OR EQUALITY? THE IMPORTANT ARGUMENT FROM REASON

Claims for the equality of the sexes, grounded in the Christian doctrine of equality of souls and in appeals to reason, were a long-standing feature of European intellectual debate since the early fifteenth century, when, by invoking Lady Reason, Christine de Pizan first challenged French male writers who demeaned women in print.[9] By the seventeenth century, this argument for sexual equality had been explicitly stated by writers such as Marie Le Jars de Gournay, in her treatise *De l'égalité des hommes et des femmes* (On the Equality of Men and Women, 1622).[10] Gournay insisted on shifting the terms of argument to emphasize the natural equality of the sexes, based on their common possession of Reason (with a capital *R*). She criticized the sexual hierarchy that had developed, insisting that women's lack of education and knowledge was to blame for the inequalities that could be observed in their condition. This "cultural" argument was destined for a brilliant future. Equality of condition did not imply sameness or imitation, however. Marie de Gournay objected strongly to the notion that the best option for women was to strive to resemble men. That, to her, was not the point. Nor has it been the point for most feminists since.

Feminist appeals to equality and reason were made throughout the sixteenth century, as Constance Jordan has beautifully documented.[11] But Londa Schiebinger argues that only with the development of Cartesian philosophy in the seventeenth century, which foregrounded the preeminence of reason and the human brain that made it possible, could feminist claims be placed on a firmer philosophical footing.[12] The Cartesian cleric François Poullain de la Barre subsequently claimed (1673) that "the mind has no sex" (*l'esprit n'a pas de sexe*). He argued that, except for genital differences, there was no significant difference between the sexes; this approach, complementing Marie de Gournay's cultural critique, opened the door for cultural explanations of women's ostensible "inferiority," unleashing a flood of publications on this subject.[13] The arguments consecrated by Poullain de la Barre reappear in a number of later tracts published in French and English, among them Montesquieu's *Persian Letters* (1721), in which the author gives the last word to Roxane, who invokes the law of nature against male law; *Woman Not Inferior to Man; or, A Short and Modest Vindication of the Natural Right of the Fair Sex to a Perfect Equality of Power, Dignity, and Esteem, with the Men*, signed by "Sophia, a Person of Quality" (1739); and *Female Rights Vindicated* by "A Lady" (1758). In this way the debate on the woman question became a central feature of the Enlightenment exploration of human society, and feminist challenges to male hegemony began to bubble up through an increasing number of fissures.

THE CRITIQUE OF INSTITUTIONALIZED MARRIAGE

Let us enter the Enlightenment debate by examining the critique of institutionalized marriage. In most European states at this time, in the aftermath of the Protestant Reformation in the sixteenth century, the formalization and dissolution of marriage remained the prerogative of Christian religious institutions. Each denomination endorsed some structural form of male control over women. The Roman Catholic Church had declared marriage to be an indissoluble sacrament, a position that some Protestant denominations never adopted (and which in consequence allowed them to tolerate divorce, rather than concocting elaborate annulment procedures in ecclesiastical courts). Moreover, churches—acting as agencies of the state—kept track of births, deaths, and marriages, and exercised moral authority over family relationships. Throughout the seventeenth century French legal authorities had exhibited interest in claiming direct control of these functions as well as in secularizing the institution of marriage, in order to exert an even more direct control over male-headed families than state officials had asserted during the previous century. Thus, in eighteenth-century France, and in those countries which modeled themselves on France, church and state appeared to be on a collision course over the control of marriage; meanwhile, dissatisfied women's questioning of conventional marriage arrangements and their complaints about husbandly abuse and misdeeds fed a stream of well-publicized lawsuits.[14] Civil divorce was one item over which agreement seemed impossible.

Male domination was also inscribed in most Protestant approaches to marriage. With the exception of the Quakers in England, who acknowledged an important degree of equality for women, most Protestant sects had reverted to Old Testament precedents to ground new assertions of male authority over married women. The leaders of Protestant churches appreciated neither Mary Astell's criticism of the submission required of English women in marriage (and her celebration of spinsterhood) in her *Reflections upon Marriage* (3d ed., 1706) nor Daniel Defoe's more scathing characterization of marriage without love in 1727 as "conjugal lewdness," a condition Mary Wollstonecraft would later label "legally prostituted."[15] This critique of arranged and loveless marriages, sometimes juxtaposed with a celebration of love itself, would reverberate through the arguments of many subsequent feminist writers in various countries, particularly in France.[16] The best-selling, much-reprinted and translated *Lettres d'une Péruvienne* (Letters from a Peruvian Woman, 1747) by Madame de Graffigny not only critiqued the French mode of marriage but invented a self-determining heroine, Zilia, an Inca princess, who ultimately renounced marriage with her French suitor in favor of friendship.[17]

By the time Montesquieu published his *Spirit of the Laws* (1748), one of the salient issues in his discussion of the structure of governments and social institutions was the subordination of women in male-headed families, and its relationship to three types of governments: republican, monarchical, and despotic. In monarchies, he postulated, women were "subject to very little restraint," while under despotic governments women were an "object of luxury," "in servitude." Under republics, "women are free by the laws and restrained by manners."[18] As critics of existing societal arrangements identified themselves increasingly with republican ideas, this set of observations provoked a new round of reflection on the woman question in terms of the "politics" of marriage. Enlightenment thinkers and writers of fiction appeared on both sides of the issue. Prominent legal theorists, notably Samuel von Cocceji, Prussian compiler of a legal code for Frederick the Great, king of Prussia, Robert Pothier, author of several influential French legal texts on marriage, and William Blackstone, commentator on the British common law, opted for circumscribing women's place in order to realize Nature's plan.[19]

On the dissenting side could be found daring writers such as Louis de Jaucourt, who in volume 6 of the enormously influential French *Encyclopédie* (1756) argued that "the reasons that can be alleged for marital power could be contested, humanly speaking." Jaucourt insisted that the authority of husbands was arbitrary: it ran "contrary to natural human equality." Men were by no means superior to women, and the extant rules were the contributions of "positive," or man-made, as distinct from "natural" law. Marriage, Jaucourt proposed, was nothing more than a contract, and as a contract it could conceivably be organized in a variety of ways by the individual parties concerned.[20] A new wave of published fiction by women novelists in France extended and deepened this critique, as Joan Hinde Stewart has ably demonstrated for the period after 1750. The actress-turned-novelist Marie-Jeanne Riccoboni, in particular, astutely explored the politics of love, marriage, and remarriage, and did not hesitate to address issues of adultery, independent widowhood, and even illegitimacy.[21] Another French novelist, Jeanne-Marie Le Prince de Beaumont, craftily seconded the case for opting out of the "uterine economy" of love and marriage, privileging mother-daughter relationships over male-female relationships, and seeking "final liberation . . . in and through the single life."[22]

THE CRITIQUE OF WOMEN'S EDUCATION

The critique of women's education became a commonplace of Enlightenment criticism. Earlier Protestant leaders and Catholic reformers of the Counter-Reformation had proposed educating girls of all social classes, primarily in the interest of encouraging their piety, by training them to read the Bible so they could inculcate Christian values in their children. Writing, on the other hand, was not encouraged. Advanced instruction for women of the upper classes was a different matter, and the critique leveled at the "learned ladies" of Elizabethan England, and especially at the *femmes savantes* of mid-seventeenth-century Parisian high society, was vicious and unprecedented, as is reflected in Molière's widely known comedies Les Précieuses ridicules (1659) and Les Femmes savantes (1672). "You've been writing! . . . You've ink stains on your fingers! Ah! Cunning Signora," Beaumarchais has Dr. Bartholo exclaim, in his comedy The Barber of Seville (1775), when he suspects his ward Rosina of writing to a suitor. "Women think they can safely do anything if they are alone."[23]

The accession of women to the still new seventeenth-century scientific learning was hotly contested in some quarters. It called forth denials that women were capable of reason, but also claims that women not only could reason, but might possess rational powers superior to those of men. Defenders of women's innate intellectual capacities, following Poullain de la Barre's claim (1673) that "the mind has no sex," reiterated and elaborated this claim in various forms throughout the following century. Nicolas Malebranche, in his treatise on the search for truth (first published in 1674), acknowledged that women's brains were characterized by "delicate" fibers, which accounted for both their great intelligence and their taste, but also made them less good at abstractions; he nevertheless acknowledged that there was no such thing as absolute masculinity and femininity. Bernard le Bovier de Fontenelle framed his best-selling *Entretiens sur la pluralité des mondes* (Conversations on the Plurality of Worlds, 1686), a work explaining the new Newtonian physics in simple language, as a dialogue between a philosopher and an aristocratic lady, the Marquise.[24]

Comparable defenses of women's reasoning capacity had already been sharply expressed by Mary Astell, in England, who in her *Serious Proposal to the Ladies* (1694) advocated founding a women's university and community for women who did not wish to marry but preferred to pursue lifelong learning in the company of other similarly disposed women. The "father" of the Spanish Enlightenment, the Roman Catholic cleric Benito Feijóo, author of *La defensa de las mujeres* (1739; in English translation, *Defense, or Vindication of the Women*, 1778), similarly insisted on the equal capacities of women and men.[25] It is in the context of this debate that studious women throughout Europe found encouragement in the 1732 conferral of a doctoral degree in philosophy by the University of Bologna on the brilliant Laura Bassi.[26]

The discussion of women's education had already taken a distinctly antifeminist and utilitarian turn in France with the publication of Archbishop Fénelon's very influential treatise *De l'éducation des filles* (On the Education of Daughters, 1687).[27] As part of a comprehensive plan for reforming the French aristocracy, Fénelon designed a program intended for daughters of the impoverished nobility, to direct them away from the frivolity of court and salon society and toward the serious business of training to become wives, mothers, and estate managers who would be useful to their husbands and families, and thereby to the French state. This tract by Fénelon—and the nearly simultaneous establishment by Madame de Maintenon, morganatic wife of Louis XIV, of the school for girls, the Maison Royale de Saint Louis, at St. Cyr—influenced the development of secular girls' education among elite families throughout eighteenth-century Europe.[28]

Following a celebrated exchange with the encyclopedist Jean Le Rond d'Alembert on the subject of women's education and place in 1758–59, Jean-Jacques Rousseau published his two most famous didactic works, *Julie; or, The New Heloise* (1761) and *Émile; or, Education* (1762), to drive home in a more popular form his bald assertion that women's education must prepare them to serve men—even as he underscored the enormous influence women could and did wield within the family.[29]

The search for abstract and speculative truths, principles, axioms in the sciences, and everything that tends to generalize ideas is not within the compass of women: all their studies must deal with the practical. Their job is to apply the principles that men discover and to make the observations that lead men to establish principles.

Rousseau's antifeminist arguments constituted a response to the many women writers who published critiques of the superficiality of girls' education during the eighteenth century and who defended women's right to reason and to acquire advanced knowledge in the best Enlightenment tradition. Many, like the pseudonymous "Sophia," had argued that in the state of nature women and men were equally reasonable creatures. "In a word, were the *Men Philosophers* in the strict sense of the term, they would be able to see that nature invincibly proves a perfect *equality* in our sex with their own."[30] Such claims recurred in radical tracts such as *Female Rights Vindicated* by "A Lady," published in London in 1758, who framed her insistence on the natural equality of the sexes and her defense of women's abilities with an attempt at a historical account of how men had subordinated women.[31] In the Paris-based *Journal des Dames* (Ladies' Magazine), the feisty *éditrice* Madame de Beaumer insisted in 1761 that "we women think under our coiffures as well as you do under your wigs. We are as capable of reasoning as you are." "In fact," she added, with what must have been a broad grin, "you lose your reason over us every day."[32] Under Beaumer's successor, Madame de Maisonneuve, the *Journal* went on to cultivate and celebrate women's intellectual prowess.

Male-dominated culture, these women knew, contrasted with what they saw as the natural (or pre-social) state of things. Some eighteenth-century feminist critics sensed then, as others have rediscovered repeatedly since, that the relationship of the sexes is a sociopolitical or "cultural" construction; they understood intuitively the distinction French philosophers, in particular, were making between "natural law" (God's law) and "positive law" (man-made law). Madame de Beaumer, addressing unnamed male critics of the *Journal des Dames*, issued this indictment:[33]

> I love this sex, I am jealous to uphold its honor and its rights. If we have not been raised up in the sciences as you have, it is you who are the guilty ones; for have you not always abused, if I may say so, the bodily strength that nature has given you? Have you not used it to annihilate our capacities, and to enshroud the special prerogatives that this same nature has bounteously granted to women, to compensate them for the material strength that you have—advantages that we would surely not dispute you—to truly appreciate vivacity of imagination, delicate feelings, and that amiable politeness, well worth the strength that you parade about so.

Madame de Beaumer and her readers were well aware of the significance of socially imposed educational norms for the cultural construction of gender, even as they acknowledged certain differences between the sexes as inherent and complementary. Their awareness was underscored by the celebrated case of the cross-dressing soldier-diplomat Chevalier d'Éon, considered to be the most famous woman in Europe, who was ordered by Louis XV to abandon male dress upon "her" return to France.[34]

Depending on the country and the cultural context, various criticisms of women's education could be and were made. British feminists repeatedly objected to the frivolity of an ornamental and "useless" education for aristocratic and wealthy girls. The 1780s works of Catharine Macaulay and Mary Wollstonecraft, among others, eloquently express this litany of complaints.[35] The Spanish reformer and educational writer Josefa Amar y Borbón argued in 1790 that a better, more substantive education for women, a cultivation of the mind and of talents, rather than of personal appearance and coquetry, would greatly enhance the quality of a couple's relationship in marriage as well as a woman's personal satisfaction in life.[36]

Well before these women critics, however, the Swedish poet and essayist Charlotta Nordenflycht had confronted Rousseau's arguments for male supremacy in a set of clever verses published in Stockholm in the early 1760s:[37]

> Woman is prevented from grasping any truth,
> people amuse themselves by laughing at her stupidity.
> But when the seeds of stupidity finally grow into sins
> then much poison is spread and much blame assigned.
> Then there is no appealing to the suppression of her intellect,
> then she is the embodiment of weakness and a woman.
> Nature, then, is blamed, and blood and heart decried
> for what has its roots in the manner of upbringing only.
> The source of a gushing well is obstructed
> and then the question asked: why does not the water flow?
> They set a trap for the Eagle's foot and break his wings,
> and then they blame him for not reaching the sun.
> Thus is the energy of women suppressed by upbringing and
>   custom,
> They are left to fight each other in stupidity's narrow arena,
> And as an ornament drag the heavy yoke of ignorance,
> Because it is seen as an affront to women to be wise and
>   learned.
> Oh, cruel tyranny, will this our world improve,
> that half of mankind is by narrow folly chained
> When lack of brains is evident in every task?

The republican thinker the Abbé de Mably would subsequently stress the strategic political importance of educating women, a cornerstone for his projects for reforming society. "The Republic," he warned in 1776, "is not composed of men alone, and I warn you that you will have done nothing if you neglect the education of women. You must choose, either to make men of them as at Sparta or condemn them to seclusion."[38] In France, the education of women had been reframed—by Mably and others—as an affair of state; it was no longer sufficient to argue that it was necessary merely for a woman's personal happiness or that of her husband. This notion of educating women for civic motherhood, by sanctioning a quasi-public role for women, would prove to be a momentous development for the history of feminism in Europe and beyond.

WOMEN'S POTENTIAL: WHAT SHOULD WOMEN BE?
WHAT COULD WOMEN DO?

Critiques of marriage and of women's education quickly led to discussion of the central issue of what women should be, of what they should be trained to do in a well-organized society. In the course of these debates, the question of women's capacities, and of public utility and practical need, resurfaced.

The developing market economy of early modern Europe opened possibilities for new roles for elite women within the family as well as opportunities for economic independence and freedom of movement for all women beyond the control of fathers, husbands, and brothers. Issues about women's options were increasingly framed in terms of "liberty" and "emancipation," in this case from familial control. The English businessman and political pamphleteer Daniel Defoe, seemingly in ignorance of Fénelon's earlier proposals, argued in his *Essay on Projects* (1697) that women should be educated to become good companions to their husbands, not "only Stewards of our Houses, Cooks and Slaves."[39] But a few women, mostly of the emerging middle classes, watching the freedoms and opportunities enjoyed by their brothers, eloquently expressed a sense of constraint, envy, and injustice. In 1779, for instance, a young German poet and housewife from Göttingen, Philippine Gatterer Engelhard, published her "Girl's Lament":[40]

> How oft with damnation
> And tears of frustration
> My gender I curse!
> Its ban ever dooms
> Us girls to our rooms;

How freely men move!
Even youngster and serf.

In her novel *Madame de Montbrillant* (a fictionalized memoir only published in the early nineteenth century), Madame d'Épinay similarly lamented the "damping down" and constraints imposed on her heroine during childhood.[41]

Women of the lower classes had always worked, and in early modern European cities many worked for pay. But the sexual division of labor that stipulated not only different, more sedentary jobs, but also lower pay for women than for men had deep roots in European societies.[42] Nevertheless, women could be found engaged in a wide range of commercial craft activities, including, rugmaking, clockmaking, taxidermy, and lens grinding—even journalism, as the *Journal des Dames* proudly reported in the 1760s.

The French monarchy had already attempted to address the "problem" of women's work in the seventeenth century by stipulating that certain trades would be reserved for women's guilds (or corporations), even as restrictions on women's entering the male trades were tightened. When these regulations were overturned during the monarchy's brief experiment in liberalizing commerce in the early 1770s, men began to infiltrate a number of lucrative women's trades. Louis-Sébastian Mercier, a writer and social commentator who thought poorly paid married women should be eliminated from the labor force and sent back to their households, nevertheless argued that single women who needed employment should have it. No enthusiast for emancipating women unconditionally, Mercier nevertheless subscribed to equity in a moral economy based on sexually separated occupations. It was absurd, he argued, for men to become women's hairdressers, to engage in needlework, to sell lingerie and items of fashion, when young women who could not find work in these suitable trades were forced to do heavy labor or resort to prostitution. He insisted, as would women pamphleteers into the mid-nineteenth century, that the monopoly of such trades should be restored to women as their rightful due.[43] The reformist playwright Beaumarchais inserted a comparable protest, this time couched in a protest against men's victimization of women, through the voice of Marceline in his subversive comedy *The Marriage of Figaro* (1784).

Women's aspirations to participate in the learned professions were highly problematic for men and rarely successful. In France Poullain de la Barre had squarely proposed the possibility of access for women to university education, including theology, medicine, and law. But even in Italy, where a few exceptional women had occupied chairs in universities since late medieval times, their role was questioned. In Padua, the Academy of Ricovrati (whose members had elected a number of French women writers to membership in absentia) sponsored a debate in 1723 between two professors on the question "whether women should be admitted to the study of science and the noble arts."[44] In Germany, Dorothea Leporin Erxleben learned of Laura Bassi's doctorate at Bologna, and determined to attempt the like at Halle. In 1742 she published a tract arguing that women should be permitted to undertake university studies. She acquired allies at Halle University and in 1754 she presented her doctoral thesis in medicine, written (as was the custom) in Latin.[45] Dorothea Erxleben was an extraordinary exception, like Laura Bassi, but news of the accomplishments of both continued to inspire other talented and ambitious women.

The universities, with their classical learning available only to men, by no means monopolized the development of the arts and sciences at this time. In other settings, a few highly intelligent women made celebrated contributions to the advancement of knowledge. Madame du Châtelet was applauded for her experimentation in physics but especially for her masterful translation into French of Newton's *Principia*. In England Elizabeth Carter received respect and praise for her translations from ancient languages. In the so-called Bluestocking circle, a cluster of well-known intellectual English women gathered regularly to discuss ideas.[46] Compilers of biographical encyclopedias of women began to insist on the contributions of learned women, as the findings of Brita Rang have demonstrated.[47]

In addition, a series of women played extraordinary roles in developing what was known at the time as the "republic of letters." The Parisian *salonnières* Madame du Deffand, Madame Geoffrin, Julie de Lespinasse, Madame Necker (and later, their counterparts in Berlin) stood strategically at the very heart of the Enlightenment project; indeed, Dena Goodman has argued that the ambitions of the *philosophes* converged with those of a small and select group of "intelligent, self-educated, and educating women who . . . reshaped the social forms of their day to their own social, intellectual, and educational needs." Goodman claims that in these new social spaces, "the primary relationship . . . was between female mentors and students, rather than between a single woman and a group of men."[48] She makes a strong case for the centrality of women's governance, through the organization of salon sociability, in the emerging French republic of letters.[49] Clever and enterprising women, including actresses and artists, could devise extraordinary opportunities for themselves through the formation of such new cultural institutions, despite their exclusion from the academies and universities. Especially in France women were playing key roles in the intellectual and cultural life of their time. This irritated critics like Rousseau, who argued that women should not even be seen in the theater in a properly organized republic, much less act in or write plays.

GENDERING AUTHORITY: CONTROVERSY OVER
WOMEN IN PUBLIC AFFAIRS

Most eighteenth-century men drew the line at the "threat" of women's participation in governance and military affairs. Poullain de la Barre's 1673 treatise, *The Woman as Good as the Man*, had put into circulation a strong and daring argument for women's capacity to fill positions of political and military authority as well as all other public offices.[50] This was a contentious claim, and one which Enlightenment writers would address frequently, especially during the highly visible reigns of Maria Theresa in Austria (1740–80) and Catherine II in Russia (1762–96). Pro-woman historians dredged up legends of the Amazons and, of course, the precedent-setting example of Joan of Arc to support arguments for women's inclusion even in military matters, while the French dramatist Marivaux would insist, in his comedy *The Colony* (1750), on their fundamental pacifism.[51] In the 1780s a cluster of utopian novels by French women writers addressing the issue of women's rule were published; only recently have these been identified and analyzed by literary scholars.[52]

Some French supporters of the principle of male rule were particularly incensed by such claims on women's behalf; had France—alone among the great powers of Europe—not excluded women from succession to the throne! "I defy you to name me a State where women have held power without destroying morals, laws, and the Government," asserted the same Abbé de Mably (who had nevertheless underscored the need for women's education) in 1776. But British sages were little better: "Nature has given women so much power that the law has wisely given them little," insisted the redoubtable Samuel Johnson.[53] Even Montesquieu noted that "except in special cases, women have almost never aspired to equality: for they already have so many natural advantages that equal power always means empire for them."[54] "Men make the laws, but women make the morals" became a familiar and oft-repeated expression of this notion.[55]

This is a different perspective on power than we are accustomed to encountering today. Some eighteenth-century male writers deemed women so powerful, so influential, so effective by virtue of their sexual allure, that only outright suppression or sequestration could keep them under control. All the more reason why men should be determined to retain a deliberate hold on *authority*. This may not have been a mere symbolic move, but rather an expression of outright fear. The most retrograde expression of this point of view was perhaps Restif de la Bretonne's tract *Les Gynographes* (1777), in which he argued that "writing and even reading should be prohibited for all women; this would offer a means to restrain their ideas and to limit them to useful household tasks."[56] In fact, the sheer volume of eighteenth-century prescriptive literature addressed to girls, exhorting them to be meek, respectful, virtuous, obedient, and the like, may be understood as a gauge of the extent to which some highly visible and articulate women were already perceived by some anxiety-ridden men as powerful forces about to escape from male control.[57]

Not all men felt that way. Madame du Châtelet's friend Voltaire had long celebrated the mixing of the sexes that contributed so much to the vivacity of French society: "Society depends on women. All the peoples that have the misfortune to keep them locked up are unsociable."[58] Voltaire ridiculed the exclusion of women from the French throne. The Marquis de Condorcet subsequently restated Poullain's claims with reference to representative government in a republic by claiming that property-owning women should be entitled both to vote and to hold office. "The facts prove," he argued in 1787, "that men have or believe they have interests that are very different from those of women, because everywhere they have made oppressive laws against them, or at the least have established a great inequality between the two sexes." Women, especially single adult women and widows, he believed, should be fully able to exercise the rights of citizenship; with respect to married women, the civil laws subordinating them in marriage should be changed. "Consider that we are speaking of the rights of half the human race," Condorcet insisted.[59] Thus did Condorcet put the issue of women's citizenship squarely on the table, just two years before the calling of the Estates-General and the beginning of the French Revolution.

WOMEN'S CIVILIZING MISSION: THE PROJECT OF FORMING FUTURE MOTHERS

Citizenship for women was still a radical idea that even the most enlightened Europeans were generally unwilling to countenance. But it was clear to some that women did have a significant role to play in the advancement of civilization as it was then understood. Indeed, more than one eighteenth-century historian attributed a central role to women in the formation of culture and the advancement of civilization, as Sylvia Tomaselli, Jane Rendall, and others have reminded us.[60] The formula, too often attributed to Charles Fourier, which identified advances in the condition of women as the index of societal progress, had many spokesmen in the 1770s and 1780s, especially among Scottish Enlightenment historians.

Side by side with such arguments, another body of prescriptive literature addressed to women expanded in the course of the European Enlightenment. This literature was also an outgrowth of the concern about women's power and influence, but it was designed to harness that power and influence on behalf of societal progress. This was the mother-as-educator, or patriotic-motherhood literature. The functionalist emphasis on educating children for specific social roles can be traced back to Renaissance civic humanism, and to reformulations in the Protestant Reformation and Catholic Counter-Reformation.[61] But in eighteenth-century Enlightenment literature this current of thought—like the prescriptive literature aimed at curbing girls' exuberance—developed increasing magnitude and impact, and attached itself, leechlike, to the secular reformulation of citizenship as nation-states emerged from the princely states and kingdoms of the Old World.

"It is so important for a household to have a virtuous and intelligent mother [*mère de famille*] that I have willingly adopted the proverb 'Women make or break households' [*ce sont les femmes qui font & qui défont les maisons*]."[62] Thus wrote the Abbé de Saint-Pierre in 1730, arguing further that the education of women should be given just as much attention as the education of men, and that well-ordered states should assure its effective organization. Several years later he proposed a plan for a network of girls' *collèges*, or secondary schools, based on the model of St. Cyr. Pierre-Joseph Boudier de Villemert, author of the much-translated *L'Ami des femmes* (Women's Friend), insisted on women's role as a civilizing force, portraying them as the complements to—and the tamers of—men, and arguing for the cultivation of their intelligence to that end.[63] Writing in 1762, Nicolas Baudeau strengthened the argument when he proposed a plan for national education that fully included female citizens: "We must pose as a fundamental maxim that the Daughters of the Nation are destined each to become within their class, *Citoyennes*, Wives, and Mothers."[64] It is in this context that we must interpret Rousseau's more subordinate, privatized vision of motherliness in the

public interest with his portraits of Julie—his vision of the new Heloise—and, of course, Sophie.[65]

The mother-educator perspective made a deep impression within the
wide circle of French influence, which included the "enlightened" des-
pots of Prussia and Russia. "I must admit being surprised," wrote Frederick the Great in 1770, "that persons of the highest class would raise their
children like chorus girls": [66]

> What! Was their destiny not to become mothers? Should one not direct
> all their instruction toward this goal, should one not inspire them early
> on against anything that could dishonor them, or make them understand
> the advantages of wisdom, which are useful and long-lasting, instead of
> those of beauty, which will pass and fade? Should one not render them
> capable of instilling good morals in their children? . . . I swear to you that
> I am often indignant when I think about the extent to which this half of
> the human race is disdained in Europe, to the point of neglecting every-
> thing that might perfect their reason.

The king's observations were echoed in 1782 by the reforming Polish
prince Adam Czartoryski, who likewise insisted on the importance of
mothers and the necessity that they be well educated, conversant with
public affairs, promoters of "citizenship, courage, capacity for public
service," and in particular that they teach their children Polish and promote Polish (not French) culture. Mothers were, for Czartoryski, the
very keystone to the future success of any Polish state.[67]

Motherhood, then, was no purely domestic matter; it was clearly seen
as a desirable and important sociopolitical or public function by these
progressive, socially minded men. Civic or patriotic motherhood could
be women's form of citizenship; indeed educating mothers could be construed as a national obligation! What may surprise modern readers is
that many elite women thought this new role quite wonderful. What
men and women of the Enlightenment were critiquing was a set of customary practices that had allegedly denied women of rank and wealth
the opportunity to mother. Consider, for instance, the critique by
Madeleine d'Arsant de Puisieux, who in 1749 had objected to mothers
who pawned off their daughters' education on uneducated governesses
or on convents.[68] Moreover, the arguments directed at women in the
1760s to encourage them to nurse their own babies, rather than employ-
ing wet nurses, struck a responsive chord among many elite women.
Rousseau was not alone in touting the virtues of breast-feeding for his
fictional role model Julie. Madame d'Épinay expressed in her fictionalized memoirs her great regret at being prevented from nursing or rearing
her own two children.[69] In the mid-1770s Madame de Montanclos raised

the theme of enlightened motherhood to new heights in the *Journal des Dames*, even as she insisted that women could both become mothers and pursue careers of their choosing.[70]

In the 1780s, in a French-language tract entitled (in translation) *How Women Should Be Viewed; or, Perspectives on What Women Have Been, What They Are, and What They Might Become*, Madame de Coicy rearticulated Madame d'Épinay's complaint, pointing out that French women of the highest ranks were not even allowed to mother; their children were taken from them, turned over first to nurses, then to governesses, then tutors. In this critique of upper-class life, she speaks of motherhood as "the most beautiful and important occupation," but one denied to women of rank.[71] In the context of the eighteenth century, breast-feeding one's own infant had become, for these women, an aspect of what Joan Hinde Stewart has since called "the struggle of these heroines for self-ownership."[72] Nor was the subversive quality of nursing as a threat to male control lost on Prussian lawmakers; under the consolidated Civil Code of 1794, healthy wives would be "required" to nurse their babies, but their husbands would be given the legal right to tell them when to stop![73]

MOVEMENTS, MOMENTS, AND OTHER

POSSIBILITIES

In her novel *Voyage de Milord Céton dans les sept planètes* (1765–66), Marie-Anne de Roumier (dame Robert) wrote:[74]

> I am always astonished that women have not yet banded together, formed a separate league, with an eye to avenging themselves against male injustice. May I live long enough to see them make such profitable use of their minds. But up until now, they have been too coquettish and dissipated to concern themselves seriously with the interests of their sex.

In 1784 the anonymous author of a one-act comedy *Le Club des dames* (The Women's Club, attributed to Madame de Genlis) called Descartes back from the grave to preside over a women's club engaged in reforming the status of women.[75]

It would certainly be misleading to make exaggerated claims either for the size of the feminist following during the European Enlightenment or for its level of organization; indeed, as Roumier Robert's utopian novel makes clear, despite many and repeated flashes of insight, there was no formally organized feminist movement as such during these years. Indeed, there were few organized reform movements of any kind in eighteenth-century Europe. Such organizations existed, at this time, only in the realm of fiction, though for men (and a few women) Freemasonry did offer one possible channel.[76]

But there was clearly a full-blown feminist consciousness in existence among some privileged women and men, and it was already encountering spokesmen for a mounting backlash. Leading Enlightenment critics participated enthusiastically in these debates, along with many other, less well-known analysts of both sexes.

My point in this chapter has been to emphasize the range and extent of claims made on behalf of women's emancipation in Enlightenment Europe, the way in which these claims were communicated primarily through the print medium, and to suggest some effects of their transmission. In at least a few European countries (where the Inquisition had long since lost its power and even secular censorship efforts were increasingly ineffective), a significant public discussion had emerged among literate women and men (aristocratic and middle-class, no doubt), out of which action for change in women's condition might be generated and find support. Such complaints and arguments for dramatic improvements in women's status, in parallel with many other reformist ideas that floated like foam on the currents of Enlightenment thinking, were ready and available to be skimmed off and acted upon if and when the time became ripe. That time came in 1789, when Louis XVI, the king of France, convened the Estates-General and inaugurated a series of dramatic political events that would become known to history as the French Revolution.

3

Challenging Masculine Aristocracy

Feminism and the French Revolution

The French Revolution (1789–95) provoked both a political and a cultural cataclysm in European history. Indeed, as the historian Margaret Darrow has aptly noted, "a Revolution that transformed time with a new calendar, space with new measurements, social identity with a new form of address (*citoyen*), and even personal identity with a host of new names like Gracchus and Égalité could hardly leave the family unchanged."[1] All existing institutions and practices were called into question, including relations between the sexes and family organization. Feminism was not "born" in 1789, but the onset of the revolution unleashed a spectacular eruption of well-formulated feminist claims; it seemed to some as if Mount Vesuvius itself had once again exploded. The gushing forth of feminist concerns articulated in France at a white heat would spread relentlessly and irresistibly throughout Europe.

Because of this outpouring, the first five years of the French Revolution provide an unparalleled historical laboratory for studying European gender politics. From the convocation of the Estates General in early 1789 (to address the serious financial and economic problems of the realm) to the formation of the estates as a National Assembly later that summer, and throughout the sequential efforts to elaborate constitutions in 1790–91 and 1792–95, feminist claims were repeatedly made and rebutted. Primed by earlier claims, including those of Condorcet, women spoke out on their own behalf, demanding personal emancipation and full citizenship—as women and as half of humanity—in the new regime that was under construction. Revolutionary men made political decisions that would position these women within public life or even exclude them from it. Both revolutionary women and men attempted to manipulate and control a complex outpouring of words, symbols, and images that swirled about "the feminine."

Within days of the convoking of the Estates General, women in France began speaking up in print on concerns particular to their sex. Perhaps the first direct published appeal was the *Pétition des femmes du Tiers-État au Roi* (Petition of Women of the Third Estate to the King), dated 1 January 1789.[2] The anonymous authors of this petition, which was dated prior to the royal edict that established the ground rules for the elections, asked, first, that women's voices be heard and that the king take up their cause. They placed no great hopes in the Estates General; indeed they seemed skeptical about the election process itself. Reflecting earlier Enlightenment complaints, the petition detailed the women's problems: a flawed education, a disadvantaged economic position (its authors objected particularly to men's usurping women's trades, especially the needle trades), and grave disabilities for women in the marriage market. "We ask to be enlightened, to have work, not in order to usurp men's authority, but in order to be better esteemed by them. . . . We ask to come out of the state of ignorance, to be able to give our children a sound and reasonable education so as to make of them subjects worthy of serving you."[3]

This petition heralded a groundswell of petitions, pamphlets, grievances, and addresses authored by, or presumed to be authored by women. Such documents, long buried in French libraries and archives, continue to be rediscovered and republished; the claims they make are remarkable. In one such text, a group of women known as the merchant flower sellers (*marchandes bouquetières*), formerly part of a Parisian female corporation that had been dissolved during the economic liberalization measures of 1776–77, detailed the problems created by that dissolution. Their trade, they argued, had been invaded by less skilled women, often women of disreputable moral character; these flower sellers argued that with such competition they could not earn enough to live on. They asked for the reestablishment of their regulated corporation, challenging the notion of individual freedom to engage in commerce; they insisted that such "indeterminate liberty" destroyed the necessary balance between well-regulated trade and their own ability to support their children.[4] These women had a firmly developed sense of their identities as tradeswomen, exhibiting what the historian Temma Kaplan has described as "female consciousness,"[5] and they understood that their problems could be resolved only through governmental action.

Two more explicitly feminist complaints were circulated sometime that spring. The first, "Remonstrances, Complaints, and Grievances of

French Ladies, on the Occasion of Assembling the Estates General,"
dated 5 March 1789, may have been a spoof. The message, however, was
politically radical: "They wish to persuade us that this respectable assembly . . . as it is presented to us, can truly represent the entire nation,
whereas more than half the nation does not sit there, is excluded from it.
This, Messieurs, is a problem, one injurious to our sex."[6]

Another pamphlet, signed by a still unidentified Madame B*** B***
from the Pays de Caux (Normandy), elaborated this point. She addressed
her words "in this moment of general revolution" to "the tribunal of the
nation," insisting that the women property owners of the Third Estate
(as well as the women fief holders and women religious of the first and
second estates, who could vote by proxy for representatives to the Estates General) also be given the opportunity to register their grievances.
Going further than the authors of the "Petition," Madame B*** B***
spoke of "the prejudices that make us slaves," and "the injustice with
which we are plucked at birth (at least in some provinces) of the goods
that nature and equity should assure us." She called for the *representation of women by women* in the Estates General ("women should be represented only by women") and sounded a sharply worded protest against
the double standard of sexual morality inscribed as "honor." "Why," she
asked, "does one sex have everything and the other nothing?"[7]

Was Madame B*** B*** responding, perhaps, to the distinction made
in July 1789 by the deputy-cleric Abbé Sièyes between active and passive
rights, active and passive citizenship, in which latter category were included women, children, foreigners, and those "who contribute nothing
to the maintenance of the public establishment"?[8] In Sièyes's formulation lay the beginning of a gendered separation that would ultimately
distinguish the French approach to citizenship from that of other nations: between *civil* (property) rights, which the revolution would accord
to single adult women in 1791, and *civic* (political) rights.

GENDERING CITIZENSHIP

When the National Assembly promulgated the Declaration of the Rights
of Man and the Citizen on the night of 26–27 August 1789, women were
not mentioned. Was "citizen" then a universal category, or were *citoyens* male, as distinct from *citoyennes*? Was *citoyenne* a paradoxical category, as one recent analyst would have us believe?[9] An implicit answer
was immediately forthcoming, when on the following day (27 August)
the National Assembly reaffirmed the so-called Salic Law, which had
been deliberately reinvented in the late sixteenth century to exclude

women from succession to the French throne. Given that the eldest child of Louis XVI and Marie Antoinette, the Princess Royal, was female, the Assembly's act was a political statement about the gender of politics in the new order. At the end of the year (22 December 1789), the National Assembly followed Sièyes's lead by distinguishing active and passive citizens, thereby purposefully omitting women from the new electorate embodying the sovereign nation.[10]

Some French women were discontent with the expression of the Rights of Man, insisting in "Motions Addressed to the National Assembly in Favor of the Sex," that "the first and most sacred of the rights of man was to make his companion happy."[11] Others insisted that women as a sex had a political role to play as *citoyennes*. In September, women of the bourgeoisie and artisan classes presented the National Assembly with gifts of their most precious jewelry, to stave off the bankruptcy of the kingdom. Such "patriotic gifts" were accompanied by invocations of historical precedents by Roman matrons and statements of principle about "heroic sacrifice."[12] British wives could not have done this; "their" property belonged to their husbands.

Then, on 5 October 1789, provoked by scarcity of bread and high prices in Paris, and led by the market women, some six thousand women marched to Versailles, in heavy rain, accompanied by members of the National Guard, to seek help from the king and the National Assembly. This march was *the* women's political event that captured the imagination of contemporaries as well as that of subsequent commentators. It cannot be considered a "feminist" event, and indeed it became antifeminists' example of choice to dispute feminist claims and perpetuate women's exclusion from political life. Edmund Burke's livid characterization of the crowd's procession back to Paris in his *Reflections on the Revolution in France* even evoked images of a witches' Sabbath: "The royal captives who followed in the train were slowly moved along, amidst the horrid yells, and shrilling screams, and frantic dances, and infamous contumelies, and all the unutterable abominations of the furies of hell, in the abused shape of the vilest of women."[13]

Though vivid, Burke's denunciation was hardly fair. There was a long tradition in France of women's participation in food riots, or what scholars now refer to as "subsistence crises." Women, considered primarily responsible for feeding their families, were empowered to protest when bread was lacking. The announced goal of the Parisian market women was to "bring back the baker, his wife, and the little apprentice [*mitron*]," on the theory that if the royal family lived in Paris, Parisians would be fed. They succeeded, amidst much astonishment, uncertainty, and considerable bloodshed fomented by members of the crowd. Henceforth, the royal family would reside in Paris, where it would effectively remain hostage to the common people. The celebrated French historian Jules Michelet later exclaimed of this event: "The men took the Bastille, and the women took the king!" ("Les hommes ont pris la Bastille, et les femmes ont pris le roi!")[14]

Not long after the women's march on Versailles, a very radical tract appeared with the title *Requête des Dames à l'Assemblée Nationale* (The Ladies' Request to the National Assembly).[15] It bears quoting *in extenso*:

> It is altogether astonishing that, having gone so far along the path of reforms, and having cut down (as the illustrious d'Alembert once put it) a very large part of the forest of prejudices, you would leave standing the oldest and most general of all abuses, the one which excludes the most beautiful and most lovable half of the inhabitants of this vast kingdom from positions, dignities, honors, and especially from the right to sit amongst you. . . .
>
> You have broken the scepter of despotism; you have pronounced the beautiful axiom . . . **the French are a free people**. Yet still you allow thirteen million slaves shamefully to wear the irons of thirteen million despots! You have divined the true equality of rights—and you still unjustly withhold them from the sweetest and most interesting half among you! . . .
>
> Finally, you have decreed that the path to dignities and honors should be open without prejudice to all talents; yet you continue to throw up insurmountable barriers to our own! Do you think, then, that nature, this mother who is so generous to all her children, has been stingy to us, and that she grants her graces and favors only to our pitiless tyrants? Open the great book of the past and see what illustrious women have done in all ages, the honor of their provinces, the glory of our sex, and judge what we would be capable of, if your blind presumption, your masculine aristocracy, did not incessantly chain down our courage, our wisdom, and our talents.

This remarkable indictment of "masculine aristocracy" was followed by six pages on women's contributions to history, drawn from the many works then circulating on the topic. But that was not all. The anonymous authors of this text continued, invoking women's talents and underscoring the power of women's sexual attractiveness to influence men, a factor that could and should be offset by the just act of incorporating women in public affairs: "Give us the possibility to work like you and with you for the glory and happiness of the French people."

The "Ladies' Request" then proposed a decree, including a preamble followed by a series of startling propositions:

Proposal for a Decree

The National Assembly, wishing to reform the greatest and most universal of abuses, and to repair the wrongs of a six-thousand-year-long injustice, has decreed and decrees as follows:

1. All the privileges of the male sex are entirely and irrevocably abolished throughout France;

2. The feminine sex will always enjoy the same liberty, advantages, rights, and honors as does the masculine sex;

3. The masculine gender [genre masculin] will no longer be regarded, even grammatically, as the more noble gender, given that all genders, all sexes, and all beings should be and are equally noble;

4. That no one will henceforth insert in acts, contracts, obligations, etc., this clause, so common but so insulting for women: That the wife is authorized by her husband before those present, because in the household both parties should enjoy the same power and authority;

5. That wearing pants [la culotte] will no longer be the exclusive prerogative of the male sex, but each sex will have the right to wear them in turn;

6. When a soldier has, out of cowardice, compromised French honor, he will no longer be degraded as is the present custom, by making him wear women's clothing; but as the two sexes are and must be equally honorable in the eyes of humanity, he will henceforth be punished by declaring his gender to be neuter;

7. All persons of the feminine sex must be admitted without exception to the district and departmental assemblies, elevated to municipal responsibilities and even as deputies to the National Assembly, when they fulfill the requirements set forth in the electoral laws. They will have both consultative and deliberative voices . . . ;

8. They can also be appointed as magistrates: there is no better way to reconcile the public with the courts of justice than to seat beauty and to see the graces presiding there;

9. The same applies to all positions, compensations, and military dignities. . . .

Nothing is known about the authors of this document or the immediate context that produced it. The wording of the text, however, ranks it among the most radical feminist statements of the revolution. The denunciation of masculine aristocracy in the "Ladies' Request" is echoed in subsequent published texts by women, while the invocation of "gender" in reference to sociopolitical constructions of the sexes rearticulates earlier Enlightenment feminist contributions. Its explicit call for an end to all the privileges of the male sex is perhaps the most radical formulation of feminist claims made during the entire eighteenth century. Ending male privilege is a different and far more confrontational formulation than demanding equal rights.

The issue of women's citizenship can thus be seen as a central issue around which the entire revolutionary era can be reinterpreted. The French feminist manifestos of 1789 issued a direct challenge to the abstraction of "universal" man. Women's citizenship looked paradoxical only through the eyes of its opponents. What these texts suggest is that revolutionary legislators would confront the provocative question of women's citizenship, as well as other intertwined issues raised earlier concerning marriage and divorce, the education of girls, women's employment, and the thorny problems of poverty and prostitution in a highly charged deliberative atmosphere. Women's complete emancipation was eminently "thinkable"—and eminently threatening.

How was citizenship for women to be thought about in 1789? Earlier in the eighteenth century, under the French monarchy, a *citizen* was customarily identified as a *subject* of the king, one practicing the same religion. Thus, to be considered a French citizen, a man needed only to exhibit signs of Catholic conformity; this effectively excluded both Protestants and Jews up to the time of the Revolution.[16] Citizenship then carried none of the connotations of free property-holding independence already identified with the British model of citizenship (which was gendered even more strongly masculine, since married English women could own no property of their own). Diderot's *Encyclopédie* (vol. 3, 1753) underscored a masculine identification, along with family headship: "This term can be accorded to women, young children, and servants only as members of a *citoyen*'s family, but they are not really citizens."[17] As the historian Dominique Godineau has underscored, "women could not be political individuals," but in the prerevolutionary context, "political individuals" represented families, not merely themselves.[18]

Once the Declaration of the Rights of Man had been formulated in 1789, citizens would be differently identified: property connotations (which had been articulated in the French context by the Physiocrats and endorsed by Condorcet) became associated with citizenship and were quickly confirmed in the electoral arrangements that distinguished between "active" and "passive" citizens, both categories of which turned out to be male. To this was added the privilege of serving in the militia— the right to bear arms—as an integral function of citizenship. This development owed a great deal to classical republican precedents, as reclaimed by the American (and earlier British) revolutionary tradition, which was familiar to educated persons in France.

Controversy over women's claims to citizenship—as women—began to heat up again in 1790, as the Constituent Assembly attempted to elaborate a new constitution for France, a task that bore fruit only in September 1791. During this debate over the first constitution, two of the most eloquent and best-known statements on behalf of women's rights and citizenship were published: Condorcet's *Sur l'Admission des femmes au droit de cité* (Plea for the Citizenship of Women, July 1790), and Olympe de Gouges's *Déclaration des Droits de la femme et de la citoyenne* (Declaration of the Rights of Woman and *Citoyenne*, in or about September 1791). These texts connected the woman question directly to the concurrent debates on the issue of black slavery in the French colonies, to the emancipation of the Jews, and, more generally, to appeals to natural rights and reason.

The Marquis de Condorcet was one of the great humanistic thinkers of the French Enlightenment and a distinguished mathematician and philosopher. He was one of the very few *philosophes* to take part in the revolutionary assemblies. Like Poullain de la Barre a century earlier, Condorcet in his short "Plea," argued that all human beings, of both sexes, possessed natural rights based on their common foundation in *reason*: [19]

> Now the rights of men result only from this, that men are beings with sensibility, capable of acquiring moral ideas, and of reasoning on these ideas. So women, having these same qualities, have necessarily equal rights. Either no individual of the human race has genuine rights, or else all have the same; and he who votes against the right of another, whatever the religion, colour, or sex of that other, has henceforth abjured his own.

Condorcet did not argue that men and women were exactly alike; indeed much in his argument refers to the distinctiveness of the sexes; his point, echoing earlier Enlightenment discussion, was about the social construction of gender: "It is not nature, it is education, it is the manner of social life, which is the cause of this difference." He squarely confronted and refuted objections based on "public utility," including the issues of women's influence and the issue of political activism diverting them from their assigned tasks. He concluded with a call to extend the vote to all women property holders.

The playwright and essayist Olympe de Gouges framed her critique in more confrontational terms: "Men, are you capable of being just? It is a woman who asks you this question. . . . Tell me! Who has given you the sovereign authority to oppress my sex?"[20] She then called for a *national assembly of women*—mothers, daughters, and sisters—and for the adoption of a Declaration of the Rights of Woman and (Female) Citizen.

Critiquing the Declaration of the Rights of Man, which had defined "the nation" as the source of all sovereignty, Olympe de Gouges reappropriated and redefined the nation as *the union of woman and man*. In seventeen separate articles, she called for equal participation and equal treatment under the law for both sexes, based on the laws of nature and reason. But she was particularly eloquent on the subjects of national education and conjugal contracts. Improvising on Rousseau's notion of the "social contract," Gouges's "Declaration" ends with an astonishingly modern "model for a social contract between a man and a woman."

Such claims did not go without comment. The radical republican journalist Louis-Marie Prudhomme, a disciple of Rousseau, confronted Condorcet's arguments, as well as claims raised in recent women's petitions. He invoked the bad effects of women's intrigues during the monarchies of Louis XV and Louis XVI as an argument against women's inclusion in the nation: "The reign of courtesans precipitated the nation's ruin; the empire of queens consummated it."[21] Women, in Prudhomme's opinion, must never, ever leave their households. In contrast, the *Journal of the Rights of Man* (10 Aug. 1791) agreed that women did have a strong claim for rights. Its editors argued, however—as had many French feminists—that these claims must be based on women's "difference" from men, not on their commonalities, based on abstract notions such as Reason.[22]

INTERPRETING "PUBLIC UTILITY" AS
DOMESTICITY FOR WOMEN

The Declaration of the Rights of Man had stipulated that civil distinctions could be based only on the principle of "public utility." The Constitution of 1791, which was finally promulgated by the Constituent Assembly in late September (following an abortive attempt by the king and queen to flee France), invoked the principle of public utility to deny claims for women's rights and citizenship based on commonalities and reason, even as it reformulated marriage as a civil contract. On the basis of women's constitutional exclusion from political rights, therefore, the defrocked clergyman and legislator Talleyrand then argued (against Condorcet and his allies) for a purely domestic "interior" role and education for women.[23] Talleyrand invoked the principle of public utility to keep women out of political life. He curtly dismissed all appeals to abstract principles, and tellingly invoked men's fear of rivalry from women to support his case.

> It is impossible here to separate questions relative to women's education from an examination of their political rights. When raising [daughters],

one must thoroughly understand their destination. If we acknowledge that [women] have the same rights as men, they must be given the same means to make use of them. If we think that their share should be uniquely domestic happiness and the duties of the household [la vie inté- rieure], they should be formed early on to fill this destiny.

Talleyrand elaborated this point at length:

It seems incontestable to us that the common happiness, especially that of women, requires that they do not aspire to exercise rights and political functions. One must seek their best interest in the will of nature. . . . The less they participate in forming the law, the more they will receive from it protection and strength; . . . especially when they renounce all political rights, they will acquire the certainty of seeing their civil rights substantiated and even expanded.

And indeed, even though the Constitution of 1791 reformulated marriage as a civil contract, in 1792 the Legislative Assembly accorded full civil (property) rights only to single adult women, even as it denied them civic (political) rights.

Across the English Channel, Talleyrand's arguments were challenged as evidence of male tyranny by Mary Wollstonecraft in her *Vindication of the Rights of Woman* (1792), a sequel to her earlier reply to Burke, *A Vindication of the Rights of Man*. Political rights were, in her view, natural rights based on common possession of reason, and subjugating women was both "inconsistent and unjust": [24]

Who made man the exclusive judge, if woman partake with him the gift of reason?
    In this style, argue tyrants of every denomination, from the weak king to the weak father of a family; they are all eager to crush reason; yet always assert that they usurp its throne only to be useful. Do you not act a similar part when you *force* all women, by denying them civil and political rights, to remain immured in their families groping in the dark? . . . But, if women are to be excluded, without having a voice, from a participation of the natural rights of mankind, prove first, to ward off the charge of injustice and inconsistency, that they want reason—else this flaw in your NEW CONSTITUTION will ever show that man must, in some shape act like a tyrant; and tyranny, in whatever part of society it rears its brazen front, will ever undermine morality.

Talleyrand's positioning of women's education and social roles as contingent on their ostensibly nonpolitical status carried the day against Condorcet, Gouges, and Wollstonecraft. But their challenges had not fallen on deaf ears. Others had already taken up the argument for women's participation in political life, such as the Dutch feminist Etta

Palm d'Aelders, who agitated on behalf of women's rights in the Parisian *Cercle social*, and the young mother of four Elizabeth-Bonaventure La-faurie, in western Gascony, who in 1791 refuted in print eight objections against women's political participation.[25] Outside France, others who had been following the revolutionary debates joined in. In an extremely radical anonymously published tract, *On Improving the Status of Women* (1792), the prominent Königsberg (East Prussia) administrator Theo-dor Gottlieb von Hippel likewise queried the grounds for eliminating women from citizenship and from full participation in governmental af-fairs. He was joined by the Swedish writer Thomas Thorild, who argued that women were first of all human beings, entitled to the same rights as men, and also that women were in fact superior to men.[26]

For quite some time "public utility" would remain contested terrain in the revolutionary gender wars. By 1793—in the face of domestic chaos, civil war, and the threat of foreign invasion—arguments about women's differences from men, reinforced by repeated appeals to the authority of Jean-Jacques Rousseau and to distinctions between public and private grounded in "Nature," would prove decisive in evicting women from civic life and in reaffirming the political necessity of their subordination in marriage.

But women who aspired to exercise a public role would not go with-out a struggle. Indeed, the slogan of "public utility" could also be wield-ed effectively by feminist women, particularly in their efforts to organize women's clubs during the early 1790s. In these clubs, organized not only in Paris by women such as Etta Palm but also in provincial towns and villages, women claimed recognition and support from public authori-ties as organizers of what we would now call social and educational work in a variety of areas—relief to the poor and the unemployed, to needy mothers, girls, and children, to the sick—often taking over where Catho-lic charitable efforts had foundered in the wake of the revolutionary secularization of the church.

If wifehood could be used to exclude women from citizenship, moth-erhood offered an incontrovertible basis for claiming the right to inter-vene in public affairs. Club women justified their clubs and their civic intervention by invoking their roles as mothers, as caretakers, and as educators.[27] One woman even argued in a letter to the National Assem-bly that motherhood should qualify women to be citizens of the State.[28] These exchanges promoted the elaboration of relational arguments based on the public utility of "civic motherhood," "mother-educators," and "social housekeeping"; such arguments would provide extremely important platforms for feminist activism in nation-building contexts throughout the nineteenth and early twentieth centuries. Not only individual claims to a common reason, but relational arguments—based in women's distinctive roles and characteristics, and their contributions to public welfare through performance of their extended familial responsibilities—could provide telling arguments against women's subordination in late eighteenth-century Europe. In fact, if we are to believe Elke and Hans-Christian Harten, the arguments on behalf of civilizing motherhood—indeed the mythologizing of motherhood and the celebration of redeeming womanhood—took on a wholeheartedly eschatological quality as the revolution proceeded toward symbolic parricide, particularly after the Convention's vote to execute the king in early 1793. In this vision of civic womanhood, "the division of roles between the sexes is not justified by relations of subordination but by principled equality that took account of differences and the natural affections that concern men as much as women."[29]

CLOSING THE WOMEN'S CLUBS: "LET THE MEN MAKE THE REVOLUTION!"

With the calling of the Convention in August 1792 to frame a new government and the September proclamation of a republic, the French debate over women and citizenship entered a new phase. Claims for women's complete equality with men were loudly and vigorously restated as the Convention undertook work on a second constitution. At first, the new republic seemed to offer promising ground for the realization of women's claims to equality as well as to participate in public service.

But the new organizations established by women, particularly those unsupervised by men, aroused suspicion among certain well-placed revolutionaries, who continued to insist that women's place was at home and that men could represent their interests quite adequately.

In the early months of 1793, following the trial and execution of Louis XVI (now vulgarly referred to as Louis Capet), the journalist Prudhomme learned of the establishment of two women's clubs in provincial cities. He criticized their practices of electing presidents, keeping minutes of their meetings, inviting local authorities to attend their deliberations, studying the social contract, and singing hymns to liberty. He lashed out against such activities in the columns of his widely read publication *Les Révolutions de Paris*:[30]

> In the name of the *patrie*, the love of which these women carry in their hearts, in the name of nature, from which one must never stray, in the

name of good domestic morals, of which women's clubs are a plague because of the dissipation that follows in their wake, we conjure the good *citoyennes* of Lyon to stay at home, to watch over their households, without worrying about reforming the catechism of Bishop Lamourette, and without having the pretension to read the social contract. We conjure them to think of the wrongs they would cause, without a doubt, to the republic, if each town, each little *burg* in France were to imitate them. There would be clubs everywhere, and soon there would be no well-maintained households.

To Prudhomme's way of thinking, as to that of many other Jacobin men, any participation whatsoever in civic life by women would distract them from their foreordained domestic duties. But the privileges of masculinity—and the maleness of citizenship—nevertheless required reassertion.

The presidents of the two women's clubs in question quickly countered Prudhomme's charges. Blandine Demoulin, president of the Dijon Société des Amies de la République, waxed particularly eloquent on the necessity for women's civic activity:[31]

> Truly, we are astonished by such language coming from you; can it be that women, who today have risen closer to the height of the revolution than even a [certain] republican, must give him lessons in philosophy and liberty? ...
>
> Among all forms of government, republican government most closely approaches nature; and in such a government each individual is an integral part of the whole and should cooperate in all that concerns the welfare of the republic; it necessarily follows that women, who are part of society, should contribute, as much as they are able, to the common good.
>
> ... Our revolution—unique in world history—requires from all citizens of the republic a tribute of work, wealth, or knowledge; [thus] it is quite natural that the *citoyennes* who are proud to be part of it should make themselves useful to the commonweal [*la chose publique*] and offer advice on ways to do so. To accomplish this in an advantageous and surer manner, they must meet. For what can individuals accomplish in isolation? It is from the fraternal meeting of *républicaines* that these astonishing effects of philosophic enlightenment have resulted, which, in freeing women from the antique prejudices that vilified them, have renewed in women the seed of the virtues they are destined to transmit to all the French from their earliest infancy....
>
> Then renounce your system, Citizen Prudhomme, which is as despotic toward women as was aristocracy toward the people. It is time for a revolution in the morals of women; it is time to reestablish them in their natural dignity. What virtue can one expect from a slave! ... Wherever women are slaves, men are subject to despotism.

Prudhomme remained unpersuaded by Madame Demoulin's eloquence (which echoed many themes developed earlier by Condorcet and Wollstonecraft), and in a final rejoinder he sought refuge in the authority of Rousseau: "You take care of your household government, and let us take care of the republic; let the men make the revolution."[32]

In April 1793, the government took a first step, formally excluding women from serving in the French armies, even as a crescendo of claims for women's civic equality reached the floor of the Convention during the constitutional debates. New tracts, including Deputy Pierre Guyomar's speech "Partisan of Political Equality between Individuals," recast the arguments of Condorcet and others to argue for citizenship as an absolute individual right, irrespective of sex or race. Guyomar argued that liberty and equality belonged equally to man and woman; if not, he insisted, "the immortal declaration of rights contains a mortal exclusion."[33] The Convention rejected Guyomar's arguments in considering the final version of the Constitution of 1793, which was finally promulgated in mid-June. This time "man" really did mean "male."

Militant Parisian women considered that revolutionary men continued to need their help, including their armed force. In May 1793 the Parisian Society of Revolutionary Republican *Citoyennes* was established, and quickly developed ties with the voting citizens of the Parisian *sections*. This group was not, strictly speaking, what we would call feminist; its members did not privilege the emancipation of women as such, but instead claimed for women a major role as defenders of the nation against internal and external subversion, a role that even carried terrorist connotations. Members of this group played a significant role in ousting the Girondins from the Convention, and boldly campaigned against profiteers and other so-called enemies of the nation.

Not surprisingly, however, the deliberate exclusion of women from positions of leadership in the new republic clearly rankled some members of the Society of Revolutionary Republican *Citoyennes*. In the one extant report of a society meeting, a woman speaker began with a rousing account of women's heroics in history to argue for women's suitability for military combat and governmental authority, and to ask that the exclusion of women from such positions be reconsidered.[34] In another meeting, as a martial standard was presented to the society by the *citoyennes* of the Section des Droits de l'Homme, this theme found its echo: "Why should women, gifted with the faculty of feeling and explaining their thoughts, see themselves excluded from public affairs? The Declaration of Rights is common to both sexes, and the difference consists in duties; there are public ones and private ones." Women's private duties as wives and mothers could be reconciled, without difficulty, with surveillance activities and instruction, in the thinking of the section's women.[35]

The fate of the women's clubs and of women's access to any political roles would ultimately turn on resolution of the far-reaching and deliberate challenge to male leadership posed by groups like the Society of Revolutionary Republican *Citoyennes*. The murder of Jean-Paul Marat in July at the hand of Charlotte Corday (who was neither Parisian nor a member of the society) had considerably heightened the Jacobins' level of anxiety about contributions to "disorder" by women in general. This event was followed by a series of confrontations during the autumn months of 1793, in which members of the society themselves embarked on a campaign of direct physical intimidation to force dissenting market women to wear not only the tricolored cockade, which had been approved for women, but also the red cap of liberty. The market women objected. They insisted that the red cap in particular was an emblem of male dress, and they retaliated against the *Citoyennes* by demanding the dissolution of all women's clubs.

With this handy excuse, the Jacobin men immediately called for a crackdown on these politically militant women in the name of public order. In a report to the Committee of General Security of the Convention, just one day later (9 Brumaire, Year II, or 30 October 1793) André Amar raised two basic questions about women's citizenship:[36] "(1) Can women exercise political rights and take an active part in affairs of government? (2) Can they deliberate together in political associations or popular societies?" Responding to them, he raised questions about women's moral and physical strength relative to that of men, and appealed to Nature's assignment of different duties to women than to men; ultimately, he argued, the important question was one of morality. The conclusion was that the Convention voted to prohibit "clubs and popular societies of women, by whatever name they are known," and to decree that "all sessions of popular societies must be public."

Two prominent historians of women's role in the French Revolution, Darline Gay Levy and Harriet Applewhite, view the Jacobin repression of 9 Brumaire as "an extreme political response to the militant citizenship that women had been practicing since 1789."[37] These scholars consider the situation up to this point to have been remarkably fluid (and my inquiry supports this view); no longer would this be the case. With this act of 1793, not only the members of the Society of Revolutionary Republican *Citoyennes* but all French women were firmly banished from political life under the new republic.

In mid-November, the Municipal Council of Paris went further than the Convention, refusing even to receive a delegation of red-capped women, and chastising their behavior. The angry procureur-syndic of the Commune, Pierre-Gaspard Chaumette, heaped scorn on the delegation:[38]

> Since when is it permitted to give up one's sex? Since when is it decent to see women abandoning the pious cares of their households, the cribs of their children, to come to public places, to harangues in the galleries, at the bar of the senate? Is it to men that nature confided domestic cares? Has she given us breasts to breast-feed our children? . . .
>
> Impudent women who want to become men, aren't you well enough provided for? What else do you need? . . . In the name of this very nature [as despots of love], remain what you are, and far from envying us the perils of a stormy life, be content to make us forget them in the heart of our families, in resting our eyes on the enchanting spectacle of our children made happy by your cares.

This profoundly antifeminist Jacobin message was hammered home by the publication two days later (29 Brumaire) in the *Feuille de Salut Public* of a vitriolic condemnation of "political women," accompanied by a reminder to women of their subordinate place in the new republican order. Invoking the three recent executions of Queen Marie Antoinette, Olympe de Gouges, and Manon Roland, and condemning their alleged treacheries and illusions, the editors issued this authoritative advice, underscoring the new republican moral order:[39]

> Women, do you wish to be *républicaines*? Then love, follow, and teach the laws that remind your spouses and children to exercise their rights. . . . Be simple in your dress; work hard in your household; never attend the popular assemblies with the idea of speaking up, but rather with the idea that your presence there will sometimes encourage your children.

At the end of November, the Paris Commune capped these admonitions with a decree abolishing women's clubs and another outlawing cross-dressing, with a view to keeping women not only at the hearth but also in skirts.[40] In May 1795 the Convention shut women out from its tribunes and from attendance at political meetings, and prohibited them from parading in the streets in groups of more than five.

The French republican regime, by confirming its definition of citizenship and political space, was henceforth gendered male. But a century of feminist claims had forced the men of the French republic to make their

arguments explicit; henceforth, proponents of excluding women would
no longer predicate their prescriptions concerning women's roles and responsibilities on arguments from public utility, as Talleyrand had done,
but on physical differences based in Nature. Learned arguments based on
"natural differences" between the sexes would henceforth be greatly
elaborated, in parallel with efforts to enforce such differences by building
categorical barriers between the public and the private spheres.

DODGING THE COUNTERREVOLUTIONARY
BACKLASH

The explosive eruption of feminist claims that characterized the early
years of the revolution subsided in the face of antifeminist efforts to stuff
the proliferating fissures with counterarguments that might effectively
reseal the crust of patriarchy. Only thus could male right to contain and
confine women politically, legally, intellectually, and emotionally be reasserted. In the face of such measures, and enveloped by the emotional
heat created by women's arbitrary exclusion from civic life, only a few
stalwart souls continued to insist openly that total equality of the sexes
might be desirable. While in hiding from the Terror, the ever hopeful
Condorcet composed his *Sketch for a Historical Tableau of the Progress
of the Human Mind* (published posthumously in 1795):[41]

> Among the advances in the progress of the human mind that will con-
> tribute most to the general happiness, we must count the thorough de-
> struction of the prejudices which have established an inequality of rights
> between the two sexes, an inequality deadly even to the party it seeks to
> favor. Justification of this principle cannot be found in any differences in
> their respective physical organizations, intellectual strengths, or moral
> sensibilities. This inequality originates solely in abuses of strength, and
> all subsequent sophistical attempts made to excuse it are futile.

But even Condorcet's friend and colleague the physician Pierre-Jean-
Georges Cabanis disagreed with him. Acknowledging that the sexes
were similar in many ways, but insisting even more on the importance
of human physiology and modes of propagation as the underpinning for
all social morality and organization, Cabanis argued (invoking "nature"
in the manner of Rousseau and Pierre Roussel, whose earlier published
opinions on these matters he explicitly admired) that men's and wom-
en's different roles, traits, and lifestyles were fundamentally determined
by their different sexual physiology, which affected their skeletal, mus-
cular, cellular, and nervous systems. Close observation of animal economy, not sheer philosophical speculation, he insisted, was required to

judge such matters. Doctor Cabanis could not resist stating that women had no place in political or civil life, and that women, including learned women (*femmes scvantes*), who thereby stepped beyond the bounds of their sexual destiny, could not possibly attract a man.[42] This influential study would be frequently reprinted; it was constantly quoted by those who opposed the higher education of women during the nineteenth century.

The French philosopher-historian Geneviève Fraisse has ably documented the backlash against women's emancipation in France during the postrevolutionary period 1800–1820, focusing particularly on the debates over and denials of women's intellectual (as well as political and economic) equality with men.[43] She singles out the remarks of the philosopher-physician J.-J. Virey, who articulated a Rousseauean position even more extreme than that of Cabanis: [44]

> Never has a woman risen through the cultivation of her intelligence to these high conceptions of genius in the sciences and literature which seem to be the most sublime conquests of the human mind. . . . Love is women's means of ruling. . . . Her sweetness is her power; her charms are her glory, precious jewels with which nature adorns her in all her magnificence.

Such remarks hardly qualify as misogyny, but in the context of the developing counterrevolution they can certainly be read as antifeminist.

One observant woman writer saw clearly where such arguments were leading. Responding to attacks on female authorship, the poet Constance de Théis Pipelet de Leury (later Princesse de Salm) attested in her long, versified "Letter to Women" (1797):[45]

> But listen now to what the wise man says:
> "Women, do you dare to speak of slavery?
> You whose mere glance can subjugate us all!
> You who enchain us, trembling at your knee!
> Your beauties, feigned tears, perfidious caresses,
> Do they not suffice to make you mistress?
> Then what need have you of further means?
> You tyrannize us! What more do you want?"
> What more do we want! Legitimate power.
> Trickery is the resource of a being oppressed.
> Stop forcing us to these unworthy ruses.
> Give us more rights, you will lose fewer.

She saw clearly through the arguments from "nature" as well:

> Let the anatomist, blinded by his science,
> Artfully calculate the power of a muscle,

> Infer, without appeal, 'twixt the more and the less,
> That his wife owes him eternal respect.

The writer Fanny Raoul, whose work was published by Constance de Salm, articulated her concern about what was happening to French women in the wake of the revolution in these damning words:[46]

> Who has been given the exercise of civil responsibilities? Men. Who has been assured the rights of property? Men. . . . Who has been given the right and privileges of paternity? Men. For whom have liberty and equality been established? Again, men. In sum, everything is by them or for them; it is therefore for them also, and for them alone, that political society has been made; women have no part in it.

This was a depressing conclusion to the odyssey toward equal citizenship that some women and men had embarked upon with such high hopes in 1789.

BEYOND FRANCE: EMANCIPATIONIST INITIATIVES AND THE EUROPEAN BACKLASH

The controversy over women's rights in the French Revolution had repercussions far beyond France. Similar scenarios and debates erupted in many different locations throughout Europe, though they never produced the same level of turbulence. Contemporary feminist historians are unearthing new evidence about claims made for women's emancipation in Belgium, the Dutch Republic, and the various states and principalities of Italy and Germany, on the heels of the events we have described above for France. Consider, for instance, the 1794 tract on women's rights published in Assisi (in Italy) by a certain Rosa Califronia, who complained that the press talked incessantly about the rights of man:[47]

> One never sees today a reasoned work on the rights of Women. Is it perhaps correct to say that the female sex is also contained in the male species? . . . Have a look at the deadly theater of France, where the RIGHTS of MAN are extolled with much noise. How many benefits for the masculine sex! What system has ever been established for women and for their rights?

More a defense of women than of their rights, this tract was complemented several years later by others, stimulated by the arrival of the French armies and republican occupations in various Italian city-states, including Milan, Rome, and Naples. One such text, a manifesto sent in October 1797 to a newspaper in Genoa, complained bitterly about the outcome of the new constitutional project, objecting in particular to clauses affecting women's rights in marriage. Its author claimed that this manifesto carried the signatures of 2,550 women.[48] In another publication, emanating from Venice and billed as "a woman citizen's speech to the Italians," the anonymous speaker complained:

> We have spent a year already, shut up inside our houses, considering your new plans and your new constitutions. Legislation has been entrusted to men; the government and the magistrature have been assigned to men, as have the embassies, treaties, courts, and armies. In short, the voices of men resound everywhere, while women hear themselves called upon only for matrimonial purposes or quasi-matrimonial purposes in relation to men. Hence, gentlemen who have embraced the new system, you think only of your own advantages and the happiness of the male sex; either you do not consider women individuals of the human race, or you are only thinking of making one half of it happy.

The author then elaborated on two propositions: first, that "women are by nature equal or even superior to men," and second, that "women have the right to take part in all public interests relating to the present reform of Italy."[49]

In 1795 a still unidentified Dutch writer (who signed only as P.B.v.W.) published his or her reflections on the French Declaration of the Rights of Man, arguing *In Defense of the Participation of Women in the Government of the Country* (1795) by condemning the exclusion of women as "arbitrariness" and "despotism." Invoking and going beyond Pufendorff's reflections on natural law, this writer argued: "I do not know from which right we have taken the domination over women upon ourselves, since many a woman has been capable of governing her husband. And who could doubt that women could do absolutely everything, as far as the mind is concerned, as well as men?"[50]

The debate over women's rights and roles even surfaced in the European musical world, as, for example, in Schikaneder's libretto for Mozart's opera *The Magic Flute* (1791). When in Act I Pamina tries to escape from her father, Zoroaster, to return to her mother, the Queen of the Night, Zoroaster remarks: "What would become of Truth and Right if I had left you with your mother?" This revealing statement is followed by his assessment of his former consort: "She is all too proud! By man your course must be decided. For by herself a woman steps beyond her sphere and is misguided." In Haydn's oratorio *The Creation* (first performed in Vienna, 1799), Adam and Eve are provided by the librettist with a duet in which Eve sings about Adam as her protector, her shelter, "my all." "Your will is my law; thus it was decided by the Creator, and to obey you will bring me joy, happiness, and glory."[51] It seems highly unlikely that these Austrian librettists were not participating—in their own fashion—in the revolutionary debate on women. Might this debate have even influenced their choice of subject matter?

Some of these interventions were of passing importance, and others have since lain forgotten in the archives and libraries of Europe; the musical interventions have been sung time and again, but only rarely contextualized. In the German city-states and principalities, however, leading philosophers who had a profound impact in their time and whose works are still read today intervened on the side of constraining women's freedom and civic participation, with serious consequences for the subsequent development of Western political philosophy and the gendering of statecraft. The writings of Kant, Fichte, and Hegel comprise part of any story about antifeminist responses to feminist impulses during and shortly after the French Revolution. To understand their resistance, however, we must first examine the important contributions of Theodor Gottlieb von Hippel, Goethe, and Schlegel.

Writing anonymously in Königsberg, East Prussia (where he was mayor), Hippel had published several contributions to the debate on the woman question. In 1792 he published his most radical tract, *On Improving the Status of Women*, which he wrote after learning that women had not been awarded citizenship rights in France. Influenced by women's history as laid out by the contemporary French writer Louise de Kéralio, by the demonstrated talent of Catherine II of Russia, by the philosophic thought of the Scotsman David Hume, and by the principle of the categorical imperative, developed by his friend the celebrated philosopher Immanuel Kant, Hippel argued that it was *unethical* to suppress women's freedom. Contradicting Jacobin prescriptions of domesticity for women, Hippel developed the case that women not only should be allowed their full freedom as individuals, but they should be able to enter the learned professions; like his Dutch counterpart P.B.v.W, he asserted that many women were clearly competent to become administrators of the state. Taking a still more extreme stand, Hippel queried: "Do I go too far in asserting that the oppression of women is the cause of all the rest of the oppression in the world?"[52]

The pros and cons of women's emancipation were debated in many arenas in the German world. The jurist Ernst Ferdinand Klein, coauthor of the Prussian legal code, questioned in 1798 whether women should have the same rights as men, arguing that men should use their power to protect the weaker sex.[53] The celebrated writer Johann Wolfgang von Goethe addressed the issues in novels such as *Wilhelm Meister* (1795–

96) and *Hermann und Dorothea* (1797), though his fictional heroes more often than not expressed the opinion that women, ruling over their households, had been dealt a better hand than men. The meanings of masculinity and femininity and their relationship to creativity and genius were explored by Wilhelm von Humboldt and Friedrich Schlegel in the mid-1790s. To Humboldt's Aristotelian reaffirmation of masculinity as active and femininity as passive, Schlegel countered with the ethical notion of a higher androgyny: "Womanhood, like manhood, should be elevated into a higher humanity. . . . Only independent womanliness, only gentle manliness are good and beautiful."[54] These writers went on to engage the issue of "free love" in fictional works such as Schlegel's *Lucinde* (1799) and Goethe's *Elective Affinities* (1809).

Immanuel Kant's views on the woman question, however, echoed those of his mentor Rousseau, and in the treatise which is considered the capstone of his philosophical system, *Anthropology from a Pragmatic Point of View* (1798), he elaborated his views on "The Character of the Sexes." The loftiness of Kant's ideals and his analysis of the transcendent possibilities of man disappeared before his acceptance of conventional views on the inferiority, submissiveness, and relative moral position of women, even as he acknowledged women's power and influence. In the *Anthropology*, woman is not to be concerned with the courage to know, or to think for herself; her primary role, like that of Rousseau's Sophie, is to advance the morality of man by manipulating him. In marriage one partner must be subjected to the other, but the traits that are marked "feminine," Kant insisted, develop as civilization advances, precisely for "the management of men."[55]

From the university in Jena, the young and recently married political philosopher Johann Gottlieb Fichte responded directly to the arguments of women's-rights advocates. In *The Science of Rights* (1796), he acknowledged that both sexes did have rights and that the usual arguments against women's exercise of rights, such as lack of education, could all be convincingly contested. He then shifted the grounds of the debate to inquire "whether and in how far the female sex *can desire* to exercise all its rights."[56] Married women, he argued, had *voluntarily* subordinated themselves by consenting to marriage in the first place; their rights are exercised by their husbands, following consultation. This left open only the question of single women, who might at any time marry. What women's rights advocates were really asking, claimed Fichte, was for the public exercise of rights, the external show of citizenship; this, he insisted, was incompatible with femininity itself—which he defined in terms of discretion, modesty, and self-renunciation. For Fichte, the issue of excluding women from the exercise of political rights was not strictly one of public utility, but was grounded in the character of the marriage relationship and in the very concept of femininity, which he viewed as strictly incompatible with public recognition. In Fichte's rigidly Aristotelian thinking, the dichotomies public/private and masculine/feminine were wholly overlaid. For a woman to act in public in her own right was to unsex herself!

With G. W. F. Hegel, these categories become central to a general theory of the state, a theory explicitly elaborated in the postrevolutionary antifeminist context. Hegel had long pondered the relationship of the sexes, especially with respect to issues of love and marriage. In his *Phenomenology of Mind* (1807), he made a case for the ethical character of the family. He remarked the tension between the community's requirements and individual self-interest within the family, pausing to note the gendered character of this tension: "Womankind—the everlasting irony in the life of the community—changes by intrigue the universal purpose of government into a private end, transforms its universal activity into a work of this or that specific individual, and perverts the universal property of the state into a possession and ornament for the family."[57] By 1821 Hegel had posited an entire sociopolitical system based on the differing physical characteristics of the sexes, which harked back to the older dichotomous distinctions active/passive and animal/plant. In a note to his *Philosophy of Right* (1821), Hegel insisted that "when women hold the helm of government, the state is at once in jeopardy, because women regulate their actions not by the demands of universality but by arbitrary inclinations and opinions."[58] In this view, which Hegel exemplified by the story of Antigone, women, because of their interests in the personal and the particular, could not be trusted to operate in accordance with the dictates of the *Ideal Universal Reason*. Therefore, they must be excluded from the operations of the state.

The German political philosophers Fichte and Hegel succeeded in writing women out of the state, but did so in elevated and dispassionate terms, and seemingly without much opposition. In England, by contrast, the reaction against women's emancipation was heated from the very beginning. There, so close to France, the debate over women's rights became inextricably entangled with the debate over the revolution itself, not least because of the way Edmund Burke had condemned the revolution, and the role of women in it, in his *Reflections on the Revolution in France* (1790). To Burke, the revolution seemed to threaten not only the notion of monarchical authority but the very principle of male authority in the family. Burke's arguments set the benchmark for what followed.

Mary Wollstonecraft challenged Burke's *Reflections* in her *Vindication of the Rights of Man* (1790), the work that initially brought her fame. Her *Vindication of the Rights of Woman* (1792) quickly followed. Although Wollstonecraft may not merit her reputation as the "first" English feminist, she became the best-remembered—and retrospectively the most maligned—advocate of women's emancipation in her time. Her language and her arguments, as eloquent as they seem in her opening volley against male tyranny, are by comparison to those of her French counterparts remarkably mild. The body of her work instead addressed the reforming of women's behavior, friendship between the sexes, notions of taste, dignified domesticity, responsible motherhood, and sexual self-control. "I do not wish [women] to have power over men, but over themselves," she exclaimed in reply to Rousseau's insistence that women's power over men would diminish as they came more closely to resemble men.[59] Women's education, viewed as the key to female empowerment and independence, remained a dominant theme in all her writings.

Mary Wollstonecraft was among the very few English writers of either sex to state the case for women's rights so outspokenly. In more covert forms Wollstonecraft's claims were expounded in domestic novels such as Charlotte Smith's *Desmond* (1792), in Thomas Holcroft's *Anna St. Ives* (1792), and in Mary Hays's *Memoirs of Emma Courtney* (1796), as well as in her own novels. Eleanor Ty has noted that political discussions were embedded in these novels, and in others by Helen Maria Williams and Elizabeth Inchbald.[60] Such political critiques could also be found in debates over girls' education, both in fictional form and in educational treatises, as is suggested by the conflicting views of writers such as Maria Edgeworth, in her novel *Belinda* (1801), and Hannah More, both in her *Strictures on the Modern System of Female Education* (1799) and in her novel *Coelebs in Search of a Wife* (1809).

The issue of women's political rights briefly reached the British Parliament in 1797, only to be dismissed out of hand. Speaking on behalf of extension of the franchise, the liberal orator Charles James Fox took pains to assure the House of Commons that unsuitable persons would not become enfranchised by the motion he proposed. He deliberately invoked the negative example of women to elucidate the necessary qualifications for the right to vote—legal and financial independence. Common reason, à la Condorcet, was to him an insignificant criterion. After complimenting the women of England, Fox preemptorily claimed that:[61]

> It must be the genuine feeling of every gentleman who hears me, that all the superior classes of the female sex of England must be more capable

than the uninformed individuals of the lowest class of men to whom the advocates of universal suffrage would extend it. And yet, why has it never been imagined that the right of election should be extended to women? Why? but because by the law of nations, and perhaps also by the law of nature, that sex is dependent on ours; and because, therefore, their voices would be governed by the relation in which they stand in society.

Never imagined, indeed! Political rights for women had certainly been imagined, not only across the Channel, but throughout Europe. But Fox's view was echoed, most influentially, by the philosophical radical James Mill, who claimed (reverting to a family model of politics) in 1814 that "all those individuals whose interests are indisputably included in those of other individuals may be struck off from political rights without inconvenience." These included children, and "also women, . . . the interest of almost all of whom is involved either in that of their fathers, or in that of their husbands."[62] Both Fox and Mill viewed women as irremediably "relative creatures."[63]

The English counteroffensive against proposals for women's emancipation became most closely associated with Hannah More's conservative evangelical Christianity as well as with the rise of English nationalism, which defined itself in opposition to the secular, revolutionary, and even libertine culture of France.[64] William Godwin's publication, following her untimely death in childbirth, of Mary Wollstonecraft's *Memoirs of the Author of a Vindication of the Rights of Woman* (1798), by mentioning her earlier affair with Gilbert Imlay and the birth of her first child out of wedlock, provided damning evidence to enemies of women's rights that to be emancipated was to be sexually wanton; Godwin's earnest attempt to justify his late wife in what by that time had become a repressive political climate ironically served only to discredit feminist claims further. The debate would simmer along underground, marked as much by what had to be read between the lines as by what was said, as the ostensibly nonpolitical novels of Jane Austen amply testified.[65]

Advocacy of women's rights in England was ultimately swamped under a flood of derisive prescriptive publications such as the evangelical Thomas Gisborne's *Enquiry into the Duties of the Female Sex* (1797) and the Reverend Richard Polwhele's venomous condemnation of feminists (and their Gallic ideas) as "a female band despising NATURE's law" in his extensively footnoted poem entitled *The Unsex'd Females* (1798).[66] By 1799, the meek, indeed almost whimpering advocacy of Mary Anne Radcliffe, on behalf of economic opportunities for "poor helpless females" and "unfortunate women," in a work vigorously titled *The Female Advocate; or, An Attempt to Recover the Rights of Women from Male Usurpation*, inadvertently illustrates the extent to which feminists were forced on the defensive.[67]

The backlash that developed in Europe against women's emancipation in the wake of the revolutionary repression was severe, and its consequences would endure for decades. It was manifested in the *Jüdisch Deutsche Monatsschrift*, published in Prague, as much as in the works of the counterrevolutionary French political theorists Louis de Bonald and Joseph de Maistre. But perhaps most important, it was fueled from the political summit. In France, Napoleon, who had crowned himself emperor in 1802, took a personal interest in the elaboration of a Civil Code that deliberately subordinated women in marriage and prescribed their obedience to their husbands in exchange for manly protection. His subsequent military campaigns carried the example of that code throughout Europe, where it served as a model to legislators of many other countries, from Italy to Poland. Although Napoleon likewise took a personal interest in girls' education, establishing schools for the daughters of his meritorious but impecunious male supporters, the members of the Legion of Honor, he did not advocate emancipatory goals: "Make believers of them, not reasoners," Napoleon wrote from the field to the Grand Chancellor of the Legion of Honor in 1807. "I am not raising vendors of style nor housemaids nor housekeepers, but wives for modest and poor households."[68] A practical education, with considerable exposure to manual labor, was prescribed for these girls—no erudition, no theatrical productions, and above all, no distinctions based on class or achievement. For boys, Napoleon established lycées and the French university system. In Italy, however, girls' lycées were established in the wake of the Napoleonic conquests.

Even in the hostile climate of Napoleon's imperial regime, feminist voices were by no means completely silenced. Feminist ideas still simmered, seeking new fissures through which to challenge patriarchal systems once again. Madame Campan, designated to organize the girls' schools for the daughters of Napoleon's legionnaires, still dreamed of a women's university. A few male voices did speak up on women's behalf even in the repressive climate of the early 1800s. One of these was the Parisian poet Gabriel Legouvé, who in 1801 published an influential 92-page poem, *Le Mérite des femmes* (The Merit of Women). Another was a certain *citoyen* Toselli in Milan, who argued that women could and should share in every societal obligation and participate in science and literature. A third was the Vicomte de Ségur, whose 1803 argument for the study of women's history, *Women: Their Condition and Influence in Society*, was immediately translated from French into English. A fourth was an obscure visionary from Franche-Comté, Charles Fourier, who in his *Theory of Four Movements and General Destinies* (1808) denounced "the absence of all justice with respect to women" and reformulated the theme that had so regularly appeared in the works of earlier Enlightenment philosophers and historians:[69]

> As a general thesis: *Social progress and historic changes occur by virtue of the progress of women toward liberty, and decadence of the social order occurs as the result of a decrease in the liberty of women.* Other events influence these political changes, but there is no cause that produces social progress or decline as rapidly as change in the condition of women. . . . In summary, *the extension of women's privileges is the general principle for all social progress.*

Fourier's restatement of this key theme in Enlightenment thought would have important repercussions throughout the nineteenth century, particularly for the development of socialist ideas.

It was the intrepid Madame de Staël, champion of liberty, declared enemy of Napoleon, and undoubtedly the best known woman in Europe during the early nineteenth century, who kept the feminist flag most conspicuously aloft during the years in which Napoleon and his armies had embarked on the conquest of Europe. "I believe a day will come," she wrote in 1800, "when philosophical legislators will give serious attention to the education of women, to the laws protecting them, to the duties which should be imposed on them, to the happiness which can be guaranteed them. . . . If the situation of women in civil society is so imperfect, what we must work for is the improvement of their lot, not the degradation of their minds."[70] The debate on the woman question, and particularly the problems faced by a woman of genius in a repressive society, the difficulty of combining love with the realization of talent, lay at the heart of her life and of her published works, including her widely-read novels *Delphine* (1802) and *Corinne* (1807). Both her life and her works would inspire a new generation of feminist activists after an armed peace—and a male-headed French monarchy—were once again restored to Europe in 1815.

PART II

The Nineteenth Century, 1815–1914

The five chapters of Part II explore the development of feminist theory and practice in the nineteenth century, in parallel with a growing antifeminist backlash. They provide an expanded, updated, and nuanced version of an interpretation that I have been developing since the early 1980s. My account pays close attention to intersections of feminist eruptions with events featured in conventional chronologies in political, intellectual, cultural, economic, and social history—including the development of representative governments, aspirations to democratization, and incipient wars. When feminist demands and criticism are placed at the center of debate, these events take on a far different meaning.[1]

Viewed in retrospect, it seems clear that this turbulent century experienced a steady stream of feminist eruptions, subdued temporarily during periods of political repression but violently explosive in times of revolutionary political upheaval—most notably in the 1830s, in 1848, in 1871, and again in the 1890s. From the 1860s on, feminist challenges developed at a steady pace, flowing expansively throughout the period of accelerating socioeconomic change that spanned the years from the 1890s to 1914.

In the early part of the nineteenth century, though, the forces of repression seemed nearly overwhelming. The shadows cast by the French Revolution and ensuing counterrevolution would repeatedly, if only temporarily, damp down the development of European feminisms, though in some areas, such as the Low Countries, Switzerland, and territories controlled by the Dual Monarchy (Austria-Hungary), overt feminist activity did not reemerge for many decades. The draconian restrictions placed on women's political activity by French Jacobins in 1793 were supplemented in the early 1800s by the framers of the Napoleonic Code, who imposed severe legal restrictions on married women. Philosophers of the state, as we have seen, attempted to rationalize women's exclusion from affairs of government. Nineteenth-century French educators would establish a national educational system with universities designed to train men for public service. Women, on the other hand, were to be silenced and trained for the household. All these measures attempted to counter—explicitly or implicitly—feminist aspirations for women's societal partnership, limits which male political leaders in other parts of Europe often adapted to their own purposes.

The postrevolutionary period on the European continent was repressive on many counts. Throughout the 1820s, in the Austro-Hungarian Empire, the states of the Germanic Confederation, or Imperial Russia, whenever tensions increased, public authorities quickly suppressed all reformist and radical publications and watched suspiciously for any signs of hostile political activism, especially female insurgency. The continental victors sought deliberately to consolidate the social order by strengthening centralized, hierarchical, male-dominated political authority in the family and in the polity, often counting on the coercive authority of established religions (which had become state-supported churches) to bolster their efforts to control "antisocial" behaviors and to insist on domesticity for women. In heavily Catholic areas of Europe especially, challenges to the authority of the male sex and its privileges became extremely unwelcome, and publications with feminist themes would be placed on the Index of forbidden books.

Not only did the counterrevolutionary backlash spawn an abundance of prescriptive laws, but it also spawned numerous "scientific" publications, by neotraditionalist and secularizing authors who sought to construct unbridgeable boundaries between the so-called public and private spheres, to articulate new and more powerful rationales for women's subordination in the family, along with attempts to demonstrate women's incapacity for other alternatives.[2] The nineteenth-century "knowledge wars" would rage with unprecedented vengeance in the postrevolutionary period, exhibiting renewed force after the upheavals of 1848. "Reason," which advocates of change had invoked in opposition to force and violence, thereby providing a powerful tool for women's emancipation, could also be reappropriated and turned against it by antifeminists, in lieu of violence. Knowledge itself could and did become a battleground in what some thought had become a war between the sexes. The stakes were high.

These repressive campaigns had the unintended effect of focusing attention on women's subordinate situation, thereby inspiring further manifestations of defiance. Women's emancipation had not only become thinkable but had begun to attract ever greater numbers of advocates. Thus the radical rearticulation of feminist claims in the social criticism of a Charles Fourier, in the widely read novels of a Germaine de Staël or her successors George Sand (pseudonym of Amantine-Lucile-Aurore Dupin, Baroness Dudevant), Charlotte Brontë, and many others, must be understood not as isolated acts of literary resistance but as tributaries to a white-hot molten flow of resistance to male privilege. The circulation of such works ensured that the flickering embers of the earlier debates would ultimately reignite, and that what James Billington once called "fire in the minds of men" would spread through succeeding generations of European women and men alike.[3]

To understand how, ultimately, feminists managed to pry open new fissures through which to launch an outpouring of protest, despite the counterrevolutionary political backlashes that marked the nineteenth century, I want to point to five offsetting and intersecting contextual developments. These developments, which lie at the core of women's history as well as the specific history of feminism that is being addressed in this book, assured the ultimate failure of antifeminists to contain or suppress feminist demands. Each of these developments has generated a vast scholarly literature to which I cannot do justice here, though I will indicate titles of particular importance in the chapter endnotes.

The first of these is the rising literacy and burgeoning education of women, which had begun in the eighteenth century but which grew dramatically during the nineteenth century, despite the fact that it still trailed behind that of men. Expanding and improving women's education, which had already become a prominent feminist theme in eighteenth-century Europe—indeed, one of particular political significance in the revolutionary context—remained at the forefront of feminist concerns. Not only did feminists continue to critique existing forms of girls' education, but they also became educators, founded schools, fought to enter universities and to acquire certification in medicine, law, theology, and other fields that would allow them to enter the learned professions and public service, and increasingly, for some, to contest antifeminist constructions of knowledge.[4] By the mid-1860s a few young women from Russia had begun to study for degrees in medicine at the university in Zurich; they were joined by French and English women at Paris, and later Edinburgh. In the 1870s women obtained formal admission to universities in England (University of London), in Ireland, and in Denmark. In the 1880s the Russian mathematician Sofia Kovalevsky obtained an advanced degree at Heidelberg, and a few women began to study at universities in Spain.

The expansion of women's primary and secondary education was, however, fundamentally linked to a second development—the growth and development of nationalism and nation-state formation. Expressions of cultural nationalism were already significant in well-established states such as France, England, and Spain, while in the politically fragmented territories of Italy and Germany, national unification movements developed around cultural nationalism: language, music, art, history, and other modes of cultural expression began to define what was "German," "Italian," "Norwegian," "Swiss," or "Czech." Even as women were held at arm's length from political participation in nations that were developing representative forms of government, national leaders adopted feminine allegories to symbolize their nations; the French personified their nation as goddesses of Liberty or Equality; Britannia, Helvetia, Hibernia, and Germania soon joined this European assembly of national allegories.[5] What, indeed, was the gender of these nations? How was it configured?

The nineteenth and early twentieth centuries witnessed independence movements and the founding of nation-states in Greece, Norway, and Finland, as well as unfulfilled aspirations to found many more, including Poland and Ukraine, parts of which were ruled by the Russian and Austro-Hungarian empires. Leaders of nationalist efforts insisted in new and varied ways on women's education, not only for purposes of promoting a citizenry schooled in its "mother tongue" but also in terms of concern about national population growth, with its implications for workforce replenishment and military strength. In the latter case, state efforts would focus increasingly on women's physical and psychological fitness for maternity in the national interest and would attempt to promote childbearing in a time of demographic transition.[6] Especially in France, but increasingly after 1900 in Germany and Great Britain, doctors and politicians began to fret anew over the possible adverse consequences for their countries of falling birth rates and high infant and child mortality. They obsessed about the physical, mental, and moral development of the national workforce, as well as the fighting force, and some even insisted that the production of future generations must become a governmental priority. Women, it became clear, mattered a great deal to men's national political aspirations; population growth was one thing they could not carry out alone.

The third significant development, and one that is closely related to issues of national aspirations, concerns the massive movement of women, many young and single, into an increasingly urbanized workforce, their work newly situated outside the household, and thus highly visible. In the 1830s France, Belgium, and parts of Germany and Switzerland, like England a few decades earlier, had entered a period of major

economic development, centered in mechanized and increasingly centralized manufacturing in the textile and metal-processing industries.
The development of industrial production and expansion of a cash economy introduced severe strains on the household subsistence economy,
and confirmed the shift in thinking about the sexual division of labor
that had been gathering ideological momentum during the eighteenth
century.[7]

Women had always worked for pay, but in some countries (led by England) politicians and economists voiced concern over the extent of participation by women—especially married women—and children in the
new industrial labor force. Lurid stories circulated in the press concerning the exploitation of workers of both sexes by manufacturers, and allegations of promiscuity and sexual harassment resulting from the mixing
of the sexes in mines, factories, and workshops aroused severe public
criticism. Opponents of women's employment reiterated that the sexes
must occupy separate physical spaces and that the place of women was
not in the paid labor force, just as it was not in political life, but in the
household, under male protection and control.

Prescriptions against women's political participation soon extended
to their economic participation. Counterrevolutionary economic theorists, trade-unionist men, and social Catholic reformers joined the chorus of political theorists who sought to institutionalize women's "enclo-
sure" and subordination in the family. In their version of "separate
spheres," they asserted that the employed male head of household (considered the breadwinner) should be paid a "family wage"—that is, a sum
sufficient to support a wife and children—while the wife managed the
household and raised the children. Such theorists urged unmarried
daughters to complete their domestic apprenticeships with their mothers, rather than seek outside employment.

Issues concerning women's employment became far more visible and
controversial as a cash economy developed and industrialization proceeded. Only landed wealth seemed to offer security either to women or
to men in these times of boom and bust, but in most European countries
such wealth was still controlled by a very few families, and then by the
male heads of households. As newly acquired family fortunes waxed and
waned with the unpredictable cycles of the market economy, single
middle-class women (a new historical phenomenon) confronted the
prospect of having to support themselves, and during the second half of
the nineteenth century, educated middle-class women flocked into the
labor force, stirring up considerable controversy as they did so. Their

married sisters, at least the more prosperous among them, might retreat into the elaboration and refinement of complex domestic households; only a few, however, could aspire to becoming ladies of leisure.[8]

In the cities and large towns of early nineteenth-century Europe, few working-class people could live according to this new ideal, though increasing numbers of skilled workers aspired to reach it. Such "separate spheres" prescriptions were for most people merely attractive ideals, impossible to realize under prevailing conditions. Women's economic contributions, whether paid or unpaid, were too important to family welfare. Ironically, however, women's household tasks would be effectively redefined as noneconomic. As a result the actual chores performed by most city women, from hauling water to cooking meals and doing laundry, became economically invisible and culturally devalued. Increasingly, the only contributions that "counted" were those that brought in cash. Women, whether married or not, had to be enabled to earn a living wage. Statisticians revealed that prostitution and unwed motherhood were on the rise, that abortion, infanticides, and suicides were increasing. Sexual morality—that is to say, women's sexual morality—became a huge issue. All these issues pointed to the problem of women's disproportionate poverty in the developing competitive market economy.

To these developments, nineteenth-century European feminists responded by demanding the recognition and reevaluation of women's domestic work, even as they fought for women's right to work outside the household, equal pay for equal work, reduced hours, better workplace conditions, unionization of women workers and supervision of women workers by female labor inspectors, and ultimately, state support for mothers and decriminalization of abortion and infanticide.[9] Socialist feminists would go further, eventually developing a multifaceted anticapitalist critique and proposing a collective restructuring of production, housework, and child care that would allow women to become equal economic partners with men. Only a few would advocate complete sexual emancipation. European feminists in the late nineteenth century were more likely to advocate sex education for women and men and a single standard of sexual morality, one that would severely curb masculine promiscuity.

Before 1848 it seemed as though socialists and feminists might be marching in parallel tracks, but in the late nineteenth century they diverged politically. The fourth significant development, then, concerns the intense rivalry that developed between feminists and socialists. This rivalry became far more acute after 1889, when Marxist-socialists founded the politically powerful Second International Workingmen's Association. Aspiring to harness a potentially massive clientele of proletarian women to the cause of international socialist revolution, in the 1890s class-conscious Marxist-socialist women created and condemned the category of "bourgeois feminism," insisting that workforce participation alone, not legal rights (whether civil or civic) or education or social reform, offered the key to women's emancipation. They insisted too that the cause of the working class must be given priority over the cause of women until the socialist revolution had been achieved.[10] Annoyed by the socialists' refusal to cooperate, feminists continued to insist that women's emancipation was all women's cause, and that all women were "sisters" in subordination irrespective of their socioeconomic class. Many believed that full political citizenship would provide women with the authority needed to break once and for all time the back of male hegemony inscribed in prevailing laws, institutions, and practices.

The fifth development, which intersects with all the others, concerns the growth both of national organized feminist movements, and of initiatives to promote a well-organized and enduring international feminist movement that would address all these issues.[11] Competing initiatives ensued, led by French and English feminists, with neo-Europeans from North America being drawn increasingly in, as well as feminists from a variety of other countries, until by 1900 a series of parallel international organizations had come into being.

The programs of national and international feminist congresses, as well as the plays, the novels, and the press of the period, attest to the range, breadth, and significance of the feminist critique. Only with the outbreak of World War I would this prolific flow of debate and demands for change be damped down by the immediacy of armed conflict. War had a way of silencing all competing discussions—at least temporarily.

CHAPTER 4 ADDRESSES the rearticulations of feminist claims during the unsettled period from roughly 1820 to the eve of the revolutions of 1848. It signals the reemergence of feminist critique in new locations as well as new formulations of older arguments. It focuses on several prominent strands of feminist thought centered around the critique of marriage institutions and around the strategic empowerment of women as citizen-mothers, or mother-educators in emerging national cultures.

Chapter 5 surveys the period from 1848 to 1870. It discusses a series of major eruptions of feminist protest on the European continent, once again beginning with revolutionary events in Paris and spreading quickly throughout the principal cities of Europe. It explores as well the emergence, following the failure of the 1848 revolutions, of another massive antifeminist backlash, particularly in Germany, as well as the articulation of feminist expressions in fiction and in the press in the outlying Scandinavian countries, and in England the beginnings of a small but well-organized feminist movement focused on women's work during the late 1850s. It examines the emergence of campaigns for women's admission to university education and the intensification of the "knowledge wars" as feminist women contested men's monopoly over formal knowledge, especially in the fields of medicine and law, both of which were repeatedly utilized by antifeminists to reinscribe women's subordination. The chapter concludes by reconsidering John Stuart Mill's extremely important contribution *The Subjection of Women* (1869) and highlights its reception throughout Europe. This work, coupled with Mill's championing of woman suffrage in the British Parliament in 1867, effectively shifted the spotlight away from France. This shift was reinforced by the defeat of the French Second Empire by a Prussian-led coalition of German states in 1870 and, in 1871, the subsequent crushing of the insurgents of the Paris Commune, who included many radical feminists, by the forces of "moral order"—all of which fostered an unfavorable political climate for French feminists during the critical early years of the Third Republic.

Chapter 6 explores a series of new developments in the history of European feminisms between the early 1870s and 1889, the latter date marking the centennial of the French Revolution and the definitive founding of an international feminist movement as well as of a rival international socialist movement. It explores also the development of a sustained feminist concern with women's work and economic well-being in an industrializing labor force, and the intensification of the rivalry between feminists and socialists in an effort to resolve the "woman question."

In Chapters 7 and 8, I trace the proliferation of "feminisms" during the period 1890–1914, an era of accelerating political and social change. This was the period in which "feminism" was named, and in which a great hue and cry was raised about the "new woman," educated, often professionally trained, increasingly economically independent, and wary of marriage as it had systematically been structured to favor male authority. In this period also, feminist concerns began to develop within organized Roman Catholicism as well as within the specifically Marxist form of social democracy embodied in the Second International.

Chapter 8 addresses in more depth questions of feminisms in developing national political cultures and nationalist contexts during the late nineteenth and early twentieth centuries, with particular emphasis on the quest for suffrage and other rights of citizenship. Case studies of smaller nations and cultures (Finland and Ukraine, Greece and Belgium) as well as larger ones (Britain, with reference to Ireland, and France) are briefly presented. Some feminists disagreed over issues that crossed national lines during this period, particularly over protective labor legislation for women workers, but others joined forces across these boundaries to develop a radical, comprehensive critique of male sexual practices, ranging from state-sanctioned prostitution to militarism.

The issues raised by European feminists in the course of the nineteenth century cut to the foundations of their respective societies; thus these issues recurred and were rearticulated with increasing force by each generation. With the expanding militarism and imperialism that characterized the late nineteenth century, the rumble of feminist protest became a deafening roar, one that could no longer be silenced. By placing antifeminists increasingly on the defensive, feminists forced their opponents to articulate explanations of their resistance. Indeed, despite—or precisely because of—the intensity of this resistance, it is possible to claim without exaggeration that the degree of support for women's emancipation in Europe increased dramatically throughout the nineteenth century. It is in this context that we must understand the claims made for the importance of feminism in the early twentieth century by Ellen Key, Madame Avril de Sainte-Croix, Millicent Garrett Fawcett, and so many others. I will repeat Key's claim here: "The struggle that woman is now carrying on is far more far-reaching than any other; and if no diversion occurs, it will finally surpass in fanaticism any war of religion or race."[12]

4

Rearticulating Feminist Claims, 1820–1848

In the period from 1820 to the new outbreak of revolutions in 1848, partisans of the critical perspective we now call feminism once again mounted a campaign to curtail, even to abolish the privileges of the male sex, to expose the prejudices that supported male privilege, to transform existing institutions, to empower women and thereby liberate them from male control. Especially in the postrevolutionary nation-states of France and England a broad spectrum of writers and social critics recast earlier Enlightenment formulations to envision a radical restructuring of the relationship between the sexes within the family and in society. Touching on a full range of legal, educational, economic, and political issues, they added full-blown demands for economic freedom and political rights, moral reform, sexual liberty, and even (in England) birth control. The issues they raised were debated not only in tracts and books but also in the pages of the *Times* of London and the *Westminster Review*, and in Paris in the *Revue des Deux Mondes*, and the *Charivari*.

This new generation of feminist challengers included such diverse contributors as Harriet Martineau, John Stuart Mill, George Sand, Flora Tristan, and Louisa Otto. They would confront the Napoleons, the Vireys, the Hannah Mores, and the Hegels who had sought to limit, constrain, and channel women's possibilities, whether in the name of the male-headed family, the "public order" of sexual and social hierarchy, or the universal subject "man."

These challengers would deploy a prolific range of arguments to make their points for liberty, equality, and justice for women: they invoked analogies to slavery, developed arguments of sexual complementarity, asserted the importance of motherhood, women's moral authority, and their unique roles as civilizers of men. In 1817, for instance, shortly after the end of the Napoleonic wars, the British poet Percy Bysshe Shelley pondered the question, "Can man be free if woman be a slave?"[1] In 1830 the Anglo-Irish Anna Doyle Wheeler argued: "When I advocate the

Rights of Women then, I do it under the most perfect conviction, that I am also pleading the cause of men by showing the mighty influence Women hold over the happiness or misery of men themselves."[2] In Paris, Prosper Enfantin proclaimed to the Saint-Simonians in 1831 that "the man and the woman, this is the social individual," and called for the re-establishment of harmony between man and woman, or as he put it, between intellect and sensuality.[3] The Berlin-based German-Jewish writer Rahel Varnhagen complained in her posthumously published letters (1834) that "men and women are two different nations in Europe," while the theologian Ludwig Feuerbach echoed Saint-Simonian arguments, insisting that "man and woman are the complement of each other, and thus united they first present the species, the perfect [hu]man."[4] In 1847, in his celebrated poem *The Princess*, Alfred, Lord Tennyson, juxtaposed the differing perspectives in a powerful dialogue between the Old King, who restated the authoritarian view of sexual hierarchy and separate spheres, and Princess Ida, who advocated women's full inclusion in life's affairs:[5]

> *The Old King:*
> Man for the field and woman for the hearth:
> Man for the sword and for the needle she:
> Man with the head and woman with the heart:
> Man to command and woman to obey;
> All else confusion.

> *Princess Ida:*
> Everywhere
> Two heads in council, two beside the hearth,
> Two in the tangled business of the world,
> Two in the liberal offices of life,
> Two plummets dropt for one to sound the abyss
> Of science and secrets of the mind;
> Musician, painter, sculptor, critic, more.

As these citations suggest, the "woman question" was very much on the minds of thoughtful Europeans. In the early 1830s, even conservative men, including some who exercised great authority over European public opinion, such as the aging French Catholic writer François-René de Chateaubriand, acknowledged the revolutionary potential of the claims being made on behalf of righting women's wrongs. In 1834 he qualified the emancipation of women as one of the major challenges to the post-revolutionary European order. Along with the economic injustices of wage labor and the redistribution of fortunes, he viewed the woman question as a key issue in the emergence of a new society, no longer organized "around groups and by families." "What aspect will [the new society] offer," he asked, "when it is individual, the way it seems to be becoming, the way one can already see it in formation in the United States?"[6]

CHARACTERIZING FEMINISM IN
A COUNTERREVOLUTIONARY CONTEXT

Despite continuing opposition, the cause of emancipating women gained strength in European societies, intersecting with efforts to free other subordinated groups, ranging from black slaves in the colonies to the "white slaves" of the European working classes, to Jews, who were still subjected to institutional discrimination in most countries other than France, and to Catholics and the Irish in militantly Protestant England. Somewhat later, the serfs of Russia and parts of the Austro-Hungarian Empire would figure in this panoply of the oppressed. But everywhere, the cause of women was recognized as the cause not of a minority, but of over half the population.

In the states of Central and Eastern Europe, advocates of women's emancipation continued to encounter stiff resistance, and opponents would place new political obstacles in their paths. Here, memory played an important role. The older male survivors who concluded the peace settlements of 1815, following Napoleon's final defeat at Waterloo, still remembered the tumultuous consequences of the Declaration of the Rights of Man and the accompanying and unsettling demands for the rights of woman; they also remembered the extraordinary phenomenon of women's political activity in the revolution, and they considered justifiable its ruthless repression during the Terror in 1793. They took note, too, of the revolutionary French government's attempt to reconstruct and reappropriate the family as a bulwark of the secular state by institutionalizing civil marriage and divorce and by equalizing inheritance laws for daughters and sons, thereby ending the favor shown to firstborn males. Nor could they passively ignore the concurrent challenge to institutionalized marriage and religious structures sounded by European male writers exploring the boundaries of freedom in passionate love. They remembered even more vividly the ensuing Napoleonic wars of conquest and appalling losses of male lives on battlefields, all in the name of "liberty." These events had shaken the political and social system of continental Europe to its foundations.

The treaties that ended the wars in 1815 had reestablished a precarious European peace. But the victorious monarchs of continental Europe

(Prussia, Russia, and Austria) did not rest content with peace treaties alone. Led by Prince Metternich, the Austrian chancellor, they also initiated a campaign to suppress the revolutionary energies and ideas that had emanated from France into Central and Eastern Europe. This counterrevolutionary campaign, epitomized by the Carlsbad Decrees of 1820, attempted to exert strict control through censorship of public speech (clamping down both on the press and on political meetings) and curtailment of public association and individual liberties. In Russia in 1797, Tsar Paul I had already altered the line of succession to the throne to reestablish male rule, in order to avert future women monarchs such as his mother, Catherine II. Under Nicholas I and his empress, Aleksandra Fedorovna (formerly Princess Charlotte of Prussia), the role of Russian empress was recast to emphasize childbearing, domesticity, and models of virtue.[7] The Russian imperial government of the 1820s became the very epitome of absolutist repression, a fortress against Western emancipationist ideas of all types.

Even in this new geography of repression, it was still possible in the 1820s to discuss some notions about women's emancipation, as can be seen in a fictional epistolary exchange on the education of daughters in Caroline Pichler's *Zerstreute Blätte aus meinem Schreibtische* (Scattered Pages from my Writing Desk, 1823), republished in Vienna in 1843.[8] Feminist initiatives also drew theoretical momentum from sporadic efforts by philosophers and poets to envision the liberation (not only moral but material as well) of individuals as freestanding, self-determining subjects. Among German philosophers, in particular, where classical notions of the public and the private had been reenergized by Hegel, a more abstract, idealistic line of thinking emerged, arguing forcefully for the ethical self-realization of the individual beyond the constraints of sexual identity or "spheres." As this transcendentalist philosophical approach to "freedom" spread through European thought, and was appropriated in the cause of women as well as men, the tensions between these very different lines of argument would begin to nourish feminist argumentation in Western European countries.

The abstract individualism of feminist argumentation in this period should not, however, be overstated. Most nineteenth-century European feminist thinkers—and their opponents—before 1848 can be characterized as relational thinkers and reformers. Most retained a holistic view of societies and agreed with their more conservative opponents that the sociopolitical relation of the sexes was the very glue that held the fabric of society together; they viewed women and men as embodied beings, marriage and sex/gender roles as inherently political and as essential for societal cohesion, but they did want to alter the sexual balance of power in family structures by ending women's subordination. Some cautiously emphasized women's *instrumental* social roles and insisted on women's special nature as a positive social force, even as they appealed to principles of liberty and equality. But the dominant notion of equality remained moral and intellectual.

In fact, complementarity of the sexes was central to feminist perspectives during this period. Most feminists accepted some type of sexual division of labor in society. What they rejected was the assertive gendering of the public/private division of spheres as male/female (postulated by political theorists from Aristotle to Rousseau, Fichte, and Hegel); this feminists deemed inappropriate, and they argued, as had Tennyson in *The Princess*, that women's influence *as women* must be felt throughout society, whether in the civic, civil and socioeconomic, or domestic spheres.

Most continental feminists in this era acknowledged the societal importance of physiological differences between the sexes and took for granted as "natural" what Adrienne Rich has since labeled "compulsory heterosexuality." In fact, some (though by no means all) political progressives who supported women's emancipation also argued for universal marriage and for an end to prostitution, though they objected strenuously to the imbalanced patterns of domination and subordination that characterized current forms of religious and civil marriage. A minority, often identified with anarchism, proposed arguments for "free love" and sexual emancipation of individuals and couples, outside the bounds of church or state regulation, and without implications for property transmission. Others, especially in England, pursued concrete reforms specific to the legal and economic emancipation of single adult women (which the revolution had already set in place in France). Demands for civil divorce were particularly vociferous in France, where the innovative revolutionary divorce laws of the 1790s had subsequently been repealed. In 1837 Flora Tristan published a blistering attack on the "despotism" and "servitude" embodied by French marriage law and the prohibition of divorce, calling for a "relationship of equals."[9]

Most feminists in this period viewed motherhood as women's particular role and responsibility, and as a strategic common ground for claiming women's solidarity across social classes and divisions. They advocated that girls be properly schooled in order to fulfill this important adult role. As the English educator Mary Maurice put it, "no woman is really able to perform the duties which devolve upon her, be her station what it may, unless she has herself been well educated."[10] Indeed, for many, maternity (not solely physical but spiritual and educational as well) could also be reimagined—in contrast to wifehood—as the vehicle for women's liberation; as the historian Ann Taylor Allen has pointed out, "spiritual motherhood" became a powerful engine for advancing women's interests and opening out their position in society. German feminists invoked Goethe's "eternal feminine" against efforts to place them on pedestals, or to cage them like canaries.[11] Such motherhood claims could even provide a means of deliberately deflecting or downplaying long-standing views of rampant and uncontrollable female sexuality, though such views would continue to trouble generations of European men.

In contrast to the anarchists, many nineteenth-century European feminists also insisted (far more than we find comfortable doing today) on the symbiotic relationship between the family and the state; indeed, in an era of dramatic development for nation-states, they optimistically wished to harness state power on behalf of women's emancipation as well as to insist on the benefits that women's power and influence could bring to bear on the state. This optimism remained intact even as emancipators envisioned a thoroughgoing reorganization of existing heterosexual relations, households, and familial institutions, including childrearing practices, housework, and the sexual division of labor—a vision diametrically opposed to the new patriarchies preferred by those who governed the mostly monarchical and militaristic states of early nineteenth-century Europe.

POLITICAL, CULTURAL, AND ECONOMIC ISSUES
IN FEMINIST ARGUMENTATION

Political memory and repression, along with motherly state building, were not the only important factors influencing the reassertion of feminist claims, however. The historical development of feminisms in Europe accompanied the emergence of literacy and mass education, and struggles to organize purely secular, national societies (often defined in opposition to the French in those countries most immediately affected by earlier French insurgency and military occupation). Feminist demands would also be articulated with reference to issues resulting from the expansive growth of an urban, commercial, and increasingly industrialized market economy that widened the chasm separating rich and poor, who seemed increasingly richer and poorer than ever before. The very vocabulary of feminism—liberty, equality, sisterhood, emancipation, liberation, rights—that had developed during the European Enlightenment and the French Revolution would take on new layers of meaning after 1830, especially with reference to new categories of political thought and behavior born in the wake of the revolution: "conservative," "liberal," "radical," and "socialist." Concepts like democracy, individualism, and socialism (the latter term coined in the 1830s by the French reformer Pierre Leroux) could be viewed either as utopian ideals or as fearful specters, even when restricted to men, in early nineteenth-century Europe. When women were incorporated, some found these concepts even more threatening.

In Restoration France, the 1820s marked a pause. One of the distinguished voices to be heard on women's behalf in those years was the Abbé Grégoire, the French cleric who during the revolution had supported the combined emancipation of Jews, slaves, and women. In 1820 he published a new treatise, *De l'Influence du Christianisme sur la condition des femmes* (The Influence of Christianity on the Condition of Women), in which he insisted on the importance of Christian doctrine for improving the status of women; going further, he favorably compared the lot of women under the Christian religion with that of their counterparts living in "idolatrous, Muslim, and savage nations."[12] Following the assassination of the Duke de Berry (the heir to the throne) that same year, a certain Thomassy argued that France, now a constitutional monarchy, should reinstate female succession to the throne, a proposal that doubtless met with very mixed reactions, given the centuries-old French tradition of excluding women.[13] In 1830 the constitutional monarchy founded in newly independent Belgium adopted that very French tradition of female exclusion from the throne.

Concerns about female rule and the meaning of queenship provoked strong responses even in England, still the most politically liberal of the victor nations. George IV's effort, also in 1820, to divorce his estranged consort, Queen Caroline, by Act of Parliament led to enormous public support for her not only as a symbol of the need for parliamentary reform but also as a standard-bearer for women's wrongs. Women, by publicly supporting Queen Caroline against George IV, were, in Thomas Laqueur's words, "striking at the very heart of sexual inequality and the double standard."[14] The symbolic significance of the subsequent long reign of Queen Victoria (1837–1901) was to a remarkable degree prefigured by the debate surrounding Queen Caroline. Although Victoria would prove personally uninterested in women's political emancipation, emphasizing domesticity and motherhood after her marriage to the prince consort, Albert, she did support efforts to promote women's education. To some, however, her very presence on the throne from

1837 on seemed to justify their demands for women's inclusion in political life. The issue of female rule was differently framed in Spain, where the succession of the young Spanish Bourbon princess Isabelle II in 1833 would be secured against the claims of her uncle Don Carlos only by some fancy political footwork on the part of her mother (the fourth wife of Ferdinand VII), despite Isabelle's acknowledged position as heir to the throne.

In England following the uproar over the Queen Caroline incident, William Thompson and Anna Doyle Wheeler published an important tract, with the outspoken title *Appeal of One Half the Human Race Against the Pretensions of the Other Half—Men—to Retain Them in Political and Thence in Civil and Domestic Slavery*. Members of radical Protestant sects known as Dissenters, Unitarians, and Quakers, such as Frances Wright and Eliza Sharples Carlyle, as well as the disciples of the textile king, social reformer, and trade-union organizer Robert Owen, began to address the woman question in their speeches and publications.[15]

The question of political rights for propertied single women quickly surfaced. But in June 1832, when the Parliament passed the landmark Reform Act, each paragraph dealing with parliamentary suffrage carried the preface "Every male person of full age, and not subject to any legal incapacity."[16] Both single adult women in possession of their own property and married women who had "surrendered" theirs to husbands were explicitly excluded from political rights. In August, a certain Mary Smith from Stanmore, county York, petitioned the British Parliament for the vote, arguing that since she paid taxes and was subject to the laws, she ought to have a voice in making them; her petition was presented by Mr. Hunt, and was quickly dismissed amid discussion of how inconvenient it would be to have both men and women on juries that had to be sequestered overnight.[17]

Neither the Chartists, who campaigned for an even broader male franchise in the 1840s, nor other laboring men were particularly supportive of women voting, as the work of Anna Clark and others establishes.[18] In fact, despite continued agitation, feminist claims for either legal or political changes met with strongly unfavorable responses in England. The exclusion of the American women delegates from the World Anti-Slavery Convention in London in 1840, which became one of the best-known "consciousness-raising" events for European feminists of the period, must be understood in this context of male objections to female political participation. In England, only one significant legal reform, establishing limited rights for mothers to custody of their own children, was realized before the 1850s, thanks to the excellent political connections and personal agitation of Caroline Norton.[19]

Meanwhile women readers, usually privileged, educated, and with sufficient leisure to read, were targeted by a proliferating and sometimes insidious prescriptive literature. These publications ranged from tracts on domestic economy and medical treatises analyzing women's reproductive functions to debates concerning their proper education. They included works of didactic fiction, poetry, and plays espousing views on the woman question that ranged from neotraditionalist to radical.

Perhaps never before in history had there been such a deluge of publications addressed to women, many of them written by women and for women. Some of these publications promoted female emancipation, but even more, it seemed, insisted on women's necessary subordination, along with their children's, in a male-headed family unit. Didactic works touted the blessings of domesticity and articulated the powerful vision of separate spheres for women and men as the wave of the civilized future. Educators, too, gave careful thought to what girls and women should read—by this time it was taken for granted that they did.

Already in the late 1830s, the redoubtable archconservative Sarah Stickney Ellis had begun to preach the doctrine of women's conscious subordination to breadwinning men in her many books on the daughters, wives, and mothers of England: "As women, then, the first thing of importance is to be content to be inferior to men—inferior in mental power, in the same proportion that you are inferior in bodily strength."[20] Eloquent feminist protests by women writers such as Marion Kirkland Reid's tract *A Plea for Women* (1843) or Charlotte Brontë's novels *Jane Eyre* (1847) and *Shirley* (1849) all testified to the fact that other women were eager to combat the counterrevolutionary arguments of the Mrs. Ellises.

Feminism in the 1830s and 1840s also addressed an important material dimension of women's subordination. First in England, then in France, Belgium, Switzerland, and several German states, social critics (mostly of middle-class background) expressed concern over the extent of participation by women and children in the new and highly visible industrial labor force, as well as over the mounting numbers of urban poor. The so-called women's work was particularly poorly paid, and working conditions were very difficult. "The most direct cause of women's misfortune," wrote Zoé Gatti de Gamond, a Belgian feminist and disciple of Fourier, in 1838, "is poverty; demanding their freedom means above all demanding reform in the economy of society which will eradicate poverty and give everyone an education, a minimum standard of living, and

the right to work."[21] The subjection of all women, she believed, was at
bottom a question of lack of resources due to defective societal organization. "Rights" for women would be hollow without first resolving the issue of their poverty.

The thrust of the precedent-setting British Poor Law of 1834 was,
however, not to pay women more, but to put men to work, in support of
their dependent wives and children.[22] As resistance to women in the
workforce grew, England also became the first nation in the world to restrict the gainful employment of women and children in mining and to
regulate it in manufacturing.[23] English women interested in challenging
male domination found more success in founding professional schools to
educate young middle-class women as teachers and governesses; such
positions were considered to be extensions of the motherly role and
therefore less threatening to men's professional interests.[24]

Looking beyond England to the United States, the French social critic
Alexis de Tocqueville recommended to his countrymen what he took to
be the American understanding of sexual equality, in which each sex
seemed to him to have its distinctive sphere of activity and respected the
other. "The Americans," he wrote enthusiastically, "have applied to the
sexes the great principle of political economy which governs the manufactures of our age, by carefully dividing the duties of man from those of
woman in order that the great work of society may be the better carried
on."[25] But such notions of separate spheres did not mean that women's
work in the "women's sphere" would be accorded economic value; instead, political economists, employers, and labor leaders fostered a more
sinister development—the valuation of men's paid labor would be accompanied by the devaluation of women's unpaid household work. The
French feminist Jeanne Deroin was quite aware of this development.
Poignantly recounting the innumerable daily tasks performed by a wife
in a working-class household, she pointed out the discrepancy to her
readers: "And they say, in speaking of her, that only her husband works;
she doesn't do anything. She has only her household and her children to
take care of."[26] The words "work" and "productivity" meant, increasingly, only paid labor—paid labor gendered masculine. Thus did assertions of women's right to work, to be well paid for their productive labor—and to redefine what was considered "productive"—claim a prominent place on the feminist agenda.

Incursions of middle-class and aristocratic women into charitable and
philanthropic work—unpaid, however much appreciated and lauded—
sometimes seemed to reinforce the notion that women and earned
money (like women and politics) might be incompatible.[27] Such charita-

ble work, however, quickly exposed them to the miseries of the poor—unemployed women workers, unwed mothers, prisoners, prostitutes. The encounters between these women of very different backgrounds frequently raised awareness among the privileged of the structural subordination and dependence of all women and encouraged their efforts to reform the structures, legal, economic, and political, that upheld these injustices. Such encounters also led to claims for private and state intervention, and—particularly in Protestant societies—the beginnings of professional training and employment in the field that would become known as social work.

CONTINENTAL UTOPIAN VISIONS

From the 1830s through the 1840s, new and stronger secular claims for women's emancipation resurfaced in France and in other continental settings. Particularly following the 1830 revolution in France, the pros and cons of women's emancipation preoccupied a considerable number of major and minor European thinkers and once again generated considerable anxiety among proponents of the old order.

On the European continent, feminist theory and action once again found their greatest stimulus in Paris, where, following a rather brief revolution, a new constitutional monarchy headed by Louis-Philippe d'Orleans replaced the legitimist Bourbon monarchy, complete with a charter of rights, a two-chambered parliament, and, briefly, reestablished freedom of the press and association. Debates over women's citizenship erupted as plans were introduced to establish a nationwide network of primary schools; that no schools were designated for girls signified, as Michèle Riot-Sarcey has pointed out, a deliberate reassertion of women's exclusion from the civic arena.[28]

In this turbulent political climate, social critics and literary Romantics once again raised questions about women's status that would be diffused and discussed by women and men in intellectual circles throughout the rest of Europe. Even the British feminists Anna Doyle Wheeler and John Stuart Mill found inspiration in France, introducing insights from Fourier and the Saint-Simonians on the woman question to their contemporaries in England.[29] Despite censorship, these ideas spread from France to the Germany principalities, the Scandinavian countries, the Italian states, the Low Countries, and Russia. Once again European feminists challenged the principle of male legal control over women in marriage, comparing it to legalized prostitution; once again they reiterated demands for female education (including the admission of women to the study of medicine), the reorganization of the household, the defense of women's trades against male intrusion, and the assertion of women's right to economic independence through paid work. In Paris "Jeanne-Victoire" argued that "until now woman has been exploited and tyrannized . . . ; half the human race cannot, without injustice, be in servitude to the other half." She called on all women—the privileged and the poor—to unite across boundaries of class on behalf of their common interests. Clarisse Vigoureux's message was aggressively confrontational, demanding "an accounting from the strong sex" for "incompetent administration" of the world's affairs. To this potent blend, advocates such as Eugénie Niboyet and Flora Tristan in France, and Carl Almqvist in Sweden, would add calls to association and cooperation.[30]

French novelists of the Romantic school, especially George Sand, author of the controversial and widely read novels *Indiana* (1832) and *Lélia* (1836), critiqued women's legal and emotional situation in marriage. In reassessing the contributions of the women writers Sand, Daniel Stern (the pseudonym of Marie-Catharine-Sophie de Flavigny, comtesse d'Agoult), and Hortense Allart, the historian Whitney Walton has persuasively argued that their feminist critiques of marriage, their reconfigurations of family arrangements, and their recasting of homes that were woman-centered add up to an alternative woman-centered political theory of society.[31] Sand's declarations of female independence stunned and inspired some readers. "I know that I am the slave and you the master," Sand's heroine Madame Delmare proclaims, in *Indiana*:[32]

> The laws of this country make you my master. You can bind my body, tie my hands, govern my acts. You have the right of the stronger, and society confirms you in it: but you cannot command my will, monsieur; God alone can bend it and subdue it. Try to find a law, a dungeon, an instrument of torture that gives you any hold on it! You might as well try to handle the air and grasp space.

Even in fictional form, this was heady stuff!

A distinctive feature of feminism in this period is its eruption in new locations, including imaginative new religious or quasi-religious frameworks linked to visionary projects for social transformation. One finds, for example, strong feminist impulses in the 1830s among the Saint-Simonians and Fourierists in Paris and among the Owenites and the Non-Conformist and Dissenting sects in England, and in the 1840s among the German Catholics and French Christian Socialists, as well as within more highly secular French socialist, and communist groups, such as Étienne Cabet's Icarians. These "utopian socialist" groups would be among the most significant in terms of their long-term impact on the formulation of issues and on subsequent emancipatory projects.[33]

The Saint-Simonians and Fourierists once again raised the explosive theme of "free love," which proposed that men and women ought to form couples only according to sexual or emotional inclination rather than submitting to the dictates of class-based family sociopolitical or economic needs; its claims were couple-based, not clan-based. Free-love enthusiasts insisted that this practice would lay the foundation for better marriages, but their opponents denounced it as a code for sexual promiscuity as well as the destruction of the male-headed family.

While calling for women to speak out on the conditions of their own emancipation in 1831, Prosper Enfantin, the acknowledged leader of the mostly well-educated Saint-Simonian men, advocated a new religious and social order, in which Catholic doctrine on the superiority of the spirit over the flesh would be set on its head. His call for a "rehabilitation of the flesh" scandalized many members, even among the sect's male leadership, and led to government prosecution for outrages to public morality. In the wake of a highly publicized trial in Paris, the word "emancipation" took on provocative, even dangerous overtones that would be difficult to dispel.

In 1832, as a response to Enfantin's call for women's voices, a small group of Saint-Simonian women founded a women's periodical, which was called successively *La Femme nouvelle* (The New Woman), *L'Apostolat des femmes* (Women's Apostolate), *La Tribune des femmes* (The Women's Tribune), and *La Femme libre* (The Free Woman). This group included Suzanne Voilquin, Désirée Veret (later known as Désirée Gay), and Jeanne Deroin, all young working women who signed their articles with their first names only—"Jeanne-Victoire," "Jeanne-Désirée"—omitting patriarchal surnames. They downplayed Enfantin's free-love doctrines (for which the Saint-Simonians had been taken to court), insisting instead on the prior importance of economic independence from men. Even as they argued specifically for women's "right" to work and to be self-supporting, they also focused (as had their eighteenth-century predecessors) on defending traditional sectors of women's employment, such as selling ribbons, from male interlopers.[34]

Though they disagreed on matters of sexual emancipation, Saint-Simonian women and men both proposed a radical notion of the complementarity of the sexes. Both viewed the male-female couple as the social individual, but the Saint-Simonian women saw maternity as the common denominator for female solidarity. Women were not simply

part of a greater whole; through maternity they possessed a unique quality that could be turned to good account in arguments for women's
emancipation. It was *LA MÈRE*—the Mother—whose revelation the
Saint-Simonians awaited while her chair stood empty, and whom they
would finally go to seek in the Orient in 1834. "Jeanne-Désirée" made
this claim in an early issue of the *Apostolat des femmes*: "Women's
banner is universal, for . . . are they not all united by the same bond, MA-
TERNITY?"[35] Suzanne Voilquin seconded the motion: "Woman, rely on
your title of *mother* to reclaim your equality from man. . . . Motherhood
is our most beautiful quality, . . . it is woman completely fulfilled."[36] A
certain Madame E.A.C. even asserted in 1834 that a child should bear
only its mother's name, and that mothers should receive state financial
support.[37] This single-minded reclamation of motherhood (outside and
beyond the dependence of wifehood) as the central feature of women's
difference, incorporating women's unique physiological capacity for
childbearing with insistence on their vital role as mother-educators, was
one of the most radical and daring features of French feminist thought in
the 1830s.

Emphasis on motherhood and the sociopolitical importance of the
mother-educator was by no means restricted to utopian feminists such
as these. Indeed, many women considered the new role appealing, and
French women educators had already proved particularly influential in
elaborating this idea. Following the important published contributions
in the 1820s of Marie-Jeanne de Campan, who headed the elite girls'
schools established by Napoleon, a trio of distinguished French and
Swiss Protestant women writers, the comtesse de Rémusat, Pauline
Meulan (later Madame Guizot), and Albertine Necker de Saussure (a
cousin of Madame de Staël) advanced strong claims for the improvement
of women's education, each insisting on the civic and social importance
of women's ostensibly domestic roles as mother-educators.[38] Male advocates made even more extravagant claims in its support, as in Louis
Aimé-Martin's influential tract *The Education of Mothers; or, the Civilization of Mankind by Women* (1834), which circulated widely in English translation as well as in French, and was reconfigured in the feminine voice by British writers such as Sarah Lewis in her tract *Woman's
Mission* (1839).[39]

Even the more conventional expressions of the mother-educator idea
were strategically important and appealing. It provided women, who
were still held at arm's length from formal political life, with a role construed as civic or political—one that transcended purely familial ("private"/"domestic") responsibilities. For urban women of the middle and

lower-middle classes, the new mother-educator model offered a ratio-nale for their importance as civilizing agents that could counteract the devaluation of the many other vital but less inspired household chores that fell to them. It also offered a strategic vehicle for demanding formal educational opportunities and special institutions for their sex, and especially for acquiring training as teachers. With this vehicle, they were ultimately able to formulate lasting claims on the state not only for adequate education but also along the lines proposed by Madame E.A.C.

In German cities, the kindergarten movement provided an important forum for feminist activity in promoting the role of mother-educators, as the work of the historian Ann Taylor Allen has demonstrated.[40] In various nationalist movements, whether Polish, Italian, Ukrainian, or, later, Finnish, women writers would repeatedly stake women's claims to full citizenship on their sociopolitical utility to the nation as mothers. Mother-educators claimed the vital role of keeping the national language alive, or of helping to revive it in the face of pressures by dominant political regimes to suppress it. In this context, however, that role could also serve antifeminist ends. Among early nineteenth-century Polish nationalists, the writer Klementyna Tanska Hoffmanova urged mothers to teach their children Polish (not French) and published extensively about Polish women's role and duties:[41]

> In my youth I saw the harm done to our sense of nationality by our in-fatuation with everything French. But having the truest and best mother in the world, in my youth I discovered the beauty of a woman's calling if she keeps to the path of her true destiny. So from the beginning of my lit-erary experience I have directed all my efforts to provide as many books as I can, in Polish, for Polish children. The intent is to familiarise them with everything Polish and to instill in growing girls the realisation that although God created them female they could be useful. My views on this are far from any advocacy of emancipation to which I am totally op-posed. I know of no need for any other philosophy for women except Christ's, nor of any other place in society than that which God deter-mined in the first days of creation: to be man's helpmate.

This emphasis on the importance of women as mothers even within neotraditional, nationalist contexts had significant reformist implica-tions. Witness the cautious efforts to reformulate relations between the sexes at the very beginnings of German Jewish reform in Hamburg. Women's role in preserving and transmitting Jewish culture was widely acknowledged to be central, but their exclusion from formal religious education and congregational governance had been firmly entrenched in custom. All this would change, thanks to the efforts of rabbis such as

Abraham Geiger, who in 1837 argued:[42]

> Let there be from now on no distinction between duties for men and
> women, unless flowing from the natural laws governing the sexes; no as-
> sumption of the spiritual minority of woman, as though she were inca-
> pable of grasping the deep things in religion; no institution of the public
> service, either in form or content, which shuts the doors of the temple in
> the face of women; no degradation of woman in the form of the marriage
> service, and no application of fetters which may destroy woman's happi-
> ness. Then will the Jewish girl and the Jewish woman, conscious of the
> significance of our faith, become fervently attached to it, and our whole
> religious life will profit from the beneficial influence which feminine
> hearts will bestow upon it.

Such claims for the importance of female cultural influence and
women's civilizing mission conferred dignity on womanhood, both
among secular rationalists and cultural nationalists and within the more
progressive sectors of religiously inspired groups, including the independent German Catholics. Our own contemporary critical perspective
(along with a not altogether unreasonable concern about the "inferioriza-
tion" of women through "difference") has too long blinded scholars to
the broader historical significance of this nineteenth-century emphasis
on sexual complementarity, of "equality-in-difference." Indeed, the celebration of the cultural significance of motherhood, as the key manifestation of sexual difference, would remain central to the feminist reconfiguration of "womanhood" and "womanliness" well into the twentieth
century.

It is important, too, to distinguish these formulations from the better-
known initiatives of French male thinkers such as Auguste Comte and
Jules Michelet, inventors of woman-centered secular religions that
placed women on pedestals from which they were forbidden to descend.
For instance, in the 1840s the philosopher-sociologist (and Saint-
Simonian renegade) Comte reconfigured his earlier "positive philosophy," in which he had invoked new scientific findings to argue against
the equality of the sexes, to reposition "Woman" as the central tenet of
his new "religion of humanity," and to subordinate politics to "morality." Moreover, he called the principle that "man should provide for
Woman" "a natural law of the human race."[43] This was an entirely different type of argument. Although Comte's formula likewise conferred a
certain dignity on Woman, seeming to enshrine her as man's muse, it
was in fact just another formula for positioning women as men's subordinates.

EXPANDING WOMEN'S "SPHERE": THE RECURRING
PROBLEM OF WORLDLY AMBITION

"Equality," wrote George Sand in her *Letters to Marcie* (1837), "is not similarity. Equal merit does not mean that one is suited to the same tasks."[44] To argue for the sociopolitical importance of women as mother-educators was to make a utilitarian argument for a distinctive public role, but at the same time to deliver a powerful statement for the moral and intellectual equality of the sexes—an equality grounded in sexual difference and complementarity. Meanwhile a different stream of argumentation was emerging. Against the printer–labor activist Pierre-Joseph Proudhon's admonition in 1846 that a woman could choose only harlotry or housewifery, some feminists in Europe would, like Tennyson's Princess Ida, claim entry to all aspects of societal life as their birthright.[45]

Civic motherhood and moral equality effectively required women to renounce some degree of worldly ambition. This was not acceptable to some feminists in this period. Early in 1837, Marie-Madeleine Poutret de Mauchamps, editor with her husband, Frédéric Herbinot de Mauchamps, of the Paris-based *Gazette des Femmes*, published a five-page petition addressed to the Institute de France. The petition requested that women be admitted to all five classes of the institute, and that they be eligible to compete for all the grand prizes, in painting, sculpture, engraving, architecture, and musical composition. The following year, she addressed another petition to the king and members of the Chamber of Deputies. In it, she demanded that women be admitted to all public courses, and that, following examinations, they be received as doctors of medicine, law, letters, and sciences. If women paid taxes to support such instruction, Poutret de Mauchamps claimed, they should be able to enjoy its benefits just as men did. "If," she added, "for selfish reasons, you reserve the exercise of these professions for men only, women will then recognize that HENCEFORTH THE CHARTER [of 1830] LIES and that they should make every effort, as you did in 1830, to change a constitution that completely excludes them from all participation in the liberal and learned professions, that deprives them of all worthy and useful instruction, and that prevents them from learning about the laws of their country."[46]

Once again, feminists had flung down the gauntlet. They asserted that women's access to knowledge—to print culture, to the arts and professions, to a public voice and presence—was a matter of politics. Feminists here contested the proposition that women could serve only as muses to male genius. "Why," asked the celebrated Paris-based woman writer Daniel Stern, "are the men of our time so afraid of a woman philosopher, and so willing to put up with a woman coquette?"[47]

Throughout early nineteenth-century Western Europe, formal educational opportunities for girls were increasing dramatically, though much schooling was still done privately or more informally at home. Yet women's learning—beyond the rudiments—was still contested as unsuitable. For them to publish under their own names was castigated as "public display," in consequence of which male pseudonyms disguised the work of many women writers, even in England and France. To deliberately attract attention to one's erudition or one's opinions was, since Rousseau, branded as vulgar, reprehensible, even promiscuous. Indeed, learned women—or even women with pretensions to expressing themselves in print—seemed to be even more highly suspect after the revolution than before; no more Laura Bassis could be identified teaching at Italian universities, though Italian academies continued to elect an occasional distinguished literary woman such as Sophie Gay or Delphine Gay de Girardin. The gifted woman mathematician Sophie Germain had kept a low public profile in 1820s Paris, though she was finally admitted to certain male scientific gatherings. George Sand spoke directly to this issue: "Women receive a deplorable education; and this is men's great crime against them." But, she added, perhaps hopefully, "the prejudice that bars women from the serious occupations of the mind is relatively recent."[48]

Even conservatives encouraged women to become civic mothers, helpmeets, and to exert their profound influence in society through quiet means. But how could women achieve in their own right? Could they be acclaimed as geniuses? Or was genius strictly a male attribute, as so many men saw fit to claim? Could they—should they?—engage themselves conspicuously with things of the mind? By the 1830s, a new generation of women scholars and women writers in France was "going public" at an ever accelerating rate, with the redoubtable Madame de Staël, now deceased, as their inspiration, and George Sand as their standard-bearer. Indeed, despite the pseudonym, Sand's example and influence extended far beyond French borders to inspire and encourage women writers throughout Europe.[49] Other women intellectuals, from Flora Tristan to Elizabeth Gaskell and Bettina Brentano von Arnim, combined social criticism with fiction to make their points about the necessity for expanding women's horizons, professionally as well as personally. In Paris in the 1840s there was even talk of nominating women writers to the Académie Française. But as Delphine Gay de Girardin (writing as

"Vicomte de Launay" in her husband's newspaper, *La Presse*) observed
ironically, bringing the debate to full circle: "Why should [women] have
a chair [at the Académie] in a country where they cannot have a throne?
Why would you accord them a pen when you have refused them a scep-
ter? Why, when they are nothing by their birth, should they be something by their genius? Why recognize a privilege for them when they are
denied all rights?"[50]

To pursue knowledge or the arts privately was one thing. But opponents charged that when a woman claimed a public voice, or displayed
her erudition, she effectively unsexed herself. That a negative, indeed
hostile, construction had been placed on women's claims to write and to
publish, to learn and to be heard, was clear from Jules Janin's snide characterization of "Bluestocking" women writers as "women men of letters," or the verse attached to an 1842 caricature of George Sand in male
costume:[51]

> If this portrait of George Sand
> Leaves the mind a bit perplexed
> It's because genius is abstract
> And as one knows has not a sex.

Christine Planté has documented the range and extent of the hostilities mounted in France by male literary critics against the "woman
author" (*femme écrivain*) during the July Monarchy, while Janis Bergman-Carton has demonstrated the severity of criticism of the "woman
of ideas" as registered in caricature and painting in those years.[52] The
shocking tactics of intimidation deployed in this highly public contest
were replicated far beyond France's borders. One anonymous British reviewer of a recently published advice book for Italian mother-educators
by Anna Pepoli remarked in 1841 that "the most insurmountable obstacle against female authorship lies in the deep-rooted antipathy, or, if we
must call it so, prejudice of the people of that country against any attempt on the part of a woman to call upon herself the gaze of the multitude or court notoriety. . . . Female authorship in Italy is looked upon as a
kind of moral hermaphroditism."[53] The tone of the article revealed the
reviewer's implicit wish to recommend this stance to his countrymen in
England as well. And indeed, in Victorian England, the path for women
writers was similarly strewn with land mines, as Deirdre David has
pointed out.[54] Anna Pepoli's quite conservative advice book for Italian
mothers was placed on the Index of Forbidden Books by the Vatican and
had to be published in Switzerland.

Women writers were even less welcome in Spain than in France, England, or Italy, according to Susan Kirkpatrick's study of women writers

in the 1840s. There the men who pioneered Spanish romanticism—the literary avant-garde, that is—seemed obsessively focused on containing women as domestic angels, "the angel in the house" (el angel del hogar). Spanish women writers, less brave perhaps than their French sisters across the border, felt it necessary to resort to highly contorted forms of self-presentation in order to justify their incursions into published space.[55] In such circumstances it was very difficult for feminist claims to be articulated.

But in Spain, Italy, and elsewhere, wherever publications in French, English, and German circulated, readers learned about the range and extent of women's ambitions and aspirations. Male privilege had been repeatedly called to account. And everywhere defenders of male privilege retaliated by attempting to discredit feminist claims and their makers by defining them as unwomanly. One had to be very brave indeed to be a feminist!

WELL BEFORE the revolutions of 1848, and in spite of a hostile political climate in most countries of Europe, clusters of women and some men sympathetic to women's emancipation had eloquently rearticulated claims to end female subordination. Once again restating claims that had flooded forth during the eighteenth-century Enlightenment, they elaborated the full range of criticisms that would characterize the movement for women's emancipation during the remainder of the century. They proposed visions of what a new society might look like in which women were men's equals. They criticized male-established marriage institutions and deplored women's legal, economic, and sexual dependence as wives; they called for divorce to end bad marriages. They attacked male definitions of womanhood, and proposed their own definitions, rehabilitating the idea of womanhood by insistence on women's potential importance as mother-educators, as physicians, as moral agents, as thinkers and doers, as artists and writers, as voters, and by consistently emphasizing the distinctive character of women's potential contributions to all aspects of society. They contested male definitions of economic life, arguing for women's right to economic independence, to restructuring the newly emerging world of extra-household employment so that it did not disadvantage women, especially as concerned childbearing. They objected to the sexual double standard that preserved the "virtue" of privileged women at the expense of poor women, and, finally, they criticized male control of political life, and claimed political representation for women based squarely on their differences from men and on the potential contribution they could make to the public weal. The elements of a thoroughgoing feminist critique of European society were clearly in evidence by 1848, but the development of an organized political movement for women's emancipation still lay a few years ahead.

5

Birthing the "Woman Question," 1848–1870

The crust of patriarchal political order rocked and trembled in 1848, the so-called springtime of the peoples. Beginning with the ouster of Louis-Philippe in Paris, protests and disturbances erupted in Berlin, Vienna, and Frankfurt, in Mainz, Meissen, Milan, Modena, Barcelona, Cologne, Prague, Venice, and Stockholm. The once redoutable chancellor of Austria, Prince Metternich, fled Vienna for exile, and the once fearsome European system of control on freedom of speech, the press, and association evaporated—though only temporarily. "Democracy" was on the march—but would it include women?

In some of these cities, feminist activity poured forth through the fissures opened by men's claims for representative government, for freedom of the press and association. Once again claiming their share of liberty, women founded newspapers and formed their own associations to demand rights and acknowledge their duties as integral members of "the people." Some demanded the right to vote on laws, freedom in marriage, including the right to divorce, and they called for educational and economic solutions to combat women's growing poverty. Others fought alongside men on the revolutionary barricades; a few even adopted male costume in order to fight against the established order. In Paris, a group of women who baptized themselves "the Vesuviennes," after the famous volcano in southern Italy, organized to parade through the streets in revolutionary bloomer costumes and tricolor sashes, whetting enthusiasm for the new order. Their "political constitution" called for men to share the housework, and demanded civil divorce.[1] They clearly believed, with the Saxon activists Robert Blum and Louise Otto, that "women's participation in the state is not just a right but a duty."[2]

The feminist honor roll for the 1848 revolutions grows ever longer. In the German-speaking world, the names of Louise Otto in Saxony, Matilda Franziska Anneke in Cologne, Kathinka Zitz-Halein in Mainz, and Karoline Perin in Vienna have joined the list of known activists in

Paris, including Jeanne Deroin, Eugénie Niboyet, Désirée Gay, and Jenny P. d'Héricourt. In most historical accounts of the revolutions of 1848, the extraordinary political activism of these women and others like them is scarcely mentioned; perhaps it seemed too disruptive to historians preoccupied by a male-centered political agenda. Even in the emerging histories of European feminism, this period and its counterrevolutionary sequel, extending from the widespread revolutions of 1848 to the literal birth of organized women's movements in the mid-1860s, remains incompletely understood. On the Continent, feminist activity in the French Second Republic (1848–51) is by now well documented.[3] Feminist historians insist on the significance of women's demands for political rights, which immediately followed the new government's proclamation in early March of "universal" suffrage and its abolition of slavery (both developments informed by earlier campaigns in England to end slavery, and to partially broaden the all-male parliamentary franchise). But historians have only recently thrown light on developments to the east of the Rhine.[4]

What does seem clear is that by 1850 counterrevolutionary forces had brutally suppressed feminist activism in most societies. But the issues resurfaced with relative rapidity in the later 1850s and early 1860s as increasing numbers of articulate women and men spoke out on the "woman question" (in French, *question des femmes*; in German, *Frauenfrage*; in Russian, *zhenskii vopros*; and in Swedish, *kvinnofrågan*), in a renewed burst of print. They argued their cases in fiction, poetry, and essays and articles in periodicals and in the daily press. These efforts might not yet qualify as an organized "movement," but their very frequency and broad geographical distribution suggest that the impulses to action would be increasingly difficult to contain, much less to eradicate.

In the 1860s the fissures in the crust of patriarchy widened and the molten lava of feminist protest against women's subordination would begin an even more sustained flow. New organizational and reformist initiatives blossomed as European feminists rephrased women's rights in terms of equal individual human rights (usually coupled with sex-based duties). They continued to develop analogies between women's emancipation and the parallel campaigns for ending black slavery in the United States and serfdom in the Russian Empire, and to address the problems of workers and the urban poor—the latter disproportionately female. Perhaps most important for the long term, the woman question took its place at the heart of the knowledge wars, providing the very core around which the new human sciences—sociology, anthropology, biology, psychology, pedagogy, and economics—would be constructed.

CHALLENGING MALE-ONLY CITIZENSHIP
IN THE FRENCH REPUBLIC

The issue of civic (or political) rights for women in 1848, particularly their demand for the vote, deserves a closer look. Most European states in the mid-nineteenth century did not have representative institutions, and in those few that did, no women could vote for parliamentary representatives. Nor, for that matter, could most men; despite the rhetorical claims for democracy, parliamentary representation, even for the propertied, was a relatively new and rare phenomenon. In the oldest parliamentary monarchy, England, as we have seen, women had been deliberately written out of the Reform Act of 1832, and even the most radical democrats, the Chartists, demanded the vote only for all men. Rare indeed were arguments like the one so eloquently expressed by the Scottish suffragist Marion Kirkland Reid, in her *Plea for Women* (1843): "The ground on which equality is claimed for all men is of equal force for all women; for women share the common nature of humanity, and are possessed of all those noble faculties which constitute man a responsible being, and give him a claim to be his own ruler." Picking up on a theme developed by feminists during the French Revolution, Reid argued that men legislated in their own interest; women's interests required representation, particularly as propertied (single) women, like men, paid taxes.[5]

The French Second Republic was the first nation-state in Europe to enfranchise all men without property or tax restrictions; this was called "universal" suffrage and "democratic." The Provisional Government boasted that:[6]

> The provisional electoral law that we have made is the most expansive that has ever, among any people on earth, called on the people to exercise the supreme right of man, his own sovereignty. The election belongs to everyone without exception. Dating from this law, there are no more proletarians in France. Every Frenchman [*Français*] of mature age [*en âge viril*] has political citizenship. Every citizen is an elector. Every elector is sovereign. The law is equal and absolute for all.

But the masculine usage of this "everyone" and "all" greatly astonished some French women. A small group of Parisian women immediately demanded to know why women had been "forgotten" and prepared a petition to the Provisional Government, insisting on the complementarity of the sexes, and making the point that if the "revolution has been made for all," women were assuredly "half of everyone," that "there could not be two liberties, two equalities, two fraternities," that "the people" is "composed of two sexes."[7] Shortly thereafter, a group constituting themselves as the Committee on the Rights of Women (Comité des Droits de la Femme) sent a delegation to the new government, demanding an explanation. "You say 'There are no more proletarians,' but if women are not included in your decrees, France can still count more than seventeen million of them."[8] The mayor of Paris, who was also a member of the Provisional Government, adroitly deferred action on this claim to the not yet elected National Assembly. But the deliberate exclusion of women exposed a serious omission at the heart of the movement for a democratic republic, demonstrating for all to see that the concept "citizen" in France had been gendered masculine.

The Parisian women, spearheaded by Jeanne Deroin and Eugénie Niboyet, refused to let the matter drop. They pursued their appeal for woman suffrage in the press and in the clubs; they also proposed nominating candidates. In *La Voix des femmes*, Deroin appealed to the National Assembly, arguing for "complete and true equality," even invoking the triumph of intelligence over brute strength and, like her English counterpart Marion Reid, the principle of no taxation without representation: "When they abolish all privileges, they will not think of conserving the worst one of all and leaving one half of the nation under the domination of the other half. They will at least give us a role in national representation."[9]

The people's delegates to the National Assembly did refuse. When Victor Considerant, a deputy and a committed Fourierist, subsequently proposed extending the municipal vote to single adult women only, he was laughed off the floor. The French Assembly's scorn for woman suffrage did not go unnoticed abroad. In London, the venerable *Times* took notice when Benjamin Disraeli (who would one day be Queen Victoria's Prime Minister) raised the issue of parliamentary suffrage for women once again in the British House of Commons during a mid-June debate on the representation of the people:[10]

I believe that in another country some ridicule has been excited by a gentleman who has advocated the rights of the other sex. (A laugh.) But, Sir, as far as mere abstract reasoning is concerned, I should like to hear any gentleman of those who will support the hon. member get up and oppose that claim. In a country governed by a woman (hear)—where you allow women to form a part of the other estate of the realm, for women are peeresses in their own right—where women possess manors, and hold law courts—and where women are by law elected as churchwardens (a laugh)—I don't see when women have so much to do in this country in state and church, why, when you come to the reason of the thing, they should not also have a right to vote.

It was in this international context that the defeat of civic rights for French women and Jeanne Deroin's subsequent candidacy for the Legislative Assembly in 1849 would take on added significance. Even in the mid-nineteenth century, such news traveled fast. In Vienna, an as yet unidentified group of women also called for political rights: "Beware of believing that we are not filled with the most lively interest in the emancipation of humanity. . . . We claim equality of political rights. Why should women not be elected to the Reichstag? . . . It would be false to call suffrage universal, if at least half of all the subjects are excluded."[11]

By mid-June 1848 (after weeks of civil disruption) the National Assembly, which was far from the revolutionary body anticipated in March, abruptly shut down all political clubs, making an explicit point of closing those organized by women. In the course of these debates over suffrage and the closing of the clubs, feminists effectively exposed the political significance of language for the politics of citizenship. In France, did *tous les français* encompass women? In England, did the term "man" or "people" encompass women? Clearly, the answer—in the electoral laws at least—was no. In England, the importance of gender politics in legal language was sufficiently recognized that in 1850 Parliament would pass an Act (thanks to the pro-woman legal reformers Lord Brougham and Lord Romilly) addressing this issue: "In all Acts words importing the masculine gender shall be deemed and taken to include females unless the contrary . . . is expressly provided," as had been the case in the 1832 Reform Act.[12] This clarification would open doors to change.

THE LANGUAGE OF FEMINIST DEMANDS

IN THE 1848 REVOLUTIONS

Feminists in the era of 1848 deployed the language of rights and equality to argue their cause. They very often argued for women's equality in terms of women's differences from men, however, rather than in terms of similarities. The concept of equality at that time was still understood primarily as a question of formal equality in the law (the right to hold property, the right to vote, for example) or of equal opportunities (to formal education, to employment). Although feminists made demands for women's inclusion in all arenas of worldly ambition a priority, they did not then understand equal rights as a synonym for "sameness" or as a demand for identical treatment for all individuals in all circumstances of societal life. Women were claiming their rights *as women*, as human beings who happened to be female, but they also claimed their womanhood with pride. In the process, some took their distance from accusations of sensuality even as they reclaimed the word "emancipation," which had stirred up controversy since the 1830s when the Saint-Simonian experiments had branded it into the public mind as a synonym for sexual promiscuity. The manifesto of the Paris-based Society for the Emancipation of Women in mid-March 1848 stated it in these terms:[13]

> The word emancipation, in its absolute and legitimate sense, signifies above all, intellectual and moral liberation [*affranchisement*]. This first and highest condition being, for both sexes, the normal basis of all social progress, carries with it all the other consequences. The word emancipation is so often abused that this explanatory note seemed necessary.

Two women exemplify the possibilities and limitations of European feminist thought and action in 1848. The French woman Jeanne Deroin and her somewhat younger German counterpart Louise Otto, from Saxony, illustrate the ways in which the cause of women's emancipation was wedded to the political and intellectual history of the times. Their respective approaches also provide insight into the national differences that emerged in the course of the nineteenth century. Both women took active roles in the revolutionary events of midcentury Europe, publishing women's periodicals during the revolutionary years, Deroin in Paris, and Otto first in Meissen (Saxony), then in Gera. Both made radical demands: Deroin advocated women's suffrage, while Otto argued for a recasting of women's educational and economic situation. Both asserted women's claims to liberty and equality as staunchly as they defended women's "difference," without perceiving these claims as in the least paradoxical or contradictory. Both were "relational" feminists, comfortable with the notion of "equality-in-difference," a term popularized by the French male feminist Ernest Legouvé.[14]

Jeanne Deroin was a Parisian working-class woman in her early forties, a seamstress and teacher, who though married and a mother used her given name rather than that of her husband, Desroches. As noted earlier, she had participated in the Saint-Simonian movement during the 1830s, contributing many articles to the Saint-Simonian women's paper, and she had subsequently absorbed many of the teachings of Charles Fourier concerning the reorganization of the household and labor. She considered herself a democratic socialist, but she gave priority to the cause of women.[15]

Writing in the women's newspaper *La Voix des femmes* (Women's Voice), founded by Eugénie Niboyet shortly after the outbreak of the Paris revolution, Deroin first called for women's formal participation in

public affairs. Even after the National Assembly closed the clubs, effectively ending all organized female political activism in France, Deroin
persisted. Even after the male voters elected Louis-Napoleon (heir of the
Bonaparte dynasty) president of the Republic, she continued to press for
women's inclusion in political life. She founded her own periodical,
L'Opinion des femmes (Women's Opinion), and in the spring of 1849, in
a serialized essay on "woman's mission," she presented her vision of
what women's participation in the public sphere needed to accomplish.[16]

Despite the disappointments of the previous year, Deroin asserted
that the revolutionary overthrow of the monarchy in 1848 and the establishment of a democratic form of government had radically changed the
conditions of political life in France. Violence and repression must
henceforth yield to participatory government. The first priority of
democratic government must be to end the struggle between women and
men. Only by abolishing male privilege (in this case, male political privilege) could the new government achieve the realization of a truly new
society. Deroin viewed privileges of sex as even more insidious than
those of class. "The abolition of the privileges of race, birth, caste, and
fortune cannot be complete and radical unless the privilege of sex is totally abolished," she wrote. Deroin argued that only by achieving full
citizenship could women effectively participate in the reconstruction of
French society.

In Deroin's view, the contributions of women and men to society
were utterly distinct. Deroin insisted on the complementarity of the
sexes, and she based her arguments for women's participation in political affairs on sexual complementarity and women's difference (both biological and social) from men—in particular, on woman's "sacred function as mother" and her "sublime humanitarian maternity." In Deroin's
estimation, woman had not only a right but a duty, given her maternal
role, to intercede in both civil and political life in order to carry out the
duty of watching over the future of her children.

Women, Deroin argued, must be called on to "teach everyone how
fraternity should be practiced," to show men the way of transcending
secular quarrels between individuals, between families, and between nations. Women had nothing less than an apostolic mission to "realize the
kingdom of God on earth, the reign of fraternity and universal harmony." Deroin never clearly elaborated her reasons for insisting on
women's ability to achieve these goals; in the existing climate of male
revolutionary violence, both physical and verbal, she seems to have considered women's moral superiority self-evident.

Deroin did more than make claims for women's participation in public life, however; she acted on her ideals. Early in 1849, she petitioned the Democratic Socialist Party to become a candidate for the Legislative Assembly. Her most vociferous opponent, the party's leading polemicist, the printer Pierre-Joseph Proudhon, was well known for his antifeminist assertion that women could be only "housewives or harlots."[17] The Democratic Socialists refused Deroin's candidacy, but she merits a distinctive place in the history of European feminism for her synthesis of ideals and activism. Not only was she the first European woman to declare her candidacy for public office under a democratized regime, but she was also one of the first women to be arrested and imprisoned for her efforts to organize joint associations of male and female workers (yet another form of political activity prohibited in mid-nineteenth-century France). In 1852 Deroin fled to England, along with other men and women who actively opposed Louis-Napoleon's tightening grip on political power. Although she kept in touch with French progressives, she spent the remainder of her life in London as a political exile.[18]

Feminist activists in the German states adopted an alternative set of arguments, although as in France they emphasized women's difference as a central tenet. There, German womanliness, in combination with social motherhood, provided the central theme. In German feminist discourse, arguments often carried nationalist overtones, emphasizing the distinctive contribution women, as women, could and must make to the building of the still nonexistent German nation, a conspicuous goal of political reformers prior to the forced unification of the many German principalities by the Prussian king in 1871. The arguments put forth by Louise Otto, a well-educated single woman of upper-middle-class background who, like Deroin, had become a political radical, exemplify this particular approach.

Based in Saxony, one of Germany's most industrialized regions, in 1849 Otto founded and edited the *Frauenzeitung* (Women's Newspaper), the longest-lived of several German revolutionary women's publications.[19] Since the mid-1840s, she had crusaded for systematic reform of the education of middle-class women and for improvements in the condition of working women in Saxony's industrial cities. Marriage, in Otto's view, was a degraded institution, merely "a support institution for the female sex." She scorned women's "characterlessness" in a culture where the building of character (*Bildung*) was considered so extremely important for educated men. Reflecting the spirit of idealist German philosophy since Kant (though Kant would hardly have applied such ideas to women), Otto emphasized "independence," not only of a moral or ethical nature ("the exercise of judgment") but also of a material or economic nature ("the exercise of action").[20]

Of particular significance to Louise Otto was her oft-repeated concern with "true womanliness," a quality quite different from, and far more potent than, the characterlessness she objected to in so many German women of her age. Her arguments for "true womanliness" carried a defensive tone, however; she constantly issued disclaimers against those who discredited the emancipation of woman "by devaluing woman to become a caricature of a man." Otto was doubtless thinking of the outspoken writer Louise Aston, who had been expelled from Berlin in 1846, following publication of her "Wild Roses."[21]

Lifestyle issues had become a sore point among German feminists, following a recent wave of *Georgesandismus*, a term used to refer to self-proclaimed "emancipated women" who appropriated the unorthodox and much-caricatured habits of the French novelist George Sand. These contentious habits included wearing male dress (still illegal—even in France—without a police permit), smoking, and engaging in liaisons with men to whom one was not married. Indeed, in Central Europe, Sand had become a symbol of all that was dangerous about French culture, and condemnations of her loose lifestyle showed up repeatedly not only among antifeminists and German nationalists, but also in the pro-woman arguments of German feminist reformers of this period. In consequence, German feminists at midcentury often demonstrated a peculiarly self-righteous and straitlaced quality. Otto's conception of "true womanhood" was, above all else, virtuous, courageous, moralistic, patriotic, and peaceable. In addition to refuting *Georgesandismus*, it represented all the things German men allegedly were not.[22]

The arguments of a Parisian male feminist confirm the emphasis being placed on "equality-in-difference." The French essayist and playwright Ernest Legouvé summed up the arguments for radical change in the legal, educational, and economic status of women in his *Moral History of Women* (1849), which he first presented in the spring of 1848 as a series of public lectures at the Collège de France, sponsored by the new republican Ministry of Public Instruction.[23] Legouvé called on men to reflect about the political implications of including women in the new regime; he charged that the 1789 revolution had failed because it was unjust to women. He advocated that the "virile" republican principles of liberty and equality must, in order to be realized, be complemented by what he called "the feminine virtue of fraternity," which "grew out of women's love." No republic, he intimated, would succeed except at this price. Legouvé's lectures and subsequent book offered a protracted argument for "equality-in-difference," a case for women's emancipation under the republic, grounded in women's distinctive physiological, mental, and emotional differences from men, and especially in their vital social role as mothers. He emphasized the importance of women's past and prospective contributions as a sex to human culture, in both private and public life. He insisted as well on the necessity for separate but equal—or parallel—tracks for women and men, linked through the institution of monogamous marriage. His explicit target was the legal subordination of women embodied in the Napoleonic Code and the inadequate education of women. He did not, however, advocate full political rights for women. In the context of 1848 pre-election politics, he proposed that "women should have a place in the State, but *a place different than that of men.*"[24]

Recent analyses of German feminism suggest that many religiously identified reformist factions were just as eager as those in France to invoke women's "difference" as a basis for equality, and to invoke female influence as a potent political tool. The research of Ann Taylor Allen on "spiritual motherhood" and of Catherine Prelinger and Sylvia Paletschek on the radical German Catholic group led by Johannes Ronge, which founded the Hamburg High School for Girls, demonstrates how imbued with radicalizing potential this notion could be, but Dagmar Herzog's findings in Baden also suggest its limits.[25]

At midcentury, however, advocates of female subordination were also invoking arguments for the importance of female influence. The secular philosopher Auguste Comte (who would be christened as the "father" of sociology and the founder of "positivist" philosophy) insisted in a new work, *System of Positive Philosophy* (1848), that equality of the sexes was contraindicated by Nature as well as by human evolution: "All history assures us that with the growth of society the peculiar features of each sex have become not less but more distinct."[26] Arguing for the subordination of politics to morality, Comte appointed women as "spontaneous priestesses of humanity," consigning them to the realm of the family, where man could support woman but should also worship her.

The Roman Catholic pope Pius IX, fleeing from the revolution in Rome in 1849, similarly invoked the positive power of educated and influential womanhood when he called for promulgation of the dogma of the Immaculate Conception of Mary. As men defected from the church, the pope seemed especially anxious to retain women's allegiance in a time of revolutionary upheaval; he understood and hoped to harness the power of Christian mothers in forming souls for the church.[27] Though they were poles apart politically, both the pope and Comte testified to their shared belief in the importance of female influence for the regeneration of European political and cultural life, as well as to the necessity of controlling and channeling it. Unlike the feminists, neither argued for women's emancipation, even in qualified terms, based on such beliefs. In the highly politicized atmosphere of mid-nineteenth-century Europe, the reinvigorated and highly elastic notions of separate spheres, female influence, civic motherhood, and mother educators could and would henceforth serve both revolutionary and counterrevolutionary ends.

Both revolutionaries and counterrevolutionaries could agree on one thing: women's civic activism, even when it was not accompanied by overt feminist claims, posed a clear threat to male hegemony. In order to douse the flames of revolution on the Continent, therefore, governments shut down women's associations and clubs and passed laws excluding women from taking an active role in the political press. During the Prague revolution, the editors of *Bohemia* attempted to forestall women's rights agitation. When a delegation of Prague women went to see the Habsburg empress in Vienna, their goal was to found a girls' school in Prague. Only one woman, Bozena Nemcová, spoke openly in favor of girls' education without disavowing rights claims. As a precautionary measure, the imperial authorities enacted a law on association in March 1849 that banned all political activity by women.[28] In 1850 the Prussian king pushed through a decree "protecting lawful freedom and order from the abuse of the rights of assembly and association," which banned women—as well as male students—from becoming members of political organizations and even from attending their meetings.[29] This law would remain in force until 1908. Measures of this type were also enacted in Bavaria, Saxony, and Brunswick, and in 1854 were incorporated into the protocols of the German Confederation. Only a few principalities and free cities escaped their rigor.

Feminist women were not silent about the failed revolutions of 1848 with respect to women's rights. In her poem "For All" (1848) Louise Otto bemoaned the exclusionary aspect of the situation in Germany:[30]

> ... on men alone rights were conferred
> In the upheavals of the revolution.
> For even though it seemed like changes had occurred
> And like the monarchy was on the brink of dissolution:
> Those new struggles were for the rights of man;
> The rights of woman were not part of their plan. ...
> The free men spoke of fraternization:
> They were citizens, not lords and slaves;
> They sang of their new affiliation

> And considered themselves a reborn race.
> But they viewed their sisters with deprecation—
> There were no rights for half the populace,
> For the cry "for all!" excluded women—
> They were denied the rights of citizens.

A similar refrain came from the pen of the Spanish poet Caroline Coronado in her meditation on "Liberty" (1852):[31]

> Young men are proud,
> Old men are happy,
> There is equality in our land,
> Liberty in the realm.
> But I tell you, sisters,
> That the law is only their law,
> Women do not count,
> Nor is there a Nation for this sex.
> Therefore, though I hear the men,
> I do not applaud for myself nor feel joy.

Thus it was not surprising, in view of the once again extremely repressive political climate of continental Europe, that organized women's movements could hardly get off the ground. The most successful initial efforts to organize took place outside Europe, in the United States, beginning with the Seneca Falls Convention in July 1848. This convention, called shortly after the forced closing of the Parisian women's clubs, rewrote the American Declaration of Independence on women's behalf. In mid-1851, the English critic Harriet Taylor Mill (who had recently married her longtime companion John Stuart Mill) expressed her admiration in the *Westminster Review* of the activism by American women who in 1850 had convened at Worcester, Massachusetts, in pursuit of their "rights." "What is wanted for women," she wrote, "is equal rights, equal admission to all social privileges; not a position apart, a sort of sentimental priesthood."[32] Jeanne Deroin and Pauline Roland, from the depths of their prison cells, appealed to the women of America in 1851: "The darkness of reaction has obscured the sun of 1848, which seemed to rise so radiantly." "No mention was made of the right of woman in a Constitution framed in the name of Liberty, Equality, and Fraternity."[33]

The great French dramatist Victor Hugo, in exile following Louis-Napoleon's coup d'état, mourned the death in 1853 of one of the women activists exiled from France as the revolution was crushed and universal manhood suffrage once again abolished. At her funeral he prophetically declared: "The eighteenth century proclaimed the right of man; the nineteenth will proclaim the right of woman."[34] On the Continent,

Hugo's prophecy would long await vindication. Not until the late 1850s and 1860s would organized efforts on women's emancipation even begin to establish a toehold.

NEW INITIATIVES, MULTIPLE FRONTS, 1850–1865

The prospects for women's political rights on the Continent had been crushed for the foreseeable future, but other initiatives emerged on multiple fronts scattered throughout Europe. Within a few years, calls for reform of marriage laws, for education and employment for women took center stage in England and in the Scandinavian countries, perhaps stimulated by the agitation for married women's property acts then under way in the United States.

English feminists quickly took action. In 1854 Barbara Leigh Smith (later Bodichon) and Caroline Norton published two stinging critiques of the legal annihilation of English wives, who were more thoroughly subordinated in marriage law than in any other European country.[35] The custom of coverture in the common law made them effectively legal nonpersons; even their personal belongings were the property of their husbands. Moreover, a full-fledged civil divorce was possible only by a special Act of Parliament, and then only following a court finding that the wife had committed adultery. Thanks to the intervention of Lord Brougham, founder of the Law Amendment Society (1844), with the help of a number of other reforming members of Parliament, action began in 1856; 1,300 English women, including some of the best-known writers, sent a petition to Parliament in March.[36] The petition argued that all women, not only more privileged women, and not only wives, were adversely affected by coverture, in a time when earnings were increasingly necessary for women of all classes. Even the relatively antifeminist journalist Eliza Lynn (Linton) supported this married women's property initiative.[37]

Parliament approved a Divorce Act in 1857, but at the expense of any resolution of the married women's property problem, which retained its central place on the English feminist agenda for another twenty years. In Mary Lyndon Shanley's summary: "Parliament did *enlarge* the rights of married women significantly in the course of the nineteenth century, but it repeatedly rejected the invitation held out by feminists to *equalize* the rights and obligations of husbands and wives."[38]

The issue of women's legal subjection was resolved more speedily in Norway and Sweden, thanks in part to two pioneering novels with feminist themes, *The District Governor's Daughter* (1854–55) by Camilla

Collett, and Fredrika Bremer's *Hertha* (1855).[39] Bremer's novel proved particularly influential in rallying support to overturn (in 1858) Sweden's Paternal Statutes of 1734, which gave fathers enormous legal authority over daughters, even as adults. By 1872 unmarried daughters in Sweden would achieve full legal emancipation. Denmark passed a similar Majority Act, giving single adult women full civil (legal) standing, in 1857.

In Italy, the achievement of national unification in 1861 raised questions about women's inclusion in citizenship as well as about their education. In 1861 a handbill signed by a group of Italian women citizens (*cittadine italiane*) from Lombardy argued that "the chief foundations [of the liberty of the nation] must be the broadest possible affirmation of the emancipation of women."[40] Unification also raised the question of laws regarding married women. To consolidate the nation, the laws of five major preexisting political regions, each of which treated the legal position of women differently, had to be harmonized in a unified code. During debates on the proposed code, the Milanese feminist Anna Maria Mozzoni argued, against the law professor Carlo Francesco Gabba, for the full civil and political emancipation of women. Neither marriage, nor motherhood, nor occupation, nor physique should disqualify women, whose natural rights were, in Mozzoni's opinion, absolute.[41] The Italian Code, enacted 1865, followed the pattern set by the Piedmontese (Albertine) Code of 1837, which itself drew heavily on the Napoleonic Code, with the major difference that its provisions for separation of property in marriage imposed less of a handicap on married women.

Efforts to reform the legal situation of married women in France had, meanwhile, to await the liberalization of the Second Empire in the late 1860s. Léon Richer and Maria Deraismes combined forces to challenge the Napoleonic Code's provisions for marital authority and the subordinate status of wives with respect to community-property law. Single adult women had long been fully emancipated in civil law, but were still subjected to administrative hassles concerning their marital status. Richer's periodical, *Le Droit des femmes* (founded 1868), would insistently promote radical change in French marriage law during the next twenty years, in the face of great resistance.[42]

In mid-nineteenth-century Russian society, married women did enjoy property rights. But young unmarried adult women were still formally subject to the legal authority of fathers; thus, personal autonomy had a far more concrete meaning than it did in France or England, where such women were legally—if not morally or economically—free of such constraints. Young Russian women of the 1860s often resorted to fictitious marriages (called "white marriages") with sympathetic and unconventional young men in order to acquire the necessary male authorization to escape from their families, pursue studies, and follow their dreams. Historian Linda Edmondson has persuasively suggested that the tight link between state and patriarchal family authority in Russia can explain why feminist agitation for personal liberty in that setting quickly developed in an antifamily and antistatist direction.[43]

Other, more organized efforts to improve other aspects of women's situation soon sprang up, especially in England, which had been far less traumatized by the 1848 revolutions than its neighbors on the Continent. There, women members of the woman-friendly National Association for the Promotion of Social Science (NAPSS), founded in 1857, spawned a host of organizations and projects aimed at improving women's condition: these included the Ladies' National Association for the Diffusion of Sanitary Knowledge, the Society for Promoting the Industrial Employment of Women and the Workhouse Visiting Society (both 1859), followed by the Female Middle-Class Emigration Society, the Victoria Press (an all-women publishing venture, which produced the *Transactions* of the NAPSS), and the National Union for Improving the Education of Women of All Classes (1871). Efforts as varied as the Married Women's Property Committee (1867), the London National Society for Women's Suffrage (1867), and the Ladies' National Association for the Repeal of the Contagious Diseases Acts (1870) all had roots in the concerns of NAPSS women members. As historian Kathleen McCrone has noted, "the roster of the [NAPSS's] female members reads like a who's who of Victorian womanhood," including many of the leading names in Victorian feminism, such as Lydia Becker, Helen Blackburn, Jessie Boucherett, Frances Power Cobbe, Emily Davies, Bessie Rayner Parkes, Barbara Leigh Smith, and Elizabeth Wolstenholme."[44]

Women's education and employment opportunities were of special concern to feminists throughout Europe during this period. In London, Barbara Leigh Smith (later Bodichon), Bessie Rayner Parkes, and their associates in the Langham Place Circle founded not only the Society for Promoting the Employment of Women (to address the needs of single middle-class women) but also the *Englishwoman's Journal*. In Paris during the early 1860s, when the imperial government authorized the admission of women to employment in state-operated concessions, including the telegraph service and tobacco concessions, Elisa Lemmonier pioneered schools for girls' vocational instruction. André Léo (Léodile Bera

Champceix) founded the society Revendication des Droits de la Femme (Demand for Women's Rights) to encourage women's education and promote legal reforms. In Berlin, the Lette-Verein (1865) was established to promote women's work, under the patronage of the Prussian crown princess, and Louise Otto succeeded in founding the "nonpolitical" Allgemeiner Deutscher Frauenverein (General Association of German Women). In St. Petersburg a local women's group also made plans for a Society for Women's Work. In 1865 the Dutch Anna-Maria (Minette) Storm van der Chijs established the first industrial trade school for girls in Amsterdam, and in 1869 Dutch activists founded a private secondary school for girls in Haarlem. In 1870 Karolina Svetla would organize the Bohemian Women's Commercial and Industrial Society in Prague.

Training schools for teachers were among the many significant undertakings. Women activists in Britain had already established schools to prepare impecunious single women of the middle classes for positions as governesses in private households and as schoolteachers. In the wake of the brief "revolution of 1868" in Spain, Madrid reformers founded a teachers' institute for women, with the intention of mounting a campaign for the instruction of girls and women, most of whom were still illiterate. Teaching children was the one position then deemed as suitable employment for women, no doubt because it could be construed as an extension of women's maternal role, and preparation for civic motherhood itself, following marriage. But even here, advocates for girls' education increasingly insisted on the importance of educating women for their own sake, as a human right, not only for the sake of their children.[45] In smaller countries such as Denmark, where traditionalists actively opposed formal education for girls, such schools were founded relatively late and then only with the most conservative rationales.

The claims made for women's right to work reached a new level of radicalism in England, with the publication by Barbara Leigh Smith of the pamphlet *Women and Work* in 1857. Combatting the mounting tide of male-breadwinner argumentation, Leigh Smith's arguments deliberately highlighted the sexual politics involved in the question of women's self-support:[46]

> Fathers have no right to cast the burden of the support of their daughters on other men. It lowers the dignity of women; and tends to prostitution, whether legal or in the streets. As long as fathers regard the sex of a child as a reason why it should not be taught to gain its own bread, so long must women be degraded. Adult women must not be supported by men, if they are to stand as dignified, rational beings before God. . . . Women must have work if they are to form equal unions.

Even more controversial than training women so that they could earn their own keep was the project of obtaining women's entry to university-level coursework and degrees. Throughout Europe, wherever higher education provided the gateway to professional careers in church and state service as well as a means of obtaining advanced knowledge, women's efforts to enter these male sanctuaries frequently provoked stiff resistance from professors and male students, as we will see below in the case of medicine.

Still bolder feminist initiatives followed as new issues emerged. Critiques of government-licensed prostitution added another highly charged issue to the feminist agenda, in the context of mounting urban social problems, especially female poverty. Since its inauguration in Paris in 1802, complete with a "morals police" agency, the state regulation system had been spreading throughout Europe, enthusiastically promoted by a combination of male physicians, public hygiene experts, and military authorities. Following Italian unification in 1860, for example, regulating prostitution quickly became a governmental priority.

In England, Parliament enacted a series of Contagious Diseases Acts in 1864, 1866, and 1869, setting up a modified system of state regulation designed to protect male military personnel from venereal diseases by controlling and inspecting female prostitutes. This program quickly led to indiscriminate police harassment of women on the streets of garrison towns, including many who were not prostitutes. These actions provoked Josephine Butler, who quickly launched a campaign for repeal of the acts. The so-called Women's Protest, signed by 124 women, and published in the *Daily News* (London) in the 1870 New Year's Day issue, pointed out not only the violation of women's civil rights inherent in the acts but also the double standard of morality these laws implicitly sanctioned: "It is unjust to punish the sex who are the victims of a vice, and leave unpunished the sex who are the main cause, both of the vice and its dreaded consequences; and we consider that liability to arrest, forced medical treatment, and (where this is resisted) imprisonment with hard labour, to which these Acts subject women, are punishments of the most degrading kind."[47] This manifesto bravely confronted a problem that well-bred "ladies," single ladies and clergymen's wives in particular, were not supposed even to know about, demanding that the "*causes* of the evil*" be addressed. Butler's efforts in particular earned feminists the epithet "the shrieking sisterhood" from the *Saturday Review* and an embarrassed "conspiracy of silence" from the British press. Undaunted, Butler founded her own periodical, *The Shield*, to spread word of the antiregulationist campaign.

Butler's campaign quickly became an international affair. Feminist writers such as Harriet Martineau in London, Julie-Victoire Daubié in Paris, and Anna-Maria Mozzoni in Milan all addressed the issue of regulated prostitution, calling for the dismantling of a system that so blatantly discriminated against women. In the course of the 1870s Butler's crusade led to the formation of an international alliance which had as its ultimate goal not only the abolition of state-regulated prostitution on the French model throughout Europe but also the so-called white slave trade itself.[48] The Contagious Disease Acts in England were finally abolished in 1886, but the abolitionist campaigns on the European continent would continue into the twentieth century.

British feminist initiatives against regulated prostitution, married women's property law, and the continuing difficulties of ending bad marriages focused attention on the problem of male sexual violence against women and children in the family. Frances Power Cobbe led the charge on this issue, first challenging "the divine right of husbands," then exposing what life was really like for some women within the sanctuary of the family in an attempt to liberalize marriage laws on behalf of aggrieved wives.[49] Such concerns also raised questions about male use and abuse of alcohol.

The women's campaign against war, increasingly viewed as another state-sanctioned form of male violence, capped the new feminist initiatives launched in the 1850s and 1860s. In late August 1854, shortly after the outbreak of the Crimean War, the Swedish novelist Fredrika Bremer published a letter in the *Times* of London. Bremer was already well known in England, thanks to the efforts of her translator Mary Howitt. Her "Invitation to a Peace Alliance" called for a peaceful international alliance of women "opposing the direful effects of war . . . and contributing . . . to the development of a state of peace, love, and well-being, to come forth when once the terrors of war shall be over, and the time of devastation has passed away." Bremer proposed uniting philanthropic Christian women across boundaries and borders, inviting them "to join hands as sisters," and to learn from one another, in order to "alleviate the miseries of the earth."[50]

Bremer's peace initiative was but one of a series of transnationalist feminist initiatives that sought to unite women in order to address general societal problems, not only to remedy their effects but, more significantly, to address their causes. These "problems" included the phenomenon of war itself. In the later 1860s, as the Prussian military campaigns of annexation and expansion with the goal of national unification got under way, the Swiss feminist-pacifist Marie Goegg would establish an International Association of Women with multiple emancipatory aims, not the least of which was to seek to forestall war itself by addressing the underlying causes of militarist values. One of Goegg's objectives was, in historian Sandi Cooper's words, "the re-education of mothers to prevent another generation of boys trained to respect the false idols of national glory through military conquest."[51] Goegg's articles and speeches were published in the short-lived periodical of the International League for Peace and Freedom, *Les États-Unis d'Europe*. The Prussian victory over France in 1870 and the Paris Commune in 1871 would put an abrupt end to Goegg's prescient pacifist-feminist project, but it would reemerge in the 1870s with new vigor.[52]

LAUNCHING THE KNOWLEDGE WARS

In 1850 a virtually unknown Danish woman, Mathilde Fibiger, published her *Klara Raphael: Tolv Breve* (Clara Raphael: Twelve Letters) under the patronage of a well-known Copenhagen intellectual, Johan Ludvig Heiberg. There she told the story of a young woman who wanted to devote herself to the pursuit of ideas. Fibiger's Clara Raphael refused marriage to a worthy man in order to achieve her goal:[53]

> For the first time in my life I feel sorry that I am not a man. How poor and empty is our life compared with theirs! Is it just that half the people should be excluded from all intellectual pursuits? Or did our Lord really create us of poorer stuff than men (as I have heard one fascinating gentleman of the neighbourhood declare in all seriousness), so that we are to be content to carry out automatically the trivial labour allotted to us in this life? Does our mind then possess no power and our heart no enthusiasm? Indeed they do, but the real life within us has not come to awareness, our spirit is captive and prejudice stands guard outside the prison.

Fibiger's volume stirred up a stormy controversy, a virtual literary war on the woman question, both in Copenhagen and throughout the Scandinavian literary world. It was a harbinger of things to come, as individual women of intellect and ambition began to articulate their desires not in terms of sexual complementarity, but in terms of self-realization outside of and beyond the highly disadvantageous constraints of marriage and family. Prior to Florence Nightingale's *Cassandra* (written in 1852 and privately published in 1860), which railed against the suffocation of privileged women in family life, *Klara Raphael* had claimed the life of the mind for women.

The issue of women's relationship to knowledge took a dramatic step forward in the years between 1850 and 1870. Feminist writers attempted to seize the high ground, claiming knowledge in their own right, and thus going beyond the old debate about women's creativity by demonstrating it. Thereby they hoped to mute questions as to whether women could create works of "genius," or should settle for being the mothers of "men of genius," as Henry Buckle would suggest in 1859.

In France, the novels of the prolific George Sand continued to pour forth from the presses, inspiring women writers all over Europe. In 1865, a flurry of pamphlet literature would propose her candidacy to the venerable Académie Française. In England Charlotte Brontë had raised the novel to new heights, with *Jane Eyre* (1847) and *Shirley* (1849), ably seconded by Elizabeth Gaskell's *Mary Barton* (1848), *Ruth* (1853), *Cranford* (1853), and *North and South* (1855); and Elizabeth Barrett Browning published her landmark epic poem *Aurora Leigh* (1855). Each of these writers placed analyses of the woman question at center stage. Subsequently, the novels of George Eliot (Marian Evans) offered new evidence in the case for women's literary genius. Artistic genius manifested itself in the massive canvases of the painter Rosa Bonheur. When France's Empress Eugénie awarded the Cross of the Legion of Honor to Bonheur in June 1865, she insisted: "It was my desire that the last act of my regency be consecrated to showing that in my eyes genius has no sex."[54]

The French Protestant feminist Jenny P. (Poinsard) d'Héricourt had used the years following the failure of the 1848 revolution to earn a degree in homeopathic medicine and become a practicing midwife, certified by the Paris Faculty of Medicine. In an 1855 article, "On Woman's Future," published in Turin in the Kingdom of Piedmont, she reminded her readers of the Saint-Simonians' earlier call for women to speak out: "Today," she wrote, "several women have disengaged themselves from the secular absorption of their sex and have developed their own individuality. These women, and I am one of them, can now reply to that call . . . and that is what I am going to do."[55]

Challenging the established wisdom, Jenny P. d'Héricourt revealed herself as a full-fledged combatant on a par with men in the knowledge wars. Invoking the law of progress, she traced out a theory of gender formation. Organic modifications, she argued, have their seat in the brain, which is "essentially modifiable." There are now women, who have had a masculine education, who are in possession of rational faculties, just as there are men who preponderantly display feelings. "It is *radically false*," she argued, "that nature made men rational and women emotional; it is education and morals that made them thus: feelings and rationality are equally distributed. . . . The brain is the instrument of progress." The mind may have no sex, but the genderless brain requires exercise to develop. No more women's nature, women's destiny, women's functions, no more women's sphere. Women, just like men, are en route to "individual independence." Finally, women must cease asking for their rights and *take them*. They must remain women, not emulating masculine habits or airs, and they must ally themselves in solidarity with other women. "Victory," d'Héricourt insisted, "will belong to those who are united by affection and a common goal, who know how to *dare* and to act."

Intellectually unleashed, as only a woman approaching fifty can be, Jenny P. d'Héricourt also challenged biblical authority, insisting that claims for the equality of the sexes based on Christian belief (much discussed in recent years) were in fact not true. Citing multiple examples from the Old and New Testaments alike, she demonstrated that "both proclaim the inferiority of woman, imposing on her the most absolute submission to her father and her husband, refusing her every right, as daughter, spouse, mother, alienating her from the priesthood, from science, from instruction, denying her intelligence, outraging her modesty, torturing her feelings, permitting the sale and exploitation of her beauty, preventing her from inheriting or owning property."[56] Catholicism, in her view, was a particular obstacle: a falling away from blind faith would be a good thing for women.

It was on the crest of these attacks that Jenny P. d'Héricourt confronted the antifeminism of her countryman from the Franche-Comté, Pierre-Joseph Proudhon, a leading spokesman for the workers' mutualist movement and the adversary of Jeanne Deroin's earlier electoral campaign. In a heated exchange Jenny challenged Proudhon's published views on the woman question since 1841. She also published his response to her, in which he argued that women's cause must not be separated from that of men, that justice could never make woman man's equal, and that the "inferiority of the feminine sex did not constitute either serfdom or humiliation, or a lessened dignity," but rather the opposite. He considered the agitation of women on women's behalf as "a madness due precisely to the infirmity of the sex, and to its incapacity to know itself and to govern itself alone."[57]

Jenny d'Héricourt quickly counterattacked, claiming that Proudhon was effectively applying a double standard for justice as concerns women. In reply, Proudhon sketched the outline of what would become his infamous "calculus" of the inferiority of women to men. The discussion terminated abruptly in March 1857, when Jenny declared Proudhon's failure to respond to her rebuttal to be his admission of defeat.

Proudhon's response was forthcoming with the publication in 1858 of his major work, *De la Justice dans la Révolution et dans l'église* (On Justice in the Revolution and in the Church), particularly the section "Love and Marriage." Singling out the would-be emancipators of woman, Proudhon claimed: "Feminine indiscretion has caught fire; a half-dozen inky-fingered insurgents obstinately try to make woman into something we do not want, reclaim their *rights* with insults, and defy us to bring the question out into the light of day."[58] Emancipation, Proudhon insisted, maintaining his earlier formula "housewife or harlot," amounted to prostitution. He then laid out the details of his calculus of women's "physical, intellectual, and moral inferiority" to men, based on the Aristotelian premises of what G. J. Barker Benfield aptly named "the spermatic economy," and what we might now call the testosterone imprint. "The complete human being," Proudhon proclaimed, "is the male." With regard to intellect, he claimed: "Genius is . . . virility of spirit and its accompanying powers of abstraction, generalization, invention, conceptualization, which are lacking in equal measure in children, eunuchs, and women. . . . To the generation of ideas as to the generation [of children] woman brings nothing of her own; she is a passive, enervating being, whose conversation exhausts you as much as her embraces."[59] In her book *La Femme affranchie* (Woman Affranchised, 1860) Jenny P. d'Héricourt returned to the charge: "We demand our right, because we are persuaded that woman has to set her stamp on Science, Philosophy, Justice and Politics."[60]

In Lausanne, Switzerland, one French woman had already begun to set her stamp on science and philosophy. In the late 1850s Clémence Royer opened a course for ladies on "woman's philosophy," defending the position that women had a special sort of genius. "What I must find," she explained in her introductory lecture, "is a form, a feminine expression of science. It is . . . a new art which I have to create," an art that could give life to the cold and virile character of science, an art that could engage women fully in scientific endeavors. "As long as science remains exclusively in the hands of men," Royer explained, "it will never go down into the depths of the family and society. . . . Why . . . should [women] be excluded from the hunt for truth?"[61] Royer went on to publish (in 1862) her French translation of Charles Darwin's *Origin of Species*, which she prefaced with a long and iconoclastic commentary. In the 1870s, following her return to France from Switzerland, Royer would become a controversial participant in the Anthropological Society of Paris.

REJUSTIFYING PATRIARCHY

Brave proclamations, these proclamations of women's integral being and capacities—and they were hotly contested from the 1850s on. Indeed, one of the least well-known features of the knowledge wars in this period is the pan-European surge of scholarly or quasi-scholarly publications justifying the necessity of patriarchy. Amid the celebrations of womanhood, the eulogies of motherhood, and the enthronement of the feminine on a pedestal, a more hostile intellectual countercurrent was developing. In addition to the widely circulated responses of Proudhon and Jules Michelet in France, the contributions of their German contemporaries Arthur Schopenhauer and Wilhelm Riehl and those of Sir Henry Sumner Maine in England and J.-J. Bachofen in Switzerland must be noted. Some of the most distinguished intellects of the nineteenth century engaged the woman question head-on, assembling their physiological, anthropological, philological, and historical expertise in defense of—or justification of—male rule. The newly emerging human sciences—sociology, psychology, anthropology—all engaged these debates.

Writing "On Women" in 1851, an aging Arthur Schopenhauer (whose mother had been a *salonnière* and a confidante of the poet-philosopher Goethe) once again invoked Nature's plan for women, which he summed up as suffering and submission. Schopenhauer, anticipating Nietzsche and others, constructed women's "difference" almost entirely in the negative. With regard to matters of the intellect, he declared, women lack reason; therefore they lack also a sense of justice. They lack an appreciation of great art, and they lack genius. Indeed, Schopenhauer claimed, "the most distinguished intellects among the whole sex have never managed to produce a single achievement in the fine arts that is really great, genuine, and original; or given to the world any work of permanent value in any sphere":[62]

> [Women] form the *sexus sequior*—the second sex, inferior in every respect to the first; their infirmities should be treated with consideration, but to show them great reverence is extremely ridiculous, and lowers us in their eyes. When Nature made two divisions of the human race, she did not draw the line exactly through the middle. These divisions are polar and opposed to each other, it is true; but the difference between them is not qualitative merely, it is also quantitative. . . . It would be a very desirable thing if this Number-Two of the human race were in Europe also relegated to her natural place, and an end put to that lady nuisance, which not only moves all Asia to laughter, but would have been ridiculed by Greece and Rome as well.

Even monogamy unduly exalts woman as being man's equal, Schopenhauer argued; the Asian peoples knew better. Women should, moreover,
not inherit property or handle wealth: "The people who make money are
men, not women; and it follows from this that women are neither justified in having unconditional possession of it, nor fit persons to be en-
trusted with its administration."

In Germany, the young journalist and social scientist Wilhelm Heinrich Riehl seconded Schopenhauer's counterattack. In reaction to the
upheavals of 1848, Riehl undertook a sociological project to discover the
"real" Germany, the traditional, patriarchal Germany of the countryside. While working on his trilogy "The Natural History of the German
People," Riehl published an essay "On Women: A Social-political
Study" in the *Deutsche Vierteljahrsschrift* in which he castigated "the
emancipated women" of 1848, who had forgotten the natural vocation of
their sex.[63] This denunciation provided the springboard for his further
discussion of male-female relations, based on biblical authority, in a
volume entitled "The Family" (1855). Cultural development, he claimed
(like Comte before him), led to increasing differentiation and distinctiveness of the sexes, not toward undifferentiated equality. Women could
be emancipated, he argued, only by making (male) heads of households,
not individuals, the representatives of the family to the state. Bachelors,
like spinsters, were, in Riehl's scheme of things, unfortunate and unen-
franchisable.

In France, the sociologist Frederic LePlay embarked on an investigation of worker and peasant households comparable to that of Riehl, with
an eye to discovering the key to social reform that would keep women in
their place as men's auxiliaries. In LePlay's view, as expressed in his treatise *Réforme social* (Social Reform, 1864), in which as yet unreformed
English marriage laws provided his model, women's place must be definitively in the household; she should have nothing to do with manu-
facture, commerce, or property. This reformer championed separation of
spheres and male breadwinners with a vengeance. LePlay's investigations into social and economic life would be complemented by the findings of Paul Bernard, winner of a competition on the history of paternal
authority sponsored in 1860 by the French Imperial Academy of Moral
and Political Sciences.[64]

Jules Michelet's popular sociophilosophical inquiries *Love* (1859) and
Woman (1860) drew heavily on recent medical research about female reproductive physiology to promote the doctrine of women as perpetual
invalids and thus to give new meaning to the term "physiological reduc-

tionism." Michelet argued that "Woman" must necessarily remain un-der man's authority within his household, her mind as well as her body fertilized by his superior attributes. In addition, he advocated cutting woman off from her family of birth, thereby rendering her totally de-pendent upon her husband. Michelet's flowery and pseudopoetic pat-riarchal doctrines, disguised in the form of marriage manuals addressed to men and widely translated, would cast an unusually long shadow throughout Europe and America during the remainder of the century.[65]

It is in light of such repressive reactions to the feminist eruptions in 1848 that these campaigns to reformulate the intellectual foundations of patriarchy—and indeed, to reassert masculinity and its prerogatives—must be reevaluated. It is in this light, too, that one must reconsider the better-known literary and philosophical campaign by poets and writers to idealize "Woman" as "the angel of the house" (angel del hogar, in the Spanish version; angelo del focolare, in Italian).[66] Rousseau's Julie, the new Heloise of the mid-eighteenth century, provided an enduring model for the "angel," but subsequent versions took culturally specific forms. The poems and essays of Coventry Patmore (The Angel in the House, 1854–63) and John Ruskin (Of Queen's Gardens, 1865) in England con-tributed to this project, as did the widely translated treatises of the French Protestant pastor Adolphe Monod, with his Woman: Her Mission and Life (in French, 1848; English, 1858; also in Danish) and the Italian Catholic prelate Gioacchimo Ventura di Raulica, author of the mul-tivolume, much-translated La Donna cattolica (1855). As for feminists, many doubtless agreed with the French women's rights advocate and popular public speaker Maria Deraismes, who in the 1860s declined "the honor of being an angel" and castigated those who so insisted on women's self-sacrificial and purely domestic role as women's worst enemies.[67]

New historical scholarship during this period focused close attention on the origins and development of human societies, particularly Euro-pean antecedents. Writing before the era of great archaeological excava-tions and on-site anthropological expeditions, these scholars had to rely on evidence drawn from early written records preserved in law and lit-erature. They prided themselves on observing a scientific, scholarly ap-proach to the past, though they wrote with an unapologetic eye on their own times. Two major works published in 1861 reveal the centrality of the woman question to theories about the history of societal develop-ment.

In Ancient Law, the British legal scholar Sir Henry Sumner Maine drew on the fruits of comparative jurisprudence to argue that since time immemorial Indo-European societies had been organized around patriarchal families, though the absolute authority of the father had been subject to increasing erosion in more recent times as the personal and proprietary freedom of individuals, especially female individuals, increased. "Ancient law," Maine wrote, "subordinates the woman to her blood-relations, while a prime phenomenon of modern jurisprudence has been her subordination to her husband. The history of the change is remarkable."[68] As family organization had ceded before the emergence of the individual, so too had contract replaced status in progressive societies. Unmarried adult women, like men, could contract as individuals.

At the University of Basel, where he was professor of Roman law, Johann-Jakob Bachofen carefully analyzed the rise and fall of matriarchy in the ancient Mediterranean world. He was deeply impressed with the significance of religion and the importance of myth as an interpretative tool. In *Das Mutterrecht* (Mother Right) Bachofen thought he had documented the overthrow of female rule by male rule, and he clearly considered patriarchy to be a superior state in social organization, representing in his mind the triumph of "mind" over "matter." His enduring contribution was to demonstrate authoritatively the existence of matrilineal kinship patterns in early Mediterranean culture, if not that of actual female governance.[69] The findings of Maine and Bachofen, supplemented by those of the Scot John Fergusson McLennan on primitive marriage, provided new rounds of ammunition with which to attack the problem of appropriately reordering the sexes in contemporary European societies. Their influence was felt in the subsequent works of such diverse writers as Friedrich Engels and Friedrich Nietzsche.

Two of the most important aspects of the knowledge wars with regard to the development of feminism in the 1860s were, first, the campaign for women's medical education, and second, the development of a well-documented critique of women's serious disadvantages with respect to paid employment.

At stake in the campaign for medical education was nothing less than knowledge of and control over women's bodies and over reproduction. Male physicians were increasingly asserting their authority in issues of gynecology and obstetrics, and building practices in these areas, the traditional prerogative of midwives. In France, where abortion had been declared a crime against the state during the French Revolution, and again criminalized in the Napoleonic Penal Code (1810), and where midwives were subjected to governmental control, the debate was complicated by concerns over feeble population growth.

The stakes were raised in the later 1850s and 1860s when prominent male physicians, particularly the public health enthusiast Ambroise Tardieu (who brought up the issue of abortion at the Academy of Medicine in early 1852, and subsequently became France's leading medical-legal authority on the subject), first, argued for changing the legal standards to ensure conviction of abortionists, and second, alleged that midwives were functioning all too frequently as abortionists—that is, as antisocial profiteers—rather than as promoters of new life.[70]

In England, Parliament passed the Medical Act of 1858, which restricted entry into the field of medicine to holders of British university degrees. This was a direct response to the recent registration of the Anglo-American Elizabeth Blackwell, who had obtained her medical degree in the United States and had interned in France. Incensed by this development, and inspired by the example of their predecessor and mentor, a few dedicated English women prepared to storm the bastions of the British medical profession. The British government's criminalization of abortion in 1861 may have also been a factor in their determination.

Meanwhile, in 1864, the University of Zurich had quietly opened its doors to women auditors. Young women from Eastern Europe, including Poland, Romania, and especially Russia, flocked to enroll at Zurich. There, science and progressive politics had linked arms in the later 1850s and 1860s, in tandem with the freeing of the serfs. But a feminist critique had begun to develop only with the publications of M. L. Mikhailov (inspired in no small part by the publications of Jenny P. d'Héricourt, whom he had met in Paris) and with N. G. Chernyshevsky's novel *Chto Delat'* (What Is to Be Done?, 1863). Some privileged women were swept into study of the natural sciences and medicine on the same wave as their male counterparts, auditing courses at St. Petersburg University. But after these universities and medical schools were closed to them in 1863–64, many left Russia to pursue their studies abroad, and Zurich gave them an initially warm welcome. This set a precedent that could not be ignored by other medical schools in Western Europe.[71]

The admission of women to the study of medicine unfolded quite differently in France. A German woman, Mathilde Theyessen, claimed the honor of becoming the first certified woman physician of nineteenth-century Europe, passing her examinations as an "officier de santé et de pharmacie" in Paris in 1865. The 1868 decision to admit women (including Elizabeth Garrett, the American Mary Putnam Jacobi, a Russian, Mlle. Gontcharoff, and the first French woman, Madeleine Brès) to the examinations of Paris Faculty of Medicine was made by Empress Eugénie (long a promoter of girls' education) and the Council of Ministers, during another short regency. When the Second Empire fell, she and the minister of education were rushing to found a women's medical school before the Russians established one in St. Petersburg. The obstacles to women's practice of medicine in France lay not in the faculties or in access to the examinations, but in the subsequent steps: their exclusion from the competitive examinations leading to hospital-based internships and residencies in medical specialties. These hurdles, controlled by the medical authorities themselves, would prove far more difficult for women physicians to clear.

Of the British aspirants to medical education, Elizabeth Garrett managed to enroll for examinations in Paris in 1868, but Sophia Jex-Blake determined to become a doctor in Britain, obtaining permission to study medicine in separate "ladies' classes" at the University of Edinburgh. "If women claim that they do need and can appreciate instruction in any or all sciences, I do not know who has the right to deny that assertion," Jex-Blake argued in 1869.[72] Three conflict-ridden years later, the University Senatus refused the women permission to register for the examinations that would lead to their degrees. The women won their lawsuit against the university, but officials subsequently stalled by appealing the decision, ultimately forcing the women to leave, after great delays and expenses. In 1877 London University became the first English university to grant medical degrees to women, following Parliament's amendment of the Medical Act the previous year to remove all restrictions grounded in sexual difference. The costs were great, but women's admission to the medical profession in England was henceforth secured.

The reactions of some university-trained men to the campaigns to admit women to medical education were astonishingly harsh. In Germany and Austria, in particular, the male academic community mobilized against women's efforts to enroll in any aspect of university study. The objections of the Munich-based medical professor Theodor von Bischoff, in his tract *Das Studium und die Ausübung der Medizin durch Frauen* (The Study and Practice of Medicine by Women, 1872) would have a lasting influence. In the later 1870s, the German professoriate in all fields would close ranks against women students in virtually all areas of study, and that opposition would last well into the 1890s.[73]

Even in England, where women won the battle for medical education, opposition to higher education continued. Opponents claimed that higher education would ruin women's reproductive capacities, or lead to nervous breakdown, and that in the process such women would somehow become thoroughly masculinized. Against such accusations as those of Henry Maudsley that the aim of higher education for women was "to assimilate the female to the male mind," Elizabeth Garrett Anderson, Britain's first female physician, insisted that "the single aim of those anxious to promote a higher and more serious education for women is to make the best they can of the materials at their disposal." "If they fail," she added pointedly, "it assuredly will not be from thinking that the masculine type of excellence includes all that can be desired in humanity."[74] Among other rights, women had the right to minds— and views—of their own.

Feminists did not need university degrees, however, to make important contributions to economic knowledge, based on systematic observation, in the debate over women's employment. In a time when both economists and labor leaders in Britain and France were arguing the case for a "family wage" that would keep women in the home, women acting as social scientists were gathering data of their own to point out the problems with the male-breadwinner model. Already in the 1840s, Flora Tristan had been surveying the issues regarding women and employment, and had offered some especially astute observations on the issue of women's inferior pay in her book *Union ouvrière* (Workers' Union, 1843): if women were given equal pay for equal work, she noted ironically, women would earn more than men, because they are more productive.

In *La Femme* (1860), Jules Michelet damned the word *ouvrière* as "impious" and "sordid," but his indignant opposition could not eradicate the phenomenon of women workers. Jules Simon's study of the woman worker, published in 1861, reignited opposition to the industrial employment of women outside the home. Simon was well informed about the many difficult social problems that had developed for working-class families in English textile-manufacturing towns and examined their counterparts in France with those problems in mind. Though historians have since shown that a surprisingly high proportion of the women employed in textiles were young and single, Simon nevertheless discussed their work exclusively as that of married women. His operating assumption was that every single woman was a prospective wife and mother of a large family whose labor-force participation, even prior to marriage, not only actively prevented the acquisition and practice of domestic skills, but also posed a deadly threat to her virtue. Like many of the liberal economists of his time, Simon advocated raising men's wages to provide a "family wage" that could support a wife and children. Any productive labor performed by women, he argued, should be done by them in their homes, where they could remain "women." "If there is one thing nature clearly teaches us," Simon asserted, echoing Michelet, Comte, and others, "it is that woman is made to be protected, to live as a girl with her mother, as a wife under the protection and authority of her husband."[75]

Julie-Victoire Daubié, the first woman to pass the French *baccalauréat* examination (1861)—which carried with it admission to university education—disputed Simon's arguments. She had prepared her book *La Femme pauvre* (The Poor Woman) for an essay competition sponsored in the late 1850s by the Academy of Lyon, and she published it in 1866. Rather than attempting, like Simon, to return working women to a dependent familial role by raising men's wages, Daubié, like her feminist predecessors, urged reforms that would permit women to become economically independent. Moreover, she called for the passage of laws that would curb sexual harassment and thereby allow women more freedom of movement in French society. She objected particularly to the intrusion of men into what she considered to be women's occupations:[76]

> Whenever we investigate carefully the causes of the poor woman's precarious state, we see that these can be attributed to an administrative centralization that arbitrarily excludes her from schools and employments, and to an irresponsible immorality that, after banishing her from the family, has loaded her down with the triple oppression of laws, institutions, and customs.

Daubié enumerated and condemned these laws, institutions, and customs in exquisite detail in her lengthy study, which tore holes in the paternalistic arguments of liberal economists such as Simon. In the 1860s, when the American Civil War had inscribed the emancipation of black slaves on the consciousness of most thinking Europeans, the studies of women's work by Bessie Rayner Parkes in England and Louise Otto in Germany likewise called for freedom for individual development through economic emancipation for women. "We want to free ourselves from the pressure of dependence," asserted Otto, "by demanding a natural sharing of labor for men and women."[77]

In 1866–67, when the debate over the woman question surfaced in the annual congresses of the newly formed International Working Men's Association, studies such as these provided ample ammunition for advocates of women's right to work. These meetings, attended by a mixture of progressive middle-class intellectuals and craft workers, engendered heated debate over women's role in the labor force and in the family. Few of the workingmen present supported the principle of women's right to work. Like so many of the learned men of that time, they preferred the notion of a "family wage" that would allow men to earn enough to support their wives and children. Here arguments from Proudhon, Simon, and Michelet were much rehearsed, commingled in the workingmen's debates with those of Marx and Engels. The consensus of the 1867 Workers' Congress, following a year of study and heated debate, was that women should be emancipated *from* work in order to remain in the family. "The greatest name on earth is the name of the father; the greatest thing is paternal authority: these are the creative and conserving elements of the family," announced the Commission's 1867 Report:[78]

> Woman, by her physical and moral nature, is naturally called to the peaceable minutiae of the domestic hearth; this is her department. We do not believe it is useful for society to give her any other charge. If the wife of the proletarian is able to become a deputy to the Chamber, the worker's soup may well be inadequately seasoned. As a mother, woman is the child's first educator, but on the express condition that the father acts as the directing agent.

In Paris, feminists objected strenuously to the First International's conclusions. In a series of public lectures held there in 1868, numerous speakers addressed the issues. The feminist socialist Paule Mink eloquently made the case for women's autonomy, for her right to work and to receive equal pay: "By denying woman the right to work, you degrade her; you put her under man's yoke and deliver her over to man's good pleasure. . . . It is work alone that makes independence possible and without which there is no dignity." But like the arguments of many of her predecessors, Mink's argument for equality and independence was cast in terms of women's differences from men:[79]

> Why can't woman be man's equal without wanting to become like him? Copying is inevitably a form of weakness; above all, one must affirm and remain oneself. Women have virtues that are their own, and men have qualities peculiar to themselves. Why meld them into a formless mass whose parts are unrecognizable? We affirm our individuality, but we want to remain women.

Far from unsexing women, Mink argued that paid employment would allow women to develop themselves to the fullest extent as female individuals.

The knowledge wars of the 1850s and 1860s had precipitated significant contributions from feminists as well as the rearticulation and reaffirmation of objections to women's emancipation from those we can call, in retrospect, antifeminists. The roles of work and family in structuring female subordination had been clearly identified. The time was ripe, then, for a publishing event that would greatly accelerate the flow of feminist thinking throughout Europe: the appearance in 1869 of John Stuart Mill's great work *The Subjection of Women*.

RECASTING THE DEBATE: MILL'S 'SUBJECTION
OF WOMEN' AND ITS DETRACTORS

In the heat of arguments over women's genius, ancient history, medical education, differential wages, and in the midst of continued romanticization of women's "sphere" by aesthetes and religious leaders, and defenses of patriarchy by sociologists and historians, the renowned British philosopher John Stuart Mill composed his most eloquent argument for women's legal emancipation from patriarchal institutions, *The Subjection of Women*. The publication of this weighty little book in 1869 was an event of truly international significance for the cause of women's rights. The London edition was quickly reprinted in New York and Philadelphia; translations appeared shortly thereafter in nearly every European language. Significantly, many of Mill's translators were women and feminists, among them the Italian Anna Maria Mozzoni, the German Jenny Hirsch, and some years later (1890s) the Spanish novelist and essayist Emilia Pardo Bazán. The rising young cosmopolitan literary critic Georg Brandes, an enthusiastic advocate of women's emancipation, prepared and promoted the Danish translation.

The woman question had been central to Mill's thinking since the early 1830s, and he remained convinced that there was no reason to admit the "necessary subordination of one sex to the other." He had finally broken off discussions with August Comte on this issue, rejecting once and for all Comte's physiological determinism on the woman question. Extending the principle he had developed in his powerful and influential tract *On Liberty* (1859), Mill suggested that all artificial or socially constructed barriers to the flourishing of the female personality should be eliminated, thereby allowing the question of "woman's nature" to be answered once and for all. Women, he argued, should be allowed the same opportunity for personal liberty, the same freedom to acquire individual dignity, as was allowed to men. He sustained his focus on the possible benefits that the development of female capacities might have for society as a whole. "The anxiety of mankind to interfere in behalf of nature, for fear lest nature should not succeed in effecting its purpose," he insisted, "is an altogether unnecessary solicitude." Confronting the basic concern of those who opposed women's emancipation, Mill threw out a challenge:[80]

> I should like to hear somebody openly enunciating the doctrine (it is already implied in much that is written on the subject)—"It is necessary to society that women should marry and produce children. They will not do

so unless they are compelled. Therefore it is necessary to compel them."
The merits of the case would then be clearly defined.

The beauty of Mill's carefully constructed and eloquent argument was
that woman's "nature" could never be properly determined until all the
legal and cultural constraints on women's full development as human
beings were removed. This line of reasoning allowed women's rights advocates to take the offensive in demanding emancipatory reforms in
women's legal status and education without having to justify such demands on the basis of women's special nature.

The Subjection of Women was widely reviewed and discussed in
print, and far beyond England, because of Mill's already great reputation
as a philosopher. One of the fiercest responses came from the eminent
German historian Heinrich von Sybel, a critic of the French Revolution,
who like so many German intellectuals totally opposed training women
for anything except marriage and motherhood.[81] In England, the reply of
Sir James Fitzjames Stephen, an unreconstructed authoritarian who had
spent many years in the colonial service in India (and the uncle of the
twentieth-century novelist Virginia [Stephen] Woolf), expressed his
adamant belief that, because of differences of physical strength and the
requirements of marriage, there could be no equality between the sexes.
In a rejoinder to Stephen, the women's rights activist Millicent Garrett
Fawcett reiterated her objections to the legal subjection of English
women in marriage, while her colleague Lydia Becker took Stephen to
task for faulty assumptions by wrongly basing his understanding of
equality on physical qualities, and in particular by applying a misguided
analogy between the subordination of women and that of children.
Equality of personal rights and of opportunity, not of condition, characterized Becker's approach to discussing the equality of the sexes.[82]

In France, Édouard de Pompéry, who shared Mill's ultimate objective,
criticized Mill for resting his case for equal rights on the ostensible
equality of faculties. Pompéry, in contrast, invoked the principle of justice: "It is not in the name of equality of faculties between man and
woman that the rights of woman should be demanded, but in the name
of human justice, which should assure to each member of society the
fullest and most complete expansion of his being." And, he added, in a
sweeping conclusion:[83]

> Slavery, serfdom, the subjection of women have been passing necessi-
> ties, along with war, theocracies, despotism, and that paternal power
> which extends to the right of life and death over every member of the
> family; but none of these institutions can find justification in rights or
> stand firm in the faith of reason.

The conservative Russian intellectual N. N. Strakhov responded to two translations of Mill's *Subjection* in a long essay published in *Zaria* (February 1870). Strakhov viewed Mill's argument for legal emancipation of women as inappropriate for Russia, but he was even more critical of the extravagant faith in human reason displayed by Russian advocates of female emancipation:[84]

> The new solution to the ancient questions, boldly put forth, amounts to the following: There is no difference between God and nature (God is merely nature personified) . . . between spirit and matter (spirit results from the behavior of matter) . . . between human beings and animals (a human being is simply an upright animal) . . . or between man and woman (a woman is some kind of beardless man, only shorter).

Other opponents, elaborating the societal implications of the new evolutionary theory proposed by Charles Darwin's celebrated *Origin of Species* (1859), asserted that even if women's legal subordination were ended, as Mill proposed, they could never reach the heights of creativity and intellect established by men. Mill's book thus launched a new round of discussion, centering on the new issue of evolutionary constraints on women's freedom, as suggested by contemporary scientific inquiries into brain size and cranial capacity, and the relation of both to body mass.

Physical anthropologists, in England, in France, in Germany and Switzerland, had already applied their new expertise in measuring skulls, both ancient and more recent, in responding to the woman question. Evolutionary theorists, led by Darwin himself, drew on the skull findings not only to assert women's difference but also to emphasize their mental as well as physical inferiority. In his second important book, *The Descent of Man* (1871), Darwin proposed the evolutionary importance of sexual selection, or choice of mate, as responsible for increasing the differentiation between men and women over time—with reference not only to their physiology but also to their mental and emotional makeup. He suggested that as women had become increasingly protected by men, they had lost the necessity of having to sharpen their wits in the unremitting struggle for survival, thereby assuring their relatively inferior development. He was clearly convinced that the results of evolutionary sexual differentiation, and the resulting male superiority, could never be undone, irrespective of the wishes of nineteenth-century women's rights advocates. Men's rivalry with other men, for women and in life's competition, and their role as breadwinners would ensure their continuing superiority. "Although men do not now fight for their wives," Darwin remarked, "and this form of selection has passed away, yet during manhood, they generally undergo a severe struggle in order to maintain themselves and their families; and this will tend to keep up or even increase their mental powers, and, as a consequence, the present inequality between the sexes."[85]

The evolutionary sociologist Herbert Spencer was also skeptical about women's ultimate potential to rival men. Once an enthusiastic partisan of women's equal right to exercise all their faculties (in his tract *Social Statics* [1851]), Spencer subsequently expressed his concern about the negative effects on women of excessive bookishness: "How many conquests does the bluestocking make through her extensive study of history? What man ever fell in love with a woman because she understood Italian?"[86] A further strong dose of Darwinism, coupled with his insistence on the importance of knowledge about the comparative psychology of the sexes as a grounding for all social science, led Spencer to assert that "adaption to the paternal and maternal duties" determined the psychology of the sexes. This difference, he argued, had evolved in response to requirements for human survival. Even so he came to more optimistic conclusions for the future than had Darwin: a lessening of women's needs to cultivate men's good will ought to "entail a less early arrest of individual evolution [for women], and a diminution of those mental differences between men and women which the early arrest produces."[87] Unlike Comte, Riehl, and others, Spencer seemed to be predicting a relative convergence over time, rather than increasing divergence, between the sexes. Mill's recasting of the question of women's emancipation had indeed stimulated a wide range of responses, many of which would deeply mark all subsequent European thought.

In May 1867 woman suffrage returned to the political agenda in England. The entire Western world witnessed the first substantive parliamentary debate on woman suffrage, initiated by John Stuart Mill and the many women activists who insisted that it become part of the electoral-reform agenda. Mill gave the campaign a further strong push, arguing the case for changing the word "man" to "person" on the floor of the House of Commons.[88] Although the amendment was defeated, the new Reform Act enfranchised a broad range of male taxpayers. A coalition of woman-suffrage advocates banded together to challenge the exclusion of unmarried female ratepayers—"no taxation without representation" seemed to offer an irrefutable argument. Historian Jane Rendall has underscored the fact that women in the early suffrage movement spoke a complex language, promoting individualist arguments to be sure, but also arguing a relational case, based on woman's civilizing mission in the struggle against barbarism and savagery, whether at home or abroad.[89]

Responding to the challenge posed by the woman question, and especially Mill's reformulation of the debate in terms of classical liberty—that is, of removing the shackles that held women down—the intellectual, scientific, and creative establishments in a number of countries began to mobilize. When coupled with feminist queries concerning the causes of prostitution and war, feminist demands—whether formulated in terms of emancipation, liberty, equality, rights, or justice—threatened the existing order of things, by challenging the holders of educational, economic, and political power. Feminist demands for self-realization and societal partnership implied a thoroughgoing reorganization of family and society; ultimately, the very practices of mating and reproduction, and the institutions that controlled them, were at stake.

Italy's first woman writer, the historian, *salonnière*, and journalist Cristina Belgiojoso, writing in the first issue of the new liberal publication *Nuova Antologia* (1866), contemplated these developments as part of the passage to a "modern society." "What would happen to the family as it is presently constituted," she queried, "if women were initiated into masculine pursuits, and shared with men public, social, and literary activities?"[90] The French liberal economist Henri Baudrillart, who objected to Mill's proposals, examined at length the question of women's emancipation in the *Revue des Deux Mondes* in 1872. Baudrillart was not one to exaggerate what was ultimately at stake:[91]

> If one accepts the terms in which [the woman question] is posed [i.e., in terms of individual liberty], one can see in it the germ of perhaps the greatest revolution the world has yet experienced. It would be nothing less than the coming into its rights of an entire sex—that is to say, half of the human species—which until now has been unjustly dispossessed. Even abolitionism, which has been devoted to eradicating the servitude of several million poor blacks from the face of the earth, would amount to little in comparison to this.

The plethora of claims for women's emancipation had flowed beyond the land of utopian dreams and had entered the promised land of political possibilities. Speaking of the "two genders" (*deux genres*) in 1868, Maria Deraismes triumphantly underscored what all could see: "Women's inferiority is not a fact of nature. . . . It is a human invention, a social fiction."[92]

Internationalizing Feminism, 1870–1890

The war declared by Prussia on France in 1870 brusquely checked the momentum of organized feminist efforts in continental Europe. This war resulted in French defeat, the fall of the Second Empire, and the unification of Germany under Wilhelm I of Prussia. Following the treaty of Frankfurt in early 1871, a brief but violent civil war, known as the Paris Commune, erupted in March. Feminist activists in Paris made a broad range of claims on women's behalf during this important episode, but their efforts were once again damped down by another wave of repressive legislation and controls. Further internationalization of the women's movements ensued, though with the initiative passing from the French, considered too revolutionary by some, to the English-speaking world. French arguments for women's emancipation, which had long emphasized partnership with men and maternal influence, increasingly exhibited assertions of absolute equality and the individual right to self-development, while British arguments, even in their most individualistic forms, show upon closer examination enduring traces of the case for equality and rights based on women's distinctive civilizing mission and duties. Meanwhile, pressures for ending women's subordination began to build in Italy, Belgium, the Netherlands, Imperial Germany, and in the Scandinavian countries. By 1889, with the commemorations of the French Revolution, considerable progress could be recorded.

WAR, REVOLUTION, AND THE QUESTION OF WOMEN IN POLITICAL LIFE

The French events of 1870–71 have occupied a distinctive place in women's history, thanks in large part to socialist historians' early fascination with European revolutions and women's participation in them.

Studies by Edith Thomas, Sheila Rowbotham, and Eugene Schulkind, published some thirty years ago, introduced a new generation of readers to women's engagement in the Paris Commune, especially to the legends that developed around the highly visible exploits of Louise Michel and the blame placed on the so-called women incendiaries, *les pétroleuses*, for allegedly torching Paris during the final days of the Commune. Other scholars have focused on interpretations of "the crowd," and the way in which mass politics became gendered female and hysteric. New studies by Kathleen Jones, Françoise Vergès, and Gay Gullickson have addressed the political implications of representation of the Communardes.[1] Here, however, I intend to focus attention on specific claims made by 1860s emancipation advocates to full participation in political decision making before and during the Paris Commune, in order to place women's activism and the ensuing legends about it within the context of feminist claims.

The Franco-Prussian War broke out in response to a diplomatic impasse provoked by Otto von Bismarck, the German chancellor, over the issue of succession to the Spanish throne, following the ouster of Queen Isabelle II in 1868. On the eve of the outbreak of hostilities in mid-July 1870, one editorialist in the Paris-based women's rights publication *Le Droit des femmes: Journal politique* issued an appeal for women's action against war: "Let us protest in the name of humanity against this pastime of princes, which causes the blood of the people to flow. . . . And here women have not only the right to interfere, it is their duty to do so. Let them protest. This is what they can do. Who will dare to say now that politics do not concern wives and mothers?" The following week, in a call for women's assistance, the editors went further: "They tell you . . . that you bear none of the burdens of war. It is one of the great arguments brought against you when you ask for equal rights with men. Show now that you know how to take your share of dangerous duties."[2]

The editors of the *Englishwoman's Review* made a somewhat different argument: "Our moral is—give women all over Europe political power, and a great peaceful influence will thus be created, which will immediately tend to diminish the frequency of wars, and may ultimately put an end to war altogether."[3] A group of German working women echoed such sentiments in September, concluding their manifesto with a call for "Peace, Bread, and Work."[4] The warring parties were unmoved by such entreaties. Within the space of six months, the German coalition invaded and defeated France at Sedan, captured the emperor Napoleon III, besieged Paris, imposed humiliating peace terms on the new provisional French government lodged at Versailles, and consolidated the unification of the German Empire in a dazzling display of diplomatic prowess and military might.

The revolt of Parisian workers and radicals against the French provisional government erupted in mid-March 1871. It was crushed by military action in late May. During its ten-week duration, women supporters made themselves conspicuous. They organized ambulance and nursing services, and established day-care facilities, secular primary schools, vocational schools for girls, and producer cooperatives for working women. They challenged the existing order of marriage, clerical control over the education of children, and especially their own occupational exploitation, which they attributed to the competition of poorly paid workers in church-sponsored workshops and prisons and to inadequate social services. Most important from our perspective, several women increasingly cast a critical eye on the male chauvinism demonstrated by their fellow Communards. These women expressed a sense of entitlement to participation as *citoyennes*, and they invoked historical memory to legitimate their demands and participation:[5]

> *Citoyennes de Paris*, we, descendants of the women of the Great Revolution, who in the name of the people and justice marched on Versailles, took Louis XVI captive, we mothers and sisters of the French people— can we tolerate any longer the fact that misery and ignorance make enemies of our children . . . ? *Citoyennes*, the hour of decision is here; the old world has had it! We want to be free!

A few days later a group of women formed a Union des Femmes, which insisted that women be included in the political work of the Commune. Everyone should be able to fight for the people, they argued. The signatories urged the leadership of the Commune to "consider all legitimate grievances of any section of the population without discrimination of sex, such discrimination having been made and enforced as a means of maintaining the privileges of the ruling class."[6] The male monopoly of political life, the insistence on relegating women to their domestic duties, on maintaining separate spheres, all were denounced as an invention of the dominators, unsuitable to "the people." The leaders of the Union des Femmes called on the government of the Commune to accord the women headquarters and meeting space, as well as printing subsidies for notices, posters, and other materials that would serve the common effort.

The Communard leadership, however, resisted the women's claims and their participation, even as members of ambulance units, which exasperated André Léo (the pseudonym used by the novelist and women's rights activist Léodile Bera Champceix): "Do they think they can accomplish the revolution without women? . . . From one point of view our history since '89 could be written under the title 'History of the Ineffectiveness of the Revolutionary Party.' The woman question would be the longest chapter."[7] The Commune's delegate for war responded publicly, offering to do whatever he could to enable the women to serve. Several days later, however, he was arrested by the Commune's Committee on Public Safety and stripped of his functions. Was this mere coincidence?

As hostilities intensified some women appropriated the uniforms of the Communards, red sashes and the rest; others carried revolvers and rifles and "manned" the barricades. Some women were killed or wounded in combat with the government troops who had been sent to quell the rebellion. The ferocity of the victors against the Communardes, manifested again during the post-Commune military trials in September, exceeded the bounds of rationality. The military prosecutor, Captain Jouanne, even blamed the imminent downfall of civilization on doctrines of women's emancipation and on women's ostensible refusal to serve as legitimate spouses! Defiant activist women, including the unmarried Louise Michel, received harsh sentences of deportation and lengthy imprisonment; others were sentenced to death. The Communard men were not alone in rejecting women's independent political activism.

Nor did others in the Western world. Elsewhere, responses to the Communardes' activities resonated with shrill hostility. In England, the ghost of Edmund Burke seemed to speak once more in the anonymous commentary published by England's *Saturday Review* in early July 1871:[8]

> The insurgence of women is a fringe of the red flag that has been flying so insolently over the city where marriage has been decreed unnecessary, fatherhood obsolete, and where women have fully attained those hideous rights for which they blindly clamour. It is certainly time to condemn every step towards the individualization of women lest they become viragoes, and their orphaned children the *gamins* of the gutter. The latent folly which would destroy family ties is but an introduction to the madness of the Paris incendiaries.

Antifeminists condemned women's employment as retrogressive; they claimed that it "unsexed" women. "Equality" was a snare; authority had been weakened; atheism, communism, utopianism seemed everywhere in evidence. "The agitation for so-called women's emancipation should be strenuously resisted. . . . To discourage subordination in women, to countenance their competition in masculine careers by way of their enfranchisement, is probably among the shortest methods of barbarizing our race," the *Saturday Review* continued. Such remarks were seconded in the posthumous publication of Proudhon's *La Pornocratie* (1875), an effusion of diatribes left over from *La Justice* and published by supporters ten years after his death. Here Proudhon postulated another widely discussed choice: not "housewife or harlot," but "the subordination of women or the debasement of men."[9] Proudhon warned young men thinking of marriage that "for a man, the first condition is to dominate his wife and to be the master."

This exacerbated climate of hostility to women's activism and demands in the early 1870s did not entirely discourage activists in other countries from pressing their own claims, but it did mean that they would distance themselves from what they perceived as French extremism. In early 1871, the Danish parliament specifically excluded women from the property-based vote. The cautious Danish women's rights advocate Pauline Worm rejected the French term "emancipation" along with the term "ladies"; even as she advocated "woman's civil rights" (*kvindes borgerret*) she rejected notions of loose morals, which she identified with French emancipationist claims. In the north, she insisted, femininity and marriage must be preserved.[10]

In 1872, the Swiss government embarked on a wholesale revision of its constitutional laws. Julie von May von Rued argued that the woman question must be addressed. Along with Rued, Marie Goegg and others in the Association Internationale des Femmes called respectfully on legislators to expand women's opportunities in Swiss society, by revising the civil code and extending women's educational opportunities: "We constitute the numerically superior portion of humanity, and the existence of man is too solidly linked to our own for him to despoil us without hurting himself."[11] Swiss men were not impressed.

Already in 1870 the Parisian suffragist Julie-Victoire Daubié had organized a petition on behalf of suffrage for single adult and widowed women, but in the chilly post-Commune political climate even such restricted initiatives would face severe resistance from the partisans of "moral order." When the French National Assembly debated a new electoral law in 1874, the deputies tried to ignore the issue of votes for women, pausing only for some sarcastic humor at the feminists' expense. Daubié died that year, leaving the suffragist cause without a champion until Hubertine Auclert took it up in 1878.

In Berlin, the issue of votes for women found an advocate in the person of Hedwig Dohm, who had been closely following the British campaigns and debates as well as developments in other parts of Europe and

America. Following German unification in 1871 and the establishment of a national system of male suffrage for electing the Reichstag, Dohm made a strong case for female suffrage in the interest of mitigating the tyranny of living under male-centered laws that women had no part in making. "For me the beginning of all true progress in the woman question lies in women's right to the vote," Dohm wrote in 1873; "the stronger the emphasis on the difference between the sexes, the clearer the need for the specific representation of women." She blamed men for willfully ignoring the necessity of women's vote, and chided them for their fears that somehow "the entire female sex might disappear along the unfamiliar path of voting rights."[12] In 1876 Dohm returned to the issue in her book *Der Frauen Natur und Recht* (Women's Nature and Right), citing historical precedents for women's exercise of political power. She disputed the range of arguments made against woman suffrage, and in the course of doing so rehearsed a litany of historic abuses of women by men, in both law and custom, in various societies: "All social arrangements, all customs and laws, Asiatic as well as European, have ever been an illustration of the text 'He shall be thy master.'" Playing with the concept of "nature," she remarked:[13]

> We cannot conscientiously blame the men for not caring to place women on an equality with themselves. We find it but natural that they should hold fast the prerogative of their sex. What rank or class ever voluntarily ceded their privileges? We find it perfectly natural that they do not care to cook or look after their children; for the presence of women in governmental affairs is to the cleverest men inseparable from the idea that they themselves must in such a case spend part of their strength in the kitchen and nursery.

Dohm, an ardent social democrat, insisted that ultimate choice lay between despotism and a democratic state. Freedom was a meaningless concept, she argued, if it was not available to women as well as to men. She called on German women, like those in England and America, to organize woman suffrage societies, arguing, much in the tradition of women activists during and since the French Revolution, that "the rights of mankind have no sex."

Hedwig Dohm found few followers in Germany in the 1870s, but as her readings and arguments attest, her enthusiasm and advocacy were fueled as much by acquaintance with developments beyond German borders as by the problems she recognized within her own society. Her writings attest to a growing development of feminist sensibility, the product of expanding literacy and book knowledge combined with increased exposure to developments beyond the Rhine and, occasionally, beyond Europe. The impact of such exposure could also be seen in the Netherlands, where the young physician Aletta Jacobs, who had studied medicine at Groningen in the 1870s, drew inspiration from English suffrage advocates to attempt to register to vote in 1882. Unlike French and British law, the Dutch constitution did not then forbid taxpaying women from voting. Jacobs petitioned, was refused, appealed, and lost, and in 1887 Dutch lawmakers added the word "male" to the constitution in order to make matters clear.[14] Jacobs would subsequently become a leader in the Dutch and international movements for woman suffrage. Thus, in spite of recurrent episodes of repression, the communication of feminist ideas across national and linguistic boundaries and the internationalization of the women's movement would become ever more conspicuous features of European history in the period 1875–90.

INTERNATIONALIZING THE WOMEN'S MOVEMENT

The movement to link women's activities across national boundaries rebounded between 1876 and 1890, though with intermittent setbacks, due to the continuing atmosphere of repression that succeeded the events of 1870–71. Despite these problems, developments of the women's press and international postal communications greatly facilitated the growth of networks; as of 1878, in a census of the women's press, the *Englishwoman's Review* qualified the woman question as "one of the leading topics of the day."[15] Improvements in transportation also contributed: coastal, river, and trans-Atlantic steamships and the ever expanding railway network brought many women and men to the international expositions held in Paris in the late 1870s and again in the late 1880s. There they would discuss many subjects of mutual concern, including women's emancipation. Women's rights advocates made a point of organizing congresses during these gatherings, facilitating personal contact and exchanges of ideas among reform-minded individuals from many parts of the world. Even so, it often took years before like-minded feminists could meet.

Following the disruptions created by the Franco-Prussian War and the Paris Commune, the intrepid Marie Goegg and her colleagues in Geneva revived the Association Internationale des Femmes. In late December 1870 they had issued an AIF membership card to Matilde Bajer of Copenhagen, which spelled out (in French) the goals of the association: "To work for the moral and intellectual advancement of woman, for the gradual amelioration of her position in society by calling for her human, civil, economic, social and political rights." The association called for "equality in salary, in instruction, in the family, and in the law."[16]

By mid-1872, however, the AIF's work experienced severe disruption, due not only to the suspicion garnered by the term "international" in the wake of the Commune, but also to an attack on the leadership of Marie Goegg. Following a schism in March, its supporters reorganized the association in June, including a change of name. The communiqué calling for a meeting in Bern, at the home of Julie von May von Rued, bore the names of fifteen women from various cities in England, Switzerland, Germany, and Italy, as well as Jerusalem; these women included Josephine Butler (Liverpool), Caroline de Barrau (La Sabartarié, near Castres), Christine Lazzati (Milan), Rosalie Schönwasser (Düsseldorf), Marianne Menzzer (Dresden), and Julie Kühne (Stettin). This new international group called itself Solidarité: Association pour la Défense des Droits de la Femme (Solidarity: Association for the Defense of Woman's Rights), and published a periodical also called *Solidarité*.[17]

Internationalist initiatives were only in temporary eclipse. With the Exposition of 1878, the internationalist initiative returned to feminists in the new but still unstable French Third Republic, proclaimed in 1875. After a series of delays, Léon Richer and Maria Deraismes (the founders in 1869 of the women's rights periodical *Le Droit des femmes*, which had subsequently consolidated with Marie Goegg's *Journal des femmes*), convened the first international congress on women's rights.

The 1878 women's rights congress, scheduled during the huge Paris International Exposition, met in the Masonic Hall (rue Cadet) over a two-week period beginning in late July. The gathering attracted a cluster of French republican political dignitaries as well as representatives from eleven other nations. Women's rights advocates came from many lands and were welcomed by France's Maria Deraismes, who reclaimed the revolutionary heritage of 1789, 1830, and 1848 for women, and by Anna Maria Mozzoni of Italy, who gave the opening address. Other registered participants, beyond those from France's immediate neighbors, included Elise Van Calcar from the Netherlands, Carl and Sophie Van Bergen from Sweden, and male participants from Brazil, Russia, and Romania. A cohort of Americans were in attendance, including Julia Ward Howe from Boston, who was named honorary co-president, and Theodore Stanton, the son of the eloquent suffrage activist Elizabeth Cady Stanton. This congress marked a new stage in the development of a truly international network among feminist activists, a network cemented at the final banquet by Antide Martin's toast: "To the international perseverance of the partisans of progress!"[18]

The congress organizers divided the agenda into five sections: historical, educational, economic, moral, and legislative. Despite a deliberate decision to avoid discussion of woman suffrage, many other controversial topics were addressed, including government-regulated prostitution and the double moral standard, equal pay for equal work, the politics of housework, government subsidies for mothers, unionization, and the relation of war to women's subordination. The published proceedings of this first congress were widely distributed and can still be read with interest today. Emily Venturi encapsulated the ambitious agenda of the congress by recounting this anecdote at the closing banquet:[19]

> Last evening a gentleman who seemed a bit skeptical about the advantages of our congress asked me, "Well, Madame, what great truth have you proclaimed to the world?" I replied to him, "Monsieur, we have proclaimed that woman is a human being." He laughed. "But, Madame, that is a platitude." So it is; but when this platitude, which everyone accepts with a smile when it is merely a question of words, is recognized by human laws, the face of the world will be transformed. Certainly, then, there would be no need for us to assemble in congress to demand the rights of woman.

The exclusion of suffrage from the 1878 congress agenda, however, provoked objections from those who insisted that political rights for women must be the foremost goal under the new French Republic. Hubertine Auclert subsequently published the speech she was not allowed to give at the 1878 congress. In this eloquent appeal, she pointed to all the reasons why French women—all nine million of them—should be able to cast their ballots: "The weapon of the vote will be for us, as it is for man, the only means of obtaining the reforms we desire. As long as we remain excluded from civic life, men will attend to their own interests rather than to ours." Women should be allowed to vote, just as they were required to pay taxes. She called on republican men to "abdicate [their] masculine kingship. It is time to proclaim equality. . . . Until you have recognized the complete right of women—civil and political rights—your struggle to obtain a greater liberty can appear to impartial witnesses and to us, the neglected half of humanity, only as a quarrel between despotisms."[20]

From the 1870s on, it would no longer suffice for women's movement leaders to issue statements of principle, however radical. Policy choices had to be made and acted upon. Strategies and tactics had begun to matter and to provoke alternative and competing organizational initiatives. The development of such internal disagreements can, in fact, be considered as a positive sign of the maturing of feminism as well as of the increasing complexity of feminist organization and arguments.

A resident for some time in Europe, and recently married to a French Protestant woman, Marguerite Berry, the now thirty-year-old Theodore Stanton set out in the wake of the 1878 congress to investigate the status of women throughout Europe. In late 1880 he began collecting material for a study intended to explain developments in the Old World to those in the New, and in 1884 he published a massive volume, *The Woman Question in Europe: A Series of Original Essays*. Except for the long essay on France, which Stanton wrote himself, contributors to this volume all addressed the status of women in their respective lands.

It is manifestly clear, from reading Stanton's transnational compendium, where the fissures had opened to release the magma of women's emancipation and where they had not. Accounts of England and France took up nearly forty percent of the book, though England—as the "Mother Country"—was accorded a place of particular honor, as was the quest for woman suffrage, which had developed most strongly in England and the United States.

Introducing the volume, the Anglo-Irish activist Frances Power Cobbe deployed the metaphor of "waves" and "tides" to characterize the varied, multiple, and overlapping embodiments of the growing women's movement:[21]

> This movement has stirred an entire sex, even half the human race. Like the incoming tide, also, it has rolled in separate waves, and each one has obeyed the same law, and has done its part in carrying forward all the rest. . . . But the crown and completion of the progress must be the attainment of the Political Franchise in every country wherein representative government prevails, and till that point be reached, there can be no final satisfaction in any thing which has been achieved.

Contributors to the volume included many who had attended the 1878 congress, but also others who had not been present but were sympathetic to or actively engaged in the struggle for women's rights. The English section included essays by Millicent Garrett Fawcett (on suffrage), Maria Grey (on the women's educational movement), Frances Elizabeth Hoggan (women in medicine), Jessie Boucherett (the industrial movement), and Henrietta O. Barnett (women as philanthropists). Writing on the German women's movement were Anna Schepeler-Lette, Jenny Hirsch, and Marie Calm, who all emphasized (as had Pauline Worm in Denmark some years earlier) the distasteful connotations of the term "emancipation" in their country. Elise van Calcar contributed a short chapter on the Netherlands, while Johanna Leitenberger wrote about the status of women in Austria. The novelist Camilla Collett provided coverage of Norway, while Rosalie Ulrica Olivecrona traced developments in Sweden, and Kirstine Frederiksen summarized the situation in Denmark. Aurelia Cimino Folliero de Luna, editor of *La Cornelia*, and Dora d'Istria (Princess Helene Koltzoff-Massalsky), both from Florence, covered the varied scene in unified Italy.

Other contributors included Concepción Arenal, who wrote pessimistically about the condition of women in Spain, while Rodrigues de Freitas, substituting for the ailing authoress Maria Amalia Vaz de Carvalho, covered Portugal. Belgium was discussed by the woman physician Isala Van Diest, and Marie Goegg wrote about Switzerland. Marie Zebrikoff described conditions in Russia, while Elise Pavlovska Oresko (Orzeszko) explained the situation of women in Poland. Bohemia was covered by Elise Krasnohorska, author and editor of a Prague woman's journal, *Zenské Listy*. The final chapter, "The Orient," was written by Kalliope A. Kehaya, the Athens-educated principal of a European-style female seminary in Constantinople. Kehaya briefly discussed the variations of women's status and condition not only among the Greeks and Turks, but also among the Jews, Bulgarians, and Armenians who resided in the westernmost parts of the Ottoman Empire.

It had become abundantly clear from the exchange of information at the 1878 congress that however much the French republican women's rights advocates hoped to maintain the symbolic lead, the axis for organizational momentum was shifting. The Anglo-American world now carried the torch on the suffrage issue, and its mostly Protestant Christian representatives seemed to be taking the lead on issues of moral reform as well. Hubertine Auclert acknowledged this shift when, in February 1884, she issued an eloquent appeal to her American counterparts May Wright Sewall and Susan B. Anthony: "We call upon you to come to our aid, as your countrymen, a century ago, besought France to help them escape the subjection of England. Will you not come to our help as Lafayette and his legion flew to yours?" Auclert appealed to the American suffragists to convene a "Universal Congress in favor of Woman Suffrage" in Paris, insisting on the importance this might have for propelling the cause "of woman's emancipation throughout the whole world."[22]

A second and somewhat overlapping international alliance, organized for the purpose of defeating government-regulated prostitution, had also taken shape in the 1870s. In the campaign against the Contagious Disease Acts in Britain, Josephine Butler had discovered that the "mother" of all governmental regulation systems was none other than that of

France, whose system of licensed brothels and inspection and patrolling of prostitutes had been imitated to a greater or lesser degree throughout Europe. Among its various effects, the French system had spawned an international network of physicians eager to spread the regulation system, as well as a robust commercial traffic in underage female flesh to feed men's taste for novelty in the brothels. To combat this horror, in the mid-1870s Butler and her associates organized an international coalition of reformers of both sexes which took the name "British and Continental Federation against the State Regulation of Vice." This group maintained its headquarters in Switzerland, holding international conferences in Geneva (1877, 1889), in Neuchâtel (1882), in Basel (1884), and in Lausanne (1887). Aimé Humbert of Neuchâtel (formerly a Prussian dependency) in Switzerland edited the federation's monthly bulletin. The group's principal associates in Switzerland, besides Humbert, were Emma Pieczynska-Reichenbach and Charles Secrétan. In France, Émilie de Morsier and Yves Guyot carried the abolitionist banners, assisted by Maria Deraismes. The ultimate goal of this coalition was the demolition, from top to bottom, of the French regulation system.[23]

The international abolitionist coalition succeeded in provoking an investigation of the Paris morals police in 1882, with the not very satisfactory result that in 1884, the French government transferred jurisdiction from the Paris municipal authorities to the Ministry of the Interior. The thousand-page report of the pro-abolitionist French physician Louis Fiaux, *La Police des moeurs en France et dans les principaux pays d'Europe* (1888), following Yves Guyot's *La Prostitution* (1882), revealed the extent of the system's abuses. Abolitionists, including Anna Maria Mozzoni, Alaide Gualberta Beccari, and Jessie White Mario (all of whom had attended the federation's first congress in Geneva in 1877), succeeded in 1888 in effecting the repeal of the Cavour Decree, which had established regulated prostitution in Italy during the 1860s. Their victory was short-lived, however. A reformed regulation system was restored in 1891 and lasted until 1958.

The international abolitionist campaign, which had become, in Butler's own terminology, a "great crusade," contributed significantly to the knowledge wars, with a burgeoning scholarly and reportorial literature on prostitution.[24] It likewise sparked scholarly interest in the culture, condition, and character of the prostitutes, and more broadly in issues of female "deviancy" and "criminality" as such. This latter development would peak in the 1890s with the publication of the widely translated *La Donna delinquante* (The Delinquent Woman) by the proregulationist Italian physicians and criminologists Cesare Lombroso and (his son-in-law) Guglielmo Ferraro, who insisted that there was such a creature as "a born prostitute." This claim would be assertively contested by feminist abolitionists. Socialist writers on prostitution would insist that the practice was merely a product of capitalist society that would disappear with the inauguration of socialism.

Feminist abolitionists did not want to wait. Their campaign spawned multiple local initiatives by city-based women's groups in rescuing and rehabilitating prostitutes, caring for released female prisoners, protecting young girls newly arrived in cities from procurers and pimps, and combatting venereal disease. They campaigned to open new areas of paid work for women, to raise the age of consent for sexual acts, and to outlaw the "white slave trade," as the traffic in women for the sex industry was then called. Besides these practical charitable efforts, as historian Mary S. Gibson has pointed out, "abolitionists preached the end of the double standard and looked toward a future that would de-emphasize sex and limit it, for both men and women, to monogamous marriage."[25] Abolitionists had come to view as a fundamental necessity the exercise by men of personal control and restraint over the sex drive, the "naturalness" of which they came to view as another kind of social fiction; sexual restraint, for both sexes, became in their view an index of mankind's progress in the long climb from barbarism to civilization. "In feminist hands, desexualization could empower women to attack the customary prerogatives of men," noted historian Judith Walkowitz.[26] But men as well as women were part of this effort to inculcate a new, single, moral standard, as, for example, in the 1880s campaign-by-lecture tour "Monogamy and Polygamy" of the Norwegian playwright Bjørnstjerne Bjørnson, following the sensation of his landmark drama En Hanske (A Gauntlet, 1883), in which he advocated premarital chastity for men.[27] According to historian Marie Neudorfl, the scandal that erupted over the Moravian Czech Thomas Masaryk's university lecture on the "unmentionable" issue of prostitution in 1884 nearly cost him his university post.[28]

These feminists could hardly have anticipated, nor could they effectively counteract at the time (given their still limited numbers and lack of political authority), the parallel campaigns for sexual repression launched subsequently by opponents of pornography, the extremist social purity campaigns, and the repressive vigilante activism that sometimes seemed to reinforce male authority over women more often than it lessened it. Such campaigns would ensue, in England, France, and elsewhere on the European continent, and they have since been evaluated by some late twentieth-century scholars as negative in the extreme.

From the 1890s on, however, these campaigns, in which many feminists participated in the name of sexual purity, would be countered by other feminist campaigns advocating sexual emancipation, stirring up controversy on a scale that had not been seen in Europe since the Saint-Simonians' "rehabilitation of the flesh" in early 1830s France.

In the United States, meanwhile, the leaders of the National Woman Suffrage Association, spurred by the European visits of Elizabeth Cady Stanton and Susan B. Anthony in 1882 (and perhaps also by Hubertine Auclert's 1884 plea), convened an international council of women to commemorate the fortieth anniversary of the 1848 women's rights convention in Seneca Falls. This body assembled in Washington, D.C., in late March 1888 for eight days of deliberations. Amidst religious services, teas, receptions, hymns (suitably revised to promote the cause of women's rights), addresses, and reports, the assembled delegates considered the topics of education, philanthropy, temperance, industries, professions, organization, legal conditions, social purity, and political conditions. Delegates were feted at the White House by President and Mrs. Cleveland, as well as at receptions hosted by Senators Palmer (Michigan) and Stanford (California) and their wives.

Although those in attendance were overwhelmingly American, a small number of women from Europe did take part in this congress: these included Isabelle Bogelot, representing the Oeuvre des Libérées de Saint-Lazare in Paris (a group that assisted women released from the Saint-Lazare prison); Alexandra Gripenberg, representing the Finnish Women's Association, and her colleague Allie Trygg; Sophia Magelsson Groth, from the Norwegian Woman Suffrage Society; Ada M. Frederiksen (of Chicago), representing the Danish Women's Association; and Margaret Moore, from Ireland. Several delegates came from England, including Alice Scatcherd (Leeds), Laura Ormiston Chant, and Margaret Dilke. Papers (subsequently published in the proceedings) were sent by Kirstine Frederiksen of Denmark, Fanny Zampini Salazaro, editor of the recently founded *Rassegna degli interessi femminile* (Women's Review) in Rome, and Josephine Butler. Many others, including Hubertine Auclert and Maria Deraismes from France, and the Russian anarchist Prince Kropotkin, sent messages of support to the congress, and these were proudly published in the conference proceedings.

Elizabeth Cady Stanton closed the congress with a challenge to men to resolve the woman question favorably, warning that otherwise "it will eventually be settled by violence."[29] Raising the political stakes for her male compatriots, she invoked the ominous image of immigrant passengers, newly arrived in the United States from Europe by steerage class on the very ship that had brought lady delegates to the congress, cautioning that "with all the elements of discontent now gathering from foreign lands, you may have the scenes of the French Commune repeated in our land":

> In all the struggles for liberty in the past women have ever taken an ac-
> tive part, and it is fair to suppose that they will do the same in the future.
> Awake to their own wrongs, as they never have been before, and exasper-
> ated with a sense of the prolonged oppressions of their sex, it requires no
> prophet to foretell the revolutions ahead, when women strike hands
> with Nihilists, Socialists, Communists, and Anarchists, in defense of the
> most enlarged liberties of the people.

Women must mobilize, Stanton argued, to attack the problems of the poor and unfortunate before they resorted to revolution: "This branch of government, regulating the morals of the people, belongs specifically to woman; and the first step to this end, is to make you believe that the happiness and prosperity of *all* the people of a nation are possible."

The year 1889 marked the centennial of the French Revolution. In midsummer two international women's congresses convened in Paris, in conjunction with the celebrations. Hubertine Auclert, then living in Algeria, was not entirely pleased by this timing: "Women should not celebrate the masculine '89; they should organize a feminine '89," she wrote in *La Citoyenne*.[30]

The French and International Congress on Women's Rights (*droit des femmes*), organized by Maria Deraismes and Léon Richer, opened on 25 June and ran through the 29th. Deraismes had asked her "eminent *consoeur*" Elizabeth Cady Stanton to serve as honorary president, but Stanton was unable to attend. In her flattering letter to the congress, she reciprocated Deraismes's equally flattering invitation by insisting that the two republics, the American and the French, must lead the world in the quest for women's rights. The rights congress was followed by the International Congress on Women's Charities and Institutions, which met with government sponsorship from 12 July to the 18th, thus centering its deliberations squarely over the French Republic's Bastille Day festivities.

Just as the 1888 congress in Washington had celebrated forty years of organized activism by American women's rights advocates, so the organizers of the Paris women's rights congress also invoked their national roots, which went back considerably further: "We were the precursors. . . . These seeds that we sowed, then subsequently neglected, others have cultivated and are already reaping their fruit."[31] It is not difficult to discern more than a hint of national rivalry in this claim, as well as an expression of friendly solidarity. At the opening session, Maria Deraismes insisted on the universal importance of the Declaration of the Rights of Man of 1789, even as she underscored how "half of humanity" had been "left out of this work of general liberation." She contrasted the rigorous exclusion of French women from political life and the closing of their clubs in 1793 with the visionary words of Condorcet concerning sexual equality. Perhaps at the time, one could excuse the revolution's failure to address the needs of women. One hundred years later, though, the men were still stalling. For this there was no excuse.[32]

The international congress heard papers presented in four sections dealing with history, economics, morals, and legislation, and its attendees formulated a set of demands addressed specifically to the French situation: the complete reform of legislation on married women's civil rights, especially as concerned property rights, equal pay for women and men teachers, access to the liberal professions, apprenticeships for women located in vocational schools rather than in workshops, suppression of the morals police and demolition of the Saint-Lazare prison, and repeal of the law that prohibited paternity suits.

The still heavily French audience was interspersed with a sprinkling of foreign delegates from Denmark and Norway, from Scotland and from England, and from Poland (including a group of students). Ellen Fries (doctor of letters) from Sweden, Marie Popelin from Belgium (a newly minted doctor of laws), Theodore Stanton (representing the National Woman Suffrage Association), and Callirhoé Parren from Athens, editor of a new Greek women's rights publication, *Efimeris ton kyrion* (Women's Journal), rounded out the delegates from abroad. Together they celebrated the prowess of academic women, especially in medicine and legal studies. According to a report by the press-clipping service, much boasted about by the organizers, this congress received more attention in the press, both in France and internationally, than any other held during the Paris Exposition. No hymns were sung, but multiple toasts were drunk, and much festivity marked the closing ceremonial banquet. Maria Deraismes paid special tribute to the press for its support of the cause. In a short toast Léon Richer insisted: "A principle has no country; truth knows no frontiers. The question of women's rights is the same everywhere; everywhere it can be summarized in two words: Equality, Justice."[33] Callirhoé Parren toasted those who, through their writings and actions, had made the "feminine question" an international question. Clémence Royer drank to the illustrious women of the past, including those nameless women who took up manual labor in order to establish human society, and invoked women's ongoing mission as peacemakers. Louise Koppe toasted the granddaughters and great-grand-daughters who would celebrate the bicentennial of 1789. Little could she know then that a number of them would become historians of women.

The warm afterglow of the 1889 internationalist vision radiated for some time. Following the congresses, the editors of *Le Droit des femmes* laid plans for a Fédération Internationale pour la Revendication des Droits de la Femme. By 1890 the paper gave increasing coverage to *le mouvement féminin* in many countries, in Europe and beyond. These efforts were complemented, early in 1890, by the founding of a Union Universelle des Femmes, complete with a bulletin edited by Marya Chéliga, a young woman of Polish descent then living in Paris. Thus, as 1890 drew to a close, supporters of women's rights throughout Europe had good reasons to be optimistic, though they would continue to confront many thorny issues as well as a resurgence of opposition.

INTERNATIONALIZING THE QUESTIONS: WOMEN'S WORK AND INFANTS' WELFARE

Among the thorniest of those issues was the question of women's work for pay, which was rearticulated within a context of growing concern over national population needs and public health. Even opponents generally conceded that single women might need to support themselves, though they continued to grumble about the fact that not all women were properly married and supported by husbands. Far more controversy swirled around the employment of married women, who, in the nationalist context of the 1870s and 1880s, were increasingly represented first and foremost as mothers—the essential providers not only of educated citizens, but in the new scheme of populationist thinking, of workers and soldiers—in short, of human capital for the consolidation of nation-states.

Concern over women in the labor force was by no means new in late nineteenth-century Western Europe, as should be clear from earlier chapters. Gender had become central to discussion of work in industrializing societies, just as it had been in the preindustrial world. Nevertheless, the increasing industrial employment of women assured that new elements would affect the shape of the discussion in the period between 1870 and 1890. Supplementing earlier arguments that had drawn in middle-class economists, working-class men, religious authorities, and feminists, a new generation of physicians and population experts weighed in on newly identified health issues related to maternity and children's well-being. Not surprisingly, these doctors strongly asserted that, for the national good, married women should not be employed, or if employed, they should not be at work when their newborns required their full attention as well as their physical nourishment in order to survive infancy.

Feminists in France continued to defend women's right to work, in the tradition of Paule Mink, Julie Daubié, and the women of the Paris Commune. "Far from thinking about removing workers [*bras* in French] from production," wrote the male feminist Léon Richer in 1877, "we must give it new ones":[34]

> What we must do is modify the present conditions of women's work; we must moralize the workshop, we must find a way of reconciling . . . the interests of the *ouvrière* with the respect due to every woman and with the obligations of mothers. . . . Woman, even when married, must be able to live from her own salary if she so desires.

Richer was no partisan of the male-breadwinner solution to women's survival, believing that all women must be able to participate freely in the market economy, independent of male breadwinners.

But the conditions surrounding women's employment in many countries remained very bad. Speaking at the 1877 Geneva congress of the International Federation for the Abolition of Regulated Prostitution, Anna Maria Mozzoni qualified Richer's optimism: "Everyone has the right to live from his work, but women seem to have more of a right to die since it is so difficult for them to find honest and sufficient work."[35] Caroline de Barrau reported that the average wage for women workers in Paris (whose employment was mostly seasonal) was about two francs per day. This was far from adequate for survival.

The organization of work was of interest to the male-dominated workers' movement as well, particularly in England. But wherever the male-breadwinner ethic monopolized discussion, labor leaders urged the regulation and limitation of working hours for women and children in factories, with the hope (not always openly expressed) that such laws would effectively regulate (and decrease) men's hours as well. They subsequently targeted non-factory-based production, or "sweated" labor, which employed even more women. The far more decentralized employment of women as domestic servants and agricultural workers (by far the majority of employed women in nineteenth-century Europe) and as home-based workers raised still more difficult issues, which would not be addressed until the twentieth century.

Several issues provoked discussions between male doctors, government officials, industrialists, and labor leaders in the early 1870s, and in every case agitation centered on issues of motherhood and morality.

These issues included continuing discussion of women's work in and around mines, night work, and an emerging set of concerns focused on maternity and wet-nursing. Not all of these provoked expressions of feminist dissent.

In England, women's underground work in mines had been outlawed in 1842, though their work at the pit face was still reluctantly conceded in the 1880s. This had set a powerful precedent for discussion by progressive legislators elsewhere in Europe. Both the French and Belgian governments restricted women's work in mines in the early 1870s. German regulations followed in the late 1870s, and Austria imposed regulations in 1884.

Women's work at night was another target of reformers. Highly industrialized Switzerland had prohibited night work for women in factories in 1877. The Russian government outlawed night work in factories for women and children in 1885, as a kind of pre-emptive strike, since there were still few factories where women might have obtained such work. Women workers were rarely if ever consulted as these restrictions were hammered into place.

Doctors, hygienists, and moralists expressed concern about the childcare practices of employed mothers in urban areas, where rates of infant mortality were disproportionately high. In 1874, French government authorities subjected the commercial wet-nursing business to additional administrative controls. In England, increased parliamentary scrutiny of baby-farming practices by employed mothers led to regulation in the 1870s. The attention focused on these problems in Western European countries generated anxiety in other national settings, provoking additional attempts at government intervention.

In 1877 the socially conservative Federal Republic of Switzerland became the first European nation to outlaw night work for women in factories and to impose an unpaid maternity leave on women workers. Historian Regina Wecker emphasizes that "the 1877 law . . . functioned as an opening wedge not only for the terms of international protective legislation but also for a retooled conception of protection: special protection for women only."[36] Imperial Germany enacted its first protective law in 1878, and this measure was followed in the early 1880s by Bismarck's comprehensive social insurance scheme, which effectively medicalized childbirth. Intergovernmental initiatives began to take shape in the 1880s and early 1890s. The intent of these measures, just as in Switzerland and Germany, was clearly to preserve the sexual division of labor in the family by designating women as a special class who needed "protection" from exploitative employment. The ultimate goal of these initiatives was to eliminate married women from the workforce, an aim in which male trade union leaders and male social Catholic employers and reformers found common ground.

By 1890 Austria and the Netherlands would also enact measures to restrict women's employment in one or more ways. The year 1890 marked the convocation in Berlin of an intergovernmental congress on worker protection, sponsored by the Swiss and German governments. This congress drew up resolutions and stimulated a flurry of subsequent legislative attempts in other countries to restrict night and Sunday work for women aged sixteen or over, to limit their working hours, to restrict women's employment in dangerous and insalubrious industries, and to forbid their employment during and subsequent to the period around childbirth. Obligatory maternity leave was mandated, but without compensation.

Feminists would disagree about how to respond to these developments, which they had helped neither to shape nor to initiate. Most feminists would adamantly defend women's right to work as they saw fit, developing several new tactical arguments around "freedom to work" to counter the protectionist pressures based on a male-breadwinner/dominator model. A second and more powerfully interventionist approach was to call for direct state financial assistance for mothers, including paid maternity leaves, so that they would not have to depend on outside employment or male breadwinners. The French socialist-feminist Léonie Rouzade argued repeatedly, though fruitlessly, in the 1880s that motherhood should become a paid social function of the state. This statist-feminist approach would pick up dramatic support in the 1890s and the early twentieth century, particularly among Scandinavian and German feminists.

A third strategy, articulated by Hubertine Auclert in response to workingmen's claims that women were taking jobs away from them, would open up a new line of feminist criticism by challenging the existing sexual division of labor. Women had a perfect right to employment, she maintained, but the precondition for women's paid work was for men to share in the unpaid additional work women were currently doing in male-dominated households. These tasks were not "women's work," she argued: "All those unproductive tasks that are assigned to women in the home are, in society, done by men for money. For money, men sweep, clean, brush shoes and clothes; for money, men sew; for money, men cook, lay and clear tables, and wash dishes. For money, men care for young children."[37] Because of the expectations for women to do household work, in addition to any paid labor they might undertake, employed women had to work far longer and harder than their husbands did. Such household work, Auclert asserted, was not currently valued in French society precisely because women were still treated as men's servants, not as their equals.

Disagreements over protective legislation for women were responsible for the emergence of the two international women's congresses held in Paris in 1889. Maria Deraismes and Léon Richer adamantly insisted on women's right to economic independence, and they objected to the choice of Jules Simon, a staunch advocate of protective legislation, as honorary president of the official women's congress. In Deraismes's opening speech at the dissenting women's rights congress she alluded to these differences between liberals, who upheld women's "right" to economic independence, and protectionists, who upheld "privileges" and supported the prohibition of women's night work: "This type of protection seems more like a restriction, an oppression, than like an advantageous concession. We know from experience that protection and liberty are two mutually exclusive terms."[38] Moreover, she noted, such "protection" could actually be quite ineffective. So her contingent had refused designation as an "official" congress under these terms and had chosen an independent path. French feminists would continue to resist protective legislation for women well into the 1890s, in company with their English counterparts associated with the *Englishwoman's Review*. But the tide was turning, and during the 1890s feminists in other countries, especially Imperial Germany, would embrace the "privileges" of state-sponsored protective legislation for women as more immediately advantageous to women workers than any number of hypothetically equal "rights" or "liberties."

COMPETING SOLUTIONS TO THE
WOMAN QUESTION

Following the Paris Commune, and amidst the flurry of feminist organizational activity, leaders of what remained of the shattered international workers' movement proposed alternative routes to the emancipation of women. Some would also advocate woman suffrage and full equality of rights, but others would focus on eliminating women and children from the labor force, regulating their hours in the interests of protecting them, or advocating state support for mothers. The more revolutionary Marxist-socialists, however, envisioned not reform, but wholesale overthrow of the capitalist mode of production.

By 1890 the unified Marxist-socialist program as concerned women

could be summarized roughly as follows: Capitalism, with its exploitation of the proletariat, lay at the root of women's subordination; only a
new socialist order, constructed by the victorious working classes, could
provide an answer to the woman question. Demands for women's rights
were increasingly portrayed as a strictly "bourgeois" or "liberal" solution (i.e., interested primarily in civil and civic rights, with a pejorative
connotation that such a solution was "reactionary"), which did not address the issue of capitalist domination and exploitation. The revolutionary overthrow of the class order and the existing property system
must be given priority; the emancipation of women would automatically follow.[39]

The First International Working Men's Association collapsed in 1876,
and the Second International was born only in 1889. In the interim years,
the German socialists succeeded in unifying competing factions (1875),
but their new Social Democratic political party was outlawed from 1878
to 1890 by the German imperial government for being, among other
things, "antifamily." These years, nevertheless, saw the publication
(originally in German) of several landmark statements on the woman
question, by leading socialist spokesmen of a Marxist persuasion, which
provided programmatic underpinning for the later movement. Two key
book-length treatises were August Bebel's *Woman in the Past, Present,
and Future*, originally published in German in 1878, and later republished as *Woman and Socialism*, and Friedrich Engels's *The Origin of the
Family, Private Property and the State* (1884). Two shorter and highly
influential statements which likewise elaborated the Marxist-socialist
position on the woman question also appeared during this period. The
first, in English, by Karl Marx's daughter Eleanor and her partner Edward
Aveling, appeared in London's *Westminster Review* (1886), and later in
pamphlet form. The second, Clara Zetkin's address to the 1889 founding
congress of the Second International, "Women Workers—and the Woman Question," was also widely distributed.

Bebel's work set out the key argument which would resonate through
the publications of all his successors; he insisted on the political primacy
of class over sex, and castigated as "bourgeois" those who would only
later be known as "feminists." "The so-called women's question is . . .
only one side of the whole social question . . . ; only in connection with
each other can the two questions reach their final solution."[40] Sex relations, for Bebel, were not the main issue, even though he insisted that
"woman was the first human being that tasted bondage . . . a slave before
the slave existed."

Bebel therefore argued—responding to feminist claims—that legal and economic equality, including women's admittance to the professions, would change nothing in the existing order of things; such advances would neither diminish wage slavery nor avert sexual slavery: "The subjection of the sex under men, the pecuniary dependence of the enormous majority and the consequent sexual slavery which finds its expression in modern marriage and in prostitution, will still remain untouched." A "complete solution" was required; anything else was merely patchwork: "By a complete solution I understand not only the equality of men and women before the law, but their economic freedom and material independence, and, so far as possible, equality in mental development. *This complete solution of the Women's Question is as unattainable as the solution of the Labour Question under the existing social and political institutions."*

Friedrich Engels, like Bebel, went well beyond the earlier proposals of Karl Marx, whose views on relationships between men and women in marriage remained relatively conventional, even as he criticized the prevailing institutional forms of the family. Engels's lengthy *Origin of the Family* built out on Marx's notes, supplementing them with material drawn from Darwin, Spencer, and Bachofen, as well as from Lewis Henry Morgan's studies of the communistic Iroquois, to probe the historical origins of women's subordination to men. His most startling and influential finding pinpointed the transfer of inheritance, once property in breeding herds and human slaves had been established in early societies, from the female to the male succession lines. Drawing heavily on Bachofen's findings on matrilinealism in ancient societies, Engels proclaimed that "the overthrow of mother-right was the *world historical defeat of the female sex."* Critical of property-based monogamous marriage, in which women were seen as systematically subordinated and dominated, he concluded that "the first condition for the liberation of the wife is to bring the whole female sex back into public industry, and . . . this in turn demands the abolition of the monogamous family as the economic unit of society."[41]

Eleanor Marx and Edward Aveling addressed their commentary on Bebel's work to British readers, again underscoring the primacy of economics in the *oppression* (following Bebel, they deliberately substituted this term for Mill's "subordination") of women; and as in the feminist critiques of the early 1830s, such as those of the Saint-Simonian women and Flora Tristan, they linked the fates of women and workers: "The position of women rests, as everything in our complex modern society rests, on an economic basis. Had Bebel done nothing but insist upon this, his work would have been valuable. The woman question is one of the organization of society as a whole." Marx and Aveling, like Bebel, criticized the women's rights advocates of their time for not seeing this, for not probing origins, for not comprehending that whatever specific reforms might be accomplished, little would be changed:[42]

> Women are the creatures of an organized tyranny of men, as the workers are the creatures of an organized tyranny of idlers. Even where thus much is grasped, we must never be weary of insisting on the non-understanding that for women, as for the labouring classes, no solution of the difficulties and problems that present themselves is really possible in the present condition of society. . . . Their emancipation will come from themselves. Women will find allies in the better sort of men, as the labourers are finding allies among the philosophers, artists, and poets. But the one has nothing to hope from man as a whole, and the other has nothing to hope from the middle-class as a whole.

Only after the revolution that would bring about the classless society would perfect equality of women with men prevail, and a material independence for women emerge that would enable them to realize their full potential as autonomous individuals. Thus was class given priority over sex.

Clara Zetkin, representing Berlin working women at the Paris labor congress of 1889, offered both a theoretical and practical appreciation of the specific issue of women's employment, grounded in her own experience as a mother and self-supporting woman. Only the work of pregnant women should be regulated, she claimed. She attempted to convince working men that the problem did not lie in women's labor competing with that of men, but that the real issue was the capitalist exploitation of women's labor. Like her predecessors, she argued that only the emancipation of labor from capital would solve this problem: "Only in a socialist society will female and male workers alike gain complete human rights." Women were prepared to be comrades-in-arms to arrive at this new society, Zetkin proclaimed, but they intended to "demand all their rights once victory is achieved."[43] Clearly the Marxist-socialists were intent on capturing the theoretical and political high ground in the matter of altering the relations between the sexes.

The argument so consistently articulated by Bebel, Engels, Marx and Aveling, and Zetkin in the 1880s would become the party "line" of the new Second International Working Men's Association and its associated national parties. For some the notion that capitalism, not male domination, was the enemy, and socialist revolution the answer, offered a compelling vision.

In consequence, relationships between socialists and feminists in

Europe would become increasingly tense from the 1890s through the early twentieth century, as we will see in Chapter 7. The German Social Democratic Party (SPD) republished Bebel's pronouncements on the woman question in a revised and expanded edition, entitled *Die Frau und der Sozialismus* (Women and Socialism), incorporating the arguments of Engels and other scholars; his arguments would be widely disseminated and translated. In 1890 Imperial Germany would repeal the Antisocialist Laws, which had severely handicapped socialist organizing since 1878; besides establishing a national social insurance program, Bismarck's government had instituted other measures designed expressly to defuse worker discontent, including protective legislation for women workers. In 1891, the emergent SPD, seeking support as a mass political party, staked out a very radical position by voting at its Erfurt congress to fight "for the abolition of class domination, of classes as such, and for equal rights and equal obligations, regardless of sex and origin. On the basis of these opinions, it fights not only against the exploitation and oppression of the workers but against any kind of exploitation and oppression in modern society, no matter whether it is directed against a class, a party, a sex, or a race." In consequence, the SPD endorsed universal suffrage without distinction of sex and "abolition of all laws that discriminate against women in public and private spheres."[44]

By 1894 Clara Zetkin, who spearheaded the newly formed German Social Democratic Women's movement, would refuse all further cooperation with representatives of the so-called bourgeois women's movement—even as she would continually remind her male comrades that their promises to women must be kept.[45] As the SPD was by far the most national party in the Second International, these political maneuvers would have an important ripple effect throughout Europe, exacerbating the relationship between feminists and socialists by attempting to place feminists on the defensive. One way to undermine feminism (and to capture its potential clientele) while purporting to emancipate women was to incorporate its demands even while adjourning their enactment.

Thus was a potent rivalry set into place between the advocates of women's emancipation and socialist theoreticians and politicians who insisted on class solidarity, encompassing both proletarian women and men. Unlike Bebel and Zetkin, many women's advocates were unwilling to wait for the success of the revolution. They expressed reservations about the entire package of revolutionary socialist goals, and particularly their order of priority; like Jeanne Deroin in 1848, they identified the imbalance in the relationship of the sexes as the core problem. Though they acknowledged the existence of class differences, and the importance of economic issues, they were troubled by continuing evidence of *masculinisme* (a newly coined French term connoting both male privilege and male arrogance) exhibited both by socialist leaders and by working-class men. They contended that women's emancipation must be pursued in the present, not postponed until after a hypothetical proletarian revolution had dethroned capitalism.

The experiences of Hubertine Auclert in French socialist circles of the 1880s offer a telling case in point. In October 1879 Auclert had sought support for woman suffrage among the delegates to the congress of the French socialist workers' movement in Marseille. In her speech there she made explicit the connection between sex and class, rephrasing in new language the long-forgotten arguments of her Saint-Simonian predecessors: "Like you [workers], we [women] have been the victims of abusive force. . . . We still endure the tyrannical force of those who are in power, to which one must add, in our case, the tyrannical force of those who now enjoy their rights. . . . A Republic that keeps women in an inferior situation cannot make men equal." Castigating "privileges of sex," Auclert demanded of the mostly male delegates: "How can you speak of equality, you who . . . wish to keep other beings under your control?" Lacking guarantees, she insisted: "I am truly afraid that human equality, as preached by every socialist school, will still mean the equality of men, and that the women will be duped by the proletarian men just as the latter have been duped by the bourgeoisie." Women were not interested, Auclert asserted, in "aiding despotism to change hands. What we want is to kill privilege, not merely to reallocate it."[46]

Delegates to the Marseille workers' congress voted to support Auclert's resolution. The honeymoon of socialism and feminism in France lasted for a few years, but the pursuit of any and all women's rights ultimately fell victim to the internecine strife in the 1880s, as reformists parted company with the more radical Marxist group that advocated collectivism and revolution. Auclert, who as a *rentière* found the collectivist program unacceptable, established her own organization and propaganda center for the pursuit of woman suffrage in republican France. In February 1881 she founded the periodical *La Citoyenne*, in which she propagandized during a ten-year period for full rights for all French women, including the vote.

Auclert's more radical counterpart Léonie Rouzade also tried to bridge the expanding chasm between socialist factions and women's rights advocates during the 1880s. As the founder of a new women's group, the Union des Femmes (named after the society established by the Communardes in 1871), and a frequent participant in workers' congresses, Rouzade claimed that women should have absolutely the same rights as men. Claims for equal education were also central to her agenda. To those who insisted (in a republic that had recently established universal military service for men) that men were entitled to rights because they were soldiers, Rouzade played the motherhood trump: "Our burden is equal in value to yours, and if one has rights for killing men, one ought to have even more rights for creating humanity!"[47] Like Auclert and Rouzade, many feminists—even those who had been sympathetic to some socialist goals—would be upset at, as well as somewhat suspicious of, the Marxist-socialists' attempts to thrust the wedge of class into the growing feminist sisterhood. They demanded full citizenship within the societies in which they lived, with the aim of changing those societies from the inside out, here and now.[48]

RECASTING DOMESTIC AND FOREIGN RELATIONS
ACROSS NATIONAL BORDERS

Henrik Ibsen's Nora first slammed the door on domesticity in 1880. Initially staged in Copenhagen and then throughout Scandinavia and Germany, *A Doll's House* provoked vigorous debate, even scandal. Within the next decade translations of this compelling play appeared in virtually every European language. Major productions were launched in London (1889) and in Paris (1894), with Europe's leading actresses portraying Ibsen's heroine. Nora's grand exit from her husband's dominion became the talk of Europe.

With Nora's declaration of independence, a woman's individual search for her freedom and her right to happiness announced itself as a major theme in the debate on the woman question. To some, Ibsen's creation epitomized the archenemy of marriage, delivering a scathing critique of the patriarchal concept of womanhood. In addition to energizing the women's movement in multiple ways, Nora's action also opened up a debate over the future relations of the sexes that would have a dramatic and profound effect on European letters, drawing in such well-known Scandinavian writers as August Strindberg, Georg Brandes, Viktoria Benedictsson, Anne-Charlotte Leffler, and Amalia Skram.[49]

Nora was not the only fictional character to challenge gender constraints and conventional expectations during these years. The nearly simultaneous publication of George Meredith's novel *The Egoist* (1879) featured a heroine, Clara Middleton, who refused betrothal to Sir Willoughby Patterne, a man who viewed women as property and ornament. Meredith's explorations of "true mating" reached a pinnacle with his

1884 novel *Diana of the Crossways*, which offered a thoughtful, if less startling and revolutionary, look at "true" marriage as a joining of two fully developed individuals. Literary analyst Elizabeth Deis has characterized Meredith's resolution as "a compromise of Victorian and modern values," honoring marriage on the one hand, but insisting on the equality of the partners on the other.[50]

Within just a few years of Meredith's novels and Ibsen's play, the South African writer Olive Schreiner, recently arrived in England, published her first novel, *The Story of an African Farm* (1883). Its heroine, Lyndall, dreamed of Napoleon and the rise of civilization instead of about her trousseau. "I am not in so great a hurry to put my neck beneath any man's foot; and I do not so greatly admire the crying of babies. . . . There are other women glad of such work," Lyndall told her married sister Em upon returning from boarding school.[51] In the course of Lyndall's musings, she dissected girls' education, marriage as a support system, the misuse of women's covert power, the need for important work to do; indeed, Lyndall was a marvelously prescient creation, wise beyond her years and, like her creator, astonishingly eloquent.

Europeans were still unaccustomed to "mere girls" speaking their minds, even in fiction. Even more scandalous was frank talk from the recently deceased. In 1887 a literary sensation was set off by the publication in Paris of the *Journal of Marie Bashkirtseff*, the diary of a Russian-born aristocrat and gifted painter living in France, who had recently died of consumption at the age of twenty-four. This revealing portrait of adolescence and young womanhood once again sparked discussion throughout European intellectual circles about the "true" nature of woman, and, among other effects, gave an enormous boost to discussion of the woman question in the newly developing fields of psychology and psychoanalysis. "Never have I rebelled so much against the condition of woman," Bashkirtseff had written in 1878 (shortly after the first international women's rights congress met in Paris). "I am not foolish enough to claim that stupid equality, which is an Utopia . . . because there can not be equality between two beings so different, as man and woman. I ask nothing, because woman has already all that she should have; but I grumble at being a woman, because I happen to be one only as far as outward appearance goes."[52]

Must self-sacrifice be the primary criterion for "womanliness"? Marie Bashkirtseff denied it; she demanded success and recognition as an artist in her own right, and worked hard to attain it. In her diary and in her life, she dared—like Schreiner's fictional Lyndall—to claim ambition and fame as her birthright, and under her own name. As the sympathetic

George Bernard Shaw put it, in commenting on the English publication of the diary and the scandal it precipitated: "The sum of the matter is that unless Woman repudiates her womanliness, her duty to her husband, to her children, to society, to the law, and to everyone but herself, she cannot emancipate herself. . . . Therefore Woman has to repudiate duty altogether. In that repudiation lies her freedom. . . . A whole basketful of ideals of the most sacred quality will be smashed by the achievement of equality for women and men."[53]

In London, a group of progressive young and mostly single women and men organized by Cambridge-educated Karl Pearson began to meet as a Men and Women's Club in 1885 to discuss the subject of sex. "Club members," observed historian Judith Walkowitz, "considered themselves part of an intellectual and political vanguard, earnestly engaged in what seemed to them—and indeed was—a revolutionary undertaking: the deliberative discussion of sexual mores and sexual passion." Nevertheless, she acknowledged, "heterosexual fantasy and ideology set the boundaries of club discussions."[54] In that time, however, frank discussions of heterosexual relations marked a singular achievement.

The campaign against the Contagious Diseases Acts in England during the last fifteen years, abetted by recent revelations of child prostitution in London, had contributed immensely to making such discussion possible and had deeply affected the views of the participating women, sensitizing them to their own sexual vulnerability. However, Pearson's social Darwinist agenda, his interest in founding "a real science of sexualogy," as he put it, and his insistence on emphasizing women's social duties (especially childbearing), rather than their liberation as individuals à la Ibsen's Nora, reportedly dampened the free expression of feminist perspectives within the group. Backing off from John Stuart Mill's radically liberal approach to ending the subjection of women, Pearson returned to "public utility" themes. Speaking as a scientist, he insisted that "we have first to settle what is the physical capacity of woman, what would be the effect of her emancipation on her function of race-reproduction, before we can talk about her 'rights,' which are, after all, only a vague description of what may be the fittest position for her, the sphere of her maximum usefulness in the developed society of the future."[55]

Coupling the reform of economic relations with the reform of sexual relations, Pearson—like his socialist colleagues—would subsequently argue that women's economic independence from men, their self-support, was a necessity; this was the precondition of full individuality and a new morality: "The economic independence of women will for the first time render it possible for the highest human relationship to become again a matter of pure affection, raised above every suspicion of constraint, and every taint of commercialism."[56] Socialism, for Pearson, held the key to a future beyond legalized monogamy. As for childbearing women, they must be supported by the state, not by individual men, even as the state set limits on their childbearing. A number of women club members were less than thrilled by Pearson's analysis and conclusions, and ultimately the club fell apart over differences of opinion and the resentment of the women members at the arrogance of men who thought they could speak for women.

It was Mona Caird's article "Marriage," in the August 1888 *Westminster Review*, however, that brought these private discussions into the public eye. Caird set off a storm of public controversy, precipitating 27,000 letters from readers throughout England to the *Daily Telegraph's* subsequent query "Is Marriage a Failure?" Caird, who had not been invited to participate in the Men and Women's Club, addressed the difficulties of communication between the sexes. She objected to the way in which (male) thinkers and philosophers discounted or ignored women's thoughts and feelings as they blamed "woman's nature" for the results of their poor education and confinement. Drawing variously on studies by Pearson, August Bebel, and others, Caird rehearsed the history of marriage as it was then understood, laying particular blame on Martin Luther (as had Pearson) for the subordination of women in a desacralized, strictly commercial form of marriage: "We shall never have a world really worth living in until men and women can show interest in one another, without being driven either to marry or to forego altogether the pleasure and profit of frequent meeting."[57] Women's economic independence and coeducation of the sexes were, according to Caird, required to move in this direction. Companionship between the sexes was also her ideal. Yet in the present institution of marriage, she argued in a second article, "disobedience . . . is a woman's first duty!"[58] Freedom must be the reigning principle in relations between the sexes, as in other relations.

It was in this context that Grant Allen invoked the national need, in his "Plain Words on the Woman Question." Ignoring the problem of "redundant" (single) women, Allen laid out the population needs of Britain, rehearsing a theme that would be widely discussed throughout Europe during the next two decades:[59]

> In every community, and to all time, the vast majority of the women must become wives and mothers, and must bear at least four children apiece. If some women shirk their natural duties, then a heavier task

must be laid upon the remainder. But in any case almost all must become wives and mothers, and almost all must bear at least four or five children. In our existing state six are the very fewest that our country can do with.

Women's emancipation, Grant Allen argued, "must not be of a sort that interferes in any way with this prime natural necessity." Women must be "trained, physically, morally, socially, and mentally, in the way best fitting them to be wives and mothers," and they must be given "the fullest and most generous support in carrying out their functions as wives and mothers." In Allen's eyes, emancipationists of the 1880s were promoting "an unsexed woman," by educating women to be men. The "self-supporting spinster" was "a deplorable accident of the passing moment, . . . an abnormality, not the woman of the future."

In other European societies, a new generation of women writers and activists addressed the woman question. Some were more "feminist" than others; few were as radical as Mona Caird. From Concepción Arenal, in Spain, for example, came a response in the early 1890s that nevertheless spoke to the Grant Allens as much as it countered the Spanish vision of the angel of the house:[60]

> It is a grave error and one of the most harmful to inculcate women with the idea that their sole mission is that of being a wife and mother; it is the equivalent of telling them that by themselves they cannot be anything. . . . [Women] must first affirm their personality, independent of their state, and persuade themselves that, single, married, or widowed, they have duties to carry out, rights to vindicate, a job to do. . . . Life is something serious, and if they take it as a game they will be unremittingly treated as a toy.

Not all women novelists of the period were as avowedly feminist as Concepción Arenal or her younger colleague Emilia Pardo Bazán, who would become Spain's most outspoken feminist in the fin-de-siècle period. The Italian novelist and journalist Matilde Serao, from Naples, who wrote compellingly from a woman's perspective and broke new ground as a reporter and critic in the naturalist or realist (verismo) school, expressed views in her works that can only be called antifeminist. Serao was herself a role breaker and a reformer, but one who consciously defended the woman's traditional role in the family as one who loves, serves, and obeys. Upholding the moral vision of Roman Catholicism, she advocated reform from above, not from below or through individual agency. As historian Judith Jeffrey Howard has remarked, "Serao's view of women nullified the possibility of improving their position because it was based fundamentally on pity and not respect for women."[61] Submission was depicted by Serao as a precondition for sainthood. Overtly feminist voices were still the exception rather than the rule in post-Risorgimento Italy, even among writers of the realist school. Fanny Zampari Salazaro insisted on the difficulties faced by Italian women's rights activists in her presentation to the 1888 Washington, D.C., meeting of the International Council of Women: "We, in Italy, have still to fight against the established pre-eminence of men and the bigotry of narrow-minded clericals who dread losing their power over women; for women, when rationally educated, will begin to think for themselves instead of meekly submitting to their authority."[62] Her efforts were at the time under attack by the Vatican ultraclerical party, and publication of her advocacy journal, *Rassegna*, ceased soon thereafter.

In France, feminist writers were far from a novelty in the 1870s and 1880s. From the novelists Germaine de Staël and George Sand to the Saint-Simonian women who had launched *La Femme libre* in the 1830s, there were plenty of precedents. In Paris during the 1880s Maria Deraismes, Hubertine Auclert, and Eugénie Potonié-Pierre continued to press for women's rights. In 1882, for example, Auclert, writing in *La Citoyenne*, congratulated the new prefect of the Seine on lifting the ban imposed by his predecessor on speeches during civil marriage ceremonies held at city hall, following Auclert's attempt to offer one. She asserted the right of *féministes*, along with "freethinkers," to criticize the marriage laws which were read aloud to the new couple during France's obligatory civil weddings, insisting that "the partisans of women's emancipation have the right to speak."[63] In May 1883 she argued that if maternity were paid (as Léonie Rouzade had been suggesting), men would try to take it over; in September 1884, she challenged the republic's National Assembly, then meeting to consider constitutional changes, to find the courage to grant French women the full civil and political rights to which they were entitled. In a petition widely discussed in the Parisian press, Auclert insisted that "a Constitution which always divides the nation into two camps, that of the kings—the sovereign men—and that of the slaves—the exploited women—would be an aristocratic, stillborn Constitution."[64]

Feminists in France had also begun to speak out on policy matters. An eloquent example is provided in Virginie Griess-Traut's "Manifesto of Women Against War" during the war scare of 1877; this was followed by her 1883 petition, submitted with Maria Deraismes and members of the Society for Ameliorating Women's Condition, which urged the French government to accept a recent American proposal for an international arbitration commission to reconcile differences between national governments that might otherwise lead to war. "Armed peace," noted the petitioners, "is no less ruinous and demoralizing than war . . . and should not constitute a normal societal state of affairs if it does not lead to a serious guarantee of maintaining the peace."[65]

Such authoritative and penetrating criticism of those in power by women would have been unthinkable in other circumstances, and it was still not possible in most countries on the European continent. Dozens, even hundreds of feminists emerged during the 1880s. They not only demanded women's emancipation but also began to criticize male-headed national governments and to call injustice by its name. Not everyone was thrilled by this development. The forty-year-old philosopher Friedrich Nietzsche, who in 1886 was on the rebound from his failed relationship with the beautiful and brilliant Russian-born Lou Andreas Salomé, disparaged these newly emergent voices: "Woman wants to become self-reliant, and for that reason she is beginning to enlighten men about 'woman as such': *this* is one of the worst developments of the general *uglification* of Europe. . . . Woe when 'the eternally boring in woman'. . . is permitted to venture forth!"[66]

An entire new generation of feminists, born between the late 1840s and the mid-1860s, had begun to emerge from the educational institutions established for women here and there throughout Europe. Clusters of young English women flocked to the new women's colleges, Girton and Newnham, established at Cambridge, and later to Lady Margaret Hall and Somerville College, at Oxford. Even as their mentors disagreed about whether the existing form of male education was the best form possible for women, a few of these women rose to the top in competitive examinations with their male counterparts. One of these was Philippa Fawcett, who took honors in mathematics at Cambridge in 1890, much to the great joy of her mother, the women's rights activist Millicent Garrett Fawcett. Others, including several Russian women who had pursued higher education in the West, distinguished themselves at academic pursuits. When in 1888 the French Academy of Science awarded its prestigious Prix Bordin to the Russian-born Sofia Kovalevskaia (who had earned a doctorate from the University of Heidelberg) for her pathbreaking work in theoretical mathematics, and the University of Stockholm then offered her a life professorship, feminists throughout Europe celebrated her victory as living proof that genius indeed had no sex.[67]

In 1880s France the new republican government founded a complete system of free, obligatory primary instruction for both sexes, supplemented by a complete structure of secular secondary education for girls that included training institutions for a new elite corps of women teachers and a higher normal school for their professors. Coeducation, particularly at the secondary level, was still considered anathema in France, even by secular men, and thus well-trained secular women teachers for girls (to replace the nuns) were deemed absolutely necessary. The curriculum established for the new *lycéennes* was deliberately designed not to lead directly to the Latin- and Greek-based *baccalauréat* degrees, and entrance to the universities and professions, though it was in other respects substantive and intellectually respectable. Ambitious French girls could still prepare privately for the state examinations, and increasing numbers embarked on university studies in their own country, a possibility still denied to their counterparts in Germany, Austria-Hungary, and many other parts of central, eastern, and southern Europe.[68]

When in 1888 the young Dr. Caroline Schultze (born Karola Szulc) submitted her doctoral thesis to the Paris Faculty of Medicine on "The Woman Physician in the Nineteenth Century," it signaled not only another triumph for women in the academy but, perhaps more important, the acceptance by at least some members of the still male-dominated academy of a woman-focused research topic. Despite objections by the renowned Dr. Charcot during Schultze's thesis defense to the "pretension" of her claim that medicine could be a womanly as well as a manly profession, Schultze's scholarly feat sparked a surge of French dissertations by women scholars on woman-focused topics as well as a series of "new woman" novels. These latter works featured female physicians and other professional women (instead of artists) as central protagonists and explored the career versus family conundrum. Schultze, who married the statistician Jacques Bertillon (future founder of the Alliance for the Growth of the French Population) and bore two daughters, later served as chief physician for the female employees of the French Postal, Telephone, and Telegraph Service.

In Ireland, Isabella Tod, founder of the Belfast Ladies' Institute, fought in 1879 for the admission of women to the university-level degree-granting examinations offered by the newly established nondenominational Royal University of Ireland. Preparation for such exams could be obtained in a variety of ways, though the male students had a clear advantage. Irish Catholic women quickly staked their claims for higher education as well. In 1888, Margaret Downes published *The Case of the Catholic Lady Student of the Royal University*, complaining that facilities were unavailable in Dublin for the exam preparation of Catholic women students, who like herself did not wish to attend the leading Protestant girls' secondary school, the Alexandra School. Ultimately, several Catholic teaching orders (which up to that point had been preoccupied by the formation of dutiful and pious wives and mothers) would establish several secondary schools for Catholic girls that would allow them to compete successfully in the examinations with their Protestant peers. As historian Eibhlin Breathnach suggests, "the capture of convent education by the English values of examination and certification is one of the most interesting developments of the period."[69] A similar competition to train girls for the French *baccalauréat* examinations developed between the Protestant and secular educators who founded the private Collège Sévigné in Paris and rival Catholic educators.

Clearly young women in the 1880s were "stepping out," to borrow Michelle Perrot's expression.[70] Not only was the new generation clearing the hurdles to secondary and higher education; a far larger number of young women, with a lesser but still significant exposure to formal education, entered clerical and office employment (what we now call skilled white-collar work), partly in the private sector and partly in government service, in the urban centers of England and France, and increasingly in Germany, the Netherlands, the Austro-Hungarian Empire, Scandinavia, and Greece.[71] Writing in 1884, Rosalie Ulrica Olivecrona, one of the founders (in 1859) of Sweden's *Tidskrift för Hemmet* (Home Review), optimistically described the new opportunities open for young women in Stockholm and other Swedish cities:[72]

> Many females now find employment in professions formerly only open to males, as, for example, clerkships in private and savings banks, in joint-stock and insurance companies, in business and railroad offices. Almost all the larger shops have female cashiers. There are instances of women acting as superintendents of branch departments of private banks, and in one town the treasurer is a lady.

These "women's occupations," or what in French are called *métiers féminins*, were initially new, economically intermediate creations; their holders were considered to be *employées*, rather than *ouvrières*; they were generally "salaried," that is to say, paid by the week or the fortnight, rather than "waged," that is, paid by the hour or day—or, as was still the case for many women workers, by the piece. Other related occupations, like teaching and nursing, could still be viewed as extensions of women's domestic responsibilities, and were less visible. This entire employment sector, expanding greatly, offered important opportunities for young, single, educated women. As the sector grew, however, and divisions of labor ensued, these positions soon became restricted in scope and in opportunities for advancement, became less well paid than equivalent men's work, and were cordoned off under male supervision. Except in England, the development of trade unions and other professional associations for women workers still lay in the future.[73]

These breakthroughs in girls' education and employment stimulated concern about women's secondary status and, thus, lent additional support to demands for women's rights. Not all employed women recognized that women faced difficulties as a group, though some did. The early women's rights organizations were as often as not the brainchildren of women of the upper middle classes who had been sensitized to women's disadvantageous situation by personal experiences in their families, through their reading and travel, and sometimes through exposure to the political activism of their fathers, brothers, or husbands. In Italy, for example, the group around *La Donna* (1868–91), led by Gualberta Alaide Beccari, pursued a woman-centered moral revolution along Mazzinian lines, while Anna Maria Mozzoni felt the time had come in 1881 to establish a Lega Promotrice degli Interessi Femminili (League to Promote Women's Interests).

In Scandinavia, the 1880s marked the nearly simultaneous founding of three national women's rights organizations, the Finsk Kvinnoförening/Suomen Naisyhdistys (Finnish Women's Association), the Norsk Kvinnesaksforening (Norwegian Association for the Rights of Women), and the Swedish Fredrike-Bremer Førbundet (Fredrike Bremer Association). The tiny country of Norway, though nominally under Swedish rule, had its own parliamentary government, in which a limited number of property-holding men could vote for representatives; their representation was enlarged in 1884, and Conservative and Liberal political parties came into existence. In response, Gina Krog in 1885 established a women-only women's suffrage association, Kvindestemmeretsforeningen, or KSF, arguing the by now familiar line that women as well as men must be consulted in the country's affairs, and that women should be enfranchised on the same basis as the men. From that time forth Norwegian feminists deliberately involved themselves in national affairs, including foreign affairs, as historian Ida Blom has demonstrated, by embarking (even as some spoke out for peace) on a successful campaign to raise money for a "women's warship," ultimately christened *Valkyrien* in 1896.[74] The Norwegian women's rights journal *Nylaende*, founded in 1887, pushed a feminist agenda until its demise in 1916, as did the Swedish publication *Dagny*, the successor to the *Tidskrift för Hemmet*.

In Sweden the Fredrike-Bremer Førbundet, founded by Baronness Sophie Adlersparre and her colleagues in 1884, had as its goal "to promote the advancement of women morally, intellectually, socially, and eco-

nomically." Adlersparre, in particular, believed that "false emancipation" (by which the speakers meant notions of sexual emancipation as
then promoted by proponents of philosophical naturalism) could best be
combatted by "true emancipation."[75] The Swedish historian Ulla Manns
has observed that sexed bodies, sexuality, and physical love counted for
less in the thought of Adlersparre and her colleagues in the 1880s than
was to be the case for their successors. Indeed, the extant vision during
the 1880s was a heavily idealized Christian feminist vision of what
Manns calls "gender transcendence," which is perhaps only another way
of describing an "individualist" feminist argument. This vision, which
was in some respects closely related to that of Josephine Butler and the
French Protestant adherents of the British and Continental Federation
Against the State Regulation of Vice, was eloquently expressed by the
Danish feminist Elisabeth Grundtvig in 1888:[76]

> If we envisage a society where lust only co-existed with love, where men
> and women live together in pure, happy marriages, helping one another
> in the work of daily life, a society where seduction, rape, prostitution and
> all the misery that follows was barely known of, where no miserable
> homeless children existed—if we imagine this, we can surely all of us
> say: this is happiness.

But in 1890 such a feminist-friendly world remained to be born.

CAUSE FOR OPTIMISM?

"The rapidity with which women in this country are obtaining an independent social and political position—the near approach of their complete emancipation—is one of the most marked features of our age." So
wrote the English author Karl Pearson in 1885. He insisted also that such
developments should not be allowed to occur piecemeal, but rather
should be guided "into such channels that [they] may gradually change
the foundations of society without at the same time depriving society of
its stability."[77] In 1889 Pearson's countrywoman Elizabeth Robins Pennell heralded "a new era in the history of female emancipation," remarking the pending admission to statehood in the United States of a territory
(Wyoming) which had already enacted woman suffrage, in addition to
the admission of two women to the London County Council.[78]

Feminist optimism was contagious, and not only in England and
France. As the two international congresses held in 1889 in Paris suggest, celebration was the order of the day, despite the rumblings of populationists, evolutionists, scientists, and military officers who did not believe women's emancipation to be in men's best interest. English femi-

nists republished Mary Wollstonecraft's *Vindication of the Rights of Woman*, who in Pennell's view was "the first woman who braved public opinion and lifted up her voice to declare that woman had rights as well as man." How mistaken Pennell was about "firsts"; how little was known in 1889, apart from Stanton's volume, about the history of feminism in England or on the European continent.[79]

Even as the feminists celebrated, opponents relaunched the knowledge wars against their claims. The "scientific" debates about women's mental capacities, about their claims to genius continued. Conclusively countering earlier antifeminist arguments about women's smaller brain size, the male feminist Dr. Léonce Manouvrier argued at the 1889 international congress on women's rights that women's brains were in fact larger in proportion to their body mass than men's. But no sooner would one argument against women's claims to equality be knocked down than another would appear. Taking issue with Darwin's more fluid notions of sexual selection, the Scottish biologists Patrick Geddes and J. Arthur Thomson, in their widely circulated study *The Evolution of Sex* (1889), persisted in delineating intellectual and emotional differences between the sexes as essential sexual characteristics. They warned that to obliterate sexual differences, "it would be necessary to have all the evolution over again on a new basis": "What was decided among the prehistoric Protozoa cannot be annulled by Act of Parliament."[80] This line was to be widely quoted during the next decades by those who insisted that women's subordination must be "natural," after all. Even among the doctors, the scientists, the novelists, the journalists, the teachers, and the clerks, vocal opponents of feminist claims could be found. As the new century approached, scientists of both sexes would roll out their heavy artillery to justify or dispute sociopolitical claims for women's emancipation.

7

Feminist Challenges and Antifeminist Responses, 1890–1914

Graphic images of sunrise, of storm clouds clearing, of women leading other women to a future of equality and freedom burst from the European women's press of the 1890s and the early twentieth century. Clémentine-Hélène Dufau's artistic poster, commissioned to launch the Parisian daily women's newspaper *La Fronde* in 1897, joined the cover illustration of the 1904 inaugural issue of *Morgonbris*, published by Swedish Social Democratic women, in epitomizing feminists' optimistic faith in the progress of their cause.

Between 1900 and 1914—a period that some would later call the *belle époque* or the birth of "modern times," but others would view as a disturbing era of massive industrialization, urbanization, militarism, imperial expansion, worker unrest, and anarchist violence—virtually every European society developed fissures through which the molten flow of feminist challenge could surge forth. As the twentieth century approached, those fissures would multiply and expand dramatically, and the flow would become a flood with many tributaries. Feminist agitation would capture public attention to an unprecedented degree; the woman question had already emerged as central to debating a broad spectrum of political and socioeconomic issues, ranging from marriage and reproduction to war and peace. In fact, feminist claims in this period would ultimately address a stunningly comprehensive range of issues, and feminists' demand for the vote was their way of insisting that women be formally included in resolving these issues.

To be sure, sisterhood still demonstrated its own rifts—along class, confessional, and even ethnic lines—but it is nonetheless true that instead of oozing slowly up through narrow fissures, feminist challenges threatened to liquefy the crust of patriarchal institutions. Its cumulative success can be gauged by the degree to which feminists and their male allies of varying political persuasions at times succeeded in coordinating their efforts at the local, national, and international levels, and by the sheer quantity of articles, tracts, and other publications intended to challenge one or another aspect of male hegemony. It can also be gauged by the vehement resurgence of the knowledge wars, which would be stoked by a new flood of publications by physicians, criminologists, psychologists, sociologists, and other "experts," many of whom (though by no means all) were committed to keeping women in what some men thought was their God-given or biologically ordained place. In fact, a surprising number of male intellectuals responded pessimistically to the birth of modern times, to which female emancipation was so central, experiencing it primarily as a crisis in masculine identity.[1]

CHRISTENING AND DEFINING "FEMINISM,"
1890–1910

The 1890s saw the popularization of the terms *féminisme* and *féministe* to describe the campaigns for women's emancipation in Europe. The two international congresses held in Paris in 1889 had paved the way for a series of further initiatives. Although Hubertine Auclert had introduced the terms in the 1880s in *La Citoyenne*, using them interchangeably with "women's emancipation" and "women's rights," the general press continued to refer to the movement for the extension of women's rights as *le mouvement féminin*, or the "woman" or "women's" movement (in Russian, *emantsipatsiya zhenshchin*).

In late 1891, this terminology began to change. In *Le Droit des femmes* (20 September 1891), Eugénie Potonié-Pierre called for the foundation of a Fédération Française des Sociétés Féministes. The group's charter appeared in the December issue, and in mid-May 1892 this federation convened its Congrès Général des Institutions Féministes, which received considerable coverage in the press, including the important Parisian daily *Le Temps*. The press and popular periodicals subsequently consecrated usage of both terms, not only in France but also in the French-language press of Belgium and Switzerland. In English, the earliest reported use of "feminist" dates from 12 October 1894, in the *Daily News* (London); "feminism" made its debut in April 1895 in a literary book review, and in 1896 the *Englishwoman's Review* gave coverage to the "feminist" congress in Paris. As late as 1901, however, a reviewer in the *Englishwoman's Review* still equated "the woman movement" with "*Feminisme*, as they style it in France."[2] By 1907, both terms had inserted themselves into the British vocabulary, as even the adamantly antifeminist E. Belfort Bax had to acknowledge.[3]

From 1893 on the expression *le mouvement féministe* also gained currency, vying with *le mouvement féminin*. In June, the *Revue Ency-clopédique Larousse* appropriated it. In 1895 Clotilde Dissard published the first issue of *La Revue féministe*. In April 1896, in Paris, a second Congrès Féministe International convened. This gathering received wide coverage in the press and contributed further to popularizing the concept of feminism, although in the French context, discussions of what was *féministe* and what was *féminin* increasingly divided sympathizers.

Reporting on the position of women in France at the September 1896 Berlin Women's Congress, Eugénie Potonié-Pierre took credit for herself and her French colleagues for inventing the word *féminisme*, and praised the press for successfully launching it. Several months later Marya Ché-liga-Loevy edited a special issue of the *Revue Encyclopédique* devoted to French feminism; it was there she made the erroneous claim for invent-ing *féminisme* on behalf of the visionary sociopolitical critic Charles Fourier, a claim that has infested French dictionaries ever since. In August 1896, the *Revue politique et parlementaire* began to publish a se-ries of articles on *féminisme* in England, Italy, the United States, Austra-lia, and Germany. This series was complemented by another series of commissioned articles in the *Revue des revues* (begun in 1895), on the condition of women in various countries, including Romania, Spain, and Russia. Henceforth, the press would keep the public well informed about issues of concern to feminists, the progress of their reform efforts, and the leading personalities of the movement. The German-born roving re-porter Käthe Schirmacher published articles about feminism in Spanish and French, as well as a book, *Le Féminisme aux États-Unis, en France, dans la Grande-Bretagne, en Suède et en Russie* (1898).

From that time forth, too, factions emerged. Splinter groups and indi-viduals espousing divergent and often competing objectives on women's behalf began to categorize themselves and their rivals through the now familiar practice of exclusionary classification, qualifying adjectives, and the formation of separate organizations and publications. By the begin-ning of the twentieth century, there were many self-described or attrib-uted feminisms in France alone: "familial feminists," "integral femi-nists," "Christian feminists," "socialist feminists," "bourgeois femi-nists," "radical feminists," and "male feminists." In the Netherlands, "ethical" feminists vied for support with "rational" feminists. Virtually everywhere, as the educator Pauline Kergomard underscored in 1897, "there is a gulf between what the antifeminists call 'feminism' and what I call 'feminism.'"[4]

Feminist publications proliferated in 1890s France. In addition to Dis-sard's *Revue féministe* (1895–97), the new arrivals included the *Journal des femmes* (1891–1911), edited by Maria Martin, a former associate of Hubertine Auclert; *Le Féminisme chrétien* (1896–99), edited by the social Catholic Marie Maugeret; the short-lived *L'Harmonie sociale* (1892–93), edited by the Guesdist-socialist Aline Valette; *La Femme socialiste* (1901–2, 1912–40), edited by Elisabeth Renaud; and the short-lived syndicalist-feminist *L'Abeille*. Perhaps the most spectacular of all was the daily newspaper *La Fronde* (1897–1903), founded by the journalist and former actress Marguerite Durand and staffed entirely by women.[5] By 1900 at least twenty-one feminist periodicals were appearing regularly in France. In Belgium, an Office Féministe Universel was established in Brussels in 1896, coupled with the publication of *Cahiers féministes* (1896–1905).

In Germany, too, a new level of publishing activism quickly developed. The venerable *Neue Bahnen*, published since 1875 by Louise Otto and Auguste Schmidt, was joined in October 1893 by the monthly review *Die Frau*, edited by Helena Lange, and in January 1895 by *Die Frauenbewegung* (1895–1919), edited by Minna Cauer and Lily von Gizycki (later Lily Braun). There, however, the term "feminism" (in German, *Feminismus*) encountered resistance, despite Potonié-Pierre's boasts in Berlin, and most continued to speak of the *Frauenbewegung*, or "women's movement," although articles about the German movement published in France by Lily Braun and Käthe Schirmacher used the term *mouvement féministe* interchangeably with *Frauenbewegung*.[6] Socialist women launched their own women-focused publications. These included *Die Arbeiterin* (The Woman Worker), founded in 1891 and edited by Emma Ihrer, and its successor, *Die Gleichheit* (Equality, 1892–1917), produced by the indefatigable and intransigent Clara Zetkin with support from the German Social Democratic Party. Only rarely did German socialist women speak of "feminism" except in disparaging and oppositional terms.

In Italy and in Spain, discussion of *feminismo* became the order of the day. Adoption of the French terms seemed to present no problem in these Latin-language cultures, where they were used routinely from 1896 on in periodicals such as the progressive *España moderna*. Even the Greek press picked up the term, transliterating it into the Greek alphabet. The same could not be said of northern Europe, where expressions connoting "woman" continued to characterize the movement. In Russia, for example, although Zinaida Vengerova used the term *feminizm* in *Obrazovanie* (1898), it was in a pejorative sense; it became customary to continue the use of other terms. The publication *Zhenshchina* (Woman) appeared in 1904, complete with a section "The Female Citizen," along with M. Pokrovskaia's *Zhenskii vestnik* (The Woman's Herald), advocating sexual equality. In Sweden, although the writer Frida Steenhoff attempted to naturalize the term *féminisme* in her *Feminismens moral* (1904), the concept *kvinnoemancipation* prevailed. In Norway the preferred terminology was *kvindersorge kvinnen*, or "women's cause women."

Among the many publications in this period, of particular interest were new efforts to document the history of feminism and/or the women's movement. In Germany, these included a series of articles published in *Deutsche Rundschau* (1896) by Gustav Cohn on *Die deutsche Frauenbewegung* (The German Women's Movement), and, of particular importance, the five-volume *Handbuch der Frauenbewegung*, edited by Helene Lange and Gertrud Bäumer, the first volume of which appeared in 1901. Echoing Theodore Stanton's 1884 *The Woman Question in Europe*, almost every article published on the women's movement in the late nineteenth and early twentieth century began with a substantive historical survey. Not all could be praised for their accuracy.

French feminists, following the earlier example of Maria Deraismes, proudly traced their origins and lineage to the revolution of 1789, thereby grounding or "naturalizing" their heritage in the face of opponents' accusations that it was a "foreign import," "un-French," part of an Anglo-Saxon, Freemasonic, Jewish, Protestant plot, or simply "American." An important contribution to this effort was Léopold Lacour's study *Trois femmes de la Révolution: Olympe de Gouges, Théroigne de Méricourt, Rose Lacombe* (1900), which appeared with the subtitle "The Origins of Contemporary Feminism." Although the widely traveled Käthe Schirmacher (who had studied in France, then attended the 1893 World Congress of Women in Chicago) persisted in locating the origins of feminism in the United States, others, including Havelock Ellis, insisted on its French revolutionary genesis. Some British feminists in the early twentieth century were quite adamant about these antecedents. "The European feminist movement was actually born in France," insisted the British socialist feminist Ethel Snowden in her book *The Feminist Movement* (1911): "Although women took a prominent part in all the activities of the Revolution, and sacrificed themselves with as much zeal as any of the men, their clubs were ruthlessly closed by the Committee of Public Safety, in the alleged interests of the public peace, but really because the women were becoming too insistent in their demands for themselves."[7] In Snowden's version, the women of revolutionary France had even inspired Mary Wollstonecraft's *Vindication of the Rights of Woman*.

Feminists, too, attempted to define feminism for the benefit of a broader public. Such definitions emphasized varying concepts, the British insisting more frequently on individual freedom and liberty, for example, whereas the French leaned more extensively on the concept of equality of the sexes, even when they used the language of liberty. Ellis Ethelmer (pseudonym of Elizabeth Wolstenholme Elmy and/or her partner Ben Elmy), while attributing the word to the French, defined it as "the movement for establishing the equality of the sexes."[8] Subsequently, in a chapter "The Meaning of Feminism," Ethel Snowden provided her definition: "the recognition, full and complete, of the humanity of women." It was about "freedom for womanhood and its equality of opportunity with manhood."[9] Who could possibly oppose such claims? she queried.

In French, the meaning of the term *féminisme* was contested.[10] Pauline Kergomard argued in 1897 that it had to do specifically with disputing the inequalities arising from the institution of marriage. By the early twentieth century, the terms of definition were shifting away from "subordination" and "oppression," increasingly emphasizing *freedom*. Contrary to the claims of the "antis," Nelly Roussel insisted that feminism was not about "masculinizing" women, or about replacing male domination by female domination; feminism "proclaims *natural equivalence* and demands *social equality* for the two factors of humankind." The sexes, in her view, were complementary; feminism was about "freedom of choice," and she emphasized the differences among women as well as differences between sexes: "We do not recognize 'The Woman,' a vague abstraction. We see around us *women*, concrete creatures with very diverse aptitudes, tastes, tendencies, temperaments." Roussel called for the recognition of individual differences, the right to full development, and justice.[11] In a 1905 brochure, *Qu'est-ce que le féminisme* (What Is Feminism?), Odette Laguerre offered this definition: "a thrust of justice that tends to equalize the rights and duties of man and woman." And, she added, "feminism is not only a thrust of justice; it is also a thrust of liberty that marks the end of Man's reign, of what Jules Bois calls 'anthropocentrism.'"[12] Feminism was increasingly defined, even in France, in terms of a woman's right to self-development and self-determination. It rested squarely on a conceptual foundation of liberty, equality, and justice, variously blended, but ultimately grounded in Enlightenment discourse.

However much disagreement there might be about defining feminism, or about whether "feminism," "women's rights," "women's emancipation," or "woman movement" best described the phenomenon, European observers did reach a consensus on the significance of the phenomenon. "Today, after a century of struggle," wrote Madame Avril de Sainte-Croix in her 1907 history, *Le Féminisme*, "the effort of women to acquire more justice and more independence seems poised on the brink of success. Feminism no longer provokes a smirk. . . . The forward march of feminism is a fact that no one can deny, a movement that no force can henceforth bring to a halt. Woman . . . has become a factor to be reckoned with."[13] In 1909 the Swedish reformer Ellen Key wrote: "The woman movement is the most significant of all movements for freedom in the world's history. The question whether this movement leads mankind in a higher or lower direction is the most serious question of the time."[14]

"NEW WOMEN" AND OTHER ANTIFEMINIST RESPONSES TO FEMINISM: THE KNOWLEDGE WARS CONTINUE

Feminists did not control the treatment provided them either in the publishing world or, more generally, in the developing knowledge industry, as their repeated efforts to clarify their goals underscore. Not all those, even among women, who engaged in debating the woman question were feminists, an observation that would become particularly salient in the period after 1890. The debate about the "New Woman" provides a case in point.

In addition to promulgating the term *féminisme*, the European press can be held responsible for promoting discussion of the "New Woman," as the educated, often single, and increasingly employed middle-class woman of the late nineteenth century became popularly known. Although the term had been circulating since the 1830s, when the Saint-Simonian women launched *la femme nouvelle* in Paris, and was picked up again in the 1860s by writers such as Chernyshevsky to characterize the young Russian women who sought education and revolution, the "New Woman" reemerged in English from a published debate between the British novelists Sarah Grand and Ouida in 1894. Grand had used the term "new woman," but when Ouida added capitalization, it was taken up in the antifeminist press, notably in *Punch*, which was also making much of "the New Humour," "the New Journalism," and "the New Art." *Punch* launched the New Woman with this verse:[15]

> There is a New Woman, and what do you think?
> She lives upon nothing but Foolscap and Ink!
> But though Foolscap and Ink are the whole of her diet,
> This nagging New Woman can never be quiet!

The New Woman was quickly reified by opponents in the satiric press as an "educated, sport-playing, cigar-smoking, marriage-hating" type, and physically unattractive to boot.[16] The images, both verbal and pictorial, had much in common with those deployed throughout Europe against George Sand fifty years before, and against Jenny P. d'Héricourt and her colleagues by Proudhon in the decade after 1848, but with the important addition of a bicycle—a new means of transportation that provided women as well as men with an inexpensive means of increasing their mobility. In 1897, Elizabeth Rachel Chapman (who approved of the women's movement, although she had reservations about freethinkers' attacks on marriage) exposed the "New Woman" as a journalistic myth, insisting that the "Real Woman" was the true friend of her sex.[17]

"New Woman" novels published in England during this period ranged from those published by male authors such as Grant Allen, George Gissing, George Meredith, and Thomas Hardy to those by Sarah Grand (pseudonym of Frances Elizabeth McFall), Mona Caird, George Egerton (pseudonym of Mary Chavelita Bright [Dunne]), and Emma Frances Brooke.[18] Not all fictional "new women" were feminists, nor were their authors; indeed, thinking about the woman question did not lead necessarily to the development of feminist consciousness, even among women who would become prominent writers and sociopolitical commentators.

The importance of these "New Woman" literary works lies precisely in the fact that their authors addressed issues that feminists had been raising, about the constraints of marriage, about work, about the possibilities and difficulties of self-realization, thereby exposing an even broader range of readers to their claims, and arguing the pros and cons with respect to the surrounding cultural context. The public impact of these novels, some of which became best-sellers, found extension in the "New Woman" theater of the period.[19] Fictional demolitions of the "New Woman" in such novels as Bram Stoker's *Dracula* (1897) and the antifeminist art and literature centered around the seductive yet menacing figure of *la femme fatale* extended the range of these works.[20] Such publications demonstrate forcefully the impact of feminist claims upon writers of imaginative fiction in Britain and may have inspired a "modernist" backlash in literature.

In France, both novelists and playwrights explored "New Woman" themes, which they often cast in terms of "the new Eve." Novels by male writers such as Marcel Prévost's *Les Demi-vierges* (1894) and *Les Vierges fortes* (1900) became best-sellers; many others commanded an important following, among them Paul Margueritte and Victor Margueritte's *Femmes nouvelles* (1900) and Paul Bourget's *Un Divorce* (1904). Choices confronting "new women" provoked controversial and widely discussed theatrical works by sympathetic male dramatists such as Paul Hervieu, Jules Case, Maurice Donnay, and Eugène Brieux. Among the important "New Woman" novels by women writers were Gabrielle Reval's *Les Sévriennes* (1900), Marcelle Tinayre's *La Rebelle* (1906), Colette Yver's *Les Cervelines* (1903) and *Les Princesses de science* (1907), and Daniel Lesueur's *Nietzschéenne* (1908). A survey of "New Woman" novels published in France between 1900 and 1914 concludes that in all the authors' attempts to portray liberated women, whether heterosexual or lesbian, "the major problem to be faced by the women characters, be it at the theoretical or practical level, is always love."[21]

Among the critics of the "New Woman," perhaps the most interesting and best-known (besides the well-known dramatist August Strindberg) was the cosmopolite Laura Marholm Hansson. Born in Riga (Latvia), of Danish and German parentage, married to a Swedish writer, and living variously in Copenhagen, Berlin, and Bavaria, Laura Marholm Hansson made a career out of critiquing the "sterile" intellectuality of the newly educated woman. Whether insensitive to or disinterested in women's subordination and the historical circumstances that underlay feminist claims for women's independence, Marholm Hansson focused on psychological issues. She insisted that "modern women" were betraying their womanliness (which she identified with instinct and nerves, and with a certain sort of "wildness," seductiveness, and fecundity, more attuned both to Nature and the Divine) through their new focus on reason and science. For Marholm Hansson claims for women's rights seemed totally beside the point with respect to women's self-realization, which was in her view ultimately about women's coming into their full womanliness. "Can it be true," she asked, "that the best women have an unnatural desire to be half men, and that they would prefer to shirk the duties of motherhood?"[22] Woman, for Marholm Hansson, was not an end in herself. Her desire to live freely was but "an illusion," she would write in her study on the psychology of woman, published in 1897. "The free life of the ego really carried out would always end in the painful void of mental and physical sterility."[23]

In the hands of antifeminists, psychological explanation became a weapon of choice. Debate over the "New Woman" provoked explorations of "the Soul of Woman," "the female ego," "the Real Women," and "women's real needs," and psychological explanations would mark not only the works of novelists and essayists, but also those of sociologists, criminologists, and other social scientists. Indeed, if science had provided a motif for individuals to transgress sexual norms in the 1860s, aesthetics, psychology, and philosophy would develop an antidote in the *fin-de-siècle* period. What was "woman" anyway? Manifestly, answers to the question would be as varied as the experiences of those who asked it.

A new set of parameters for this intense psychological exploration of the woman question were set in Central and Eastern Europe, by writers in the German and Russian languages. A number of them were either outright enemies of feminism, or did not see how the type of feminist claims being made in England and France, and the proposed political solutions, changing laws, and so forth, might make sense in differing sociopolitical contexts. Some were proponents of the Modernist aesthetic, intensely individualistic, sometimes mystical, and with a heavily introspective bent.

In an article "La Femme russe," the Russian Jewish-born writer Zinaida Vengerova characterized her subject as having "a mystic soul and an active mind." After many years living in the West, Vengerova had concluded that what distinguished Russian women writers from those in Western Europe was that, whether they adhered to the realist or the symbolist school, they were not preoccupied by feminism: "They did not have the feeling and vocation of being especially and uniquely women and were not inspired by women's rights more than anything else. . . . They participated in the general literary movement." This, in her opinion, was a great advantage. "The Russian woman is the freest in Europe . . . she is above all else a human being, equal to others."[24] In Russia, the enemy was tradition and routine, not a civil code or the exclusion of women from political or economic life. Freedom, from Vengerova's perspective, was something found within, not in relation to external constraints. In a subsequent article, she insisted that such inner freedom was something that Russian women had and French women didn't. That wives and daughters were wholly under the legal authority of husbands and fathers throughout their lives did not seem to trouble Vengerova.

The Russian socialist Aleksandra Kollontai complained in her essay "Novaya Zhenschchina" (New Woman) in 1913 that "new women" had not received their due in Russian literature. Old types still prevailed. A wholly new type of heroine commanded the attention of writers: "heroines with independent demands on life, heroines who assert their personality, heroines who protest against the universal servitude of woman in the State, the family, society, who fight for their rights as representatives of their sex. Single women are the ones who more and more determine this type."[25] She then provided a remarkable catalog of such fictional heroines from the imaginative literature of Germany, Scandinavia, and France, characters who offered a laboratory for researching a woman for whom "love" was not the be-all and end-all of existence:[26]

> Thus does the new woman present herself to us: self-discipline instead of emotional rapture, the capacity to value her own freedom and independence rather than impersonal submissiveness, the assertion of her own individuality instead of the naïve effort to internalize and reflect the alien image of the "beloved." The display of the right to family happiness instead of the hypocritical mask of virginity, finally the assignation of love-experiences to a subordinate place in life. Before us no longer stands the "wifie," the shadow of the husband—before us stands the personality, the woman as human being.

In the German-speaking world, the "New Woman" became the subject of novelists and playwrights, among them Gerhard Hauptmann in the play *Einsame Menschen* (Lonely People, 1891) and Grete Meisel-Hess in her novel *Die Intellectuellen* (The Women Intellectuals, 1911). But perhaps the most startling works stimulated by debates on the "New Woman" and feminism were those in sexual psychology and moral philosophy. Centered in the relationship of masculinity to femininity, and grounded in Kantian ethics, the works of several highly influential writers addressed the pros and cons of feminism, going well beyond the boundaries of the "womanly woman" discussions of the late 1880s.

The abstractions of most aestheticists, psychologists, and philosophers in the German tradition acted to problematize, relativize, and downgrade feminist claims for sociopolitical change in relations between the sexes. Perhaps the most disturbing challenger of feminist aspirations was the young Otto Weininger in Vienna. His controversial, best-selling treatise *Geschlecht und Character* (Sex and Character, 1903) grew out of a doctoral dissertation in philosophy. It was quickly translated into English, Russian, and a number of other languages. "Weininger," according to literary scholar Gisela Brude-Firnau, "sees the central problem of all ethics in the relationship between the sexes. For him it is . . . woman who is the cause of the problem; she embodies sexuality. Therefore, it is also she who impedes the ethical salvation of humanity and indeed the process of becoming authentically human altogether."[27] Guiltless Adam was again blaming Eve for temptation, corruption, and sin. What was more, Weininger not only castigated "the feminine" as bad for women as well as for men, but he connected it with notions of "Jewishness" and "servility."

Most of Weininger's book was actually cast as a reflection on women's emancipation, which he interpreted in a new and unusual way. "A woman's demand for emancipation and her qualification for it are in direct proportion to the amount of maleness in her," he asserted at the beginning of his chapter "Emancipated Women." By "emancipation," however, he meant not changes in women's legal, educational, or economic status, but rather "the deep-seated craving to acquire man's character, to attain his mental and moral freedom, to reach his real interests and his creative power." All women who exhibited aspirations in this direction, Weininger maintained, were not true women but intermediate types, "partly bisexual, partly homo-sexual." "It is only the male element in emancipated women that craves for emancipation. . . . The female principle is not conscious of a necessity for emancipation." "Away with the whole 'women's movement,' with its unnaturalness and artificiality and its fundamental errors," Weininger trumpeted, alleging further on that the entire movement was a "revolt from motherhood towards prostitution." The real solution, and the route to woman's freedom, he insisted, was for "man to free himself of sex."[28] No wonder Weininger committed suicide at the age of twenty-three. Nevertheless, his polarized typology of masculine/feminine, where the "masculine" represented everything positive and active, and the "feminine" everything bad (though hardly passive), exerted a direct, extended, and adverse influence on European intellectual life, not least among writers such as Franz Kafka, James Joyce, and D. H. Lawrence.

In her *Zur Kritik der Weiblichkeit* (To Critics of Femininity), published in 1905, the Viennese writer Rosa Mayreder countered Weininger and his supporters, turning the focus on masculinity itself. "The true origin of the change which is taking place in the position of the female sex will never be rightly understood," she wrote in a chapter entitled "On Masculinity," "so long as the change in the conditions of life of the male sex remains unconsidered. . . . One of the most important factors in the rise of the feminist movement is probably to be found in the change which is taking place in the male sex." She pointed out the extent to which the concept of "Woman" was "a product of the masculine brain, an eternal illusion, a phantom capable of taking all forms without ever possessing a single one." And, she insisted: "Nothing is of greater importance to women than to battle against the abstractions into which they are constantly being converted by masculine thought. . . . They must battle against woman as a fetich."[29]

New parameters for comprehending the "New Woman" were set by Havelock Ellis's painstaking investigations of human sexual physiology and psychology. Ellis was as impatient as Mayreder with male fetishizing of femininity and sought to deploy science to get closer to under-standing female sexuality as well as male sexuality. Of particular impor-tance are his work *Man and Woman: A Study of Human Secondary Sexual Characteristics* (1894), his pioneering investigation of *Sexual Inversion* (1897), and his subsequent study *The Sexual Impulse in Women* (1902), which redirected attention to the particularities of women's sexuality in its own right.

In sharp contrast to the antifeminist, even misogynous Weininger, Ellis took a progressive and multifaceted approach to the analysis of sexual questions. His interest lay in demystifying, through assiduous comparative research, an area in which there still existed so much ignorance and willful misunderstanding. Although Ellis did his work in England, many of his findings were first published in the United States or in Germany, where publishers were not subject to the notoriously strict English censorship laws concerning sexual matters.

Havelock Ellis's work was undoubtedly inspired by feminist questions, which were probably heightened by his close yet failed relationship with the novelist Olive Schreiner and by his friendship with members of the London Men's and Women's Club. His approach was undoubtedly intensified by his medical training and his experiences as a practicing obstetrician. These concerns are evident in his remarks in "The Changing Status of Women," an essay Ellis claims was originally published in the late 1880s. His feminism, however, was qualified; he did not claim absolute equality for women: "It is necessary to remember, he remarked,[30]

> that the kind of equality of the sexes toward which this change of status is leading, is social equality—that is, equality of freedom. It is not an in-tellectual equality, still less is it likeness. Men and women can only be alike mentally when they are alike in physical configuration and physio-logical function. Even complete economic equality is not attainable.

Moreover, he argued for the social importance of reproduction, "the end and aim of all life everywhere," and insisted that "every healthy woman should have, not sexual relationships only, but the exercise at least once in her life of the supreme function of maternity, and the possession of those experiences which only maternity can give."[31]

Ellis remained open to obtaining further and better knowledge. A few years later, addressing those who insisted that homosexuality among "new women" was increasing, or that a "third sex" was developing, Ellis asserted that "the modern movement of emancipation—the movement to obtain the same rights and duties as men, the same freedom and re-sponsibility, the same education and the same work—must be regarded as, on the whole, a wholesome and inevitable movement." But, he cautioned, "these unquestionable influences of modern movements cannot directly cause sexual inversion, but they develop the germs of it." He believed that the inclination to "inversion" "occurs with special frequency in women of high intelligence who, voluntarily or involuntarily, influence others."[32] Ellis remained convinced that motherhood was women's highest calling, but his works also fed into an increasing concern with lesbian sexuality.

It was given to another German intellectual, the Berlin-based Jewish-born sociologist, philosopher, and cultural theorist Georg Simmel, to underscore the fundamental *masculinisme* of European civilization and thereby to highlight the feminist dilemma. Like Weininger and so many other German philosophers, Simmel was working from the perspective of Kantian moral philosophy, but unlike either Kant or Weininger, he seemed far more sympathetic to feminist aspirations as well as to issues of individual development and personal relations: not surprisingly, he had read and reviewed Theodor-Gottlieb von Hippel's radical works of the 1790s and had occasionally contributed to debates on the woman question in the German press.[33]

Discussing the notion of "objective culture" in his 1911 essay "Female Culture," Simmel stipulated that it was "thoroughly male": "It is men who have created art and industry, science and commerce, the state and religion." What is "Human" is identified with "Man." This is why women's contributions to the "artifacts of culture" were invariably weighed in a scale comparing them (usually negatively) to the accomplishments of men. In other words, what we now call gender lay at the center of culture, though as Simmel indicated, it was generally unnamed and unrecognized. Simmel provocatively raised the question of what an "autonomous femininity" would be and how the contents of an "objective female culture" might look, were such possible.[34]

Simmel subsequently addressed the implications of male cultural dominance for female subjectivity. The "relationship between masculinity and femininity," which Simmel specified as "the fundamental relativity in the life of our species," was, he indicated, a relationship of power, and within it "Woman" invariably came out on the short end. Psychically, woman was differently positioned than man with respect to objective culture, which meant in the end that she was more self-contained, more confined in her bodily and psychic femininity than her male counterpart. Constantly qualifying his conclusions, and offering complex and lengthy arguments, Simmel offered feminists no answers and ultimately little hope, though he exhibited considerable sympathy in what to him seemed ultimately woman's insoluble, even tragic dilemma.[35] In this highly German, highly ethical, and highly fatalistic perspective, "new women" and especially feminists were fighting an unwinnable battle.

If such highly intelligent sympathizers as Simmel ultimately took the tragic view, two other transnational entities in European society greeted feminism as a serious threat and political rival, with profound implications for the extant male-dominated order. Both the Roman Catholic Church and organized Social Democracy, for differing reasons, contested aspects of the claims being made for women's emancipation, even as their male leadership sought to enroll women under their organizational banners. Each was profoundly affected by feminist claims, even as each insisted on harnessing women in an effort to counteract feminist "separatism." The Vatican objected to feminist claims with respect to their ultimate end, contesting claims for women's independence from the God-given, male-headed family. Social Democrats objected not to these ends, but to the means; in the view of the leadership of the Second International, as we have seen, class struggle, not women's liberation, must take priority in the fight for a new society. Women's independence from the family could come only through paid labor, a position that church authorities found extremely objectionable.

CONTESTING WOMAN'S PLACE WITHIN
ROMAN CATHOLICISM

Feminist eruptions broke out in the most diverse locations during the late nineteenth century. Even the Roman Catholic Church would become a venue for debating feminist claims during the reforming papacy of Leo XIII (1878–1903). This pope had already restated the church's position on issues of marriage and divorce in 1880.[36] In 1891 Leo XIII issued the encyclical letter *Rerum Novarum*, known in English as "On the Condition of the Workingmen." Leo XIII drafted this male-centered statement as an explicit response to socialist doctrines, asserting the necessity of private property as the foundation of the family, and invoking the "natural right" of personal ownership to counter socialist proposals for the community of goods. He staunchly defended the male-breadwinner model, so dear to English political economists: men, as heads of families, should toil to support their wives and children, and should be able to pass on their accumulated property to their descendants. Moreover, the encyclical continued, women and children should not be expected to do the same work as men, adding that "a woman is by nature

fitted for homework, and it is that which is best adapted at once to preserve her modesty, and to promote the good bringing up of children and
the well-being of the family."[37]

The pope's pronouncements were elaborated by the British Cardinal
Manning, archbishop of Westminster, who invoked contract theory (not
biblical authority) to underscore his point about Christian marriage in
industrial society. He insisted that women who married had contracted
"to fulfill with [the husband] the duties of wife, mother, and head of his
home." Working for pay in addition meant that a wife could not fulfill
these prior contractual duties. Additionally, Manning insisted that
"there can be no home, where a mother does not nourish her own infant." "Where the domestic life of a people is undermined," the cardinal
warned, calling for a more equitable distribution of male salaries, "their
social and political life rests on sand."[38] There was no room in this view
for the possibility that women workers might be—or wish to remain—
single, or that women's employment might be anything but a disaster for
them and for the next generation. A far stronger set of objections to
women's emancipation was published by the antifeminist Viennese
priest Father Augustin Rösler, in a lengthy tract, "The Woman Question
from the Standpoints of Nature, History, and Revelation," initially published in German in 1893 and widely translated, distributed, and reprinted in Catholic circles.[39]

A polite but firm objection to such views on women's employment
came from Marie Maugeret, editor of the monthly periodical *Le Féminisme chrétien* in Paris. Maugeret spearheaded the development of Christian feminism in France, insisting that feminism was a cause "that belongs to no one class of society, to no one part of humanity more than
another, but to the entire society and to all humanity."[40] Feminism, she
affirmed, could be nicely reconciled with Christian morality.

At the head of the demands of Christian feminism, she asserted, was
women's "right to work": "We admit no restriction, no limitation, no
regulation of this freedom, and we protest with all our energy against any
law that, under the fallacious and hypocritical pretext of 'protecting' us,
takes away our right, the most sacred of all, to earn our living honestly."
Moreover, she demanded that the salary of the woman worker remain
her own personal property, and that the propertied woman be granted
continuing control of the property she brings to marriage, noting that "it
is against the husband who so often dissipates the resources of the community property, and not against the fatigues of labor, that women need
laws of 'protection.'"[41] Her efforts were seconded by a series of initiatives
to reform the Catholic education of girls, including the publication by a

remarkable convert from Protestantism, the Comtesse d'Adhémar, of the educational treatise *La Femme catholique et la démocratie française* (1900).

Maugeret meanwhile established a controversial Catholic women's federation, which took the name Fédération Jeanne d'Arc, and in 1900 this group held its first congress, separate and distinct from the two more secular feminist congresses held that year in Paris. In 1903 she collaborated in the publication of *La Femme contemporaine*, a periodical edited by Abbé Jean Lagardère. This review adopted a more progressive view on the woman question; although it continued to place the interests of the family before those of the individual, male or female, it nevertheless presented a positive perspective on women's intellectual and professional possibilities. Abbé Lagardère would prove to be a staunch ally in the fight to instill more progressive views on the woman question within the church, as would A. D. Sertillanges, author of *Féminisme et christianisme* (1908).

In 1906, Maugeret succeeded in getting the delegates to the Congrès Jeanne d'Arc to approve resolutions for the representation of women in politics, and, going further, for full political rights for women. Her actions were sharply contested by the women of the Ligue Patriotique des Françaises, whose leaders continued to insist that the existing order— and particularly female subordination in marriage—had been established by God, not men. Still Maugeret and her followers persevered, picking their way through a thicket of Catholic opposition to their efforts. They also confronted what they considered to be hostility from the Jewish and Protestant women who led the secular feminist organizations in France and who, in their eyes, seemed bent on rejecting Catholic cooperation. Tensions between Catholics and the republican establishment in France were at their highest point in the early twentieth century, because of the anticlerical republican government's deliberate and ultimately successful move (in 1904) to separate church and state. In consequence, the bonds of sisterhood in France would long remain fractured along confessional lines.

Feminism began to bubble up within newly formed Catholic women's organizations after 1900 in Belgium, Italy, Austria, Ireland, and Spain as well as in France. These groups attracted thousands of Catholic women, far more than their secular feminist counterparts. In Italy, the woman question became a subject of discussion in *Cultura sociale*, published by the social Catholics, and Luisa Anzoletti and Adelaide Coari took up the cause of Christian feminism, developing a "minimum feminist program" in 1907 at the first Italian feminist congress in Milan.[42] Feminist aspirations succeeded in capturing the attention of Pope Pius X, the successor to Leo XIII, who in 1906 spoke out against women's direct participation in politics during an interview with an Austrian feminist novelist, Camille Theimer. This interview made headlines in the *Neues Wiener Tageblatt* and in the international press. In 1909 this pope further elaborated his views, convoking a pontifical audience with leaders of the Italian Unione delle Donne Cattoliche, the Ligue des Femmes Françaises, and the Ligue Patriotique des Françaises in which he insisted that it was an error for women to seek "the same rights and social role as men." "Women," he stated, "are under men's authority. . . . However, a woman is neither a slave nor a servant of men. She is a companion, helper, associate. . . . Their functions are different but equally noble and have a unique goal: to raise children and form a family."[43]

Such pronouncements notwithstanding, Catholic feminists in several countries continued their campaigns for women's rights. Although loath to tackle the issues around marriage and sexuality that characterized secular feminist challenges, they vigorously pursued issues relating to women's education, their participation in social action, and especially employment issues affecting single women, including the founding of many trade unions and benevolent societies for women workers. These campaigns continued after the outbreak of war in 1914.

In England, a more radical Christian feminist group formed in 1911, also adopting Joan of Arc as its guiding saint. The members of the new Catholic Women's Suffrage Society (founded 1911) celebrated the "New Eve," and even quarreled with a bishop over the church's stance on marriage. In 1914 the group began to publish a newspaper to promulgate its advanced views.[44] Their obstinate support for suffrage precipitated objections from the rival Catholic Social Guild. One guild member, Margaret Fletcher, published a study guide for Christian women entitled *Christian Feminism: A Charter of Rights and Duties*, in which she criticized the position of the Catholic Women's Suffrage Society, even as she affirmed a woman's right to choose celibacy rather than marriage and proclaimed that "Christian inspiration lies at the root of all Feminism."[45]

By 1917, in the heat of war, the Vatican seemed to realize that the issue of women's emancipation was not going to go away. Benedict XV, objecting to secularists' attempts to "snatch the woman from the maternal solicitude and the vigilance of the Church," declared:[46]

> With the decline in Religion, cultured women have lost with their piety, also their sense of shame; many, in order to take up occupations ill-

befitting their sex, took to imitating men; others abandoned the duties of the housewife, for which they were fashioned, to cast themselves recklessly into the current of life.

This situation had led, in Benedict XV's view, to "that deplorable perversion of morals" which the war had so greatly exacerbated. After the war, modesty in dress for women would become one of this pope's pet campaigns, along with a qualified endorsement of women's action in the world, which some interpreted as lukewarm support for woman suffrage. Catholic leagues explicitly supporting the vote for women and political action would be established in countries such as France, where women did not obtain the vote immediately after World War I.

Most Catholic feminists, however, were less bold than those in England, refusing to critique the institution of marriage, bowing to doctrinal pronouncements from the Vatican on its sacramental character and on the evils of civil divorce. The Catalan Catholic feminist Dolors Monserdá de Macia clarified her position on this issue in her *Estudi feminista* (1909), after reading Sertillanges:[47]

> It is not in my mind to speak against or detract in the slightest way from the submission that women, by natural law, by the mandate of Jesus Christ, and by their willing acceptance on contracting matrimony have to have for men, as this submission is altogether necessary . . . for the correct running of the family and society.

Nevertheless, like Marie Maugeret in France, Spanish Catholic feminist women such as Monserdá would remain firm advocates of single women's right to work and married women's right to participate fully in resolving societal problems. They would increasingly join in Catholic social action efforts to ameliorate women's difficulties.

CONTESTING THE SECOND INTERNATIONAL'S
ANSWERS TO THE WOMAN QUESTION

In the period 1890–1914 feminists operating within a socialist context faced a different set of issues, both doctrinal and practical in character: the problem was how best to assert claims for sexual equality in a situation where the leadership of the Second International, though enthusiastically paying lip service to feminist claims, continually invoked instead the necessity of acting first on the claims of the working class. It was an article of faith among Marxist-socialists that private property was the source of women's oppression. Having reduced the "woman question" to an economic issue, they believed it was logically necessary to proceed first and foremost against capitalism and the private-property regime. This point had been made over and over in the earlier works of Bebel, Engels, and Zetkin, as we have seen in Chapter 6.

Socialist feminists were not invariably eager to wait until after the revolution for results. Moreover, they also faced a serious problem of sexism within the broader social-democratic and workingmen's movements. The British suffrage advocate Millicent Garrett Fawcett, though no socialist, put her finger on one problem:[48]

> Many socialists cannot divest themselves of the idea of property in marriage. Marriage, as they see it, consists in a man seizing or becoming possessed of a woman, and keeping her as his private property to the exclusion of all other claimants. To drop this notion of property, and to rise to the idea of mutual fidelity, mutual responsibility, mutual duties, mutual rights, is something which is beyond men. It is an instance of the confusion arising from the use of the theory and the language of the market or of economics where such theory and language are totally inapplicable.

In France, on the first day of May 1893, members of the Fédération Française des Sociétés Féministes deposited a "Cahier des doléances féminines," or statement of grievances, at town halls. This tract called for the proclamation of "human rights," beginning with "the right to life," by which its authors meant the right to earn a living. Its authors advocated access for women to every profession, career, and vocation, a salary sufficient to assure existence, and equal pay for equal work in every sector of employment. The manifesto also called for the opening of all educational establishments to both sexes, the abolition of all articles of the French Civil Code which maintained women's inferiority to men, women's inclusion in governmental affairs, and social assistance for all who could not or could no longer work.

This list of grievances, in its published form, accompanied a brochure entitled *Socialisme et sexualisme: Programme du Parti Socialiste Féminin*, which argued—as did the Second International—that economic solutions were central to resolving both socialist and feminist claims. Offering in addition a thoroughgoing critique of patriarchy, however, the authors of this pamphlet blasted *masculinisme*, objected to competition between the sexes in the workplace, and affirmed the emancipation of women as fully sexual, reproductive individuals. This pamphlet and a sequence of articles in *L'Harmonie sociale* and other publications such as *Le Travailleur* were the work of Aline Valette. In addition to her charitable work directed at salvaging women ex-prisoners and prostitutes, Valette was an active member of the Parti Ouvrier Français, the purportedly "Marxist" party organized by Jules Guesde and Marx's son-in-law

Paul Lafargue; in fact, she served as the party's permanent secretary from
1896 until her death in 1899.[49]

Valette insisted, as had other socialists since 1889, that the feminist
program was fully contained in the socialist program: "The feminist
movement . . . is a revolutionary movement of the first order; the emancipation of woman its goal, itself a revolution."[50] Her survey of women
in the industrial labor force, published in *La Fronde* beginning in late
1897, not only detailed the immense surge of industrially active women
in France but pointed to their handicaps: lack of unionization, omission
from the electorate for *conseils de prud'hommes* (who judged labor disputes) as well as from political representation. Employed women num-
bered 4,415,000 strong; they must become aware of the power they represent, Valette insisted. They must be able to earn an honorable living;
starvation wages presented as "pin money" would no longer do, nor
would the continuing restriction of women workers to certain miserably
paid jobs: "Woman's dignity and independence, like that of man, has no
surer guarantee than work."[51] This work should be adequately paid and
well organized. Valette insisted on women's right to employment, but
she also believed that women were fundamentally maternal and sought
ultimately to return them to the home, though her new vision of motherhood was far more radical than that espoused either by the Roman
Catholic Church or by most socialist men.

French socialists were not unified as a political party until 1904, in
contrast to their German counterparts, and thus in the early 1890s feminists and socialists seemed to find it easier to cooperate. Most of the battles over the place of feminist demands with respect to socialism that
would mark the Second International were played out first in the German Empire, within the framework of the German Social Democratic
Party (SPD). The German battles found their echoes in a number of other
national settings, including France and Italy, where the Zetkin/Bebel
line of argument against cooperation with feminists would be vociferously articulated by Louise Saumoneau and Anna Kuliscioff, and Russia,
where the party line would be elaborated by Aleksandra Kollontai.

In contrast to France and England, "liberal" thinking had a rather
tenuous hold in German political culture, and in the later nineteenth
century it was far more clearly identified with a "national liberalism."
Following unification in 1871, under Bismarck, Imperial Germany operated as a federation of states ruled by a male emperor, with a male line of
succession. Prussia remained a highly militarized, authoritarian police
state; as in Russia and other areas of Eastern Europe, "freedom" (*Freiheit*)
meant something far closer to "ethical" or "philosophical" freedom than

to political liberty and rights as these were understood—more concretely—in France and England. Outside socialist or liberal circles, which offered the only fissures through which feminist protest could seep, there was virtually no discourse of "rights" of the sort that characterized Western European debates, nor did the notion of "citizenship" carry the same signification. As in other European societies which had not experienced a "liberal" revolution, citizenship was still seen as a subject's reward for service, including military service, rather than a right. In an age of increasing militarization and universal manhood conscription, this amounted to a substantial obstacle for women. The SPD had successfully captured the discourse about "equality," or *Gleichheit* (a word that also connotes "likeness" or "sameness" in German), and had absorbed many of the earlier concepts identified with French and English socialist idealism, though rejecting such "utopian" notions in favor of Marxian "scientific" solutions.

Thus, despite the existence of a shadowy historical tradition of feminist protest with roots in the European Enlightenment and in the revolutions of 1848, there was still little general recognition in German lands of the possibility that women's subordination might be a sociopolitical and cultural, not a "natural" product. Many nineteenth-century German women—and men—believed that women were creatures very different from men, and that God had ordained their subordination; Goethe's concept of the "eternal feminine" reigned supreme, and indeed carried more positive than negative valences. The male-headed family had been thoroughly "naturalized" and endowed with enormous moral authority by the earlier writings of legal and social theorists such as Savigny and Riehl. Not all believed, with Laura Marholm Hansson and church authorities, whether Catholic or Evangelical (Lutheran) Protestant, that women could best realize themselves by submitting to the inevitable, in a situation where they were almost wholly dependent upon men's good will. But the climate of public opinion was such that only a few, such as Louise Otto-Peters or Hedwig Dohm, dared speak out or act on such radical notions. Even then, most dissenters framed their views in "economic, social, or cultural" terms, or what Ute Gerhard calls "depoliticized ways of thinking."[52]

Bismarck's antisocialist laws were not renewed in the early 1890s, but the Prussian law on coalitions still forbade the participation of women in political associations, as did the laws of various other German states (with some exceptions, such as the city-state of Hamburg and the former duchies of Baden and Württemberg). Thus, when the Bund Deutscher Frauenvereine (BDF: Federation of German Women's Organizations) was established in 1894, its leadership defined its goals in extremely cautious terms. Composed of groups including the older German Women's Association (established in the 1860s), and a variety of charitable, educational, and philanthropic groups, the BDF did not extend a welcome to the women of the "revolutionary" SPD, who had in any case explicitly and repeatedly reiterated their refusal to cooperate, in the interests of proletarian solidarity, with any "bourgeois" (bürgerliche) women's movement.

In the early 1890s the BDF viewed women's "rights" and especially woman suffrage as taboo; they rated educational, economic, and charitable issues as far more important. The emphasis on girls' education should not surprise us; as the British observer Alys Russell noted in 1896, looking at higher education especially, "Germany was found to offer fewer opportunities to women than any other country in Europe except Turkey."[53] The federation's first petitions to the government addressed issues of regulated prostitution and factory inspection; educational opportunities for girls as well as the advancement of women teachers dominated its agenda. The first president of the BDF, Auguste Schmidt, insisted that BDF members were working not for themselves but for the "general welfare"; the rhetorical emphasis was not on rights but on "duties" (Pflicht), and, what was more, Frauenrechtlerinnen, "women's righters," were anathema.[54] These BDF women may have been entering the "public sphere," but their initial leadership was by no means willing to be identified with feminist demands.

This situation began to change in the mid-1890s. In Berlin there were a few outspoken advocates of "rights" who were not afraid of suffrage, and who were also familiar with French and English precedents, if not with their own. One of these, Lily von Gizycki (later Lily Braun), bravely spoke out on behalf of suffrage in late 1894, then in early 1895 founded—with Minna Cauer—a periodical, Die Frauenbewegung, which emphatically called on women of the left and right to cooperate in pursuit of women's rights and woman suffrage by signing and submitting a petition to the government.

For this Von Gizycki was taken to task in harsh terms by the SPD's spokeswoman Clara Zetkin, who referred to the radicals' project in Die Gleichheit as "fuzzy stupid dreams about harmony" and asserted that "the 'woman's cause,' to the extent that it means the emancipation of the female masses, the proletarian women, is indeed the cause of a party, and of one party only—the Social-Democratic one."[55] Von Gizycki countered by noting that in contrast to women's rights advocates in other countries, and to the social democratic women in Germany, the bürger-

liche women's movement had no political party behind it to press its demands; hence its cautious approach. This notwithstanding, she insisted: "The women's movement demands *not alms, but justice* for the female sex. It demands open access to the universities, changes in the laws that treat women as second-class people, and constitutional recognition of the woman as a citizen with equal rights." And, she added pointedly, "I doubt that humanity can be led closer to this goal [the maximal possible well-being of all] when those in the vanguard turn around and beat with sticks against those who do not step exactly into their footprints; and I particularly doubt whether the example thus given by the leader [Clara Zetkin] is a fruitful one."[56]

In 1896 Minna Cauer, Lily Braun (who had remarried following the death of her first husband, Georg von Gizycki), and their associates organized in Berlin (during the Berlin Exposition) the first international women's congress to be held in Germany; it was at this congress that Eugénie Potonié-Pierre from Paris made her claims for *féminisme*. They also organized a mass meeting in Berlin to protest the implications for women of the new German Civil Code, following it up with a protest petition addressed to the government.

The events of 1896 greatly energized German feminists, and their subsequent political activity greatly concerned Clara Zetkin, since some leading party men, leaning in a reformist direction, had greeted it with some sympathy. At the SPD congress in October, Zetkin lectured her comrades on the impossibility of women's solidarity across class lines: "There is a women's question for the women of the proletariat, of the middle bourgeoisie, of the intelligentsia, and of the Upper Ten Thousand; it takes various forms depending on the class situation of these strata."[57] Women must remain in solidarity with the proletariat, not engaged in separatist action.

In 1899, following an unsuccessful attempt to radicalize the BDF by inserting legal and political demands into its program, this group of self-styled "radicals" founded the Verband Fortschrittlicher Frauenvereine (League of Progressive Women's Organizations), which remained independent of the BDF until 1907. In 1902 they also organized the Deutscher Verein für Stimmrecht (German Association for Woman Suffrage), which affiliated almost immediately with the BDF and hastened its endorsement of the vote. Many of these women, including Marie Stritt, who became president of the BDF, were also active in the Bund für Mutterschutz (League for the Protection of Mothers) and vocal participants in the efforts to reform marriage, sexual mores, and the conditions for motherhood itself. Indeed, as elsewhere in Europe, a woman-centered and expansive reformulation of motherhood became central to the program of most German feminists, moderate, radical, and socialist alike.[58]

By 1907 the now far more courageous BDF produced a sweeping program statement, including sections on education, economic life, marriage and the family, and public life, community, and the state, which insisted that its members worked "for the women of all classes and parties." Its professed goal was "to bring the cultural influence of women to its complete development and free social effectiveness" by seeking "a transformation of ideas and conditions" in these areas.[59] The BDF insisted on the recognition of the cultural importance of women's "vocation" in marriage and motherhood, and at the same time insisted on the importance of women's paid vocational work, equal pay for equal work, reform of marriage laws, the necessity of combatting prostitution, and the inclusion of women in all aspects of public life, up to and including the local, church, and political franchise. This sweeping program insisted on the full realization of women's potential within a relational framework.

The SPD women, led by Clara Zetkin, responded by floating a proposal for unrestricted woman suffrage, in parallel with unrestricted suffrage for men. Delegates to the first conference of European socialist women, held during the Stuttgart congress of the Second International in August 1907, passed a resolution calling on the member parties to support a wholly inclusive suffrage. For Zetkin, however, the fight for woman suffrage could never be considered a goal in itself; it was always presented as a means to the greater end of "the proletarian struggle for liberation."[60] Still, the very fact of acceptance of this "bourgeois" feminist goal, stated in its most radical form of universal suffrage for both sexes, could be seen as a compromise with the SPD's earlier revolutionary position.

Some French socialist feminists took a dim view of the continued insistence by the SPD-dominated Second International on noncooperation with "bourgeois" feminism. The physician-activist Madeleine Pelletier, editor of La Suffragiste, argued that feminism, by achieving political and social equality of the sexes, could benefit all women; she saw nothing wrong with a proletarian/socialist feminism operating in parallel with its counterpart: "The proletarian woman is twice a slave; the slave of her husband and the slave of the boss; the success of feminist claims would assure that she would only be once a slave; that would already be progress."[61] Hubertine Auclert was less sanguine: "There cannot be both a bourgeois feminism and a socialist feminism because there are not two female sexes."[62]

In 1910, the proposal for an international women's day, at the Second Congress of Socialist Women, held in conjunction with the Copenhagen congress of the Second International, was presented as a specifically and exclusively socialist celebration. The resolution submitted by Clara Zetkin and her colleagues made the point:[63]

> In agreement with the class-conscious, political and trade union organizations of the proletariat of their respective countries, the Socialist women of all countries will hold each year a Women's Day, whose foremost purpose it must be to aid the attainment of women's suffrage. This demand must be handled in conjunction with the entire women's question according to Socialist precepts.

Another variation on the competition between so-called "bourgeois" or citizenship feminists and Marxist-socialist feminists would be played out in Russia, where a very significant feminist initiative developed during the revolutionary years 1905–6. *Pace* the dismissive claims made by Zinaida Vengerova, it had become apparent that women in Russia were severely disadvantaged from the perspective of Western standards of civil and political liberty. True, married women in the Russian Empire could control their own separate (landed) property, which was almost invariably not the case in Western Europe. But in a system in which both daughters and wives were formally subject to male authority throughout their lives, this had little practical significance. Based on these property rights, such women could exercise a very limited franchise (usually by proxy, through a male relative) in local governmental affairs. It was also the case that important opportunities for women's higher education had opened in the 1870s, but these had been repeatedly compromised by government interventions and shutdowns of educational institutions during the 1880s and 1890s. Even so, more and more Russian women had obtained an advanced education. As Russia industrialized, however, increasing numbers of women were entering the new industrial workforce, especially in major cities such as St. Petersburg and Moscow, and this would raise other issues about pay and property. The mere mention of such reforms, however, stirred up strong resistance. A campaign by legal reformers to revise marriage and family law "provoked such strong conservative and clerical resistance that little improvement in women's legal status had been achieved by the fall of the old regime."[64]

At the beginning of the twentieth century, the Russian autocracy still exercised highly effective controls on speech, association, and local initiative through its extensive bureaucracy and secret police. Organizing possibilities for women and men alike were minimal. There was hardly any "public sphere" in the sense of that term further to the west. Indeed, even after 1905 censors were alert to "emancipation of women" as a risky topic, and, as historian Linda Edmondson has pointed out, "feminism" was one foreign term that the intelligentsia did not import. The Russkoe Zhenskoe Vzaimno-Blagotvoritel'noe Obshchestvo (RZhVBO, Russian Women's Mutual Philanthropic Society), founded in 1895 in St. Petersburg, had been planning a women's congress since 1902, but its efforts were continually thwarted by the Ministry of Internal Affairs, which not only insisted on limiting its agenda to philanthropy and education issues, but also demanded prior submission of congress papers for official approval; the Philanthropic Society finally canceled its congress. Russian women's rights activists never received the crucial governmental authorization necessary to establish a National Council of Women.

In such an environment it was not altogether surprising that some aspiring reformers had turned in frustration (and would return) to exalted notions of social revolution and to terrorist methods, including assassinations of public officials. Such revolutionary alternatives were historically enshrined in memories of the populist movement of the 1860s and 1870s, and subsequently in memories of socialist secret societies, led by Russian intellectuals in exile. Only in 1905, following the massacre of Bloody Sunday (9 January in the Gregorian calendar), did feminist demands for civil and political rights find an opening.

The new 1905 law on associations did permit the establishment of registered (controlled) associations, and in late February the Soiuz Ravnopravnosti Zhenshchin (SRZh, Union of Equal Rights for Women) was organized by a group of educated Moscow women. By May it had established twenty sections in various Russian cities. But when two women delegates from this group showed up at the founding congress of the all-encompassing Union of Unions in early May, the response was: "How did women get here? This must be some misunderstanding."[65]

The SRZh platform, elaborated in Moscow at its first congress in early May, presented a wide range of feminist demands, associated with the general cause of changing the political character of Russia. "The struggle for women's rights is indissolubly linked with the struggle for the political liberation of Russia," the program read. Delegates called for the convening of a constituent assembly, "on the basis of universal, direct, secret suffrage without distinction of sex, nationality or religion, with the preliminary establishment of inviolability of the person and the home, freedom of conscience, speech, assembly and association, the reinstatement of the rights of all those suffering for their political and religious beliefs." It supported claims for cultural and national self-determination within the Russian Empire, and for "the equalisation of peasant women's rights with men's in all future agrarian reforms." Additional claims called for equal opportunities in education and in vocational choices, and the "abolition of all exceptional laws relating to the question of prostitution and demeaning women's human dignity." Further and finally, it called for an immediate end to the war with Japan.[66]

Other new women's groups, such as the Society for Mutual Aid to Working Women, in Saratov on the Volga (long a center of dissident thinking), had also insisted on equal suffrage: "Both as members of families and as citizens, women must take an active part in deciding questions of war and peace."[67] Many other women's groups throughout Russia would subsequently formulate and publish demands for change in their condition, including equal rights.

Suffrage and civil rights for women, however, proved to be extremely controversial, just as in France in 1789 and 1848. The tsar's October Manifesto, which accorded limited civil rights and acceded to demands for a representative assembly, pointedly ignored the issue of rights for women. Newly formed political parties, including the liberal Constitutional Democrats (Kadets), repeatedly proved reluctant to endorse such principles, though many Kadet leaders acknowledged their sympathetic support. When provisions for the election of the first state Duma (Parliament) were finally elaborated, women were excluded even as men were enfranchised. This was becoming an all-too-familiar scenario in European history. Even peasant women acknowledged the problem. An indignant women's petition to the first Duma from Voronezh province pointed out that the representative from Voronezh had "announced in the Duma that peasant men only acknowledged women's work in the family and claim that women themselves do not want any rights." Echoing demands that could be traced back for centuries, the petitioners insisted: "There are no women delegates in the Duma who could speak for the women, so how does he know? He is wrong, as he would know if he had asked us. We, the women from Voronezh province . . . understand well that we need rights and land just as men do."[68]

The Women's Union for Equal Rights finally succeeded in pressuring the male representatives to debate woman suffrage in the Duma in early June 1906. The Women's Mutual Philanthropic Society had collected some four thousand signatures in a petition for women's equal rights, and in support of the women's petition Deputy Lev Petrazhitskii presented an eloquent argument on behalf of enfranchising women. However, this would be the first and last such debate. In early July the Duma was abruptly closed down by government troops, then dissolved.

Even during 1905-6 Russian feminists confronted opposition on virtually every side of the newly emerging political spectrum, from Muslims, Orthodox clergy, and ultraconservative peasants on the right, to the Social Democrats and Social Revolutionaries on the left. When the St. Petersburg supporters of the Union of Equal Rights organized their founding section meeting on 10 April 1905, Aleksandra Kollontai, on behalf of the Russian Social Democrats, made an attempt to disrupt it. "In those years," Kollontai wrote later, "the bourgeois women's movement posed a serious threat to the unity of the working-class movement." She and her associates "warned the working women against being carried away by feminism and called on them to defend the single revolutionary worker's banner." Their resolutions, "outlining principles of proletarian class unity" were, however, "decisively defeated."[69] Other radical and social revolutionary women joined the St. Petersburg SRZh's council, but did not stay long; they withdrew from the union in the spring of 1906.

Russian social democrats, like their German counterparts, possessively defended their claim to the proletariat, including its women, as their exclusive constituency. Even as the women of the SRZh were drawn increasingly to the left of the political spectrum, the resistance of the social democratic women, whether Menshevik (moderate) or Bolshevik (radical), seemed to grow. Social democratic women in Russia, as in Germany, insisted that class struggle must take precedence and opposed efforts of the *ravnopraki* (equal-righters) to attract "their" working-class women to support the feminist cause, not wishing to have them "infected," as Kollontai put it in retrospect, by the "poison of feminism."[70]

The thinking and maneuvering of Kollontai, like that of Clara Zetkin, from whom Kollontai sought advice in 1906, set the subsequent tone for social democratic approaches to the woman question in Russia. Her efforts to sabotage feminist efforts reveal the enormous resistance feminism faced from organized socialism in Europe during the early twentieth century, as well as the depth of the socialist parties' fears of feminist competition for the loyalties of working-class women. Opposed to the efforts of the "bourgeois" feminists in Russia, Kollontai nevertheless wanted to incorporate efforts for the emancipation of women into the Russian socialist program in order to recruit women for social democracy. But none of the social democratic men of whatever faction seemed particularly interested or understanding, and indeed, they reproached *her* for being a "feminist," despite her expressed hostility to organized feminism and to "separate" women's issues.

The clash between feminists and social democrats reached a showdown during the All-Russian Congress of Women, held in December

1908 in St. Petersburg. Facing down Kollontai and the Working Women's delegation's insistence that the woman question could not be resolved outside social democracy, *ravnopraki* spokeswomen insisted that women of all classes shared common problems, problems having their root in male domination. The vote, argued Anna Kal'manovich, was just the beginning, a means to realize a broader program:[71]

> Even the proletarian to whom the contemporary order gives so little joy [would lose] a slave; the wife who serves him, brings up his children, cooks and launders. Perhaps this is why [social democrats] instinctively and unconsciously do not hurry to realize [their program of equal rights for women], and are willing to bequeath the task to future generations.

The Kadets promoted women's rights as window dressing, Kal'manovich insisted at the Congress, but the social democrats were the same: "Regardless of what men call themselves—liberals, conservatives, or social democrats—they cannot be depended upon to give women freedom."[72]

This type of analysis was not welcomed by female social democrats such as Kollontai, but she was forced to leave the congress abruptly and flee the country in order to avoid arrest. Her statement was read by another member of the women workers' delegation:[73]

> There is no independent woman's question; the woman question arose as an integral component of the social problem of our time. The thorough liberation of woman as a member of society, a worker, an individual, a wife, and a mother is possible therefore only together with the resolution of the general social question, together with the fundamental transformation of the contemporary social order.

Kollontai's subsequent publication *The Social Basis of the Woman Question* (1909), a critical evaluation of the Russian feminist movement and the social democratic response, was her legacy. She remained in exile in Western and Central Europe until 1917. With the All-Women's Congress a thing of the past and Kollontai out of the country, the Russian social democrats, with only a few exceptions, "lost virtually all interest in women workers."[74]

What seems clear from Kollontai's early career is that other causes (social democratic party work; antiwar work with the Bolsheviks), invariably and repeatedly took precedence over women's emancipation. Only in exile did she begin to develop the more detailed and nuanced analysis of women's subordination to men that would emerge in her later writings. In the revolutionary years 1918–19, following the Bolshevik seizure of power in Russia, Lenin would put Kollontai in charge of the new Communist Party women's section, the Zhenotdel, which during its short life was charged with developing the revolutionary government's program for women. "The main thrust of all this activity," Kollontai later wrote, "was to implement, in fact, equal rights for women as a labor unit in the national economy and as a citizen in the political sphere and, of course, with the special proviso: maternity was to be appraised as a social function and therefore protected and provided for by the State."[75] The consequences of this approach would mark eastern—and northern—Europe for over half a century.

8

Nationalizing Feminisms and Feminizing Nationalisms, 1890–1914

The rise of nation-states and nation-centered thinking since the French Revolution had opened new channels within which feminist action could develop. Aspiring patriotic and nationalist groups sought—quite successfully—to enlist women's energy on behalf of aspiring statehood, providing them with carefully channeled opportunities to act in the public domain and, occasionally, offering them the hope of eventual decision-making power. At the same time, these male-dominated groups could set in place new barriers, even fostering backlashes with peculiarly national cultural characteristics. Women's lot was closely tied to the making of nations: the Bohemian Czech writer Josefa Himpal Zeman insisted, speaking to the 1893 World's Women's Congress, that "whatever they do, for whatever they may long, [the women] never forget their obligation to the nation, and are first patriots and then women."[1]

During the nineteenth century, as the previous chapters suggest, in cities and towns throughout Europe, feminist challenges coursed along an explosive trajectory. Feminists and feminist organizations multiplied rapidly, developing identities and characteristics that were culturally distinctive and context-specific—what historian Amy Hackett has baptized "national feminism."[2] Recent scholarship has paid increasing attention to the particularities of feminist political cultures, which more often than not developed their case in a series of relational arguments framed in terms of rights and duties, to the nation, to men, to children.

Internationalist efforts likewise developed, spinning a dense web of contacts between women of different nations and cultures. If Roman Catholicism and the Second International Working Men's Association took strong and internationally influential positions, pro and con, on the emancipation of women in the late nineteenth century, the now increasingly visible independent feminist international organizations accelerated their activity, calling a series of general conferences and joint ventures in Paris, London, Berlin, Brussels, and Rome.[3] Feminists also participated in other conferences dedicated to specific topics, such as promoting popular education, combatting alcoholism, fostering protective legislation, advocating eugenics, organizing workers, and preventing war. They placed many highly controversial issues on the table for discussion in this period, including sex education, contraception, abortion, and regulated prostitution and the white slave trade. They published and publicized their proceedings and resolutions, and attracted expansive coverage in the press.[4]

At the 1899 Conference of the International Council of Women in London, and at the 1904 conference in Berlin, prosuffrage activists began to press for international mobilization and a unified front. The International Woman Suffrage Alliance (IWSA), born in 1902, henceforth spearheaded this initiative, encouraging the establishment of suffrage societies and active campaigns in each of its member countries. Both for those who lived in societies that had established some form of representative government and for those whose societies aspired to do so, the campaign for woman suffrage symbolized women's fight for inclusion, for a decision-making role that would allow them to shape the future of the national states in which they lived, or hoped to live.

FEMINISM AND NATIONALISM: FOUR CASE STUDIES
IN ASPIRING NATION-STATES

In the territories under the rule of the Habsburg and Russian empires such as Bohemia, Poland, Hungary, Finland, and the Ukraine, among peoples aspiring to nationhood, the molten stream of feminist lava would flow most expansively through the openings provided by the politics of cultural nationalism. Poland, Bohemia, and Hungary were all old kingdoms which had lost their sovereignty in the course of earlier territorial conflicts; Ukrainians and Finns had developed distinctive cultures but had never achieved sovereign status as nations. Feminists in those societies (as among other peoples aspiring to independence such as the Norwegians, Catalonians, Latvians, or Estonians) would stake their claims with reference to building a culture and a nation. In Greece (Hellas), which had staged a successful national movement for independence from the Ottoman Empire in the early nineteenth century, feminism erupted amidst men's search to define Greek ethnic and cultural identity with respect to Western Europe. In each case, advocates of women's emancipation determinedly and overtly positioned themselves with respect both to specific internal circumstances and to external influences as well. In each case, feminists promoted women's education and full citizenship as central to the realization of the national project. Here I will consider the cases of Finland, the Ukrainians, Greece, and Belgium.

A particularly successful example of a national feminism is offered by the small Nordic nation of Finland, the first country of Europe in which all women, along with all men (age twenty-four and above for both sexes), obtained the unrestricted suffrage as well as eligibility for office. In 1809 Finland, after being ruled by Sweden for six centuries, had become a quasi-autonomous duchy with its own representative institutions, governed by the tsar of Russia, who also carried the title of grand duke of Finland. Consequently, the politics of Finnish cultural autonomy were defined, on the one hand, in relation to the small but long-dominant Swedish minority, and on the other, with respect to the much larger and more powerful autocratic Russian Empire. A reading of John Stuart Mill's *Subjection of Women* in the 1880s had stimulated the founding of the women's organization Suomen Neisyhdistys (known to Swedish-speaking Finns as Finsk Qvinnoforening).

Achieving women's rights with respect in the politics of national identity probably owed less to Mill, however, than to the struggle for independence from Russia and the political clout of the Finnish socialists. In this struggle, the Finns made use of the French revolutionary idea of mother-educators in the service of the national cause, a concept that had by the 1890s permeated the politics of nationalism throughout nineteenth-century Europe. Women leaders of the Finnish-speaking majority played a vital and highly visible role in the nationalist struggle, by deliberately teaching the Finnish language to their children and promoting Finnish culture through the founding of schools and newspapers. As the novelist and longtime women's rights advocate Baronness Aleksandra Gripenberg explained it to the World's Congress of Representative Women in 1893: "The leading men appealed to the mothers, through whom the idea was to go to the coming generation by the education of the children in their native tongue. The women did not remain indifferent, and for them this movement became the plow which prepared the field for another great idea—that of their own rights."[5] The establishment of coeducational schools in the 1880s provided a further vehicle for young people of both sexes to study together and overcome old prejudices.

The politics of feminism in Finland was egalitarian and thoroughly relational, celebrating the "feminine" in relation to the "masculine." In some ways comparable to their German counterparts, Finnish feminists claimed "maternalist" and "womanly" qualities in both a social and a cultural sense. In an 1897 speech to the Finnish Diet, Gripenberg expressed the concept this way: "In other words, femininity is motherhood in the deepest meaning of the word. That this be given its true value in that greatest of all homes, society, is the primary task of women's rights work, it is the essence of all our efforts, even though it is often misunderstood by our opponents and by our ostensible friends."[6]

Viewing the political implications of the Finnish cultural campaign with alarm, in 1899 the Russian autocracy launched a Russification campaign, thereby provoking a crisis that mobilized Finns of both sexes in a fight for their rights and for national and cultural self-determination. This effort culminated in a great national strike in late October 1905, which, combined with the revolutionary events developing in Russia at that time, forced the tsar to offer the Finnish Diet significant concessions, including virtual independence and democratic suffrage for both sexes. In contrast to Russia, all political factions in Finland supported woman suffrage; women had been voting at the municipal level for decades already. The national vote was openly acknowledged as a "reward" for the women's important role in the nationalist effort.

Finland's 1906 woman suffrage victory was enthusiastically announced to her envious European colleagues by Alexandra Gripenberg, who was subsequently elected to the Finnish parliament:[7]

> Our victory is in all cases great, and the more so as the proposal has been adopted almost without opposition. The gratitude which we women feel is mingled with the knowledge that we are much less worthy of this great success than the women of England and America, who have struggled so long and so faithfully, with much more energy and perseverance than we.

The suffrage victory in Finland, helped by the significant organizational muscle and support of the socialists, served as a rallying point for the intensification of suffrage campaigns by feminists throughout the Western world, ultimately stimulating the reorientation of socialist and Catholic policy on the question. Clusters of women were elected to the Finnish Diet in subsequent elections, and in 1909, equal rights and duties for both sexes were incorporated into the Finnish constitution. Their agenda for reform encompassed twenty-six points, including dramatic changes empowering married women in property and guardianship law, the employment of women in state service, as parish midwives, sanitary inspectors. Only in 1917, however, after many more episodes of resistance to the Russian tsardom, did the Finns obtain complete independence as a nation-state.

A less successful nineteenth-century feminist eruption situated in a cultural-nationalist context occurred in Ukrainian women's groups, which engaged, in association with Ukrainian men, in a lengthy but ultimately futile attempt at building a nation. The Ukrainian people then lived under the jurisdiction of two vast and very different multiethnic empires, the Russian and the Austro-Hungarian (mostly in Galicia), in both of which they were a politically insecure ethnic and religious minority. Among Ukrainians, neither women nor men had "rights" within the sovereign entities under which they lived; their shared goal was self-determination and recognition for their entire community. Nevertheless, within the Ukrainian national movement, sexual discrimination sometimes raised its ugly head, and a few Ukrainian women invented an indigenous feminist politics in response to male leaders' attempts to exile them to the kitchen when the women thought they should be included in making political decisions. They became, in historian Martha Bohachevsky-Chomiak's words, "feminists despite themselves."[8]

Indisputably the most important figure in the Galician Ukrainian women's movement was Natalia Ozarkevych Kobryns'ka, whose thinking on the woman question had been stimulated not only by the Ukrainian question but also by her extensive exposure to German and English debate on the woman question. Her father, a member of the Ukrainian Catholic clergy, also served as a deputy to the Reichsrat in Vienna. As the eldest child and only daughter, Kobryns'ka read widely (evidently including works in German, in German translation, in Polish, and in Russian), and was familiar with the writings of Chernyshevsky, John Stuart Mill, and Marx and Engels, among many others.

Kobryns'ka focused especially on the need for women's education and economic independence, and in the mid-1880s she had organized a women's association in Stanyslaviv whose goal was to introduce women to critical reflection through literature. In the 1890s she published a series of women's almanacs, *Nasha dolia* (Our Fate), in which she advocated women's organization, self-help, greater educational and economic opportunities, and woman suffrage. A convinced but not a dogmatic socialist, she (like so many others) argued in print with Clara Zetkin, asserting the legitimacy and necessity of so-called bourgeois feminism, and remarking that men, whether socialist or not, did not automatically work on behalf of women's emancipation. "It is a pity," she wrote, "that the age-long slavery of women is etched as a scar in the concepts of men, so that women must struggle not only against the social order, which keeps them in slavery, but also with the prejudices of men."[9]

To ease the burdens of women, Kobryns'ka worked to establish central kitchens and Ukrainian-language day-care centers for mothers in the peasant villages who worked in the fields, which would among other things make it possible to counter Polish Catholic efforts to supply such services (and thereby influence children away from Ukrainian culture). She also organized petitions, in particular an April 1890 petition to the Reichsrat in Vienna (signed by 226 Ukrainian women) demanding higher educational opportunities for women of the lands under Austrian rule, in support of a comparable demand made by Czech feminists, with whom she subsequently tried to develop alliances.[10] Her father presented the petition to the Reichsrat, but it was never discussed. The wording of this petition set the educational demand in a far broader context, fully comparable with understandings of women's subordination in Western Europe:[11]

> The woman's question is without any doubt the most important movement in our century. While other issues relate to some one part of society, this movement touches half of the whole human race. . . . The present social system differentiates between man and woman on all levels of spiritual and economic life. Conflicting . . . interests in community and private life make it possible for the men who control the public realm to overlook even the most justified wishes and needs of women.

Kobryns'ka's efforts were not welcomed by men of the Ukrainian intelligentsia, who castigated her for not supporting their efforts uncritically. She in turn denounced "the blind faith of our women in male authority and the tragic economic dependence of women upon men."[12] The next generation of women was standoffish: their publication *Meta* (Aim), founded in 1908, was subtitled "a journal of progressive Ukrainian women," but its editors were unwilling to express avowedly feminist aims. Patriotism, not feminism, remained uppermost; Ukrainian sovereignty was the goal, though when it materialized briefly in 1917, in consequence of the Russian Revolution, it would be short-lived. In 1920 the Ukrainian Republic would once again be swallowed up by a larger state, this time by the newly founded Union of Soviet Socialist Republics (USSR).

The kingdom of Greece offers a sharply contrasting case study in the relationship of feminism with nationalism. Following the revolution for independence from Ottoman rule in the early 1820s, and the importation of a Bavarian prince as king, the new Greek state had positioned itself as "East of the West, or West of the East," in historian Eleni Varikas's terms.[13] There, feminist discontent found an opening through a language grounded in the Greek independence movement itself, which drew deliberately and heavily on that of the French Revolution, and through a history that increasingly elaborated an image of a historical Greece, and Athens in particular, as the very birthplace of democracy.

After several earlier rumblings, Greek feminism erupted in the 1890s, following the launching in Athens in 1887 of the weekly all-woman publication *Efimeris ton kyrion* (Ladies' Journal), edited by Callirhoé Siganou Parren. The *Ladies' Journal* appeared as an eight-page weekly until 1908, when it switched to a bimonthly schedule, maintained until early 1916. Parren was both multilingual (in addition to Greek, she spoke English, French, Italian, and Russian) and well traveled. Born in Crete, she had been a schoolmistress in cities of the Greek diaspora (in Russia and in the Balkans) and had married a French journalist, Jean Parren, who had established the French press agency in Constantinople before the couple moved to Athens. She was thus thoroughly cosmopolitan as well as positioned on the cutting edge of the communications revolution. Many of her collaborators had been educated at a private girls' school in Athens, which had been founded in the era of the war for independence by an American couple. These were remarkable and energetic women, and they articulated radical demands.

Parren, who had embarked on a world history of women, was not above adapting Greek history to her own feminist ends. When she spoke to delegates at the 1893 World's Congress of Representative Women in Chicago, she cleverly invoked the "unknown" women's history of Athens. In addition to its meaning "light, progress, civilization, letters, art, science," it also meant "the predomination of the goddesses in Olympia, and the predomination of woman in society . . . with the same civil rights as men." It was the women, she asserted, who chose the goddess of wisdom, Athena, over Poseidon, the god of the sea, as protectress of the city. Moreover, she claimed, "the golden age" of Greece "is due to Aspasia." As for modern Greece since independence: "The women are preserving its language, its customs, and its traditions. The Christianity which they embraced, and for the improvement of which they have worked more than all else, as orators, reformers, and apostles, has given to them strength for the great work of patriotism."[14] This was clearly an appeal designed to tempt the West and to appeal to the thousands of American feminists present at the Chicago congress.

Parren and her associates explicitly disclaimed seeking the legislative vote. This decision was tactical and deliberately calculated to demonstrate moderation while demanding radical changes in opportunities for education and employment. She would later refer to critics of feminist aspirations and goals as "oriental misogynists." After the Finnish women had obtained the vote in 1906, however, Parren's disappointment revealed itself viscerally:[15]

> Look at these happy mortals who are no longer constrained to supplicate male legislators, who are no longer constrained to beg for reforms. As for us, the so-called queens of the household who wear crowns of thorns . . . we will continue for a long time to submit to our fate, even if we are enslaved to tyrannical and imbecilic masters.

In the interim, Parren and her colleagues were actively engaged in promoting the works of women writers, in recovering women's history, and in establishing vocational schools for women, Sunday schools, and philanthropic endeavors of all kinds designed to enhance opportunities for Greek women: "We are fighting so that women will take their emancipation into their own hands."[16] In the process of celebrating women and combatting Greek men's chauvinism, Parren and her associates put the blame on men:[17]

> Ever since Greece has existed, archaic Greece and the Greece of colonies, free Greece and slave Greece, it is man who has assumed and still assumes the government, the hegemony, the tyranny, the absolute power. It is man, and not woman. Thus, if social affairs go badly, the responsibility rests on those who govern and not on the governed.

These Greek feminists insisted on a sort of transvaluation of values, rendering women irresponsible for the current political mess, but positioning them as the ethical carriers of Greek salvation.

In each of these small aspiring countries, feminists confronted the shifting fortunes of a political life over which they had no power. In 1909 a military takeover shifted the climate for feminist activity in Greece, a scenario that would recur more than once in the twentieth century. The authoritarianism of the Russian state and the turbulence of the 1917 revolution would weigh heavily on the possibilities open to feminists in Russia and in the Ukrainian community. Before 1914, only the Norwegians and the Finns, through a combination of favorable political circumstances, were able to realize some of their goals with the advent of sovereignty. Elsewhere feminists would be continually confronted with preemptive national agendas.

A fourth case study is provided by Belgium, which had achieved independence in 1831, after centuries of Spanish, then Austrian and Dutch rule. In order to prevent French designs on Belgium, the great powers had established a constitutional monarchy under international protection. With a population split between French and Flemish culture, with a heavy preponderance of conservative Catholics and a small contingent of anticlerical liberals, governed by French laws incarnated by the Napoleonic Code, anti-Dutch, and increasingly industrialized, Belgians had to invent a more positive national identity.

Women's education long preoccupied would-be feminists in Belgium. In the 1890s, a feminist movement had begun to gather supporters among the French-speaking population, thanks to the efforts of Marie Popelin, the first Belgian woman to earn a law degree, and her attorney-colleague Louis Frank. Popelin had attended the 1889 international feminist conferences in Paris, and by 1892 she succeeded in founding a Ligue Belge du Droit des Femmes (LBDF, Belgian League for Women's Rights) on the model established in France by Maria Deraismes and Léon Richer. The Ligue's constituency of progressive French-speaking educators, lawyers, liberals, and freethinkers, and its close contacts with Paris-based feminists, assured that Ligue members would undertake parallel action to reform women's status in marriage under the Napoleonic Code, and to work for girls' secondary education. Under a Catholic-dominated government, it was perhaps not possible to do more. Refusing to acknowledge class struggle as a priority, Belgian feminists entered into an initially friendly competition with the Belgian Workers' Party (POB).[18]

In its 1894 Charter, the Belgian Workers' Party had enthusiastically endorsed woman suffrage and the end to all discriminatory laws, pressed by Emilie Claeys and other Flemish-speaking working-class socialist feminists. But in 1902, party leaders struck a deal with the Liberal Party to challenge Catholic political control by advocating universal manhood suffrage; one condition of the agreement was to hedge on the party's principled commitment to woman suffrage. The POB leadership called on its women to publicly place their suffrage quest on hold. They did so reluctantly, though not without strenuous objections. The Belgian Workers' Party, in one historian's scathing judgment, "was quick to betray women's cause at the first notes of the electoral siren-song."[19] This opportunistic move did not go unnoticed by other social democrats and feminists throughout Europe.

FEMINISM AND NATIONALISM IN ESTABLISHED NATION-STATES

These smaller cultures and aspiring nations were by no means the only ones to produce "national feminisms." The major European powers—England, France, and Germany—were engaged in precisely the same sort of exercise. Although many feminists were active internationalists, they were also centrally engaged with their own political cultures. French feminists insisted on their identification as *Françaises*—French women—increasingly so, as they reclaimed their past and pursued civil and political rights within the framework of the highly centralized, secular French nation-state.[20] Publications with such titles as *The English-woman's Review* and *The Englishwoman* deliberately underscored the point for English feminists. "German feminists were," in one historian's words, "acutely aware that they were Germans as well as women."[21] No one could dare claim, in the face of feminist activity in the early 1900s, that women had no countries.

The issue on which virtually all feminists agreed by the first decade of twentieth century was that women, including married women, must have the suffrage and full citizenship in their respective nation-states. It had, however, become increasingly apparent to activists on the European continent, as it had already become clear in the English-speaking world several decades before, and to French feminists since 1789 and 1848, that male-dominated governments—particularly democratizing governments responsive only to male voters and the newly developing political parties that sought to represent them—could be extremely resistant to sharing their newfound power with women. In some provinces of the Austro-Hungarian Empire, where the vote was still property-based and women had been voting through male proxies, female taxpayers were deliberately stripped of their vote; when this happened in Lower Austria in 1889, it stimulated feminist organizing among Austrian teachers. In Bohemia, it provoked Czech-speaking feminists to campaign for a woman representative in the Reichsrat in Vienna.[22]

Feminists first demanded the democratic parliamentary suffrage at the outset of the French Revolution. But it had been obtained only by women living on the periphery of the Anglo-American world—in the western United States (beginning with Wyoming in 1869), in New Zealand (1893), and in Australia (1894, 1899). In Europe, woman suffrage seemed to be far more controversial, and although some women could vote on local issues, only Finland (1906) and Norway (1913) enfranchised women at the national level before 1914.[23] Instead, some national governments succeeded in closing loopholes that had allowed women to vote. Adding the word "male" to electoral qualifications seemed to have become an ominous pastime.

Suffragists constantly developed new arguments in support of women's participation in national political life. Different national contexts called for different rhetorical strategies and political tactics. In England, following defeat in 1867 of John Stuart Mill's amendment to the Parliamentary Reform Bill, in 1869 single adult women had nevertheless been granted the franchise in municipal and school elections. When the national parliamentary vote came up again in 1892, William Gladstone, the supremely influential British Liberal Party leader and four-time prime minister, argued against giving the vote to women, claiming that even unmarried women must be "saved" from "the whirlpool of public life."[24] Susan Elizabeth Gay responded on behalf of the Women's Liberal Federation:[25]

> No, Sir, it is not by depriving woman, or any portion of womanhood, of just rights, that you can preserve 'her delicacy, purity and refinement,' it is not by accentuating sex that you can promote the 'elevation of her own nature'; it is by upholding that which makes her a human being in its full sense, free of choice, with issues as vast as those you possess yourself; a soul as divine; an immortality as profound. . . . In carrying the idea of womanly dependence beyond the domain of sentiment . . . and converting it into a system of religious and legal oppression and moral inequality, a foul wrong has been perpetrated, not only on womanhood but on the entire race, whose excessive and perverted sexual instincts show the natural consequences.

The British campaign for the vote quickly became the most spectacular, because of the militant campaign led by Women's Social and Political Union (WSPU), which supplemented the activities of the National Union of Woman Suffrage Societies (NUWSS), headed by Millicent Garrett Fawcett.[26] These campaigns engaged thousands of middle-class and working-class women in the years between 1906 and 1914. Indeed, the WSPU campaign, with its massive parades, its deliberate and well-publicized acts of violence against property, and its focus on defeating candidates of every political party that refused to support woman suffrage, riveted world attention. In this "suffragette" (as distinct from "suffragist") campaign, orchestrated by Emmeline Pankhurst, her daughters Christabel and Sylvia, and the Pethick-Lawrences, so-called feminine propriety (though not femininity) was definitively renounced. As Emmeline Pankhurst put it in her court testimony of 1908, following her arrest for "disorderly conduct": "We have tried to be womanly, we have tried to use feminine influence, and we have seen that it is of no use . . . ; we are here not because we are law-breakers; we are here in our efforts to become law-makers."[27] The British women's campaign for the vote ranks as the feminist movement's most stupendous media event, and the repressive measures instituted by the British government against the suffragettes aroused the indignation of women and men around the world.

In the years 1910–14 the fate of woman suffrage in the British Parliament was tightly tied to the fate of Home Rule for the Irish. The Irish suffrage campaign, though less spectacular than that in England, was in some respects even more dramatic. The stakes were extremely high. Since 1801, the Irish, under British rule (some called it colonization), their own parliament abolished, had become increasingly committed to national self-determination. But Irish society was divided politically between Unionists and Nationalists, and religiously between Protestants (who tended to be Anglo-Irish, residing in Ulster) and Catholics (more often of Celtic descent, poorer, and concentrated in the more southerly counties). For many decades, the Nationalists had struggled for constitutional Home Rule, a campaign that a more radical minority increasingly wished to press toward complete national independence. Irish women had faithfully supported such efforts. Along with men, Irish women had been granted the local vote in 1898, and numerous moderate women's suffrage societies promoted the cause of parliamentary suffrage.

Yet in the early twentieth century the Irish Party—the M.P.'s who represented Ireland in the British House of Commons (and who held the balance of power from 1910 to 1914)—refused either to support woman suffrage as such or to endorse it as part of the Home Rule settlement which they had determined to negotiate with the Liberal British ministry then in power. Irish Party leaders were notoriously opposed to giving women the vote; the quest for Home Rule, they insisted, must not be compromised by raising the question of women's votes. Besides, leaders claimed, the Irish themselves, not the British House of Commons, should decide such issues. They feared priestly—that is, Roman Catholic—influence over women voters.

The Irish feminists quickly recognized that the most serious obstacle to their enfranchisement lay among their own parliamentary representatives. Consequently, in 1908, Irish nationalist suffragettes Hanna Sheehy Skeffington and Margaret Cousins founded the militant Irish Women's Franchise League (IWFL), including both Nationalist and Unionist women, drawing inspiration from the English WSPU, and they set to work.[28] The IWFL program insisted particularly on including a woman suffrage clause in any Home Rule Bill that the Commons might endorse. In 1911 the group, "believing that, in the interests of the country as a whole, women ought to be admitted to a share in the government of Ireland," spelled out its specific demand, "that the proposed Home Rule

Bill shall provide for the election of the members of an Irish Parliament upon the Local Government Register, which includes women as well as men."[29]

In April 1912 the Irish M.P.'s at Westminster torpedoed the Conciliation Bill, which would have enfranchised property-holding and taxpaying women, most of whom were single or widowed; immediately thereafter the Home Rule Bill—without any woman suffrage proviso—was brought to the floor. They had, in effect, sold out Irish women for Male Home Rule. "No self-respecting woman can be satisfied with any self-government Bill which makes her sex a disqualification for citizenship," angrily insisted Margaret Cousins.[30]

Thus began an increasingly hostile and violent campaign by the IWFL, during which its members, like WSPU militants in England, organized mass demonstrations, broke windows, and went to jail, insisting that they were political prisoners. In the wake of a media blackout on their activities, IWFL members founded their own news publication, *The Irish Citizen*.

At the other extreme on the Irish question stood the nationalists of Sinn Fein, who advocated an independent Irish republic. This group was a small though increasingly enthusiastic minority in the early twentieth century, but its leaders did advocate full equal rights for women, even promising to restore the Celtic rights of women that the English occupation had obliterated—but only after the revolution. The IWFL leadership was, however, skeptical of such claims for support of women's rights, including suffrage, by leaders of Sinn Fein. In the circumstances, they claimed, Irish women needed the vote immediately.

With the founding in April 1914 of the Cumann na mBan, the women's auxiliary to the paramilitary nationalist Irish Volunteers group (which later became the Irish Republican Army), other suffragists, led by Constance (Gore-Booth) Markievicz, insisted—much like the Irish Party M.P.'s and in opposition to the IWFL—that the cause of national liberation must come first. The IWFL women in turn accused them of "crawling servility" and "slavishness" to their menfolk, thereby precipitating a feud that would long endure.[31] Following the Easter Uprising of 1916, and the republican proclamation, however, the Cumann na mBan would take a far more proactive stance on women's issues, including a leading role in educating women to use the vote they felt they had by then fully earned; in support of Sinn Fein and the aspiring Irish Republic. IWFL activists like Hanna Sheehy Skeffington, whose husband had been murdered by British soldiers during the uprising, spoke on behalf of Cumann na mBan. Irish women ultimately obtained the vote in 1918, and following a bloody civil war, woman suffrage was confirmed in the constitution of the new and independent Irish Free State in 1922.

Of all the national suffrage campaigns, the French effort produced the most disappointing results. Its failure was due not to the hegemonic significance for French republicans of the "universal subject," "Man [*l'homme*]," as some recent historical accounts have suggested, but to sheer, bullheaded political resistance by legislators in a regime that had already established unrestricted male suffrage.[32] Suffrage had again been placed on the political agenda in 1900. Many feminists, especially those of the new generation, agreed with Hubertine Auclert that the reason important reforms in the laws governing women's situation were not being enacted was precisely because women had no political power. As René Viviani, deputy and future prime minister, declared to the assembled delegates at the 1900 Paris women's rights congress: "In the name of my relatively long political and parliamentary experience, let me tell you that the legislators make the laws for those who make the legislators."[33] There was no arguing with this point; women must have the vote to realize the full program of feminist demands.

In Third Republic France, the question of woman suffrage had become enmeshed with an emotional discussion on overall electoral reform through proportional representation, brought on by an ever growing concern for the future of parliamentary democracy under "universal" manhood suffrage. Republican political leaders considered the Third Republic besieged, both on the Catholic monarchist and secular nationalist Right and on the socialist and social revolutionary Left. They feared adding voting women to this mix, especially since they believed most women, as Catholics, would probably vote for right-wing antirepublican candidates.

In contrast to their counterparts in Britain and in Ireland, French feminists never engaged in dramatic public demonstrations or committed deliberate acts of violence against property; only two small incidents of public protest have been recorded. Instead they turned to organizing: in 1909 Jeanne Schmahl, Cécile Brunschwicg, and Marguerite Witt-Schlumberger founded the Union Française pour le Suffrage des Femmes (UFSF), affiliated with the International Woman Suffrage Alliance, to spearhead the drive for the vote. That same year a parliamentary committee headed by sympathizer and Radical Party deputy Ferdinand Buisson reported on a suffrage proposal that would give the vote to all women, single or married, at the municipal level only. Similar to the measure enacted in England in the late 1860s, it would have amended the wording of the 1884 municipal elections law, "tous les français . . . ," by adding the words "des deux sexes." Alternative proposals were to add "sans distinction de sexe" or "hommes et femmes." As of 1913 French feminists were highly optimistic that this measure would pass; in July 1914 they staged their first major suffrage demonstration in Paris.

At the international level, the officers of the International Woman Suffrage Association thought they saw the end in sight. In her presidential address at the IWSA's 1913 congress in Budapest, the American Carrie Chapman Catt voiced an optimism that many among the dominantly European delegates shared:[34]

> When movements are new and weak, Parliaments laugh at them; when they are in their educational stages, Parliaments meet them with silent contempt; when they are ripe and ready to become law, Parliaments evade responsibility. Our movement has reached the last stage. The history of the past two years has demonstrated that fact beyond a shadow of a doubt. Parliaments have stopped laughing at woman suffrage, and politicians have begun to dodge! It is the inevitable premonition of coming victory.

RECONCILING WOMEN'S WORK AND MOTHERHOOD
WITH POPULATION CONCERNS: NATIONAL AND
INTERNATIONAL CONTEXTS

Feminist concerns cut across national boundaries, even though solutions would necessarily have to be found within the particular legal and cultural circumstances that prevailed in both aspiring and established nation-states. In addition to pursuing suffrage and full citizenship, feminists sought solutions to other significant issues that also cut across national boundaries, yet required national solutions. One of the most important was the complex set of issues surrounding women's employment, motherhood, and national population concerns.

Since at least the eighteenth century, some feminists had been defending women's right to employment, and in the early nineteenth century others had added demands for equal pay for equal work, shorter hours, more humane working conditions, and state support for mothers. These issues provoked varying responses from Catholics, socialists, labor leaders, mainstream politicians, physicians, hygienists, and other concerned observers. As male-headed mass political parties and labor unions emerged in the late nineteenth century and began to court supporters, women's employment and its surrounding conditions again became the subjects of intense debate. If some treated women's work for pay as a necessity for sustaining their aspirations to independence, others viewed it either as a tragic consequence of poverty brought on by an economy that failed to sustain male breadwinners, or, more radically, as an unfortunate consequence of capitalist greed. Whatever the perspective, however, most commentators agreed that women's employment had serious implications for their potential as mothers, with respect to both the bearing and the rearing of children. This was quite a different and more specifically physical perspective on motherhood than the societal motherliness or "maternalism" invoked by feminists in their quest for citizenship.

The new element in the equation by the early twentieth century was "depopulation," a peculiarly male form of anxiety about national futures which arose in a context of mounting national and imperial economic and military competition; this competition engaged all the great and would-be great powers of Europe.[35] Significantly, reproduction was the one vital factor that men did not and could not entirely control (though the passage of laws criminalizing abortion and infanticide, and attempts to silence those who promoted or attempted to distribute contraceptive information, suggest the extent to which they tried). Such concerns about national population strength, coupled with concern about "degeneration"—both physical and mental—in the existing population, confronted feminists with a troubling set of concerns that had to be addressed. Especially in France—the first nation in Europe to pass through the "demographic transition" to smaller and better-planned families— but increasingly after 1900 in Germany and Great Britain, members of the educated classes began to fret anew over the possible adverse consequences for their countries of falling birthrates, high infant and child mortality, and, with respect to that specific context, women's health, a linked set of subjects that continued to fuel the knowledge wars.

While the French population stagnated, successive republican coalition ministries stepped in to simplify the legal requirements for marriage, and even encouraged women teachers (who were state employees) to marry and bear children while continuing their teaching careers. Meanwhile, France's competitors had caught up. In Imperial Germany (as also in England some decades earlier), population growth had been spectacular during the last half-century, reaching some sixty million. By 1900 adult women outnumbered men by about a million; marriage for these "surplus" women was quite impossible, and employment a necessity for their survival. In some smaller countries, especially those in Scandinavia, heavy emigration to the New World had begun to deplete an already small population. Spain, defeated in 1898, lost its overseas possessions in Cuba and the Philippines; Spanish army officials designated the Virgin Mary as commander-in-chief, and Spanish intellectuals began to address the neglected education of women. England had suffered defeat in the Boer War in South Africa, and its officials began to doubt the fitness of its military recruits and, by extension, the potentially adverse consequences of British mothers' workforce participation.[36] Leaders of other national governments began to interrogate the physical, mental, and moral development of the workforce, as well as the fighting force, and some even insisted that not only the production of future generations but attention to the "manliness" of men must become a governmental priority, one that required women's sustained presence in the home. Symptomatic of this point of view was the British Minister of War, Lord Cromer; speaking at a 1910 anti–woman suffrage rally in Manchester, he warned his audience: "The German man is manly, and the German woman is womanly. . . . Can we hope to compete with such a nation as this, if we war against nature, and endeavour to invert the natural roles of the sexes?"[37]

In such a climate, debates over women's employment throughout Europe reached a new level of intensity. Opponents of women's emancipation interpreted feminist assertions of women's right to gainful employment, especially in "masculine" professions, as a threat to the demographic and economic well-being of the nation-state as well as to the physical and psychological health of women themselves. Working women, they argued, did not bear and could not raise healthy children. Women's claims for "rights" threatened to interfere with their maternal "responsibilities" to society and the state. What was more, opponents of women's emancipation invoked the threat of "individualist" feminist arguments, arguing that that unmarried "independent" women might become a "third sex." Indeed, they seemed to believe that emancipated women threatened both men's virility and national security.

Throughout Europe women were entering the workforce in unprecedented numbers, and their work was becoming far more visible than before. They could and did work night shifts, thanks first to gas, then to electric lighting. Young single women, who had always predominated in the workforce, were supplemented by increasing numbers of married women and mothers of young children. England and Belgium had seen sizable proportions of employed women since the early nineteenth century. In England alone, some two million women worked in protected industries by 1912. In Germany, especially in the latter third of the nineteenth century, millions of women, mostly young and unmarried, surged into the new industrial labor force. The number of women employed in industrial production alone mounted from 390,000 in 1882 to 1.5 million in 1895 and 2.1 million in 1907. In France, there were nearly 619,000 industrial women workers in 1899, 758,000 in 1911, and 764,000 in 1912.[38]

Industrial employment was by no means the biggest employment sector for women, however; domestic servants were far more numerous, and the white-collar sector was rapidly expanding. Agricultural employment of women remained very significant. But women working in industry were by far the most conspicuous. Employment in factories and workshops placed women in situations where they were clustered together and beyond the direct supervision of the male family authorities. Sometimes, to reach their workplaces, they had to go out alone in the dark. Although working conditions varied enormously from one industry to another, some of the most egregious abuses, from safety issues to sexual harassment, could be found in industrial settings. Such issues alarmed defenders of the male authoritarian family.

During the period 1890–1914, feminists began to disagree publicly over one significant issue: that of state legislation specifically designed— by male legislators—to "protect" industrial women workers in the interest of their reproductive and domestic roles. Such legislation variously barred women as a sex from hazardous industries (such as those engaged in lead-based or mercury-based processing, or phosphorus- related production), restricted their working hours, or prohibited employment on nights or weekends. As historian Ulla Wikander has rightly insisted, "the controversy over protective legislation for women was closely connected to key questions for the women's movement of the time, such as woman's position in the family, her duties in society, the gender division of labour, competition with men for work, woman's nature, [and] motherhood."[39]

In France, proposals for protective legislation for women workers had emerged in governmental circles during the mid-1880s, sponsored by a coalition of social Catholics, disciples of Frédéric LePlay's secular program for social reform, and secular socialists. A pathbreaking 1890 intergovernmental congress, convened in Berlin by the Swiss and German governments, stimulated a flurry of attempts by male legislators in various countries to restrict night and Sunday work for women aged sixteen or over, to limit their working hours, to restrict women's employment in dangerous and insalubrious industries, and to insist on obligatory and unpaid maternity leave.

Feminists objected that work in dangerous industries was bad for workers of both sexes, not only for women. They welcomed obligatory maternity leave for women workers, as did most social democrats—but they insisted unsuccessfully that women on mandatory leave be compensated for their lost wages. Proposals to restrict hours and prohibit night work, on the other hand, were diversely viewed. Some thought, optimistically, that hours restrictions for women in industry would automatically entail the same shorter hours for men's work; others objected categorically to discrimination based solely on the sex of the worker.

After considerable controversy, the French legislature in 1892 broke with its long-held noninterventionist principles to pass a law specifically regulating the employment of adult women. The new law not only restricted the daily hours of women's work in industry but forbade women's employment at night (when work, notably in the printing trades, was often much better paid).[40] Leading liberal republican political economists, armed with alarming medical evidence about the alleged deleterious effects of married women's employment on the survival and development of their babies, sacrificed their noninterventionist principles to argue that *all* women workers needed the state's protection. For some men, whether Catholic or secular republican, there seemed to be more to the agenda than merely "protecting" women workers; Paul Leroy-Beaulieu publicly castigated the feminist movement for diminishing women's interest in marriage and maternity by tempting them with "men's jobs."[41] Émile Faguet, an increasingly regular critic of feminist aspirations, insisted in the *Journal des Débats* in late 1895: "The strong nation, the nation of the future, will be that in which women have no profession other than their traditional role. The access of women to masculine professions is initially the sign, and eventually the cause of a formidable national degeneration."[42]

Both in France and in England rebuttals to such assertions flew thick and fast. Women went to work not for amusement, Marya Chéliga-Loevy retorted, but for survival. Countering antifeminist claims that feminists were "masculine" single women, she pointed out that the majority of women attending meetings of the Fédération Française des Sociétés Féministes were mothers; they well understood the legal liabilities women faced in French society.[43] French socialist feminists such as Eugénie Potonié-Pierre were particularly insistent that women's right to earn their own living was the bedrock of their emancipation. In England, where women's labor in certain industries had been subject to increasing controls since the 1840s, feminists such as Jessie Boucherett and Helen Blackburn expressed their concern that some aspects of the new regulations and special conditions specified by the Factory Act of 1895 would simply discourage employers from hiring women at all: "The kindly legislator who wishes to protect women because they are helpless and ignorant, only makes that helplessness greater by treating them as hopelessly helpless."[44] Many English feminists, including Olive Schreiner, Edith (Mrs. Havelock) Ellis, and Rebecca West, agreed in principle that women—of whatever class—should not live as parasites on men. Indeed, Olive Schreiner's 1899 essay "The Woman Question," which she reworked in her influential treatise *Woman and Labour* (1911), became a classic statement on that subject. Edith Ellis concurred: "Woman," she wrote, "must cease to be either a parasite or a slave and be economically free. To be economically free is to be rid of the necessity to be a prostitute or a parasite."[45]

The British Fabian socialist Beatrice Webb countered feminist opposition to provisions in the Factory Act of 1895 that restricted working hours for industrially employed women, arguing that "in the life of the wage-earning class, absence of regulation does not mean personal freedom." The labor force was sharply segregated, she pointed out, and the fact was that (in England, at least) women only rarely competed with men for the same jobs: "The real enemy of the woman worker is not the skilled male operative, but the unskilled and half-hearted female 'amateur' who simultaneously blacklegs both the workshop and the home."[46] Factory-organized labor and unionization were, in Webb's mind, the keys to proper conditions for women's labor. Home-based production (or "homework," as it was then called), on the other hand, should be formally discouraged.

Disagreements, even polarization, over aspects of protective labor legislation for women became a central feature of international women's congresses during the next fifteen years. For instance, at the International Congress of Women held in London in 1899, the French representative Camille Bélilon briskly defended the principle of women's right to work and reiterated her opposition to protective legislation, which she and her colleagues perceived (perhaps not wrongly, in the French context) as a conspiracy by male workers to handicap women in the labor market and thereby force them back into the household. The combination of political pressures against married women's employment in the wake of the papal statements on marriage and work, coupled with populationist responses to the declining birthrate, led feminists to mount a principled defense. French feminists of all nuances objected to any restrictions on women's work where men's work was not similarly restricted. Comparable positions were taken by Alexandra Gripenberg in Finland, by Emilie Claeys in Belgium, by Wilhelmina Drucker in the Netherlands, and by Paolina Schiff in Italy.

German feminists disagreed. At the congresses, they staunchly supported protective legislation for women, though within the context of an ideally complete sexual division of labor, based on the "special quali-ties" of each sex. Alice Salomon, of Berlin, opposed recent proposals emanating from the Catholic Center Party in Germany that would en-tirely eliminate married women from the labor force, insisting much like her French counterparts that "economic independence from men can alone procure social equality for women." But she did support spe-cial legislation for women, particularly laws limiting their working hours, on the grounds that such measures would soon lead to the inclu-sion of men. Salomon was convinced that there was no real threat to women's employment, and that there were certain "peculiar skills" women had that men didn't. In her view, protective legislation "will produce for the labouring classes what we must struggle to attain for all classes of humanity—a division of work according to sex on account of special qualities; it will put in place of a mechanical or organic division of work a division according to characters and constitutions!"[47]

Speaking after Salomon, the English Fabian socialist Beatrice Webb strongly endorsed certain aspects of protective legislation in the national interest: "We assert that in some cases legislation specially adapted to the particular needs of women, and not of general application, is perma-nently desirable . . . as a question of economic principle." Competition with men was not the issue, she reiterated:[48]

> What injures women as a class in their struggle to obtain employment, is not their occasional competition with men, but their reckless underbid-ding of each other. . . . We must . . . get rid of this idea of sex rivalry. . . . Without the enforcement of such minimum conditions as will protect every set of workers, whether men or women, from physical and mental deterioration, the nation will not reach its maximum strength, and women, therefore, will fail to attain their maximum development.

Despite attempts by Webb and others to recast the issues in dispas-sionate and highly scientific economic terms, sex rivalry in the work-place—and the bad faith of the ostensible male protectors, whatever their political affiliation—remained a burning issue. In France, this issue came to a head in the printing industries during the *fin-de-siècle* period. Male printers staged many strikes in response to the hiring of women in the shops at lower wages, and during one particularly difficult strike ac-tion in Nancy in 1901, the union of women compositors organized by *La Fronde*'s Marguerite Durand sent in some of its members as strikebreak-ers to teach the male printers' unions a lesson.[49]

Selective regulation was another issue. Noting in 1906 that prostitu-tion was not on the list of night work assignments to be prohibited to women, the Russian feminist M. I. Pokrovskaia questioned the motives of both socialists and liberals who supported restrictive legislation: "O male hypocrisy! . . . The protection of women's work is preached not for the sake of the spiritual and physical health *of the woman herself*, but in the name of state, sexual, and family goals. The woman requires protection, not as a person but as a sexual apparatus, as a slave obligated to serve the needs of others."[50]

In tandem with discussions of protective legislation for women workers generally, the Catholic-inspired campaign to eliminate the employment of married women's work quietly continued to gather momentum. In combination with the efforts of trade unionists to impose a "family wage" for men, this campaign had a formidable potential to curb women's independent labor, one which would ultimately be proposed in several Western European countries before World War I. In 1912 a coalition of feminists in the Netherlands successfully defeated an initiative, known as the Heemskerk Law, which would have dismissed all married women schoolteachers and civil servants.[51]

One celebrated case in France around 1912 highlights the nastiness that characterized the printer's union's attempts to combat women's work, as well as the complexity of the questions involved. Emma Couriau, a printer like her husband Louis, had applied to join the local printers' union in Lyon. The French printers had long been among the most vociferous opponents of women's employment. Their skilled trade was increasingly threatened by a combination of technological and organizational changes that allowed employers to recruit women at lower wages. Not only did the Lyon local deny Emma Couriau's application, despite the fact she was at the time earning union wages, but its members voted to expel her husband because he had "permitted" his wife to work. French feminists rallied behind the Couriaus as they appealed the decision at the national level. Only the feminists rallied to Emma Couriau's support, scheduling a mass rally in late December 1913 with the slogan "Do women have a right to work?" The socialist women "refused, fearing, according to their leader Louise Saumoneau, to engage in 'antimasculinist' action."[52] Although the leadership of the national union (the Confédération Générale du Travail, or CGT) ultimately supported Emma Couriau's right to work and to join the union, incidents like this confirmed French feminists in the view that they must obtain the vote in order to break men's hold on political power.

At the 1913 international women's congress held in Paris, delegates again debated the issue of protective legislation for women. It was not regulation as such that feminists opposed, but specifically regulations they considered to be discriminatory and disadvantageous to women workers, including those who were married. They particularly criticized the 1906 Bern Convention, which had called on all governments to prohibit women's night work. In a lengthy report, Louise Compain recounted reservations reported by correspondents throughout Europe. In Denmark feminist organizations and women's unions had succeeded in persuading their government to reject the Bern accords. In the Netherlands, Compain cited the case of a Maastricht industrialist who, following governmental adoption of the convention, had swiftly fired all his married women workers. In France, however, earlier hour limitations on women's work had led to the establishment of a ten-hour day for men, women, and children alike. There, at least, Beatrice Webb's hope of achieving uniform regulation for both sexes had been realized. Other countries would adopt uniform hour laws a few years later.

After heated debate, delegates to the 1913 congress voted to reject the conclusions of the congress's commission report, which had endorsed protective legislation for women. The counterresolution argued "that the exceptional laws regulating the work of women, should be abolished and replaced by a law of equal protection to be applied to the whole working population without distinguishing between the sexes."[54] According to one feminist commentator, Jane Misme, this decision flew in the face of the opinion of "practical feminism"; but according to another, Jeanne Crouzet-Benaben, it was necessary in order to command support for the subsequently discussed principle of "work for equal pay."[55]

There were two exceptions to the protective legislation issues that divided feminists. These concerned proposals for paid maternity leave, both before and following childbirth, and for the endowment of motherhood. On the first proposal, feminists from every shade of the political spectrum to the left of the Catholics tended to agree; on the second, a range of opinions could be identified.

The issue of how parturient women should be sustained during the late phases of their pregnancies and the formative years of their infants was—and remains, along with the more recent and radical questions as to who should care for children, and why mothers only—a fundamental question with respect to societal organization. By the early twentieth century, two schools of thought had arisen: first, the more conventional view, that mothers, married or unmarried, should be supported by the breadwinner fathers of their children, and, second, the opposing view that motherhood should be "endowed" by the state, and mothers and infants supported by a "mother's wage," financed by taxes on the generality of (mostly) male wage earners. This latter position threatened patriarchal wisdom about the necessity of male authority in the family. Both these views made the assumption that caring for infants was women's work. Even most socialist women, who advocated community-financed day care for working mothers once children had reached a certain age, were of the opinion that babies needed their mothers, and that the community should support them economically.

The complexity of this issue can be grasped only by exploring the debate over motherhood among feminists at the end of the nineteenth century, and placing it against claims then being made by socialists that all women should be incorporated into the workforce, as well as against allegations by antifeminists about the ostensible masculinization or "unsexing" of the "new woman." "The feminist vision of motherhood," which some now refer to as "maternalism," was not, as historians Gisela Bock and Pat Thane have made clear, "the acceptance of a 'traditional' female role, but a call for reform—from some even for revolution—in the situation of mothers, of women and of society at large. Rather than having motherhood imposed upon them, they sought to keep it within women's own control and to improve its conditions."[56] They also sought to deploy it as an emancipatory strategy within a "relational feminist" framework. Within the context of national state formation and development, where population and economic growth were becoming issues of widespread concern, this position constituted a trump card, one which could be played with great efficacy in all sorts of issues. All maternalist feminists insisted on women's differences from men, their "uniqueness" as a sex, grounded in their motherly nature (even if they had no children of their own), as their central qualification for full participation in sociopolitical decision making. A woman's identification as mother—in contrast to that as wife, which still subordinated her—offered an incontrovertibly powerful platform on which to base claims for emancipation and societal recognition.

Even British proponents of woman suffrage in England, such as Millicent Garrett Fawcett, elaborated a maternalist position, as is suggested in the published version of her speech "Home and Politics": "If men and women were exactly alike, the representation of men would represent us; but not being alike, that wherein we differ is unrepresented under the present system." It was precisely because women were mothers, either actual or potential, and designated as the homemakers and child rearers, that they required representation—and participation in governmental affairs: "We want the home and the domestic side of things to count for more in politics and in the administration of public affairs than they do at present."[57] Social housekeeping and what Fawcett referred to as "true womanliness" were becoming the order of the day. Both were grounded in women's capacity for mothering or caretaking.

Policy-oriented issues concerning motherhood featured prominently on the agenda at the April 1896 Congrès Féministe International (International Feminist Congress) in Paris, where they provoked a confrontation among three factions: those who espoused legalizing paternity support suits by unmarried mothers (which were illegal in France); those who, like Léonie Rouzade, advocated state recognition and financial incentives for mothers; and those who opposed state intrusion of any kind into the reproductive arena and called for unrestricted access to contraceptive information and devices. "Motherhood is women's principal social function and deserves to be subsidized by the State," argued Rouzade.[58] These conflicting claims would foster significant political consequences. The month following the feminist gathering, the statistician and demographer Dr. Jacques Bertillon and his associates founded the Alliance Nationale pour l'Accroissement de la Population Française (National Alliance for the Growth of the French Population), and only three months later the neo-Malthusian anarchist Paul Robin founded the Ligue de Régéneration Humaine (League for Human Regeneration) expressly to promote the practice of birth control by the working class as a weapon against the French state.

In 1896 the Swedish writer Ellen Key also began to lecture on "The Misuse of Women's Power [Missbrukad Kvinnokraft]." Her arguments offered another controversial contribution to continental feminist thought about motherhood and work. In the published version of these lectures, Key argued that women's energy should not be "misplaced" in outside work (as Clara Zetkin and others in the Second International argued) but instead should be channeled into a new and powerful type of mothering. Key's theoretical work was not confined to short articles and newspapers, but also took the form of book-length meditations, such as The Century of the Child (originally published in Swedish, 1900), Love and Marriage (1904), The Woman Movement (1909), and The Renaissance of Motherhood (English edition 1914). These works were circulated, quoted, translated, and argued about throughout Europe and America; Key's thinking had a major impact on feminist and antifeminist thought and action in Germany, in Scandinavia, and in the English-speaking world.[59]

Key's arguments were in some respects closely related to the social motherhood arguments promulgated by Jeanne Deroin and some other mid-nineteenth-century continental advocates of women's emancipation. But Key gave them a distinctive twist, as well as a pessimistic edge.

She invoked both women's biological nature and the extant division of labor between the sexes in the family, according to which women not only bore but also reared the children. Concerned about what she saw as a growing number of "emancipated" women who wished to avoid having children in order to "live their life," Key countered that "real liberation for women is . . . impossible; the only thing possible is a new division of burdens."[60]

Key diverged from other women writing on the question of state-organized, state-subsidized institutional child care for women in the workforce. Such proposals as those of Léonie Rouzade had roots in the visions of social thinkers from Plato to Charles Fourier, and in the 1890s they were again stimulating discussion and a limited amount of action as national governments began to address the sociopolitical consequences of women's employment. Key had visited some child-care institutions established in response to such demands, and what she saw horrified her, thus provoking her exploration of the complex problems posed for women by motherhood in modern Western industrial societies.

The strategic significance of Key's contribution lay in her successful synthesis of a rigorously "relational" approach to sociopolitical problems, based on acknowledgment of women's difference, with "individualist" claims for women's fulfillment and self-realization. Key proposed that women could achieve their maximum development as individuals through their contributions to society as mothers. But she also argued that the conditions for motherhood must be totally restructured in order for this to occur, and that motherhood must be revalued and sanctioned, both politically and economically, by the nation-state.

Economic support of individual women by individual men during their childbearing years, which Key viewed as the ultimate foundation for women's subordination, should be removed one step from individual male control by vesting it in the government. Though supported by the collectivity, child care should take place in the home, in the biological mother's charge, not in institutions; it should not become a direct responsibility of the collectivity. Indeed Key argued—developing the logic of earlier "civic motherhood" arguments—that the state ought to recognize formal training of women for this role as women's equivalent of military service for men.

At the same time, she called boldly for open recognition of the sexual side of love, including acknowledgment of women's erotic nature and sexual pleasure, a feature of her arguments that endeared her to commentators such as Havelock Ellis in England but scandalized those who righteously defended conventional morality. She also promoted eugenic and evolutionary thinking with regard to motherhood, even as she strongly opposed what she called "amaternal" thinking: "Motherliness is not a spontaneous natural instinct, but the product of thousands of years not merely of *child-bearing*, but also of *child-rearing*; . . . it must be strengthened in each new generation by the personal care which mothers bestow upon their children."[61]

Reframed in this way, motherhood became "a political strategy" for feminist activism. In a variety of European countries feminist activists established institutions designed to assist and empower women as mothers, and to address the causes of maternal and child distress, especially among the poor and working class. "Arguing for the centrality of the maternal role in society," historian Annarita Buttafuoco has argued, in examining the Italian case, "meant foregrounding the responsibility of the state towards mothers and children as integral, essential elements of the nation itself."[62] The resulting philanthropic activity can be seen less as charity than as politics. In Italy in the 1890s a group of Milanese women organized the Lega par la Tutela degli Interessi Femminile (League for the Defense of Women's Interests) to press for a maternity insurance fund based on the mixed support of women workers, workingmen's organizations, wealthy women, and the state. Related fund experiments in other cities, including Turin and Rome, led to proposals (voiced at the Union Femminile's first national congress in 1908) for a national maternity fund. Such a fund was finally established in 1912 by the government, following much pressure from feminists, who still had no vote. But the measure took a form that both feminists and many women workers found unsatisfactory. The latter refused their cooperation, even striking to make their point. Employers were also reluctant to cooperate. Only after a number of changes were made in 1917, heeding women's complaints, did the fund begin to realize its promise.

Proposals to support motherhood even more broadly—by freeing women from unwanted dependence upon men—were most vociferously promoted in Germany, where partial post-partum maternity benefits for women industrial workers had been enacted as sick benefits, beginning in 1878, under Bismarck's worker-insurance program. The Bund für Mutterschutz (League for the Protection of Mothers), led by Helene Stöcker, Lily Braun, Adele Schreiber, and their associates in the radical wing of the German women's movement, urged in its 1905 *Manifesto*:[63]

> All protection of children that does not at the same time protect mothers is inadequate . . . for the mother is the source of the child's life and essential to its survival. Whatever guarantees her rest and care during her delivery, ensures her economic security in the future, and shields her from

the scorn ... of her fellow human beings, creates the basis for the welfare of the child.

In order best to combat infant mortality, the Bund urged that motherhood be protected not just for married women but also for unmarried mothers, whose newborns died in far greater proportion due to their mothers' lack of resources. This stand outraged the defenders of conventional morality.[64]

Leaders of the Bund für Mutterschutz did support women's employment, though they did not insist on it as a necessity. This group repeatedly petitioned the German Reichstag, arguing not only for more extensive maternity provisions for industrially employed women, but also that the government should recognize maternity as a national service for which *all* mothers should be duly compensated. "It is the duty of the state," they affirmed in a 1907 petition, "to create new ways which will allow the mother to work without damage being done to the whole nation."[65] They argued that working women who took maternity leave must be able to return to their jobs without penalty, receive full financial compensation for the period of their leave, and collect the payments in their own right. Citing not only women's own health, but the importance of healthy soldiers to defend the nation, the Bund called for "protection of the mother during the time she gives to the state the citizens upon whose existence the state rests."

Emboldened by this debate, other German feminists began to take radical positions on a variety of associated issues. In 1907 the leadership of the once meek Bund Deutscher Frauenvereine (Federation of German Women's Associations, or BDF), presided over by Marie Stritt, who was also a member of the Bund für Mutterschutz, developed a major statement, "Goals and Tasks of the Woman's Movement." This program did not endorse full state support for mothers, including the unmarried, but in other respects it was as radically woman-centered as that of the Mütterschutzbund: "The demands of the Woman's Movement are based on the existence of thoroughgoing mental and physical differences between the sexes. It deduces from this fact that only by the cooperation of men and women can all the possibilities of cultural progress be realized."[66] Upholding the sanctity of marriage, the BDF nevertheless insisted that "the vocational work of women is an economic and moral necessity"; its leaders demanded a single standard of sexual morality, called the fathers of illegitimate children to account, denounced regulated prostitution, and insisted on obtaining the vote at every level of society—in the church, in the community, and in the state.

In 1910 Marie Stritt's leadership of the BDF was challenged over her advocacy of access to birth control for all women. A coalition of more conservative women defeated her bid for reelection. In other countries, however, feminists succeeded in keeping such radical notions on the agenda for discussion. In Norway, Katti Anker Møller advocated both state support of motherhood and contraceptive access and women's control over their own bodies: "We love motherhood, we want to promote motherhood, but it should be voluntary and the responsibility should be all ours."[67]

The motherhood trump would be played even more dramatically by feminists within the population-conscious political climate of Third Republic France, just as the government was beginning to address the ongoing decline in the national birthrate.[68] Shortly after 1900, the feminist freethinker and birth-control advocate Nelly Roussel, a colleague of Paul Robin, would turn the debate in a new direction by eloquently insisting not only on state support for motherhood, but also on women's right to control their own fertility.

Nelly Roussel, married and mother of three young children, emerged as a powerful public speaker for the French feminist movement in 1903, following her letter to La Fronde on the subject of population politics:[69]

> Doesn't it seem to you, ladies, that our "repopulators" consider woman a bit too much like a sort of machine for producing cannon fodder, which must work without a break until it is completely worn out. . . . Such a conception of their sublime role cannot but disgust all conscious mothers! Feminism should proclaim above all else "liberty for motherhood," the first, the most sacred, and nevertheless—what an inconceivable aberration—the least discussed and the least respected of liberties.

Roussel's subsequent interventions took the form of published letters, articles, theatrical presentations, and collections of articles. She appealed to women of all classes to "declare war on today's society," and called for a complete revision in the French laws governing marriage. In one celebrated oration, at a 1904 feminist gathering denouncing the centennial of the French Civil Code, Roussel even invoked the threat of a birth strike against the patriarchal state and its populationist schemes:[70]

> Beware, oh Society! The day will come . . . when the eternal victim will become weary of carrying in her loins sons whom you will later teach to scorn their mothers or daughters destined—alas!—to the same life of sacrifice and humiliation! The day when we will refuse to give you, ogres, your ration of cannon-fodder, of work-fodder, and fodder for suffering! The day, at last, when we will become mothers *only when we please*.

Like Ellen Key and the leaders of the Bund für Mutterschutz, Roussel centered her arguments for women's emancipation in motherhood—

demanding that its terms be rendered far more favorable to women. Like Key, she wanted "freedom" for women, but she emphatically insisted on the political implications of the connection between women, children, and the male-dominated and increasingly militaristic nation-state. Like Rouzade, she demanded the establishment of motherhood as a "social" or state function with concomitant rights.

Roussel took every opportunity to criticize *masculinisme*. Critical of socialist party opposition to birth control, she addressed her arguments to women of every class, and worked closely with French birth-control advocates in their efforts to extend contraceptive information to women of the working class. From Roussel's perspective, all women were "oppressed"; women of all classes pursued the same goal of emancipation, if with different arguments. Women, she insisted, had far more in common than did men of different classes, because whatever their class, they shared a common oppression. Women were, in her view, still society's "eternal victims."[71]

OFF WITH THE GLOVES: CHALLENGING MALE PRACTICES

It is, of course, true that feminists did not succeed in their bid for political rights before 1914. But they had succeeded in one very significant respect: all Europe was responding to the challenges that women's emancipation posed. This is not an inconsiderable achievement. Redefining motherhood was one aspect of their breakthrough; challenging male practices was another.

In 1912 Lily Braun addressed the problems women faced in coupling motherhood with "professional and work conditions that necessarily were attuned to the man's needs and capabilities." She pointed to the crushing load created by this triple burden of remorseless maternity, undervalued housewifery, and underpaid employment:[72]

> The women's movement started so harmlessly; its pioneers never tired of assuring us that they would not touch any institution hallowed by tradition and custom, and it turns out to be revolutionary in the profoundest sense of the word. And, instead of arriving at its final goal, once its first demands—the economic, legal, and political equality of the woman—have been fulfilled, it will only then begin to face its greatest task. On its solution will depend not only the future of women but the future of the human race.

Prophetic words, indeed! Braun's history may have been incomplete, but her analysis cut to the core of the challenge now posed by European feminist analysis and activism. Indeed, it had become apparent that the woman question was also the man question; both masculinity and femininity, as previously constructed in European societies, and their synergistic relationship, in all its problematic aspects, was henceforth due for radical renegotiation.

All the talk about motherhood, spiritual or corporeal, when juxtaposed with national populationist and imperial expansionist goals, made some men extremely nervous. In France, some began to moan about the possibility of "race suicide," and in England others articulated still more ominous threats to female demands for self-determination. In Imperial Germany, the leader of the National Liberal Party, Friedrich Naumann, waxed lyric in his own way on the subject of motherhood: "All other women's work makes way for the work of motherhood. . . . The youthfulness of nations depends on whether their girls want to become mothers."[73] During a royal visit to Königsberg in 1910, Kaiser Wilhelm himself lectured German women on their duties to the nation:[74]

> They should learn that the primary task of German women lies not in the area of assemblies and associations, not in the attainment of would-be rights, by which they could be like men, but in quiet work in the home and in the family. . . . It is a matter not of . . . attaining one's goals at the expense of the fatherland, but of concerning oneself solely and exclusively with the fatherland.

Such men did not mean the same thing by "motherhood" that most maternalist feminists did, irrespective of their particular cultural or national context.

Indeed, expressions of male anxiety that women's reproductive capacity—even their sexuality—might escape from men's control seemed increasingly conspicuous. In France and Norway, as the arguments of Nelly Roussel and Katti Anker Møller underscored, making babies as a duty to others, whether on behalf of the male-dominated church or the male-dominated state, was a role that some feminists categorically rejected, as much as they would otherwise honor and value maternity. Thus it was that in the early years of the twentieth century, some feminist critics in European societies became even bolder and more explicit in naming the obstacles that faced women with respect to sexual responsibility and reproductive control.

Feminist critics joined wholeheartedly in what became a war of ideas and knowledge over issues surrounding sexuality, birth, and social responsibility that had, by 1900, emerged definitively from behind a veil of taboo. The fight to end state-regulated prostitution and to confront men's violence toward women in particular had energized feminists not only to combat the double moral standard but also to attack male sexual practices. They deliberately reclaimed women's control over their lives as sexual beings, over their own fertility, and over their children, born and unborn. These were demands about individual choice, about individual autonomy for women; thus they had revolutionary societal implications, and they would be vehemently contested. Some demanded autonomy for woman-as-female-individual, while others demanded their share of human autonomy, a freedom that transcended and submerged any specific sexual identity.

Many women mobilized their very considerable intellectual skills to critique prevailing male practices with respect to marriage, sexuality, violence, and militarism. And they did not mince words. It is particularly among this group of feminists, many of whom still drew on "maternalist" notions with respect to other issues, that one can locate a series of thoroughly libertarian "individualist" arguments on behalf of women's emancipation. In England, especially, where feminists could build off the previous generation's campaign against regulated prostitution and male sexual violence, some radicals developed eloquent arguments for complete sexual emancipation.

Mona Caird's dissection of marriage and motherhood as currently conceptualized in England was devastating. In her 1894 novel *Daughters of Danaus* she traced the itinerary of Hadria, a bright young woman whose promise and talent were ultimately crushed by societal demands of marriage and motherhood, enforced by unremitting pressure from family members. Having fled from her entire family, like Ibsen's Nora, Hadria resists her sister-in-law's appeal to return home, arguing that:[75]

> Motherhood, in our present social state, is the sign and seal as well as the means and method of a woman's bondage. It forges chains of her own flesh and blood; it weaves cords of her own love and instinct. . . . Motherhood . . . , among civilized people, represents a prostitution of the reproductive powers, which precisely corresponds to that other abuse, which seems to most of us so infinitely more shocking.

In Italy, the much-translated novel *A Woman* by Sibilla Aleramo, published in 1906, echoed this critique of motherhood in its story of an unhappily married woman who sought existential freedom at great personal cost:[76]

> Why do we idealise sacrifice in mothers? Who gave us this inhuman idea that mothers should negate their own wishes and desires? The acceptance of servitude has been handed down from mother to daughter for so many centuries that it is now a monstrous chain which fetters them. . . . What if mothers refused to deny their womanhood and gave their chil-

dren instead an example of a life lived according to the needs of self-respect?

In France, the most outspoken feminist critic of male-devised controls on women's sexuality and reproductivity was undoubtedly the young physician Madeleine Pelletier.[77] In a context in which the concern over a declining birthrate was triggering severe resistance to feminist demands, Pelletier began to articulate a series of uncompromising claims for women's reproductive freedom. Claiming chastity for herself, she eloquently argued the case for the destruction of the male-dominated family, a feminist education for girls, woman suffrage, and for a woman's right to love as she pleases and to abortion as a "last resort," when other preventive measures proved inadequate. As things stood in France, Pelletier pointed out in her 1912 tract *L'Émancipation sexuelle de la femme* (The Sexual Emancipation of Woman), "woman is only an instrument man uses for his pleasure; he consumes her like a fruit." Unwanted pregnancy and shame should not be women's inevitable fate. She asserted that "it is up to the woman, and the woman alone, to decide if and when she wants to be a mother."[78] Pelletier explicitly denounced male sexual violence against women, challenging French society to accord them complete sexual emancipation as individuals, and she called for the repeal of Article 317 of the French Penal Code, which outlawed abortion.

Debate in Germany proceeded along somewhat parallel lines.[79] Feminists quickly responded when populationist physicians (such as the Dutch doctor S. R. Steinmetz, writing in a German-language periodical) condemned feminism as an obstacle to the numerous progeny required from "the most competent and talented women" by "humanity, our race, our culture," and when German governmental authorities began enforcing Article 218 of the new Civil Code, a clause that outlawed abortion, and succeeded in increasing the number of convictions.[80] In 1908, the Bund Deutscher Frauenvereine debated whether or not to call for the repeal of Article 218, and although the decision was negative (moderates had packed the meeting by inviting representation from religious women's groups, both Protestant and Jewish), the BDF did agree to support a modification of the penalty and to medicalizing abortion decision-making in ways that would include other women besides the reluctant mother in the process. Apparent throughout the debate was that feminists agreed across the board that both abortion and infanticide were "desperate responses to the sexual victimization of women by men."[81] When in 1913 two neo-Malthusian socialist physicians demanded a "birth strike" (reminiscent of the threat posed earlier in France by Nelly Roussel), the feminists of the Bund für Mutterschutz, who demanded state support for all mothers, including the unmarried, were less than enthusiastic. Social Democratic women, led by Clara Zetkin, found this suggestion equally objectionable, opposing such a strike as counterproductive to the ultimate victory of the proletariat, and even defending monogamous marriage. The abortion-repeal issue would not soon be settled.

Sex education and contraception took on more significance as feminist issues. In 1897, the Swiss feminist and abolitionist Emma Pieczynska-Reichenbach published a sex education manual for girls, *L'École de la pureté* (The School of Purity), which was translated into thirty-four languages and found many imitators.[82] Young women needed to know what lay ahead of them; physiological knowledge, Pieczynska-Reichenbach argued, could be combined with moral purity. In the Netherlands, the suffragist physician Aletta Jacobs promoted the use of the diaphragm, or Dutch cap (called the Mensinga technique) by her female patients. Writing in the pages of *Zhenskoe delo* (1910) in Russia, Sofiya Zarechnaya linked birth-control measures to women's emancipation. Women's "choice" would increase the value and dignity of maternity, argued some; others insisted that "quality" of children must take precedence over "quantity."

Venereal disease, considered a blight on the health of women and children, offered another salient feminist target. German feminists launched a campaign for required premarital health examinations, which would help to protect women from the ravages of venereal disease—spread, they believed, mainly by unclean husbands who had engaged in promiscuous and unprotected sexual activity prior to marriage. Concern about women's health, blended with issues over fitness to reproduce, surfaced in Norway, where the eugenicist reformer Dr. Alfred Mjøen petitioned the Norwegian parliament, demanding amendment of the marriage laws to include an alternative proposal for a premarital declaration of sound health by both parties to the marriage.[83]

The issue of venereal disease and its transmission by men to unsuspecting women was posed more bluntly by the young English suffrage militant and law graduate Christabel Pankhurst. Following a series of sex scandals that rocked Britain during the period of suffragette militancy and persecution, Pankhurst issued a scathing attack on male vice. Syphilis and gonorrhea carried dire consequences for innocent women and children. "The cause of sexual disease," Pankhurst insisted, "is the subjection of women. Therefore to destroy the one we must destroy the other. . . . Here we have the woman question in perhaps its most urgent and acute form."[84] The essence of Pankhurst's solution was "Votes for

Women and Chastity for Men." Going still further, Christabel Pankhurst called for the education of men to their duties: "Fatherhood, fa-
ther-craft, and the duties and responsibilities of paternity are, or rather
ought to be, the question of the day. . . . If men were conscious of their
paternal duty prostitution would be at an end."[85]

Campaigning against sexual vice and male violence against women
raised a more general issue—that of organized male violence. War and
militarism had for some time been the targets of extensive feminist
criticism. In the 1870s and 1880s feminists such as Marie Goegg and Virginie Griess-Traut, who had become active in the peace movement, had
initiated protests in times of war, presenting women, the givers of life, as
peacemakers. In the late 1890s a very significant critic of male violence
in war emerged, the Austrian writer Bertha von Suttner. Challenging the
double standard in sex and love, and revulsed by society's hypocritical
castigation of unwed mothers and their "illegitimate" offspring, Suttner
developed her critique of organized warfare: "While you glorify death
and even murder so much that you know nothing greater and proclaim
nothing more loudly than the fame of battles—there exists among you
nothing that is more reviled, nothing that must be done more secretly
than the creation of life."[86]

Suttner's powerful best-selling novel, *Lay Down Your Arms!* (first
published in 1889 as *Die Waffen nieder!* and widely translated), developed her critique of male violence, its facade and its futility, by presenting the story of a young woman, married to an Austrian military officer,
who through the experiences of her widowhood and motherhood came
to condemn the senseless slaughter war entailed. She led her readers behind the curtain of military pomp and circumstance to explore the ugli-
ness of war's residue:[87]

> No more thunder of artillery, no more blare of trumpets, no more beat of
> drum; only the low moans of pain and the rattle of death. In the trampled
> ground some redly-glimmering pools, lakes of blood; all the crops de-
> stroyed, only here and there a piece of land left untouched, and still cov-
> ered with stubble; the smiling villages of yesterday turned into ruins and
> rubbish. The trees burned and hacked in the forests, the hedges torn with
> grape-shot. And on this battle-ground thousands and thousands of men
> dead and dying—dying without aid.

Addressing these horrors, she launched a celebrated campaign for disarmament that would eventually be honored by the Nobel Peace Prize.

Such efforts inspired a number of other more conspicuously woman-
centered ventures, such as the League of Women for International Disarmament (founded in 1897 by Princess Gabrielle Wiszniewska), whose

manifesto called on women to undertake a "war against war," and another group led by the German activist Margarethe Lenore Selenka, which organized an international petition with a million women's signatures to endorse the aims of the May 1899 Hague Peace Conference.[88] Many ardent feminists were also active in the peace movement, though not all peace activists were feminists.

In direct response to such feminist claims, in the early twentieth century a new and nervous male backlash began to manifest itself. In Germany, Heinrich von Treitschke, in his two-volume study *Politics* (1899–1900), denounced the idea of female emancipation as "calamitous" and defended monogamous marriage, private property, and the male-headed family as the necessary foundation of the state.[89] In France, in a series of yearly antifeminist diatribes, some of which won prizes from the Académie Française, Théodore Joran denounced feminism, along with socialism, as "an anti-French disease." Joran's works regularly featured arguments such as, "Feminism is above all else revolt, discord, disorganization, jealousy of our masculine nature."[90] The cult of womanhood, he reminded his readers, was a French invention, the destruction of which would effectively lead to war between the sexes.

More unsettling than either the bluster of Treitschke or the bravado of Joran were works that blended expressions of warrior mentality with antifeminism and even misogyny. Reassertions of masculinist warmongering in the early twentieth century were sometimes constructed as responses to the "feminization" of modern society. A particularly virulent expression of this perspective was Filippo Tommaso Marinetti's "Futurist Manifesto," published in *Le Figaro* (Paris) in 1909:[91]

> We will glorify war—the world's only hygiene—militarism, patriotism, the destructive gesture of freedom-bringers, beautiful ideas worth dying for, and scorn for women. We will destroy the museums, libraries, academies of every kind, will fight moralism, feminism, every opportunistic or utilitarian cowardice.

Was this mere adolescent bluster, or was it evidence of "a crisis of masculine identity"?[92] Must male identity be built, as Otto Weininger's work suggested, on the repression of the feminine element? And what of the feminine element? Another Futurist writer, Valentine de Saint-Point, argued that both men and women of the early twentieth century lacked virility. What women needed was not "rights" but an infusion of spilled blood, of instinct; she called for a resurgence of heroic warriors, warrior women, and ferocious mothers. Then masculinity and femininity would reassume their proper places. "*Let Woman rediscover her cruelty and violence, which assure that she will tear apart the van-*

quished." Sentimentalism, softness, compassion, humane values were the enemy: feminist claims, to Saint-Point, incarnated these. "Feminism," she concluded, "is a political error . . . a cerebral error, which woman's instinct recognizes as such."[93]

Echoing the concerns of Bertha von Suttner, and seemingly speaking to the assertions of Marinetti and Saint-Point, Olive Schreiner spoke eloquently of women's difficult relation to war:[94]

> Men have made boomerangs, bows, swords, or guns with which to destroy one another; we have made the men who destroyed and were destroyed! We have in all ages produced, at an enormous cost, the primal munition of war, without which no other would exist. There is no battle field on earth, nor ever has been, howsoever covered with slain, which it has not cost the women of the race more in actual bloodshed and anguish to supply, than it has cost the men who lie there. *We pay the first cost on all human life.*

War would end only, in Schreiner's view, "when intellectual culture and activity have made possible to the female an equal share in the control and governance of modern national life." The woman-centered rationale of a Schreiner would find many advocates in the century's second decade. But not enough to stave off disaster. During the nineteenth century, there may have been fewer and shorter wars than previously, but arms budgets constantly mounted. "'Peace,'" historian Sandi Cooper has pointed out, "was, in effect, a period of preparation for war."[95]

Writing in opposition to the three-year military-service law proposed in France, Fanny Clar tried to warn her audience about the prospects ahead: "We are before a precipice, over the edge of which the European nations dizzily lean and are about to slide, if . . . they don't straighten up and pull back from the chasm. . . . War is hideous!"[96] The following year, at a huge rally in support of woman suffrage held at the National Theater in Rome during the May 1914 congress of the International Council of Women, the French attorney Maria Vérone passionately called for a "war against war."[97] Then on 28 June 1914 (Vidovdan, the Serbian nationalist anniversary), a Serbian nationalist assassinated the Austrian archduke, heir to the throne, in Sarajevo. Soon thereafter, the interlocking diplomatic alliances fell into place, the guns began to blast, and the blood began to flow.

The Twentieth Century

"In the past," argues the sociologist Gisela Kaplan, "social questions, including women's liberation, have always disappeared from the political agenda when major political events seemed to demand a nation's complete attention."[1] "Disappeared" may put the case too mildly, and "social questions" hardly captures the political import of the issues raised by feminists. It would seem more accurate to label women's emancipation a "political" rather than a "social" question, and to substitute the term "erased" for "disappeared." These substitute terms better describe what happened (at least temporarily) to feminist claims under conditions in which women, even voting women, still wielded little formal political power and where feminist views remained unwelcome. This has been the case in European societies well into the twentieth century, the era of war, revolution and backlash par excellence.

The guns of August 1914 signaled the end of one turbulent era and the beginning of another, an era in which the politics of nation-state building and international rivalries at once acknowledged and began to threaten the possibilities for success of European feminism in myriad and unforeseeable ways. It almost seemed as if those who controlled the guns were attempting to dynamite closed the fissures in the crust of patriarchal institutions that feminists had succeeded during the previous decades in forcing open so wide. Could it be that one of the unspoken objectives of this war was to dam off, even to quench, the dangerous, molten outpouring of feminist aspirations that had so captured the attention of Europeans, and indeed, of the world?

What more compelling political event could there be than war? The new, highly mechanized and increasingly technological modern warfare of the twentieth century, a warfare that requisitions massive national resources in the service of armed might, has repeatedly and powerfully served—perhaps far more than earlier wars—to reposition the sexes by refocusing all eyes on male endeavor and male valor in the service of the nation-in-arms. Feminists were well aware of its implications for relations between the sexes. Two British antiwar suffragists summed up war's effect in early 1915: "In war time only men matter."[2] In 1923 the Austrian feminist activist and writer Rosa Mayreder remarked: "Theoretically, war represents the most extreme product of masculinity, the final and most terrible consequence of absolute masculine activity. The naturally feminine cannot assert itself as something with equal rights beside this greater external intensification of masculinity."[3] As non-combatants in wartime, women were symbolically thrust "behind the lines," even as they remained subject to mobilization in supporting roles to serve the national interest. Both during the war and in its aftermath, women, like men, would be subjected to new and innovative forms of surveillance and control.[4]

Couple the effects of war with those of the Russian Revolution, the surfeit of women in the postwar European population, the intensified efforts at national mobilization, and the factional disputes between male-dominated parties of the Right and of the Left (some would say, of tradition and movement, but this dualism is perhaps too simple) for control of the state that characterized the 1920s and 1930s, in tandem with economic upheaval and mounting militarism that would provoke a second World War, and the momentum of feminism would be seriously disrupted, its course abruptly changed. Owing to this complex of conditions, Part III of this book might be entitled "Feminism Besieged."

Besieged, yes; but also partially triumphant. For it was not the case that feminism achieved no advances during the first half of the twentieth century. Surely, the granting of suffrage to women in most European states counts as a considerable victory, as does the election of a few women to public office, and their promotion to government executive positions.[5] Delivering the first speech to be given by an elected woman representative in a German parliament, Marie Juchacz, perhaps too optimistically, claimed:[6]

> Political equality has given my sex the possibility to fully develop its powers. . . . The Woman Question, as things stand now in Germany, no longer exists in its old sense. . . . Political struggle . . . will play itself out in other forms from now on. We women now have the opportunity to let our powers have an effect within the framework constructed by ideology and by freely chosen party groupings.

As a committed social democrat Juchacz was perhaps too sanguine that extant ideologies and party groupings would sufficiently promote emancipatory ends for women. Nevertheless, legislatures composed of mostly men and a few women did secure the enactment of programs to support needy mothers, the consolidation of women's access to higher education and professional opportunities, the amendment of marriage laws, the implementation of divorce laws, and ultimately, the demolition, later in the century, of legal restrictions of women's reproductive freedom. Exceptionally gifted women "worthies," activists and writers, won new kinds of public recognition for their contributions, ranging from honorary university doctorates and government orders of merit to the Nobel Prizes for Peace (Bertha von Suttner, 1905; Jane Addams, 1931), Literature (Selma Lagerlöf, 1909; Grazia Deledda, 1926; Sigrid Undset, 1928), Chemistry (Marie Curie, with her husband, Pierre, 1903), and Physics (Marie Curie, 1911; Irène Joliot-Curie, with her husband, Frédéric, 1935). Even so, one must not underestimate the extent to which such women's "progress" and recognition, along with feminist gains, would be constantly threatened, as the somber essays on "the nationalization of women" in the fifth volume of *A History of Women in the West*, edited by Françoise Thébaud, make abundantly clear.[7]

Indeed, from the 1920s through the 1930s, and the beginnings of a new war, European feminists confronted a variety of difficulties that were closely tied to national and international politics, and to the nationalization of women. Not the least of these was the expansion of government efforts to design a national population politics, based in the maternal bodies of women.[8] Defenders of the "traditional" (i.e., male-dominated) family would propose restrictions on women's educational opportunities at the university level, which feminists would vigorously contest.[9] Women's workforce participation—their "right to work"—was effectively consolidated during this period, and concurrent efforts undertaken to ease the burdens of their domestic labor (as well as to celebrate it) were paralleled by efforts to promote and consolidate women's participation in labor unions and professional organizations.[10] Nevertheless, particularly with the onset of the severe economic depression that began in 1929, antifeminist opponents continued vociferously to oppose women's employment outside the home in the name of jobs for men. They preferred what they considered to be a "natural" gendered division of labor, in which male household heads earned the bread and dictated the terms, while women raised the children and did the cooking and the housework, subordinate to the orders of their menfolk. They refused to believe that this "natural" order of things could also be culturally constructed.

On the cultural front, concerns about "restoring" the old prewar gender order would also mark the antifeminism of many "traditionalists."[11] The knowledge wars would continue as the new "science" of psychoanalysis began to consider women's psychological health—or lack of it— with respect to men and maternity. And in literature and the arts the development of "modernism," and abstract and "avant-garde" forms of cultural expression, would blur, even obscure, many of the feminist insights that had been so eloquently conveyed by writers of both sexes in the earlier realist and naturalist literary modes.[12]

By the end of World War I, prohibitions on association for women had lapsed in most European countries, and women's organizational activity dramatically increased. The "women's movement" consisted of an increasingly broad band of specialized groups, of which only a few highly visible councils and associations could be considered "feminist." Increasing numbers of women's organizations developed within organized religious bodies, Protestant, Catholic, and Jewish.[13] They likewise developed in a variety of secular settings ranging from charitable enterprises to patriotic societies. Moreover, in countries that had enfranchised women, newly formed political parties of all persuasions from Right to Left began to exhibit interest in recruiting women and carefully channeling their political activity. The rivalry of feminists and socialists throughout Europe developed in new forms, following the Bolshevik Revolution in Russia and the aggressive campaign to recruit women sponsored by the Communist Third International.[14] Noncommunist feminists stepped up their efforts to join together across national borders, dramatically expanding the number of international feminist and/or women's associations, and consolidating their joint efforts both to promote laws that would secure married women's nationality, end regulated prostitution, and defend women's employment at all levels, and to work for peace, appropriating to the extent that they could do so the framework of the League of Nations.

Part III of this book, consisting of four chapters, explores these developments in the history of European feminisms from World War I to the beginning of the Cold War.

In Chapter 9, I focus on how the earlier feminist campaigns were short-circuited by the outbreak of war and by the ensuing Russian Revolution. Many feminists opposed armed violence and militarism, and the active commitment of a cohort of feminists to antiwar activities and to ensuring a lasting peace form an important topic in the history of feminisms during this period. In parallel, the partial triumphs of patriotic feminists in influencing several critical aspects of the Treaty of Versailles offer new insights into the process and outcome of the peace negotiations, showing what women could—and could not—accomplish when they attempted to influence public policy making at the highest levels.

With the triumph of the Bolsheviks during the Russian Revolution,

the new Union of Soviet Socialist Republics enacted—at least on paper—
an unprecedented set of changes designed to transform the household,
family, and work, even as its government deliberately silenced the prewar generation of feminists, most of whom opposed the Bolsheviks.
Echoing the long-standing party line of the Second International, "feminism" as such was treated scornfully by the leaders of the new revolutionary Russia, who continued to insist that scientific socialism provided all the necessary answers to the "woman question."

In Western and Central Europe, many new nations and a few old ones
enfranchised women, leading to a dissolution of the massive prewar
campaign for suffrage and many shifts in—and fragmentation of—
feminist energies. Serious disagreements arose as to the appropriate path
to follow, and the politics of "equality-versus-difference" was born. The
antifeminist backlash would reemerge with particular force in medical
and psychoanalytic circles.

Chapters 10 and 11 explore the difficulties faced by feminist activists
in a series of national settings, with particular reference to fascism,
which can be understood, despite its "modern" aspects, as both an anticommunist and an antifeminist reactionary politics. The "gender" of
fascisms throughout Europe seems unmistakably well marked.[15] Chapter 10 considers developments in postwar England and in Italy before and
during Mussolini's installation of a fascist regime in 1922, then in Austria and Hungary, the successor states of the old Austro-Hungarian Dual
Monarchy, and finally in Germany, from the Weimar Republic to the
Third Reich. Chapter 11 continues this exploration of feminisms embedded in national political cultures, examining further the relationships between feminisms, nationalisms, socialisms, and burgeoning an-
tifeminisms in the varying scenarios provided by a sequence of smaller
and midsized nation-states often neglected in accounts of European history, namely Portugal, Ireland, Spain, and Sweden.

Chapter 12 shifts to consider the activity and successes of European
feminists in working within and influencing the new international organizations, the League of Nations and the International Labour Office,
established in the wake of the Treaty of Versailles. Here I insist on the
dramatic effectiveness of feminist activists in pressing for a League inquiry into the status of women in its member countries, their significant
interventions on the side of peace and disarmament. But I also highlight
the increasing commitment by the leaders of international organized
feminist groups to a new terminology of "humanism" rather than "feminism," as the menace of fascism and Nazism begins to threaten far more
than "merely" the rights of women. Antifascist "Popular Front" coali-

tions formed by progressives and socialists with national communist political parties had the effect of shifting or inflecting the vocabularies of many feminists as well as their political emphases. In contrast to its resurgence after 1918, organized international feminism barely survived World War II, since not only was its aging leadership disorganized through dispersement, but some leaders were also imprisoned or executed, and precious records of its achievements and difficulties were, all too frequently, lost.

With the outbreak of World War II, women in a variety of European countries took a prominent through usually unacknowledged role in the movement to resist fascism, which was very often spearheaded by the communist parties.[16] Increasingly, women—especially younger women—were defining themselves as active participants in their communities and countries, but without particular reference or awareness of a politically independent feminism that had fought so long to obtain the rights that could now be almost taken for granted. The Cold War pitted communist states against capitalist states, both claiming "democracy" as their own; as women became increasingly incorporated into these disputes, feminists would experience increasing difficulties in attracting an independent following or garnering the recognition they deserved for past achievements.

The Epilogue reviews the problem of history and memory for feminism following the end of one dramatic and difficult historical period and the beginning of another.

9

Feminism Under Fire

World War I, the Russian Revolution, and the Great Backlash, 1914–1930s

When war broke out on the European continent in early August 1914, it halted the momentum of the burgeoning international women's movement, just as it derailed the now better-known socialist workers' movement. Most feminists in France, England, and other European countries placed their suffrage efforts on hold. Few remained as intransigent as the women of the Irish Women's Franchise League (IWFL), who resisted strenuously:[1]

> The European war has done nothing to alter our condition of slavery. It has only served to make us realise more deeply and poignantly than ever the utter helplessness and defenselessness of our position as political outcasts in attempting to stem the tide of masculine aggression and brute force.

FEMINIST DILEMMAS: LOYALTY TO THE NATION? OR OPPOSITION TO THE WAR?

At the outset of the war, when it was a question of rallying round the flag, individuals who identified with their countries found it exceedingly difficult to resist the enthusiasm for war. Patriotic outrage and eagerness for decisive action even infected many feminists, who devoted themselves conspicuously to the patriotic effort, perhaps with an eye to "earning" or "being rewarded by" the vote. This was initially true for women in Belgium and France, the countries invaded by the German army, and for their British allies. In parallel with Emmeline and Christabel Pankhurst and Millicent Garrett Fawcett in England, Cécile Brunschvicg and Marguerite Durand (the latter closely associated with the French prime minister René Viviani) called on feminists in France to support the Allied war effort. Gertrud Bäumer, president of the BDF (Federation of German Women's Associations), adopted an even stronger pro-war position, as did her counterparts in Austria. It was supposed to be a short war, after all. Only after several months, as victory for either side remained elusive, did serious doubts begin to find expression.

By late 1914 other feminists and dissenting radical socialists had launched parallel actions against the war. In early November 1914 the British suffragist Mary Sheepshanks protested in the IWSA publication *Jus Suffragii* against "wholesale self immolation," "massacre and devastation," the "orgy of blood" unleashed by the war, and called for women to "earnestly study the causes of the present criminal madness."[2] Clara Zetkin addressed an "unauthorized" appeal "To the Socialist Women of All Countries," which did not survive the German censorship of *Die Gleichheit*. From Stockholm, where she had gone from Berlin, the Russian Bolshevik Aleksandra Kollontai echoed Zetkin's (and Maria Vérone's) appeal, calling for a "war on war" in mid-November 1914. Echoing the earlier antiwar critiques of Bertha von Suttner and others, she insisted that "the war is not only booty, power, and devastation, not only suffering, unemployment, and poverty; it is also the unleashing of all the wild passions among humanity, it is the triumph of raw force, it is the justification for all the cruelty, conquest, and degradation which militarism brings in its wake."[3] In February 1915, the German feminist and pacifist Lida Gustava Heymann published her appeal "Women of Europe, When Will Your Call Ring Out?":[4]

> Towns of the highest civilisation, homes of simple human happiness, are destroyed; Europe's soil reeks of human blood. The flesh and blood of men will fertilise the soil of the waving cornfields of the future on German, French, Belgian, and Russian ground. Shall this war of extermination go on? Women of Europe, where is your voice? . . . Can these things not rouse you to blazing protest?

In April 1915 C. K. Ogden and Mary Sargent Florence published their eloquent pamphlet *Militarism versus Feminism: An Enquiry and a Policy Demonstrating That Militarism Involves the Subjection of Women.*[5] Censorship of publications could not entirely stifle expressions of feminist antiwar sentiment.

Government leaders quickly discovered that women were far from irrelevant to the war effort; soldiers alone would not suffice. During the first months of the war, for the "Defense of the Realm," British government leaders imposed martial law and called on women to keep the home fires burning and the war economy going. Some governmental authorities also suspended protective labor laws (including restrictions on hours and night work for women), placed soldiers' wives under police surveillance (to ensure that they did not spend their separation allowances on drink), reestablished or strengthened systems of regulated prostitution to "service" soldiers, or, alternatively, placed curfews on women in order to protect soldiers from venereal disease. In Cardiff, Wales, five prostitutes were court-martialed under the Defense of the Realm Act for breaking curfew and sentenced to sixty-two days' detention. Feminists singled out such restrictions: in *Votes for Women*, one British suffragist observed acidly that "it does not seem to have occurred to the military rulers of Cardiff that in protecting the troops from the women they have failed to protect the women from the troops, or that they might have accomplished both ends by closing the streets to soldiers instead of to prostitutes."[6] From this suffragette perspective, there was but one solution to such violations of human rights: woman suffrage.

French populationist postcards promoted procreation by solders during their home leaves, and at the other extreme, contributors to French publications battled over whether babies born to French women raped by German soldiers during the invasion could be considered French citizens.[7] (The consensus was that they could be so considered.) German military authorities installed condom-vending machines for their troops, while the imperial government formulated population policies to stimulate the birthrate, curb the circulation of contraceptive information, and enforce legal action against abortionists and their clients. In fact, as historian Cornelie Usborne has remarked, "the wartime powers of the military authorities and the growing regimentation of public life offered the Wilhelmine state an opportunity to intervene in decisions of family size and sexuality which today would be regarded as an intolerable interference with basic human rights."[8] Defeat and the socialist revolution which established the Weimar Republic staved off enactment of other intrusive aspects of the populationist program. But the agenda was clear. The German physician Alfred Grotjahn put the point forcefully: reproduction was "the only female contribution to war and military power which equals . . . men's wartime national service"; it was "indispensable for our national ascendency."[9]

Early in 1915, convened by Dr. Aletta Jacobs of the Netherlands and Jane Addams from the United States, feminists gathered despite great obstacles at The Hague for an International Congress of Women, "to discuss what the women of the world can do and ought to do in the dreadful times in which we are now living." As Jacobs insisted in the conference call, "we feel strongly that at a time when there is so much hatred among nations, we women must show that we can retain our solidarity and that we are able to maintain a mutual friendship."[10] She and her associates called on governments to acknowledge the necessity of involving women in political decision-making and called for a "conference of neutral nations as an agency of continuous mediation for the settlement of the war."[11] In order to facilitate their discussions, the organizers insisted that the congress not discuss the explosive issue of blame for starting the war, focusing instead on feminist demands for principles to guide a peace settlement. Their efforts in this direction, accompanied by a series of visits to government leaders on both sides of the war, were applauded by many statesmen at the time. Socialist women of the Second International separately contested the war, meeting at Bern in March 1915, though with far less fanfare and fewer attendees (25–28) than the suffragists. Clara Zetkin, Louise Saumoneau, and their associates, however, continued to insist—with Lenin—that capitalism and imperialism, lying behind and propelling militarism, constituted the real enemy. Socialists, women and men alike, remained firmly committed to viewing male hegemony as a secondary problem.

However they might feel on the subject of capitalism, feminist women expressed heartfelt skepticism about militarism as such, its *masculinisme* and its violence, especially its violence against civilians. At the 1915 Hague Congress Lida Gustava Heymann insisted pointedly on an aspect of wartime male violence that others hesitated to name: "We know that women are being raped and we protest against it, for worse than death, worse than hell, worse than demons is the rape of women. . . . We do not want statements saying that we women are protected by war. No, we are being raped by war!"[12]

In England the British suffragist Helena Swanwick denounced militarism in these words: "War is waged by men only, but it is not possible to wage it upon men only. All wars are and must be waged upon women and children as well as upon men." To Swanwick, war exemplified the "physical-force argument," which by valuing physical force over moral suasion effectively ensured male domination over women: "If destructive force is to continue to dominate the world, then man must continue to dominate woman, to his and her lasting injury."[13] Severing her long association with English suffragists, especially Millicent Garrett Fawcett, who, in company with the Pankhursts, had unconditionally endorsed the war effort, Swanwick threw her energies into the Union for Democratic Control and the Women's International League. In Dublin, also opposing the Pankhursts' pro-war stance, Francis Sheehy Skeffington made an even more provocative assertion: "War is necessarily bound up with the destruction of feminism," and "feminism is necessarily bound up with the abolition of war." "The woman who does not . . . discourage recruiting, has an imperfect understanding of the basis of the feminist movement. The woman who deliberately encourages recruiting is betraying that movement—though her name be Christabel Pankhurst."[14] Even Sylvia Pankhurst disagreed with her older sister's pro-war stance. She critiqued the British government's call for women's war service, given that the same government still refused women full citizenship. She also called on feminists to monitor the conditions for national service by women, and to ensure that women obtained not only the vote but fair wages, inclusion in the adjudication of labor disputes, and safeguards concerning work hours and conditions. Women's loyalty to the nation must, in Sylvia Pankhurst's view, be materially rewarded.[15]

On the Continent, governments were far less tolerant of antiwar dissent. In France, one of the most outspoken antiwar protesters, the schoolteacher Hélène Brion, was arrested and tried for treason in 1918 by a French military court for questioning the war and distributing antiwar propaganda. At her trial she proclaimed: "I am first and foremost a feminist. And it is because of my feminism that I am an enemy of war. . . . War represents the triumph of brute strength, while feminism can only triumph through moral strength and intellectual values."[16] But as in England and Germany, feminists could be found on both sides of the issue: in Italy, the attorney and suffragist Teresa Labriola (later credited as "the foremost theoretician of Latin feminism") threw all caution to the winds, waxing philosophical about the ethical nation—the state—and the reconfiguration of gender relations that must characterize it in the future.[17]

After four bloody years, the loss of some ten million men dead and some twenty million wounded, the warring powers concluded an armistice on 11 November 1918. Following the Americans' infusion of resources and manpower on the side of the Allies in 1917, Imperial Germany had collapsed, and its allies were not far from doing the same. Even the winning nations were strained to the limit of their endurance. "At least," remarked the IWSA's Mary Sheepshanks, "organised international suicide is over."[18]

INFLUENCING THE PEACE SETTLEMENT

As the victorious Allies assembled in Paris to draw up the terms of the peace, IWSA women activists from the Allied nations determined to make their presence felt. Noting the extent to which organized labor interests were gearing up to do likewise, the clear-sighted Mary Sheepshanks spelled out in *Jus Suffragii* "What Women Should Demand of the

Peace Congress": assuring woman suffrage; defending women's economic freedom; putting a stop to government-regulated prostitution;
raising the age of consent; and enacting a radical reform of marriage laws,
including the question of married women's nationality. "Who," she
asked, "is going to safeguard the claims of women" if not women themselves?[19]

Representatives of the IWSA-affiliated Union Française pour le Suffrage des Femmes (UFSF) wrote to President Woodrow Wilson in January
1919 requesting a meeting with him, which was granted on the opening
day of the Interallied Women's Conference (10–16 February). The delegates asked for Wilson's help in establishing an International Women's
Commission parallel to the International Labour Commission, as well
his support in gaining political representation; in the meantime the
feminists organized a de facto women's committee to draft specific proposals. They organized meetings with virtually all the Allied plenipoten-
tiaries to gain support for the Women's Commission, took tea with the
French president Raymond Poincaré and his wife at the Elysée Palace,
and met with the French prime minister Georges Clemenceau, who
countered the proposal for a Women's Commission proposal with the
suggestion to include women in the work of the Peace Congress wherever their interests seemed pertinent. This idea prevailed; the Supreme
Allied Council authorized "that women's organizations could be heard
by Commissions occupying themselves especially with questions touching on women's interests."[20] "Women's interests" in this construction
meant, however, the special interests of women and children, not issues
of war and peace or women's suffrage. Thus, the feminists' agenda would
not be fully realized, and their cries of victory must be viewed as relative.
Even this concession from the Allies, however, must be viewed as a major breakthrough for the principle of women's active participation in
public affairs.

The men of the Allied powers kept their word. The following month
(18 March) a joint delegation of feminists from the International Council
of Women and the International Woman Suffrage Association appeared
before the Commission on International Labour Legislation, chaired by
the American labor leader Samuel Gompers; their visit made front-page
news in Paris and was heralded by Madame Jules Siegfried as "a red letter
day in the history of the feminist movement."[21] On 10 April, a third
delegation of feminists met with the Commission on the League of Nations, chaired by Woodrow Wilson. At this meeting, they asked that
women be included in all permanent commissions of the League, as well

as in the bureaus and official delegations. They further demanded that countries entering the League renounce the trade in women and children and support women's freedom of choice in marriage, and they asked that the League issue a statement of support for the principle of woman suffrage.[22] Provision would be made for women's inclusion, but the commission considered the latter requests as raising issues that would unduly complicate the launching of the League.

The Allied leaders did deliver on a few of the feminists' demands. The final version of the Treaty of Versailles (Preamble and Articles 389 and 427) did stipulate certain provisions for equal rights, notably equal pay for equal work (strongly demanded by the IWSA and a group of activist women known as the International Correspondence, coordinated by the Dutch feminist Martina G. Kramers), and it made specific provision for the inclusion of women in the work of the International Labour Organization and the League of Nations.[23]

Another group of feminists—participants in the Second International Congress of Women, meeting in Zurich in mid-May 1919 (the successor conference to the 1915 meeting at The Hague)—expressed their displeasure with other major aspects of the treaty, the terms of which were released to the public during their conference. In their view, the draft treaty met neither the conditions laid down earlier in Woodrow Wilson's Fourteen Points nor the guiding principles ratified by the feminist internationalists in 1915 (which many feminists considered to be the underpinning of the Fourteen Points):[24]

> By guaranteeing the fruits of the secret treaties to the conquerors, the terms of peace tacitly sanction secret diplomacy, deny the principles of self-determination, recognize the rights of the victors to the spoils of war, and create all over Europe discords and animosities which can only lead to future wars.

Unfortunately, they were right! These feminist internationalists founded the Women's International League for Peace and Freedom, an organization based in Geneva that continues its work to this day (and about which more will be said in Chapter 12).

In some European nation-states, women's displays of patriotism and loyalty to the war effort, along with their sacrifices, would be rewarded by the vote in 1918–19, and women voters would begin to stream to the polls. Adult women outnumbered men in a number of countries, and the gap would only be increased by the enormous number of military casualties. In March 1917, the British House of Commons had endorsed a partial extension of the parliamentary vote that included single women over

thirty who held either property or university degrees. In the elections of
1919, however, the Tories (conservatives) won, to the considerable distress of some woman suffrage advocates.

In France, following the conclusion of peace in 1919, the Chamber of
Deputies would hold its first formal debate on the woman suffrage question. Pro-suffrage deputies, secular and Catholic, by an overwhelming
margin amended a proposal for municipal suffrage to grant the vote at
every level to "all French citizens without distinction of sex." The
Chamber of Deputies unanimously endorsed this sweeping measure.
However, the feminist celebration would have to wait. The French Senate stonewalled, successfully and repeatedly blocking the Chamber's repeated passage of woman suffrage measures for nearly thirty more years,
fearing that women would vote on the right and against the republic.
Even without French women voting in 1919, an all-male electorate
handed right-wing and nationalist forces a sweeping victory in the first
parliamentary elections to follow the armistice.

Denmark had proudly enfranchised its women in 1915. In Italy the
legislature voted favorably on a long-promised woman's suffrage bill in
1919, but it never became law. In 1920 Belgium enfranchised the mothers and widows of soldiers killed in the war. For Irish women, a war of
independence, followed by a bitter civil war, lay ahead.

In the defeated nations, first Weimar Germany, then the new states
(Czechoslovakia, Austria, Hungary, Poland) created by the peace treaties
from the remains of the Austro-Hungarian Empire, women along with
men were given the vote by fiat in the new democratic state constitutions. In the new Weimar Republic of Germany, forty-one women were
elected to parliament and for the first time took their place as actors on
the national political stage; the National Assembly would include some
very well-known feminists, such as Alice Salomon, Gertrud Bäumer,
and social democratic women such as Luise Zietz and Marie Juchaz. Indeed, the Weimar government could boast of the highest percentage of
elected women in all Europe. Very quickly, the patterns of female political activism and voting became the subject of intense and often un-
friendly scrutiny (as we shall see in Chapters 10 and 11).

REVOLUTION IN RUSSIA AND THE TRANSFORMATION
OF HOUSEHOLD, FAMILY, AND WORK

Amidst the flurry of anticipation and celebration surrounding the war's
end and suffragist victories in Western and Central European countries, a
series of extraordinary political events in Russia would have a profound

impact on the future of European feminisms. Coupled with the impact of the war, these events, which became known as the Russian Revolution, would irrevocably change the context in which feminist demands would be articulated, weighed, and considered in Western and Central Europe, as well as the context in which noncommunist socialists would develop their own programs with respect to the emancipation of women.

In early 1917, the Russian Empire—fighting on the Allied side—collapsed under the weight of severe challenges brought on by the World War, including disastrous shortages of goods, inflation, and famine. On International Women's Day (23 February on the Russian calendar; 8 March on the Western calendar), women began to strike, calling for bread and peace. Their agitation soon drew reinforcements from men in the labor unions and various dissident factions who began to articulate political demands. In contrast to the uprising of 1905, when the czar's troops had fired on demonstrators, however, in 1917 the army went over to the side of the protesters. Within a very short time, the emperor Nicolas II had abdicated, and a provisional government had been formed.

The new government lifted the prohibitions on speech and assembly and promised a constituent assembly and civil equality—without mentioning sex as a category to be addressed. This "omission" was taken up by feminists of the League for Equal Rights, which then called on women to come together in support of their own political emancipation. Within only a few weeks, on 19 March, the League organized a huge demonstration of women who marched through the streets of the new Petrograd, "replete with two brass bands playing the Marseillaise, red banners, placards and several 'Amazons on horseback'" (as historian Linda Edmondson has described the events), to the Tauride Palace to meet with the new government. Dr. Poliksena Shishkina-Iavein issued the feminists' challenge: "We declare that the Constituent Assembly, in which only one half of the population will be represented, can in no wise be regarded as expressing the will of the whole people, but only half of it." Two days afterward, a delegation of feminists received assurance that woman suffrage would be part of the proposed electoral law, but they insisted that this assurance be provided in writing. In April an All-Russian Women's Congress convened to form a Republican Union of Democratic Women's Organizations, despite efforts by Bolshevik women to disrupt the proceedings.[25] Writing in *Zhenskii vestnik*, the feminist Mariia Pokrovskaia confronted the Bolsheviks, objecting to their program and denouncing their methods.

Indeed, this scenario of revolutions that "forgot" about the women was becoming an all-too-familiar feature in European history. What was different in 1917 was that, first, the new Russian government had finally included the women, giving the right to vote to "Russian citizens of both sexes who have reached the age of twenty by the day of the elections."[26] The other significant difference was that Russian feminists had competition on the political Left. In the ensuing months the women's organizations and publications all supported the new government and the continuation of the war effort, which included the formation of the controversial and much-publicized "women's batallions."[27]

The promised elections were eventually held, but the Constituent Assembly was as quickly dissolved. In mid-October 1917 the Bolsheviks seized control of the government, insisting that they would conclude a separate peace with Germany, much to the consternation of Imperial Russia's former allies in the West. A new and more extreme kind of revolution had arrived. The moment had come for the communist revolutionaries to deliver on their longtime promises, not the least of which was that of emancipating women as part of the great project of reorganizing society. The Bolsheviks, even Aleksandra Kollontai, were not (as we have seen) feminists as such—and like other Marxist socialists in the tradition of Bebel and Zetkin they routinely castigated feminists as "bourgeois" and "separatist," with a rhetorical finality that precluded further discussion. Class struggle and class solidarity remained their ideological and strategic priorities. Once in control, the Bolsheviks, who renamed themselves as the Communist Party, dissolved independent feminist organizations, shut down feminist publications, and silenced feminist activists: only a few resisted the Bolsheviks; the rest evidently withdrew into private life or left the country. Indeed, the new rulers consigned the very memory of the rival feminist movement and its adherents to oblivion, even as they appropriated parts of its program. "From the Bolshevik standpoint," Edmondson argues, "the feminists had done no more than tinker with the system; equality between the sexes was the exclusive achievement of Soviet rule."[28]

To give the Bolsheviks credit, they did accomplish an extraordinary set of reforms in the position of women—at least on paper—particularly in the area of marriage and family law, which they completely secularized and refashioned. They established divorce by mutual consent and civil marriage by decrees in mid-December 1917. The Family Code promulgated in December 1918, offered, according to historian Wendy Goldman, "the most progressive family and gender legislation the world had ever seen."[29] By November 1920, the Bolshevik regime had legalized and medicalized abortion on demand and had envisioned steps to address the troubling issue of prostitution, insisting on the necessity of independent paid employment for all women.

In late 1917 Aleksandra Kollontai had been appointed People's Commissar for Social Welfare and set about making maternity a "social function" of the state, protecting women as workers, and promoting their equal rights. Her program for maternity insurance, encompassing "a fully paid maternity leave of eight weeks, nursing breaks and factory rest facilities, free pre- and post-natal care, and cash allowances" has been praised as "the crowning legislative achievement for women workers" of the entire regime.[30]

In mid-November 1918, just a year after the Bolshevik seizure of power, a new congress of women was convened at the behest of Kollontai, Inessa Armand, and their collaborators, to confirm that women's emancipation—Bolshevik-style—was no mere separatist project. At the All-Russian Congress of Working Women and Peasants, Lenin himself called for an end to women's domestic slavery and drudgery, to the double standard of sexual morality, and to prostitution. He viewed women as "the feminine section of the proletarian army," deserving entirely equal rights, including speedy divorce and the equal recognition of children whether born in or out of marriage. Women must be fully involved in the revolutionary effort. "The aim of the Soviet Republic," Lenin declared, "is to abolish . . . all restrictions of the rights of women." "Our law wiped out, for the first time in history, all that made women inferior."[31] Serious challenges remained, however, among them the questions of educating a mostly illiterate populace, of combatting poverty as well as ignorance, of liberating women from domestic drudgery by developing "social economy." But the commitment was total, as Inessa Armand pointed out soon thereafter:[32]

> As long as prostitution is not destroyed, as long as the old forms of the family, home life, childrearing are not abolished, it will be impossible to destroy exploitation and enslavement, it will be impossible to build socialism. If the emancipation of women is unthinkable without communism, then communism is unthinkable without the full emancipation of women.

Some enthusiasts were ecstatic, opponents appalled, at Kollontai's 1918 tract *Communism and the Family* (the substance of her speech at the 1918 congress), in which she laid out the Bolshevik program, arguing the case for social construction of what were once considered immutable institutions:[33]

> We have only to read how people lived in the past, and we shall learn immediately that everything is subject to change and that there are no customs, nor political organizations, nor morals, which remain fixed and inviolable.... The family ... has frequently changed its form.

Away with "superannuated rubbish," she declared. Had they read further, critics might also have found much to admire in Kollontai's vision of the future, in which the family was not "abolished" but transformed—and women's roles were redefined by the availability of public kitchens, public laundries, and state provision for child care so mothers could honorably support themselves and their children—and where women and men could be "lovers and comrades," outside structures that formalized relationships characterized by domination and subordination. This was a vision in which the bugbear prostitution—legalized or clandestine—should surely cease to exist. In other words, a monogamous free union, beyond property considerations, and with a full range of societal support services was Kollontai's ideal for women—and men. Lenin's speech to the conference of nonparty working women in late September 1919 confirmed this vision. Lenin insisted particularly on the "unproductive," "savage," and "arduous" character of housework. "Even when women have full rights, they still remain downtrodden because all housework is left to them."[34]

These demands were, of course, firmly rooted in nineteenth-century European progressive thought, well before Bebel, Kollontai, or Lenin had taken them up, but the leadership of the new Union of Soviet Socialist Republics intended to make their realization national policy. Given the unfavorable conditions prevailing in 1918, such a program would prove exceedingly difficult to realize, as Lenin, Kollontai, and others freely acknowledged at the time. The distance between revolutionary intent and the profound social change necessary to realize its objectives would remain far greater than anyone at the time could imagine.

In mid-1919, following the Eighth Party Congress, the Communist Party finally (though, it appears, reluctantly) conceded the establishment within the Central Committee of a women's bureau or "Section for Work among Women," known as Zhenotdel, the goal of which was to coordinate with all other ministries and to organize the political education and professional mobilization of the "backward" masses of women, in order to bring them aboard the communist project. It was headed first by Inessa Armand, then, following her death in late 1920, until 1922 by Kollontai. Meanwhile the civil war raged on, and living conditions continued to erode dramatically.

With the establishment of the Zhenotdel, these fiercely committed communist women fought for additional support within the party, extracting a strong endorsement of their work from the Ninth Party Congress in March 1920, founding a theoretical publication, *Kommunista*, to supplement the more popular *Rabotnitsa*. During the summer they managed to acquire support for a secretariat at the Comintern (Communist International) level, following the Comintern's split with the more moderate social democrats, who now controlled what was left of the Second International. A fierce enemy of the social democrats, the German independent socialist Clara Zetkin was by this time working in Moscow, where she set up the secretariat in late 1920 to press for international agitation and propaganda among women, publishing her celebrated interview with Lenin, in which he commissioned her to develop the program for international work. "You are to work out the leading theses on communist work among women," Lenin told Zetkin. "You must lay stress on the unbreakable connection between woman's human and social position and the private ownership of the means of production. This will draw a strong, ineradicable line against the bourgeois movement for the 'emancipation of women.'"[35]

"We want no separate organisations of communist women!" Lenin concluded. But that did not mean that there would be no women's organizations whatsoever. Systematic work among women must be done to bring them on board the Bolshevik project, but this work would be securely lodged within the framework provided by the Communist Party. Thus, Lenin added, "we must have our own groups to work among them, special methods of agitation, and special forms of organisation. This is not bourgeois 'feminism'; it is a practical revolutionary expediency."[36]

Within Russia Zhenotdel staff members set to work, and outside Zetkin encouraged affiliated communist parties to embark on efforts to recruit women. The new publication *L'Ouvrière* in France, for example, was founded by the new Parti Communiste Français (PCF) in response to her orders. But even in Russia lack of budgetary resources continually hampered the effectiveness of Zhenotdel's efforts to organize and train women, and opponents in the party at the local level continued to suspect "feminism" at the core of Zhenotdel efforts and refused to support them. In early 1922, Kollontai was removed from her position at Zhenotdel for political reasons and was reassigned to the Soviet trade delegation to Norway. Her publications on "winged eros," or higher forms of erotic love between men and women, in 1923 sealed her fate in Russia, and her work and ideas increasingly fell into discredit. In 1923 the Zhenotdel was accused of "feminist tendencies" by the Twelfth Party Congress. "Deviationism" became increasingly suspect, as the communist regime, especially following the death of Lenin and the advent of Stalin, committed itself to salvaging the nuclear family, to population growth, and to enforcing "socialism in one country" by totalitarian means. Even Zetkin's international operations would be shut down in 1926, although she continued to fulminate against the "bourgeois" tendencies of the noncommunist socialists in the West. The 1926 Marriage Law would mark a giant step back from the audacious Family Code of 1918. In 1930 the Zhenotdel was dissolved on the grounds that it was no longer needed.[37] Ultimately, the visionary changes in women's situation promoted by Kollontai and her associates would never be fully realized in the USSR, though the vision endured long after institutional pressures and budgetary shortfalls had irrevocably betrayed it.

Echoes of the Bolshevik experiment with respect to women resonated throughout Europe, both in the short-lived revolutions that broke out in Munich, in Vienna, in Berlin, and in Budapest, and in the backlash regimes that succeeded these revolutions, particularly in Eastern Europe. Feminists in Western Europe were eager to see for themselves what miracles the Bolsheviks had wrought. To some, the reality seemed less appealing than the promise. Like Hélène Brion, Louise Bodin, and other socialist-feminist militants, the cross-dressing French suffragist physician Madeleine Pelletier had enthusiastically welcomed the Bolshevik victory; as a delegate to the 1920 Socialist Party Congress at Tours, Pelletier voted to join the new Third (Communist) International. She reviewed the works of Lenin and Trotsky in *La Voix des femmes* (Louise Bodin's radical feminist publication, which the new communist-affiliated Parti Socialiste Unifié (PSU) subsequently abandoned in favor of *L'Ouvrière*). In late July 1921, lacking an official French passport, but endorsed by the French communists, Pelletier left for Russia "disguised as a woman" (as she put it), sneaking across international borders with the help of party supporters. Once there, she encountered famine, disease, abandoned children, misery of all sorts. She met with Kollontai, and disputed her view that citizens owed children to the state. She disapproved of the Zhenotdel, opposing (as she had in France) the idea of separate sections for women. She was appalled at the sexist attitudes she encountered in the new Bolshevik utopia, as much as by the truly serious problems that confronted the new regime. She had rejected sewing as her contribution to volunteer labor demanded of foreign visitors. "At all the women's gatherings I attended, it was a question only of organizing children's colonies . . . it was a matter of saving the children from the Volga regions from death. Nevertheless, in the men's meetings, one discussed many more general subjects, which meant that the women's meetings had less interest."[38]

Chastened and relieved, Pelletier returned to Paris, where she published a memoir of her trip. Her "adventurous journey" convinced her that she was, strictly speaking, a "theoretical revolutionary" though no less an "integral feminist," an anarchist who hated the bureaucratic procedures that continued to exist in the new Russia, as well as the seeming fatalism of the people in the face of appalling conditions and emerging governmental terror. Writing in La Voix des femmes, she concluded that in Russia women's emancipation would be the last battle to be won. By 1925 the French Communist Party, increasingly subject to the dictates of Moscow, acted to marginalize Pelletier; by 1926 she had broken with the party, returning to the more congenial milieu of French anarchism.

If the reality was harsh and the Bolshevik government under Stalin increasingly diffident about throwing its resources behind women's emancipation, the mirage created between 1917 and 1920 remained powerful and assiduously promulgated in Western Europe. By the early 1930s the Russian-born Austrian writer Fannina Halle had drawn up an impressive account of "the humanization of woman" in her book Women in Soviet Russia, first published in German (1932), then in English (1933). Echoing the official line, she insisted that "the process of emancipation now going on in Russia differs from all earlier ones in the recorded history of mankind in that it is carried out according to plan and on an unprecedented scale. . . . Here for the first time the feminist question is conceived as part of the great social question."[39] The British feminist Winifred Holtby, who was particularly enthusiastic about the prospects opened to women by the introduction of socialized housekeeping and child care, pointed out that "the communist theory has quite unambiguously stated the complete equality of status of men and women, and the Soviet Government has attempted with varying degrees of success to put this theory into practice. The rest of the world may march hither and thither along intersecting paths; Moscow has a plan." As Holtby indicated in her 1934 book Women and a Changing Civilization:[40]

> The whole attitude of mind is new—that it is right for women to work, right for them to produce children, that the state is served equally by tractor drivers and by kindergarten teachers and that both may be mothers; that the state should encourage this double rôle as a service, and not discourage it as a dangerous and self-indulgent experiment—all this is surely new. . . . One must permit at least a few generations to pass before considering the scheme as a failure.

It was precisely the sweeping character of the plan and its unprecedented scale, along with its perceived feminism (however unjustifiable), that made some fearful. The enthusiasm of Halle, Holtby, and other European feminists was not widely shared by current decision-makers. In fact, implicit rejection of Soviet Russia's revolutionary proposals for reconfiguring marriage, familial organization, and women's and men's roles would become a determining theme in the antifeminist backlash that characterized much of the 1920s and 1930s. What was more, explicit rejection of the Bolshevik experiment with women's liberation would become central to the programs of emergent authoritarian political parties, factions, and movements in the postwar period.

BACKLASH: REKINDLING THE KNOWLEDGE WARS

The combined effect of the relatively long and extremely costly war and the Bolshevik program for women's liberation was to trigger yet another enormous political and cultural backlash against the emancipation of women. In order of magnitude, this was certainly on a par with earlier backlashes that had followed the French Revolution, the multiple European revolutions of 1848, and the Paris Commune in 1871. The difference was that the combination of the war experience with a half-century of education and economic participation had brought far more women into the public arena. "Modern" woman—antithetical to the "angel in the house" but also to the motherly new woman that feminists had promoted prior to the war—was now becoming a reality in much of Western Europe. Both femininity and masculinity were undergoing reconfiguration, whether anyone liked it or not.[41]

In consequence, all further feminist campaigns for ending women's subjection or, put more positively, for obtaining their rights had to be rethought and pursued in the shadow of renewed loud, insistent, and repetitive rearticulations of women's obligations and role. In some countries, notably in Eastern Europe, where feminist eruptions had only begun to occur, they were swamped and almost completely extinguished. In others, where they were more extensive, considerable regrouping and cautionary reformulating of demands took place. Political developments, new developments in the knowledge wars (particularly in psychology and psychoanalysis), and contemporary movements in "modernist" literature and art all fed this mushrooming backlash, which was heavily reported in the contemporary press.

Even in France, where the government of the Third Republic was officially committed to the principles of liberty, equality, and justice for all, feminists continued to face serious obstacles with respect to suffrage. As feminists pushed for final Senate confirmation of the outgoing Chamber of Deputies' resounding support of woman suffrage, the French prime minister Georges Clemenceau, calling for Senate ratification of the Treaty of Versailles in October 1919, sketched his vision of France's future in the postwar world:[42]

> The treaty doesn't say that France engages itself to have many children, but that is the first thing that should have been included. For if France turns its back on large families, you could jolly well put the most beautiful clauses you want in the treaties, you could jolly well take all the cannons in Germany, you could jolly well do whatever you please, but France would be lost, because there would be no more Frenchmen.

Four times in the 1920s and 1930s the French Senate would refuse to ratify the Chamber of Deputies' repeated endorsement of women's voting; the possible adverse (read Catholic or antiparliamentary nationalist) consequences of women's votes for the future of the secular republic continued to worry men of the French Left. Even the progressive men of the Ligue des Droits de l'Homme (League for the Rights of Man) would continually hedge when it came to issuing an unqualified endorsement of full woman suffrage, though they continued to endorse equality of the sexes in principle. At the Ligue's 1924 convention, its vice-president, Victor Basch, apologized for the nonneutrality of the term *Homme* (Man) in the organization's title, but was unwilling to go beyond an endorsement of municipal suffrage for women.[43]

Meanwhile, by the early 1920s French republican legislators had set in place prohibitions on contraceptive information and sales (condoms, deemed necessary for "hygiene," were excluded from the ban) and had "decriminalized" abortion, in the hope that by substituting stern judges for lenient juries, more convictions could be obtained. These French efforts were accompanied by a program of Medals for Motherhood, which offered a model to many other postwar states. Some governments subsequently inaugurated official Mother's Day celebrations to honor mothers of large families and to promote natality.[44]

European antifeminist rhetoric grew more shrill. In England, readers were treated to such highly charged tracts as the Dublin-based Arabella Kenealy's *Feminism and Sex Extinction* (1920), in which the author alleged that the goal of feminism was the abolition of all sex difference, and the subjection of Man. The sexual division of labor, she argued, was fundamental to societal order; to claim, as had Olive Schreiner, that women could have all labor for their province was, in Kenealy's eyes, quite wrongheaded. Women, in this postwar period, must be convinced to "surrender freely all the essentially masculine employments into which mischance has cast them."[45] There were "Feminists" and "Femininists," claimed Kenealy, and the former were hermaphroditic; the whole development she saw as antievolutionary.

In the 1920s, the knowledge wars developed a new twist when psychological and psychiatric analysts joined generations of antifeminist physicians in taking the measure of feminism. Dr. Gina Lombroso (daughter of the Italian physician-anthropologist Cesare Lombroso and wife of Gugliegmo Ferrero, whose views on the woman question were anathema to most feminists) weighed in from Milan with *L'Anima della donna* (The Soul of Woman, 1922), which explored what its author called "the tragic consequences of woman's alterocentrism" or other-directedness.[46] Dr. Karl Abraham published his important article "Manifestations of the Female Castration Complex" (first presented in 1920), in which he posited that women who had interests outside their families were suffering from "penis envy."[47] This latter term, along with the more general notion that women were becoming more "virile," would enjoy a long life in international psychoanalytic circles, particularly (though by no means solely) in the works of Sigmund Freud, who would finally confront the woman question in his important paper "Some Psychological Consequences of the Anatomical Distinction between the Sexes" (originally published in German in 1925, and in English translation in 1927).[48]

Such ideas would quickly find elaboration in speculations about what was "wrong" with modern womanhood by Helene Deutsch, in her strongly antifeminist *Psychoanalyse der weiblichen Sexualfunctionen*, published in Vienna in 1925 (and subsequently in English translation as *The Psychology of Women: A Psychoanalytic Interpretation* in 1944), and by her colleague C. G. Jung, who spoke in 1927 of "psychic injury" and "mental masculinization of the woman," as well as in the later, more speculative works of Freud.[49] Not even the counterhypotheses put forward by the courageous German feminist psychoanalyst Karen Horney in the 1930s, insisting that it was not the penis but the social power accompanying the penis that women wanted, could dislodge the new Freudian psychoanalytic paradigm as it developed in the English- and German-speaking world.[50] Alfred Adler was among the very few European psychoanalysts who wholeheartedly supported women's emancipation. In his important treatise *Menschenkenntnis* (1927; translated in the same year as *Understanding Human Nature*) he argued that "so long as we cannot guarantee every woman an absolute equality with man we cannot demand her complete reconciliation with life, with the facts of our civilization and the forms of our social life."[51]

But few European psychological investigators were as profeminist as Horney and Adler. In Paris, Léontine Zanta's sensitive exploration of the *Psychologie du féminisme* (Psychology of Feminism, 1922), in which she posited sharp differences between Latin and Northern women and their respective feminisms, was introduced by the novelist Paul Bourget, who explained to prospective readers that feminism was merely another manifestation of "individualism," itself a product of the social instability and rootlessness that had become such unappetizing features of modern society. Mary Louise Roberts has explored the discourse that swirled around the so-called modern woman in French society during the decade following the war, posing war veteran Pierre Drieu la Rochelle's extravagant 1927 plaint, "this civilization . . . no longer has sexes," as emblematic, and adding that "the blurring of the boundary between 'male' and 'female'—a civilization without sexes—served as a primary referent for the ruin of civilization itself."[52]

But who might be held responsible for "blurring" these boundaries? Who had become the real target of the 1920s culture wars? Was it the apolitical Parisian "modern woman," who cropped her hair and sought out personal pleasure? Or was she—more likely—merely a surrogate for the committed pro-rights and antiwar "feminist," whom many confused with the new Bolshevik woman? Both of them claimed all labor for their sex, state support for motherhood, and control over their own fertility. Whoever it was, feminism very often became the scapegoat. In the view of one critic, the German Ehrhardt F. W. Eberhard, manager of the German League against Women's Emancipation and author of *Feminismus und Kulturuntergang: Die erotischen Grundlagen der Frauenemanzipation* (1924; 2d ed. 1927), feminism itself was synonymous with cultural decline and decadence. Another critic, the Norwegian professor Knud Asbjørn Wieth-Knudsen, in a tract published in Danish, then in English and in French, attempted to prove, through the mobilization of dense layers of physiological, psychological, sociological, and historical data, that women must be subordinated to men; to emancipate them was to do them no favor, nor was it in the interests of preserving civilization.[53] Dr. Robert Teutsch, in his 1934 survey of the woman question in France, entitled *Le Féminisme*, insisted that women must be put back in their place: "Females who do not want to live as real women, conscious of the duties their dignity requires, must sooner or later be corrected . . . or sent back to the unworthy ranks from whence they came. It is one of the only ways to save our society from certain sources of moral putrefaction."[54] Indeed, civilization would henceforth be identified with patriarchy by some antifeminist psychoanalytic writers, including Freud—an identification that would ultimately stimulate the initial phases of the revisionary thinking of the French analyst Jacques Lacan, who, in the words of Carolyn Dean and in the best French manner, "believed that paternal authority was not a natural force but a cultural product."[55]

That the war had seriously aggravated European men's general sense of insecurity is attested by innumerable published writings from war veterans in the 1920s and early 1930s. But in view of the Bolshevik effort to realize sexual equality in the Soviet Union, that effect would be greatly magnified. In addition, the centuries-long symbolic leadership of French feminist argumentation and effort, already challenged by Anglo-American leadership in the international women's movement, would be seriously eroded, though not eclipsed, by the proponents of the new Soviet experiment. These developments, which evoked a potent combination of antiemancipatory secular responses, would contribute directly to a climate of opinion fearful of any disruption in the "traditional" relations of the sexes. In such a climate, an aggrieved and defensive nationalism would thrive, one in which militant fascism could sometimes find a foothold. Both integral nationalists and fascists adopted antifeminist views on the woman question as their own. "Fascism," as Peter Nathan insisted unequivocally in his 1943 study *The Psychology of Fascism*, "is an over-valuation of masculinity. It is an attempt to make a man's world. . . . Fascism is a mighty façade attempting to cover up [men's] innermost secret fear of being weak, unmanly, impotent. The denial of weakness is its whole purpose, and the clue to all its deeds. . . . Fascism . . . is a great anti-feminist movement."[56]

10

Feminist Dilemmas in Postwar National Political Cultures

England, Italy, Austria, Hungary, and Germany

In the wake of the war trauma and casualties, and with the end of the massive temporary mobilization of women as workers and volunteers for the war effort, debates on the woman question continued to occupy a central place in European political and cultural life. In the postwar reframing of feminist demands, a growing schism developed between those who would insist on women's absolute rights as individuals and those who emphasized women's responsibilities to society as mothers or as workers. In national contexts, were women "persons in their own right," or were they mere cogs—female cogs—in the societal machinery? What should be the relation between women, the family, and freedom in European nation-states? How would feminists frame their answers to these questions, as opponents sought to reduce women to mere breeding machines, to confine them to "separate spheres," or to treat them as a reserve army of labor, turning the tables on feminists' earlier encompassing claims to "mother" all society even as they demanded their rights as individuals?

Feminists throughout Europe debated these issues intensely in the postwar period. Several facts remained paramount: adult women outnumbered adult men in virtually every European country that had participated in the recent World War, and birthrates had continued to decline. Moreover, as political democratization proceeded on a seemingly irresistible course, government leaders had become extremely interested in the size, strength, and well-being of the populations under their control, though they were often reluctant to spend undue amounts of money on measures designed to alleviate perceived shortfalls in these areas. These facts provide a key to understanding how the relationship between women's employment, motherhood, and politics unfolded in the newly emergent nations of Europe during the 1920s and 1930s, and how addressing that relationship could potentially lead to dramatic changes in the configuration of nation-states. They also provide a means of understanding just how threatening radical feminist claims for sexual and reproductive freedom, including birth control, could be to the leaders and supporters of authoritarian, male-dominated regimes.

Remasculinization efforts were apparent everywhere during the immediate postwar period. Governments systematically forced women war workers out of the labor force so that jobs would be available to returning soldiers. Political leaders contemplated initiatives to control and direct reproduction in the interests of national population growth. Both neotraditionalist nationalist regimes and the new fascist authoritarian regimes of the 1920s and 1930s would explicitly combat emancipationist demands by and for women.

As economic conditions eroded in the late 1920s and the European political climate careened toward extremes on both the Right and the Left, it would become increasingly difficult for feminists to hold their ground, and even more so to get their proposals moved to the front burner of the national political stove. The old formula of equal rights and equal opportunities for women no longer seemed (to some) to elicit stirring responses to the new and complex problems of the postwar, postsuffrage world. In particular, the complicated set of problems surrounding employment and motherhood took on far greater political significance.

NATIONAL POLITICAL CULTURES IN THE
POSTWAR YEARS

This chapter and the next comprise a series of case studies in which expressions of feminism within a variety of European nation-states will be briefly examined, along with societal responses to feminist demands. Two "victor" nations, England and Italy, will be considered first, followed by the principal "defeated" nations, Austria, Hungary, and Germany. The subsequent chapter will investigate feminist developments in several other nation-states which were less immediately affected by the war—two smaller and nominally Catholic countries, Portugal and Ireland, and the larger Catholic nation of Spain—followed by the contrasting case study of Sweden, a small but highly democratized Protestant country.

If British feminists, who were perhaps the most outspoken of European feminists following their suffrage triumphs in 1919 and 1928 (when all women obtained the vote), could disagree so bitterly over strategies and tactics with respect to work and motherhood, feminists in other national settings on the Continent experienced even more difficulties. In some countries, the fissures through which the feminist magma had flowed in earlier situations were virtually dammed, the very memory of the eruptions and their locations erased. For some activists on the political Left who thought that the Bolsheviks had answered the woman question, it would become more stylish to be communist than feminist; for others, who valued both the mother's unique role in the rearing of children and aspects of women's unpaid labor in the household, Bolshevik solutions to the woman question seemed distinctly inappropriate, if not downright repugnant. In both instances, the question of how to mobilize women on behalf of their own emancipation was far from answered. In the meantime, political parties, labor unions, and other professional and volunteer associations (both single-sex and "mixed" groups) began to compete for women's attention and support. The war had ensured that women had entered Europe's public life, but not that they would seek emancipation as the feminists understood the term, nor either that they would appreciate the role feminism had played in forcing open the doors of modern life to them.

To this set of factors, we must add the rise of new antifeminist political formations in the period from 1919 to 1939. The Israeli historian Zeev Sternhell has claimed that fascism was "neither Right nor Left," by which he meant "above parties."[1] With respect to the woman question, however, it can be said that many political parties and virtually all the varieties of fascism produced in the 1920s and 1930s were profoundly antifeminist, just as they were profoundly anti-Bolshevik. These two characteristics alone should serve to suggest that fascism, along with these parties, falls definitively on the political Right.

Even before fascism took hold, however, the paramilitary dictatorships established in some European countries in the interwar period were decisively partisan to the reconsolidation of male authority over women; virtually all objected specifically to women's public roles (including the professions, and many forms of paid employment) and to their participation in political life. In this they marked themselves as even more conservative than the Roman Catholic Church, which in 1919 had ended its opposition to woman suffrage and political participation—although they shared the Vatican's position (formulated in the papal encyclical *Rerum Novarum* of 1891, and restated in 1931 in its successor, *Quadragesimo Anno*) on the primacy of male breadwinners.[2] The cases of Italy, Hungary, Austria, Spain and Portugal, Ireland, Belgium, and Germany all provide variations on this common theme.

This particular feature of European political life in the decades after

World War I would make the work of secular feminists and their organizations within national political cultures exceedingly difficult, even in the newly established nations with democratic constitutions. One cannot adequately assess the feminist organizational initiatives of the interwar period (with reference to democratic initiatives) without recognizing the increased hostility of the national political environments in which they attempted to achieve their goals. The situation became difficult for them even in countries where women had already been accorded the vote. In countries where women still lacked formal political citizenship, it became still more difficult—indeed, virtually impossible, as the following case studies will demonstrate.

ENGLAND

The development of English feminism during the period 1920–40 is perhaps the best-chronicled to date by historians.[3] During the 1920s and especially in the 1930s, following attainment of the vote for all women in 1928, English feminists began to disagree sharply over how to reformulate their political agendas. Already in 1925, in an editorial published in *The Woman's Leader and the Common Cause* entitled "What Is Feminism?" (which discussed a heated exchange between Lord Ampthill and novelist Rose Macaulay in the *Morning Post* on the subject of whether feminism had been a "failure"), the editorialist recounted Rose Macaulay's definition: "Attempts of women to possess privileges (political, professional, economic, or other) which have previously been denied to them on account of their sex." But, the writer added, "this is not enough":[4]

> The mere throwing open to women of all privileges, political, professional, industrial, social, religious, in a social system designed by men for men is not going to carry us all the way to our feminist ideal. And what that ideal is, becomes clear when we define feminism as *"the demand of women that the whole structure and movement of society shall reflect in a proportionate degree their experiences, their needs, and their aspirations."*

This included, in the writer's estimation, the social recognition of motherhood as having an equal claim "to be economically produced and legally protected."

Embedded in these lines was the thinking of Eleanor F. Rathbone, Member of Parliament, who had succeeded Millicent Garrett Fawcett as president of the now renamed National Union of Societies for Equal Citizenship (NUSEC; formerly the NUWSS). For nearly two decades

Rathbone had been insisting that *women's needs* should be dealt with in *women's terms*. Her important book *The Disinherited Family* (1924) had laid out her views on the woman question in the guise of an appeal to those in postwar England who, like their French colleagues, were concerned about the low birthrate and the shrinking power of the nation. Sylvia Pankhurst, in her small book *Save the Mothers* (1930), joined the campaign by calling on the government to supplement the voluntary provisions of the 1918 Maternity and Child Welfare Act with an effective nationally funded maternity-care system. In the wake of the Soviet Russian measures on behalf of maternity, however, even Rathbone's proposal for a family-endowment act, with an allowance to be paid to the wife/mother rather than to a wage-earning husband, encountered serious resistance, even though—as historian Susan Pedersen has underscored—it was based on allocations established during the war to support British soldiers' wives.[5]

Significant opposition to family endowment came from within the English feminist movement itself, spearheaded initially by Fawcett, who cautioned that such payments to women would undermine men's sense of responsibility as husbands and fathers. By degrading men's roles as economic providers, endowment would thereby destroy rather than stabilize the family, Fawcett affirmed. Rathbone, in her rejoinder to Fawcett, "The Old and the New Feminism," castigated the strictly egalitarian approach that had for so long been the most visible feature of British feminism. Closer in her arguments to the continental feminists of prewar Germany and France, she insisted that:[6]

> At last we can stop looking at all our problems through men's eyes and discussing them in men's phraseology. We can demand what we want for women, not because it is what men have got, but because it is what women need to fulfil the potentialities of their own natures and to adjust themselves to the circumstances of their own lives. . . . The achievement of freedom is a much bigger thing than the breaking off of shackles.

In 1927, the English feminist movement fractured over these issues of work-related protective legislation and endowment of motherhood. Tensions that had long been building manifested themselves as schism. In a period when nearly half the women in England were still without a political voice (though all would finally obtain it in 1928), Eleanor Rathbone's brand of "new" feminism and the pursuit of state support for mothers made the advocates of formal legal equality for women extremely uneasy. Indeed, some English partisans of individual equality viewed all legal "protection" or privileges for mothers or for working women as a trap. This view characterized the feminists associated with the Six Points Group and with the publication *Time and Tide* and its editor-benefactress, Margaret Haig Thomas Mackworth, Viscountess Rhondda. Following the franchise victory in 1928, Lady Rhondda wrote that "the real task of feminism" was to "wipe out the overemphasis on sex that is the fruit of the age-long subjection of women. The individual must stand out without trappings as a human being."[7] To such advocates of pure equality in the law and in the workplace, it seemed reprehensible for other feminists to play the motherhood trump in the way it had been and would repeatedly be played, for instance, in France and Germany, and later in Sweden and other Scandinavian countries.

The schism between these two approaches to feminism, one highly relational and woman-centered and the other highly individualistic, subsequently became encapsulated in the somewhat misleading formulation "equality versus difference." In truth both factions desired equality, but they understood the term somewhat differently. The split between them would be reinforced and reified by subsequent developments, in particular the construction of an explicitly dependent motherhood and wifehood in the British welfare state after World War II. This later set of developments has profoundly affected interpretations of the interwar period by late twentieth-century historians such as Jane Lewis, Susan Kingsley Kent, and Susan Pedersen. Indeed, according to historian Susan Kingsley Kent, "by the end of the 1920s, new feminists found themselves in a conceptual bind that trapped women in 'traditional' domestic and maternal roles, and limited their ability to advocate equality and justice for women."[8] The British experience has not often been evaluated with reference to developments on the motherhood front that lay beyond England's borders. Had this been done, it might also be possible to affirm that the "old" feminists found themselves in a conceptual bind that trapped women in a strict-constructionist version of equality as sameness, a legalistic formula that did not allow for acknowledgment or expression of sexual differences created and reinforced by women's experience of maternity except within a separate-spheres model of sexual relations.

Indeed, by the 1930s, the term "feminism" (if not the complex of changes for which it stood) was being repudiated by some activist English women, especially those of a younger generation. Ray Strachey complained about this in her preface to the 1936 stocktaking work *Our Freedom and Its Results*:[9]

> Modern young women know amazingly little of what life was like before the war, and show a strong hostility to the word "feminism" and all which they imagine it to connote. They are, nevertheless, themselves

the products of the women's movement and the difficult and confusing conditions in which they live are partly due to the fact that it is in their generation that the change-over from the old to the new conception of the place of women in society is taking place.

In *Three Guineas* (1938) Virginia Woolf even proposed incinerating the word "feminist"—"an old word, a vicious and corrupt word that has done much harm in its day and is now obsolete."[10] Not only suffrage, but the "chief" right of women—in Woolf's eyes, the right to earn an independent living—had been won; thus, in her view, the term was no longer needed. Even so, Woolf—already the author of many path-breaking novels as well as a provocative study of the plight of women writers, *A Room of One's Own* (1929)—had written one of the most unequivocally radical and far-reaching "feminist" tracts of all time. *Three Guineas* eloquently joined the issue of sex discrimination in the professions with that of racism and other forms of discrimination, all as mutually reinforcing sources of war. But Woolf's annihilation of the terms "feminism" and "feminist" served to discredit them just as effectively as if her book had been censored by Clara Zetkin or Aleksandra Kollontai.

ITALIAN FASCISM AND ITS IMITATORS

After its unification in 1861, Italy was governed by a parliamentary monarchy. A very limited male franchise had been established in 1882. Women had no votes, and their legal situation in marriage was severely circumscribed. Switching to the Allied side late in the World War, Italy emerged as a victorious power. Within only a few years, the Italian nation became the first country in Europe to empower a fascist government. Mussolini's "march on Rome" in late October 1922 and his appointment as prime minister were generally considered the means of ending the chaos that had marked Italian politics after the war.

It became clear during its first few years that "Mussolini's regime stood for returning women to home and hearth, restoring patriarchal authority, and confining female destiny to bearing babies," even as it celebrated the "New Italian Woman."[11] Italian fascists, perhaps inspired by at least one aspect of the Russian communist experiment, deliberately set out to harness women to the purposes of the new fascist order. Historian Victoria De Grazia points out that "every aspect of being female was . . . held up to the measure of the state's interest and interpreted in light of the dictatorship's strategies of state building."[12] Or, as the goals for female youth groups would express this goal in 1929, young women must prepare "to serve the Fatherland as the greatest Mother, a Mother of all good Italians."[13]

This deliberate appropriation of female energy by the Italian state was by no means foreordained at the outset, but it did create a dilemma for Italian feminists. Prior to Mussolini's arrival in power, suffragists had invited the International Woman Suffrage Association to hold its 1923 meeting in Rome, in an effort to stimulate support for the enactment of woman suffrage, a goal that seemed tantalizingly near at hand. Italian suffrage was still restricted even for men: the 1912 electoral law had expanded the electorate from three million men to five million, but accommodated only those over thirty who could read and write and all those over twenty-one (whether literate or not) who had served in the military. The June 1919 Fascist Party electoral program, like those of other political parties, including the Futurists, had advocated full suffrage for women over the age of twenty-one, along with eligibility to hold office, anticipating that the parliament was soon expected to grant votes for women. Early fascism welcomed women as supporters, many of them former socialists like Mussolini himself, even though the party did little to recruit them actively. Early in 1922, however, guidelines for the newly emerging women's groups insisted on their subordinate character. Continued movement to the Right was reinforced by what De Grazia has termed the "exaggerated masculinism" of veterans' and nationalist groups, and by the explicitly antifeminist positions of the Roman Catholic Church.

Meanwhile Mussolini teased the feminists by dangling various forms of suffrage in front of them. In mid-May 1923 he addressed the opening session of the IWSA, promising some categories of women (widows and mothers of male war casualties; university-educated women) access to suffrage at several levels, beginning with the municipalities: "I do not believe that enfranchising women will have catastrophic consequences . . . but in all probability it will have beneficial results because women will bring to the exercise of these new rights their fundamental virtues of balance, equilibrium, and prudence."[14] Not long afterward, however, the fascist government suspended all municipal elections and appointed *podeste* (prefects) to rule the towns. In early January 1925, following the assassination in May 1924 of the socialist deputy Matteotti and the subsequent secession of the opposition deputies, Mussolini dissolved the parliament and unleashed squadrons of *Fascisti* against the opposition. In 1926 *il Duce* would do away with elections altogether.

Even as late as 1925, however, these games around the vote for women continued. The well-known antifeminist journalist Matilde

Serao questioned what the Italian suffragists thought they were doing in continuing to advocate woman suffrage. She warned of the danger that lay ahead:[15]

> Have you ever considered, oh suffragists, that the majority of women are crassly ignorant? . . . they don't read a newspaper, open a book, they are only interested in conversations that come out of gossip? Have you ever considered that these feminine masses are impermeable to ideas and to knowledge, that they flee from thinking, from reflecting, and from judging? Look out, suffragists, if you want to explain to them local and state-wide law . . . as they do in the kindergartens, with children, teach them a little summarizing lesson, and then make them repeat it. A kind of catechism, tit for tat.

Surely, Serao did not number among these women her intellectual peers, including the novelist Grazia Deledda, Nobel laureate for literature in 1926.

In 1925, by his Law of 8 June, Mussolini mobilized "all citizens, men and women, and all legally constituted organizations" for the "moral and material defense of the nation. . . subject to military discipline."[16] Women, like other bodies, might ultimately be treated as a corporate interest group of the Italian fascist state. In December of that year, L'Opera Nazionale per la Protezione della Maternità e dell'Infanzia (ONMI) was founded, a welfare organization for mothers and infants. The widely distributed ONMI publication *Maternità ed Infanzia* celebrated the virtues of maternity in the national interest.

Earlier that year, the editors of a profeminist paper in Genoa, *La Chiosa*, sought to defend economic equity for women, but in vain: "We wish to ask our good Fascist *camerati* what you have done recently for women's rights, to educate and elevate women? In fascism there seems to be a spirit of inexplicable, yet ferocious antifeminism."[17] Not long afterwards, *La Chiosa* was abruptly turned into a fashion magazine. The profascist journalist Ester Lombardo declared in the *Almanacco della donna italiana* for 1927 that the "feminist movement in Italy no longer exists . . . [having been] gobbled up by the Fascist Revolution."[18] Not quite: the regime had still bigger goals; as one fascist writer pointed out in 1929, "it will be to our credit if we can extend the restraints we've applied to women in politics to other fields, above all to art and literature."[19] If the existence of women's creativity could no longer be contested in the same old ways, its evidence would have to be blotted out!

In May 1927, Mussolini had laid out his goals for an increase in the national population, from forty million to sixty million. The Italian *donna nuova* or "new woman" had been redefined as the prolific mother, not the working mother of the Russian Bolshevik experiment. By 1931 Italian women were being enrolled in women's sections, or *fasci femminili*, which were positioned as auxiliaries under the control of men's groups. In this they were comparable to parallel Catholic women's organizations, which by virtue of the 1929 treaty with the Vatican were permitted a continued existence. Also in 1931, laws against the circulation of contraceptive information were incorporated into the new penal code. Women's wages had been cut to half those offered to men, women were restricted to low-level jobs, and married women were encouraged to leave employment; family allowances were introduced and made payable to fathers. As historian Bonnie Smith has wryly commented: "The Fascist government did not really oppose women's working. It only opposed their having good jobs and being well paid."[20]

By 1932, Mussolini was speaking openly about his antifeminist and anti-Malthusian views: "My notion of woman's rôle in the State is utterly opposed to feminism. Of course I do not want women to be slaves, but if here in Italy I proposed to give our women votes, they would laugh me to scorn. As far as political life is concerned, they do not count here." But, he added, "we do as much for mothers as any country in Europe."[21] This included unwed mothers. Indeed, among the measures put in place were taxes on bachelorhood and benefits for Italian women living outside Italy if they would return home to have their babies, with the promise of reimbursing them for both their travel and their confinement. Multiple benefits for large families were included; fruitful mothers of a sixth child would receive a portrait of Mussolini himself! But work outside the home for married women was deemed unacceptable. (This in a state where around 50 percent of the labor force was female in the immediate postwar period.) "Work," Mussolini announced in August 1934, "where it is not a direct impediment, detracts from reproduction. It forms an independence and consequent physical and moral habits that are incompatible with childbearing."[22]

Italy under fascism was not a nation willing to foster women's emancipation; indeed, fascist priorities precluded emancipation for either sex. If, as most scholars claim, there was no coherent sexual politics at the outset of the fascist movement, there is little doubt that what developed in the course of its first ten years in power amounted to a relatively consistent and comprehensive, if not startlingly innovative, antifeminist program. Italian feminists adapted to it, sacrificing their earlier convictions to the patriarchal, authoritarian regime that promised to bring glory to their country and their people, but which also separated them from the international feminist movement. After 1936, as De Grazia explains it, "with the militarization of the regime, the formation of a new generation of cadres and followers with no recall of historical feminism, and finally, the outlawing of the surviving bourgeois feminist groups in 1938, . . . the emancipationist tradition [was] finally obliterated."[23] Even though the fascist regime never succeeded in eliminating women completely from the labor force, and even though the birthrate did not significantly increase, the intentions of the state and its supporters with respect to women's place in the new order were clearly demarcated. These intentions sustained a threatening atmosphere, weighing heavily on women's options in Italy, and influencing developments beyond Italy's borders.

Elsewhere in Europe, admirers of Mussolini's new regime, including his forthright opposition to woman's emancipation, quickly began to second his views publicly. One such admirer was the French nationalist Pierre Taittinger, founder of the Jeunesses Patriotes (Patriotic Youth) in France, one of the many fascist leagues that had begun to spring up outside Italy. Taittinger was not, however, above calling on French women—in a deceptive parody of women's rights rhetoric—to assist in the work of the movement through its women's sections: "Our great ancestors took the Bastille. But they did not take all the Bastilles. There is one they left standing: that of masculine supremacy. . . . They bestowed upon themselves the Rights of Man. They forgot the Rights of Woman."

Lest this remark be mistaken for an appeal for women's active participation in political life, however, Taittinger (who did support women's suffrage) quickly clarified his intentions, sounding astonishingly like the revolutionary antifeminist journalist and separate-spheres advocate Prudhomme in 1793: women should not engage in "battles of the forum." Theirs was a separate sphere: "We call to our side all those women who have a happy life to defend. . . . They have no need to profess inflammatory opinions. They live quite simply their little *chez soi* which is their interior and that great *chez soi* which is France. We have no need of amazons, nor of . . . bombthrowers."[24]

Such appeals would become a staple of Mussolini's imitators. In England, Sir Oswald Mosley, the leader of the British Union of Fascists (BUF) and advocate of procorporatist anticommunist agitation, insisted in 1932:[25]

> The part of women in our future organisation will be important, but different from that of the men; *we want men who are men and women who are women.* . . . The logic of the situation seems to demand some Corporate organisation and representation of motherhood. . . . Fascism, in fact, would treat the normal woman and mother as one of the main pillars of

the State, and would rely upon her for the organisation and development of one of the most important aspects of national life.

In BUF publications such as *Blackshirt* and *Fascist Quarterly*, debate swirled for several years around the issues of whether a British fascism intended to return women to the home.[26]

To Mosley and others like him, who seemed to circumscribe women's "place," Virginia Woolf would issue an eloquent reply:[27]

> There . . . is the egg of the very same worm that we know under other names in other countries. There we have in embryo the creature, Dictator as we call him when he is Italian or German, who believes that he has the right, whether given by God, Nature, sex or race is immaterial, to dictate to other human beings how they shall live; what they shall do. . . . Should we not help [the woman] to crush him in our own country before we ask her to help us to crush him abroad? And what right have we . . . to trumpet our ideals of freedom and justice to other countries when we can shake out from our most respectable newspapers any day of the week eggs like these?

An excellent question indeed!

AUSTRIA AND HUNGARY

"Eggs like these" were being hatched daily in the successor states to the venerable and vanquished Austro-Hungarian Empire. Indeed, in the new states the difficulties created for feminist aspirations by postwar conditions and the peace settlements were far less tractable than in Western Europe. While the war was still in progress, in 1916, the Austrian social democrat Klara Mautner had heralded the importance of women's war work for launching a new stage in women's possibilities: "The war signifies a turning point in the history of women. It has concluded the debate over the 'natural profession' of women. . . . The epoch of the woman as homemaker, wife and mother is definitely at an end."[28]

Mautner was unduly optimistic. When the war ended, employed women were forced out of the labor market in Austria just as emphatically as in the victorious nations, and the need for their presence in the home was just as adamantly reasserted. Such measures had the approval of the union leader Anna Boschek, who had been active in the social democratic women's movement since the 1890s. Despite this setback, following the demise of the Dual Monarchy, feminists of all political persuasions could be pleased with the fact that the December 1918 Constitution of the new Austrian Republic fully enfranchised women. (Universal manhood suffrage had already been accorded in 1907, under the monarchy, an event which had stimulated the Austrian campaign for woman suffrage.) The pro-suffrage social democrat Adelheid Popp was exultant:[29]

> The hour has come. . . . We can cherish the hope that, through the entry of women into political life, and through their cooperation in legislation, needs will be eliminated which now exist and which press especially hard on women. . . . The machine has destroyed the earlier idea of feminity [sic]. It has created the economically productive woman. . . . The sufferings of the war have sharpened the mental capability of women and awakened and strengthened their own political interest. . . . The great time has now begun, in which the word of the women will be heard.

Women activists in the new Austria could also be pleased when eight women deputies (out of 170) were elected to the Constituent Assembly in 1919, and ten to the National Assembly in 1920. The first elected president of the Republic of Austria was Michael Hainisch, son of Austria's "first" feminist, Marianne Hainisch, founder and president of the Bund Österreichischer Frauenvereine (BÖFV, Federation of Austrian Women's Societies). What was more, the Social Democratic Party governed Vienna, where they would carry out a singularly ebullient program of municipal reforms, including the building of vast blocks of modern workers' housing. Again, Adelheid Popp had great hopes for the power of the ballot in women's hands: "The vote is only a weapon with which the struggle for the complete transformation of society may be served. The hegemony of the male sex . . . will be eliminated."[30]

None of these developments signified that a feminist program could or would be enacted. The two major parties, the Social Democrats and the Christian Social Party, held significantly different views on the woman question. Thus, women deputies of competing political persuasions found themselves quite powerless to realize a common program. Feminist commitments, when they existed, gave way before the conflicting priorities set by the political parties and enforced on individual deputies through party discipline. Social Democratic women's priorities, which in addition to equal pay and other employment issues included legal abortion and access to contraceptive information, were anathema to women affiliated with the dominant Christian Social Party, who endorsed the Catholic line on the sexual division of labor in marriage (male breadwinners, female housewives/mothers) and repulsed all suggestion of interference with God's will in reproduction. In Vienna, however, a group of women teachers, journalists, and academics founded the Catholic Women's Organization of the Archdiocese of Vienna to advocate women's right to work. Such divisions assured that any hope of achieving solidarity of women's interests would be illusory.

The new parliamentary republic of Austria had under seven million inhabitants, about a quarter of whom lived in Vienna; most Austrians were nominally Roman Catholic, and many were practicing believers and social conservatives. The new national territory had been created by the victorious Allies from the German-speaking "leftovers" of the former Austro-Hungarian Empire, shorn of South Tyrol and of its access to the Adriatic Sea. By contrast, its neighbor to the north, the equally new Republic of Czechoslovakia, had acquired a population of some fifteen million, including Bohemia, which encompassed most of the former empire's industrial and resource base, along with a mixed population of Czech- and German-speaking inhabitants, and, to the east, the agrarian and mineral-rich lands of Moravia and Slovakia. Austria's neighbor to the east, the new Hungarian Republic, whose former territories had also been severely truncated to the benefit of Czechoslovakia, Poland, Romania, and Yugoslavia, encompassed a mostly rural population of about eight million.

The intense ethnic and linguistic nationalist identification of the German-speaking Austrians with the new German Republic was thwarted by the peace treaties, which specifically forbade a merger that might in other circumstances have offered the most sensible solution to their dilemma. Thus, the primary political issue for the leadership of the Austrian Republic in the postwar period was to assure its economic and political viability as an independent state: whether it should or could attempt to remain independent (as argued by the "patriotic" faction) or whether it should simply aspire, against the terms of the peace treaties, toward incorporation into an expanded Germany (as advocated by the highly vocal "nationalist" faction). The Social Democrats repositioned themselves as the Sozialdemokratische Arbeiterpartei Deutschösterreichs (German-Austrian Social Democratic Workers' Party), as did a new Jewish women's organization, the Jüdischer Frauenbund für Deutsch-Österreich, founded in 1922. Such designations raised highly problematic issues about what or who in Austria was properly "German": was it culture and language, or ethnicity and race? Historian Johanna Gehmacher has pointed out in her study of German nationalism among Austrian women that "Austrian Germano-nationalism cannot be understood unless one analyzes its indestructible link with racial antisemitism which lies at the core of the concept of 'ethnic community.'"[31] What had once been the center of a cosmopolitan, multiethnic, multicultural empire, encompassing many Slavic peoples, Jews, Hungarians, and Germans, became a far more exclusionary and frustrated Germano-centered society in the wake of defeat.

From the initial elections of 1919 until the suspension of Austria's parliamentary government in 1934, no political party ever held a majority. Throughout the 1920s the Christliche Sozialpartei (Christian Social Party), allied with the German nationalists of the Großdeutsche Volkspartei (German People's Party, GDVP), controlled the national parliament and ministries. All parties were conscious and wary of one salient fact: in the new Austria, women voters outnumbered men voters. The Christian Social Party pushed for national compulsory voting, in order that Catholic political interests might benefit from women's ostensible conservatism. Although this decision was ultimately left to local control, differential voting patterns for the sexes were patrolled by the use of different-colored envelopes for men's and women's ballots; separate counting was formalized in 1923. With women casting some 60 percent of Christian Social votes, it was understandable that claims were made that this in fact *was* a "women's party," even though it continued to lose women's votes up to 1930, at which point the Social Democrats attracted more women voters than any other party. Women's votes became increasingly important to the male-dominated political parties, though not women's representation or forceful action on "women's issues." It proved exceedingly difficult, for instance, to place women high on the party electoral lists, especially outside Vienna. By 1930 even the women activists within the Christian Social Party had begun to complain about this omission and to demand representation by women deputies.

The majority of women who were elected deputies in the 1920s were Social Democrats, among them Gabriele Proft, Therese Schlesinger, and Adelheid Popp. Popp, a longtime Social Democratic activist, was, along with Proft and Schlesinger, an ardent advocate of women's advancement—and of women's values: women should vote and take part in politics, she had claimed in 1911, "exactly because we are womanly and motherly."[32] Popp had taken over Clara Zetkin's former role as women's advocate in the now reformist Socialist International, following Zetkin's adherence to the Communist Party after the Russian Revolution. For Popp women's issues were important *as such*, and thanks to Popp and Schlesinger, the Social Democratic women were extremely active on women's behalf. After some controversy, their *Arbeiterinnen Zeitung* (Women Workers' Paper) became *Die Frau* (The Woman) in 1924, catering more broadly to all "women's interests," not only those of women workers. In 1926 the Austrian Social Democratic women succeeded in winning party ratification for a sweeping program for change in the status of Austrian women. Among its demands were "for women full opportunity for the development of their personality," and "a greater respect for the social function of woman as mother and housewife and protection against the double burden of work in employment and household."[33] The Social Democratic women also called for the repeal of Article 144 of the Austrian penal code, which outlawed abortion, and they advocated free circulation of contraceptive information. Such claims were marked by a defiant anticlerical, even anti-Catholic bias. Another prominent Social Democratic woman activist, Käthe Leichter, produced an important series of investigations of working women's lives, *Der Weg zur Höhe: Die sozialdemokratische Frauenbewegung Österreichs* (Working Their Way Up: The Austrian Social Democratic Women's Movement, 1930), which was published along with Adelheid Popp's résumé of women's progress.

Despite their relative success, these Social Democratic Party women—like their Christian Social Party counterparts—continued to face significant opposition within their own party. As historian Thomas Hamer described it, "rank and file opposition . . . was as strong in the postwar period as it had ever been. . . . The pull of tradition combined with the fear of wage competition to override the efforts of the women and their supporters."[34] For decades the antifeminism of the socialist workingmen would foreclose effective action on behalf of women's emancipation.

If Social Democratic women activists had appropriated the rhetoric of struggle, the rhetoric of peace and harmony resided with the middle-class feminists of the BÖFV. Its leaders, which included many liberal Jewish and Christian women, continued to press for better schooling and more opportunities for girls—including vocational education and entry into the professions—and an end to armed conflict. What they shared with their Social Democratic counterparts as well as with their Catholic counterparts was the relational language of maternalism: Gisela Urban had already underscored this forcefully in 1913 when she insisted that women wanted "to complement the work of man and to make it more fruitful for both sexes, especially through the victory of the idea of motherhood in all the walks of life for the future generations."[35]

In 1930, the BÖFV published its own collective retrospective history and progress report, *Frauenbewegung, Frauenbildung und Frauenarbeit in Österreich* (Women's Movement, Women's Education, and Women's Work in Austria), prefaced by Marianne Hainisch and including a number of younger contributors, such as Stephanie Braun and Ilse Schuller Mintz, who had earned university doctorates since Austrian universities had begun to enroll women students in 1897. These feminists, ranging from moderate to radical, were not aligned with any extant political party, which may have freed them from some of the internal party difficulties faced by the Social Democratic Party women, but also made government enactment of their proposals more difficult. They were utterly unsuccessful, for example, in achieving reform of the laws governing married women's status, established by the Civil Code of 1811.

In December 1929 the BÖFV organized the Österreichische Frauenpartei (Austrian Woman's Party), along with a publication, *Das Wort der Frau* (The Voice of Women), in an effort to bridge the gap between the two major political parties and to promote peace and international disarmament as well as a range of changes in Austrian women's legal and economic situation. The small party coalition they supported did promote women candidates in 1930, but the resulting election of Dr. Phil. Maria Schneider, a fervent German nationalist and advocate of a corporatist state (in 1934 she joined the National Socialist Party), who positioned herself as the defender of women's interests, may have been a bittersweet victory.[36] In the deteriorating political and economic climate that developed from 1930 on, the failure of the Credit Anstalt, Austria's major bank, heightened the effects of the world economic depression, and paramilitary groups began to organize discontented men throughout the country. Austria's parliamentary government, whose male leaders had increasingly flirted with fascism and corporatist solutions to their impasse, capsized to dictatorship in 1934. In these circumstances, even a moderate feminist program faced serious obstacles, and feminist organizations had to tread carefully. Even Maria Schneider's 1931 bill to establish Chambers of Home Economics, backed by the BÖFV, did not succeed in winning parliamentary approval.

Still in 1932 the Frauenpartei vice-president Helene Granitsch believed, no doubt idealistically, that female politics could "*save the world from hatred*—to put in the place of the *business-politician* the arguments of *humanity* and to let the management of *idealism* take the place of the regency of *materialism*, as it complies with the principle of *motherly love* and *justice.*"[37] But this was not to be. By 1933, Frauenpartei spokeswomen were thinking increasingly in terms of representing women as an interest group in a refurbished corporate Austrian state. Following the dissolution of the Austrian parliament in early 1934 and the crushing of social democratic uprisings, the new authoritarian government dissolved all democratic organizations, including the Catholic women's organization and the BÖFV. The subsequent success of National Socialism in Austria and the *Anschluss* with Nazi Germany in 1938 merely sealed the fate of feminist activism in Austria. Austrian Nazi women had openly opposed women's emancipation, and their leaders moved quickly to absorb all other women's organizations into their own.

The new Hungarian state had also gotten off to a shaky start. Defeat had led to dismemberment by the imposed Treaty of Trianon. Women's enfranchisement was accompanied by two failed attempts at revolutionary governments between late 1918 and late 1919. The first, a liberal republican regime headed by Count Mihály Károlyi, had posted the first woman ambassador—the feminist Rozsika Schwimmer—to Switzerland. The second was Béla Kun's Bolshevik regime. The failure of both helped to assure the hegemony in the 1920s of the old ruling elites. The new regime, ultimately constituted as a parliamentary kingdom with no king, headed by the distinguished Admiral Horthy (the former commander-in-chief of the navy of the Austro-Hungarian Monarchy) as regent, had established constitutional equal rights and a restricted suffrage that included some qualifying women of age thirty and above. But the new nationalist government, supported by the emergent Christian National Party, promptly set about restricting access to university education, by imposing a quota system designed to exclude Jews and women (especially Jewish women) from the liberal professions in favor of Hungarian men.

The new women's coalition that sprang up to protest this ban called itself the National Association of Hungarian Women. It was strongly nationalistic, Christian, and right-wing; its leadership succeeded in reinstating Hungarian women's admission to universities, but at the expense of Jews of both sexes. According to its leader, the writer Cecile Tormay, it had "nothing in common with international feminism": "It is not an outgrowth of a foreign movement. . . . It sprang from the Hungarian soil, it is as native as Hungarian wheat."[38] The 1930 Association statutes read:[39]

> The Association incorporates all Hungarian women, Catholic or Protestant, who insist on Christian belief and love the Hungarian nation. Nothing else was required from the members, but that they should not be influenced by demagogic agitators, but to demand courageously and persistently that their representative should be a good Christian Hungarian person and a member of that party which is fighting for Christian ideas.

In the decidedly anti-Bolshevik climate of the time, Hungarian nationalists staked out a strongly anti-Semitic—and increasingly anti-

German—identification to argue the case for Hungarian women. These ultranationalist women made it a point to distinguish themselves from the most internationally visible segment of the prewar Hungarian feminist movement, the Feministák Egyesülete (Association of Feminists), whose leading members, Rozsika Schwimmer and Vilma Glücklich, had put women's votes on the Hungarian political agenda in 1913 when they hosted the International Women's Suffrage Alliance conference in Budapest. Assimilated Jews and Germans had been the backbone of the Hungarian commercial and industrial middle class—and of the prewar women's movement—but both were increasingly demonized in the highly nationalistic climate of the now truncated, bitter, resentful, and unwelcome postwar Hungarian state. The prewar feminists, who came predominantly from educated women in these now contested groups, never recovered their earlier momentum; their leaders were either in exile or working outside Hungary at the international level, particularly in the peace movement. Vilma Glücklich returned to Hungary in 1926, and she and her colleagues, including Eugenie Miscolczy Meller, organized lectures and events, kept up their international contacts, and organized their association's twenty-fifth anniversary in 1929. But they were unable to rally support to contest the 1925 parliamentary electoral law, which imposed an additional educational requirement on women voters. Nor were they able to make any headway in efforts to reform the marriage laws.

Under the Horthy regency, several elections were held for the unicameral parliament, and two women were in fact elected to serve, including the Social Democrat Anna Kéthly. Women voters were of interest to the parties, but strictly as supporters. When the authoritarian Party of National Unity mobilized, to the right even of the Christian National movement, it attempted to organize women corporately in a women's section. Clearly, in the Hungarian case, such interwar party-based women's movements only selectively espoused what could be considered feminist goals, and all too often, it seemed, to the detriment of other categories of citizens.

In Austria, in Hungary, and especially in Germany, feminist aspirations would face increasing opposition. Nevertheless, there would be some surprises, as will be seen in the case of Germany. In general, however, one can say that throughout the postwar successor states, the fissures that had permitted the flow of feminist magma to the surface would be narrowed, even sealed off, as bulldozers operated by patriarchal, authoritarian, nationalist drivers plowed them over and filled them in, in the name of "national protection."

GERMANY—FROM THE WEIMAR REPUBLIC
TO THE THIRD REICH

In the new German Republic, controversy over feminist objectives would manifest itself in particularly acute fashion. In the early twentieth century, the middle-class German *Frauenbewegung* had developed a radical feminist edge, focusing on issues of sexual emancipation and advocating state support for unmarried mothers. Its rival, the women's group of the German Social Democratic Party (SPD), had positioned itself against the *Frauenbewegung* as the "true" defender of women's interests by insisting on women's economic independence through paid labor as the key to equality and emancipation. In the broader society, a separate-spheres family model with a male breadwinner and a woman exclusively in the home was vigorously promulgated by German neotraditionalist nationalists. The war experience had generated considerable nostalgia for this latter vision of family life.[40]

Prewar German feminists (like their counterparts in other European countries) had elaborated a concept of "spiritual" or "extended" motherhood that empowered women as mothers and nurturers (applicable to women that were single and childless as well as to married mothers) to act throughout society and claim a significant role in the nation. While this concept retained notions of women's special qualities and strengths, it was not at all contiguous with the notion of separate spheres that restricted women to domesticity and private life. In progressive hands, it provided a powerful and empowering vision. This vision still inspired German feminists in the 1920s. BDF activist Agnes von Zahn–Harnack described it this way: "Organized Motherhood . . . not only sends women into the nursery schools, kindergartens and schools, but also into the ministries and parliaments. . . . This is not the oft-praised division of labor, man:mind, woman:heart . . . but the humanization of work, the humanization of the sciences, the humanization of contact among peoples."[41]

In postwar Germany, however, as in many other war-torn European countries, the polarized view of the sexes based on a thoroughgoing sexual division of labor still had many supporters. Before the war, Germany had its share of committed antifeminists, including the emperor Wilhelm II himself, who was well known throughout Europe as the forceful advocate of the "three K's"—*Kinder, Kirche, Küche*—for women. Germany had its patriarchal League for Large Families as well. German antifeminists also included some remarkably articulate women, such as Kathinka von Rosen and Ida von Meerheimb. In response to the growing momentum generated by the pre-1914 women's movement, significant antifeminist organizations had taken root, notably the Deutsche Bund zur Bekämpfung der Frauenemanzipation (German League for the Prevention of Women's Emancipation, 1912–20), whose motto was "Genuine manliness for men; genuine femininity for women."[42] This league was concerned that "equal rights would lead to a 'feminization and a weakening of the state itself,'" and sought to confine working women to "female professions."[43]

Following defeat in 1918 and the peaceful revolution that ousted the Hohenzollern dynasty, some German feminists, like those in Austria, had reason to celebrate on at least one front: they obtained the vote. Women of twenty and over were enfranchised in late 1918 and voted for the first time in early 1919 for the Constituent Assembly. But the conditions in which this "success" was realized were equivocal, as historians Renate Bridenthal and Claudia Koonz have pointed out:[44]

> The right to vote had been given to women in the hope that women voters would help to ensure the defeat of Bolshevism and to provide a progressive, liberal image of Germany at the Paris Peace Conference. When the crisis of 1918–1919 subsided, so did loyalty to *all* of the Weimar reforms, which had been dictated by opportunism, not idealism.

According to the new electoral law, candidates would be elected on party lists and by proportional representation. Men's and women's votes were to be counted separately. In this country of some sixty million people, following war losses, women outnumbered men absolutely; the 1925 electorate showed 21.0 million women electors, compared with 18.8 million male electors.[45] Electoral results would ultimately reveal that, as in Austria, the religiously affiliated parties of the Center and Right profited most from women's votes; the new German Communist Party (KPD) would profit least. The reorganized Social Democratic Party (SPD), which proudly insisted on its record in supporting women's true emancipation through work, benefited less than its leaders had hoped, despite the fact that the SPD did include a number of women on its party lists. As in Austria, SPD supporters did elect the largest delegation of women deputies to the Reichstag. Under the Weimar Republic's list-based electoral system, however, no deputy held a personal mandate. Voters supported the party and its program, not the individuals that represented it. Unless the party was willing to throw its full weight behind legislation, its individual deputies had little scope for independent action.[46]

In 1919 the new Constituent Assembly of the Weimar Republic, heavily populated by social democratic deputies, produced a constitution that explicitly incorporated—at least on paper—equal rights for both sexes (Articles 109, 119, 128), including the vote for women and their admission to public office. The earlier woman suffrage organizations soon disappeared, in contrast to their counterparts in England, which reformulated their mission without dissolving themselves. Was this decision, in the German case, simply the consequence of political naïveté? How could feminist activists not realize that there was no legal mechanism for translating these constitutional clauses into effective legislation?

The new Reichstag welcomed forty-one women deputies, representing various political parties, but preponderantly the SPD. Some of the new deputies were feminists of varying degrees, including Gertrud Bäumer, former president of the BDF, and Toni Sender, an Independent Social Democrat and socialist-feminist from Frankfurt. As time went on, these women deputies found it difficult to come to agreement on a common platform or even to work together. They did cooperate in two significant areas, however, supporting measures to enhance protective legislation and maternity benefits as well as measures to foster civic equality. Like their Austrian counterparts, these women deputies disagreed sharply over issues concerning equality for married women, especially in the workplace, and over protection for unwed mothers and their children. Both Catholic and Evangelical (Protestant) women deputies balked at supporting "immorality" and employment guarantees for married women, whom they believed should be at home.

Even though they collectively constituted some 10 percent of the deputies, women in the Reichstag "owed their seats . . . to a political system which was entirely male dominated": "Whatever their loyalties to specifically women's issues, they could not count on being returned to the legislature if they threatened party unity or broke with party discipline in voting."[47] Nor did their female constituents necessarily support women's emancipation, at least that form of emancipation advocated by the Social Democratic Party leadership. The hoped-for coalition of women voters on behalf of women's ostensible common interests never came together during the short life of the Weimar Republic; again like their Austrian counterparts, women voters in Germany did not even support the political parties that had been most favorable to women's rights before the war. Historian Richard J. Evans underscored the point: "[German] women as a whole put party loyalty before their real or supposed interests as women, even . . . on issues that vitally affected these interests."[48]

In retrospect, this outcome is not totally surprising. The period of the

Weimar Republic (1919–33) was "a roller-coaster ride into chaos," marked by drastic inflation, continued hunger, periodic political crises, and above all growing resentment against the imposed peace settlement.[49] The leaders of the male-dominated political parties confronted a series of extremely tough problems; nevertheless, they did not welcome contributions by the women deputies in efforts to resolve them. In the world beyond parliamentary politics, many German women found themselves overburdened, even overwhelmed, by circumstances that seemed entirely beyond their control; less politically experienced, and more economically exploited, than their male contemporaries, they developed a certain nostalgic vision of the status quo ante to accompany a keen sense of wounded German pride: "The women of the Weimar Republic failed to embrace their putative emancipation and even rejected it politically. . . . The home was to the German woman what the workshop or small business or farm was to the German man. It meant status, independence, respectability, and security. It was, in short, territory to be defended."[50]

Given this deep-seated antifeminism among German women and men, feminists in German women's organizations found themselves in difficulties. The once radical BDF (Bund Deutscher Frauenvereine) had thrown itself behind the war effort, becoming increasingly nationalistic and chauvinistic, and continuing in this vein following the Allied victory and the installation of the new republican regime. Its new program of 1919, as Richard J. Evans has pointed out, "breathed a strongly *völkisch* nationalistic spirit."[51]

Objecting to the harsh terms of the Treaty of Versailles in 1919, the BDF leadership refused for several years to take part in the postwar meetings of the International Council of Women. Its revised program did not champion women's emancipation, but emphasized the family institution and an "appropriate" sexual division of labor, and charitable work—not paid labor—for women. Gone was the demand for state support for unmarried mothers and their children; gone were the demands for sexual emancipation and a new sexual ethics promoted by the Bund für Mutterschutz. Even so, critic Marie Diers argued in 1920 that the women's movement had gone too far (during the war) in promoting women's "competition" with men: "The over-emphasis and over-valuation of individual parts hopelessly disturb the perfection of the whole."[52] This was the state of the organization that Renate Bridenthal has described as having "an ideological profile so low as to bring its feminist credentials into question."[53]

During the 1920s the BDF became increasingly a federation of relatively conservative corporate economic interest groups, ranging from the enormous National Federation of German Housewives to the Rural Housewives' Federation, along with the women's white-collar employees' association and the female postal workers' union.[54] The BDF's one great success, in 1927, was to achieve the abolition of regulated prostitution; in the interim, its campaigns opposed the liberalization of sexual morality that characterized Weimar culture, particularly that associated with loose life in the capital city of Berlin.

Under Gertrud Bäumer's successors as president of the BDF, Marianne Weber (1919–31) and Agnes von Zahn–Harnack (1931–34), the organization's drift toward the right continued. Characteristically, von Zahn–Harnack's 1928 historical account of the German women's movement "almost totally ignore[d] the radical wing of feminism."[55] For the BDF, campaigns for the legal actualization of women's constitutional equal rights—in a republic in which rights acknowledged on paper had no teeth behind them—had become past history: the Civil Code of 1895 (enacted in 1900), which gave husbands so much power over wives in marriage, was never amended; the campaigns for equal pay and professional parity were effectively abandoned, and employment of married women was not defended. Efforts to magnify women's political clout by mobilizing their votes, particularly through the establishment of a women's political party (*Frauenpartei*) came to nothing (though such women's parties did materialize, however briefly, in Sweden and in Austria, and more enduringly in the United States). Some Germans believed, when they looked at the election results, that *all* the political parties had become *Frauenparteien*, since women's demographic strength gave them a potentially preponderant voice in every single one. Yet German women never spoke at the polls in a feminist voice during the years of the Weimar Republic.

In the early 1930s, as Germany again plunged into economic depression, the two housewives' associations voted to leave the BDF. Lacking its earlier numerical strength, the BDF never protested government measures in 1932 to dismiss married women from the civil service, ostensibly to combat severe male unemployment. Indeed, by then, German citizens, frustrated by the ravages of the depression and by the ineffectiveness of their parliamentary system in resolving any of the outstanding problems, increasingly pondered notions of state corporatism along the lines already proposed in Mussolini's Italy, in Hungary, and elsewhere. In these circumstances, the BDF could think of no more effective strategy than to advocate (as the BÖFV in Austria had also proposed) that women might constitute one such corporation within a postparliamentary state.

Renate Bridenthal's generalization about the BDF does not, however, cover all aspects of German feminism. Radical feminists of the so-called left wing of the German women's movement, who were ardent suffragists before the war, had long since been expelled from the BDF for their antiwar agitation and internationalist stance during wartime. In the 1920s two leaders of this faction, Anita Augspurg and Lida Gustava Heymann, continued their agitation from Munich, even founding a new monthly journal, *Die Frau im Staat* (1919–32), to foster women's participation in national affairs. They and their supporters actively participated in the Women's International League for Peace and Freedom (WILPF), founded in the wake of the 1919 Zurich women's congress. When Hitler came to power in 1933, Augspurg and Heymann were traveling in Italy, and quickly decided to seek refuge in Switzerland rather than return to Germany. Other radical feminists, many of them Jewish, left the country voluntarily or were forced into exile. The women of the German WILPF were among the few who put up some resistance to the Nazi regime. But resistance was difficult; any woman, feminist or not, who openly resisted might find herself under arrest and in a concentration camp—just like a man.

Confessional feminist efforts were considerably more constrained in their political action than the Augspurgs and the Heymanns would have liked. Parallel to the Catholic and Evangelical Protestant women's federations, Jewish women had their own BDF-affiliated organization, the Jüdischer Frauenbund (Jewish Women's Federation, JFB: 1904–38), headed by Bertha Pappenheim.[56] This organization worked for equal rights for women within the Jewish community; although Jewish women, like all other German women, could vote in local and national elections after 1918, they were still (like Evangelical Protestant women in their churches) denied a voice in Jewish communal affairs, especially in regard to leadership positions. The JFB also established a number of social services specifically for Jewish girls and women—including refuges for unwed mothers and improved vocational training—many of these intended for recently arrived girls from poor Eastern European Jewish families. In addition, its members dedicated considerable effort to combatting regulated prostitution and the so-called white-slave trade, which shortly before the war came to be called the "traffic in girls and women" and increasingly stocked houses of prostitution in cities and ports around the world, particularly in Argentina and in the Middle East.[57]

The JFB's founder, Bertha Pappenheim, was born in Vienna, but her mother was from a Frankfurt family, and the two women returned there in 1889. Even as a girl Pappenheim recognized that boys were deemed more important and that the education of girls left a great deal to be desired. As a young woman, suffering from the monotonous existence of a marriageable upper-class Viennese daughter, she was treated by Dr. Josef Breuer in the early 1880s and contributed to the "talking cure" therapy, which Breuer and Sigmund Freud went on to pioneer as psychoanalysis. When she was forty, she wrote a play on women's rights and translated Mary Wollstonecraft's *Vindication of the Rights of Woman*, which she had somehow discovered, into German.

In founding the JFB in 1904, Pappenheim was determined to establish an independent Jewish women's organization, not an auxiliary to a male organization such as the B'nai B'rith sisterhoods. In particular, the JFB would be Jewish, but not Zionist; to combat anti-Semitism it would emphasize working with non-Jewish women, particularly within the framework of the BDF. The JFB eventually included around 25 percent of Jewish women in Germany, most of whom were middle-class housewives and not nearly as committed to women's rights as Pappenheim: in September 1926, one member insisted in the JFB publication that "we are not the so-called emancipated women": "We definitely do not want to be quasi-men and do not want to compete with men or displace them. On the contrary, we want to remain particularly womanly, particularly feminine women. We want to carry softness, warmth, love, and motherliness into life wherever we can."[58] The defensive tone in this statement is manifest and speaks to the tensions that existed within the organization; building self-worth through womanly social work was one thing, but mounting outspoken challenges, both within and outside the Jewish community, was quite another. The JFB persisted, insisting in 1924 that "the Jewish community needs our collaboration more than ever": "We are unanimous in our fight . . . for our rights! Not because we are power hungry. Not because we are suffragettes, but because we are convinced that women's work is necessary for the cultural development of the Jewish community and that we can accomplish good . . . in official communal posts precisely because we are women." By 1927, the JFB had succeeded in getting votes for women in the *Gemeinden* of six out of seven major German cities, though not in Berlin. Nevertheless, in Marion Kaplan's judgment, "the conflict between Judaism and feminism was one the JFB could never resolve to its own satisfaction."[59] In respect to feminist convictions, Bertha Pappenheim and her close associates Henriette Fürth and Ottlie Schönewald remained well out in front of their troops.

As was the case elsewhere in Europe in the 1920s, concern over the issue of population and the falling birthrate had a significant effect on German feminist action during the Weimar Republic. Imperial officials had begun to fret about the declining birthrate well before the war—in much the same manner as French authorities had several decades earlier—and quickly placed blame on fertility control and abortion, and more generally on women's emancipation. During the war this concern had turned to panic, and the government began to formulate an unrepentantly interventionist pronatalist policy. Despite the inauguration of a state maternity benefit for the wives of men in military service, financial support for unwed mothers, and prohibitions against publicity and distribution of contraceptives and abortificants, by 1918 the birthrate had dropped still further, to half the prewar level. The fall of the imperial government in 1918 thwarted a nearly successful attempt to ram through a series of harsh measures, mostly directed at regulating women's sexual practices.

Feminist responses to these efforts were guarded, but did protest the exclusive emphasis on faulting women. Historian Cornelie Usborne reports that, for once, bourgeois and socialist women cooperated in sending a delegation to protest the repressive 1918 Reichstag bill. But spokeswomen for the BDF nevertheless supported many features of the government program, even as they tried to turn it to women's advantage by demanding more substantive support for mothers. What is clear is that "fertility control, more than anything else, created the concept of the New Woman, which was to play so prominent a part during the Weimar Republic."[60] But the birthrate decline continued until 1933, when at 14.3 births per 1,000 women it became the lowest in all Europe, and the number of miscarriages reported by women who already had children seemed suspiciously high to populationists.

The Weimar government did make significant contributions to supporting mothers and children, though the dramatic difficulties created by inflation and depression severely limited their impact. Women newly arrived in government following their enfranchisement helped to achieve a qualitative and effective approach to maternity, far different from the repressive system envisioned before and during the war. In 1919 SPD deputy Adele Schreiber called for increased state support in order that "maternity no longer oppresses and burdens the individual woman but becomes the concern of the public at large."[61] In 1925, Anna-

Margarete Stegmann, a physician and also an SPD deputy, delivered her maiden speech in the Reichstag on maternity and reproductive freedom: "We must grant people freedom to develop and give women control over their own bodies."[62] Socialists and feminists agreed that punitive approaches to the population problem must be replaced by social welfare approaches. Family allowances for state employees and civil servants, plus family wages for male workers, were among the proposals initiated under the Weimar government. Thus did protection of mothers became a signal feature of politics on the Left, including the SPD and the KPD, as well as on the Right, although with a very different emphasis.

Abortion, however, remained the thorniest, most controversial issue for feminist activists. Both the SPD and the KPD attempted from the early 1920s on to attract women voters through opposing antiabortion laws; thanks to pressure from party women, intermittent rallies and other forms of organized protest had developed. In early 1930, however, as the economic crisis deepened, the Catholic Center party controlled the government, forcing deep cuts in welfare programs. In the encyclical *Casti Connubii* (31 December 1930) the pope spoke out yet again on "family" issues, condemning all nonreproductive sexuality and any and all measures to thwart pregnancy.

In response the KPD launched a massive campaign to attract women supporters by challenging the Vatican and pointedly advocating the legalization of abortion. Campaigners determined to revoke Article 218 of the 1871 Penal Code (revised in the direction of lighter penalties in 1926), which criminalized this act, inflicting harsh penalties on the aborting woman as well as on those who assisted her. Sex reformers, women physicians, radical feminists, pacifist feminists, Social Democrats, and many others rallied in support of this campaign. The KPD conspicuously dangled the example of Bolshevik Russia's success story before the Weimar government it challenged and sought to bring down in the name of the proletarian revolution. In this instance, a still-minority political party was deliberately deploying a "woman's issue" to achieve a broader goal; no longer were the German communists, as historian Anita Grossmann has pointed out, maintaining their earlier exclusive focus on women as workers. Once unleashed, however, the movement accelerated well beyond the KPD's ability to control it.

When two conspicuously pro-abortion physicians were arrested in Stuttgart, in February 1931, the campaign began in earnest. One of these physicians, the communist Friedrich Wolf, had authored a controversial play, *Cyankali*, whose closing line was "A law that turns 800,000 mothers into criminals every year is no longer a law." This line became "the battlecry of a growing movement."[63] Indeed, the movement grew to very serious proportions, incorporating newspaper surveys, cultural events, and massive street demonstrations, in addition to anti-218 posters by important women artists such as Alice Lex-Nerlinger. The International Women's Day celebration organized by the KPD on 8 March featured 1,500 demonstrations throughout Germany; the communist women's movement emphatically articulated its position on the issues of abortion and contraception: "We women refuse to let ourselves be regarded as baby machines and then additionally to serve as slaves in the production process. . . . Our slogan is not 'back into the family,' but equal wages for equal work."[64] In mid-April a mass rally sponsored by the KPD featured the two incriminated physicians, who challenged their audience to seek freedom for birth control and better lives. The second of the arrested physicians, Dr. Else Kienle, developed a strongly feminist position in her prison journal, published in 1932: "Of what use is suffrage to woman if she is still to remain a helpless baby machine?"[65] Others called for an entirely new sexual code as well as an acceptance of societal responsibility for motherhood. Conspicuously, the leadership of the BDF stayed on the sidelines, even as the repeal movement peaked and ultimately quieted down. Article 218 remained in force until the 1970s.

What energy German feminism might still have had was abruptly terminated by the coming to power in 1933 of Adolf Hitler and his Nationalsozialistische Deutsche Arbeiterpartei (National Socialist German Workers' Party, NSDAP; for short, Nazi Party).[66] By 1930 the Nazis had become the second largest political party in Germany; among other concerns, the party stood for reinstituting harsh penalties for abortion, and had introduced a measure to that effect in the Reichstag in March of that year. Though never debated, its wording made the Nazi position sufficiently clear:[67]

> Whosoever undertakes to stem artificially the natural fertility of the German people to the detriment of the nation or makes propaganda for it or who contributes or threatens to contribute to racial deterioration and degeneration by mixing with members of the Jewish or coloured race will be punished with penal servitude for racial treason.

In February 1933, following Hitler's appointment as chancellor, the Nazis immediately suppressed or dissolved all feminist organizations, along with the Socialist and Communist parties, labor unions, and any other independent organizations that might provide rallying points for potential opposition. They shut down birth-control clinics and instituted marriage loans.

The BDF—saving what little honor remained to it in the face of an ultimatum from Lydia Gottschewski, head of the Nazi Frauenfront—voted to dissolve itself in order to avoid being taken over. The Nazis had several years earlier (1931) established their own party women's section, the NS-Frauenschaft, which firmly subordinated all organized women's activities to male party direction under Gregor Strasser. Under the Third Reich, women's organizational activism would be strictly channeled into the programs established by male political leaders and run by committed Nazi women such as Gertrud Scholz-Klinck.

Historian Gisela Bock has emphasized that attitudes about race, not sex, were what made Nazism novel: "Nazi sexism was largely traditional, whereas Nazi racism was both novel and deadly."[68] What is important for understanding Nazism from the perspective of a history of European feminisms, however, is that Nazism was not merely "traditional," but explicitly antifeminist as well as anticommunist; its national socialism was of a very particular kind. Nazi leaders actively developed their response to feminism, one which, as in Italy, was elaborated over time and with respect to the particular issues raised by the upheaval of war and defeat—women's employment and reproductive issues.

Already in 1921 the NSDAP had established a rule barring women from party leadership positions.[69] In his lengthy programmatic statement *Mein Kampf* (1925), Adolf Hitler addressed the "woman question" only obliquely. In order to combat prostitution ("a disgrace to mankind") and syphilis ("this plague"), Hitler argued, a nation should foster early marriage, which should serve "the one greater aim, the propagation and preservation of the species and the race," but for this to be possible, better housing and a host of related social reforms must be put into place. Eugenics and solid physical education were all necessary to promote better marriages and better children.[70] Decrepit Germans would beget only more decrepit Germans. This was not the traditional sexism of the Christian churches, nor was it the antifeminism of the nineteenth century. It was a reformulated antifeminism born of anti-Bolshevism and anti–Social Democracy, in which Jews/Bolsheviks (these categories blended together in Nazi discourse) were blamed for taking women out of the realm of the family, marriage, and the home by insisting on their independent employment and on making family limitation possible.

In the mid-1920s, a small group of committed and energetic Nazi women objected to the party's exclusion of women from leadership functions. Their 1926 arguments in the party paper, the *Völkischer Beobachter*, articulated claims for equal participation in all areas of their party's proposed new society; none other than Alfred Rosenberg, the

Nazi party ideologue, countered their claims by insisting (in terms reminiscent of the earlier arguments of Hegel and Treitschke, or even Prudhomme during the French Revolution) on the importance of the *Männerbund*, or men's bonding, as the basis of the state, out of which women should be kept. Rosenberg elaborated the Nazi position in 1930: "Emancipation of woman from the women's emancipation movement is the first demand of a generation of women which would like to save the Volk and the race, the Eternal-Unconscious, the foundation of all culture, from decline and fall. . . . But there must be clarity on one point: only man must be and remain a judge, soldier, and ruler of the state."[71]

In April 1932, Hitler responded to a delegation of women's organizations who had expressed concern over the future of equal rights for women as accorded by the Weimar constitution: "What has the Revolution of 1918 actually done for women? All it has done is to turn 50,000 of them into blue stockings and party officials. Under the Third Reich they might as well whistle for such things. Every woman then will get a husband for herself."[72] This was a remarkable claim for a political party leader to make in a country that still had an absolute surplus of some two million women. The antifeminist arguments of Rosenberg, Hitler, Goebbels, and others were widely noticed abroad as well as at home. For example, in a particularly informative 1934 anti-Nazi tract published in England, Hilda Browning compared and contrasted programmatic statements made by Nazis and by communist leaders in the USSR about women's emancipation. The overall Nazi message as concerned solutions to the woman question could not have been more explicit.

With Hitler's coming to power and the deliberate suppression of feminist activity, the harnessing of women to the aims of the authoritarian Nazi state manifested itself in particularly malignant fashion. The party's perspective on the position of women received further elaboration. It featured, to be sure, a consistently and blatantly antifeminist view of sex roles, insisting on separate spheres and childbearing for women, but it also insisted on the cultivation of women's physical strength and beauty. The importance of women's *auxiliary role* in the Third Reich was repeatedly spelled out by National Socialist spokesmen. "There is no place for the political woman in the ideological world of National Socialism," reiterated Engelbert Huber in 1933; "the German resurrection is a male event."[73] Hitler himself spoke at length on the subject in his address to the NS-Frauenkongress (National Socialist Women's Conference) in 1934: "The phrase 'emancipation of woman' is the product of Jewish intellect, and its content is stamped with that same intellect." Man's world was the state; woman's "world is her husband, her family, her children, and her home," so necessary to the men's world: "We feel it is not correct for a woman to invade man's world." Hitler's emphasis was on "duties," not on "rights." Woman "must be the complement of man"; the sexes must "go hand in hand through life, combating together, just as Providence has ordained and for which purpose Providence created them both."[74] It is not clear just what he thought was "Jewish" about feminist ideas, which had—as we have seen—a long and solid basis in European thought.

Although Hitler envisioned a certain kind of sexual complementarity, his vision was consistently framed as a relation of male domination and female subordination, leavened by glorification; this was the very antithesis of the "spiritual motherhood" throughout society envisioned by earlier German feminists. The Nazi view was systematically underscored by Hitler's minister for propaganda and public enlightenment, Dr. Josef Goebbels, in February 1934: "Woman's proper sphere is the family. There she is a sovereign queen. If we eliminate woman from every realm of public life, we do not do it in order to dishonour her, but in order that her honour may be restored to her."[75] Gertrud Scholtz-Klink, who was subsequently chosen by Strasser to head the Nazi women's organization, was reliably racist as well as an advocate of separate (and subordinate) spheres. The work of the NS-Frauenschaft was "to cooperate in our Führer's work of reconstruction," beginning with the work of the Reich Maternity Service and the Women's Labor Service. In contrast to the earlier women's movement, "in principle we permit only Germans to be leaders of German women and to concern themselves with matters of importance to Germans. . . . We have never demanded, nor shall we ever demand, equal rights for women with the men of our nation."[76] Scholtz-Klink repeatedly reminded Nazi women that national needs must take precedence over women's special interests.

Hitler, Goebbels, and Scholtz-Klink were responding not only to a challenge from a perceived feminist enemy from without, now associated with "Jewishness" and Bolshevism, but also to a challenge led by a small group of articulate feminists within the Nazi Party. Historians Leila Rupp, Richard Johnson, Jost Hermand, and Liliane Crips have variously told the story of these "Nazi feminists," whose challenges were finally crushed.[77] As Richard Johnson points out, these Nazi women were both racist and elitist, yet within the Nazi framework their claims were undeniably feminist: they argued, in Tennysonian style, for "two heads in council." Their views were most dramatically stated in a collection of essays published shortly after Hitler's seizure of power in early 1933, *Deutsche Frauen an Adolf Hitler* (German Women to Adolf Hitler), edited by Irmgard Reichenau. In this work, the longtime Nazi sympathizer Sophie Rogge-Börner squarely stated the claim that "a *Volksgemeinschaft* [community] of Germanic blood cannot in the long run be led and controlled only by men."[78] Her arguments were seconded in 1934 by Lydia Gottschewski, in a lengthy tract, *Männerbund und Frauenfrage: Die Frau in neuen Staat* (Male Association and the Woman Question: Woman in the New State). These Nazi women claimed equal partnership in the new regime; they fingered sexism and male domination as the *origin* of the decadence that Nazism decried. Sophie Philipps argued that "in the politics of the new Germany the active political influence of the woman is indispensable."[79] Invoking matriarchy and equal sharing of governance in a pre-Judeo-Christian Teutonic warrior society, these women called for a return to such a configuration of power. It was not excessive masculinity that new times called for, but a new, androgynous being, argued Irmgard Reichenau. In the periodical *Die Deutsche Kampferin* (The German Woman Warrior, 1933–37), Sophie Rogge-Börner and her associates persisted in demanding the inclusion of women in the power structure of the Third Reich, as well as individual self-determination. They objected to the emphasis on marriage and motherhood:[80]

> To acquire a husband is not every girl's goal; just any man will not satisfy a girl who is a really valuable member of the community of our people. Such girls would refuse to play the part of breeding cattle. . . . Nowhere do we find a divine or natural law allowing one of the sexes to claim all the pleasant, honourable, well-paid and leading positions for itself, and leaving the menial, hard and badly-paid jobs to the other.

In September 1934, the *Deutsche Kämpferin* criticized the Nazis' reintroduction of state-regulated brothels: "How can a community of people be brought about when the law allows one half of the community to treat the other half as a marketable commodity, and when the female portion alone is under control, and may eventually be punished, as a result of outrages against decency committed by both of them?"

This sort of overt feminist criticism was unwelcome, and Nazi male leaders soon countered. At the 1935 Party Days, as Hitler was mounting his war effort, he again spoke to the NS-Frauenkongress, collapsing feminism with Marxism:[81]

> The so-called granting of equal rights to women, which Marxism demands, in reality does not grant equal rights but constitutes a deprivation of rights, since it draws the woman into an area in which she will necessarily be inferior. . . . I would be ashamed to be a German man if in the event of a war even only one woman had to go to the front. The woman has her own battlefield. With every child that she brings into the

world, she fights her battle for the nation. The man stands up for the Volk, exactly as the woman stands up for the family.

In 1936, at the height of German rearmament and defiance of the Treaty of Versailles, Hitler spoke out again against the notion of the German woman warrior: "So long as we possess a healthy manly race—and we National Socialists will attend to that—we will form no female mortar battalions and no female sharpshooter corps. For that is not equality of rights, but a diminution of the rights of woman."[82]

In 1937 the Nazi regime silenced Rogge-Börner's publication, *Die Deutsche Kämpferin*. Apart from religious women's organizations, Scholtz-Klink and the Nazi women's organization remained the only game in town for activist women during the Third Reich. Even when women were recalled to the labor force as Hitler headed toward total war in the late 1930s, it was not in the interest of their emancipation but in the further service of the reinvigorated German nation as *Männerbund*. In the 1940s Hitler would even requisition male labor from defeated and Nazi-occupied countries such as France to keep the Third Reich's war production going, rather than conscript women as the English would ultimately do. Jews, on the other hand, were deemed disposable both as breeders and as workers; between 1941 and 1945 the Nazis executed millions of Jewish women and children right along with Jewish men, Gypsies, Bolsheviks, social democrats, and other "undesirables."

11

More Feminisms in National Settings

Portugal, Ireland, Spain, and Sweden

The question is often posed as to whether the Nazi phenomenon in Germany was unique or whether it simply offers an extreme case of more general European cultural developments. This historical survey of feminisms with respect to the major political events of the times should make it clear that there were a number of parallel developments, and that a central concern for those who organized right-wing movements of a nationalist sort, including fascist and national-socialist movements, and those who supported these movements, was to put a stop to feminist aspirations and to channel women's movements for their own ends. Their commitment to male dominance and their hostility to feminism is deliberate, sustained, and central to their common projects.

Attempts to preserve male hegemony in European settings figured significantly in the development of both aggressive and defensive nationalisms, as well as fascisms, as is revealed by case studies of two small, predominantly Catholic countries, Portugal and Ireland, and a far larger nation, Spain. Where aggressively right-wing movements were muted, and where the hold of Catholicism was less significant, and the society more secularized, feminists had an easier time, as the case of Sweden will suggest. In most of these cases, but especially in Spain and Sweden, feminist approaches were confronted with both opposition from and co-optation by social democratic and communist activists, enthusiastic about the experiment in reshaping sexual relations in the USSR and emboldened by the Third International's attempt, at least theoretically, to export the Russian model.

PORTUGAL

In the rural, Catholic nation of Portugal, the First Republic replaced an old monarchical state in 1910, at which point a tiny but enthusiastic organized feminist movement established itself in Lisbon in conjunction with demands for manhood suffrage. Portuguese men were enfranchised in 1911. The Liga Republicana das Mulheres Portuguesas (Republican League of Portuguese Women), in which Adelaide Cabete and Ana de Castro Osório played significant parts, agitated for women's inclusion in the work of the new republic, and for the sustained education of women about democratic principles. This group, which had hundreds of members, also worked for a divorce law, for the economic autonomy of married women, and for a number of other legal reforms that would pave the way for women's future as "autonomous and conscious individuals."[1]

Realization of these initiatives was cut short by World War I, during which the Portuguese government joined the side of the Allies, particularly to assist England. In contrast to the major combatant countries, war casualties did not precipitate a national trauma; in 1920, Portugal had a population of about six million, most of whom were relatively unschooled in democratic ways. A military coup d'état took control of the republic in 1926, and with Antonio de Oliveira Salazar's imposition of an authoritarian regime, most feminists found themselves in opposition to the "New State," whose principles were unhesitatingly Catholic, nationalist, and corporatist. The Salazarist constitution of 1933 granted equal rights—except for sexual equality—pleading the importance for women's exclusion from such rights based on "differences resulting from their nature and from the good of the family."[2] Only women who had completed secondary or higher education could vote, and they could also be elected—but in a single-party system, where no choice existed, this amounted to a Pyrrhic victory. The three women deputies elected in 1933 were conservative, Catholic, and single.

As in Italy under Mussolini, and subsequently in Germany under Hitler, Salazar's administration permitted only officially organized women's associations such as the Obra das Mães para a Educação Nacional (OMEN, Mothers for National Education) and the Mocidade Portuguesa Feminina (MPF, Portuguese Young Women's Organization). After World War II (in which Portugal remained neutral), the "unofficial" National Council of Portuguese Women was dissolved by government order, as was the Portuguese women's peace association. The "real reasons" for their dissolution, according to historians Anne Cova and Antonio Costa Pinto, had to do with their members' outspoken participation in the emerging clandestine resistance to Salazar's "New State."[3]

Not only was coeducation at the primary schools abolished, but the constitution of 1966 reestablished the principle of marital authority exercised by husbands. In the meantime feminist advocates found their articles censured or relegated to the women's page in daily papers. Only in the concluding years of Salazarism in the early 1970s did the adverse situation change and feminist activism and protest reemerge in Portugal.

IRELAND

The new Republic of Ireland, established in the early 1920s, provides a well-documented case study of tensions between feminism and nationalism. In the eighteenth century Ireland had enjoyed its own parliament, but since 1799 (with the failure of the Irish independence movement, which was aided by revolutionary France) the Irish had been roughly treated as a sort of English colony, with the result that a strong movement for the rebirth of Irish culture and Home Rule, with an eye toward independence, developed during the late nineteenth century. As we have seen in Chapter 8, this aggressively nationalist movement flourished in the early twentieth century, and it was paralleled by a highly vocal feminist movement focused firmly on obtaining suffrage for all Irish women.[4]

Ardently nationalist Irish women were concerned about channeling the suffragist fixation. In her much-quoted speech "Women, Ideals and the Nation" (later reprinted as *Call to the Women of Ireland*), the militant Irish nationalist feminist Constance (Gore-Booth) Markievicz warned women against joining suffrage societies that did not prominently feature national independence as a goal: "'A Free Ireland with no Sex Disabilities in her Constitution' should be the motto of all Nationalist women. And a grand motto it is." She compared the Irish cause with that of the Russians combatting the tsar and the Poles' search for independence. (Markievicz's husband, Casimir, was of Polish descent.) Ireland was being governed as "an alien province": "England is now holding by force three civilised nations, . . . Ireland, India and Egypt, not to consider her savage territories and South Africa." Markievicz called on her younger countrywomen to put their nation before their sex: "The old idea that a woman can only serve her nation through her home is gone, so now is the time; on you the responsibility rests . . . you must make the world look upon you as citizens first, as women after."[5]

The Proclamation of the Irish Republic, issued during the Easter Uprising of 1916, stipulated equal political rights for Irishmen and Irishwomen:[6]

> The Irish Republic is entitled to, and hereby claims, the allegiance of every Irishman and Irishwoman. The Republic guarantees religious and civil liberty, equal rights and equal opportunities to all its citizens and declares its resolve to pursue the happiness and prosperity of the whole

nation and of all its parts, cherishing all the children of the nation equally.

The Easter Uprising was followed by a state of undeclared war with England. Thanks to the brutality of the English repression, in which all the male leaders of the uprising, including the feminist pacifist Francis Sheehy Skeffington, were executed and many others imprisoned, the Irish independence movement led by the Sinn Féin Party gained great popular support. Militarism on behalf of independence was contagious. Enthused by the example of Constance Markievicz and others, many Irish women became activists for independence along with the men.

Ironically, Irish women obtained the vote from the British Parliament before they had a sovereign nation to call their own. The Irish parliamentary delegation continued to oppose women's inclusion. With the passage of the Representation of the People Act in early 1918, the British Parliament enfranchised Irish women thirty and over as well as their English counterparts; men were enfranchised at the age of twenty-one. The women of Cumann na mBan, the women's organization associated with the Irish nationalist party, Sinn Féin, made haste to bid for women's votes to support the cause of Irish independence:[7]

> Irishwomen, your country calls to you to do your share in restoring her to her rightful place among the nations. . . .
> The Sinn Féin Party stands for an Ireland developing all her resources industrial and agricultural, and able to provide well paid employment for all Irishmen and Irishwomen.
> An Ireland collecting her own taxes, and spending them in the country which produced them, for the development of that country.
> An Ireland free from the bad of England's war debt.
> A prosperous Ireland—prosperous as Denmark, Holland, Norway and Sweden are prosperous.
> An educated and enlightened Ireland.
> An independent Ireland.

Sinn Féin was the only political party to nominate women candidates in the 1918 general election; two were elected, including Constance Markievicz, who was by then a prisoner of the English government. She never took her seat, and instead became minister of labor in the rebel Irish republican government.

Nationalism triumphed during the years of war with England over the question of independence. In the final issue of the suffragist publication *Irish Citizen* (late 1920), the now widowed Hanna Sheehy Skeffington, who had poured her energy into the Irish Women's Franchise League, regretfully described how the Irish women's movement had become a casualty of the war: "Women became patriots or heroes' wives or widows, rather than human beings, so now in Ireland the national struggle overshadows all else."[8]

In late 1921 Ireland's twenty-six southern counties, with a population of under three million, successfully obtained Home Rule—that is to say, legislative independence—though remaining under the administrative umbrella of the British Commonwealth, with a London-appointed governor-general. An oath of allegiance to the king was still required of representatives; this alienated all of the more radical Sinn Féiners, who advocated nothing less than a fully independent Irish Republic. In 1922 the Constitution of the Irish Free State (*Saorstat Éireann* in Gaelic) established a two-house parliament, and Article 3 proclaimed: "All citizens shall, as human persons, be held equal before the law, without distinction of sex." Women and men twenty-one and over could vote and hold office. But in the Irish Free State, as in the earlier suffrage struggle, it seemed that the greatest enemies of women's full emancipation were Irish nationalist men, not the least of whom was Eamon De Valera, who would play a major role in Irish politics as prime minister and foreign minister during the next twenty years. The 1922 constitution, in the judgment of historian Rosemary Cullen Owens, was "the last piece of progressive legislation affecting women until recent times."[9] There was no shortage of targets for Irish feminists to redress, beginning with the singularly dispossessed situation of wives in civil law.

Between 1922 and 1937, eleven women served in the Dáil (House of Representatives) and in the Seanad (Senate); most of them were either widows or sisters of men earlier active in Irish political life, and few of them applied a feminist perspective to legislation. As historian Mary Clancy has underscored, "women representatives are not necessarily progressive merely by virtue of gender, but . . . factors such as conservative political orientation, religion, and class must also be taken into consideration."[10] Only senators Jennie Wyse Powers and Kathleen Clarke, both veteran Sinn Féiners (Wyse Powers had long been vice-president), spoke out sharply in the legislature when various restrictive measures were debated.[11] On matters concerning divorce, access to contraceptive information, raising the age of consent for girls, the legal situation of unmarried mothers, and prostitution—all discussed in the legislature during the 1920s and 1930s—most women deputies kept an exceedingly low profile. Efforts to restrict women's employment, particularly by barring women from the civil service in various ways (1925) or by curbing their employment in industry (1935), were combatted by the two women senators, who repeatedly criticized the failure of Irish nationalist men to stand together with Irish women. Feminist opposition was alive and well in a cluster of Irish women's groups, but it was all too little represented in the new Irish parliament.

Irish feminists strongly opposed legislative efforts to exempt women from jury service in 1924 and again in 1927. Historian Maryann Gialanella Valiulis has remarked the symbolic importance of the debate over women's right to sit on juries: "What was at issue was women's demand to participate in the public, political life of the country and, on a broader level, women's post-colonial identity. . . . The first indigenous government of the Irish Free State sought to eliminate women from public life, to take away from women rights which they already possessed."[12] In 1924 the issue was exemption on demand, because many women seemed reluctant to serve on juries. The resolution sent to all members of the Dáil by the Irish Women's Citizens' Association insisted "that women have no right to evade the duties and responsibilities involved in citizenship"; to exempt them on grounds of their sex alone would be "unfair to the men citizens and derogatory to the women."[13] In 1927 the government went still further, calling for complete removal of women from jury service, given that most women did apply for exemption. The government argued that keeping lists of exemptions and non-exemptions was too expensive, that providing public facilities for women jurors was inexpedient. The minister of justice, Kevin O'Higgens, went further to criticize those women who defended women's jury service as "advanced propagandist women," "self-appointed spokeswomen," and not representative of women in general, who he claimed had no interest in serving on juries. Women's rights groups strongly objected; they insisted that "access to jury service was a 'constitutional right which no Minister can tamper with without violating Article 3 of the Constitution of the Irish Free State.'"[14] What would be targeted next? The vote itself?

Outside Parliament, a most important debate took place on this issue in the Dublin press. Feminists such as Hanna Sheehy Skeffington publicly countered the government ministers' arguments; they argued, further, that no women's groups had been consulted. In the Senate, Jennie Wyse Powers insisted that passage of this disqualification law would arrest women's public spirit, which had been developed during the previous fifty years when "the men who led political movements and carried them in the main to success utilised women in order to achieve their object."[15] In the continuing press debate, women's groups and individuals also pressed arguments for sexual complementarity, or "equality-in-difference," as reasons why women brought something unique to jury service. Spokeswomen for groups as diverse as the Irish Women Workers' Union (IWWU) and the Save the Children Fund insisted on women's civic presence as jurors, whatever the crime and whoever the accused. Nor would women "neglect" their homes if called to jury duty: "Surely the argument of the neglected home and husband has become too thin and poor to be referred to save by way of joke in any civilised country."[16] The government did introduce an amendment that would allow women to volunteer, which promptly led to unflattering remarks about what kind of "respectable" women would possibly serve. The bill passed, as amended. The opposition coalition simply did not have the votes to stop it.

New obstacles would soon be placed in the path of Irish feminists by Roman Catholic Church authorities. Even before the papal encyclicals of the early 1930s reinforced their views, Irish Catholic sociologists spoke out against women's work. For example, the Jesuit Edward Cahill wrote in 1925:[17]

> It is the duty of a Christian State to remedy, by prudent legislation, the abuses which have driven an excessive number of women into industrial employment outside the home. . . . In a Christian State women should be excluded even by law from occupations unbecoming or dangerous to female modesty. The employment of wives or mothers in factories or outside their own household should be strictly limited by legislation.

The counties of the Irish Free State had hardly any factories, and a very low rate of female employment. But trouble was anticipated. Thus, in 1935, passage of the Conditions of Employment Act, which severely restricted female employment opportunities, ensured that the Irish Free State would be blacklisted by the International Labour Office of the League of Nations on grounds of sex discrimination in its employment conditions. It was exactly this sort of thing that Louie Bennett's Irish Women Workers' Union had been organized to prevent.[18]

In 1937 came the effort of Prime Minister Eamon de Valera to rewrite the constitution, establishing the independence of the Irish Republic by fiat. The new constitution was pressed through during the crisis in British politics surrounding the abdication of Edward VIII. The Irish Free State became Eire, or Ireland, and the governor-general was replaced by an elected Irish president. Although the new constitution retained language stipulating equal political rights for men and women, sexual equality abruptly ended there. The words "without distinction of sex" were excised from Article 40.1, which then read: "All citizens shall, as human persons, be held equal before the law." This phrase, shorn of its earlier qualification, was followed by De Valera's addition: "This shall not be held to mean that the State shall not in its enactments have due regard to differences of capacity, physical and moral, and of social function." Once again, the argument from "utility" or "expediency" had sneaked in. In the Irish case, as earlier in France, it marked out a straight path to separate—and in this case, subordinate—spheres.

For feminists, the most controversial aspects of the new constitution lay in three articles. Article 41.2 read as follows:[19]

> (1) In particular the State recognises that by her life within the home, woman gives to the State a support without which the common good cannot be achieved.
> (2) The State shall, therefore, endeavour to ensure that *mothers* shall not be obliged by economic necessity to engage in labour to the neglect of their duties in the home.

This section was followed by Article 45, section 4.2, which read: "The State shall endeavour to ensure that the strength and health of workers, men and women, and the tender age of children shall not be abused and that citizens shall not be forced by economic necessity to enter avocations unsuited to their sex, age or strength." A further measure effectively banned divorce, but this measure was supported at the time by many Irish women, including the feminists who took an active part in Irish political life.

Such proposals could be read—as Eamon De Valera repeatedly insisted—as simply a tribute to the unpaid labor of wives and mothers, and as a conscientious effort to fend off problems with respect to industrialization. But in the broader context of 1930s Europe, following the papal encyclicals of 1930 and 1931 (which had tremendous importance in Catholic Ireland), the stepped-up effort in various countries to remove married women (considered to be "double earners") from the labor force, and particularly the fascist insistence on women's place as outside political and economic life, these measures read somewhat differently. What still surprises is that not one of the three women deputies to the Dáil—the "silent sisters" as Hanna Sheehy Skeffington called them—raised their voices in protest. Again, what opposition there was came from feminists outside.

The press, meeting, and letter-writing campaign mounted by Irish feminists ensured that the public could make no mistake about the problems inherent in the language of the proposed new constitution. Gertrude Gaffney, writing in the *Irish Independent* (7 May 1937), argued that "any curtailment of women's rights as citizens is going to send the whole body of intelligent women eventually into the arms of Communism, which at least promises them fair play." And, she added:[20]

Women are in the majority in this country, and if they let themselves be robbed of the rights that it has taken so long to win they are not only themselves going to suffer for their indifference, but their daughters will suffer more, for their chances of securing work in the future will be reduced by more than half of what they are at present, and bringing them up at all will be a sheer liability.

Mary S. Kettle, who chaired the Joint Committee of Women's Societies, reinforced Gaffney's concern, insisting that "if these Articles (40, 41, 45) become law, no woman who works—be it in trade, factory or profession—will have any security whatsoever."[21]

Louie Bennett, head of the Irish Women Workers' Union, wrote an open letter to the prime minister to protest the proposed wording. The addition to Article 40.1, she insisted, was "a phrase capable of wide interpretations highly dangerous not only to women, but to classes or groups of men and women both. . . . In a period of Fascist ideology such as the world is now experiencing normal workers cannot fail to look with suspicion upon so vague a phrase in so vital a document as this proposed Constitution." As for Article 45, section 4.2, Bennett added, it "opens the door to Fascist legislation of a very objectionable type."[22] The objections by other leading feminists expressed at a protest rally sponsored by the university women's association were only published in July in *Prison Bar*, a small-circulation periodical edited by the venerable Irish cultural nationalist and reformer Maud Gonne MacBride. The protests of Irish feminists were subjected to a blackout in the mainstream Irish press.

Alerted by Irish feminists, international women's groups protested directly to the prime minister's office (Department of the Taoiseach). The chair of the executive committee of the London-based Six Point Group, Betty Arendale, argued that "these clauses are based on a fascist and slave conception of woman as being a non-adult person who is very weak and whose place is in the home." And, she added: "Ireland's fight for freedom would not have been so successful if Irish women had obeyed these clauses. . . . If you would only help the women to be free instead of clamping these tyrannous restrictions on them you would be doing a great service to women and to Ireland."[23] Margery Corbett Ashby, president of the International Alliance of Women for Suffrage and Equal Citizenship, wrote to De Valera of her group's concerns about "any wording which may subsequently be interpreted as permitting discriminations against the woman citizen."[24] Despite the Irish feminists' campaigns against the new constitutional wording, however, the constitutional referendum passed with the objectionable paragraphs intact. Four veteran feminists ran for the Dáil in 1943 on an independent ticket, hoping to rally the support of women voters against the discriminatory clauses and other laws, thus laying the basis for a women's party, but they were resoundingly defeated.

This defeat was enduring. It was only in the 1970s that agitation to ameliorate women's status in Ireland was rekindled. Until then, the fissures through which feminist magma could flow in Ireland were virtually sealed. Despite the significant advances made by Irish feminists in the last twenty years, the objectionable clauses are still embedded in Ireland's constitution in the 1990s.[25]

The Irish case exemplifies what could happen in a new, nominally republican and democratic state where women had acquired political and civil rights but, because of the prevailing political and religious culture, coupled with continuing economic difficulties, did not see the need—or did not have the energy—to use these rights for emancipationist ends, despite vigorous efforts by their feminist sisters to mobilize them in opposition to the masculinist politics of republican men.

SPAIN

Spain, with a population in 1930 of 23.5 million, was a larger and more diverse country than either Portugal or the Republic of Ireland. Still dominantly rural and Catholic, it was a federal state of discrete regions united by an old, ostensibly constitutional, but faltering monarchy; from 1923 to 1930 the corrupt parliamentary government was suspended, and Spain was governed by a military dictatorship under General Miguel Primo de Rivera. During Primo de Rivera's regime, protective labor legislation for women was enacted, including paid maternity leave for women industrial workers and prohibition of night work (which brought Spanish law into line with the Washington Convention of 1919). Catalan separatist activities, problems in Spanish Morocco, and labor unrest at home troubled the regime. Illiteracy, poverty, infant mortality, rampant prostitution, and discriminatory laws provided a broad agenda for the feminist movement. The 1930s, however, would be particularly turbulent on the political front, with the fall of Primo de Rivera in late 1930 and the proclamation of the Second Republic in mid-April 1931. These developments opened fissures through which feminist claims flowed profusely.[26]

Among urban, educated women in Spain, *feminismo* was alive and well before 1923. From the Lyceum Club, which united educated feminist women in Madrid, to publications such as the book *Feminismo, feminidad, españolismo* (1917), published by María Lejárraga under the name of her famous playwright husband, Gregorio Martínez Sierra, Spanish women readers had become acquainted with developments in international feminism.[27] The Asociación Nacional de Mujeres Españolas (National Association of Spanish Women, ANME; founded 1918) began its thirty-six-point program with a declaration in favor of defending Spain's national territory, presumably against regional movements for autonomy in Catalonia, Galicia, and the Basque country. The ANME program called for major changes in marriage law, in family law, in women's access to the judiciary and professions, including medicine, to equal opportunity and equal pay, for more public schools, and a host of other transformative reforms in Spanish institutions.[28] Other significant feminist organizations included the Cruzada de Mujeres Españolas (Spanish Women's Crusade) and the Liga Internacional de Mujeres Ibéricas e Hispanoamericanas, both spearheaded by the writer and teacher Carmen De Burgos Seguí.

Women's groups with feminist leanings (of the relational type) also accompanied the Catalan, Basque, and Galician nationalist/regionalist autonomy movements, where emphasis was placed on women's education and on their role as carriers of language and culture, much in the same manner as in the earlier Ukrainian, Finnish, and Czech nationalist movements. In the judgment of historian Mary Nash, "the [Spanish] feminist movement covered a wide spectrum in its objectives, policies, and strategies, which ranged from demands for education and work facilities to the right to vote to a redressal of discriminatory laws," even though "it was not at all comparable to the vast mobilizations of the first wave of feminism in other countries."[29] Nevertheless, "feminism was in the air," and intense debate on the woman question often proceeds without "vast" mobilization.

Socialist feminism was likewise in evidence, thanks to the efforts of propagandists such as Maria Cambrils, who in her *Feminismo socialista* (1925) argued the by now familiar case that only socialism could resolve the woman question. An important recruit to the Partido Socialista Obrero Español (PSOE, Spanish Socialist Party) was the young Margarita Nelken, who had become very critical of women's situation in Spain— their lack of education, their exploitation as laborers, their legal impotence, their sexual ignorance. In 1919 Nelken first published an important perspective on these issues, *La Condición social de la mujer en España; su estado actual; su posible desarrolo* (The Social Condition of the Spanish Woman: Current Status and Possible Development). A

committed socialist who had read Bebel as well as Mill (though evidently not, at that time, Marx or Engels, Zetkin, Lenin, or Kollontai), she
also joined the Unión General de Trabajadores (UGT, Workers' General
Union) to bring attention to the problems of poor laboring women and
children, and was commissioned by the dictatorship to launch a full investigation. Following a sojourn in the countryside of Extremadura, during which Nelken helped organize peasant strikes, in 1931 she published
La Mujer ante las Cortes constituyentes. For Nelken, who returned to
Madrid, where she chaired the Spanish Socialist Party's Committee on
Women's Affairs after April 1931, economic opportunity (not political
rights) provided the key to resolving women's problems; she argued that
"feminism is, above all, an economic question, of liberty, of dignity and
of a place to work."[30]

With the fall of the monarchy and the proclamation of the Second Republic in April 1931, however, the issue of political rights for women
surged to the forefront. Historians Danièle Bussy Genevois, Judith
Keene, and Frances Lannon and others have underscored the importance
of female figures in the revolutionary symbolism and ideals appropriated
from the French Revolution by the leadership of the Second Spanish Republic.[31] The Cortes Constituyentes opened on 14 July—Bastille Day—
1931; the republic was incarnated as a woman, "Liberty" leading the
people, in the manner of Delacroix's famous painting. Pro-feminist secular liberals insisted that the incorporation of equal rights for women
would crown Spain's emergence as a modern, secular, democratic European nation. In May women who met certain qualifications had been
authorized to stand for office, along with priests and government employees, despite the fact that Spanish women did not yet have the national vote. (A limited number of women had been granted the municipal vote in 1924 by Primo de Rivera, but as in Italy, elections had been
suspended.) The Second Republic adopted a system of proportional representation, modeled on that of Weimar Germany, with electoral lists
that favored party formation. In the absence of woman suffrage, few parties sought to address issues that women cared about; this was clear from
complaints expressed in late June in *L'Opinio* by a Catalan women's
group:[32]

> It is time to end flattering promises. There have been some for everybody
> except us. The candidates and their friends have had this lapse which
> may come to be regretted. Only *Esquerra Catalana* has remembered to
> say that it will accord careful protection to mothers and children. That is
> not what we want: we do not ask for protection; we want our rights to be

recognized and equal to those of men. Now that it is time to structure a people, let it not seem that there are only men on earth.

In June 1931 two distinguished women were elected as deputies (out of 470 seats) to the Constituent Assembly, or Cortes Constituyentes: Clara Campoamor Rodríguez represented the Radical Party, and Victoria Kent Siano, the Radical Socialist Party. In October they were joined by Margarita Nelken, representing the Socialist Party, but she could not take her seat until she received naturalization papers (her father, a German Jew, and her French mother had settled in Málaga).

Members of the ANME campaigned vigorously for inclusion of the women's vote in the new republican constitution. So did Spanish Catholics, on the ground that women's vote would prove beneficial—as indeed it had in certain other dominantly Catholic postwar nations—to the socially conservative program of the church. This was precisely what skeptics among the strongly secular Liberal Republicans—and Socialists—feared, however much they may have supported the concept of equal suffrage in principle. As in so many European countries in the 1930s, women outnumbered men in Spain, even though this nation—which had remained neutral in World War I—had not suffered major war losses. Fear of women's numbers, their illiteracy, and the threat of clerical influence on their politics dampened the enthusiasm of men on the Left who should, in theory, have been most supportive.

During the constitutional debates of 1 October, the public was treated to a floor fight between two of the women deputies, Clara Campoamor and Victoria Kent, over the paragraph that became Article 36, on the subject of women's votes. Campoamor, an attorney who served on the constitutional commission and also represented the new Republic of Spain to the League of Nations, argued the pro-suffrage position, and Kent, a well-known defense attorney who had been appointed director-general of the Spanish prison system, argued against women's immediate enfranchisement, which she nevertheless supported in principle. This debate between two women deputies over women's political rights was a political "first" for European history. All earlier parliamentary suffrage debates had been the exclusive province of men.[33]

Victoria Kent argued that Spanish women were not "ready" and that to enfranchise them immediately was to endanger the very survival of the fragile republic. She had seen little evidence of women's mobilization on the new regime's behalf: "I believe that . . . postponement would be the most beneficial. . . . It is dangerous to concede the vote to women."[34]

Clara Campoamor rebutted Kent, arguing from principle. In earlier debates she had insisted on showcasing the opportunity available to Spain to take the lead among the Latin countries of Europe in enfranchising women, and had also fended off an attempt to take the equal-suffrage clause out of the constitution, placing it instead in a more easily changed electoral law. Against Kent she pointed out, amid heckling from her own male party colleagues, that the same criticisms Kent made of women were also true of many men, yet nobody pointed to them or threatened to withdraw their vote: "Precisely because the Republic means so much to me, I understand what a grave political error it would be to cut women out of the right to vote."

Invoking the principles of the French Revolution (if not the practice), the observations of Fichte in 1796, the appeals of Victor Considerant in 1848, Campoamor argued:[35]

> Do not forsake the woman who, if she is not progressive, places her hope in the Dictatorship, or the woman who thinks, if she is progressive, that her hope for equality can only be achieved in Communism. Do not commit, Honourable Deputies, a political error which has such grave consequences. Save the Republic, support the Republic by attracting and drawing into it this female force which anxiously awaits the moment of redemption.

The motion passed by a margin of 161 to 121, with 183 male deputies absenting themselves, including the Socialists. Going against her own party's position on woman suffrage effectively derailed Campoamor's political career. In 1936 she sorrowfully left Spain for exile abroad.

The new constitution of the Second Republic, ratified in December 1931, did enfranchise all women and men over the age of twenty-three. It also separated church and state, secularized marriage law and introduced civil divorce, and initiated a host of other dramatic and potentially radical changes in Spanish civic life, including the outlawing of regulated prostitution. Thus did the republican government, liberal and emphatically secular, if not adamantly left-wing, antagonize the conservative and authoritarian forces on the Right. The ensuing 1933 elections were a disaster for the republicans, and not surprisingly, many on the Left blamed women's votes for these results. The republic's difficulties increased dramatically, and the forces of the Right began to organize their challenge.

In July 1936 civil war broke out, following the mutiny of troops behind General Francisco Franco, in the name of what came to be called "national Catholicism." The stakes were high. Both the republican and the monarchist factions quickly began to receive infusions of materials, manpower, and advice from the USSR (on the republican side) and from fascist Italy and Nazi Germany (on Franco's side), in addition to assistance—and sometimes interference—from various other enthusiastic left-wing European and even North American nationals, including the redoutable anarchist-feminist Emma Goldman.

During the civil war, the magma of feminism would erupt vigorously and repeatedly. Of particular interest for the history of feminism is the Federación de Mujeres Libres (Free Women's Federation), founded in May 1936 by a small group of intellectual women anarchists (Lucía Sánchez Saornil, Mercedes Comaposada, and Amparo Poch y Gascón) on behalf of working-class women.[36] This group spun out from an anarcho-syndicalist workers' union, the Confederación Nacional del Trabajo (CNT), following an extended debate in the CNT publication *Solidaridad Obrera* during the fall of 1935, concerning the sexism of the *compañeros*. As if in response to the complaint of Victoria Kent and the invocation of Clara Campoamor for women to rise in support of the republic, this group soon boasted of some twenty thousand members in local groups scattered throughout Spain. The Mujeres Libres dedicated themselves less to the survival of the republic than to social revolution. The group's leaders positioned themselves boldly with respect to their male anarcho-syndicalist associates.

The announced goal of the Mujeres Libres was to combat the "triple enslavement to which [women] have been subject: enslavement to ignorance, enslavement as women and enslavement as workers."[37] The Mujeres Libres were skeptical of comprehensive claims being made by anarchist and other men for dramatic social change:[38]

> Revolutionary men who are today struggling for their freedom fight alone against the world, against a world opposed to desires for freedom, equality and social justice. Revolutionary women, on the other hand, have to fight on two levels; first they must fight for their external freedom. In this struggle, men with the same ideals are their allies in an identical cause. But women also have to fight for their inner freedom, which men have enjoyed for centuries. And in this struggle, women are on their own.

As Mary Nash points out, "the Mujeres Libres was groundbreaking in its demand for institutional autonomy" within the anarchist movement. Its leadership disputed the views of longtime female anarchist intellectuals such as Federica Montseny, who "did not believe there was any specific woman question."[39] Although Montseny, like the Socialists, had frequently discussed the woman question, she, like them, typically argued that both sexes were oppressed, that making women like men was not the answer, and that women must first shape themselves up. Or, as she put it in a much-quoted 1924 article: "Feminism? Never! Humanism? Always!"[40] When Montseny became the republic's minister of health and social assistance in late 1936, she focused on organizing women's volunteer welfare and relief services in support of the republic's military efforts.

Despite their radical views on most feminist questions, the women of Mujeres Libres never called for legalized abortion or the circulation of contraceptive information. It was only in Catalonia, where medical men of anarchist persuasion came into power during the mid-1930s, that such efforts were briefly institutionalized. In Spain, given the sustained conservative Catholic opposition and the turbulent political climate, however, these issues had never been among the top priorities of organized feminism.[41]

In the tense and agitated environment of civil war, the anarchists and the socialists were not alone in placing feminist claims in second place. Many other left political groups—for example, the Agrupación de Mujeres Antifascistas (AMA, Antifascist Women's Organization, a sort of popular-front combination coordinated by the Spanish Communist Party) or the Feminine Secretariat of the Dissident Marxist Party (POUM)—put the revolution and combatting fascism ahead of any emancipationist goals for women. Their appeals were directed to a sacrificial maternalism rather than to independent womanhood. Thus, by their insistence on placing women's freedom first, the Mujeres Libres struck a dissonant note, as had the Saint-Simonian women a century earlier in France, Irish suffragists in the early twentieth century, and other independent feminist groups throughout history; they extolled the fact that their monthly publication, Mujeres libres was produced and published exclusively by women. They organized schools to teach women to read and write, and to acquire vocational training; and they organized day-care facilities for women workers and centers for refuge and retraining of former prostitutes, as well as many other types of woman-centered social services. This did not mean, however, that the Mujeres Libres claimed the feminist label; far from it. Like their counterparts in the socialist and communist movements (and the Zhenotdel in the USSR) they (wrongly) identified "feminists" as strictly middle-class. In practice, however, and despite their rhetoric, they were thoroughly and unrepentantly feminist in their aspirations and activities.

Antifascist alliance groups did not, on the whole, offer an explicitly feminist agenda. Groups such as the AMA sought to mobilize women, but primarily in auxiliary roles: "Women were rarely addressed in their own right as rational beings who could reject fascism as individuals but rather as mothers and spouses to whom fascism was presented as a threat to home and family."[42] Nevertheless, there were feminists engaged in this alliance who did insist on raising questions about the "separate-spheres" parameters of women's participation. Astrea Barrios, for example, questioned what she perceived as the marginalization of women within the movement:[43]

> Given the moment of danger . . . the Government and the authorities must remember that women in Spain . . . are citizens with broad civil rights. . . . The allegation that women lack preparation for certain tasks is inadmissible; women, just like antifascist men . . . cannot tolerate the existence of professional impediments, when those impediments serve to open the way for the common enemy: fascism. Did our comrades know how to use arms on the 19th of July? No; and yet, they went to the front line. . . . Women will have the same experience in whatever posts they are assigned.

Creating women's sections of other organizations was not a problem limited to the parties of the Left; this problem manifested itself also on the Right. An intriguing example is the Sección Femenina of the Falange, organized by Pilar Primo de Rivera, daughter of the former military dictator. The Sección Femenina was the very antithesis of Mujeres Libres; founded in 1934, it had more than half a million members by the time of Franco's victory in early April 1939, and would soon provide the sole channel for women's organization in Spain under Franco's rule. As historian Victora Enders has pointed out, "every woman who desired state employment, a passport, a driver's license, or even a fishing license passed through the six months' required social service of the *Sección Femenina*."[44] Its program was intensely nationalist, intensely Catholic, and based in a thoroughly Catholic notion of separate, hierarchically arranged roles for the two sexes; it seemed to embody antifeminism. The "true duty of women to the Patria," Pilar Primo de Rivera announced during a 1938 lecture, "is to form families . . . in which they foster all that is traditional":[45]

> What we will never do is to put ourselves in competition with [men] because we will never attain equality with them and instead will lose all the elegance and all the grace indispensable for harmonious living together. . . . These women, formed thus with Christian doctrine and National Syndicalist style, will be useful to the Family, the Municipality and to the Syndicate . . . these women will know how to give—as they are giving now with their entire will—their fiancées, their husbands, their sons and brothers to the Patria.

As Enders insists, "to be considered 'feminist' was anathema to the *Sección Femenina*."[46] But Pilar Primo de Rivera, like her English predecessor Sarah Stickney Ellis, thought "feminist" meant aping men; she was perfectly comfortable with reforms, including radical ones, that would enhance the situation of women within "traditional," subordinate roles—that is, as mothers and homemakers, who would prepare their sons for service to the Catholic nation. The employment of married women and mothers was, however, strongly disapproved; for them, the "angel in the house" had been reinstalled as the guiding model. Yet the female leadership of the Sección Femenina was required to remain single.

Service and self-abnegation, not personal empowerment, was the path laid out for all Spanish women, including single women, by the Sección Femenina. The Y of Isabella of Castille, signifying a yoke, was chosen as the preferred symbol of service. Under this yoke, over the course of two generations, the women of the Sección organized countless educational and social service initiatives outside the home on behalf of Spanish women, inadvertently laying the groundwork for the rebirth of Spanish feminism of the 1970s and 1980s. Might we interpret their seeming submissiveness to the dictates of the male-dominated Falange as merely a cover for doing important, potentially feminist work beyond the boundaries of the household?

A cover was surely needed if feminist work was to be done. The post–civil war climate was hardly auspicious; the fissures had been thoroughly blocked. Many feminist militants had left Spain for exile; others apparently ceased their activities. Under the Franco regime, abortion (which had been legalized in Catalonia in 1936) was redefined in January 1941 as a "crime against the state" rather than "against human life." As in Italy under Mussolini, Franco deliberately linked the notion of population growth to Spain's aspirations to great-power status; all efforts to limit fertility were interpreted as threats, not only to God's will but to the growth and prosperity of the Spanish nation. Mothers must do their duty!

By 1945 the Franco regime had undone much of the secular legislative reform accomplished under the Second Republic. In the new law code, Fuero de los Españoles, the family was recognized as "a natural and fundamental institution of society, with rights and duties anterior and superior to all positive human law": "Matrimony will be one and indivisible."[47] In conformity with the doctrine of the church, divorce was again made illegal. Coeducation of the sexes in schools ceased. Male authority in marriage was restored. Fathers were mandated to feed, educate, and instruct their children, subject to state control. Family allowances were initiated, payable to male breadwinners. Marriage loans, along the Nazi model, were initiated, and birth premiums paid. However, no racial discrimination developed in conjunction with these policies, as in Germany; that had been taken care of by the reconquest of Spain from the Moors and the "blood purification" programs initiated in the late fifteenth century, which expelled both Moors and Jews and punished those who attempted to convert to Catholicism in order to remain. Despite all these and other measures, Mary Nash concludes that "Franco's pronatalist discourse and legislative policies were unsuccessful in enforcing pronatalist practice among Spanish women."[48] The times were just too difficult. Nevertheless, in historian Frances Lannon's assessment, "it would be hard, and wrong, to evade the conclusion that one of the important issues at stake in the Spanish Civil War was the future position—legal, economic, and cultural—of women."[49]

SWEDEN

A far different trajectory for feminism developed in northern Europe, especially in Sweden. In the early 1930s Sweden, with 6.2 million inhabitants, was the most populous of the Scandinavian nations; governed by a parliamentary monarchy, it was still, in the postwar period, a relatively poor, heavily agricultural country, though one with a highly literate and culturally cohesive population, and with a Protestant Christian religious culture institutionalized in a state church.

During the last half-century, finding little opportunity at home, many Swedes had emigrated, principally to North America; those who remained began to limit the size of their families, which resulted in a dramatic decline in the birthrate (to below replacement level). As urbanization and industrialization accelerated, many town-dwelling Swedish women, both single and married, found new forms of employment in the industrial and commercial sectors. When the Great Depression hit, however, vastly increasing unemployment in Sweden as in so many other countries, those who insisted that male breadwinners should have priority for employment attempted to force women out of the workforce, even as they sounded alarms about natality.[50]

Sweden had remained neutral in the Great War, but because of the country's geographic proximity to the new regimes in Germany and Russia, Swedish public opinion remained keenly sensitive to and somewhat fearful of the progress of revolutionary events, even as its leaders were increasingly attuned to developments in the United States. Perhaps in efforts to forestall revolution at home, several important advances were effected on women's behalf in the immediate postwar period. In 1918 the government abolished regulated prostitution. In 1919 universal suffrage in local elections was accorded to both sexes, and in 1921, all women as well as all men received parliamentary suffrage. In 1920 married women obtained full legal capacity; no longer would they require marital authorization to work, to study, or to engage in commercial transactions. In 1923 women achieved equal access to certain civil-service positions, and in 1929 Sweden established its first round of motherhood insurance, building out of a series of mutual insurance societies organized before the war, to partially subsidize women who had lost work or wages because of childbearing. In 1931 this insurance scheme was extended to provide subsidized maternity leave for all industrial women workers.

Although the term "feminism" had (as has been mentioned) never been accepted in Sweden, a tradition of feminist (kvinnosakskvinne, or "woman's cause" in Swedish) eruptions could be traced, dating back to Charlotta Nordenflycht in the 1760s, to C. J. L. Almqvist in the 1830s, and in the 1850s to the novelist and reformer Fredrika Bremer, after whom the major Swedish feminist organization had been named. By the mid-1920s, however, perhaps in consequence of the many reforms already realized in women's status (which also included educational equality), the "woman's cause" was popularly perceived (perhaps wrongly) as of interest mostly to single, childless women (with the suspicion that they might be man-hating lesbians, in the Strindberg mode). Even so, the school for women's citizenship founded in 1925 by radical liberal "women's-cause women" flourished at Fogelstad, the farm-home of Elizabeth Tamm, a Liberal deputy to the Swedish parliament, as did the group's weekly publication, Tidevarvet. Their long-term success (1925–54) in training women to contribute to political life offset their failed attempt to get women voters to support "women's lists" in the 1927 elections.[51]

In Sweden, the emphasis was placed (as in France) on women and men working together; family and community interests were insistently invoked as taking precedence over the desires of individuals. Singling out "women's issues" or pointing to instances of male domination was viewed by many Swedes as provocative and unnecessary, a deliberate act of separatism that could not be tolerated in a small, culturally cohesive country. Yet as the Fogelstad women pointed out in 1928: "We cannot accept politics in its present form. We don't recognize money and force as the irreducible foundation of social development. We want to cooperate with men. . . . But where are the radical men in Sweden's land?"[52] If there were few on the political Left, there were certainly even fewer on the Right.

The central issues for Swedish feminists in this postwar, postsuffrage period, as elsewhere, were those of paid work, motherhood, and reproductive freedom. But there were serious differences of perspective on how to arrive at workable solutions. As historian Sondra Herman characterized the situation, "where socialist women looked for ways the state could transform the home, the radicals of Fogelstad looked for ways the home should transform the state."[53] Herman insists, too, on the rural, even environmental, outlook of the woman-centered Fogelstad feminists, whereas the social democratic women were concerned more particularly with the problems of urban working women.

Indeed, the Swedish feminists of Fogelstad contributed a new dimension to European feminism, when in 1940 Elizabeth Tamm and Elin Wägner published their joint work, *Fred med Jorden* (Peace on Earth), which emphasized women's connections to the earth and to prepatriarchal times, rural women's skillfulness, and the importance of women's gatherings to discuss current issues. Wägner elaborated on these themes in her long essay *Väckerklocka* (Alarm Clock, 1941), an antifascist, antimilitarist work of what Herman calls "matriarchal history and political theory . . . . intended to awaken women to solidarity and action while warning them about the implications of modern progress."[54] Wägner would subsequently be elected to the Swedish Academy, its second woman writer, following the great novelist Selma Lägerlof. The thread of Swedish antimilitarist ecofeminism represented by Wägner's writings, which is wholeheartedly relational and based on qualities deemed particular to women, has experienced a rebirth in today's Sweden.

In parallel to the Fogelstad feminist-pacifist tradition ran another strand of Swedish feminist thinking, more closely associated with social democracy, though far less ideological and far more pragmatically presented than was the case for social democratic solutions during the Second International. In the 1930s, a few progressive Swedes began to pioneer a novel resolution to the dilemma in which many employed women found themselves. In combination with programs to industrialize and modernize the country, Sweden's Social Democratic Workers' Party, which was both more nationalist and more populist (and less ideologically Marxist) than some of its counterparts, threw itself behind Gunnar and Alva Myrdal's unusual combination of pro-natalist and socialist suggestions (outlined in their 1934 book *Crisis in the Population Question*) for resolving women's problems of combining employment with motherhood.[55]

Although the more explicitly feminist features of the Myrdals' program would not be enacted before the 1960s, it nevertheless launched a series of state-propelled reforms that would ultimately meet many women's practical needs, as well as the nation's needs, and ensure the Social Democratic Party's political success during the next fifty years. If the Swedish reforms developed with an eye to the neighboring Bolshevik experiment, or sought to short-circuit attempts of right-wing thinkers to return women to the private sphere, such references remained scrupulously understated. Whether omission of these related international developments was disingenuous or deliberate is not discussed by scholars. The Social Democratic focus on Sweden as a *Folkhem* (People's Home), though it did imply an ethnic and cultural solidarity and had some impact on immigration policy, never developed the more sinister racial exclusiveness of contemporaneous Nazi proposals for the seemingly identical notion of *Heimat* or *Volksheim*.

Alva Myrdal explicitly opposed the "new feminism" advocated by the British M.P. Eleanor Rathbone, in which it was proposed that stay-at-home motherhood be endowed by the state; responding to a debate in *Tidevarvet* (16 September 1933), Myrdal argued that such a system was "antiquated."[56] Instead, the Myrdals, starting from a firm social democratic commitment to women's economic independence as well as to family planning, succeeded in using the national anxiety over depopulation as a springboard for pioneering an emancipatory solution to the "woman question." As historian Yvonne Hirdman characterized it: "Motherhood, or rather children, were used as blackmail to achieve better conditions for women. . . . Stealing [the population question] and filling it with 'leftist' content was . . . a brilliant move."[57] Drawing selectively on the legacy of the earlier Swedish reformer Ellen Key, who had emphasized women's maternal as well as intellectual and professional drives, and on the discussions of women's concerns in Social Democratic Party women's groups (views not then shared within the party at large), and implicitly opposing the well-known Nazi solution of sending women back to the home, Alva Myrdal boldly proposed (in contrast to Key) that rearing children in a well-organized collective setting, while permitting employment for mothers, would offer a solution superior to the home-based care of individual mothers for individual children, and better for both.

While Gunnar Myrdal served as secretary to the Royal Population Commission, established in May 1935, Alva Myrdal worked from 1935 to 1938 as secretary to the Women's Employment Commission, chaired by the feminist M.P. Kerstin Hesselgren, who had also chaired an earlier committee on maternity issues and who represented Sweden to the League of Nations. In the course of this work, Alva Myrdal attempted to reverse the view commonly held by many Swedish socialists—that married women should not be permitted to remain in the labor force—by insisting that in the national interest women workers should be aided, not penalized, if and when they married and bore children. As she summarized the new approach in 1938:[58]

> For economic reasons the married women must have the opportunity to contribute to the support of the family, and for ideological reasons they must have freedom to work in order to feel contentment and security. The change may be symbolically formulated thus, that while the right of married women to earn a living was formerly discussed, the right to marriage and motherhood is now proclaimed for women in paid employment.

In order to implement such a policy, she advocated a government-sponsored support system for women that included not only sex education, family planning, and organized child care, but also modification of domestic labor and even of domestic architecture (collective houses). The committee's Report on the Employment of Married Women recommended:[59]

1. Rejection of all bills restricting or denying married women's right to work in public or private enterprise; no firing of women because of betrothal, marriage, pregnancy, or motherhood;

2. Prohibition of all bribes designed to induce married or pregnant women to resign;

3. Strict enforcement of the 1923 Eligibility Act giving women equal entry to most civil-service posts; reexamination of female exclusion from religious, judicial, and military offices;

4. Vocational and professional education for girls, emphasizing agriculture and the skilled trades;

5. Increasing the possibilities for part-time work;

6. Consideration of married women's right to keep their birth-given names;

7. Community care for minor children of both employed mothers and homemakers.

During the ensuing "mothers and babies parliament," following the elections of 1936, the Swedish parliament enacted legislation to allow pregnant women to keep their jobs. Contraception was legalized (by overturning the restrictive law of 1910), though abortion was still subjected to restrictions. In 1937 maternity relief benefits were made payable to mothers. But resistance to the more radical of the Myrdals' proposals remained strong, even in Social Democratic Party circles, and notions of the "professional housewife" quickly displaced those of the emancipated woman worker/mother, once the Myrdals left Sweden in 1938 for a second stay in the United States.

The approach advocated by the Myrdals would ultimately triumph as official policy in Sweden, though only in the course of several decades. Alva Myrdal recounted in her book *Nation and Family* (published in Swedish in 1940) that women in the workplace had been placed on the defensive, especially by the fallout from the Great Depression: "In this crucial moment the population argument was wrenched out of the hands of the antifeminists and instead used as a new and formidable weapon for the emancipation ideals. The old debate on married women's right to work was turned into a fight for the working woman's right to marry and have children. The change in public opinion concerning women's problems brought about by this reformulation of the issue was tremendous." And, she noted: "The gain was purely a gift to [the feminists]. . . . What is protected is women's right to have those very children that society also wants."[60]

Where Alva Myrdal's solution went beyond the Soviet Russian solution for women's economic independence, coupled with social services, was to insist that, along with facilities for child care and social supports for the household, the division of labor within the family must also be renegotiated. Women must not have to serve a "double shift." In particular, boys must be trained in domestic work, so that as men they could be helpful around the house; they should also participate in parenting. Thus, current indoctrination to sex roles must be addressed, and roles themselves radically reorganized. This was truly revolutionary, and it was deliberately cast in terms of social engineering; it was pragmatic, nondoctrinaire, and framed exclusively in terms of Sweden's national interest. Economic independence for women, yes; but healthy heterosexual partnerships and healthy children counted too. This program would become a central feature of Swedish life from the 1960s on.

NATIONALISMS, FEMINISMS, AND SEXUAL POLITICS, 1920S–1940

It should be clear from the preceding case studies that national politics and population issues greatly conditioned the circumstances open for feminist successes in the 1920s and 1930s. It should also be clear that not all European women were feminists. Nor could all women's movements be considered feminist movements; indeed, some women's organizations—such as the various Central European housewives' associations or church-affiliated and patriotic women's organizations like the Ligue Patriotique des Françaises and the Sección Femenina of the Falange, just to name a few—could be understood as comprising an antifeminist women's movement. Yet even these organizations would contribute, over the long term, to changing the lives of many women, single and married, young and old, by engaging them in activities outside their households, in charitable work, social work, and reform efforts. These activities could—and sometimes did—lead some participants to an understanding of women's collective subordination and to the development of a full-blown feminist consciousness, and beyond feminism to a recognition of other related forms of social injustice.

The Roman Catholic Church took the measure of the feminist challenge. In Catholic women's organizations, feminist consciousness continued to bud, but blossomed at a slower rate, despite the importance of such relatively militant organizations as the British Catholic woman suffrage society, St. Joan's Social and Political Alliance, and the Union Féminine Civique et Sociale in France. The Vatican came to realize that women's emancipation—particularly in the form advocated by the leadership of the "godless" USSR, but also that which followed from the sheer development of literacy, women's education, and capitalist economic growth—threatened its authority, and Catholic popes increased both their recognition of women's importance and their attempts to guide Catholic women and their organizations in the proper direction.

Pius XI issued important encyclicals in the early 1930s, supplementing them with his *Divini redemptoris* (1937), which not only condemned communism but restated Catholic arguments on male authority in the family. But his successor, Pius XII (1939–58), would circulate no fewer than *seventy-two* messages to the faithful on the woman question, covering issues from dress codes to women's submission in marriage and efforts to refocus their attention on home and children. In a landmark radio broadcast from Vatican City, in October 1945, Pius XII would outline the political and social obligations that, in the church's eyes, underlay "woman's dignity"—her unique role in the domestic sphere, her control of the education of children:[61]

> Every woman has . . . the obligation, the strict obligation in conscience, not to absent herself but to go into action in a manner and way suitable to the condition of each so as to hold back those currents which threaten the home, so as to oppose those doctrines which undermine its foundations, so as to prepare, organize and achieve its restoration.

These obligations would include using the vote appropriately, taking full advantage of civil rights, even campaigning for measures that would bolster and reinforce the Catholic vision of the family. On one thing both secular feminists and the Catholic hierarchy would agree: "No wise woman," remarked Pius XII, "favors a policy of class struggle or war. Her vote is a vote for peace."[62]

The Vatican would remain adamantly opposed to practices that might limit the size of families. Secular feminists, in contrast, held mixed views on population-related issues, including women's right to control their own bodies and "free love," as sexual emancipation was called in the 1920s and 1930s. Sex reform, availability of birth control and sex education, and campaigns to legalize abortion became an increasingly important area for action by some secular feminists—though not by most major feminist associations—during these years. Interest in such issues had received a significant impetus from measures adopted in Bolshevik Russia following the revolution, as was discussed in Chapter 9.

On the European continent, some national governments would aggressively contest campaigns aimed at realizing dramatic changes in sexual control, and feminists not identified with the radical Left would proceed cautiously. The potential divisiveness of this issue revealed itself in a 1917 exchange in *Jus Suffragii*, the organ of the International Woman Suffrage Alliance, over the issue of family limitation, following the French suffragist and pro-natalist Marguerite de Witt-Schlumberger's denunciation of neo-Malthusian teachings as "selfish." Her allegation led to a flurry of dissenting letters to the editor from England and the Netherlands. W. W. Rutgers-Hoitsema, from the Netherlands, who coupled her feminist work with an active role in the Dutch Neo-Mathusian League, argued that at least while the war continued, and in the interests of solidarity in achieving woman suffrage, "difficult, complicated, and especially most delicate problems, partly national, partly international—such as patriotism, Chauvinism, internationalism, Neo-Malthusianism, depopulation, repopulation, immigration, emigration, colonisation, imperialism, etc.,—should not be raised nor discussed in our dear International Woman Suffrage paper."[63]

In the wake of the USSR's legalization and medicalization of abortion, this issue—along with the now seemingly more moderate solution of family planning—attracted considerable attention among secular feminists in the Anglophone and Scandinavian countries. Throughout Scandinavia the Norwegian-born Elise Ottesen-Jensen campaigned vigorously for sex education, contraceptive availability, and social support for mothers.[64] In England, Dr. Marie Stopes pushed for accessible birth-control information for women, and by the early 1930s the Anglican Church in England arrived at a qualified endorsement of family planning. In England Stella Browne promulgated women's sexual liberation and the legalization of abortion, asserting vehemently in the face of populationist arguments that women had the right not to have children. Few British feminists were prepared openly to endorse Stella Browne's liberationist arguments.[65]

On the Continent, other feminists were far from enthusiastic about legalizing abortion. In 1919 socialists in Basel, Switzerland, had gained a majority on the Grand Council, and proposed decriminalizing abortion. Swiss suffragists called a mass meeting of women's organizations to oppose the measure. Anna Löffler-Herzog argued that "if abortion is authorized, not only . . . is woman depreciated in her quality of creator [*créatrice*] and guardian [*gardienne*] of life, but she is revalued as an object of men's sexual avidity." She considered this to degrade women—to threaten their maternal feelings and to render them "incapable of fulfilling their civilizing mission."[66]

Löffler-Herzog's reservations about the meaning of thoroughgoing sexual emancipation for women were shared by many feminists, who continued to believe that controls should instead be placed on expressions of male sexuality. The French women's advocate Madeleine Vernet remarked in 1920, recanting her earlier espousal of *amour libre*, "what is currently called 'free love,' far from aiding the emancipation of woman, is most often a new source of servitude and suffering for her."[67] Sexual love, she had concluded, was ultimately an individual problem; sociopolitical changes through education and economic reorganization seemed to her far more crucial. Even in the 1930s not all feminists agreed on the meaning or importance of sexual freedom for women, even if they acknowledged women's sexuality as an aspect of their being that demanded expression. Most would have supported Nelly Roussel's contention that women must have the right to control their own bodies, but they could disagree sharply on the potential of the practice of "free love" without regard for pregnancy. Although sex-education and birth-control campaigns grew in importance over the long term, in the short term the protection of motherhood and other societal changes of direct immediate benefit to women often took priority. Some feminists even thought there was altogether too much emphasis on sex and, for women, on getting past virginity. Winifred Holtby remarked ironically in 1935: "Today, there is a far worse crime than promiscuity: it is chastity. . . . I think we shall one day get over this somewhat adolescent preoccupation with the human body and its miscellaneous experiences."[68]

Government sanctions against contraceptive practices and abortion meanwhile grew more pronounced in some nations. In 1920, the French government had prohibited all circulation of information regarding contraception or abortion, while criminalizing the sale of instruments or materials that could be used for abortive purposes. The communist-feminist Louise Bodin acidly remarked of the 1920 measure: "The social prison of woman has been furnished with one more bar; such is the justice of men."[69]

In Weimar Germany, as we have seen in Chapter 10, in the face of opposition from both Catholic and Protestant clergymen, the medical establishment, and secular advocates of repressive legislation, some German feminists in 1931 joined the communist campaign for the repeal of Article 218 of the German Penal Code, which in 1871 had criminalized abortion. Their efforts would be bitterly opposed by the National Socialists, who not only closed down birth-control clinics but in 1943 would initiate a death sentence for repeat abortionists. In the 1940s, under Nazi occupation, the Vichy government in France would reclassify abortion as an act of high treason and would subsequently execute one defiant practitioner for crimes against the state.[70]

"I HAVE SEEN a revolution in social and moral values which has transformed the world I live in. It is a direct result of that challenge to opinion which we call the Women's Movement." So wrote the British feminist Winifred Holtby in 1935. "I am well aware," she noted, "of the imperfections of the movement":[71]

> I have seen what happened in Germany, where the pendulum of reaction has swung back so violently that all that had been gained seems lost again. I know that Great Britain has dependencies in Africa and the Far East still untouched by any sense of the humanity of women. . . . I know that we still have plenty to do.

The position of Englishwomen, in her opinion, had been transformed beyond all measure. Feminism was by no means finished, just because the vote had been won.

Others on the Continent and in Scandinavia measured the distance traveled. In summing up the situation of European women and feminist triumphs in 1934, Bertie Albrecht divided them into five categories:[72]

1. The Nordics, "who, slowly educated and emancipated, conscious of their rights and dignity have merited and obtained emancipation." In this category Albrecht included Swedish, English, and Dutch women.

2. The women of Russia, "who passed brusquely from slavery to ab-

solute equality—social, legal, civic, and economic [*de traitement*]. These women have rapidly adapted to their new condition thanks to an intensive cultural program organized by the government."

3. The "women" who have acquired all the theoretic liberties, but who, because of lack of education, ambition, and self-respect are incapable of deploying their rights and getting the laws applied. The governments do nothing for their social education." In this category Albrecht included Romania, Spain, and Poland.

4. The "curious group of fascist women who (like the Germans) have lost all their acquired rights, and whom one amuses and flatters by parades and paramilitary fuss, but whom one treats and considers simply as national resources."

5. "The most amorphous group, that of women who have no rights and who demand none. Habituated to their state of inferiority, their ambitions do not go beyond the hatmaker's boutique. They remain in the tradition of the nineteenth century." In this group (despite considerable evidence to the contrary) Albrecht included her own French countrywomen and the Belgians.

She concluded by noting that "in countries where women have equal rights, the practice of birth control is legal." And, adding a twist to Fourier's observation of 1808, she remarked that "one can currently judge the degree of dignity accorded to women in a country by the state of the birth-control question in that country."

But on many other fronts, dramatic progress had been made throughout Europe. The opening of educational opportunities for European women had been confirmed; literacy and schooling continued to increase. Feminists had called for dramatic changes in marriage and property laws, and for changes in laws concerning children born outside marriage. Demands for women's economic emancipation—as symbolized by equal employment opportunity and equal pay for equal work—had been vocalized everywhere, and were being insisted on even as opponents sought to fight the Depression by eliminating married women from the workforce. Proposals to restructure the domestic division of labor had been strongly suggested, particularly in Sweden. Equity for women in the developing state welfare programs was under intense discussion. That campaigns for sexual emancipation of women, though far and away the most contentious issue for feminists in the interwar period, could even be broached; that national governments were now striking back against proposals to legalize contraceptive measures and to decriminalize abortion; that religious bodies had accelerated their attempts to channel and control women's activities—all this signaled the extent of the successes achieved since 1700, when a chorus of feminist voices had begun to challenge women's subordination in print. Wherever one looks, feminist agitation was under way on a variety of fronts.[73]

Indeed, many tasks remained for feminists even in those nations that had enacted provisions for women's equal rights and the vote. One response, which could stand in for many others in the period, was elaborated by Karen Johnsen of Denmark. In a collection of essays published in 1937 (and in English translation in 1939), Johnsen observed that, even following the granting of constitutional equality in 1915, the tasks of the Danish women's movement were by no means at an end:[74]

> The Women's Movement, besides endeavouring to get the remaining unreasonable inequalities removed, now has the task of seeing that the position of equality the Law has given women is also conformed with, and that the legal provisions are carried out in actual life. Furthermore, the Women's Movement must try to counteract the tendency originating from the Fascist and Nazi countries—wherever it appears—to force the woman (especially the married woman) back into her old position of inequality. Having attained to her present legally-safeguarded status, it would be unthinkable for the Danish woman to revert to the old conditions.

Moreover, in social legislation, as the president of the Danish Council of Women, Kirsten Gloerfelt-Tarp, pointed out, "there is . . . a certain idea that the wants and requirements of women are less than those of men": "Thus Old Age Pensions and Disablement Benefit are a little lower for women than for men, for example; the National Insurance Act fixes the basic pension for single women at about 93% of that paid to single men."[75] Women's individual needs were no less, she asserted, than those of men. Such thinking as this would generate new resistance among male-centered thinkers who would shape national welfare states throughout Europe, culminating in the reforms and social programs of the late 1940s and 1950s. It would significantly influence the development and expansion of planned-parenthood programs and underpin the Swedish effort to reorganize sex roles in the 1960s.

12

Globalizing and Politicizing European Feminist International Activity, 1919–1945

Feminisms in Europe had become deeply intertwined with the growth and development of nation-states, on both the political and the economic front. Indeed, in the aftermath of World War I feminists achieved a level of involvement with national political life that they had only dreamed of a decade earlier. Not only were women voting, forming associations, joining political parties, standing for and being elected to parliaments, but a few were called upon to serve as cabinet ministers.

Following the precedent set by Aleksandra Kollontai, named People's Commissar for Social Welfare in late 1917 for the Bolshevik revolutionary government in Russia, first Constance Markievicz in Ireland (for the rebel Irish republican countergovernment) and then Margaret Bondfield in the United Kingdom (under the Labour Party in 1929) headed their respective ministries of labor. In Denmark, Nina Bang served as minister of education under a Social Democratic cabinet (1924–26). None of these political women considered herself a feminist before all else, but they all did attend to women's issues within their respective nationalist, socialist, and labor parties. Many more women served on municipal councils and even, in a few cases, as mayors of major cities. In 1939, just as war threatened once again to sweep through Europe, the Irish senator and revolutionary widow Kathleen Clarke would be appointed Lord Mayor of Dublin.

Women's increasing involvement as nominally full-fledged citizens—even their election to parliaments and their affiliation with political parties—by no means assured that other feminist objectives for ending women's subordination could be attained, or even that these objectives could be kept in the conceptual foreground of political life. Even the appointment in 1936 of three French women as ministerial undersecretaries by Léon Blum, leading Socialist and head of the French Popular Front government, would include but one dedicated feminist, the suffrage leader Cécile Brunschvicg. Still, this appointment had enormous symbolic significance in the nation where feminists had made the earliest demands for political rights and representation and where a recalcitrant Senate repeatedly refused to enfranchise the female majority of its population, fearing that their votes would undermine the secular Third Republic.

Such ministerial appointments, combined with the nomination of some feminists to governmental commissions and their hotly contested entry into national civil services, were symbolically crowned when a few women received appointments to ambassadorial posts. The short-lived Károlyi government in Hungary nominated suffragist Rozsika Schwimmer as ambassador to Switzerland (a nomination refused by the Swiss government) and the USSR would send Aleksandra Kollontai to Norway as its minister and then appoint her as ambassador to Sweden (a posting that would allow Kollontai to survive the Stalinist purges of the 1930s). Such appointments signaled the arrival of women, and to a very limited degree, of woman-concerned (if not necessarily feminist) thinking, in the highly masculine and closely guarded field of international relations. The few sympathetic governments that took a chance on such appointments forced others to reconsider their resistance. Nevertheless, such appointments came slowly; as I have suggested in earlier chapters, the postwar backlash against feminist aspirations to emancipation from male control was extensive and prolonged, even in the most ostensibly liberal European societies. Women's "firsts" in the national political arena could still be easily counted, and the resistance to their entry into government service, especially at senior levels, must not be underestimated.

There was, however, another front on which feminists could pose their demands. Throughout the first half of the twentieth century, activist women from a number of European countries expanded their organizational activities at the international level, beyond and to some extent outside control by governments or political parties. Charlotte Perkins Gilman, an American observer at the Seventh Biennial Meeting of the International Woman Suffrage Alliance (IWSA), held in Budapest in 1913, marveled that "women, for the first time in history, are moving in large bodies and for purposes of social benefit. . . . It is a phenomenon of our own time; of immense importance."[1] Following a triumphal procession of delegates from Berlin to Budapest via Dresden, Prague, and Vienna, the IWSA Congress celebrated the arrival of ceremonial greetings, embodied in a silk banner, from Chinese feminists. Feminism was quickly becoming a global affair.

In the 1920s and 1930s the Atlantic-seaboard bias of European feminism would be increasingly diffused by the formation of smaller coalitions within Europe such as the Petite Entente des Femmes (Little Entente of Women) by feminists from Greece, Czechoslovakia, Yugoslavia, Romania, and Poland, who organized their own meetings in Bucharest (1923), Belgrade (1924), and Athens (1925).[2] Feminist Eurocentrism would be further diluted by the much-welcomed appearance at European conferences of visitors and delegates from many areas of the non-Western world, including China, Japan, and India, and by increasing communication concerning women's issues and feminist gatherings in Argentina, in Cuba and in the Yucatan, in Korea, and in several developing nation-states in the Middle East, notably Egypt and Turkey. In 1923 the IWSA Congress in Rome elected the Egyptian feminist Huda Shaarawi as vice-president. In 1931 French feminists organized a third États-Généraux du Féminisme on the subject of colonialism; in early 1932 the French suffragist Germaine Malaterre-Sellier convened a Mediterranean women's conference in Constantine, Algeria.[3] In 1935 the International Alliance of Women (IAW; formerly IWSA) would proudly hold its triennial conference on the easternmost edge of Europe, in the great ancient capital city of Istanbul.

This dynamic expansion of the feminist movement, begun well before World War I, had not stopped, even in wartime. European and North American feminists (organized as the Women's Peace Party) convened at The Hague in 1915 and again in Zurich in 1919 to protest the war, celebrate the peace, combat militarism, and press for women's full inclusion in the world's business. In addition to suffrage and full citizenship, feminists worked on a broad agenda for change. They sought to expand women's educational opportunities (sometimes in the face of efforts to restrict them), to achieve thoroughgoing marital law reform, to address a variety of issues concerning women's employment (especially women's right to work and pay equity), to promote (or, in some cases, to oppose) protective labor legislation, and to challenge the alcohol and the drug trades, regulated prostitution, and what would become known as the international traffic in women and girls. Feminists also sought to change the laws governing the nationality and citizenship of women who had married men of different nationalities, to amend discriminatory laws regulating the status of children born out of wedlock, and to enact laws that would enhance the protection of children. Sex education, family planning, and the more controversial issues surrounding reproductive control continued to figure on the feminist agenda at the national (and, more rarely, at the international) level. Feminists continued to work hard for disarmament and world peace.

In the 1920s and 1930s a new and unprecedented surge of activism erupted on behalf of women's emancipation at the international level. European women—increasingly equipped with advanced university degrees in law, philosophy, medicine, and history—stood at the forefront of these expansive efforts. Their activities (both intellectual and political) are only now being properly documented by historians. Referring mainly to British and American activists (who continue to dominate accounts by English-speaking scholars), historian Carol Miller rightly insists that "feminists' international work was intended to bolster national campaigns to advance the status of women, and as such was not as detached from national goals as has been previously suggested" by historians such as Brian Harrison and Richard J. Evans.[4]

This was even more true for feminists from continental European countries, whose international activism amounted to far more than a mere complement to the work of their British and American counterparts. That they had some degree of success in making their case during the Paris peace talks in 1919, and in participating in the first International Labour Conference in Washington, D.C. (October 1919), speaks volumes about the impact of feminist perspectives and activism in international affairs during the immediate postwar period. By 1926 one American activist's report on European feminist initiatives at the League of Nations enthusiastically proclaimed, "Feminism More Effective in Europe than America."[5]

COALITION BUILDING AND DIVERGING
APPROACHES

If multiple streams of feminist magma flowed in the interwar period, they did not invariably flow in the same direction or at the same speed; indeed, in their abundance, they even threatened at times to collide and to compete for pathways. Sometimes feminists hesitated and lost ground when women's lack of political power to enforce decisions made on paper became apparent, or when, in an age of mass politics and political party discipline, they could not mobilize an independently minded mass of supporters to rally behind a unified program of women's political interests. It became quite apparent that not all women were feminists, and not all women's movements were feminist in intent. In nations where the vote had been won, even those who professed a feminist commitment could disagree on priorities, objectives, strategies, and tactics. The split during these years between advocates of protective labor legislation for women and advocates of absolute equality of legal rights proved particularly difficult to bridge. On a more philosophical plane, the ensuing tension between feminism and humanism became, as will be discussed later in the chapter, particularly acute.

Differences in approach to what constituted "feminist" remedies for the problems specific to women industrial workers, which had developed in the rivalry with Marxist-socialist women in the Second International since the late nineteenth century, were thrown into sharp relief by the Bolshevik revolution. These differences intensified during the first International Labour Conference in 1919 and became even more acute during the 1920s, following the Communist–Social Democratic split at Tours in 1920. In 1921 the International Federation of Working Women (IFWW) was founded by European social democratic and labor women, an outgrowth of the international congresses called by a coalition of women's trade union organizations in 1919 and 1921. The goals of the IFWW were "to examine all projects for legislation proposed by the International Labour Conference of the League of Nations" and "to promote the appointment of working women on organizations affecting the welfare of the workers."[6] The IFWW, however, proved relatively short-lived. It was absorbed by the new Socialist International, just as the prewar women's labor organizations were also reabsorbed into the male-dominated trade unions in the name of solidarity.

Another, more enduring, international women's group sympathetic to the efforts that the USSR claimed to be launching on behalf of women workers (especially those who were mothers) was the International Co-operative Women's Guild (ICWG), founded in 1921 in Basel, Switzerland, by British co-operator Margaret Llewelyn Davies and her associates. In the early 1920s, the ICWG was often referred to as the "Mothers' International," since its membership consisted primarily of working-class housewives and their middle-class advocates. More deeply rooted than their response to developments in the new Soviet state were the positions ICWG leaders had developed since the late nineteenth century during the decades prior to the internationalization of the original British Women's Co-Operative Guild (WCG). These women did not challenge the sexual division of labor, but did insist on the importance for society of women's work in the household as wives and mothers, and especially as consumers, and they did advocate a public voice for the legitimate concerns of such housewifely women.[7] In England, the WCG had worked since the 1880s for a number of measures to improve the lives of ordinary women, including the payment of maternity benefits directly to mothers, and this proposal became an international concern in the postwar period, as working-class women flocked to join the guild—and the Labour Party—following the women's suffrage victory. Reproductive control also figured in the WCG's agenda, and in 1934 this group even signaled its approval of legal abortion. The mother body of ICWG also took a deep interest in issues of peace and disarmament, and in 1938 sponsored an international congress of women in Geneva to protest the looming threat of war.

Three extremely important loci of international feminist activity in Europe during the 1920s and 1930s were the International Council of Women (ICW), the International Woman Suffrage Alliance (IWSA, which, in the mid-1920s, reconstituted itself as the International Alliance of Women for Suffrage and Equal Citizenship, known as IAWSEC, or simply as the IAW), and the newly formed Women's International League for Peace and Freedom (WILPF, or WIL).

Each organization held regular congresses in European cities, usually in alternating years, with occasional overlap in personnel. Paris and London often became the sites for executive sessions in the 1920s and 1930s, but congresses were spread throughout Europe (Oslo, Vienna, Dubrovnik, Edinburgh, Geneva, Rome, Berlin, Copenhagen, Interlaken, Zurich, Vienna, Dublin, Prague, Grenoble, Luhacovice, Luxembourg), occasionally in North America (Washington, D.C., and Philadelphia), and uniquely (IAW, 1935) in Istanbul.

As historian Leila J. Rupp has underscored, these three international women's organizations were all closely related; most of their leaders were not only acquainted with one another, but often on friendly and interactive terms.[8] Operationally, these three organizations exemplified three distinctive approaches. The International Council of Women (ICW), the oldest, was a loose federation of women's groups which left matters of national action strictly to the initiative of the affiliated national councils. With respect to international issues, during the 1920s and 1930s the ICW focused particularly on the traffic in women and on married women's nationality, issues which cut decisively across national boundaries. The more specifically "political" IWSA/IAWSEC/ IAW had established itself in 1904 as a spin-off "daughter" organization of the ICW, focusing expressly on obtaining woman suffrage. After the postwar suffrage victories, the IAW suffered to some extent from a split identity, encompassing as it did national bodies whose representatives wanted to move "beyond suffrage" and others who had not yet obtained it. Following a change in name and orientation in 1926, the IAW organized its Committee on Peace and the League of Nations, sponsoring a series of January conferences on the "Cause and Cure of War." WILPF, which had formed following World War I as an outgrowth of the Women's Peace Party, the IWSA spin-off group that had organized the Women's Peace Congresses of 1915 and 1919 (discussed in Chapter 9), could be seen as the "granddaughter." Of the three groups, WILPF was the only one that set policy at what historian Jo Vellacott calls the "transnational" level, and expected its nationally affiliated "sections" to follow its lead in pursuit of various initiatives on behalf of peace and freedom.[9] Although the presidents of these groups were dominantly American or British, most members of the international boards and many of the most active workers were feminists from the European continent.

In 1925 these three associations joined with several others to establish a Joint Standing Committee of Women's International Organizations, with the aim of engaging more women in the business of the League of Nations and the International Labour Organization (ILO), as well as lobbying in both these bodies on behalf of women's issues. Madame Avril de Sainte-Croix, of France, long active in international feminist affairs, served as the Joint Committee's official delegate to the League. By 1931, when the Liaison Committee of Women's International Organizations was established, it also included a number of other groups that aspired to represent an international membership extending well beyond Europe. Among them were the International Federation of Business and Professional Women; the International Federation of University Women, the International Federation of Women Magistrates and Barristers, St. Joan's Social and Political Alliance, the World Union of Women for International Concord, the World's Women's Christian Temperance Union, and the World's Young Women's Christian Association. Others, not then represented in the Liaison Committee, included the International Cooperative Women's Guild (mentioned above), several international Catholic women's social action groups, the Equal Rights International, the Inter-American Commission of Women, and the All-Asian Conference of Women. By 1936, according to Magdeleine Boy's doctoral thesis, twenty such groups appeared under the rubric "Feminism" in the League of Nations' most recent listing of international organizations.[10] This "inter-international" feminism, as the Dutch feminist Willemijn Hendrika Posthumus–van der Goot later called it, would make important contributions during the years ahead.[11]

FEMINIST ACTIVISM IN GENEVA: THE LEAGUE OF

NATIONS AND THE ILO

In the 1920s the two major venues for international action by feminist groups were the newly established League of Nations and the International Labour Organization, both headquartered in Geneva. Both were open to women's active participation, thanks to measures successfully incorporated in the 1919 Treaty of Versailles at the urging of European and American feminists. Article 7 of the League's Covenant stated that "all positions under or in connection with the League, including the Secretariat, shall be open equally to men and women."[12] The IWSA president, Margery Corbett Ashby, heralded this brief statement as "women's great charter in the League."[13]

The League's host country, Switzerland, was remarkable in Europe not only for its scenic beauty but also for obstinately delaying women's vote and full citizenship at the federal level until 1971. "How is it," wrote Emilie Gourd, editor of *Mouvement féministe* (Geneva), in 1914, "that Switzerland, which is certainly one of the most advanced countries in all that concerns democratic institutions and social reforms, is so backward in what concerns women's political rights?"[14] In November 1918 Swiss socialists endorsed woman suffrage, and suffragists demanded total revision of the Swiss federal constitution to that effect; this was rejected in favor of local decisions. In June 1920 the IWSA held its World Congress in Geneva to stir up enthusiasm for enfranchisement, but between 1919 and 1921, six Swiss cantons, including Geneva, resoundingly defeated proposals for local women's suffrage.[15]

Swiss feminists were a small but active group, both at the national and international levels. In 1920 Pauline Chaponnière-Chaix, president of the Swiss Council of Women, was elected president of the ICW; her countrywoman Klara Ragaz, from Zurich, held a series of important leadership positions in the WILPF. But from the outset, the Swiss women's lack of full citizenship in their own country cast a certain shadow over feminist activities in Geneva—the birthplace of Rousseau and celebrated as such. Sporadic resistance from some of the male delegates and bureaucrats at the League of Nations and the ILO further challenged feminist ingenuity in accomplishing their goals.

Feminist activists enthusiastically embraced the founding of the League and the ILO. As they established their operations in Geneva, they prodded and poked at every possible opportunity and on all pertinent issues. The latter included items under the jurisdiction of the League's Maritime Committee (which had under its purview the government-established brothels in port cities) and the Mandates Committee (which could address questions concerning women's status in territories supervised by League-appointed nominees). The WILPF even established a permanent headquarters in Geneva, with an office and a staff that monitored and sought to influence activity at the League headquarters. The WILPF's Maison Internationale became a familiar rendezvous point for internationally active feminists.

The League of Nations absorbed a series of earlier ventures in international cooperation. At the outset, it seemed to hold great promise not only as a vehicle for achieving world peace and promoting more cordial labor-capital relations, but also for advancing women's rights. Most European nations, with the exception of the powers defeated in the war, quickly became members and sent delegations to Geneva. Germany, Austria, and Hungary came in later, as did the newly established USSR.

The League's Secretariat and Assembly offered possibilities for political action that feminist activists were quick to take up, even as they complained about the relative scarcity of women in official positions and as delegates. Their successes were publicized in D. M. Northcroft's successive editions of the brochure *Women at Work in the League of Nations* (1923, 1926, 1927) and in international feminist periodicals. From the outset, the three Scandinavian countries all sent women to Geneva, either as delegates to the League of Nations' General Assembly or as technical advisers. Henni Forchhammer, longtime president of the Danish Council of Women (1913–31) served for many years as a technical adviser to the Danish delegation, as well as on the ICW executive board. She worked particularly in the fight against trade in women and children. Dr. Kristine Bonnevie, zoology professor and women's rights activist, served repeatedly as a substitute delegate for Norway. She was named to the Commission on Intellectual Cooperation, along with the French physicist and Nobel laureate Marie Curie. Kerstin Hesselgren, successor to the longtime substitute delegate from Sweden, Anna Bugge Wicksell, was one of the few women to serve as a full General Assembly delegate for an extended period of time. She would play a vital role in the 1930s in securing the League's support for an examination of the status of women worldwide.

In the 1920s other feminists arrived as national delegates to the League of Nations Assembly. Helena Swanwick, a longtime suffrage and peace activist, and editor of *Foreign Affairs*, was twice appointed (1924, 1929) as a delegate by Labour governments in Britain. Following Germany's admission, Dr. Gertrud Bäumer served as technical adviser to the German delegation in the 1920s. In 1931, Clara Campoamor, suffragist and a newly elected member of the Spanish Republic's parliament, served as a delegate. In 1933 Germaine Malaterre Sellier became a technical adviser to the French delegation. In 1935, Aleksandra Kollontai, still ambassador of the USSR to Sweden, made her appearance as a substitute delegate at the League Assembly, following the Soviet government's 1934 admission. The Countess Albert Apponyi represented Hungary. In 1938 Bodil Begtrup became a member of the Danish delegation. In Geneva, aristocrats sat side by side with social democrats, and women from amazingly different backgrounds worked together to achieve their common aims.

Princess Gabrielle Radziwill from the new state of Lithuania looked out for feminist interests as an employee of the League's Secretariat, while Dame Rachel Crowdy served as a Chief of Section. A number of French feminists, such as Marguerite de Witt-Schlumberger and Madame Avril de Sainte-Croix, obtained governmental appointments to League commissions, while others such as Gabrielle Duchêne and Andrée Jouve (who headed the French section of WILPF) also participated actively in its international work. As historian Siân Reynolds has remarked of these enterprising (but still disenfranchised) women, "exclusion from national politics gave a certain desperate energy to French women's participation in international initiatives," and pointed "towards the conclusion that women's presence at Geneva could be a displaced form of participation in national politics."[16]

In the 1930s the League's publication series reflected some successes for feminist pressure politics. Not only had women's issues become visible within the League, but feminists had also secured the League's collaboration and effective publicity in some of their endeavors. By the end of the decade, League publications included a wide range of titles concerning women's peace work, married women's nationality, and women's status worldwide.[17]

The International Labour Organization, chartered as an integral component of the postwar treaties and linked to the League, was also open to non–League members. The ILO had a unique tripartite structure, consisting of government, employers, and employees; the employees were dominated by representations of trade unions. For all practical purposes, male-dominated trade union interests effectively controlled the ILO's agenda.

The ILO mandate (encompassed in Article 395 of the Treaty of Versailles) specifically called for the hiring of female as well as male staff members in its Geneva headquarters, known as the International Labour Office (Bureau International du Travail). It also stipulated (thanks to feminist insistence) that with respect to issues regarding women's employment, knowledgeable women should be included among the appointed technical advisers and that women should be encouraged to serve as labor inspectors at the national level. Despite these equal-opportunity measures, many ILO officials and delegates persisted in sharing the still dominant male trade union and employer view, which deemed that men ought to be the breadwinners and occupy the positions of authority; thus, despite their "inclusion," women staffers did not have an easy time advancing at the ILO. Even Marguerite Thibert, the prodigiously industrious ILO researcher, with her French doctorate in history and her dedication to women's issues, was never promoted to head an ILO division.

Of foremost interest to feminists was the provision in the ILO Charter (Article 427 of the Treaty of Versailles) stating "the principle that men and women should receive equal remuneration for work of equal value."[18] Determining "equal value" would prove a difficult task indeed. This solemn proclamation of what we now call the principle of comparable worth long took a back seat to other continuing issues on the ILO's agenda, in particular the protection and regulation of labor. Nonetheless ILO Studies and Reports soon included the brief report *International Protection of Women Workers* (1921). By 1931 a longer study appeared, *The Regulation of Women's Work*, and in 1939 the massive, 570-page *The Law and Women's Work: A Contribution to the Study of the Status of Women* was produced in tandem with the League's inquiry into the legal status of women (about which more will be said below). ILO researchers were keenly aware of the conflicting approaches to women's work issues, and their observations were reflected in various ILO publications, including articles in the *International Labour Review*. Remarking on the introduction by the Norwegian delegation in 1919 of the principle of absolute equality in labor legislation, the 1921 report noted:[19]

> [1913] was the first appearance of this essentially feminist principle in an international labour conference. Until that time the desirability of special protection for the weaker members of the working community had never been questioned. Since that time there has always been one section of opinion which lays particular stress on the equal competition of men and women, and which does not wish to destroy this equality by placing women in an inferior economic position merely in order to secure certain material advantages for them in the organisation of labour.

Norway withdrew for a time from the ILO; among its objections figured the ILO's commitment to differential legislation for women.

From the time of the ILO's founding meeting (1919) and the ensuing

Washington Convention—a document that reinscribed the ban on women's night work established by the Bern Convention in 1906 and that endorsed other forms of "protective" legislation concerning women workers—the ILO and its policies came under close and continued feminist scrutiny.[20] A 1924 scholarly study by the young French attorney and women's rights activist Andrée Lehmann, *De la réglementation légale du travail féminin (Étude de législation comparée)*, laid out the parameters of the existing comparative legislation as well as the international regulations then in force, and discussed the efforts of feminists to reshape both. Dedicating her work to the ICW activist Maria Vérone, attorney and president of the French League for Women's Rights, Lehmann argued that sexual difference must not be construed as inferiority and that the right to work was the most sacred of rights, for women as for men.

The Washington Convention of 1919 was viewed as unacceptable by such radical individualist, or "equal rights," feminists, both in France and in England. They remembered with indignation the mass firings of women workers following the end of the war and objected vociferously in the 1920s to efforts to bar women from certain positions. They continued vehemently to oppose any restrictions on women's employment as well as to challenge the guiding assumption that such restrictions (no night work, limited hours) were necessary so that "women workers" (presumed by the protectionists to be married and mothers) could properly fulfill their housework and child-care responsibilities. They were upset with the implicit corollary that male workers were the breadwinners and had no such responsibilities. They argued that women should be free to support themselves as they saw fit and to do whatever they chose with their lives. Most of these fervent partisans of unqualified equal rights and equal opportunity in employment were themselves single, middle-class, educated professional women who objected to prevailing notions of a sexual division of labor.[21]

Defenders of the Washington Convention included the more "relational" feminists, who tended to be sympathetic to the difficulties of daily life for those female workers who were also wives and mothers, and who thought in terms of specific rights for women as a distinct sex with distinct societal responsibilities, capable of making distinct contributions. Many of these feminists had themselves been active in the labor movement or were sympathetic to some aspect of solidarist, socialist, or communitarian thinking. They staunchly insisted upon the continuing need for protective legislation. Even more vociferous in its insistence on invigorated provisions for protecting maternity was the leadership of the reorganized International Conference of Socialist Women, which met in Hamburg in 1923. Still further to the Left, communist sympathizers, such as Madeleine Vernet in France, demanded that maternity itself be institutionalized as a remunerated "social function" of the state, comparable to men's compulsory military service. This argument, long made by some European feminists (as has been indicated in earlier chapters), had acquired a new, heavily politicized context since the Russian Revolution. Others, such as Dora Russell, in England, a supporter of motherhood endowment, insisted in 1925 that motherhood be treated as "work"—"the most dangerous of all trades and the most neglected and despised."[22]

These strongly held differences of opinion among feminists over legal and economic equality and especially over the biases apparent within the ILO soon developed into open hostilities, particularly at the 1923 (Rome) and 1926 (Paris) world congresses of the IWSA. These hostilities were signs of disagreement not merely over strategies and tactics on a single issue, but ultimately over the central objectives of feminism and how best to achieve them. Provoked by an attempt of the American-based National Women's Party (whose leaders took the radically egalitarian view on women's equality) to affiliate with the IWSA, a move opposed by the already affiliated League of Women Voters (whose leaders supported protective legislation), the New York World headlined the dissidence "Rival Suffragists Take Row to Paris. Feminism Is Real Issue."[23] Radical equality in civil and political law was one thing, but total equality in the workplace clearly posed far more complex issues. What did women want? What did women need? Who spoke for which women? Which women did feminists speak for? These were not problems that feminists had had to confront in earlier centuries. The outbreak of disagreements over them was, ironically, a product of feminist accomplishments to date.

Indeed, the schism provoked over protective legislation at the 1926 Paris conference led to the founding of two new international groups, Open Door International (1929), which opposed protective legislation for women, and Equal Rights International (1930), which advocated unqualified legal equality, including equality in the workplace. The latter group was composed of British and American individualist feminists (affiliated in their respective countries with the Six Point Group and the National Women's Party). They insisted on "rights equal to those of men" in law and no discrimination in the workplace. They pursued an Equal Rights Treaty within the framework of the League of Nations, while their opponents—including most of those we would call relational feminists, who strongly advocated maternal protection and increased benefits for mothers, especially employed mothers—continued to emphasize the need for recognition of women's unique position with respect to reproduction. The latter insisted on maintaining the standards for protective legislation established by the Washington Convention.

In the 1930s, however, the ground for debate shifted as attacks mounted on women's employment in the wake of the massive world depression, which had begun in 1929. When in late 1931 distinguished scientists such as the French physician and Nobel laureate Charles Richet called for the forcible eviction of all women from the workforce as the solution to both the French birthrate crisis and male unemployment, feminist activists strenuously objected.[24] Academically trained feminists such as the French attorney Suzanne Grinberg, the economist Fernande Dauriac, and the ILO's Marguerite Thibert countered claims that women had taken "men's jobs" by publishing well-documented studies of women's employment, showing that women's employment had not increased to any great extent since the early twentieth century but instead had been redistributed, with increasing numbers of women employed in the tertiary (service) sector.

To allay the specter of "competition," Thibert argued in extremely measured language in an influential article published in the ILO's *International Labour Review* in 1933 that women and men were not, in the vast majority of cases, competing for the same jobs; indeed, except for civil-service positions, she pointedly observed, most employed women held jobs that no man would want.[25] With abundant documentation drawn from a number of European countries as well as from the United States, she demonstrated that measures to prohibit paid employment for women (particularly married women) were ultimately counterproductive and would not create jobs for men, and that equal pay and better access to unemployment benefits for women workers would go far to remedy some of the problems they faced. "If a solution of this kind [eliminating women from the workforce] is to be described as a remedy for unemployment," Thibert insisted, "it must be postulated in advance that the right to work, to earn one's livelihood by one's own activity, is an exclusive prerogative of the masculine portion of humanity, instead of being recognised as a fundamental right of every human being."[26] Thibert can be credited for insisting firmly on this perspective in the very halls of the ILO. Despite such reasoned and well-documented arguments, several governments (such as that of Belgium, where conservative Catholics wielded considerable political power) persisted in promulgating (though in fact not enforcing) regulations that gave hiring preference to men.

In addition to women's employment, a second strand of activity for feminists at Geneva addressed not only the issue of regulated prostitution but also the international traffic in women and children. According to its founding covenant (and again thanks to the lobbying efforts of the Allied feminists in 1919), the League of Nations was authorized to take up this particularly thorny issue. This development in some sense institutionalized and extended the campaign to combat regulated prostitution throughout Europe, which before the war had been led by the International Abolitionist Federation, founded by Josephine Butler in the mid-1870s. ICW leaders had become increasingly preoccupied with this issue since 1900, and now leaned hard on the new League to do something about it.

The extent of this seemingly endemic problem in European countries had been underscored, once again, by the 1910 International Convention for the Suppression of the White Slave Traffic, subsequently signed by twelve European nations, plus Brazil. At the Fifth International Congress for the Suppression of the White Slave Trade, held in London during late June and early July 1913, European and American feminists joined forces in denouncing commercialized vice as a heinous crime, and in demanding that their respective governments establish commissions to investigate the situation. In 1914 appeared a thick and thoughtful survey, *Prostitution in Europe*, undertaken by Abraham Flexner on behalf of the New York Bureau of Social Hygiene. Flexner had emphasized that the low status of women, combined with the unquestioned toleration of male promiscuity (the "boys will be boys" attitude), exacerbated the problem of prostitution in Europe, but that governmental regulation and state-sponsored brothels did not provide a satisfactory answer.[27]

In 1920 the League of Nations' General Assembly authorized the polling of all member governments concerning the international trade in persons that fed prostitution. The survey revealed that many countries had not complied with the 1910 Convention and it proposed, among other measures, that the age of consent for girls be raised to twenty. The ICW had also taken on the issue of "white" slavery, pointing out that sex slaves were not exclusively white, and raising other issues of redefinition. Accordingly, in June 1921, the League of Nations addressed the problem at a conference held in Geneva, attended by delegates from thirty-four nations. There the words "traffic in women and children" were officially substituted for "white slave traffic," thereby reframing the issue. This change in vocabulary recognized that the problem of prostitution concerned the exploitation of women of many differing races and ethnicities around the globe. At stake was not only municipal regulation of prostitutes, but the more recent phenomenon of legally protected extraterritorial districts (known as capitations) established for the sex trade by and for Europeans in port cities such as Alexandria and Port Said in Egypt, and in India. Other results of this meeting included the revisiting of the issue of ending state-regulated prostitution, and a further international Convention to this effect which was ultimately ratified by most participants by 1925.

But the problem would not go away. The IAW (formerly IWSA) also took a strong position on the issue of the sex trade. Egyptian feminists, in particular, used the IAW as a forum to attack these protected enclaves for prostitution in their own country. According to Saiza Nabarawi, in an address to the 1926 IAW congress in Paris, "all measures taken by our government [to combat prostitution] are condemned to failure from the start" because of the immunity accorded to the capitations.[28]

An Advisory Committee to the League of Nations, which included a number of persons committed to resolving the problem of the organized international trade in prostitutes (spearheaded by the American representative, Dr. Grace Abbott), called for further detailed investigation. This resulted in a newly appointed body of experts, which in early 1927 issued a lengthy two-part report entitled *Report of the Special Body of Experts on Traffic in Women and Children*. The investigators had attempted to go beyond government sources and to secure firsthand information from persons directly engaged in the prostitution business such as pimps, madames, traffickers, and prostitutes. The close association of this business with traffic in drugs, alcohol, and obscene publications had become very apparent to the investigators, as was its intimate link to the problem of inadequate wages available to women workers. The report revealed that the international traffic encompassed the transport of women from Europe to Central and South America, and from Europe to the Middle East, particularly Egypt:[29]

> The facts . . . show that the international traffic in women is still an ugly reality and that it continues to defy the efforts to suppress it made both by Governments and voluntary agencies. It assumes new forms as restrictions are increased. It is therefore a menace to society and a challenge to greater efforts in the future.

This difficult issue would continue to arouse feminist indignation, ultimately into the present.

INQUIRING INTO THE STATUS OF WOMEN
WORLDWIDE

Among the many feminist initiatives at the League of Nations, undoubtedly the most impressive was the project of persuading the League Assembly in the mid-1930s to undertake a worldwide survey of the status of women. Historian Carol Miller rightly insists: "It was a real achievement for women's groups to have convinced League member states that the position of women in society could be construed as a problem for international attention. . . . Inter-war women's groups had irrevocably challenged the notion that the status of women was a purely 'national' issue."[30] Leila Rupp concurs: "It was through the League of Nations that feminist internationalists succeeded in putting their issues on the international agenda. . . . Just being there mattered."[31] Being there meant that feminists could effectively place political pressure on the national delegations, many of which included prime ministers and other ranking government officials; being there allowed feminists to maneuver within—and thereby influence—the international bureaucracy. Being there allowed feminists the opportunity to speak out in a forum that would mightily magnify their collective voice, thanks to the coverage of the League's activities by the international press, radio reports, and the new cinematic documentary newsreels.

In spite of repeated frustrations and setbacks, feminists from both hemispheres would succeed brilliantly by the mid-1930s in piggybacking the cause of women's emancipation onto the framework of the League. Following an initial defeat in attempts to win acceptance for the principle of independent nationality for married women during the League of Nations' conference debates over nationality and codification of international law in the early 1930s, feminists from Europe joined hands with their counterparts from Latin America and the United States in pressing for a League-sponsored inquiry into the comparative legal status of women. They were greatly assisted in these efforts by members of the Pan-American Federation for the Advancement of Women (which had been founded in Baltimore in 1922, in conjunction with the Pan-American Union) and subsequently by activists affiliated with the official Inter-American Commission of Women (IACW). The latter, founded in 1928 during the Sixth International Conference of American States in Havana and chaired by the American activist Doris Stevens, immediately launched a survey of the status of women in Latin America and pressed for enactment of an Equal Rights Treaty. At the next Conference of American States in 1933, the IACW succeeded in persuading the participating nations to endorse a proposal for women's equal rights and independent nationality known as the Montevideo Convention on the Nationality of Women. This measure, plus the Montevideo Equal Rights Treaty, would provide the needed wedge—and the standard—for a full-fledged inquiry into the legal status of women by the League of Nations. Ultimately, this initiative would directly confront the protectionist feminist politics implanted in the ILO since 1919.

During the League General Assembly's sixteenth session in September 1935, issues concerning the nationality and status of women were extensively discussed in the prestigious First Committee (Constitutional and Legal Questions). In a lively exchange, the committee heard eloquent endorsements of League action by Henni Forchhammer (Denmark), Aleksandra Kollontai (USSR), Johanne Reutz (Norway), Kerstin Hesselgren (Sweden), Madame C. A. Kluyver (Netherlands), and others. Despite objections from Swiss and Hungarian delegates who insisted that such issues were strictly matters of national concern, the First Committee endorsed a preliminary inquiry into the political and civil status of women. This initiative received approval from the General Assembly on 27 September. Employment issues were deliberately excluded from this initiative.

Responses drifted in during 1936 and 1937, and were duly published by the League of Nations. In addition to the reports from thirty-eight countries around the world (of which twenty-four were European), of particular interest was the fact that reports from international women's organizations were also solicited and included in the League publications. These reports offer precious testimony about the status of women and the organizational initiatives of world feminism in the late 1930s. Among the reports of unusual interest are "Status of the Women of Native Races," undertaken by St. Joan's Social and Political Alliance, and the report on the status of woman as "Wife, Mother and Home-maker" by Equal Rights International. A coalition of international women's organizations (including ICW, WILPF, the Inter-American Commission of Women, Equal Rights International, and the All-Asian Conference of Women) went further, proposing that the General Assembly revise the Covenant of the League in the direction of equal rights: "We wish, in presenting this proposal, to state our belief that only in a League of Nations in which women participate equally with men will the highest expression of a new world order be possible."[32]

During the eighteenth session of the League in September 1937, the General Assembly considered Kerstin Hesselgren's report on the results of the inquiry to date and voted favorably on a resolution to establish "a committee of experts of both sexes" to prepare a comprehensive study on the issues of women's political and civil status. Issues concerning women's employment were treated separately but in parallel, in a bulky 570-page report from the ILO, subsequently published as *The Law and Women's Work* (1939).

World War II seriously delayed reporting results of the inquiries launched by the League of Nations in the late 1930s. The committee of experts published its initial progress report in January 1939, at a time when the threat of war hung heavily over Europe. League records show that a 186-page report, "Legal Status of Women: A Survey of Comparative Law (Fourth Provisional Edition)," was issued in typescript in Rome in 1942, but it was evidently neither published nor distributed. Following the war's end, the League of Nations was dissolved, and haste was made to organize its successor.

However, neither the woman question nor the international women's organization lobbyists would go away, as will become clear at the end of this chapter. The ongoing concern with women's rights—as part and parcel of human rights—would be fully engaged by the League's successor, the United Nations.

CONFRONTING MILITARISM AND WAR

In our own time, some contemporary theorists have argued that women are no more naturally peaceable creatures than their male counterparts, and that the identification of feminism with pacifism and especially with maternalist claims may be a false route for late twentieth-century feminists.[33] Those who advance such a line of argument clearly possess no historical memory of the turbulent and militaristic history of Europe in the nineteenth century and the first half of the twentieth, nor do they acknowledge the stance of feminists in that time toward issues of war and peace. These earlier events render perceptions of historical (if not "natural") connections between women and peace, and between feminism and pacifism, virtually unquestionable. Nor do such theorists seem aware of the relationship between lines of argument connecting women and civility to the powerful eighteenth-century arguments for women as a civilizing force that informed so much of eighteenth- and nineteenth-century feminism, and subsequently the "social feminism" of the early twentieth century. As Naomi Black notes, "an important part of the social feminist rationale has always been the relationship of women to violence and especially to war."[34] We can perhaps appreciate the contemporary relevance of such rationales as we assess the sexual politics in today's Bosnia or Afghanistan, where women have been deliberately singled out as victims of personal violence—male violence—designed to humiliate enemy men sexually in military contests that read as throwbacks to brutal male warfare in earlier centuries. In such contests, women have overwhelmingly been the victims of male violence, not the perpetrators of violence.

In the aftermath of World War I and especially in the 1930s, when renewed militarism and warmongering by aggressively masculinist regimes in Europe reached a peak, when population politics became a subject of great national concern, and when racial and ethnic exclusionism was promulgated as national policy by National Socialists in Germany, it is hardly surprising that feminist international activity focused deliberately on issues of peace, conflict resolution, and disarmament, or that feminists rallied to antifascist coalitions and to the defense of peace, democracy, and freedom. Well before 1914 such feminist initiatives on behalf of peace had already reached a high degree of development with the spectacular contributions of the antiwar novelist Bertha von Suttner and many others. The protestations of Lida Gustava Heymann at the Hague Conference in 1915, linking war with rape, were seconded by those IWSA suffragists who in 1919 founded the Women's International League for Peace and Freedom (WILPF).

After World War I, feminist antiwar activism found organizational expression in the WILPF, which historian Sandi E. Cooper wryly characterizes as "the first woman's association organized across national boundaries devoted to ending man's oldest profession."[35] The WILPF's concerns were shared by most groups, including the ICW, the IWSA/IAW, and the International Co-Operative Women's Guild.

The WILPF was undoubtedly the most ambitious, broadest-scope international women's organization in operation during the interwar period. In the name of the linked causes of peace and freedom, WILPF took up issues that ranged from defending the rights of minorities (particularly in areas such as South Tyrol, ceded to Italy by the 1918–19 treaties), combatting anti-Semitism, and documenting the situation of political prisoners to ending the opium trade and securing international control of waterways and aviation. Unlike the ICW and IWSA/IAW, WILPF was bold enough to make transnational policy for its entire organization at the top rather than leaving policy initiatives to national sections (though this procedure would be hotly contested in the early 1930s). WILPF sent investigators to Indochina and China, and into the successor states of Eastern Europe to document abuses and seek remedies to practices that adversely impacted women. WILPF was also the group with the most conspicuous North American presence, thanks to the extended involvement and high visibility of its founders and original organizers, the Americans Jane Addams and Emily Greene Balch. Both subsequently received the Nobel Peace Prize (Addams in 1931 and Balch in 1946), the most prestigious of international awards for contributions to peace. The postsuffrage ambitions of these distinguished women from the United States, coupled with a heavy influx of energetic British pacifist feminists such as Mary Sheepshanks, and French antiwar activists Gabrielle Duchêne and Camille Drevet, no doubt shaped the WILPF's agenda in the direction of such political issues. As historian Linda Gordon underscores, "it remains important to have women lead organizations that take on the greatest issues of what was once the man's world."[36]

In consequence, however, the WILPF became unique among international women's organizations of the interwar period in its approach; although the WILPF spoke incessantly on behalf of women, it actually mentioned issues directly concerning women rather infrequently. During the first ten years following World War I, the WILPF's initially explicit feminist aims, in which the "full equality of women" had once figured proudly, were overshadowed by an even more ambitious commitment to ending the use of all violence and force. Its 1926 revised Statement of Aims read:[37]

> The W.I.L.[P.F.] aims at uniting women in all countries who are opposed to every kind of war, exploitation and oppression, and who work for universal disarmament and for the solution of conflicts by the recognition of human solidarity, by conciliation and arbitration, by world cooperation, and by the establishment of social, political, and economic justice for all, without distinction of sex, race, class, or creed.

WILPF's work for peace and social transformation would take a variety of forms. In all cases WILPF women acted as though they fully belonged on the stage of international affairs, as stateswomen in their own right. For example, following the signing of the Kellogg-Briand Pact outlawing war as a tool of national policy in late August 1928 (shortly before the September opening of the fall session of the League of Nations General Assembly), Mary Sheepshanks briefed WILPF members on the pact's significance, noting wisely that "the test of the genuineness of the pact will be the readiness to disarm of those who sign it."[38] In early September the WILPF sent a deputation of fourteen women, representing ten nationalities, to the Assembly in support of convening a disarmament conference at the earliest possible opportunity. Their memorial statement urged the League to call the conference quickly and asked participating governments to "send to that Conference delegates instructed to make every sacrifice necessary for the transition from a state of organisation for war to a state of organisation for peace."[39]

WILPF's formal representations were seconded and given a more overtly feminist spin by activists affiliated with other, more outspokenly feminist organizations. In France, a small group of equal-rights activists from several nations, including the American National Women's Party leader Doris Stevens, Britain's Viscountess Rhondda, and the French feminist activists Maria Vérone (president of the Ligue Française pour le Droit des Femmes) and Germaine Malaterre-Sellier, organized a demonstration at Rambouillet, where the French president was entertaining signatories to the Kellogg-Briand Pact. The women demanded simultaneous ratification of an equal-rights treaty. This was an early stage of the (earlier-mentioned) initiative that would result in the 1933 Montevideo Treaty and ultimately inspire the League's formal inquiry into the status of women. Some of these demonstrators were arrested and were roughed up by French police before being released. But they had made their point with the men of the international diplomatic community and—significantly—with the international press.

By 1929 seven of the fifteen women delegates, substitute delegates, and technical advisers to the League of Nations were WILPF members. The significance of such representation may not have been lost on Aristide Briand, then the French prime minister. Yet, in the course of his speech to the League's General Assembly in September, he chose to acknowledge women's growing importance to peace not by recognizing the growth in participation of politically active women at the League but rather by appealing to the world's mothers—as mother-educators—to inoculate their children against the seeds of hatred then being planted by warmongers. In France, Maria Vérone, who reported annually in the mass-circulation newspaper L'Oeuvre on the gains made by feminists at the League, remarked acidly that in France, where women were still effectively disempowered both in civil and political law, they could hardly be called upon to meet Briand's challenge against the contrary opinion of husbands or fathers; she used the occasion once again to call on Briand's government to act on women's enfranchisement.[40]

In early 1931, with the failure of the Austrian bank, the Credit Anstalt, the world economic depression deepened, and peace began to seem more fragile as the militaristic Japanese regime launched its invasion of China. This set of developments, though halfway around the world, made an enormous impression on knowledgeable Europeans, and greatly influenced the thinking of feminists in Geneva. In that year, too, feminists and pacifists concerned themselves with ensuring that women would be represented at the 1932 World Disarmament Conference, which was scheduled to open in early February.

European feminists such as Maria Vérone were thrilled when, in late December 1931, the American president, Herbert Hoover, appointed a woman delegate, Mary Emma Woolley, the president of Mount Holyoke College, to represent the United States. By the time the disarmament conference opened, Woolley would be joined by four other women, including Margery Corbett Ashby from England, Dr. Paulina Luisi from Uruguay, Anna Szelagowaska from Poland, and Winnifred Kidd from Canada. All five, *Jus Suffragii* proclaimed for all to hear, were active feminists, and they were duly feted at a special dinner hosted by the Women's Disarmament Committee. Such women's participation was illuminated by the rosy glow from Jane Addams's recently awarded Nobel Peace Prize.

This committee, organized as a joint committee of the international women's organizations, had, in anticipation of the disarmament conference, launched a worldwide campaign to collect signatures for a huge petition of women for peace. Dutch feminists Cor. Ramondt Hirschmann and Rosa Manus coordinated this massive effort. On the 6th of February, amidst much fanfare and coverage in the press and by cinema, and with elaborate ceremony, the women's committee delivered truckloads of petitions for peace and disarmament, signed by eight million women from around the world, to the floor of the disarmament conference. Six million of these signatures had been collected by national sections of WILPF. It was an enormous effort. "Behind each of these names," declared Mary A. Dingman, president of the World's Young Women's Christian Association, as she presented the petition to the conference, "stands a living personality, a human being, oppressed by a great fear, the fear of the destruction of our civilisation, but also moved by a great will for peace, that cannot be ignored and must not be denied."[41] "If women could make politics," insisted the German feminist and IAW activist Adele Schreiber, in describing the proceedings, "we would do away with war; there would be no more bitter feeling between the belligerent countries!"[42] It may have been due to the mellow mood created by this massive women's peace initiative that the League of Nations was able to move forward on the 1931 proposal of the Spanish delegation requesting its Council to "consider the possibility of studying means of associating feminine action and feminine feeling with the work of the League of Nations by effective and direct collaboration."[43]

That feminists could not keep this initiative going was due more to the pressure of world events than to their own shortcomings. By late

January 1933, when Hitler became chancellor of Germany, it had already become clear to everyone that the disarmament conference was going nowhere. There were too many military and industrial representatives among the delegates and not enough genuinely peace-minded men and women. Instead of reducing armaments, the Draft Disarmament Convention presented to the conference delegates actually increased the permissible allotted quotas for weaponry and manpower. The weapons manufacturers and dealers seemed to have triumphed over the peacemakers. WILPF's executive committee, meeting in Geneva in mid-April 1933, vigorously denounced the draft convention, and issued several statements, including a "Statement on Fascism," calling on women to "unite, or accept war or Fascism."[44] In the interim two of the mainstays of WILPF activism in Germany, Lida Gustava Heymann and Anita Augspurg, had sought refuge in Geneva from the National Socialist regime, alerting their associates to the imminent dangers posed to all feminists—as well as to socialists and Jews—by Nazism.

In the meantime the USSR, which had since reentered international politics, had taken the lead in fostering an international cooperative effort among socialists, communists, and other parties of the Left to oppose fascism, a politics encompassed under the appealing rubric "Popular Front." Alarmed by the prospect of advancing Bolshevism, in early July 1933, the Swiss government attempted (unsuccessfully) to expel WILPF's current international secretary, the French war widow and feminist pacifist Camille Drevet, a close associate of Gabrielle Duchêne, on the ground that she was a communist sympathizer.

In September 1933, the WILPF executive committee—spearheaded by Duchêne and her associates in the WILPF French section—decided to convene a mid-November meeting of representatives from international women's organizations to engage women in the campaign against fascism. WILPF by this point had effectively accepted the Third International's definition of fascism as "the modern form of capitalism, of big industry, of high finance," a definition that had manifestly taken on flesh at the disarmament conference. WILPF's officers went on to insist that "every inch won by Fascism, under whatever guise, is ground lost to women."[45] WILPF's leaders viewed 1933 as a decisive moment, as decisive as 1915, for women to speak out against fascism and war, and their perspective was validated by Nazi Germany's abrupt withdrawal in October from the disarmament conference and also from the League of Nations itself. The work undertaken by the French WILPF women was in large part educational, intended—particularly in the wake of concern about women's voting for right-wing parties—to alert working women and peasant women throughout Europe to the dangers of fascism, but also to alert them to the defense of their rights. Duchêne and her French associates subsequently threw their energies into organizing the new World Committee of Women against War and Fascism, which held its founding congress in August 1934.

In September 1934, the WILPF again met in congress at Zurich. In the course of a contentious debate about the organization's goals and future, a majority of delegates voted to restate the organization's goals in even broader fashion than in 1926, including "their determination to study, make known, and abolish the political, social, economic and psychological causes of war, and to work for a constructive peace." More controversial—though entirely understandable in the stressful circumstances of that year—was WILPF's endorsement of "social transformation": "the inauguration of a new system under which would be realized social, economic and political equality for all without distinction of sex, race or opinion. They see as the goal an economic order on a world-wide basis and under world regulation founded on the needs of the community and not on profit."[46] WILPF had, by this revised statement (written in the third person plural), deliberately aligned itself with the anticapitalist Left—if not wholeheartedly with the politics of the Third International. The gender identity of the perpetrators of violence and exploitation remained unstated, even though "sex" was still conspicuously listed prior to "race" or "opinion." Implicitly, the feminist insistence on ending the subordination of women had become diluted, one issue among others in a comprehensive and reprehensible pattern of domination and exploitation.

During the later 1930s the feminist claim receded still further as other, more "general" issues rose to the forefront for WILPF. It seems significant that WILPF submitted no separate statement in 1937 to the League of Nations' inquiry into the status of women, though it did participate in a joint statement made by the Collaborative Committee on Women's Nationality. In fact, due to controversy over the protective labor legislation issue, delegates at the 1937 Luhacovice (Czechoslovakia) congress could not agree on a resolution concerning women's equal status, except to repeat "with strength [a] belief in women's liberty in all shades of life" and protest "against all attempts to reduce women's right to decide in their own affairs."[47]

Between 1936 and 1939 as prospects for peace grew increasingly dim, feminist peace activists, like their nonfeminist counterparts, found themselves increasingly frustrated and helpless before the aggressive designs of Mussolini's Italy in Ethiopia, the intervention of fascist and communist outsiders supplying weapons to the competing parties in the Spanish Civil War, and, in 1938–40, the successive incursions of Hitler's armies into Austria, Czechoslovakia, and within only a few months Poland, Belgium, Norway, Denmark, and France, while the USSR moved into Finland and eastern Poland. Amidst this turn to violence, feminist women could do little to halt the flood tide of war, except to bear witness. Already in September 1935 the Disarmament Subcommittee of the Liaison Committee of the Women's International Organizations petitioned the League of Nations to insist that the member countries carry out their obligations:[48]

> We . . . call on the Governments represented in the League to respect faithfully two fundamental principles of the Covenant, namely the settlement of all dispute by peaceful means and the obligation to maintain the territorial integrity and political independence of every State Members.

The Subcommittee likewise telegraphed Mussolini, appealing to his leadership in seeking a "civilized" solution in Ethiopia rather than using force. Mussolini, however, had other intentions and invaded Ethiopia in October 1935, just as the League of Nations General Assembly adjourned. Feminist interventions grew increasingly anguished in tone: Swedish delegate Kerstin Hesselgren's 1936 speech to the General Assembly (as the Ethiopian crisis deepened and the League failed to act) is exemplary. Claiming to speak in the name of "women in many parts of the world," she expressed her frustration with the League of Nations' seeming inability to stand up to blatant aggression:[49]

> Fifty nations give in to one aggressor. Fifty nations let a small Power, one of the Members of the League, fall to the ground. However can we, after this, expect that any small nation can have any hope for the future?
>
> A few years ago the League of Nations asked for the collaboration of women. We answered by pleading, by millions all over the world, for disarmament. What was the result? Not disarmament, but rearmament all over the world. . . .
>
> In many countries the authorities are afraid of the low birth rate. How could it be otherwise? How could women wish to bear children into a world that is so hopeless, so insecure? I have heard numbers of women say this. You may well say that conflict and war have always existed, and that children have been born into the world all the same. That is true; but war has never taken such horrible forms as now. . . .
>
> I can give no advice. I can only voice the intense anguish of women all over the world, and urge you to use every wit and every power to find a solution.

But no solution was found. And, in truth, war had been ongoing in Europe, and not only in Ethiopia, since the fascists of Italy and Germany and the Bolsheviks began to deliver arms to Spain. There was little that feminists, or indeed any women then in political life, could do, except to fall in line with military preparedness or to invoke the Lysistrata strategy. The protest of Eleanor Roosevelt, wife of the American president, following the bombing of Barcelona in the spring of 1938, echoed Hesselgren's plea; it was widely quoted in the European press: "Why the women of every nation do not rise up and refuse to bring children into a world of this kind is beyond my comprehension."[50] Her cry from the heart would be echoed many times by women in and beyond Europe during these dark years. But words could not stop the military juggernaut. And it is hard to know whether any women actually refused to bear children as a political act.

In the shadow of the storm about to have its force unleashed throughout Europe by the neighboring National Socialist government in Germany, IAW delegates gathered in Copenhagen, Denmark, in July 1939, to reaffirm their commitment to democracy and to ponder the future. Following Hitler's invasion of Poland in September 1939, and with it the formal outbreak of World War II in Europe, feminists felt powerless to continue their international work. In October 1939, the IAW president Margery Corbett Ashby wrote in *Jus Suffragii / The International Women's News*:[51]

> The catastrophe which has been hanging over Europe for so long has burst upon us. . . . As human beings, as nations, as individuals even we must acknowledge defeat and failure, blindness and negligence. . . . Before the God whom the great majority of all peoples acknowledge in their hearts, and before the judgement of the future we stand arraigned and we can only bow our heads.

Drained by economic difficulties and the sheer exhaustion of campaigning for so many years against the odds, feminists in 1940 did not attempt to protest this war; they knew which side they were on. On the eve of the Nazi occupation of Denmark, Norway, the Netherlands, and Belgium in the spring of 1940, the president of the ICW, Marthe Boël of Belgium, pleaded with members not to "allow the fine spark of international solidarity alive in their hearts to become extinguished, or the human bond linking the peoples together to be completely torn asunder."[52] By June, with the capitulation of France, Britain was the only sizable democracy at war with the authoritarian Axis powers. "The problem," wrote Margery Corbett Ashby in late 1940, as she looked back on the IAW's

Copenhagen meeting of the previous year, "was no longer how to force democracies logically to include women, but how to protect democracy itself": "We called on women, while fighting their own battle, to fight for all mankind and to keep alive the belief in democracy. It was the last flicker of light before silence and darkness shut out our companions."[53]

Yet in spite of the myriad hardships brought on by the war and despite the demise of the League of Nations, some planning for what might come after the war began to emerge, and feminist interest in that planning developed apace. Even amidst the hostilities, the realization of a few feminist goals and reports of women's advances mitigated the gloom: in January 1940, *Jus Suffragii* reported that in France, the legal profession had been opened to women in the French colonies and that a French governmental decree had suppressed forced marriages in France's African colonies. Romania had elected its first woman senator, and Turkey had elected fourteen women to its National Assembly. In the USSR, a woman had been named head of the international airlines.

Meanwhile, combatant governments mobilized women as participants in the war effort, both in civilian and military capacities. In Nazi Germany, however, Hitler refused to call for all-out mobilization of women, preferring instead to forcibly import foreign male labor, especially from occupied France; German women's war work was encouraged only in a voluntary capacity. The Allied democracies felt they could not afford such reservations. In early December 1941, the British prime minister, Winston S. Churchill, called for a resolution that would extend obligatory national service "to include the resources of woman-power and man-power still available." Married women would not be compelled to serve, though those without children would be encouraged to do so. But unmarried adult women between the ages of twenty and thirty would be enrolled in the uniformed fighting forces and in civil defense. "Women are already playing a great part in this war, but they must play a still greater part," Churchill argued before the House of Commons. "The technical apparatus of modern warfare gives extraordinary opportunities to women. These opportunities must be fully used."[54] In the USSR women entered combat on virtually the same terms as men in an effort to turn back the massive Nazi invasion.[55]

The integration of women into the national war efforts (a process already initiated during World War I), and their central role in assuring the survival of those around them during the subsequent fighting, military occupations, and resistance efforts, suggested that many women identified closely with their national cultures. A few dedicated pacifist feminists such as Vera Brittain in England continued to oppose war, but they were the exceptions. To combat the Axis aggression, women would join the Resistance: they would also organize in France as wives of prisoners of war; they would build bombs and ships and airplanes. National governments discovered that women were indispensable; indeed, their value as "manpower" would be increasingly appreciated by leaders of nation-states, who would nevertheless continue their attempts to control and channel women's activities. As Gertrude Bussey and Margaret Tims would sum it up a generation later in their 1965 history of the WILPF, women became "directly involved, no less than men, in all the violence and degradation of total war: victims of air-raids and concentration camps, partisans in the resistance movement, conscripts for war-service alongside their brothers, forced labourers in arms factories—how tragic was this culmination of the struggle for women's rights!" But they added: "And how essential, therefore, to carry on the fight and rectify the false values by which the new rights had been won!"[56]

Despite antifeminist efforts to restore "normalcy," women's role in the post–World War II world would never again return to what it once had been. European women had become full-fledged citizens of a sort that the earliest feminists might never have anticipated. Following war's end in 1945, the various women's international groups reconstituted themselves, ever so haltingly. They mourned the loss—to concentration camps, to execution by the Nazis—of some of their most stalwart militants, such as the faithful IAW campaigner Rosa Manus and WILPF activists including the Czech senator Frantiska Plaminkova, and the Hungarian stalwarts Eugénie Miscolczy Meller and Melanie Vambery. A few, among them Virginia Woolf, had committed suicide. Others, including longtime activists like Maria Vérone, Cécile Brunschvicg, Lida Gustava Heymann, and Anita Augspurg, had succumbed either just before or during the war to illness, deprivation, or old age. Yet among many of the surviving feminists in the victor states, hopes soared that they might have a role in building a better peacetime world, a world in which more heed would be paid to the rights and contributions of women.

"FEMINISM"? OR "HUMANISM"?

Citizenship in the nation-state and in the workplace became realities for women in many European societies in the interwar period. During these years, the goals and aims of feminism were reformulated and new meanings elaborated in response to new challenges. No longer was women's legal and material subordination to men the most obvious centerpiece of feminist activity; indeed, after 1918, in a mostly postsuffrage Europe (the glaring exceptions being France, Italy, Belgium, and Switzerland), the term "feminism" did not seem, in the view of some women's movement activists, nearly encompassing enough. Margery I. Corbett Ashby, the English president of the IAW, had summed up this new view in 1928 when she argued: "It is a fact which cannot be ignored that women are not only feminists in a perpetual state of protest against restrictions and disabilities, they are also to an increasing extent, keen citizens, peace workers, reformers and educators. The greatest freedom won by women is surely precisely this equal right with men to effective interest in the whole of life."[57]

Such a view had been developing for some time, mainly among the postsuffrage English-speaking feminists, and despite the resurgent back-lashes against women's emancipation, it blossomed in postsuffrage contexts. Already in 1913, Helena Swanwick had suggested, in her preface to *The Future of the Women's Movement*, that "humanist" was a better term than "feminist" for the emancipatory goals she and her associates envisioned.[58] Conversely, the term "feminist" might be extended to encompass all human rights. Such chords had been struck repeatedly during the English controversies over feminism in the 1920s (as we have seen in Chapter 10), and as women were pulled increasingly into the political and economic life of their respective nations, they were played once more during debates in the late 1920s and 1930s among supporters of the international women's organizations over the controversial issue of protective labor legislation for women workers.

In France as well, critics such as academician Henri Joly argued that feminism was strictly derivative of humanism: "The idea of humanism had, among other advantages, that it did not postulate any separation between the interests of man and those of women."[59] This French writer (like many socialists) viewed feminism as all too exclusively about women's "separate" interests, rather than about the joint interests of men and women (or class interests). Such a statement would have been familiar to anyone who had confronted socialist views on the subject since the founding of the Second International in 1889, but it took on an even more intriguing political charge in a context in which women comprised more than half the population and were feared as a potentially threatening political majority. The questionable view it encapsulates—that feminism is "separatist"—remains alive and well in France today, where it continues to impede the establishment of women's history and women's studies in French university settings. The fact that "men's separate interests" had dominated European societies for so many centuries went unnoticed by the Henri Jolys of Europe; they were "given," representing the interests of "man." Women's interests could, in this context, be construed as exclusive, divisive, and dangerous.

In the late 1920s, following the schismatic developments of its 1926 congress in Paris and an ensuing 1927 study conference in Amsterdam, adherents of the newly renamed International Alliance of Women heatedly debated the meaning and scope of the concept "feminism." Setting off a series of exchanges in *Jus Suffragii* that continued through most of 1928, one disenchanted "equal rights" activist, C. Nina Boyle, voiced her alarm about the IAW's embrace of pacifists and social reformers, whom she viewed as "the two most dangerous rivals and foes of Feminism."[60] Rather than joining in the clamor for peace and endorsing protective legislation for women workers, Boyle thought the IAW should remain focused specifically on abusive marriage customs and laws, and on violence against women—or what she subsequently underscored as "desperate conditions, under which women suffer hideous personal and sexual coercion."[61]

It was in this context that Corbett Ashby defended the Alliance's position of multiple interests in a world in which some women had arrived at full citizenship. She went on to insist that "a feminist is no less a feminist because she has reached a point at which she dare develop every side of her human nature and natural interests. . . . [A]ll our work must be done from a feminist angle and by feminist inspiration."[62] The following month, the aging German activist Marie Stritt joined the debate, arguing for the intimate connection between feminism and pacifism, and for a broad understanding of feminism: "Feminism . . . means nothing else than the struggle against violence in every form—means right and justice instead of violence and injustice."[63] This was a breathtakingly encompassing agenda, but it also threatened to neutralize or diffuse continuing campaigns on behalf of issues specific to women.

In the course of this 1920s debate, one point was clarified: that at least for the IAW, working at the international or transnational level, issues concerning free love, birth control, and "marriage slavery" were ruled out of bounds on grounds that they had religious implications as well as national (or cultural) implications, both of which the IAW leaders considered to lie beyond their association's internationalist mandate. "It must advise and aid very gently, but wait for the women themselves of each nation to move effectively," cautioned the former IAW president, the American suffragist Carrie Chapman Catt. The "great problems" of the world were, however, within its mandate: "Peace is proper work for feminists," Catt argued. But she also clarified another point, the exclusive identification of feminism with the suffrage cause (historically erroneous, but nonetheless solidly embedded in the popular mind): "I feel that I have personally moved on and become a humanist since the vote came to me. . . . I have not ceased to be a feminist nor to be less sympathetic with protests against women's wrongs."[64]

In the *Jus Suffragii* issue for June 1928, the British equal-rights feminist Helen A. Archdale, who sympathized with Nina Boyle's concerns, criticized the "admission" of both Corbett Ashby and Catt that they had moved on to "humanism":[65]

> A humanist is . . . one who cares for the joys and sorrows of all humanity, and works directly on their cure. A feminist is one who works for the advancement of women's intellectual and social status. . . . Peace, for which nearly all our hearts are full of longing, is the business of humanity, of men and women; co-operation, not separation, should be its strength. Equality, defined as we all know as feminism, is the special business of women; the burden of acquiring it must be mainly theirs. I share cordially the deep regret expressed by your correspondents that the I.W.S.A. has deserted feminism for humanism, knowing that each such extravert to humanism is rejecting feminism.

By December, Archdale (who, along with Lady Rhondda, founded the Open Door Council in 1926 and became a force in Equal Rights International) was arguing that there could be only one kind of feminist: "Feminists believe in equality [for women] and will accept nothing less."[66]

When the IAW met in Berlin in 1929, its members ratified a "Restatement of Policy after 25 Years," which reaffirmed its commitment to suffrage work and peace work, and emphasized equality in economic, moral, and legal rights. Significantly, neither this "Restatement" nor the *History* compiled and published by Regine Deutsch for the IAW anniversary celebration included the word "feminism."[67]

By the 1930s many whom we might view historically as feminists disagreed on what "equality" meant and even on whether "women" should be considered distinct from "men," based on their physiology and reproductive roles, or whether any perceived "difference" should be erased or glossed over in pursuit of legal "rights equal to those of men." Particularly in the English-speaking world, older notions of "equality-in-difference" faded from view before the polarization that would increasingly oppose absolute legal "equality" for individuals to sex-specific needs perceived to flow from women's distinctive "difference."

In consequence of these disagreements, the term "feminist" was claimed by and became identified more exclusively in the public mind with partisans of the legalistic "equal rights." (This faction was led by the Americans Alice Paul and Doris Stevens, and their British counterparts from the Six Point Group, in the new group known as Equal Rights International.) These women fiercely opposed protective legislation for women on principle, pressing instead throughout the late 1920s and early 1930s for enactment of an international equal-rights treaty. Despite the efforts of Eleanor Rathbone and others to delineate a "new feminism" that took women's differences and unique contributions and functions as mothers into account, the term "feminist" migrated and stuck to the more adamantly egalitarian faction. No doubt this context explains Virginia Woolf's interest in incinerating the word.

Debates in the IAW's *Jus Suffragii* and publications by other international women's groups continued to delineate other and varied understandings of "feminism," broadly extending the meaning of feminism to encompass a very broad struggle for human rights and social justice. This line of thinking would be rearticulated far more vigorously in the 1930s, as the menace of fascism to human rights became increasingly pronounced. With the rollback in opportunities for women imposed by fascist regimes—and particularly in Nazi Germany, where assaults on the civil liberties of Jews and other "undesirable" minorities, including Gypsies and the handicapped, were already well known to the international feminist community—organizations such as the WILPF would broaden their mission to encompass "the inauguration of a new system under which would be realized social, economic and political equality for all without distinction of sex, race or opinion."[68]

Developments in world politics during the late 1930s brought the confusion and contentiousness about feminism—and the rearticulation of positions—to a head. These can be studied in the rhetoric of the IAW president Margery Corbett Ashby. In late 1936 Corbett Ashby had insisted that feminism should not be set aside, as had been done in 1914, in the face of "more than medieval savagery in Abyssinia, Palestine and Spain." But she offered a broad and diffuse definition of feminism, which, she declared, "is the faith of women who believe in individual freedom and responsibility":[69]

It is but the women's side to the great doctrine of freedom of thought and speech, of ordered self-discipline, of self-government, of free loyalty to the community, of equal opportunity and mutual assistance which in the last century effected a world wide change from medieval to modern conceptions and produced the most amazing progress in science, health, standard of living and amenities of any century known to us. Because our material power has outgrown our spiritual conceptions we are allowing our inventions to bring torture and death, poverty and tyranny instead of happiness, health, riches and freedom. . . . If we insist on our rights as human beings we are fighting the battle of every man who suffers for his race, his creed, his class or his opinions.

In this interpretation, which would become increasingly the standard in IAW rhetoric, women's rights *were* human rights; the one stood for the other. Was "humanism" en route to becoming "the feminism that dare not speak its name"?[70]

Hitler's invasion of neighboring Czechoslovakia in 1938 and the looming threat to Poland sealed a definitive shift in IAW rhetoric from feminism to humanism. By June 1939 humanism had once again taken the high ground. In speaking of the dramatic changes that had ensued for women since the early twentieth century, and the ways in which women had entered the work for social reform and peace as well as seeking equality, Margery Corbett Ashby underscored that the aims of feminism had seemed relatively straightforward when democracy was in the ascendant. But with the nefarious political developments of recent times and particularly the precarious economic situation created by the Great Depression, democracy was besieged: "The equal status and equal influence of women must be seen as more than ever necessary, but we cannot, we dare not be only feminists, we must be humanists as well in order to preserve in society the very rights in which we would share."[71] Corbett Ashby's French colleague and IAW vice-president Germaine Malaterre-Sellier seconded the argument: equal rights for women were no longer the main point. "True feminism imperiously requires, as a vital necessity, that women, fraternally united beyond all questions of nationality, political party, or religious beliefs, come to the rescue of democracy wherever it is threatened—and, alas, this is in a growing number of countries." Saving women's rights was equated, in Malaterre-Sellier's view, with saving civilization itself: "The Copenhagen Congress must organize women's action for the defense of human values in order to save Peace and Civilization."[72]

At its July 1939 congress in Copenhagen, IAW delegates bravely restated their organization's understanding of feminism in measured yet stirring language, recasting the challenge in terms of "the fundamental principles concerning the relations between individual and state, and between states," and "the responsibilities which their feminist conviction entails." Its "Declaration of Principles," subsequently published in English and French, concluded with a heartfelt statement that provides a fitting epigraph for our chapter:[73]

> The woman's battle is that of all mankind. There can be no freedom for women when freedom is no longer a recognised right of every individual. There can be no justice nor economic freedom for women, when all justice is dependent on the will of an oligarchy.
> Now we live through difficult times in which life based on our principles is at stake. Therefore, women, with men, true to their fundamental principles, must defend a system which will lead to greater justice, freedom, real peace, general prosperity, and more happiness for all.

For IAW activists, ending women's subordination in particular had become inextricably entangled with, or coterminous with, the broader cause of defending freedom, individual and collective, for women and men alike, and of working for democracy. Women had become citizens. As "women's issues" became "human issues," what would be the fate of feminism?

SEARCHING FOR THE FUTURE OF FEMINISM

When the war ended in 1945, the conundrum of feminism and humanism would be revisited in a new setting—the United Nations (UN). The shock impact of the Holocaust against the Jews and other atrocities committed during the World War II years had refocused the attention of world leaders on the issue of human rights. Despite a paucity of feminists—or indeed even of women delegates (14 women and 521 men)—at its April 1945 founding meeting in San Francisco (or, for that matter, at the first session of the General Assembly in early 1946), the Preamble to the UN Charter of June 1945 affirmed and specified "faith in fundamental human rights, in the dignity and worth of the human person, in the equal rights of men and women, and of nations large and small."[74] Behind this choice of words lies John Stuart Mill's 1867 proposal to change the word "man" to "person" in the British parliamentary electoral law, but—significantly—the equal rights of "men and women" are explicitly mentioned in the UN Charter; no mistake could be made about the Charter's intent.

In this new context, the prior work of the "equal rights" feminists on women's issues at the League of Nations in the 1930s found its reward. Their successors in the late 1940s continued to press the point. But the broader humanist current also had its representatives. A subsequent declaration by women representatives, alternates, and advisers to the first General Assembly of the United Nations, presented to the delegates by

Eleanor Roosevelt early in 1946, emphasized "joint efforts" of men and women, "common ideas of human freedom," and called on women to take part in the "work of peace and reconstruction as they did in war and resistance."[75]

In the spring of 1946, the Commission on Human Rights, a division of the UN Economic and Social Council (ECOSOC), established a sub-commission, but soon bowed to feminist pressure to create later that year a full-fledged Commission on the Status of Women, with a far more extensive mandate to inquire into "improvements in political, civil, educational, social and economic fields." Influential in this development were the Danish feminist and social democrat Bodil Begtrup, who became the Commission's first chair, and Latin American feminists. In December 1946, Begtrup and other Scandinavian feminist delegates pushed for the General Assembly's adoption of a resolution urging that member states who had not yet done so "fulfill the purposes and aims of the Charter . . . by granting to women the same political rights as to men."[76] They intended to revive the examination of the worldwide status of women begun by the now defunct League of Nations (thanks to earlier feminist activists) and to carry the reforms proposed during the 1930s to fruition.

The UN Commission on the Status of Women took up its investigation in January 1947. Its work would eventually provide the model for many national commissions (and even regional and local commissions) on the status of women throughout the world. Many landmark UN measures—including the 1948 Universal Declaration of Human Rights, the 1952 Convention on Women's Political Rights, the 1967 UN Covenants on civil and political rights and on economic, social, and cultural rights—have their origins in the work of this Commission. Finally, in 1975, a resurgent women's rights movement would help bring to fruition what the Commission on the Status of Women had been recommending since 1946–47—the International Women's Year in 1975 and the International Decade of Women. All of these post–World War II developments owe a large debt to the bold initiatives launched during the interwar period by European and American feminist activists and organizations working on behalf of women's issues at the League of Nations. The work of the UN Commission on the Status of Women continues to this day.

Although IAW president Margery Corbett Ashby thought in early 1946 that "at this stage it would be dangerous to set up a 'women only' committee to deal with sex differentiation,"[77] it soon became clear to some (among them the social democratic women of the 1930s who had for so long emphasized class rather than sex differences) that even in the UN, and despite every principled pronouncement, if feminists did not insist on specifying and making visible women's rights and women's representation, nobody else would. The new terminology adopted was that of "the status of women" and "human rights." However, the terms "equal rights" and "women's rights," and the earlier languages of "feminism" that lay behind them, were not entirely forgotten. They would eventually resurface through new fissures.

Epilogue

Reinventing the Wheel?

In July 1949, when delegates of the International Alliance of
Women convened in Amsterdam, the congress theme was
"Human Rights and Human Needs." The IAW publication, *The International Women's News* (formerly *Jus Suffragii*), heralded the 1948 United
Nations Declaration of Human Rights as "a magnificent feminist victory."[1] The program for the future seemed evident: implementation of
these principles. And yet, this would clearly not be so simple, as IAW
leaders were deeply aware: "Alas, our experience shows that these declarations of principles remain a dead letter unless public opinion in each
country insists on their implementation." "Democracy without women," in Christine Fauré's more recent phrase, would not do; still less democracy without feminist watchdogs.[2]

But how to implement the victory was precisely the problem. It
seemed that women's international organizations and feminist activists
still had to insist that governments fulfill their obligations to the equality of women and men under the UN Declaration. In the postwar nations
of Western, Central, and Southern Europe, the disadvantaged legal status
of women in marriage remained high on the list of problems that called
out for remedies, as did the relationship of married women to paid employment and to the social benefits being elaborated by mostly male
politicians in the newly developing welfare states. The long-standing issues of state-regulated prostitution and the international traffic in
women and children took a step forward with the abolition in 1946 of
the notorious and long-contested "French system" of government-endorsed brothels in Paris (thanks in particular to the campaigns of Paris
municipal councilor Marthe Richard) and by the subsequent 1949 International Convention "for the Suppression of the Traffic in Persons and of
the Exploitation of the Prostitution of Others," under the auspices of the
United Nations, which deliberately employed the newly fashionable
gender-neutral language of human rights.

FEMINISTS CONFRONT THE COLD WAR
AND PARTY POLITICS

In the rush to return to normalcy following the end of World War II, however, and despite the gains described above, it would not be so simple to mobilize European women to insist on their rights when there were so many other pressing problems to be addressed. Amid the bombed-out ruins of half of Europe, and especially in Germany, Poland, and points east where so many had been murdered in the name of Nazi racial policies, and others slaughtered in the devastating air attacks inflicted by the Allies in order to bring down the Third Reich, many women simply found themselves overwhelmed by the twin projects of survival and reconstruction. Ironically, they also came to personify, in these circumstances, their very nations; "their role in the community's survival was unusually visible."[3] Whether identified with the winning or the losing powers, or with civilian resistance efforts in Nazi-occupied countries, many women found themselves in much the same situation as their French predecessors who, during the revolution of 1789, had marched on Versailles to complain about the high price of bread and the difficulty of feeding their families. Faced with the overwhelming effort to reconstitute shattered families and lives, what approach could possibly mobilize European women on behalf of further steps toward their own liberation? Was it, as Mary Wollstonecraft and other feminists had earlier perceived, that women themselves—women who did not think as feminists did, who were frivolous, ill-educated, shortsighted—were the problem? More likely, most European women were simply exhausted by the effects of what male diplomacy and warmongering had recently put them through. Small wonder that "peace and bread" might have more appeal than any campaign for liberty, equality, rights, and justice, or that they might opt for solidarity with the decimated ranks of their menfolk.

The need for a fresh rallying theme for feminist activism was reflected in a thematic reorientation of the IAW by its new president, Dr. Hanna Rydh, archeologist, member of the Swedish Parliament and president of the Fredrika Bremer Association. In contrast to her predecessor, Margery Corbett Ashby, whose individualist feminism elided into a humanism beyond sex, Rydh proposed a more relational approach at Amsterdam, one based on specificity of function and approach: "Women must unite in something greater than national or race loyalties, and that is the motherhood of the whole wide world."[4] It was a tall order, indeed.

IAW activists were not, however, alone in seeking new ways to rally women's support. In postwar Europe, many political party organizations would vie for women's allegiance, seeking to present an attractive picture of women's future under their auspices, and in the process tailoring their offerings to attract more conventional women, especially housewives. Indeed, feminists continued to face serious rivals, and undoubtedly the most serious of these rivals would be the resurgent Communist Party. Reinvigorated by the impressive participation of communists in the antifascist resistance movements of France, Italy, Yugoslavia, and elsewhere, and by the Soviet Union's military alliance with the Western powers against Nazi Germany (an alliance which, following the Yalta accords between Roosevelt, Churchill, and Stalin, had successfully gained the USSR great latitude for its ensuing military occupations, followed by political takeovers, throughout Eastern Europe), communists relaunched their organizational initiatives to draw women in. Soviet communists under Stalin had long since renounced the most sexually radical aspects of programs articulated by Aleksandra Kollontai and others in the wake of the 1917 revolution, and had reverted to notions of bolstering marriage and conventionally structured families, educating girls and boys for appropriate sex roles, and emphasizing women's roles as mothers as well as workers; in the USSR abortion had been outlawed once again in 1936, even as socialized maternity and collective solutions to infant care and domestic services long provided by women were made a state priority. One enthusiastic proponent of the Bolshevik approach, George N. Serebrennikov, had boasted in 1937 that "the U.S.S.R. is the only country in the world where full equality for women has not only been proclaimed, but is also being made an actuality."[5] This message would be insistently repeated, though actual achievements would lag far behind.

The war inflicted severe population losses and economic damage on the USSR. The Soviet Family Law of 1944, in addition to strengthening the programs devoted to enhancing benefits for mothers, also established a series of honors—"the title 'Heroine Mother,'" and "the institution of the order 'Motherhood Glory' and the 'Motherhood Medal.'"[6] The Third International's initiatives to win Europe for communism, Soviet-style, would be launched not only by military occupations followed by invasions in Eastern Europe, but in the West by concerted attempts at persuasion, especially in France and Italy, where women had at last gained full national citizenship rights.

French women obtained the vote in March 1944—due less to General Charles de Gaulle (who generally gets the credit) than to the Gaullist government-in-exile's Consultative Assembly, which met in Algiers in March 1944, even before D-Day and the liberation of Paris by Allied forces. The initiative was pressed by a few insistent women delegates from the Resistance, notably Lucie Aubrac, along with prosuffrage male communist resistance figures.[7] Once again, for feminists, being there mattered. The French communists, whose party (PCF) had been outlawed during the Vichy period, had incontestably played a major role in organizing the antifascist Resistance. They strongly advocated woman suffrage, arguing publicly that women had earned it through their resistance activism (and hoping privately that they would rally to the PCF program for a new and transformed France). However, despite continuing concerns that women were more numerous than men (by about one million), constituting 62 percent of eligible voters, fear of communism seemed to serve as an even more powerful motivator for other French delegates' acquiescence in supporting woman suffrage. Politicians further to the Right were convinced that the majority of women would in fact vote conservatively, as had been argued for more than a century as a reason for not enfranchising them. These men would not be disappointed in this hope, as subsequent elections were to prove. A subsequent study by Mattei Dogan and Jacques Narbonne, published in 1955 as part of a UNESCO inquiry into women's voting patterns, indicated that married women voted rather like their husbands, but that single women and older widows did tip the balance in a conservative direction. Dogan and Narbonne would add that in France the notion of a women's political party or faction was "inconceivable."[8]

In late 1946 a clause giving women equal rights in law was incorporated into the constitution of the new Fourth Republic; it would be reconfirmed in 1958 by de Gaulle's Fifth Republic. Women's rights, including their right to work, had arrived—along with their stated obligation (in the new republic of workers) to do so. Equal pay for equal work became law in mid-1946, followed by the opening up of the French civil service to women. Once again, strong pressure for such reforms on the work front came from the PCF, led by Maurice Thorez and his companion-in-arms, Jeannette Vermeersch. While the PCF was outlawed, they had taken refuge in the USSR, returning to France in 1944. Vermeersch would play an unchallenged role in French and international Communist Party women's activism during the next quarter-century.[9]

Vermeersch and her associates had emerged as leaders in the French communist girls' youth group organized in the 1930s. In June 1945 they outlined their vision and program at the first congress of the newly established Union des Femmes Françaises (UFF). At the congress Claudine Michaut laid out the "duties of the French woman," among which were "to give children to France, to found a home, to raise her children mor-

ally, to inculcate in them a taste for work, filial respect, love of country
and a civic sense; [her duties] are thus above all those of the woman—
mother of a family, honest, a quality worker, a citizen informed about
and conscious of the national interest."[10] This tripartite identity did not
sound much like the image of the sexually emancipated Bolshevik woman painted by Kollontai at the outset of the 1917 revolution, and it was
even less like the 1920s image of the militant citizen-heroine tractor
driver, but this mother-centered program promised to serve the UFF in
mobilizing women who were primarily housewives, not workers, and to
gain their support for the Communist Party's vision of France's future.[11]

This set of population-conscious postwar developments, coupled
with the UFF's founding of the Women's International Democratic Federation (of which more below), put other French political parties on notice. Soon they too began to issue appeals to women, offering them both
visions and directives, in a battle not only for their votes but also for
their minds and souls. The new and important Christian Democratic
Mouvement Républicain Populaire (MRP) published its assessment of
the "woman problem" in 1946, contesting the longtime communist assertion that equality of the sexes carried with it identity of function,
conspicuously in the workforce: "Others think . . . that equality does not
presuppose identity and that within this equality, differences of function
should be respected." Reconstruction in France implied both an economic and a reproductive aspect, according to the MRP; the question
was how to build a "humane" economy. "Natural law" must be respected, and that meant that married women "should consecrate themselves first of all to domestic labor and to maternal functions."[12] With
the male-breadwinner model (referred to as the single salary) as its ideal,
MRP spokeswomen believed there was still much that could be done to
improve women's situation: clearing and elimination of slums, more
and better home-economics training, mass-produced household appli-
ances, more household help, expanded and improved child-care and kindergarten facilities, collectives for laundry, mending, cleaning, and in
the countryside, improved child-care facilities during the times of intensive agricultural labor, so that farm women could work in the fields or
help with the mass feeding of farm help.

In June 1947, with the French Communist Party no longer included in
the Fourth Republic's ministry, and only months before the Moscow-
based Cominform reasserted its hostility to Western "imperialism," and
especially to the United States, a different but recognizably familiar program was elaborated at the eleventh congress of the PCF. Condemning
the demand of "reactionaries" for women in the home, the communist

program elaborated by Jeannette Vermeersch reemphasized women's economic contribution through employment, calling also for a greater rate of participation by women in the party and in positions of authority. Women must involve themselves in identifying capitalism as the enemy and in overthrowing it. Echoing the now hallowed party line (firmly established, as should be clear from earlier chapters, during the late nineteenth century by the writings of August Bebel, Friedrich Engels, and Clara Zetkin, and promulgated incessantly by both the Second and Third Internationals), the report *Les Femmes dans la nation* (Women in the Nation) reiterated that women's emancipation would come about only through their paid labor, and that only socialism could realize their total emancipation, in tandem with that of men. Everywhere capitalism exploited women, not only in the workplace but also in the household: "Far from us is the backwardness of feminism, of suffragettes and feminists, which had a progressive role in the past. But that does not mean that one must ignore the particularly difficult position of women and the special forms of organization that permit us to gather them together. . . . Thus we must gain still more women to the cause of socialism, of communism, to the cause of Lenin and Stalin."[13] Such would be the language of postwar communism in Europe.

In the French Fourth Republic, women could not only vote; they could run for office and were initially elected, not only in local government positions. But at the national level, based on an electoral system that featured proportional representation and political-party lists, elected women remained few and far between. Seventeen of the thirty-three women elected to the National Assembly in 1946 represented the PCF; the next most numerous group of women deputies—including Germaine Poinso-Chapuis, who became a minister—represented the Christian Democratic MRP. There were a sprinkling of Socialist Party women deputies as well. But only nine elected women served in both constituent assemblies and in the Fourth Republic's three legislatures, and significantly, none of them came from the ranks of Third Republic feminists. Another small cluster of women would be elected to the Senate (Conseil de la République) during this period, and a few served as cabinet ministers. In every case, the women were specifically assigned to deal with "women's issues," that is, issues affecting health, welfare, or children. The direction of the women's vote would become a pawn in party politics; the prevailing idea seemed to be to keep French women happy but to keep them out of "serious" positions of political authority such as foreign affairs, defense, finance, agriculture, colonial matters. The political analyst Maurice Duverger pointed to the ploy in 1955: "The essentially competitive reasons for the elimination of women are indeed masked by a very effective justification mechanism. The argument is that politics is, by nature, a field essentially suited to men, to which women should be admitted only in exceptional circumstances and then only within strictly defined limits." And, he added:[14]

> This is basically the same attitude as that of a mother country which admits the natives of the colonies to certain administrative and technical posts, without allowing them to take part in political leadership proper, or as that of certain employers who allow their workers to take part in the direction of the social welfare side of the business but not in its economic direction. In spite of appearances, it is fundamentally anti-equalitarian, for it tacitly assumes that man's aptitudes are polyvalent, while those of women are monovalent.

In such circumstances, the flag of an independent (i.e., non-party-affiliated) feminism would be kept aloft in France by activists such as the indefatigable attorney Andrée Lehmann, who (succeeding Maria Vérone, who had died in 1938) would head the Ligue Française pour le Droit des Femmes from the mid-1940s until 1971. She would also serve as vice-president of Open Door International and of the International Alliance of Women, which latter organization she would represent to UNESCO. But a feminist political presence outside party politics would become increasingly difficult to sustain, as the parties energized their efforts to mobilize women's support through their own sections. By the early 1950s, even the Radical Party (which had blocked woman suffrage for so many decades) had formed its own women's section—and this section would be headed by the feminist attorney Marcelle Kraemer-Bach.[15]

As elsewhere in Europe, population issues and economic rebuilding, not women's liberation, were the most pressing items (besides decolonization) on the agenda of the new Fourth Republic. Further reforms in the legal status of married women languished until the mid-1960s. But in 1946, a full-scale system of state-supported maternity allowances was set in place—payable in cash to the mothers. The very important benefit of free maternity care, prenatal, delivery, and postpartum, was included in the social-security medical-benefits package. Birth premiums were established for each child born; in addition, prenatal allowances payable to the woman to cover her expenses during pregnancy were added, with the explicit intention of discouraging abortion. Crèches and nursery schools (écoles maternelles) were established. All these measures, in fact, addressed the combined demands of pro-natalists and many feminists as well during the previous thirty years. But government officials strongly resisted the language of the long-enunciated socialist-feminist, then communist, formula "maternity as a social function" of the state. In 1948, according to Andrée Lehmann, French women gave birth to 864,000 children, the highest number since the early twentieth century. The postwar baby boom was under way. Historian Claire Duchen has since underscored that, in the short run, "the vote and admission of women to the world of politics [in France] paradoxically demobilised them rather than offering a new impetus to—and a new forum for—discussion of women's rights."[16]

COMPETITION FROM THE COMMUNIST WOMEN'S INTERNATIONAL

In the interim, the French communist women had launched a new and enterprising international initiative. In December 1945 the Union des Femmes Françaises (UFF), hosted an International Congress of Women in Paris. In the course of this congress was born yet another international organization of women—the Women's International Democratic Federation (WIDF: Fédération Démocratique Internationale des Femmes, or FDIF, in French; Internationale Demokratische Frauenförderation, or IDFF, in German).[17] The WIDF, with backing from Moscow, would subsequently achieve consultative status as a nongovernmental organization (NGO) at the United Nations, and would attempt to co-opt WILPF's national sections in the fight against resurgent fascism and for peace. The WDIF founding congress in Paris was described by IAW president Margery Corbett Ashby as "a series of passionate demonstrations of women's essential solidarity in their hatred of fascism, their desire for social welfare, their immense pride in their new national liberty and newly acquired citizenship."[18] The program, she added, "was as advanced as regards equality as the most old-fashioned feminist could require." Yet to these women, "who had stepped out from six years of isolation," this meeting seemed—to Corbett Ashby's amazement—as if it were "the first international gathering ever held." Militant antifascist delegates from Russia, Hungary, Romania, Bulgaria, Yugoslavia, and Spain (including such celebrated heroines of the antifascist resistance as Dolores Ibarurri of Spain, Anna Pauker of Romania, and Nina Popova of the USSR) set the tone for the conference, and among these militant women, memory of interwar European feminism, as it had existed prior to the Nazi conquests or at the international feminist level, was dim—if indeed it registered at all.

But the feminist international organizations had changed as well, temporarily muting their distinctive, once vigorous voices. In the postwar IAW as well as in the WILPF, claims for human rights had effectively absorbed and eclipsed the earlier vocabulary of women's rights. There, as in the United Nations itself, personhood—the woman as individual—had triumphed, at least rhetorically speaking. This did not mean that claims for "women's rights" would long remain in total obscurity; against the "rights of man" one could emphatically reassert the "rights of woman," thereby underscoring once again the false universality of the term "man."

This did not happen right away. But in the 1950s, in an ironic twist, claims for women's rights would erupt once again during a series of congresses convened by the newly established procommunist WIDF, which by 1953 claimed to be the largest of all international organizations of women. After holding feminist claims at arms' length for so many decades, the communist women's international in effect annexed—without batting an eye—the earlier feminist program and the language of "women's rights"!

During the early years of the Cold War, the president of WIDF was Eugénie Cotton, a French physicist and director of the prestigious Higher Normal School for Women at Sèvres (which trained all the professors who trained female teachers in France). Cotton was not a card-carrying Communist Party member, but her left-wing credentials were such that she also presided over the UFF; the secretary-general of the WIDF was the French resistance figure and parliamentary deputy Marie-Claude Vaillant Couturier, a ranking French Communist Party activist. At the WIDF-sponsored World Congress of Women in Copenhagen in June 1953, WIDF raised the banner of women's rights, in language wholly reminiscent of the great eruptions of French feminist protest since the French Revolution. WIDF supplemented its appeal to the "women of the whole world" by a "Declaration on the Rights of Women"—a declaration that conspicuously omitted the word "feminism" even as it addressed a wide-ranging series of discriminatory issues for women "as mothers, workers and citizens."[19] Promoting International Women's Day on 8 March, and organizing subsequent world congresses of mothers (from 1955 on), the WIDF and its nationally based flanking organizations focused particularly on the needs and aspirations of women workers and trade unionists, and like the WILPF and the IAW—which remained active in the noncommunist world—campaigned to foster world peace and a safe environment for children. "Feminism"—even its memory—was obliterated, but "Women's Rights" were alive and well on the world screen, this time in harness to an anticapitalist, anti-imperialist sociopolitical program spearheaded by the Soviet Union.

BUILDING THE WELFARE STATES

France and the USSR by no means monopolized programs benefiting women and children, however. We have seen in earlier chapters how women's and children's welfare had long since preoccupied European nation-states, with feminists developing widely different, even conflicting positions with respect to state intervention aimed unilaterally at protecting women workers. Germany had already put an impressive system into place, beginning in the late nineteenth century. The USSR had raised the stakes considerably, issuing a challenge that all postwar European states would be forced to address. Already during the 1930s the Swedish Social Democratic Party had developed a comprehensive and progressive series of state programs within the framework of population policy that would enhance both population growth and the quality of working women's lives in postwar Europe. Such programs would inspire other nation-based efforts to develop welfare programs, to facilitate national population growth, and to redistribute wealth.

In England, the end of the war brought to fruition the elaboration of a particular type of welfare state under the Labour government, based on measures formulated during the war by Sir William Beveridge. As political analyst Jane Jenson has underscored, the plan was based on the male-breadwinner model favored by the trade unionists; and that entailed, in the words of the Beveridge Report (1942), the "recognition of housewives as a distinct insurance class of occupied persons with benefits adjusted to their special needs." Viewing marriage as a partnership and putting "a premium on marriage, in place of penalising it," the report stated, both as an assumption and as an assertion, that "in the next thirty years housewives as mothers have vital work to do in ensuring the adequate continuance of the British race and of British ideals in the world." Thus, "during marriage most women will not be gainfully employed."[20]

Although a system of minimal family allowances was enacted in England, it was a far cry from the program advocated in the 1900s by the German Bund für Mutterschutz or since the mid-1920s by Eleanor Rathbone's "new feminism," intended to provide economic independence (from men) for women as mothers. As Rathbone had made clear already in 1934, "the economic dependency of the married woman is the last stronghold of those who, consciously or unconsciously, prefer woman in subjection, and that perhaps is why the stronghold is proving so hard to force."[21] But the "new feminism" advocated by Rathbone never gathered sufficient political support to override the almost overwhelming dedication of British politicians and trade unionists to the male-breadwinner model, as historian Susan Pedersen has made clear in brilliant comparative study.[22] In contrast to France, married women's access to social benefits in England would come principally and explicitly through the gainful employment of their husbands. That this was not immediately perceived as a problem is suggested by Vera Brittain's rhapsodic enthusiasm for the new welfare state in 1953: "In it women have become ends in themselves and not merely means to the ends of man."[23]

In postwar Germany, following the Nazi defeat, as historian Robert Moeller has shown, the elaboration of policies concerning the relationship of the sexes, and in particular the situation of women, lay at the base of reconstruction efforts. In addition to the overwhelming problem of survival and rebuilding, German women outnumbered men by some four million in the aftermath of the war. Under the Allied Occupation, and the new German Federal Republic, the Communist Party remained outlawed, as it had been under the Third Reich; but the resurgent Social Democratic Party (SPD), which was permitted, argued for full equality of the sexes—in the law, at least—while its principal adversary, the Christian Democratic Party (CDU), espoused a conservative Christian understanding of the family unit, with a sharp sexual hierarchy and division of labor in marriage.

Even though the SPD attorney Elisabeth Selbert, from Kassel, succeeded in inserting a clause guaranteeing equal rights for the sexes in the 1949 Basic Law (Article 3, Paragraph 2), politics of the family were such in postwar Germany that no individual emancipation for women—especially married women—could be institutionalized. A young feminist sociologist, Helge Pross, wrote in 1958 that "asking about the social status of woman in the Federal Republic today is about the same as rummaging around idly in an antiques store for social problems." Yet, she argued, women must be allowed to support themselves through paid work, to have careers, to live beyond and outside the confines of the male-dominated family.[24] But this was not to be. Moeller concludes his study in these words: "In the process of political self-definition that marked West Germans' exit from the ruins of the Third Reich, 'woman's place' was reasserted and reified, not redefined."[25] Women's organizations there were, by the drove, but as historian Annette Kuhn and her collaborators have pointed out, women's "organizations" had replaced the (feminist) women's "movement."[26]

DEBATING THE WOMAN QUESTION AND
OBLITERATING FEMINISM

Such developments as have been sketched above—and one could chroni-
cle comparable developments in many other countries—would mark the
early years of the Cold War period, when so many European countries,
even as they sought to elaborate their own political and cultural futures,
hung suspended in the encompassing power struggle that developed between the USSR and the United States and its NATO allies. This struggle laid yet another level of meaning over internal political struggles
(generally polarized between social democratic and Christian democratic political parties) that affected the possibilities for realizing feminist ends.

Thus, despite the United Nations' insistent emphasis on human
rights and equality of the sexes, it would be increasingly difficult during
these difficult postwar years either to promote "human rights" or to focus exclusively on "women's rights." Due to the hegemony of competing political parties in Western European nations, feminists had difficulty finding space in which to work effectively for *women's* rights.
With the exception of the Swiss, European women had attained political
citizenship, and theoretically at least, single adult women enjoyed formal equality before the law; however, the status of married women with
regard to laws governing property and employment remained compromised, even as states set in place elaborate benefit systems for mothers
and children, in the name of the family. In Western European states, constitutional promises of equality of the sexes before the law seemed insuf-
ficient to undo existing systems of inequality, as long as governments
and parties put other priorities first, and as long as women voters did not
pressure their governments to guarantee an end to married women's
continued subordination to men, or to ensure an unrestricted range of
life choices. East of the so-called Iron Curtain, in the postwar societies
dominated by the USSR—which by 1950 encompassed the new German
Democratic Republic (DDR), Czechoslovakia, Poland, Hungary, the Baltic republics of Lithuania, Latvia, and Estonia, and Yugoslavia, Romania,
and Bulgaria—the single-party system and severe governmental constraints on the "public sphere" of association and expression meant that,
effectively, there was no space for women's organizations other than
Communist Party–sponsored ones. Organized feminism, along with
"public space" itself, had been deliberately extinguished and co-opted in
these countries. Only in the wake of the 1989 collapse of the Soviet sys-

tem has inquiry into the history and repression of pre-1945 feminist activity even become possible.[27]

The debate on the woman question did not die during the 1950s, yet neither did it flourish. In the decades following the war, the magma of feminism would simmer just under the surface of postwar institutional arrangements, sometimes finding crevasses through which to issue reminders that patriarchal, authoritarian societal arrangements must never remain unquestioned. Indeed, a steady barrage of important publications appeared, all addressing one or another aspect of the woman question.

Among the best-known of these, in retrospect, was Simone de Beauvoir's now classic two-volume treatise, *Le Deuxième Sexe* (The Second Sex, 1949), which would be celebrated for its grounding in existential philosophy (positing a dualism in which "woman" served as man's "Other") and for its insights into the social construction of femininity. Beauvoir's work would also be roundly condemned for its author's visceral hostility toward marriage and maternity and for her insistence (echoing Aristotle and Otto Weininger) that men embodied the "active" principle and women the "passive" principle, and that the solution to women's dilemma lay only in transcending the "immanence" of "femininity" and in socialism (Beauvoir was not then an acknowledged feminist).[28] The work quickly gained a place on the Vatican's Index of Forbidden Books, even as it was pointedly ignored by the communist women of the UFF. Its most celebrated assertion, which introduced the second volume and was destined for a brilliant future—"One is not born, but rather becomes a woman"—revived an idea that had in fact characterized French debate on the woman question since at least the eighteenth century, reminding readers yet again that "woman" was a cultural construction, a "gender" as much as a "sex."[29]

The Second Sex was by no means the sole contribution to European debate on the woman question during the 1940s and 1950s, although it was perhaps the most learned, controversial, and widely translated publication of the period. The young British sociologist Viola Klein had already published her wide-ranging analysis *The Feminine Character: History of an Ideology* (1946), in which she critiqued the earlier contributions of Havelock Ellis, Otto Weininger, Sigmund Freud, and various experimental psychologists to the formulation of constraining notions of "femininity." The Belgian Catholic philosopher Jacques Leclercq expostulated for some 395 pages in *Marriage and the Family: A Study in Social Philosophy* (1940 in French; 1945 in English). The distinguished

French educator Paul Crouzet's *Bachelière ou jeune fille* appeared the same year as Beauvoir's *Second Sex*, and developed the author's contrasting concerns that "equal or not to men, women are *different than them*": "The education of girls must be considered in relation to the *feminine personality*, with the goal of awakening, developing and affirming the *feminine vocation*. This vocation in the natural order is that of spouse and mother."[30] This, from the husband of Jeanne Crouzet Ben-Aben, who had campaigned for equal educational opportunity for French girls. Like Beauvoir, Crouzet understood that gender was a social construction: all the more reason why it must be constructed appropriately. In the immediate postwar setting, Crouzet's construction may have seemed more appealing to many young women than was Beauvoir's resistance to maternity and motherhood.

In Western Europe, the stream of publications addressing the woman question continued throughout the 1950s and into the 1960s. Among these, we can point to several particularly significant works, both in favor of emancipation and against it. The Parisian attorney and women's rights activist Andrée Lehmann addressed "The Role of the French Woman at the Midpoint of the Twentieth Century" (1950). The Dutch philosopher Frederik Jacobus Johannes Buytendijk, responding in part to Beauvoir, undertook a phenomenological and psychological inquiry concerning *De Vrouw* (1951), which was subsequently published in German and French translations (1953, 1954, respectively). Political scientists took an interest in how women were voting, thanks primarily to a survey initiated by UNESCO in 1952; among the works published in response to this inquiry were Maurice Duverger's important comparative study *The Political Role of Women* (1955) and Mattei Dogan and Jacques Narbonne's *Les Françaises face à la politique* (1955). Initially stimulated by a survey conducted by the International Federation of University Women (IFUW), in 1956 the Swedish social democrat Alva Myrdal and her junior partner Viola Klein published their influential analysis *Women's Two Roles: Home and Work*, which—perhaps deliberately— did not address the causes of conflict between these two roles.[31] Although the communist regimes to the east had effectively shut down access to such works in the satellite states of Eastern Europe, throughout Western Europe the debate on relations between the sexes found fissures through which to simmer and bubble along until the baby boomers learned to read and grew to maturity.

The story of feminism was by no means over. In the late 1960s feminist resistance once again exploded in Western European societies, led by young women who had enjoyed more educational opportunities than any previous generation. Some, engaged in left-wing politics, found the Communist Party's position on the woman question inadequate, while others took inspiration from developments in the United States, where feminism had emerged once again in the early 1960s in the wake of the civil rights movement. Most knew very little or nothing of the historical struggles of their feminist predecessors, with the singular exception of Beauvoir's rather unflattering account; they had no historical feminist consciousness, in Gerda Lerner's phrase. They began from the "Year Zero" to reinvent feminism. And the story of their reinvention has now begun to spawn a whole series of retrospective accounts.

REINVENTING THE WHEEL? OR BUILDING A HISTORICAL SPRINGBOARD

Why reinvention? Why not memory? Why not history? Surveying the broad sweep of European history and the geography of feminist eruptions between 1700 and 1950, it seems clear that the impulse to reposition women under male control has recurred repeatedly and each time has been more vigorously challenged. Indeed, striking manifestations of feminist resistance can be documented in every generation of the European past from the Enlightenment to the Atomic Age. Fundamentally, what feminism has been—historically speaking—about is *enabling* women within the context of a male-defined and male-dominated society, even as feminists have attempted to alter the definition, to eliminate the domination, and thereby to transform the society they live in. It is, as I claimed at the beginning of this study, about equalizing the balance of power between the sexes.

We still have a great deal to learn about the history of feminisms not only in European countries but throughout the world. We are seeing recurrent patterns that we are only beginning to understand. We are learning more about the intricacies of constructing—and reconstructing—patriarchal institutions, about the particular conditions that force fissures to open, the molten lava of feminist protest to erupt, and about the advances and retreats in women's situation that allow it to flow and ebb—or the resistances that force it to recede—over time. But of one thing we can be certain: the history of this pathbreaking, multifaceted, centuries-long feminist tradition in European societies can teach us all a great deal. Knowledge and historical memory can be used to address problems as they arise and to avoid mistakes in the future. They can be powerful tools for assuring that efforts to subordinate women are met with sustained resistance. In short, they can provide a springboard.

Amnesia, particularly historical amnesia, may well be the worst enemy of those women, broadly speaking, who continue to be thought of—
or who all too often think of themselves—as "the Other" rather than as
half of humanity. If I could put copies of the thousands of historical
feminist texts I have consulted into the hands of every literate woman
not only in Europe or the Americas, but also in many other parts of the
world where feminism has had far less opportunity until recently to find
expression in print, the very earth might rumble as the fissures grew to
vast chasms. Perhaps the crust of patriarchy might liquefy and dissolve,
instead of being cnly intermittently breached, generation after generation, by a magma that subsides all too quickly—almost deferentially—
after each partial success.

These feminist forebears do not have to be from my own village, my
own country, my own group, in order for me to appreciate the magnitude
of their contribution. Their legacy is one common to all those who continue to insist that women are "half of humanity," half the human race,
rather than the "auxiliary sex," as Helena Swanwick put it, or the "second sex," in the words of Simone de Beauvoir. Women's rights are human rights, as the Beijing Declaration put it so nicely in 1995. Or, to
quote Hedwig Dohm, "human rights have no sex."

The long, rich history of European feminisms from 1700 to 1950 is a
heritage that belongs to all of us, women and men alike, wherever in the
world we live, whatever the color of our skin or our ethnicity, whatever
our religion or our national origin. What we have learned since 1970
about the history of feminisms in Europe constitutes a precious legacy
for all of us who insist on challenging male domination, on reshaping relations between the sexes in ways that empower women. It is less a
question of "inventing a tradition" than of retrieving and reclaiming a
once well-buried but surprisingly well-documented aspect of the past.
Moreover, we have an obligation not only to contemplate this newly rediscovered history ourselves but to assure its transmission, to the best of
our ability, to our daughters and our sons, to our grandchildren, and their
posterity. Not only does this mean transmitting it to our colleagues in
other fields of history, in women's studies, and in feminist theory: this
means working in the schools and on the schools, and educating teachers
and members of our communities to be knowledgeable in this historical
material.

What is at stake here is not merely a more systematic knowledge of
the complex history of the European past, of events that took place in
particular cultural configurations that may never be repeated. What is at
stake is access to knowledge that can help us, women and men, Europe-

ans, neo-Europeans, Asians, Africans, Indians of the subcontinent, people of all backgrounds and persuasions who have been touched by the "woman question" in some aspect of our lives (as indeed, we all have been), to learn to live more amicably with one another—to build futures in which partnership and mutual respect, not institutionalized dominance and subordination, nor physical, psychological, or symbolic violence, become the norm. Women and men need to stand side by side as partners, not face to face as antagonists. Men need to learn that telling women who they are and what they need to be, using force to ensure their submission, will no longer be tolerated.

The construction—and transmission—of a feminist memory, a feminist past, as it were, is not simply an academic exercise; it is a kind of guidebook. This book is therefore a political guidebook, a political act. In our 1983 documentary interpretation *Women, the Family, and Freedom*, which provided the springboard for this book, Susan Groag Bell and I wrote: "Reinventing the wheel is hardly necessary. It is more efficient to build on what is already in place."[32] We now know far more than we did in 1983 about feminism's history; indeed, there seems to be far more evidence available than we ever dreamed then of finding. There is still a great deal more to learn. The challenge, then, is to inform ourselves about what has been "already in place," the victories, the mistakes, the challenges, and to use this knowledge as a springboard to future feminist thought and action. We have far more important things to do than continually to reinvent the wheel.

Reference Matter

Notes

PROLOGUE

1. For a discussion defining feminism and delineating the subject of study in historical feminisms, see Chapter 1 below.

2. Madame Avril de Sainte-Croix, *Le Féminisme* (Paris: V. Giard & E. Brière, 1907), p. 6. This writer's first name has been given variously as Ghénia and as Adrienne.

3. Millicent Garrett Fawcett, "Introduction," in H. M. Swanwick, *The Future of the Women's Movement* (London: G. Bell, 1913), xii.

4. Ellen Key, *Love and Marriage*, transl. Arthur G. Chater (New York: G. P. Putnam's Sons, 1911), p. 214. Originally published in Swedish as *Lifslinjer af Ellen Key*, 1904.

5. Simone de Beauvoir, "Introduction," in *The Second Sex*, transl. and ed. H. M. Parshley (New York: The Modern Library, 1968; originally published in 2 vols. in French, 1949), xix.

6. Dale Spender, "Introduction," in *Time and Tide Wait for No Man* (London: Pandora Press, 1987), p. 2.

7. The two books in question are Richard J. Evans, *The Feminists: Women's Emancipation Movements in Europe, America and Australasia, 1840–1920* (London: Croom Helm; New York: Barnes & Noble, 1977), and Jane Rendall, *The Origins of Modern Feminism: Women in Britain, France, and the United States, 1780–1860* (London: Macmillan, 1983; New York: Schocken, 1984). See my discussion of these earlier works and others in "Challenging Male Hegemony: Feminist Criticism and the Context for Women's Movements in the Age of European Revolutions and Counter-Revolutions, 1789–1860," paper presented at the conference on women's movements in nineteenth-century Europe, Stuttgart/Birkach, 31 May–4 June 1995, in press.

8. See the insightful discussion of these issues in Marilyn J. Boxer, *When Women Ask the Questions: Creating Women's Studies in America* (Baltimore: Johns Hopkins University Press, 1998), chap. 6.

9. For France, see Françoise Thébaud, *Écrire l'histoire des femmes* (Fontenay Saint-Cloud: ENS Éditions, 1998); for many other European countries, see the essays in *Writing Women's History: International Perspectives*, ed. Karen Offen, Ruth Roach Pierson, & Jane Rendall (London: Macmillan; Bloomington: Indiana University Press, 1991).

10. See Miriam Schneir, *Feminism: The Essential Historical Writings* (New York: Random House, 1972), and Alice Rossi, ed., *The Feminist Papers* (New York: Columbia University Press, 1972; Bantam Books, 1973). See also Julia O'Faolain & Lauro Martines, eds., *Not in God's Image* (New York: Harper & Row, 1973), and Susan Groag Bell's *Women: From the Greeks to the French Revolution* (Belmont: Wadsworth, 1973; 2d ed., Stanford: Stanford University Press, 1980). It was the acknowledged dearth of available documentation available for teaching European women's history to American students who did not read continental European languages that provoked Susan Groag Bell and myself to publish our two-volume documentary interpretation *Women, the Family, and Freedom: The Debate in Documents, 1750–1950* (Stanford: Stanford University Press, 1983; hereafter *WFF*).

11. See the references listed in the editors' introduction to *Writing Women's History: International Perspectives*, xxvi, and xxxix n. 7. Information concerning developments in the 1990s can be gleaned from the publications of the group Women's International Studies Europe (WISE), including their newsletter *WISE Women's News* and the quarterly *European Journal of Women's Studies*. See also the quarterly *Feminist Collections* published by the Women's Studies Librarian, University of Wisconsin System, Madison, and new items in the three women's history and gender history journals *Journal of Women's History, Women's History Review*, and *Gender & History*, as well as in the bibliographies I have published in the newsletters of the International Federation for Research in Women's History (IFRWH).

12. Contrast this situation with the lament of Richard David Sonn about the placement of anarchism in the "HX" series, only after Marxism, socialism, and utopias. See Sonn, "Introduction," in *Anarchism* (New York: Twayne Publishers, 1992).

13. "Estudien, estudien ustedes Historia, damas y caballeros españoles, antes de accusar de extranjerismo à un feminista": G. Martínez Sierra (María Lejárraga Martínez Sierra), *Feminismo, feminidad, españolismo* (Madrid: Renacimento, 1917), p. 132.

14. F. Š(mahel), review of Katherine Walsh's *Ein neues Bild der Frau im Mittelalter?* in *Ceský Casopis Historický* (Czech Historical Review), 91:1 (1993), p. 147; as transl. Jitka Malečková, "Gender, Nation and Scholarship: Reflections on Gender/Women's Studies in the Czech Republic," in *New Frontiers in Women's Studies*, ed. Mary Maynard & June Purvis (London: Taylor & Francis, 1996), p. 96.

15. See the provocative analysis by Joan W. Scott, *Gender and the Politics of History* (New York: Columbia University Press, 1988), but also the long-awaited study by Bonnie Smith, *The Gender of History: Men, Women, and Historical Practice in the West, 1800–1940* (Cambridge, Mass.: Harvard University Press, 1998).

16. Dr. Lucie Charewiczowa, "Est-il fondé d'écrire une histoire spéciale de la femme?" in *La Pologne au VIIe Congrès International des Sciences*

Historiques, Varsovie 1933 (Warsaw: Société polonaise d'histoire, 1933), pp. 309, 311.

17. *Vie sociale* (published by CEDIAS, Musée Social, Paris), no. 8–9 (1988), p. 367.

18. *Die Frauenfragen in Deutschland: Strömungen und Gegenströmungen, 1790–1930, sachlich geordnete und erläuterte Quellenkunde*, ed. Hans Sveistrup & Agnes von Zahn–Harnack (Burg-bei-Main: A. Hopfer, 1934).

19. The Archive of the German Women's Movement in Kassel publishes an informational periodical, *Ariadne*.

20. See, in English, Ineke Jungschleger, *Bluestockings in Mothballs: 50 Years International Archives for the Women's Movement* (Amsterdam: IAV, 1987). For a published catalog of holdings through the late 1970s, including works in a variety of languages, see *Catalog of the International Archives for the Women's Movement* (Boston: G. K. Hall, 1980). On the recuperated Dutch materials, see Mineke Bosch, "Historiography and History of Dutch Feminism, 1860–1919," unpublished paper, Stuttgart/Birkach, 1995.

21. For further information about European women's history archives, see Leila J. Rupp, "Introduction" to her *Worlds of Women: The Making of an International Women's Movement* (Princeton: Princeton University Press, 1997).

22. See Claudia Wirz, "Ein historisches Gedächtnis für die Frauen," *Neue Zürcher Zeitung*, 20–21 March 1998; forthcoming in English translation "A Historical Memory for Women" in the *Journal of Women's History*, 12: 1 (Spring 2000).

23. Marie von Ebner–Eschenbach, *Aphorismen aus einem zeitlosen Tagebuch altweibersommer Parabeln und Märchen* (1880), in her *Gesammelte Werke*, 9 (Munich: Nymphenburger Verlagshandlung, 1961), as transl. G. H. Needler in the *Longman Anthology of World Literature by Women 1875–1975*, ed. Marian Arkin & Barbara Shollar (New York & London: Longman, 1989), p. 5.

24. Eleanor Rathbone, "Foreword," to Erna Reiss, *Rights and Duties of Englishwomen: A Study in Law and Public Opinion* (Manchester: Sherratt & Hughes, 1934), viii.

25. Review of *Josephine Butler* by K.B. in *Jus Suffragii/The International Woman's Suffrage News*, 22:5 (Feb. 1928), 71.

26. Review of *The Cause* by K.B. in *Jus Suffragii/The International Woman Suffrage News*, 23:2 (Nov. 1928), 19.

27. Among the first historical studies born of Women's Liberation in contention with male-dominated New Left socialism and communism in a British setting were Sheila Rowbotham's *Women, Resistance and Revolution: A History of Women and Revolution in the Modern World* (London: Penguin, 1972) and *Hidden from History: Rediscovering Women in History from the Seventeenth Century to the Present* (London: Pluto Press, 1973). The French socialist-feminist tension similarly underlies the differing ap-

proaches of Charles Sowerwine's *Les Femmes et le socialisme: Un Siècle d'histoire* (Paris: Presses de la Fondation Nationale des Sciences Politiques, 1978; originally a Ph.D. dissertation at the University of Wisconsin, Madison), and Marilyn J. Boxer's unpublished Ph.D. dissertation, "Socialism Faces Feminism in France, 1879–1913" (University of California, Riverside, 1975), parts of which have been published as articles. Such tensions also shaped the important analyses of earlier nineteenth-century conflicts in England, among the Owenite socialists, and in France, among the Saint-Simonians, respectively by Barbara Taylor, *Eve and the New Jerusalem: Socialism and Feminism in the Nineteenth Century* (London: Virago, 1983; New York: Pantheon, 1983), and Claire Goldberg Moses, *French Feminism in the Nineteenth Century* (Albany: SUNY Press, 1984). Both these works were also based on doctoral dissertations.

28. The phrase comes from Heidi Hartmann's much-quoted article in the collection *Women and Revolution: A Discussion of the Unhappy Marriage of Marxism and Feminism*, ed. Lydia Sargent (Boston: South End Press, 1981). "Fatal Attraction" is, of course, the title of a recent film.

29. See Dorothy Kaufmann, "Uncovering a Woman's Life: Edith Thomas (novelist, historian, *résistante*)," *The French Review*, 67:1 (Oct. 1993), 61–72.

30. See Evelyne Sullerot, *Histoire de la presse féminine en France, des origines à 1848* (Paris: A. Colin, 1966), and the more general *La Presse féminine* (Paris: A. Colin, 1966).

31. On Pieroni Bortolotti's contributions, see Paola di Cori, "Franca Pieroni Bortolotti: Una Storia solitaria," *Memoria*, no. 16 (1986), 135–39.

32. See *Les Femmes et la Révolution française*, ed. Marie-France Brive, 3 vols. (Toulouse: Presses Universitaires du Mirail, 1989–91), and the small catalog *Les Femmes et la Révolution française: Bibliographie établie par Simone Blanc* (Paris: Bibliothèque Marguerite Durand, 1989).

33. See, among other contributions: Gabriella Hauch, *Frau Biedermeier auf den Barrikaden: Frauleben in der Wiener Revolution 1848* (Vienna: Verlag für Gesellschaftskritik, 1990), and "Die Wiener Achundvierzigerinnen," in *1848—"das tolle Jahr": Chronologie einer Revolution* (Exhibition catalog, Historische Museum der Stadt Wien, 1998), pp. 44–51; Ulla Wischermann, *Frauenpublizistik und Journalismus: Vom Vormärz bis zur Revolution von 1848* (Weinheim: Deutscher Studien Verlag, 1998); and essays by Michèle Riot-Sarcey, Bonnie S. Anderson, and myself in the forthcoming proceedings (ed. Jean-Luc Mayaud) of the February 1998 Colloquium on the 1848 revolutions, held at the Assemblée Nationale in Paris.

34. Kathleen Jones's thoughtful study *Compassionate Authority: Democracy and the Representation of Women* (New York & London: Routledge, 1993), based on discussions of authority primarily by European political theorists, should be supplemented by a parallel historical account of European feminists' critiques of male authority and its direct links to military might and organized violence. See also Marlene LeGates's discussion of authority and power in her excellent book *Making Waves: A History of*

Feminism in Western Society (Toronto: Copp Clark/Addison Wesley, 1996), pp. 12–13. I have also addressed these issues in an unpublished essay, "Women and the Problem of Political Authority in France."

35. See my essays "Going Against the Grain: The Making of an Independent Scholar," in *Voices of Women Historians,* ed. Eileen Boris & Nupur Chaudhuri (Bloomington: Indiana University Press, 1999); "A Comparative European Perspective: Comment on [Judith Bennett's] 'Confronting Continuity,'" *Journal of Women's History,* 9:3 (Autumn 1997), 105–18; "Reflections on National Specificities in Continental European Feminisms," *University College Galway Women's Studies Centre Review,* no. 3 (1995), 53–61; and "Feminism and Sexual Difference in Historical Perspective," in *Theoretical Perspectives on Sexual Difference,* ed. Deborah L. Rhode (New Haven: Yale University Press, 1990), pp. 13–20, with notes, pp. 265–66.

36. Susan Stanford Friedman, "Making History: Reflections on Feminism, Narrative, and Desire," in *Feminism Beside Itself,* ed. Diane Elam & Robyn Wiegman (New York & London: Routledge, 1995), p. 29.

37. The quote is from LeGates, *Making Waves,* p. 3.

38. Margaret Camester and Jo Vellacott, "Introduction," in *Militarism versus Feminism: Writings on Women and War* (London: Virago, 1987), p. 2.

39. Audre Lorde, "The Master's Tools Will Never Dismantle the Master's House," in *Sister Outsider: Essays and Speeches* (Freedom, Calif.: The Crossing Press, 1984).

CHAPTER 1: THINKING ABOUT FEMINISM IN EUROPEAN HISTORY

1. For a more extended discussion, see Karen Offen, "On the French Origin of the words *Feminism* and *Feminist,*" *Feminist Issues,* 8:2 (Fall 1988), 45–51. A slightly earlier and different usage of *féminisme* can be found in French medical literature, referring to a "weakening" or feminization of the male body during illness; see Ferdinand-Valère Faneau de la Cour, *Du Féminisme et de l'infantilisme chez les tuberculeux* (Paris: n.p., 1871; I owe this reference to Geneviève Fraisse). As Faneau de la Cour's brief medical thesis was completed and published in the midst of France's 1870 defeat (by Prussia) and subsequent civil war in 1871, it seems unlikely that its title or content had much public impact.

2. These issues are explored in greater detail in Karen Offen, "Defining Feminism: A Comparative Historical Perspective," *Signs: Journal of Women in Culture and Society,* 14:1 (Autumn 1988), 119–57. See also Karen Offen, "Feminism," in *Encyclopedia of Social History,* ed. Peter N. Stearns (New York: Garland, 1993), 271–73. For a discussion of feminism as individualistic in the U.S. context, see Nancy F. Cott, *The Grounding of Modern Feminism* (New Haven: Yale University Press, 1987).

3. These points, and the arguments that follow, were originally developed in Offen, "Defining Feminism." In France, Geneviève Fraisse has led

the way in thinking through, from a formal philosophical perspective, a theoretical framework for a history of feminism based in concern about the "universal subject," man; this is not, however, the framework I have chosen to adopt, as it does not lend itself to the sociopolitically based kind of cross-national comparative perspective I am developing here. See in particular Fraisse's essay "Feminist Singularity: A Critical Historiography of the History of Feminism in France," in *Writing Women's History*, ed. Michelle Perrot (Oxford: Blackwell, 1992; orig. French publ. 1984), pp. 146–59.

4. The word "oppression" can be repeatedly found in American feminist rhetoric, from the 1848 "Declaration of Sentiments" at Seneca Falls to the Red Stocking Manifesto in 1969. It is also featured in Marxist-feminist analyses, as, for example, Michèle Barrett, *Women's Oppression Today: Problems in Marxist Feminist Analysis* (London: Verso, 1980), or Lise Vogel, *Marxism and the Oppression of Women: Towards a Unitary Theory* (New Brunswick: Rutgers University Press, 1983). "Oppression" is also the term employed by Gerda Lerner, *The Creation of Feminist Consciousness* (New York: Oxford University Press, 1993), and by Marlene LeGates, in her thoughtful survey *Making Waves: A History of Feminism in Western Society* (Toronto: Copp Clark/Addison Wesley, 1996).

5. See Offen, "Defining Feminism."

6. Thus, I do not subscribe to the notion that only women can be feminists. The European past offers too many remarkable examples of men who wholeheartedly championed women's emancipation, often in very radical ways, ranging from François Poullain de la Barre in seventeenth-century France to the chevalier de Jaucourt, the marquis de Condorcet, and Theodore Gottlieb von Hippel in late eighteenth-century France and Prussia, and Charles Fourier, Ernest Legouvé, John Stuart Mill, and August Bebel in nineteenth-century France, England, and Germany. For an explicit statement of the "women only" claim, see Naomi Black, *Social Feminism* (Ithaca: Cornell University Press, 1989), and for an implicit statement, see Lerner, *Feminist Consciousness*.

7. I am not posing here any "essential" notion of womanliness, though I do insist—as did feminists in the time period under consideration—on women as embodied persons both physically and emotionally distinct from men.

8. The formulation "equality" versus "difference" that has characterized so much internal debate within European feminisms in the twentieth century is not only unfortunate, but altogether unhelpful when it comes to understanding the issues historically. I have discussed the development of this formulation, born during the conflict that arose over protective labor legislation for women workers between the 1890s and 1930s, at greater length in "Reflections on National Specificities in Continental European Feminisms," *University College Galway Women's Studies Centre Review*, 3 (1995), 53–61, and in the later chapters of this book.

9. Judith Bennett has introduced the concept of "patriarchal equilibrium" to convey the complexity and fluidity of patriarchy as a system. See

her essay "Confronting Continuity," *Journal of Women's History*, 9:3 (Autumn 1997), 73–94, and the ensuing forum. The chapters in this book will highlight both the challenges to male hegemony and the resistance to these challenges in a set of male-dominated systems that had become surprisingly vulnerable.

10. Rosalind Delmar, "What Is Feminism," in *What Is Feminism? A Re-Examination*, ed. Juliet Mitchell and Ann Oakley (Oxford: Basil Blackwell, 1986), p. 17.

11. For alternative starting points, see Richard J. Evans, *The Feminists: Women's Emancipation Movements in Europe, America and Australasia, 1840–1920* (London: Croom Helm, 1977); Jane Rendall, *The Origins of Modern Feminism: Women in Britain, France and the United States, 1780–1860* (New York: Schocken, 1984); Claire Goldberg Moses, *French Feminism in the Nineteenth Century* (Albany: SUNY Press, 1984); Geneviève Fraisse, *La Raison des femmes* (Paris: Plon, 1992), esp. pt. 2; and Joan Wallach Scott, *Only Paradoxes to Offer: French Feminists and the Rights of Man* (Cambridge, Mass.: Harvard University Press, 1996).

12. See the contributions in *Perspectives on Feminist Political Thought in European History: From the Middle Ages to the Present*, ed. Tjitske Akkerman and Siep Stuurman (London & New York: Routledge, 1998).

PART I: THE EIGHTEENTH CENTURY

1. See, most recently, the essays in *Femmes et pouvoirs sous l'Ancien Régime*, ed. Danielle Haase-Dubosc & Éliane Viennot (Paris & Marseille: Rivages, 1991); *Die europäische Querelle des Femmes: Geschlechterdebatten seit dem 15. Jahrhundert*, ed. Gisela Bock & Margarete Zimmermann, vol. 2 of *Querelles: Jahrbuch für Frauenforschung* (Stuttgart: J. B. Metzler, 1997); *Perspectives on Feminist Political Thought in European History: From the Middle Ages to the Present*, ed. Tjitske Akkerman & Siep Stuurman (London & New York: Routledge, 1998); and *Women Writers and the Early Modern British Political Tradition*, ed. Hilda L. Smith (Cambridge: Cambridge University Press, 1998). On the significance of Poullain de la Barre, see in particular Siep Stuurman, "Social Cartesianism: François Poul-[l]ain de la Barre and the Origins of the Enlightenment," *Journal of the History of Ideas*, 58:4 (Oct. 1997), 617–40, and Stuurman, "L'Égalité des sexes qui ne se conteste plus en France: Feminism in the Seventeenth Century," in *Perspectives on Feminist Political Thought*, pp. 67–84.

2. Approaches with which I am taking issue include, notably, Paul Hoffmann's magisterial *La Femme dans la pensée des lumières* (Paris: Éditions Ophrys, 1977), which nevertheless remains invaluable for its extraordinary bibliography. The pessimists whose arguments I also address include Joan Kelly-Gadol, "Early Feminist Theory and the *Querelle des femmes*, 1400–1789," *Signs*, 8:1 (Autumn 1982), 4–28; and the essays by Abby Kleinbaum, "Women in the Age of Light," and by Elizabeth Fox-Genovese, "Women and the Enlightenment," in the first and second editions of *Becoming Visible: Women in European History*, ed. Renate Bridenthal et al. (Boston:

Houghton Mifflin, 1977, 1987, respectively); and Michèle Crampe-Casnabet, "A Sampling of Eighteenth-Century Philosophy," in *Renaissance and
Enlightenment Paradoxes*, ed. Natalie Zemon Davis & Arlette Farge (Cambridge, Mass.: Harvard University Press, 1993), pp. 315–47. Characteristic of
many treatments in the 1970s and 1980s by the "first wave" of feminist
scholars are a shared impatience with the notion that any arguments for
equality based on sexual difference—or sexual complementarity—could
possibly be considered "feminist" and an *a priori* Marxist-socialist skepticism that anything positive for women could have emerged from "bourgeois culture."

I here rejoin and expand upon an earlier and more positive current of interpretations concerning feminism and the French and English Enlighten-
ments advanced in the 1970s and early 1980s by literary scholars including
Katherine B. Clinton and David Williams, and especially by Jane Rendall, in
*The Origins of Modern Feminism: Women in Britain, France, and the
United States, 1780–1860* (London: Macmillan, 1983; New York: Schocken,
1984). For an important reconsideration of French Enlightenment culture
and women's contribution to it, see Dena Goodman, *The Republic of Letters: A Cultural History of the French Enlightenment* (Ithaca: Cornell University Press, 1994), and Goodman, "Women and the Enlightenment," in
the third edition of *Becoming Visible*, ed. Bridenthal et al. (Boston: Houghton-Mifflin, 1998), pp. 233–62.

For a powerful indictment of patriarchal thinking and positioning of
"woman" as nonsubject in German Enlightenment thought, see Barbara
Becker-Cantarino, "Patriarchy and German Enlightenment Discourse:
From Goethe's *Wilhelm Meister* to Horkheimer and Adorno's *Dialectic of
Enlightenment*," in *Impure Reason: Dialectic of Enlightenment in Germany*, ed. W. Daniel Wilson & Robert C. Holub (Detroit: Wayne State University Press, 1993), pp. 48–64. The pertinent texts by Kant, Fichte, Hegel,
and other pre- and postrevolutionary male philosophers are reproduced in
translation in *Visions of Women*, ed. Linda A. Bell (Clifton: Humana Press,
1983).

3. New texts are emerging all the time. For studies that are responsible
for recuperating some of them, see Christine Fauré, *La Démocratie sans les
femmes* (Paris: Presses Universitaires de France, 1985), translated as *Democracy Without Women: Feminism and the Rise of Liberal Individualism
in France* (Bloomington: Indiana University Press, 1991); the essays in *Going Public: Women and Publishing in Early Modern France*, ed. Elizabeth
C. Goldsmith & Dena Goodman (Ithaca: Cornell University Press, 1995);
and the works cited in Chapter 2 below.

4. Works pertaining to the "knowledge wars" include the immense
study by Linda Timmermans, *L'Accès des femmes à la culture (1598–1715)*
(Paris: Honoré Champion, 1993); Londa Schiebinger, *The Mind Has No Sex?
Women in the Origins of Modern Science* (Cambridge, Mass.: Harvard University Press, 1989); and Thomas Laqueur, *Making Sex: Body and Gender
from the Greeks to Freud* (Cambridge, Mass.: Harvard University Press,

1990). See also Elizabeth A. Williams, *The Physical and the Moral: Anthropology, Physiology, and Philosophical Medicine in France, 1750–1850* (Cambridge: Cambridge University Press, 1994), chaps. 1–3.

5. For example, Lieselotte Steinbrügge, *The Moral Sex: Woman's Nature in the French Enlightenment* (New York: Oxford University Press, 1995; originally published in German as *Das moralische Geschlecht: Theorien und literarische Entwürfe über die Natur der Frau in der französischen Aufklärung* [1992]). Other influential works that address male thinking about women, primarily in political theory, include Joan B. Landes, *Women and the Public Sphere in the Age of the French Revolution* (Ithaca: Cornell University Press, 1988), which examines the period by exploring the gender gaps in the subsequent theories of Jürgen Habermas on the origins of "publicity" (*offentlichkeit*); and Carole Pateman, *The Sexual Contract* (Cambridge: Polity Press; Stanford: Stanford University Press, 1988). See the important correctives to Landes's account by Keith Baker, "Defining the Public Sphere in Eighteenth-Century France: Variations on a Theme by Habermas," in *Habermas and the Public Sphere*, ed. Craig Calhoun (Cambridge, Mass.: MIT Press, 1992), pp. 182–211; and Dena Goodman, "Public Sphere and Private Life: Toward a Synthesis of Current Historiographical Approaches to the Old Regime," *History & Theory*, 31:1 (1992), 1–20. An important earlier work, Fauré's *Democracy Without Women*, also offers a corrective, as does Tjitske Akkerman's study *Women's Vices, Public Benefits: Women and Commerce in the French Enlightenment* (Amsterdam: Het Spinhuis, 1992). Further correctives can be found in Sarah Maza, *Private Lives, Public Affairs: The Causes Célèbres of Prerevolutionary France* (Berkeley & Los Angeles: University of California Press, 1993); and in Sarah Hanley, "Social Sites of Political Practice in France: Lawsuits, Civil Rights, and the Separation of Powers in Domestic and State Government, 1500–1800," *American Historical Review*, 102:1 (Feb. 1997), 27–52.

6. See Joel Schwartz, *The Sexual Politics of Jean-Jacques Rousseau* (Chicago: University of Chicago Press, 1984). More recently see Penny Weiss, "Rousseau, Antifeminism, and Woman's Nature," *Political Theory*, 15:1 (Feb. 1987), 81–89, who argues that Rousseau deliberately posited domesticity for women as a cultural construction, in the interests of social and political utility; another argument in the same vein is Paul Thomas, "Jean-Jacques Rousseau, Sexist?" *Feminist Studies*, 17:2 (Summer 1991), 195–217, who correctly insists that "women's capacity to redeem or corrupt men is at the center of Rousseau's concerns." What seems clear is that Rousseau considered "woman" as a powerful and potentially dangerous "Other." A new work that considers Rousseau's female interlocutors is Mary Seidman Trouille's *Sexual Politics in the Enlightenment: Women Writers Read Rousseau* (Albany: SUNY Press, 1997).

7. On this question, my reading supports the more optimistic position advanced in 1975 by Jane Abray, "Feminism in the French Revolution," *American Historical Review*, 80:1 (Feb. 1975), 43–62, and in *Women in Revolutionary Paris, 1789–1795*, ed. Darline Gay Levy, Harriet Branson

Applewhite, and Mary Durham Johnson (Urbana: University of Illinois Press, 1979), and Elisabeth G. Sledziewski, "The French Revolution as the Turning Point," in *Emerging Feminism from Revolution to World War*, ed. Geneviève Fraisse & Michelle Perrot (Cambridge, Mass.: Harvard University Press, 1993), pp. 33–47, as against the more pessimistic assessments of Landes, *Women and the Public Sphere*; Madelyn Gutwirth, *The Twilight of the Goddesses: Women and Representation in the French Revolutionary Era* (Berkeley & Los Angeles: University of California Press, 1992); Candice E. Proctor, *Women, Equality and the French Revolution* (Westport: Greenwood Press, 1990); and other scholars who view women's demands for equality and citizenship as doomed from the outset, or by the hegemony of the "universal subject." Lynn Hunt's thought-provoking book *The Family Romance of the French Revolution* (Berkeley & Los Angeles: University of California Press, 1992) does concern itself with gender issues, but focuses primarily on male patriarchal discourses. An important German-language collection is *Sklavin oder Bürgerin? Französische Revolution und neue Weiblichkeit, 1760–1830*, ed. Viktoria Schmidt-Linsenhoff (Frankfurt: Jonas Verlag/Historisches Museum Frankfurt, 1989). For a survey of recent French- and English-language book-length publications, see Karen Offen, "The New Sexual Politics of French Revolutionary Historiography," *French Historical Studies*, 16:4 (Fall 1990), 909–22.

8. I have been making this argument since the 1980s, initially in *WFF*, and subsequently in articles on the "Theory and Practice of Feminism in Nineteenth-Century Europe," in the second and third editions (1987, 1998) of *Becoming Visible*.

9. For eloquent statements of the argument for the hegemony of the "universal subject" and what amounts to a brief for the logical inevitability of women's exclusion, see Pierre Rosenvallon, *Le Sacre du citoyen: Histoire du suffrage universel en France* (Paris: Gallimard, 1992), and its echo in Joan W. Scott, *Only Paradoxes to Offer: French Feminists and the Rights of Man* (Cambridge, Mass.: Harvard University Press, 1996). Careful contextual historical work in the feminist debates of the revolution does not support such an argument, as I trust the ensuing chapters will make clear. Neither philosophical statements, in and of themselves, nor "logic" can be effective in the absence of advocates who have the authority to persuade others of their merit—and/or their political utility!

10. Williams, *The Physical and the Moral*.

CHAPTER 2: RECLAIMING THE ENLIGHTENMENT

FOR FEMINISM

1. Francis Steegmuller, *A Woman, a Man, and Two Kingdoms* (New York: Alfred A. Knopf, 1991), xiii.

2. This term appears in *Requête des dames à l'Assemblée Nationale* (1789), repr. in *Les Femmes dans la Révolution française, 1789–1794*, presented by Albert Soboul, vol. 1 (Paris: EDHIS, 1982), unpaginated.

3. See Londa S. Schiebinger, *The Mind Has No Sex? Women in the Origins of Modern Science* (Cambridge, Mass.: Harvard University Press, 1989); also see Schiebinger, "Why Mammals Are Called Mammals: Gender Politics in Eighteenth-Century Natural History," *American Historical Review*, 98:2 (April 1993), 382–411; and Lisbet Koerner, "Goethe's Botany: Lessons of a Feminine Science," *Isis*, 84:3 (Sept. 1993), 470–95.

4. "When I say man [*l'homme*], I mean all human creatures; when I say a man [*un homme*], I am designating only a human creature of the masculine gender [*du genre masculin*], and when I say a woman [*une femme*], I am designating a human creature of the feminine gender [*du genre féminin*]": Louise-Florence-Pétronille de Tardieu d'Esclavelles, marquise de La Live d'Épinay, *Les Conversations d'Émilie* (Paris, 1776; orig. publ. Leipzig, 1774), p. 11. The marquise's work responded to Antoine-Léonard Thomas, *Essai sur le caractère, les moeurs et l'esprit des femmes dans les différens siècles* (Paris, 1772), and Denis Diderot, "Sur les femmes," in Grimm's *Correspondance littéraire, année 1772*. Both these works were widely circulated and extensively translated.

5. See especially Constance Jordan, *Renaissance Feminism: Literary Texts and Political Models* (Ithaca: Cornell University Press, 1990); Christine Fauré, *Democracy Without Women: Feminism and the Rise of Liberal Individualism in France* (Bloomington: Indiana University Press, 1991; orig. French publ. 1985). For England, see Hilda L. Smith, *Reason's Disciples: Seventeenth-Century English Feminists* (Urbana: University of Illinois Press, 1982); and the essays in *Women Writers and the Early Modern British Political Tradition*, ed. Hilda L. Smith (Cambridge: Cambridge University Press, 1998).

6. Roger Chartier, *The Cultural Origins of the French Revolution*, transl. Lydia G. Cochrane (Durham: Duke University Press, 1991), p. 69. See also the essays in *Going Public: Women and Publishing in Early Modern France*, ed. Elizabeth C. Goldsmith & Dena Goodman (Ithaca: Cornell University Press, 1995); and Carla Hesse, "French Women in Print 1750–1800: An Essay in Historical Bibliography," *Studies on Voltaire and the Eighteenth Century*, vol. 359 (Oxford: The Voltaire Foundation, 1998), pp. 65–82.

7. Nancy K. Miller, *The Heroine's Text: Readings in the French and English Novel, 1722–1782* (New York: Columbia University Press, 1980), p. 155.

8. See Jeanne Hageman, "Elizabeth Wolff & Agatha Deken," in *Women Writing in Dutch*, ed. Kristiaan P. Aercke (New York & London: Garland, 1994).

9. Christine de Pizan, *The Book of the City of Ladies* (ca. 1405), transl. Earl Jeffrey Richards (New York: Persea Books, 1982).

10. See the recent reprint, Marie de Gournay, *Égalité des Hommes et des Femmes, 1622*, preface by Milagros Palma (Paris: côté-femmes, 1989).

11. Jordan, *Renaissance Feminism*.

12. Schiebinger, *Mind Has No Sex?*, esp. pp. 169–70, 176.

13. François Poullain de la Barre, *The Woman as Good as the Man; or, The Equality of Both Sexes* (1673), transl. A.L., ed. with introd. Gerald M. MacLean (Detroit: Wayne State University Press, 1988). See also Siep Stuurman, "Social Cartesianism: François Poulain de la Barre and the Origins of the Enlightenment," *Journal of the History of Ideas*, 58:4 (Oct. 1997), 617–40. On women Cartesians in France, see Erica Harth, *Cartesian Women: Versions and Subversions of Rational Discourse in the Old Regime* (Ithaca: Cornell University Press, 1992). See also Carolyn C. Lougee, *Le Paradis des Femmes: Women, Salons, and Social Stratification in Seventeenth-Century France* (Princeton: Princeton University Press, 1976).

14. See Sarah Hanley, "The Monarchic State in Early Modern France: Marital Regime Government and Male Right," in *Politics, Ideology, and the Law in Early Modern Europe*, ed. Adrianna E. Bakos (Rochester: University of Rochester Press, 1994), pp. 107–26; Hanley, "Social Sites of Political Practice in France: Lawsuits, Civil Rights, and the Separation of Powers in Domestic and State Government, 1500–1800," *American Historical Review*, 102:1 (Feb. 1997), 27–52; and Sarah Maza, *Private Lives, Public Affairs: The Causes Célèbres of Prerevolutionary France* (Berkeley & Los Angeles: University of California Press, 1993).

15. Mary Astell, *Some Reflections Upon Marriage* (1700). The third edition, *Reflections Upon Marriage* (1706) is reprinted in *The First English Feminist: Reflections on Marriage and Other Writings by Mary Astell*, ed. with introd. Bridget Hill (New York: St. Martin's Press, 1986); Daniel Defoe, *Conjugal Lewdness; or, Matrimonial Whoredom: A Treatise concerning the Use and Abuse of the Marriage Bed* (1727), repr. ed. with introd. M. E. Novak (Gainesville: Scholar's Facsimiles & Reprints, 1967); Mary Wollstonecraft, *A Vindication of the Rights of Woman* (New York: Norton, 1967; originally published 1792), p. 104. On the issue of married women's subordination in England around 1735, see Barbara J. Todd,"'To Be Some Body': Married Women and *The Hardships of the English Laws*," in *Women Writers*, ed. Smith, pp. 343–61.

16. See Joan DeJean, "Notorious Women: Marriage and the Novel in Crisis in France, 1690–1715," *Yale Journal of Criticism*, 4:2 (1991), 67–85. Important additions to the literature are Joan DeJean, *Tender Geographies: Women and the Origins of the Novel in France* (New York: Columbia University Press, 1991), and Joan Hinde Stewart, *Gynographs: French Novels by Women of the Late Eighteenth Century* (Lincoln: University of Nebraska Press, 1993).

17. Françoise de Graffigny, *Lettres d'une Peruvienne* (1747); see the new English edition, *Letters from a Peruvian Woman*, transl. David Kornacker (from the 1752 edition), and introduced by Joan DeJean and Nancy K. Miller (New York: Modern Language Association, 1993).

18. *The Spirit of the Laws, by Baron de Montesquieu*, transl. Thomas Nugent (New York: Hafner, 1959; orig. publ. 1749). See esp. bk. 7, sect. 9, pp. 102–3.

19. *The Frederician Code* (Edinburgh, 1761), pt. 1, bk. 1, tit. 8, pp. 37–39 (orig. German publ. 1750); Sir William Blackstone, *Commentaries on the Laws of England*, 11th ed., (London, 1791), bk. 1, chap. 15: pp. 433, 442–45 (lectures presented at Oxford, 1756; orig. publ. Oxford, 1765–69). Pertinent parts have been republished in *WFF*, vol. 1, as docs. 4 & 5.

20. Louis, chevalier de Jaucourt, "Femme (Droit Nat.)," in *L'Encyclopédie*, 6 (Paris, 1756), 471–72; transl. KO, in *WFF*, vol. 1, doc. 6.

21. See Joan Hinde Stewart, *The Novels of Mme Riccoboni* (Chapel Hill: University of North Carolina Press, 1974).

22. On Le Prince de Beaumont, see Stewart, *Gynographs*, p. 47.

23. Pierre-Augustin Caron de Beaumarchais, *The Barber of Seville* (1775), in Beaumarchais, *The Barber of Seville/The Marriage of Figaro*, transl. with introd. John Wood (London: Penguin, 1964), p. 64. My thanks to Nina Gelbart for calling these lines to my attention.

24. Bernard le Bovier de Fontenelle, *Conversations on the Plurality of Worlds*, transl. H. A. Hargreaves, introd. Nina Rattner Gelbart (Berkeley & Los Angeles: University of California Press, 1990).

25. Benito Jerónimo Feijóo y Montenegro, *Three Essays or Discourses on the Following Subjects: A Defense or Vindication of the Women, Church Music, A Comparison between Antient and Modern Music. Tr. from the Spanish of Feyjoo by a Gentleman* [John Brett] (London, 1778). On the Spanish debates on women's education and related issues, see Margarita Ortega López, "'La Defensa de las mujeres' en la sociedad del Antiguo Regimen: Las aportaciones del pensamiento illustrado," in *El Feminismo en España: Dos Siglos de Historia*, ed. Pilar Folguera (Madrid: Editorial Pablo Iglesias, 1988), pp. 3–28; and Sally-Ann Kitts, *The Debate on the Nature, Role and Influence of Woman in Eighteenth-Century Spain* (Lewiston: Edwin Mellen Press, 1995).

26. On the career of Laura Bassi, see Paula Findlen, "Science as a Career in Enlightenment Italy: The Strategies of Laura Bassi," *Isis*, 84:3 (Sept. 1993), 441–69; and Gabriella Berti Logan, "The Desire to Contribute: An Eighteenth-Century Italian Woman of Science," *American Historical Review*, 99:3 (June 1994), 785–812.

27. François de Salignac de La Mothe, archbishop Fénelon, *Treatise on the Education of Daughters*, in *Fénelon on Education*, ed. H. C. Barnard (Cambridge: Cambridge University Press, 1966; orig. French publ. 1687).

28. See Lougee, *Paradis des Femmes*, chaps. 11–13.

29. Jean-Jacques Rousseau, *Émile; ou de l'éducation* (1762; repr. Paris: Gallimard, 1969), bk. 5, p. 572; as transl. in Michèle Crampe-Casnabet, "A Sampling of Eighteenth-Century Philosophy," in *A History of Women: Renaissance and Enlightenment Paradoxes*, ed. Natalie Zemon Davis & Arlette Farge (Cambridge: Harvard University Press, 1993), p. 329.

30. Sophia, a Person of Quality (pseud.), *Woman Not Inferior to Man; or, A Short and Modest Vindication of the Natural Right of the Fair Sex to a Perfect Equality of Power, Dignity, and Esteem, with the Men* (1739); partially reprinted in *WFF*, vol. 1, doc. 1; quote, p. 27.

31. *Female Rights Vindicated* by "A Lady" (London: G. Burnet, 1758). My thanks to Gary Kates for bringing this text to my attention.

32. Madame de Beaumer, in the *Journal des Dames* (Nov. 1761), as transl. Nina Rattner Gelbart in *Feminine and Opposition Journalism in Old Regime France* (Berkeley & Los Angeles: University of California Press, 1987), p. 107.

33. Madame de Beaumer, "Avant-Propos," *Journal des Dames* (Mar. 1762), in *WFF*, vol. 1, doc. 2; quote, p. 28. This text is discussed fully in Gelbart, *Feminine and Opposition Journalism*, chap. 3.

34. See Gary Kates, *Monsieur d'Eon Is a Woman: A Tale of Political Intrigue and Sexual Masquerade* (New York: Basic Books, 1995).

35. See the texts by Catharine Macaulay-Graham, *Letters on Education* (1787), and Mary Wollstonecraft, *A Vindication of the Rights of Woman* (1792), in *WFF*, vol. 1, docs. 11 & 12. Wollstonecraft also published on women's education in the 1780s.

36. Josefa Amar y Borbón, "Prologo," in *Discurso sobre la educación física y moral de las mugeres* (Madrid: B. Cano, 1790; repr. Madrid: Ediciones Cátedra, 1994). Thanks to Constance A. Sullivan for pointing out to me that the 1784 version of this text, often cited and reproduced, is fictive. See Sullivan, "The Quiet Feminism of Josefa Amar y Borbón's 1790 Book on the Education of Women," *Indiana Journal of Hispanic Literature*, 2:1 (Fall 1993), 49–73.

37. Hedvig Charlotta Nordenflycht, *Fruentimrets Försvar, emot J. J. Rousseau medborgare i Geneve* (1761); commissioned translation from the Swedish by Stina Katchadourian (1991), with assistance from the Marilyn Yalom Fund, IRWG.

38. Gabriel Bonnot de Mably, *De la Législation, ou principes des lois* (Amsterdam: n. p., 1776), pt. 2, bk. 4, chap. 1, pp. 154–55.

39. Daniel Defoe, *Essay on Projects* (1697; facsimile of 1st ed., Menston: Scolar Press, 1969), p. 302.

40. "Girl's Lament" (1779), from *Gedichte von Philippine Engelhard geb. Gatterer* (1782); transl. Walter Arndt, in *Bitter Healing: German Women Writers from 1700 to 1830; An Anthology*, ed. Jeannine Blackwell & Susanne Zantop (Lincoln: University of Nebraska Press, 1990), p. 195.

41. Louise-Florence-Pétronille de Tardieu d'Esclavelles, marquise de La Live d'Épinay, *Histoire de Madame de Montbrillant*, ed. Georges Roth, 3 vols. (Paris: Gallimard, 1951; orig. publ. 1818).

42. On the history of women's work in eighteenth-century Europe, see in particular the recent contributions by Olwen Hufton, "Women, Work and Family," in Davis & Farge, eds., *A History of Women*, vol. 3, pp. 15–45; and Elizabeth Fox-Genovese, "Women and Work," in *French Women and the Enlightenment*, ed. Samia I. Spencer (Bloomington: Indiana University Press, 1984), pp. 111–27. See also Merry Wiesner, *Women and Gender in Early Modern Europe* (Cambridge: Cambridge University Press, 1993); Bridget Hill, *Women, Work and Sexual Politics in Eighteenth-Century England* (London and New York: Basil Blackwell, 1989); the essays in *European*

Women and Preindustrial Craft, ed. Daryl M. Hafter (Bloomington: Indiana University Press, 1995); and Olwen Hufton, *The Prospect Before Her: A History of Women in Western Europe, 1500–1800* (New York: Alfred A. Knopf, 1996). On the "hardy feminism of the women's guilds' petitions" in mid-eighteenth-century Paris, see Judith G. Coffin, "Gender and the Guild Order: The Garment Trades in Eighteenth-Century Paris," *Journal of Economic History*, 54:4 (Dec. 1994), 768–93 (quote, 786); and Cynthia Maria Truant, "Parisian Guildwomen and the (Sexual) Politics of Privilege: Defending Their Patrimonies in Print," in *Going Public*, ed. Goldsmith & Goodman, pp. 46–61.

43. Louis-Sébastian Mercier, *Tableau de Paris*, vol. 9 (Amsterdam, 1788), pp. 177–78.

44. On the 1723 debate, see Paolo Mantegazza, "Il Problema dell'educazione della donna nel 1723," *Nuova Antologia*, 124:16 (16 Aug. 1892), 689–701.

45. Dorothea Christiane Leporin, frau Erxleben, *Gründliche Untersuchung der Ursachen, die das weibliche Geschlecht vom Studieren abhalten, darin deren Unerheblichkeit gezeiget und wie möglich, nöthig und nützlich es sey, dass dieses Geschlecht der Gelahrheit sich befleisse* (Berlin: Rüdiger, 1742; repr. [with afterword by Gerda Rechenberg] Hildesheim and New York: Georg Olms Verlag, 1975). To my knowledge, this treatise has never been translated into English. My thanks to Kay Flavell and Peter Petschauer for introducing me to Dorothea Leporin Erxleben.

46. See Sylvia Harcstark Myers, *The Bluestocking Circle: Women, Friendship, and the Life of the Mind in Eighteenth-Century England* (Oxford: Clarendon Press, 1990).

47. See Brita Rang, "A 'Learned Wave': Women of Letters and Science from the Renaissance to the Enlightenment," in *Perspectives on Feminist Political Thought in European History*, ed. Tjitske Akkerman & Siep Stuurman (London: Routledge, 1998), pp. 50–66.

48. See Dena Goodman, "Enlightenment Salons: The Convergence of Female and Philosophic Ambitions," *Eighteenth-Century Studies*, 22:3 (Spring 1989), 329–50; quotes, 332–33. See also further discussion in Goodman, *The Republic of Letters: A Cultural History of the French Enlightenment* (Ithaca: Cornell University Press, 1994).

49. See Dena Goodman, "Governing the Republic of Letters: The Politics of Culture in the French Enlightenment," *History of European Ideas*, 13:3 (1991), 183–99.

50. Poullain, *Woman as Good*, pp. 123–24.

51. Pierre Carlet de Marivaux, *La Colonie*, in *Le Mercure* (June 1750), transl. Peter V. Conroy, *Signs*, 9:2 (Winter 1983), 339–60. On the Amazons, see Abby Wettan Kleinbaum, *The War Against the Amazons* (New York: New Press [McGraw-Hill], 1983).

52. See Josephine Grieder, "Kingdoms of Women in French Fictions of the 1780s," *Eighteenth-Century Studies*, 23:2 (Winter 1989–90), 140–56.

53. Mably, *De la Législation*, p. 155; Samuel Johnson to the Reverend

Dr. Taylor, 18 Aug. 1763, as repr. in *The Letters of Samuel Johnson, LL.D.*, ed. George Birkbeck Hill, vol. 1 (Oxford: Clarendon Press, 1892), p. 104. I am grateful to Lisa Jadwin for this latter reference.

54. Montesquieu, *Mes Pensées*, in *Oeuvres complètes*, vol. 1 (Paris: Gallimard, 1949), p. 1076.

55. See, for example, the exchange between Adelaide ("Les hommes font les lois") and Bayard ("Les femmes font les moeurs") in the play *Le Connetable de Bourbon* (1769) by Jacques-Antoine-Hippolyte Guibert: *Oeuvres dramatiques de Guibert . . . Publiés par sa veuve* (Paris: Persan, 1822), vol. 10, p. 22.

56. Nicholas-Edmé Restif de La Brétonne, *Les Gynographes; ou Idées de deux honnêtes femmes sur un projet de règlement proposé à toute l'Europe pour mettre les femmes à leur place, & opérer le bonheur des deux sexes* (The Hague: chez Gosse & Pinet, 1777), vol. 1, p. 183. On Restif, see Ginevra Odorisio Conti, "*Les Gynographes* de Restif de la Brétonne: L'Utopia antifeminista di uno scrittore ginofilo," *OZ: Rivista Internazionale di utopie*, no. 3 (1995), 83–99.

57. Perhaps the most notorious example is *A Father's Legacy to His Daughters*, by the Scottish physician Dr. John Gregory (London: W. Strahan, T. Cadell; Edinburgh: J. Balfour, W. Creech, 1774), which was widely republished both in England and in North America and was subsequently denounced by Mary Wollstonecraft. For many others, see *Women in the Eighteenth Century: Constructions of Femininity*, ed. Vivien Jones (London: Routledge, 1990).

58. Voltaire, "À M. le Chevalier Falkener (Seconde épître dédicatoire)," *Zaïre: Tragédie en cinq actes* (1736), in *Oeuvres complètes de Voltaire*, vol. 1, *Théatre* (Paris, 1877), p. 551.

59. Condorcet, *Lettres d'un bourgeois de New Haven à un citoyen de Virginie* (1787), in *Oeuvres de Condorcet*, ed. A. Condorcet O'Connor & F. Arago, vol. 9 (Paris, 1847), p. 15; transl. KO.

60. See Jane Rendall, "The Enlightenment and the Nature of Women," in Jane Rendall, *The Origins of Modern Feminism* (New York: Schocken, 1984); Sylvia Tomaselli, "The Enlightenment Debate on Women," *History Workshop*, no. 20 (1985), 101–24.

61. See Hilda Smith, *Reason's Disciples*, chap. 2.

62. Charles-Irénée Castel, abbé de Saint-Pierre, "Projet pour perfectionner l'éducation des filles" (1730), in *Oeuvres diverses de Monsieur l'abbé de Saint-Pierre* (Paris: Briasson, 1730), p. 96.

63. Pierre-Joseph Boudier de Villemert, *L'Ami des femmes* (1758); in English transl. as *The Ladies Friend from the French of Monsieur de Gravines* (London: W. Nicoll, 1766 [there were also American editions]); in Italian, *L'Amico delle donne* (Lucca, 1763; Venice, 1764).

64. Nicolas Baudeau, "De l'Éducation nationale," *Ephémérides du Citoyen, ou Chronique de l'esprit national*, 4:4 (12 May 1766), transl. KO, in *WFF*, vol. 1, doc. 17.

65. Jean-Jacques Rousseau, *Julie* (1761) & *Émile* (1762), bk. 5.

66. Frederick the Great, "Lettre sur l'éducation" (1770), in *Oeuvres de Frédéric le Grand*, vol. 9 (Berlin: Chrétien-Frédéric Voss, ca. 1850), pp. 143, 145; transl. KO.

67. Prince Adam Kazimierz Czartoryski, "Drugi List Imc Pana Doswiadczynskiego do przyjaciela swego wzgleden edukacji corek," in his *4 Listy Imco Pana Doswiadcaynskiego* (4 Letters by Mr. Experience; Warsaw, 1782); repr. in *Zrodla Do Dziejow Wychowania i Myscli Pedagogicznej*, ed. Stefan Wolosyn (Warsaw: Panstvrowe Wydawnictwo Naukowe, 1965), pp. 695–98. This reference was furnished and translated by Bogna Lorence-Kot.

68. Madame de P***, *Conseils à une amie* (n.p., 1749).

69. D'Épinay, *Histoire de Madame de Montbrillant*.

70. Madame de Montanclos, in Gelbart, *Feminine and Opposition Journalism*, pp. 187–88.

71. Madame de Coicy, *Les Femmes comme il convient de les voir ou aperçus de ce qui les femmes ont été, de ce qu'elles sont, et de ce qu'elles pourraient être*, 2 vols. (London and Paris: Bacot, 1785), p. 60.

72. Stewart, *Gynographs*, pp. 201–3.

73. *Allgemeines Landrecht für die Preussischen Staaten*, ed. C. F. Koch (Berlin 1862; orig. publ. 1792–94), pt. 2, tit. 2, arts. 67 and 68, as transl. in *WFF*, vol. 1, doc. 7.

74. Marie-Anne de Roumier, dame Robert, *Voyage de Milord Céton dans les sept planètes; ou Le Nouveau Mentor . . .* (The Hague & Paris: chez tous les libraires, 1765–66); quotation as transl. Nina Gelbart in *Feminine and Opposition Journalism*, p. 146.

75. Anon. (attributed to Stephanie-Félicité du Crest, comtesse de Genlis), *Le Club des dames; ou le retour de Descartes: Comédie en un acte en prose* (Paris: Au Bureau de la Bibliothèque des Romans, 1784).

76. See Margaret Jacob, "Freemasonry, Women, and the Paradox of the Enlightenment," in Margaret Hunt et al., *Women and the Enlightenment* (New York: Haworth Press, 1984), pp. 69–93; repr. as chap. 5 in Margaret Jacob, *Living the Enlightenment: Freemasonry and Politics in Eighteenth-Century Europe* (Oxford: Oxford University Press, 1991), pp. 120–42; Janet Burke, "Freemasonry, Friendship, and Noblewomen: The Role of the Secret Society in Bringing Enlightenment Thought to Pre-Revolutionary Women Elites," *History of European Ideas*, 10:3 (1989), 283–94; and Janet Burke and Margaret Jacob, "French Freemasonry, Women, and Feminist Scholarship," *Journal of Modern History*, 68:3 (Sept. 1996), 513–49.

CHAPTER 3: CHALLENGING MASCULINE ARISTOCRACY

1. Margaret Darrow, *Revolution in the House: Family, Class, and Inheritance in Southern France, 1775–1825* (Princeton: Princeton University Press, 1989), p. 11.

2. *Pétition des femmes du Tiers-État au Roi, 1er janvier 1789*, as transl. in *Women in Revolutionary Paris, 1789–1795*, ed. Darline Gay Levy, Harriet Branson Applewhite, and Mary Durham Johnson (Urbana: University of Illinois Press, 1979), pp. 18–21.

3. *Pétition*, p. 20.

4. *Doléances particulières des marchandes bouquetières fleuristes chapelières en fleurs de la Ville et faubourgs de Paris* (1789), as transl. in *Women in Revolutionary Paris*, pp. 22–26.

5. See Temma Kaplan, "Female Consciousness and Collective Action: The Case of Barcelona, 1910–1918," *Signs*, 7:3 (Spring 1982), 545–66.

6. *Remonstrances, plaintes et doléances des Dames Françoises, à l'occasion de l'assemblée des États-généraux*, par M.L.P.P.D. St.L. (dated Paris, 5 March 1789). Repr. in *Les Femmes dans la Révolution française, 1789–1794*, présentés par Albert Soboul (Paris: EDHIS, 1982), vol. 1, no. 5; quote, p. 2.

7. *Cahier des doléances et réclamations des femmes, par Madame B*** B***, Pays de Caux, 1789*, repr. in *Cahiers de doléances des femmes en 1789 et autres textes*, préface de Paule-Marie Duhet (Paris: des femmes, 1981), pp. 47–51; transl. KO.

8. Emmanuel-Joseph Sièyes, *Préliminaire de la constitution: Reconnaissance et exposition raisonnée des Droits de l'Homme et du Citoyen* (Versailles, July 1789), as repr. in Sièyes, *Écrits politiques*, ed. Roberto Zapperi (Paris: Éditions des archives contemporaines, 1985), p. 199; transl. William Sewell.

9. See Joan Wallach Scott, *Only Paradoxes to Offer: French Feminists and the Rights of Man* (Cambridge, Mass.: Harvard University Press, 1996).

10. See the discussion of this and related points in Christine Fauré, *Democracy Without Women: Feminism and the Rise of Liberal Individualism in France* (Bloomington: Indiana University Press, 1991), chap. 5; and in Sarah Hanley, "La Loi salique," in *Encyclopédie politique et historique des femmes*, ed. Christine Fauré (Paris: Presses Universitaires de France, 1997), pp. 11–30.

11. *Motions adressées à l'Assemblée Nationale en faveur du sexe* (Paris: Imprimerie de la Veuve Delaquette [1789]); repr. in *Femmes dans la Révolution française*, vol. 1.

12. *Discours prononcé par Mme Rigal, dans une assemblée de femmes artistes et orfèvres, tenue le 20 septembre, pour délibérer sur une Contribution volontaire* (n.p., n.d. [1789]); transl. in *Women in Revolutionary Paris*, pp. 31–33.

13. Edmund Burke, *Reflections on the Revolution in France* (1790); quote from the Dolphin edition (New York: Vintage, 1961), p. 85. For a recent reinterpretation of the women's march on Versailles, see Kerstin Michalik, *Der Marsch der Pariser Frauen nach Versailles am 5. und 6. Oktober 1789: Eine Studie zu weiblicher Partizipationsformen in der Frühphase der Französische Revolution* (Pfaffenweiler: Centaurus, 1990).

14. Jules Michelet, *Les Femmes de la Révolution* (Paris: Delahays, 1853; repr. Paris: Éditions Carrère, 1988 [introd. Françoise Giroud]); quote, p. 92 (1988); transl. KO.

15. *Requête des Dames à l'Assemblée Nationale* (1789), repr. in *Femmes dans la Révolution française*, vol. 1, no. 19; transl. KO.

16. See Jeffrey Merrick, "Conscience and Citizenship in Eighteenth-Century France," *Eighteenth-Century Studies*, 21:1 (Fall 1987), 48–70; William H. Sewell, Jr., "Le Citoyen/la citoyenne: Activity, Passivity, and the Revolutionary Concept of Citizenship," in *The Political Culture of the French Revolution*, ed. Colin Lucas, vol. 2 (Oxford: Pergamon, 1988), pp. 105–23; and, for earlier notions, Charlotte Wells, *Law and Citizenship in Early Modern France* (Baltimore: The Johns Hopkins University Press, 1994).

17. "Citoyen," in *L'Encyclopédie*, vol. 3 (Paris, 1753), p. 488.

18. See Dominique Godineau, *Citoyennes tricoteuses* (Paris: Alinea, 1989), pp. 14–15.

19. Marie-Jean-Antoine-Nicolas Caritat, marquis de Condorcet, "Sur l'Admission des femmes au droit de cité," *Journal de la Société de 1789*, 3 July 1790; English transl. John Morley (1870), repr. in *WFF*, vol. 1, doc. 24.

20. The "Declaration" is part of Olympe de Gouges, *Les Droits de la femme* (Paris, 1791); transl. Nupur Chaudhuri, with SGB & KO, in *WFF*, vol. 1, doc. 26. On Gouges, see Olivier Blanc, *Une Femme de libertés: Olympe de Gouges*, ed. revue et augmentée (Paris: Syros, 1989).

21. Louis-Marie Prudhomme, "De l'influence de la révolution sur les femmes," *Les Révolutions de Paris*, 9, no. 83 (5–12 Feb. 1791), 227. Significantly, it was the antifeminist Prudhomme who published (and perhaps commissioned) Louise de Kéralio Robert's *Les Crimes des reines de la France* (1791); on this work, see Carla Hesse, "Revolutionary Histories: The Literary Politics of Louise de Kéralio (1758–1822)," in *Culture and Identity in Early Modern Europe*, ed. Barbara Diefendorf & Carla Hesse (Ann Arbor: University of Michigan Press, 1993), 237–59.

22. *Journal des Droits de l'homme*, no. 14 (10 Aug. 1791), as repr. in *Collections des matériaux pour l'histoire de la Révolution de France: Bibliographie des journaux*, ed. F.-J. Deschiens (Paris, 1829), pp. 242–43; transl. KO.

23. Charles-Maurice de Talleyrand–Périgord, *Rapport sur l'instruction publique, fait au nom du Comité de constitution, à l'Assemblée nationale, les 10, 11, et 19 septembre 1791 (Projet de décrets sur l'instruction publique)* (Paris, 1791); quotes interspersed on pp. 115–20; transl. KO.

24. Mary Wollstonecraft, *A Vindication of the Rights of Woman, with Strictures on Political and Moral Subjects* (1792). Page references are to the 1967 Norton Library edition, with an introduction by Charles W. Hagelman, Jr.; quote, "Dedication," pp. 3–4. See Virginia Sapiro, *A Vindication of Political Virtue: The Political Theory of Mary Wollstonecraft* (Chicago: University of Chicago Press, 1992); and *The Works of Mary Wollstonecraft*, ed. Janet M. Todd & Marilyn Butler, 7 vols. (London: Pickering & Chatto, 1989).

25. *Discours sur l'état de nullité dans lequel on tient les femmes, relativement à la Politique; dédié à M. Carra, par Elizabeth-Bonaventure Lafaurie, Patriote et Démocrate, Mère de quatre enfans, dont elle en allaite*

un actuellement . . . (16 mai 1791) (Dax: Chez René Leclercq, 1791). Thanks to Suzanne Desan for forwarding a copy of Lafaurie's text.

26. Theodor Gottlieb von Hippel, *On Improving the Status of Women*, transl. and ed. with introd. Timothy F. Sellner (Detroit: Wayne State University Press, 1979); orig. publ. in German as *Über die bürgerliche Verbesserung der Weiber* (1792). Thomas Thorild, *Om qvinnokönets naturliga höghet* (On the Natural Dignity of the Female Sex: Copenhagen, 1793; repr. Stockholm: Bokförlaget Rediviva, 1978). Thanks go to Helena Wedborn, Women's History Collection, University of Göteborg Library, Sweden, for forwarding a copy of this text, and to Stina Katchadourian for her translation.

27. See the *Prospectus pour le Cercle patriotique des Amies de la Vérité* (Paris: Imprimerie du Cercle social, 1791), p. 1. Translated by Stephanie Whitlock, with assistance from the Marilyn Yalom Fund. "In the new order of things that we owe to liberty, each individual can and must serve his country. . . . Maternal cares and concerns are inseparable from the love of humanity." See Gary Kates, "'The Power of Husband and Wife Must Be Equal and Separate': The *Cercle Social* and the Rights of Women, 1790–91," in *Women & Politics in the Age of the Democratic Revolution*, ed. Harriet B. Applewhite & Darline G. Levy (Ann Arbor: University of Michigan Press, 1990), pp. 163–80.

28. Mentioned by Hippel, *On Improving the Status of Women*, p. 121. The text, from the session of 29 March 1790, can be consulted in *Archives parlementaires*, 1ᵉ série, t. 12 (Paris, 1881), p. 402.

29. Elke Harten & Hans-Christian Harten, *Femmes, Culture et Révolution*, transl. from the German by Bella Chabot, Jeanne Etoré, and Olivier Mannoni (Paris: des femmes, 1989), p. 9.

30. Louis-Marie Prudhomme, "Club de femmes à Lyon," *Les Révolutions de Paris*, 19, no. 185 (19–26 Jan. 1793), 234–35; transl. KO. According to Suzanne Desan, revolutionary women's clubs can be traced for fifty-six French towns and villages; see her article "'Constitutional Amazons': Jacobin Women's Clubs in the French Revolution," in *Recreating Authority in Revolutionary France*, ed. Bryant T. Ragan & E. A. Williams (New Brunswick: Rutgers University Press, 1992), pp. 11–35, 177–86.

31. Rejoinder from Citoyenne Blandin Demoulin, *Les Révolutions de Paris*, 19, no. 189 (16–23 Feb. 1793), 367–71; transl. KO.

32. Response by Prudhomme, *ibid.*, 371–72; transl. KO.

33. Pierre Guyomar, *Le Partisan de l'égalité politique entre les individus, ou problème très important de l'égalité en droits et de l'inégalité en fait* (Paris, 1793), published in annex to Session of 29 April, Convention Nationale, in *Archives parlementaires de 1787 à 1860*, 63 (Paris, 1903), 591–99.

34. Speech by Soeur Monic, as quoted in the account in Pierre-Joseph-Alexis Roussel, *Le Château des Tuileries* (1802), vol. 2; translated and reprinted in *Women in Revolutionary Paris*, pp. 166–71. The veracity of this account has since been questioned by John R. Cole, "Debunking Roussel's

'Report on the Society of Revolutionary Republican Women,'" *French Historical Studies*, 21:1 (Winter 1998), 181–91. The use of history to prove a point about women's qualifications would, however, have been quite typical of the time.

35. "A Laudatory Address to the Revolutionary Republican Women," in *Women in Revolutionary Paris*, p. 176.

36. The following quotations from Amar's report to the Convention are taken from the translation in *Women in Revolutionary Paris*, pp. 214–16.

37. See Darline Gay Levy & Harriet B. Applewhite, "Women and Militant Citizenship in Revolutionary Paris," in *Rebel Daughters: Women and the French Revolution*, ed. Sara E. Melzer & Leslie W. Rabine (New York: Oxford University Press, 1992), p. 96.

38. An English translation of Chaumette's remarks, from the official minutes of the Conseil-général, Commune de Paris, 27 Brumaire, *Gazette Nationale, ou Le Moniteur Universel*, no. 59, Nonidi, 29 Brumaire, l'an II (repr. in the *Réimpression de l'Ancien Moniteur*, vol. 18, p. 450), can be consulted in *Women in Revolutionary Paris*, pp. 219–20. I have amended this translation slightly.

39. Editorial, *La Feuille de Salut public*, as repr. in *Gazette National, ou Le Moniteur Universel*, 29 Brumaire, l'an II (mardi, 19 novembre 1793, vieux style), *Réimpression de l'Ancien Moniteur*, vol. 18, p. 450; transl. KO.

40. The decree read by Chaumette to the Commune de Paris, session of 7 Frimaire (27 Nov. 1793), was reported in *La Gazette Nationale*, 30 Nov. 1793, p. 281.

41. Marie-Jean-Antoine-Nicolas Caritat, marquis de Condorcet, *Esquisse d'un tableau historique des progrès de l'esprit humain* (1795), ed. Monique et François Hincker (Paris, 1966), pp. 274–75; transl. KO.

42. Pierre-Jean-Georges Cabanis, "Cinquième mémoire: De l'influence des sexes sur le caractère des idées et des affections morales," *Rapports du physique et du moral de l'homme*, 2d ed., 2 vols. (Paris: Crapart, Caille et Ravier, An XIII [1805]), vol. 2, pp. 357–58; transl. KO.

43. See Geneviève Fraisse, *Muse de la raison: La Démocratie exclusive et la différence des sexes* (Aix-en-Provence & Paris: Alinea, 1989); in English as *Reason's Muse: Sexual Difference and the Birth of Democracy* (Cambridge, Mass.: Harvard University Press, 1994).

44. J.-J. Virey, "Femelle, femme, féminin," in *Nouveau Dictionnaire d'histoire naturelle* (Paris: Deterville, 1816–19), vol. 11 (1817), p. 337; transl. KO.

45. Constance-Marie de Théis Pipelet de Leury (later Princess de Salm-Dyck), "Épître aux femmes" (Letter to Women: 1797), transl. Dorothy Backer in *The Defiant Muse: French Feminist Poems from the Middle Ages to the Present: A Bilingual Reader*, ed. Domna Stanton (New York: The Feminist Press, 1986); quotes, pp. 113, 115. See Elizabeth Colwill, "Laws of Nature/Rights of Genius: The *Drame* of Constance de Salm," in *Going Public: Women and Publishing in Early Modern France* (Ithaca: Cornell University Press, 1995), pp. 224–42.

46. F. R.*** (Fanny Raoul), *Opinion d'une femme sur les femmes* (Paris: Giguet, 1801), pp. 68–69; transl. KO.

47. Rosa Califronia, contessa romana (pseud.?), *Breve difesa dei diritti delle donne, scritta da Rosa Califronia, contessa romana* (Assisi: n.p., 1794), p. 3; commissioned translation by Mary S. Gibson with assistance from the Marilyn Yalom Fund.

48. "[Sull'egoismo mascolino] Agli estensori del giornale," *Il Defensore della Libertà* (Genoa), 21 Oct. 1797, repr. in *I Giornali giacobini italiani*, ed. Renzo De Felice (Milan: Feltrinelli, 1962), pp. 470–71; commissioned translation by Rhoda Hanafi (MY Fund).

49. *La Causa delle donne: Discorso agl'italiani della cittadina*** (Venice: G. Zorsi, 1797), republished in *Giacobini italiani*, ed. Delio Cantimori & Renzo De Felice, vol. 2 (Bari: Laterza e Figli, 1964), pp. 455–64; commissioned translation by Rhoda Hanafi (MY Fund). Feminist texts from Milan and Turin have also been located and republished by Elisa Strumia in her thesis, "Il Dibattito sulla donna nell'Italia del periodo giacobino (1796–99): Il Piemonte e la Repubblica cisalpina" (Turin: Faculty of Letters, University of Turin, 1983–84).

50. P.B.v.W., *Ten betooge dat de vrouwen behooren deel te hebeen aan de regeering van het land* (Harlingen: V. van der Plaats, 1795), 16-page pamphlet, republished by Judith Vega in "Het Beeld der vryheid: Is het niet use zuster?" in *Socialisties-Feministiese Teksten*, no. 11, ed. Selma Sevenhuijsen et al. (Baarn: Amboboeken, 1989), pp. 104–11. A commissioned English translation by Sarah Lewis (MY Fund), "In Defense of the Participation of Women in the Government of the Country," introduced by Judith Vega, appeared in the *Journal of Women's History*, 8:2 (Summer 1996), 144–51.

51. See, respectively, the librettos of Wolfgang Amadeus Mozart, *The Magic Flute*, and Franz Joseph Hayden, *The Creation*.

52. Hippel, *On Improving the Status of Women*, in Sellner transl., p. 188. Both of Hippel's works are now available in English, thanks to Timothy F. Sellner.

53. Ernst Ferdinand Klein, "Muss das weibliche Geschlecht mit dem männlichen durchgehend gleiche Rechte haben?" *Annalen der Gesetzgebung und Rechtsgelehrsamkeit in den Preussischen Staaten*, 17 (1798), pp. 202–13. Thanks go to Ute Gerhard for transmitting a copy of this text.

54. Friedrich Schlegel, "Über die Diotima" (1795), in *Friedrich Schlegel, seine prosaischen Jugendschriften*, 2d ed., ed. J. Minor, 2 vols. (Vienna, 1906), vol. 1, p. 59; orig. publ. in *Berlinische Monatsschrift*, vol. 26 (July–Dec. 1795); as transl. SGB, in *WFF*, vol. 1, doc. 16, p. 71.

55. Immanuel Kant, "The Character of the Sexes," in *Anthropology from a Pragmatic Point of View*, transl. Victor Lyle Dowell, rev. ed. Hans H. Rudnick (Carbondale: Southern Illinois University Press, 1978), pp. 216–20; repr. in *WFF*, vol. 1, doc. 27, p. 113.

56. Johann Gottlieb Fichte, *The Science of Rights* (1796), transl. A. E. Kroeger (London, 1889; repr. London: Routledge & Kegan Paul, 1970), p. 440.

57. G. W. F. Hegel, *The Phenomonology of Mind* (1807), transl. J. B. Baillie, 2d rev. ed. (New York: Macmillan, 1931), p. 496.

58. *Hegel's Philosophy of Right* (1821), transl. T. M. Knox (Oxford: The Clarendon Press, 1942; repr., 1967), note to para. 166, p. 263.

59. Mary Wollstonecraft, *A Vindication of the Rights of Woman*, p. 107. See also above, n. 24. For further comparison of Wollstonecraft's views with those of her French contemporaries, see Karen Offen, "Was Mary Wollstonecraft a Feminist?: A Contextual Rereading . . . ," in *Quilting a New Canon: Stitching Women's Words*, ed. Uma Parameswaran (Toronto: Sister Vision, 1996), pp. 3–24.

60. See Eleanor Ty, *Unsex'd Revolutionaries: Five Women Novelists of the 1790s* (Toronto: University of Toronto Press, 1993).

61. Charles James Fox, speech in the debate on Mr. Grey's motion for a reform of Parliament (1797), in *The Parliamentary History of England*, vol. 33 (London, 1818), pp. 726–27; as repr. in *WFF*, vol. 1, doc. 30.

62. James Mill, in *Encyclopedia Brittanica*, 5th ed., supplement (London, 1814), s.v. "Government"; as repr. in *WFF*, vol. 1, doc. 31.

63. The term is used by Françoise Basch, *Relative Creatures: Victorian Women in Society and the Novel*, transl. from the French by Anthony Rudolf (New York: Schocken, 1974).

64. On aspects of the connections between gender politics and mounting English chauvinism, see Gerald Newman, *The Rise of English Nationalism: A Cultural History, 1740–1830* (New York: St. Martin's Press, 1987); Leonore Davidoff and Catherine Hall, *Family Fortunes: Men and Women of the English Middle Class, 1780–1850* (Chicago: University of Chicago Press, 1987); and Linda Colley, *Britons* (New Haven: Yale University Press, 1992).

65. See Marilyn Butler, *Jane Austen and the War of Ideas* (Oxford: The Clarendon Press, 1975); and Claudia Johnson, *Jane Austen: Women, Politics and the Novel* (Chicago: University of Chicago Press, 1988).

66. Richard Polwhele, *The Unsex'd Females: A Poem Addressed to the Author of Pursuits of Literature* (London: Cadell and Davies, 1798; repr. New York: Garland, 1974), p. 6.

67. Mary Anne Radcliffe, *The Female Advocate; or, An Attempt to Recover the Rights of Women from Male Usurpation* (London: Vernor & Hood, 1799; repr. New York: Garland, 1974 [Edinburgh, 1810]).

68. Napoleon I, "Notes sur l'établissement d'Écouen," addressed to the comte de Lacépède, grand chancellor of the Legion of Honor, 15 May 1807, as repr. in Gabrielle Reval, *Madame Campan, assistante de Napoléon* (Paris, 1931); transl. KO, in *WFF*, vol. 1, doc. 23.

69. Charles Fourier, *Théorie des quatre mouvements et des destinées générales* (1808), 3d ed. (1846), republ. in *Oeuvres complètes*, vol. 1 (Paris: Éditions Anthropos, 1966); quote, pp. 132–33, transl. KO, in *WFF*, vol. 1, doc. 9. On Fourier's ideas, see Jonathan Beecher, *Charles Fourier: The Visionary and His World* (Berkeley & Los Angeles: University of California Press, 1986).

70. Madame de Staël, *De la littérature*, 2d ed. (Paris, 1800), as transl. in *An Extraordinary Woman: Selected Writings of Germaine de Staël*, transl. and introd. Vivian Folkenflik (New York: Columbia University Press, 1988); quotes, pp. 201, 205. On Staël, see the articles in *Germaine de Staël: Crossing the Borders*, ed. Madelyn Gutwirth et al. (New Brunswick: Rutgers University Press, 1991).

PART II: THE NINETEENTH CENTURY

1. For earlier interpretation and scholarly bibliography published prior to 1986, see the overview chapters and bibliography in *WFF* and my 1987 article, "Liberty, Equality, and Justice for Women: The Theory and Practice of Feminism in Nineteenth-Century Europe," in *Becoming Visible: Women in European History* (Boston: Houghton-Mifflin, 2d ed., 1987), which includes a lengthy bibliographical essay. In the endnotes to these chapters, I will refer primarily to original sources or to scholarly works of particular interest published since 1986. More recent scholarship on nineteenth-century European feminism will also be listed in the Select Bibliography, including a series of invaluable published documentary collections. These chapters have also greatly benefited from a series of unpublished articles prepared for a 1995 conference on nineteenth-century European feminism organized by Bianka Pietrow-Ennker & Sylvia Paletschek in Stuttgart; a volume of proceedings is in preparation.

See also the essays and bibliography in *A History of Women in the West*, ed. Georges Duby & Michelle Perrot, vol. 4: *Emerging Feminism from Revolution to World War*, ed. Geneviève Fraisse & Michelle Perrot (Cambridge, Mass.: Harvard University Press, 1993). This volume, to which many leading European historians of women have contributed, contains a thoughtful essay by Anne-Marie Käppeli on nineteenth-century feminisms, "Feminist Scenes," pp. 482–514. Where pertinent, supplementary essays that have appeared in the Dutch, German, Spanish, and Italian editions of the Duby-Perrot collection will be cited below.

2. On antifeminist knowledge production, see, for Germany, Silvia Bovenschen, *Die imaginierte Weiblichkeit: Exemplarische Untersuchungen zu kulturgeschichtlichen und literarischen Präsentationsformen des Weiblichen* (Frankfurt: Suhrkamp, 1979); Karin Hausen, "Family and Role-Division: The Polarisation of Sexual Stereotypes in the Nineteenth Century . . . ," in *The German Family*, ed. Richard J. Evans & W. R. Lee (Totowa: Barnes & Noble, 1981); the essays in Ute Frevert, ed., *Bürgerinnin und Bürger: Geschlechterverhältnisse im 19. Jahrhundert* (Göttingen: Vandenhoeck & Ruprecht, 1988); and Claudia Honegger, *Die Ordnung der Geschlechter: Die Wissenschaft vom Menschen und das Weib, 1750–1850* (Frankfurt-am-Main: Campus, 1991). See also Sigrid Lange, ed., *Ob die Weiber Menschen sind: Geschlechterdebatten um 1800* (Leipzig: Reclam, 1992). An extraordinarily rich collection of documents on legal issues pertaining to marriage, etc., can be consulted in Ute Gerhard, *Verhältnisse und*

Verhinderungen: Frauenarbeit, Familie und Rechte der Frauen im 19. Jahr-hundert (Frankfurt-am-Main: Suhrkamp, 1978).

For philosophical and medical debates in France during the Napoleonic era, see Geneviève Fraisse, *Reason's Muse: Sexual Difference and the Birth of Democracy*, transl. Jane Marie Todd (Chicago: University of Chicago Press, 1994), and for literary and artistic reconstructions of woman in the postrevolutionary backlash, see the essays in *Rebel Daughters: Women and the French Revolution*, ed. Sara E. Melzer & Leslie W. Rabine (New York & Oxford: Oxford University Press, 1992).

For nineteenth-century male efforts to reposition women, see Stéphane Michaud, *Muse et madone: Visages de la femme de la Révolution française aux apparitions de Lourdes* (Paris: Seuil, 1985); for attacks on women writers, see Christine Planté, *La Petite Soeur de Balzac: Essai sur la femme auteur* (Paris: Seuil, 1989), and Janis Bergman-Carton, *The Woman of Ideas in French Art, 1830–1848* (New Haven: Yale University Press, 1995).

For "scientific" efforts to rationalize women's inferiority in England, see Cynthia Russett, *Sexual Science: The Victorian Construction of Woman-hood* (Cambridge, Mass.: Harvard University Press, 1989), and Ornella Moscucci, *The Science of Woman: Gynaecology and Gender in England, 1800–1929* (Cambridge: Cambridge University Press, 1990). Additionally, for a longer view of medical men's efforts to reposition and subordinate women, see Thomas Laqueur, *Making Sex: Body and Gender from the Greeks to Freud* (Cambridge, Mass.: Harvard University Press, 1990).

For nineteenth-century British economic thought, see the first part of Michèle A. Pujol, *Feminism and Anti-Feminism in Early Economic Thought* (Aldershot, Hants.,: Edward Elgar, 1992). See also Anna Clark, *The Struggle for the Breeches: Gender and the Making of the British Working Class* (Berkeley & Los Angeles: University of California Press, 1995), and essays on the economic thought of Harriet Taylor Mill and others in Mary Ann Dimand, Robert W. Dimand, & Evelyn L. Forget, eds., *Women of Value: Feminist Essays on the History of Women in Economics* (Aldershot, Hants.: Edward Elgar, 1995).

3. See James Billington, *Fire in the Minds of Men: Origins of the Revolutionary Faith* (New York: Basic Books, 1980), who only addresses "the role of women" as an afterthought.

4. Schooling of girls raises a number of important political questions for feminist history, among which are the clientele, the teachers, the curriculum, and who is organizing and financing which schools, at what level, and to what end. On English girls' literacy and education in the nineteenth century, see Kate Flint, *The Woman Reader, 1837–1914*, rev. ed. (Oxford: Clarendon Press, 1994). For France, see Françoise Mayeur, *L'Éducation des filles en France au XIXe siècle* (Paris: Hachette, 1979), and Linda L. Clark, *Schooling the Daughters of Marianne* (Albany: SUNY Press, 1984); see also Mayeur's essay "The Secular Model of Girls' Education," in *Emerging Feminism*, pp. 228–45, and on training of teachers, Jo Burr Margadant, *Madame le Professeur: Women Educators in the Third Republic* (Princeton:

Princeton University Press, 1990). For Germany, and German-speaking lands: James C. Albisetti, *Schooling German Girls and Women* (Princeton: Princeton University Press, 1988); Marie-Claire Hoock-Demarle, "Reading and Writing in Germany," in *Emerging Feminism*, pp. 145–65; Juliana Jacobi, "Zwischen Erwerbsfleiss und Bildungsreligion: Mädchenbildung in Deutschland," in the German edition of *History of Women*; James C. Albisetti, "Female Education in German-Speaking Austria, Germany, and Switzerland, 1866–1914," in *Austrian Women in the Nineteenth and Twentieth Centuries*, ed. David Good et al. (Providence: Berghahn, 1996); Ursi Blosser & Franziska Gerster, *Töchter der Guten Gesellschaft: Frauenrolle und Mädchenerziehung im schweizerischen Grossbürgertum um 1900* (Zurich: Chronos, 1985); and Ilse Brehmer & Gertrude Simon, eds., *Geschichte der Frauenbildung und Mädchenerziehung in Österreich* (Graz: Leykam, 1997).

On Italy, see Simonetta Soldani, ed., *L'educazione delle donne: Scuole e modelli di vita femminile nell'Italia dell'Ottocento*, 2d ed. (Milan: Franco Angeli, 1991). See also, on the attitude of the Roman Catholic Church, Adriana Valerio, "Patienza, vigilanza, ritiratezza: La questione femminile nei documenti ufficiali della chiesa (1848–1914)," *Nuova DWF*, no. 16 (Spring 1981); and Michela De Giorgio, "The Catholic Model," in *Emerging Feminism*, pp. 167–97. On Spain, see Pilar Ballarín, "La construcción de un modelo educativo de «utilidad doméstica»," in the Spanish edition of *A History of Women*, vol. 4, and Gloria Espigado Tocino, *Aprender a leer y a escribir en el Cádiz del ochocientos* (Cádiz: Universidad de Cádiz, 1996). On Greece, see Eleni Varikas, "Subjectivité et identité de genre: L'Univers de l'éducation féminine dans la Grèce du XIXe siècle," *Genèses*, no. 6 (Dec. 1991).

For the Netherlands, see Cornelia Wilhelmina (Mineke) Bosch, *Het Gesclacht van de Wetenschap: Vrouwen en joger oonderwijs in Nederland, 1878–1948* (The Gender of Science: Women and Higher Education in the Netherlands) (Amsterdam: SUA, 1994). See also Mineke Van Essen & Mieke Lunenberg, eds., *Vrouwlijke pedagogen in Nederland* (Nijkerk: Intro, 1991). For Russia, see Christine Johanson, *Women's Struggle for Higher Education in Russia, 1855–1900* (Kingston: McGill–Queen's University Presses, 1987), and for Poland, the articles in "Kobieta i edukacja," ed. Anna Zarnowskiej (Zarnowska) & Andrzeja Szwarca, 2 vols., *Kobieta*, 2 (1992).

For Ireland, see Mary Cullen, ed., *Girls Don't Do Honours: Irish Women in Education in the 19th and 20th Centuries* (Dublin: Women's Education Bureau, 1987), and on the network of girls' private schools in Sweden, see Gunhild Kyle, *Svensk flickskola under 1800-talet* (Göteborg: Kvinnohistoriskt Arkiv, 9, 1972), and Christina Florin, "Schoolboys, Schoolgirls and the Swedish State" (unpubl. paper, Bielefeld, 1993). For Belgium, see Luc Courtois, *L'Éducation des étudiantes à l'Université de Louvain* (Louvain-la-Neuve: L'Université, 1987).

5. The historiography on nationalism, nation-building, and population concerns is immense. Here I will only point to some works of particular in-

terest for exploring the gender of nations and states from a feminist stand-point. Others can be located in the chapter endnotes.

For studies of how images of women function as national symbols in male-dominated societies, see, for France, Maurice Agulhon, *Marianne into Battle: Republican Imagery and Symbolism in France, 1789–1880*, transl. Janet Lloyd (London: Cambridge University Press, 1981), and *Marianne au pouvoir: L'Imagerie et la symbolique républicaines de 1880 à 1914* (Paris: Flammarion, 1989). See also the following exhibition catalogs: Ian Jeffrey, Isabelle Julia, & Alain Sayag, eds., *La France: Images of Woman and Ideas of Nation, 1789–1989* (London: South Bank Center, 1989); Georg Kreis, *Helvetia - im Wandel der Zeiten: Die Geschichte einer nationalen Repräsentationsfigur* (Zurich: Verlag Neue Zürcher Zeitung, 1991); *Les Révolutions de 1848: L'Europe des images*, 2 vols. (Paris: Assemblée Nationale, 1998), and *Mythen der Nationen: Ein europäisches Panorama*, ed. Monika Flacke (Berlin: Deutsches Historisches Museum, 1998). On women as cultural symbols in Russia, see Joanna Hubbs, *Mother Russia: The Feminine Myth in Russian Culture* (Bloomington: Indiana University Press, 1988).

6. For insight into the operation of feminist aspirations within national-ist frameworks and national unification efforts, as well as the gendering of nation-states, see Bogna Lorence-Kot, "Klementyna Tanska Hoffmanowa, Cultural Nationalism and a New Formula for Polish Womanhood," in *History of European Ideas* (special issue on "Women, Society, and Culture," ed. Karen Offen), 8:4/5 (1987); Lorence-Kot, "A New Vision for Polish Women: Handmaidens to the Nation?" in *Views of Women's Lives in Western Tradition*, ed. Frances Richardson Keller (Lewiston: The Edwin Mellen Press, 1990); Martha Bohachevsky-Chomiak, *Feminists Despite Themselves: Women in Ukrainian Community Life, 1884–1939* (Edmondton: Canadian Institute of Ukrainian Studies, University of Alberta, 1988); Linda Edmondson, *Feminism in Russia, 1900–1917* (Stanford: Stanford University Press, 1984); and Ann Taylor Allen, *Feminism and Motherhood in Germany, 1800–1914* (New Brunswick: Rutgers University Press, 1991). See also Christiane Veauvy & Laura Pisano, *Paroles oubliées: Les Femmes et la construction de l'État-nation en France et en Italie, 1789–1860* (Paris: Armand Colin, 1997); also published in Italian, 1994; Eleni Varikas, "La Révolte des dames: génèse d'une conscience féministe dans la Grèce du XIXe siècle (1833–1907)," thèse du troisième cycle, University of Paris VII, 1986; published in Greek, 1987; and Marie Neudorfl's book on nineteenth-century Czech feminism (see Bibliography, p. 519).

On the convergence of nationalism, imperialism, feminism, and population issues, see Anna Davin, "Imperialism and Motherhood," *History Workshop*, no. 5 (Spring 1978), 9–65; Karen Offen, "Depopulation, Nationalism, and Feminism in Fin-de-siècle France," *American Historical Review*, 89:3 (June 1984), 648–76. See also Michael S. Teitelbaum & Jay M. Winter, *The Fear of Population Decline* (Orlando: Academic Press, 1985); John R. Gillis, Louise A. Tilly, & David Levine, eds., *The European Experience of*

Declining Fertility, 1870–1970: The Quiet Revolution (Oxford: Blackwell, 1992); and the special forum "Population and the State in the Third Republic," ed. Rachel G. Fuchs, in *French Historical Studies,* 19:3 (Spring 1996).

7. For a range of case studies in the intersections of gender and class issues during industrialization, see Laura L. Frader & Sonya O. Rose, *Gender and Class in Modern Europe* (Ithaca & London: Cornell University Press, 1996). Earlier debates can be tracked in the essays in *European Women and Preindustrial Craft,* ed. Daryl M. Hafter (Bloomington: Indiana University Press, 1995).

See also the recent interpretative analyses of women workers, the industrial capitalist economy, and the sexual division of labor by Laura Levine Frader, in *Becoming Visible,* 2d ed. (Boston: Houghton-Mifflin, 1987), pp. 309–33; a revised version, with additional bibliography, is "Doing Capitalism's Work: Women in the Western Industrial Economy," in *Becoming Visible,* 3d ed. (1998), pp. 295–325. See also Joan W. Scott, "The Woman Worker," in *A History of Women,* vol. 4, ed. Fraisse & Perrot, pp. 399–426; and in the same volume, Michelle Perrot, "Stepping Out," pp. 449–81.

On aspects of nineteenth-century women's paid and unpaid work in various European societies, see, for Spain, Mary Nash, "Identidad cultural de género, discurso de la domesticidad y la definición del trabajo de las mujeres en la España del siglo XIX," in vol. 4 of the Spanish edition, *Historia de las mujeres,* ed. Duby & Perrot. For England, see Sonya O. Rose, *Limited Livelihoods: Gender and Class in Nineteenth-Century England* (Berkeley & Los Angeles: University of California Press, 1992); Deborah Valenze, *The First Industrial Woman* (New York: Oxford University Press, 1995), and the book by Anna Clark, mentioned above. For France, see Michelle Perrot, ed., "Métiers de femmes," special issue of *Le Mouvement social,* no. 140 (July–Sept. 1987), and on women's unions see the essays in *Clio: Histoire, Femmes et Sociétés,* no. 3: *Métiers, corporations, syndicalismes* (1996). On Russia, see Rose Glickman, *Russian Factory Women: Workplace and Society, 1880–1914* (Berkeley & Los Angeles: University of California Press, 1984). On unionization efforts, see the essays in *The World of Women's Trade Unionism: Comparative Historical Essays,* ed. Norbert C. Soldon (Westport: Greenwood Press, 1985).

On issues of women's poverty, morality, and intervention efforts with regard for poor mothers on the Continent, see, for the earlier part of the century, Frances Gouda, *Poverty and Political Culture: The Rhetoric of Social Welfare in the Netherlands and France, 1815–1854* (Lanham: Rowman & Littlefield, 1995). For the later part, see the essays in Elinor Accampo, Rachel G. Fuchs, & Mary Lynn Stewart, eds., *Gender and the Politics of Social Reform in France, 1870–1914* (Baltimore: The Johns Hopkins University Press, 1995), and Leora Auslander & Michelle Zancarini-Fournel, eds., *Différence des sexes et protection sociale (XIXe–XXe siècles)* (St. Denis: Presses Universitaires de Vincennes, 1995). See also, for France, Rachel G. Fuchs's remarkable studies, *Abandoned Children: Foundlings and Child Welfare in Nineteenth-Century France* (Albany: SUNY Press, 1984), and

Poor and Pregnant in Paris: Strategies for Survival in the Nineteenth Century (New Brunswick: Rutgers University Press, 1992). On claims for women's rights and issues of maternity, see Anne Cova, *Maternité et droits des femmes en France* (Paris: Anthropos, 1997).

On the debuts of protective legislation for women workers, see the comprehensive set of European essays in *Protecting Women: Labor Legislation in Europe, the United States, and Australia, 1880–1920*, ed. Ulla Wikander, Alice Kessler-Harris, & Jane Lewis (Urbana: University of Illinois Press, 1995). On policies addressed to mothers, see *Maternity & Gender Policies: Women and the Rise of the European Welfare States, 1880s–1950s*, ed. Gisela Bock & Pat Thane (London: Routledge, 1991).

8. On issues particular to middle-class women, the construction of separate spheres, and efforts to demolish them, see Bonnie G. Smith, *Ladies of the Leisure Class: The Bourgeoises of Northern France in the Nineteenth Century* (Princeton: Princeton University Press, 1981); Leonore Davidoff & Catherine Hall, *Family Fortunes: Men and Women of the English Middle Class, 1780–1850* (Chicago: University of Chicago Press, 1987), and Marion A. Kaplan, *The Making of the Jewish Middle Class: Women, Family, and Identity in Imperial Germany* (New York & Oxford: Oxford University Press, 1991). On controversies surrounding middle-class women's entry into the Dutch labor force, see Francisca DeHaan, *Gender and the Politics of Office Work: The Netherlands 1860–1940* (Amsterdam: Amsterdam University Press, 1998).

9. On prostitution, rescue work, and feminist efforts to abolish regulated prostitution on the Continent, see Edward Bristow, *Prostitution and Prejudice: The Jewish Campaign against White Slavery, 1870–1939* (Oxford: Clarendon Press, 1982), and Laurie Bernstein, *Sonia's Daughters: Prostitutes and Their Regulation in Imperial Russia* (Berkeley & Los Angeles: University of California Press, 1996); and Anne-Marie Käppeli, *Sublime croisade: Éthique et politique du féminisme protestant, 1875–1928* (Carouge-Geneva: Éditions Zoé, 1990). On Italy, see Mary Gibson, *Prostitution and the State in Italy, 1860–1915* (New Brunswick: Rutgers University Press, 1986), and Annarita Buttafuoco, "Motherhood as a Political Strategy: The Role of the Italian Women's Movement in the Creation of the Casa Nazionale di Maternità," in the Bock-Thane volume.

On English and Irish feminist efforts to address prostitution and contest male promiscuity as irresponsible, see Lucy Bland, *Banishing the Beast: English Feminism and Sexual Morality, 1885–1914* (New York: The New Press, 1995), and Sheila Jeffreys, *The Spinster and Her Enemies: Feminism and Sexuality, 1880–1930* (London: Pandora Press, 1985). See also the essays by Philippa Levine, "Consistent Contradictions: Prostitution and Protective Labour Legislation in Nineteenth-Century England," *Social History*, 19:1 (Jan. 1994), 17–35, and, on Ireland, Maria Luddy's "Prostitution and Rescue Work in Nineteenth-Century Ireland," in *Women Surviving*, ed. Maria Luddy & Cliona Murphy (Dublin: Poolbeg, 1990).

On other aspects of female organizing, from philanthropy and charity to feminist politics, see Catherine M. Prelinger, *Charity, Challenge, and Change: Religious Dimensions of the Mid-Nineteenth Century Women's Movement in Germany* (Westport: Greenwood Press, 1987); the essays in Kathleen D. McCarthy, ed., *Lady Bountiful Revisited: Women, Philanthropy and Power* (New Brunswick: Rutgers University Press, 1990), especially, on Russia, Brenda Meehan-Waters, "From Contemplative Practice to Charitable Activity: Russian Women's Religious Communities and the Development of Charitable Work, 1861–1917." For Ireland, see Maria Luddy, *Women and Philanthropy in Nineteenth-Century Ireland* (Cambridge: Cambridge University Press, 1995). For France, see Evelyne Lejeune-Resnick, *Femmes et associations (1830–1880)* (Paris: Publisud, 1991); Sylvie Fayet-Scribe, *Associations féminines et catholicisme: De la charité à l'action sociale, XIXe–XX siècle* (Paris: Les Éditions ouvrières, 1990). For Sweden, see Brita Åkerman, ed., *Vi Kan, Vi Behovs: Kvinnorna Går Samman i egna förengar* (We Can, We Are Needed: Women Enter Their Own Associations) (Stockholm: Akademiklitteratur, 1983).

10. For analyses of early nineteenth-century socialist feminism in England and France, see Barbara Taylor, *Eve and the New Jerusalem: Socialism and Femininsm in the Nineteenth Century* (New York: Pantheon, 1983; rev. ed. Cambridge, Mass.: Harvard University Press, 1993), and Claire Goldberg Moses, *French Feminism in the Nineteenth Century* (Albany: SUNY Press, 1984); see also Susan K. Grogan, *French Socialism and Sexual Difference: Women and the New Society, 1803–1844* (London: Macmillan, 1992); and the essays and texts in Moses & Leslie Rabine, *Feminism, Socialism, and French Romanticism* (Bloomington: Indiana University Press, 1993).

For the later nineteenth century, see my remarks in the Introduction and the discussion and the extended notes in Chapters 6 and 7. See also Lise Vogel's study *Marxism and the Oppression of Women: Toward a Unitary Theory* (New Brunswick: Rutgers University Press, 1983), especially chaps. 4–8; had I discovered Vogel's work earlier in my research, I could have saved myself a lot of effort.

11. Two complementary studies of early international feminist networking are: Bonnie S. Anderson, *Joyous Greetings! The First International Women's Movement* (New York: Oxford University Press, 2000), and Margaret H. McFadden, *Golden Cables of Sympathy: The Transatlantic Sources of Nineteenth-Century Feminism* (Lexington: University of Kentucky Press, 1999). For the later nineteenth and early twentieth centuries, see the superb study by Leila J. Rupp, *Worlds of Women: The Making of an International Women's Movement* (Princeton: Princeton University Press, 1997).

12. Ellen Key, *Love and Marriage*, transl. Arthur G. Chater (New York: Putnam, 1911), p. 214; orig. publ. in Swedish 1903, in German 1904, and in French 1906.

CHAPTER 4: REARTICULATING FEMINIST CLAIMS

1. Percy Bysshe Shelley, *The Revolt of Islam* (1817), canto 2, verse 43. On Shelley, see Barbara Charlesworth Gelpi, *Shelley's Goddess: Maternity, Language, Subjectivity* (New York: Oxford University Press, 1992).

2. Anna Doyle Wheeler, "Rights of Women: A Lecture delivered by Mrs. Wheeler last year, in a Chapel near Finsbury Square," *The British Co-Operator*, 1:1 (April 1830), 13. My thanks to George Offen for fetching a copy of this text in London. On Wheeler, see Margaret McFadden, "Anna Doyle Wheeler (1785–1848): Philosopher, Socialist, Feminist," *Hypatia*, 4:1 (Spring 1989), 91–101; and Dolores Dooley, "Anna Doyle Wheeler (1785–c. 1850)," in *Women, Power and Consciousness in 19th Century Ireland*, ed. Mary Cullen & Maria Luddy (Dublin: Attic, 1995), pp. 19–53.

3. Prosper Enfantin, "Extrait de la parole du Père dans la réunion générale de la famille, le 19 Novembre 1831," *Oeuvres de Saint-Simon et d'Enfantin*, vol. 47 (Paris, 1878), as transl. KO, in *WFF*, vol. 1, doc. 34.

4. *Rahel: Ein Buch des Andenkens für ihre Freunde*, ed. Karl Auguste Varnhagen von Ense (Berlin: Duncker und Humblot, 1834), vol. 1, p. 312; as transl. Doris Starr Guilloton in "Toward a New Freedom: Rahel Varnhagen and the German Women Writers before 1848," in *Woman as Mediatrix*, ed. Avriel H. Goldberger (New York: Greenwood Press, 1987), p. 136; Ludwig Feuerbach, *The Essence of Christianity* (1841), transl. George Eliot (1854; New York: Harper & Row, 1957), appendix 15.

5. Alfred, Lord Tennyson, *The Princess* (1847), Part V, lines 427–31 and Part II, lines 155–61. The contextual study by John Killham, *Tennyson and the Princess: Reflections of an Age* (London: Athlone Press, 1958), is still extremely helpful. This poem subsequently inspired Gilbert & Sullivan's musical *Princess Ida*.

6. François-René, vicomte de Chateaubriand, "L'Avenir du monde," *Revue des Deux Mondes*, 15 April 1834, 236–37. Chateaubriand may have been heavily influenced in this view by his much younger mistress from 1829 to 1831, Hortense Allart, who subsequently published *La Femme et la démocratie de notre temps* (Paris: Delaunay, 1836).

7. See Richard Wortman, "The Russian Empress as Mother," in *The Family in Imperial Russia*, ed. David L. Ransel (Urbana: University of Illinois Press, 1978), pp. 60–74.

8. Caroline Pichler, "Über weibliche Erziehung" (1823), in *Zerstreute Blätter aus meinem Schreibtische, neue Folge* (Vienna: A. Pichler's sel. Witwe, 1843). Commissioned translation from the German by Barbara Hyams (MY Fund).

9. Flora Tristan, *Pétition pour le rétablissement du divorce à Messieurs les députés, le 20 décembre 1837* (Paris: Impr. de Mme Huzzard, 1838); as transl. in *Early French Feminisms 1830–1940: A Passion for Liberty*, ed. Felicia Gordon & Máire Cross (Cheltenham: Edward Elgar, 1996), pp. 44–46. Scholarship on Tristan is well developed. A number of full-length works by Flora Tristan, including *The Worker's Union*, are now available in English translation; see also the collection *Flora Tristan: Utopian Feminist*, transl.

and ed. Doris Beik & Paul Beik (Bloomington: Indiana University Press, 1993).

10. Mary Maurice, *Mothers and Governesses* (1847), as quoted in *WFF*, vol. 1, doc. 47, p. 175.

11. See Ann Taylor Allen, "Spiritual Motherhood: German Feminists and the Kindergarten Movement, 1848–1911," *History of Education Quarterly*, 22:3 (Fall 1982), 319–39.

12. Abbé Henri Grégoire, *De l'Influence du christianisme sur la condition des femmes* (1821), repr. in *Oeuvres de l'abbé Grégoire*, vol. 13 (Nendeln: Krauss-Thomson, 1977); quote, chap. 1, p. 5; transl. KO.

13. Thomassy, *De la Nécessité d'appeler au trône les filles de France* (Paris: A. Egron, 1820). The younger brothers of the executed King Louis XVI reestablished the "legitimate" Bourbon monarchy; the dead king's only surviving child, a daughter, remained under her uncles' guardianship.

14. See Thomas W. Laqueur, "The Queen Caroline Affair: Politics as Art in the Reign of George IV," *Journal of Modern History*, 54:3 (Sept. 1982), 417–66; and Anna Clark, "Queen Caroline and the Sexual Politics of Popular Culture in London, 1820," *Representations*, no. 31 (Summer 1990), 47–68.

15. On all these groups, see Barbara Taylor, *Eve and the New Jerusalem: Socialism and Feminism in the Nineteenth Century* (London: Virago, 1983). On Thompson and Wheeler's work, see especially Dolores Dooley, *Equality in Community: Sexual Equality in the Writings of William Thompson and Anna Doyle Wheeler* (Cork: Cork University Press, 1996).

16. "An Act (2 William IV, c. 45) to Amend the Representation of the People in England and Wales, 7 June 1832," in *English Historical Documents*, ed. David C. Douglas, vol. 11, *1783–1832*, ed. A. Aspinall & E. Anthony Smith (Oxford: Oxford University Press, 1959), doc. 303, arts. 19 and 20.

17. Mary Smith's petition was presented and discussed in the House of Commons session of 3 August 1832; see *Hansard's Parliamentary Debates*, 3d ser., vol. 14 (3 July–16 Aug. 1832), p. 1086.

18. See especially Anna Clark, *The Struggle for the Breeches: Gender and the Making of the British Working Class* (Berkeley & Los Angeles: University of California Press, 1995).

19. The efforts of Caroline Norton, who fought back when her husband charged her with adultery and absconded with their children, resulted in changing the law on child custody; see her tract *The Separation of Mother and Child by the Law of 'Custody of Infants', Considered* (London: Roake and Varty, 1838), excerpted in *WFF*, vol. 1, doc. 41.

20. Sarah Stickney Ellis, *The Daughters of England: Their Position in Society, Character and Responsibilities* (London: Fisher; New York: Appleton, 1842). Excerpts from the protests of Reid and Brontë can be consulted in *WFF*, vol. 1, docs. 44, 54, 68, 81, and 83.

21. Zoé Gatti de Gamond, *Fourier et son système* (Paris: Capelle, 1841–42); as transl. in Bonnie G. Smith, *Changing Lives* (Lexington: D. C. Heath,

1989), pp. 174–75. Gatti de Gamond's work was originally published in 1838.

22. See Pat Thane, "Women and the Poor Law in Victorian and Edwardian England," *History Workshop*, no. 6 (Autumn 1978), 29–51.

23. See Angela V. John, *By the Sweat of Their Brow: Women Workers at Victorian Coal Mines* (London: Croom Helm, 1980); and Sonya O. Rose, *Limited Livelihoods: Gender and Class in Nineteenth-Century England* (Berkeley & Los Angeles: University of California Press, 1992).

24. On girls' schooling and the growth of the teaching profession in England, see the essays in *Lessons for Life: The Schooling of Girls and Women, 1850–1950*, ed. Felicity Hunt (Oxford: Basil Blackwell, 1987); and *The Private Schooling of Girls, Past and Present*, ed. Geoffrey Walford (London: Woburn Press, 1993).

25. Alexis de Tocqueville, *Democracy in America*, vol. 2 (New York: Vintage, 1959), pp. 222–25.

26. Jeanne Deroin, "Le Travail des femmes," *Almanach des Femmes* (1852); transl. in *Victorian Women: A Documentary Account of Women's Lives in Nineteenth-Century England, France, and the United States*, ed. Erna Olafson Hellerstein, Leslie Parker Hume, & Karen M. Offen, assoc. eds. Estelle B. Freedman, Barbara Charlesworth Gelpi, & Marilyn Yalom (Stanford: Stanford University Press, 1981 [hereafter *VW*]), p. 305. On Deroin, see Moses, *French Feminism*; and additional references in the notes to Chapter 5 in this work. An indispensable new study in French is Michèle Riot-Sarcey, *La Démocratie à l'épreuve des femmes* (Paris: Albin Michel, 1994).

27. Perspectives on philanthropy differ: a useful discussion of the issues in France can be found in Evelyne Lejeune-Resnick, *Femmes et associations (1830–1880)* (Paris: Publisud, 1991).

28. See Riot-Sarcey, *Démocratie à l'épreuve*, pp. 94–99.

29. On French influences, see particularly Iris Wessel Mueller, *John Stuart Mill and French Thought* (Urbana: University of Illinois Press, 1956); and Patricia Thomson, *George Sand and the Victorians* (London: Macmillan, 1977). In a series of articles in the early 1830s, Wheeler introduced Saint-Simonian ideas to Owenites in the pages of *The Crisis*.

30. "Jeanne Victoire," "Appel aux femmes," *La Femme libre*, no. 1 (1832), p. 1, as transl. in *WFF*, vol. 1, doc. 36, pp. 146–47; Clarisse Vigoureux, *Parole de Providence* (1834; repr. Seyssel: Champ Vallon, 1993), p. 94. See also Carl Jonas Love Almqvist, *Sara Videbeck*, transl. Adolph Burnett Benson (New York, 1919; orig. publ. as *Det Går An* [Stockholm, 1839]); Eugénie Niboyet, "Prospectus" for *Le Conseiller des femmes* (dated 1 Oct. 1833); Flora Tristan, *Union ouvrière* (Paris: Prévot, 1843).

31. See Whitney Walton, "Sailing a Fragile Bark: Rewriting the Family and the Individual in Nineteenth-Century France," *Journal of Family History*, 22:2 (Apr. 1997), 150–75.

32. George Sand, *Indiana* (1832); from the 1900 translation by George Burnham Ives, in *WFF*, vol. 1, doc. 37; quote, p. 149.

33. See Barbara Taylor, *Eve and the New Jerusalem: Socialism and Feminism in the Nineteenth Century* (New York: Pantheon, 1983; rev. ed., Cambridge, Mass.: Harvard University Press, 1993); Moses, *French Feminism*; Sylvia Paletschek, *Frauen und Dissens: Frauen im Deutschkatholizismus und in den freien Gemeinden 1841–1852* (Göttingen: Vandenhoeck & Ruprecht, 1990); and Susan K. Grogan, *French Socialism and Sexual Difference: Women and the New Society, 1803–44* (London: Macmillan, 1992). On the Icarians, see Diana M. Garno, "Gender Dilemmas: 'Equality' and 'Rights' for Icarian Women," *Utopian Studies*, 6:2 (1995), 52–74.

34. See Moses, *French Feminism*, chap. 3. A selection of Saint-Simonian women's texts in English translation, coupled with interpretative essays, can be consulted in Claire Goldberg Moses and Leslie Wahl Rabine, *Feminism, Socialism, and French Romanticism* (Bloomington: Indiana University Press, 1993).

35. "Jeanne-Désirée," "Amélioration du sort des femmes et du peuple par une nouvelle organisation du ménage," in *L'Apostolat des femmes*, no. 5 (3 Oct. 1832), p. 38.

36. Suzanne Voilquin, "Preface" to Claire Démar's *Ma Loi d'avenir* (1834); as repr. in Claire Démar, *L'Affranchissement des femmes* (Paris: Payot, 1976), p. 164. Démar, in fact, took exception to the Saint-Simonian emphasis on the maternal, arguing instead a radical libertarian/individualist feminist line; see Eleni Varikas, "'A Supremely Rebellious Word': Claire Démar, a Saint-Simonian Heretic," in *Die Marseillaise der Weiber*, ed. Inge Stephan & Sigrid Weigel (Hamburg: Argument-Verlag, 1989), pp. 89–103.

37. Madame E.A.C., *La Femme est la famille* (Paris: chez Gautier, 1834), pp. 8–9.

38. See Margaret H. Darrow, "French Noblewomen and the New Domesticity, 1750–1850," *Feminist Studies*, 5:1 (Spring 1979), 41–65, and Barbara Corrado Pope, "Revolution and Retreat: Upper-Class French Women after 1789," in *Women, War, and Revolution*, ed. Carol R. Berkin and Clara M. Lovett (New York: Holmes & Meier, 1980), pp. 215–36.

39. See Elizabeth Helsinger, "Sarah Lewis and 'Woman's Mission'," in *The Woman Question: Society and Literature in Britain and America, 1837–1883*, ed. Elizabeth K. Helsinger, Robin Lauterback Sheets, and William Veeder (Chicago: University of Chicago Press, 1983), vol. 1, *Defining Voices*, pp. 3–20.

40. See Ann Taylor Allen, *Feminism and Motherhood in Germany, 1800–1914* (New Brunswick: Rutgers University Press, 1991).

41. See Bogna Lorence-Kot, "Klementyna Tanska Hoffmanova, Cultural Nationalism and a New Formula for Polish Womanhood," *History of European Ideas*, 8, no. 4–5 (1987), 435–50; quote, p. 445.

42. Rabbi Abraham Geiger, "Die Stellung des weiblichen Geschlechtes in dem Judenthume unserer Zeit," *Wissenschaftliche Zeitschrift für jüdische Theologie* (1837), as transl. in W. Gunther Plaut, *The Rise of Re-*

form Judaism: A Sourcebook of Its European Origins (New York: World Union for Progressive Judaism, 1969), p. 253.

43. See the excerpts from Auguste Comte's *Cours de philosophie positive* (1839) and *Système de politique positive* (1848), repr. in *WFF*, vol. 1, docs. 62 and 63. For a more favorable interpretation of Comte's subsequent arguments, see Mary Pickering, "Angels and Demons in the Moral Vision of Auguste Comte," *Journal of Women's History*, 8:2 (Summer 1996), 10–40.

44. *Lettres à Marcie* (1837), repr. in George Sand, *Les Sept Cordes de la lyre—Lettres à Marcie—Carl, etc.*, new ed. (Paris: Michel Lévy frères, 1869; 1st ed., 1843), pp. 228–29. See Naomi S. Schor, "Feminism and George Sand: Lettres à Marcie," in *Feminists Theorize the Political*, ed. Judith Butler & Joan W. Scott (London: Routledge, 1993), pp. 41–53.

45. Concerning Proudhon's antifeminism, see Pierre-Joseph Proudhon, *Système des contradictions économiques, ou Philosophie de la misère* (1846), in *Oeuvres complètes de P.-J. Proudhon*, new ed., ed. C. Bouglé and H. Moysset, vol. 2 (Paris: M. Rivière, 1923); excerpts as transl. in *WFF*, vol. 1, doc. 52.

46. *La Gazette des Femmes; Journal des droits politiques et civils des françaises*, 1 Jan. 1837 and 1 Jan. 1838; quote, issue of 1 Jan. 1838, 4.

47. Daniel Stern, "Esquisses morales: Pensées sur les femmes," *La Revue indépendante* (25 Sept./10 Oct. 1847), 193.

48. Sand, *Lettres à Marcie*, pp. 230–31.

49. Sand's influence as far away as Russia is documented by Martin Malia, *Alexander Herzen and the Birth of Russian Socialism 1812–1855* (Cambridge, Mass.: Harvard University Press, 1961), chap. 11. See also Thomson, *George Sand and the Victorians*, for her influence in England; and Penny Brown, "The Reception of George Sand in Spain," *Comparative Literature Studies*, 25:3 (1988), 203–44.

50. Delphine Gay, *Lettres parisiennes*, vol. 3 (Paris: M. Lévy, 1857), letter of 23 March 1844, p. 303; transl. KO.

51. Jules Janin, "Le Bas-bleu," in *Les Français peints par eux-mêmes* (Paris: L. Curmer, 1842), pp. 201–31; quote, p. 202. The verses quoted here are from the caption for a caricature by Alcide Lorenz, *Miroir drolatique* (1842), reproduced and translated in Janis Bergman-Carton, *The Woman of Ideas in French Art, 1830–1848* (New Haven: Yale University Press, 1995), pl. 19, p. 48.

52. See Christine Planté, *La Petite Soeur de Balzac* (Paris: Seuil, 1989); Bergman-Carton, *Woman of Ideas*, esp. pp. 216–18.

53. Anonymous review of *La Donna saggia ed amabile* by Anna Pepoli, widow of the marquis de Sampieri (1838), in the *Foreign Quarterly Review*, 27:55 (Oct. 1841), 94.

54. See Deirdre David, *Intellectual Women and Victorian Patriarchy* (Basingstoke: Macmillan, 1987).

55. See Susan Kirkpatrick, *Las Romanticas: Women Writers and Subjectivity in Spain 1835–1850* (Berkeley & Los Angeles: University of Cali-

fornia Press, 1989). On the even grimmer situation of women writers before 1848 in the German states, see the essays in *Out of Line / Ausgefallen: The Paradox of Marginality in the Writings of Nineteenth-Century German Women*, ed. Ruth-Ellen Boetcher Joeres & Marianne Burkhard, *Amsterdamer Beiträge zur neuren Germanistik*, vol. 28 (Amsterdam: Rodopi, 1989).

CHAPTER 5: BIRTHING THE "WOMAN QUESTION"

1. See the brochure *Les Vésuviennes, ou La Constitution politique des femmes, par une société des françaises* (Paris: Imprimerie d'Edouard Bautruche, 1848), Bibliothèque Nationale Lb⁵³.1298. This publication lays out a list of women's rights and duties. On this group, and how they were represented, see Laura S. Strumingher, "The Vésuviennes: Images of Women Warriors in 1848," *History of European Ideas*, 8, no. 4–5 (1987), 451–88.

2. Louise Otto's affirmation in November 1843 of women's right and duty to participate in affairs of state responded to the initial proposal by Robert Blum in his *Sächsische Vaterlandsblätter* (22 Aug. 1843). The circumstances of Otto's reply are discussed by Bonnie S. Anderson in her forthcoming book (pers. comm., 1998).

3. On 1848 feminisms in France, see Claire Goldberg Moses, *French Feminism in the Nineteenth Century* (Albany: SUNY Press, 1984), chap. 6; S. Joan Moon, "Woman as Agent of Social Change: Woman's Rights during the Second French Republic," in *Views of Women's Lives in Western Tradition*, ed. Frances Richardson Keller (Lewiston: Edwin Mellen Press, 1990), pp. 323–59; and Michèle Riot-Sarcey, *La Démocratie à l'épreuve des femmes* (Paris: Albin Michel, 1994), pp. 183–261. Joan Wallach Scott fishes for paradoxes and contradictions in "The Duties of the Citizen: Jeanne Deroin in the Revolution of 1848," in her book *Only Paradoxes to Offer: French Feminists and the Rights of Man* (Cambridge, Mass.: Harvard University Press, 1996), pp. 57–89.

4. Scholarship on German-speaking women's movements often treats of feminists in the context of a broader women's civic activism, but the two terms should not be confused. The most comprehensive account to date of women's activism in Vienna (but which takes account of developments in other German-speaking areas) is Gabriella Hauch, *Frau Biedermeier auf den Barrikaden: Frauenleben in der Wiener Revolution 1848* (Vienna: Verlag für Gesellschaftskritik, 1990). See also *Schimpfende Weiber und patriotische Jungfrauen: Frauen im Vormärz und in der Revolution 1848*, ed. Carola Lipp (Moos & Baden-Baden: Elster Verlag, 1986); Catherine M. Prelinger, *Charity, Challenge, and Change: Religious Dimensions of the Mid-Nineteenth-Century Women's Movement in Germany* (Westport: Greenwood Press, 1987); Sylvia Paletschek, *Frauen und Dissens: Frauen im Deutschkatholizismus und in den freien Gemeinden 1841–1852* (Göttingen: Vandenhoeck & Ruprecht, 1990); Ann Taylor Allen, *Feminism and Motherhood in Germany, 1800–1914* (New Brunswick: Rutgers University Press, 1991); Stanley Zucker, *Kathinka Zitz-Halein and Female Civic Activism in Mid-Nineteenth-Century Germany* (Carbondale: Southern Illinois Univer-

sity Press, 1991); and Dagmar Herzog, *Intimacy and Exclusion: Religious Politics in Pre-Revolutionary Baden* (Princeton: Princeton University Press, 1996).

5. Marion Kirkland Reid, *A Plea for Women* (1843), as reprinted in *WFF*, vol. 1, doc. 68; quote, p. 233.

6. "Le Gouvernement provisoire, au peuple français," proclamation du 16 mars, reproduced in *La Commune de Paris*, no. 10 (18 March 1848); transl. KO.

7. "Les Femmes au Gouvernement provisoire et au peuple français," dated 16 March 1848, and signed by Antonine André de Saint-Gieles and a number of others, published in *La Voix des femmes*, no. 3 (23 March 1848); also republished in Maïté Albistur & Daniel Armogathe, *Grief des femmes* (Paris: Éditions Hier & Demain, 1978), vol. 1, pp. 277–79.

8. Pamphlet *Les Femmes électeurs et éligibles* (Paris: J. Dupont, 1848), Bibliothèque Nationale Lb^{54}.423; also partially reproduced in Albistur & Armogathe, *Grief*, vol. 1, pp. 280–81. For the full texts, in French and English translation, of the documents cited here and immediately above, see Karen Offen, "Women and the Question of 'Universal' Suffrage in 1848: A Transatlantic Comparison of Suffragist Rhetoric," *NWSA Journal*, 11:1 (Spring 1999), 150–77.

9. Jeanne Deroin, "Aux Citoyens français," *La Voix des femmes*, no. 7 (27 March 1848); transl. *WFF*, vol. 1, doc. 70.

10. Benjamin Disraeli, speech during the 20 June 1848 debate in the House of Commons on the reform of representation: *Hansard's Parliamentary Debates*, 11 & 12 Vic., 1847–48, vol. 99 (29 May–30 June 1848), p. 950. Also reported in *The Times* (London), 21 June 1848.

11. "Briefe an einen Clubb," in Hauch, *Frau Biedermeier*, pp. 139–40; transl. Gabriella Hauch in an unpublished AHA paper, "Gender Battles and Bourgeois Revolutions: European Women in 1848/49," Jan. 1998.

12. "An Act for Shortening the Language Used in Acts of Parliament" (1850), *Hansard's Parliamentary Debates*, 13 & 14 Vic., 1850, vol. 113, c. 21; as quoted in Erna Reiss, *Rights and Duties of Englishwomen: A Study in Law and Public Opinion* (Manchester: Sherratt & Hughes, 1934), p. 195.

13. "Manifeste, Société pour l'Émancipation des Femmes," dated 16 March 1848 (Paris); copy in Archives Nationales, BB^{30}.307, no. 6802.

14. On the development of this concept, see Karen Offen, "Ernest Legouvé and the Doctrine of 'Equality in Difference' for Women: A Case Study of Male Feminism in Nineteenth-Century French Thought," *Journal of Modern History*, 58:4 (June 1986), 452–84.

15. On Deroin, see the works listed in n. 2 above.

16. Deroin's "Mission de la femme dans le présent et dans l'avenir" appeared in the issues of 28 January, 10 March, and 10 April 1849; transl. *WFF*, vol. 1, doc. 77. Quotations in the ensuing paragraphs are all from this text.

17. See Pierre-Joseph Proudhon, *Système des contradictions économiques, ou Philosophie de la misère* (1846); transl. *WFF*, vol. 1, doc. 52. In the 1850s Proudhon would develop a lengthy—and utterly cynical—argu-

ment for women's inferiority. See English translations in *WFF*, vol. 1, docs. 52, 84–85, and 95.

18. See Riot-Sarcey, *Démocratie à l'épreuve*, on Deroin's later life; and especially Vaughan B. Baker, "Jeanne Deroin: The Years in Exile," in *Proceedings of the Western Society for French History: Selected Papers of the Annual Meeting, 1997*, vol. 25, ed. Barry Rothaus (Greeley: University Press of Colorado, 1998), pp. 142–55.

19. On Otto, see Ruth-Ellen Boetcher Joeres, "Louise Otto and Her Journals: A Chapter in Nineteenth-Century German Feminism," *Internationales Archiv für Sozialgeschichte der deutschen Literatur*, 4 (1979), 100–129; and Catherine M. Prelinger, "The *Frauen-Zeitung* (1849–52): Harmony and Dissonance in Mid-Century German Feminism," *History of European Ideas*, 11 (1980), 245–51. For collections of Otto's texts, see Ute Gerhard, Elisabeth Hannover-Drück, & Romina Schmitter, eds., *"Dem Reich der Freiheit werb' ich Burgerinnen": Die Frauen-Zeitung von Louise Otto* (Frankfurt-am-Main: Syndikat, 1980); *Die Anfänge der deutschen Frauenbewegung: Louise Otto-Peters*, ed. Ruth-Ellen Boetcher Joeres (Frankfurt-am-Main: Fischer Verlag, 1983); and *Louise Otto-Peters: Politische Denkerin und Wegbereiterin der deutschen Frauenbewegung*, ed. Ilse Nagelschmidt & Johanna Ludwig (Dresden: Sächsische Landszentrale für Politische Bildung, 1996).

20. English translations of the Otto texts referred to here can be consulted in *WFF*, vol. 1, docs. 48, 78, and 89.

21. See Hans Adler, "On a Feminist Controversy: Louise Otto vs. Louise Aston," *German Women in the Eighteenth and Nineteenth Centuries*, ed. Ruth-Ellen Boetcher Joeres & Mary Jo Maynes (Bloomington: Indiana University Press, 1985), pp. 193–214.

22. On *Georgesandismus*, see Chapter 4.

23. Ernest Legouvé, *Histoire morale des femmes* (Paris: Gustave Sandré, 1849). This influential work went through ten French editions and was translated into Spanish (1860), English (1860), Russian (1862), and Swedish (1867), and partially into Italian.

24. Ernest Legouvé, "Au citoyen Directeur-Gérant de *La Commune*," *La Commune de Paris: Moniteur des Clubs*, no. 30 (Friday, 7 April 1848), 1.

25. See the works cited above in n. 4.

26. Auguste Comte, "The Influence of Positivism upon Women," in his *General View of Positivism*, transl. J. H. Bridges (London, 1875; reprint: Stanford, n.d.); originally published in volume 1 of Comte's *Système de politique positive* (Paris, 1848); reprinted in *WFF*, vol. 1, doc. 63 (quote, p. 223).

27. Pius IX, "Ubi Primum," 2 February 1849, in *Pontificis maximi acta*, vol. 1 (n.p., n.d.); English text in *Papal Documents on Mary*, comp. William J. Doheny & Joseph P. Kelly (Milwaukee, 1954), pp. 1–5; reprinted in *WFF*, vol. 1, doc. 79.

28. On attempts to forestall feminist outbreaks in Prague, see Stanley Z.

Pech, *The Czech Revolution of 1848* (Chapel Hill: University of North Carolina Press, 1969), chap. 9.

29. The Prussian Decree on Associations, 11 March 1850, is translated in *WFF*, vol. 1, doc. 86.

30. Louise Otto, "Für Alle" (1848), transl. S. L. Cocalis and G. M. Geiger, in *The Defiant Muse: German Feminist Poems from the Middle Ages to the Present*, ed. Susan L. Cocalis (New York: The Feminist Press, 1986), p. 57.

31. Caroline Coronado, "Libertad," *Poesias* (1852 ed.), republished in Susan Kirkpatrick, *Las Románticas: Women Writers and Subjectivity in Spain, 1835–1850* (Berkeley and Los Angeles: University of California Press, 1989), pp. 319–20; commissioned translation by Maria-Cristina Urruela (MY Fund).

32. Harriet Taylor Mill, review essay on *The New York Tribune for Europe* (issue of 29 Oct. 1850), *Westminster Review*, no. 109 (July 1851); reprinted, with John Stuart Mill's introduction, as "Enfranchisement of Women," in his *Dissertations and Discussions* (1859), and again under the latter title in John Stuart Mill and Harriet Taylor Mill, *Essays on Sex Equality*, ed. Alice S. Rossi (Chicago: University of Chicago Press, 1970); also in *WFF*, vol. 1, doc. 88. A recent reassessment is Gail Tulloch, *Mill and Sexual Equality* (Hemel Hempstead: Harvester Wheatsheaf; Boulder: Lynne Rienner, 1989).

33. Jeanne Deroin and Pauline Roland, "Letter to the Convention of the Women of America," 15 June 1851, published in English in *History of Woman Suffrage*, ed. Elizabeth Cady Stanton, Susan B. Anthony, & Matilda Joslyn Gage, vol. 1 (New York: Fowler & Wells, 1881), pp. 234–37; reprinted in full in *WFF*, vol. 1, doc. 87.

34. Victor Hugo, "Sur la Tombe de Louise Jullien" (1853), *Oeuvres complètes de Victor Hugo* (Paris: Éditions Hetzel-Quantin, 1880–89), vol. 44, p. 92.

35. Barbara Leigh Smith (Bodichon), *A Brief Summary in Plain Language of the Most Important Laws of England Concerning Women, Together with a Few Observations Thereon* (London: J. Chapman, 1854), excerpted in *WFF*, vol. 1, doc. 90; and Caroline Norton, *English Laws for Women in the Nineteenth Century* (printed for private circulation, 1854). See Sheila R. Herstein, *A Mid-Victorian Feminist: Barbara Leigh Smith Bodichon* (New Haven: Yale University Press, 1985).

36. The petition was republished by Caroline Cornwallis in her article "The Property of Married Women," *Westminster Review*, 66 (Oct. 1856), 336–38; it is also reprinted in Lee Holcombe, *Wives and Property: Reform of the Married Women's Property Law in Nineteenth-Century England* (Toronto: University of Toronto Press, 1982), pp. 257–38.

37. Eliza Lynn Linton, "One of Our Legal Fictions," *Household Words*, 9 (April 1854); cited in Mary Lyndon Shanley, *Feminism, Marriage, and the Law in Victorian England, 1850–1895* (Princeton: Princeton University Press, 1989), p. 29.

38. Shanley, *Feminism, Marriage, and the Law...*; quote, p. 17.

39. Camilla Collett, *Amtmadens dötre* (Christiania, 1854–55); Fredrika Bremer, *Hertha; eller, En själs historia* (Stockholm, 1854). *Hertha* has long been available in English, thanks to the translation of Mary Howitt (New York and London, 1856). Collett's novel is now also available in English: *The District Governor's Daughter*, transl. Kirsten Seaver (Norwich: Norvik Press, 1991).

40. *Alla camera dei deputati* (Milan: Tipografia Ciminago, 1861), in the archives of the Museo del Risorgimento, Milan; as quoted by Annarita Buttafuoco, "Motherhood as a Political Strategy: The Role of the Italian Women's Movement in the Creation of the *Cassa Nazionale di Maternità*," in *Maternity & Gender Politics*, ed. Gisela Bock & Pat Thane (London: Routledge, 1991), p. 193.

41. For the Gabba-Mozzoni debate, see Judith Jeffrey Howard, "Visions of Reform, Visions of Revolution: Women's Activism in the New Italian Nation," in *Views of Women's Lives*, ed. Keller, , pp. 432–50, as well as the translated documents in *WFF*, vol. 1, docs. 122, 123. On Mozzoni, see Franca Pieroni Bortolotti, *Alle origini del movimento femminile in Italia, 1848–1892* (Turin: Giulio Einaudi, 1963), chap. 2; and the collection of her texts, *Anna Maria Mozzoni: La Liberazione della donna*, ed. Franca Pieroni Bortolotti (Milan: Gabriele Mazotta, 1975).

42. On Richer and Deraismes, see Patrick Kay Bidelman, *Pariahs Stand Up! The Founding of the Liberal Feminist Movement in France, 1858–1889* (Westport: Greenwood Press, 1982); and Moses, *French Feminism*, chaps. 8 and 9. See also Laurence Klejman & Florence Rochefort, *L'Égalité en marche: Le féminisme sous la Troisième République* (Paris: des femmes and Presses de la Fondation National des Sciences Politiques, 1989).

43. See Linda Edmondson, "The Women's Movement and the State in Russia Before 1917," paper presented at the University of Bielefeld, April 1993. For an important earlier interpretation, see Richard Stites, *The Women's Liberation Movement in Russia: Nihilism, Feminism, and Bolshevism, 1860–1930* (Princeton: Princeton University Press, 1978); and more recently, Bianka Pietrow-Ennker, *Russlands "Neue Menschen": Die Frauenemanzipationsbewegung von den Anfängen um 19. Jahrhundert bis zur Oktoberrevolution*, Habilitationsschrift, University of Tübingen, 1994.

44. On this NAPSS web of organized reform efforts, see Kathleen E. McCrone, "The National Association for the Promotion of Social Science and the Advancement of Victorian Women," *Atlantis*, 8:1 (Autumn 1982), 44–66; quote, p. 47.

45. See Giuliana di Febo, "Origines del debate feminista en España: La Escuela krausista y la Institución Libre de Enseñanza (1870–1890)," *Sistema*, no. 12 (Jan. 1976), 49–82.

46. Barbara Leigh-Smith (Bodichon), *Women and Work* (London: n.p., 1857), originally published in the *Waverley Journal*; reprinted in *Barbara Leigh Smith Bodichon and the Langham Place Group*, ed. Candida Lacey (London: Routledge and Kegan Paul, 1987): quote, p. 41.

47. "The Women's Protest," originally published in *The Daily News* (London), 1 Jan. 1870. Reprinted in Josephine E. Butler, *Personal Reminiscences of a Great Crusade* (Westport, Conn.: Hyperion Press, 1976; from the "new edition" of 1910–11), pp. 9–10, and in *Harriet Martineau on Women*, ed. Gayle Graham Yates (New Brunswick: Rutgers University Press, 1985), pp. 265–67, in conjunction with Martineau's accompanying letters to the *Daily News*.

48. See Judith R. Walkowitz, *Prostitution and Victorian Society: Women, Class, and the State* (Cambridge: Cambridge University Press, 1980); and Anne-Marie Käppeli, *Sublime Croisade: Éthique et politique du féminisme protestant, 1875–1928* (Carouge-Geneva: Éditions Zoé, 1990).

49. On Cobbe, see the essays in *Woman's Work and Woman's Culture*, ed. Frances Power Cobbe (London: Macmillan, 1869); and Deirdre Raftery, "Frances Power Cobbe (1822–1904)," in *Women, Power and Consciousness in Nineteenth-Century Ireland*, ed. Mary Cullen & Maria Luddy (Dublin: Attic Press, 1995), pp. 89–123.

50. Fredrika Bremer, "Invitation to a Peace Alliance," *The Times* (London), 28 August 1854.

51. Sandi E. Cooper, "The Work of Women in Nineteenth Century Continental European Peace Movements," *Peace and Change*, 9:4 (Winter 1984), 11–38; quote, p. 16.

52. On Marie Goegg's efforts, see Franca Pieroni Bortolotti, *La Donna, la pace, l'Europa: L'Associazione internazionale delle donne dalle origini alla prima guerra mondiale* (Milan: Franco Angeli, 1985); and Susanna Woodtli, *Du Féminisme à l'égalité politique: Un Siècle de luttes en Suisse, 1868–1971* (Lausanne: Payot, 1977).

53. Klara Raphael (pseud. of Mathide Fibiger), *Klara Raphael: Tolv Breve* (1850), as translated in Inga Dahlsgård, *Women in Denmark Yesterday and Today* (Copenhagen: Det Danske Selskab, 1980), p. 80. For the beginnings of Danish feminism, see Erwin Kurt Welsch, "Feminism in Denmark, 1850–1875," Ph.D. dissertation, Indiana University, 1974 (Univ. Microfilm 74-13548).

54. Quoted in Bonheur's account in Anna Elizabeth Klumpke, *Rosa Bonheur, sa vie, son oeuvre* (Paris: Flammarion, 1909), p. 264.

55. Jenny P. d'Héricourt, "De l'avenir de la femme," *La Ragione* (Turin), no. 54 (27 Oct. 1855), 26–31, and no. 56 (10 Nov. 1855), 59–64. Quotes, pp. 31, 59–61, 64. On d'Héricourt, see Karen Offen, "A Nineteenth-Century French Feminist Rediscovered: Jenny P. d'Héricourt, 1809–1875," *Signs*, 13:1 (Autumn 1987), 144–58; and Alessandra Anteghini, *Socialismo e femminismo nella Francia del XIX secolo: Jenny d'Héricourt*, Quaderni dell'Istituto di Scienza Politica, Università di Genova, Pensiero politico 10 (Genoa: ECIG, 1988).

56. See her series of four articles, "La Bible et la question des femmes," in *La Ragione* (Sept.–Oct. 1857); quote, issue of 24 Oct. 1857, pp. 38–39. A slightly different version had appeared the previous August as a single article in the *Revue philosophique et religieuse* (Paris).

57. Proudhon's letter, quoted in "M. Proudhon et la question des femmes," *Revue philosophique et religieuse*, 6:21 (Dec. 1856), 7.

58. P.-J. Proudhon, *De la Justice dans la Révolution et dans l'église* (1858), in *Oeuvres complètes de P.-J. Proudhon*, new ed., ed. C. Bouglé and H. Moysset, vol. 12 (Paris, 1935), transl. KO, *WFF*, vol. 1, doc. 95; all quotes are from this latter source.

59. *WFF*, vol. 1, *ibid*.

60. Jenny P. d'Héricourt, *La Femme affranchie* (1860), in English translation as *A Woman's Philosophy of Woman, or Woman Affranchised; An Answer to Michelet, Proudhon, Girardin, Legouvé, Comte, and Other Modern Innovators* (New York: Carleton, 1864; reprint, Westport: Hyperion Press, 1981), and excerpted in *WFF*, vol. 1, doc. 98; quote, *WFF*, vol. 1, p. 346.

61. Clémence Royer, *Introduction à la philosophie des femmes, cours donné à Lausanne par Mlle A.C.R.: Leçon d'ouverture* (1859), transl. Sara Miles, in an appendix to her Ph.D. dissertation, "Evolution and Natural Law in the Synthetic Science of Clémence Royer" (University of Chicago, 1988); quoted with permission from Miles, pp. 397, 405, 407. On Royer, see Geneviève Fraisse, *Clémence Royer, philosophe et femme de sciences* (Paris: Éditions la Découverte, 1985); Joy Harvey, "'Strangers to Each Other': Male and Female Relationships in the Life and Work of Clémence Royer," in *Uneasy Careers and Intimate Lives: Women in Science, 1789–1979*, ed. Pnina G. Abir-Am & Dorinda Outram (New Brunswick: Rutgers University Press, 1987); and Joy Harvey, *"Almost a Man of Genius": Clémence Royer, Feminism, and Nineteenth-Century Science* (New Brunswick: Rutgers University Press, 1997).

62. Arthur Schopenhauer, "On Women," in *Studies in Pessimism: A Series of Essays*, sel. and transl. T. Bailey Saunders, M.A. (London: Swan Sonnenschein, 1893), pp. 105–23 (quotes, pp. 105–6); originally published as "Über die Weiber," chap. 27 of Schopenhauer's *Parerga und Paralipomena: Kleine philosophischen Schriften* (1851).

63. R. (Wilhelm Heinrich Riehl), "Die Frauen: Eine social-politische Studie," *Deutsche Vierteljahrsschrift*, 1852, no. 3, pp. 236–96.

64. See Paul Bernard's winning study, *Histoire de l'autorité paternelle en France* (Montdidier: Radenez, 1863).

65. Jules Michelet, *Love*, transl. J. W. Palmer (New York: Carleton, 1860; orig. publ. Paris, 1859); and Jules Michelet, *Woman (La Femme)*, transl. J. W. Palmer (New York: Carleton, 1873; orig. publ. Paris, 1860); both excerpted in *WFF*, vol. 1, docs. 97, 98. An important feminist analysis is Thérèse Moreau, *Le Sang de l'histoire: Michelet, l'histoire et l'idée de la femme au XIXe siècle* (Paris: Flammarion, 1982).

66. See Carol Christ, "Victorian Masculinity and the Angel in the House," in *The Widening Sphere*, ed. Martha Vicinus (Bloomington: Indiana University Press, 1977); and Susan Kirkpatrick, *Las Románticas: Women Writers and Subjectivity in Spain, 1835–1850* (Berkeley & Los Angeles: University of California Press, 1989).

67. Maria Deraismes, "La Femme et le droit," public address given in the late 1860s, published in *Ève dans l'humanité* (Paris, 1891); quote pp. 16–17, as excerpted and translated in *VW*, doc. 25ii, p. 140. *Ève dans l'humanité* has since been republished with a preface by Laurence Klejman (Paris: côté-femmes, 1990).

68. Sir Henry Sumner Maine, *Ancient Law: Its Connection with the Early History of Society, and Its Relation to Modern Ideas*, 6th ed. (1876; orig. pub. 1861); in *WFF*, vol. 1, doc. 101 (quote, p. 374).

69. Johann-Jakob Bachofen, *Myth, Religion, and Mother Right*, transl. Ralph Manheim (Princeton: Princeton University Press, 1967), originally published as *Das Mutterrecht: Eine Untersuchung über die Gynakokratie der alten Welt nach ihrer religiösen und rechtlichen Natur* (Stuttgart, 1861); excerpted in *WFF*, vol. 1, doc. 102.

70. For the information on the importance of Tardieu to this debate, I am indebted to the Ph.D. dissertation of Nancy Robin Jaicks, "Angel Makers: The Crime of Abortion in Nineteenth-Century Lyon" (Columbia University, 1993). He also strongly opposed homosexuality.

71. The most recent study of the Zurich women is Thomas Neville Bonner, "Rendezvous in Zurich: Seven Who Made a Revolution in Women's Medical Education, 1864–1874," *Journal of the History of Medicine*, 44:1 (Jan. 1989), 7–27. See also Bonner's book *To the Ends of the Earth: Women's Search for Education in Medicine* (Cambridge, Mass.: Harvard University Press, 1992).

72. Sophia Jex-Blake, "Medicine as a Profession for Women," in her *Medical Women*, 2d ed. (Edinburgh, 1886); the essay was originally published in 1869. Excerpted in *WFF*, vol. 1, doc. 133, quote, p. 475.

73. On German opposition, see James C. Albisetti, *Schooling German Girls and Women: Secondary and Higher Education in the Nineteenth Century* (Princeton: Princeton University Press, 1988); and Patricia Mazón, "Academic Citizenship and the Admission of Women to German Universities, 1865–1914," Ph.D. dissertation, Stanford University, 1995.

74. Elizabeth Garrett Anderson, "Sex in Mind and Education: A Reply," *Fortnightly Review*, n.s., 15 (May 1874); quotes, p. 583.

75. Jules Simon, *L'Ouvrière*, 4th ed. (Paris, 1862); transl. KO in *WFF*, vol. 1, doc. 126, p. 458.

76. Julie-Victoire Daubié, *La Femme pauvre au XIXe siècle* (Paris, 1866); transl. KO in *WFF*, vol. 1, doc. 127, p. 459. The second edition of Daubié's *Femme pauvre* (3 vols., 1870) has now been reprinted (Paris: côté-femmes, 1992–93). A fine analysis of the Simon-Daubié exchange is Joan W. Scott, "'L'Ouvrière! Mot impie, sordide . . .': Women Workers in the Discourse of French Political Economy, 1840–1860," in *The Historical Meanings of Work*, ed. Patrick Joyce (Cambridge: Cambridge University Press, 1987), 119–42 & 282–85 (notes).

77. Louise Otto, *Das Recht der Frauen auf Erwerb: Blicke auf das Frauenleben der Gegenwart* (Hamburg, 1866); transl. SGB in *WFF*, vol. 1, doc. 129, p. 465.

78. The First International Working Men's Association, Lausanne Congress 1867, "Rapports lu au Congrès ouvrier réuni du 2 au 8 septembre 1867 à Lausanne," in *La Première Internationale: Recueil des documents*, ed. Jacques Freymond, vol. 1 (Geneva, 1962); transl. KO in *WFF*, vol. 1, doc. 131, pp. 469–70.

79. Paule Mink, "Le Travail des femmes, discours prononcé par Mme Paul [*sic*] Mink à la réunion publique du Vauxhall, le 13 juillet 1868," Bibliothèque Nationale, microfiche RP.12236; transl. KO in *WFF*, vol. 1, doc. 132, pp. 472–73. Thanks to Marilyn J. Boxer for providing a copy of this posted speech.

80. John Stuart Mill, *The Subjection of Women* (New York, 1869); quoted in *WFF*, vol. 1, doc. 105, pp. 392, 393. This work has been frequently reprinted.

81. Heinrich von Sybel, *Über die Emanzipation der Frauen* (Bonn: Cohen & Gohn, 1870).

82. James Fitzjames Stephen, *Liberty, Equality, Fraternity*, 2d ed. (1874; orig. publ. 1873), ed. with introd. and notes R. J. White (Cambridge: Cambridge University Press, 1967); Millicent Garrett Fawcett, *Mr. Fitzjames Stephen on the Position of Women* (London: Macmillan, 1873); and Lydia E. Becker, *Liberty, Equality, Fraternity: A Reply to Mr. Fitzjames Stephen's Strictures on Mr. J. S. Mill's 'Subjection of Women'* (Manchester: A. Ireland, 1874). A new edition of Stephen's tract has been published by the University of Chicago Press, 1991.

83. Édouard de Pompéry, "L'Assujetissement des femmes, par Stuart Mill," *La Philosophie positive*, 6:5 (March–April 1870); transl. KO in *WFF*, vol. 1, doc. 108 (quotes, p. 406).

84. N. N. Strakhov, "Mill (zhenskii vopros)," *Zaria* (Feb. 1870), reprinted in Strakhov, *Borba s zapadom v nashei literature*, 2d ed., vol. 1 (St. Petersburg, 1887), p. 176; as cited and translated in Linda Gerstein, *Nikolai Strakhov* (Cambridge, Mass.: Harvard University Press, 1971), p. 123.

85. Charles Darwin, *The Descent of Man and Selection in Relation to Sex* (New York, 1879; orig. publ. London: John Murray, 1871), p. 565; repr. in *WFF*, vol. 1, doc. 110, p. 411.

86. Herbert Spencer, *Education: Intellectual, Moral and Physical* (London, 1861), p. 279.

87. Herbert Spencer, "Psychology of the Sexes," *Popular Science Quarterly*, 4:1 (Nov. 1873), 30–38; quotes, 31, 36.

88. For the transcript of Mill's speech and the ensuing debates, see *Hansard's Parliamentary Debates*, 30 Vic., vol. 187, 20 May 1867, pp. 817–45; excerpted in *WFF*, vol. 1, docs. 135, 136. See also Bruce L. Kinzer, Ann P. Robson, & John M. Robson, *A Moralist in and out of Parliament: John Stuart Mill at Westminster, 1865–1868* (Toronto: University of Toronto Press, 1992).

89. See Jane Rendall, "Citizenship, Culture and Civilization: The Languages of British Suffragists, 1866–1874," in *Suffrage and Beyond: Interna-*

tional Feminist Perspectives, ed. Caroline Daley & Melanie Nolan (Auckland: Auckland University Press; London: Pluto Press; New York: New York University Press, 1994), pp. 127–50.

90. Cristina Belgiojoso, "Della presente condizione delle donne e del loro avvenire," *La Nuova Antologia*, no. 1 (31 Jan. 1866), 96–113 (quote, 100); transl. in Beth Archer Brombert, *Cristina: Portrait of a Princess* (New York: Alfred A. Knopf, 1977), p. 229. Belgiojoso's contributions to nation-building in Italy are documented in Christiane Veauvy & Laura Pisano, *Paroles oubliées: Les Femmes et la construction de l'état-nation en France et en Italie, 1789–1860* (Paris: Armand Colin, 1997).

91. Henri Baudrillart, "L'Agitation pour l'émancipation des femmes en Angleterre et aux États-Unis," *Revue des Deux Mondes* (1 Oct. 1872), 652; transl. KO.

92. Deraismes, "La Femme et le droit," in *Ève dans l'humanité* (repr. ed., 1990), pp. 21–42 (quotes, pp. 26, 39); transl. KO.

CHAPTER 6: INTERNATIONALIZING FEMINISM

1. Recent feminist scholarship on the women in the Paris Commune includes: Kathleen B. Jones & Françoise Vergès, "Women of the Paris Commune," *Women's Studies International Forum*, 14:5 (1991), 491–503; Jones & Vergès, "'Aux Citoyennes!': Women, Politics, and the Paris Commune of 1871," *History of European Ideas*, 13:6 (1991), 711–32; and Gay L. Gullickson, *Unruly Women of Paris: Images of the Commune* (Ithaca: Cornell University Press, 1996).

Still valuable are the contributions of Edith Thomas, *The Women Incendiaries* (New York: George Braziller, 1966); and Eugene Schulkind's penultimate article, "Socialist Women in the 1871 Paris Commune," *Past and Present*, no. 106 (Feb. 1985), 124–63. On the impact of the women Communards on the subsequent "crowd" literature, particularly the influential antifeminist interpretation of Gustave LeBon, see the works of Susanna Barrows and Robert Nye.

2. *Le Droit des femmes*, 13 July 1870; transl. in *The Englishwoman's Review of Social and Industrial Questions*, n.s., 1:4 (Oct. 1870), 248.

3. *Ibid.*, 249.

4. "Friedensruf an die Frauen Deutschlands," Sept. 1870; reprinted in *Dokumente der revolutionären deutschen Arbeiterbewegung zur Frauenfrage* (Leipzig: Verlag für die Frauen, 1975), pp. 25–26.

5. "Appel aux citoyennes de Paris par un groupe de citoyennes," 11 avril 1871, *Journal officiel de la République française sous la Commune* (Paris, 1871; also in *La Sociale*, no. 13 [12 April 1871]); transl. in *The Paris Commune of 1871: The View from the Left*, ed. Eugene Schulkind (London: Jonathan Cape, 1972; New York: Grove Press, 1974), pp. 171–72.

6. From the *Journal officiel . . . sous la Commune*, 14 April 1871; transl. Schulkind in *Paris Commune*, pp. 172–73.

7. André Léo, "La Révolution sans la femme," *La Sociale*, no. 39 (8 May

1871); transl. KO. The best work on André Léo is Fernanda Gastaldello, "André Léo: Quel Socialisme?" (laureate thesis, University of Padua, 1978–79).

8. "The Probable Retrogression of Women," *Saturday Review*, 32:818 (1 July 1871), 10–11; quotes, 11.

9. P.-J. Proudhon, *La Pornocratie, ou les femmes dans les temps modernes* (Paris: A. Lacroix, 1875); quotes, pp. 379, 430.

10. Pauline Worm, "Kvindesagens fortid og fremtid [The Past and Future of the Woman's Cause]," *Faederlandet*, 8 April 1872; a longer version with the same title was published in *Nordisk maanedsskrift*, 1872, pp. 19–63. See Erwin K. Welsch, "Feminism in Denmark, 1850–1875" (Ph.D. dissertation, Indiana University, 1974), 197–202.

11. Julie von May von Rued, *Die Frauenfrage in der Schweiz: Zur Bundesrevision am 12. Mai 1872* (Biel, 1872); Petition of the International Association of Women, in *L'Espérance* (Geneva), 9 March 1872, reprinted in Beatrix Mesmer, *Ausgeklammert, eingeklammert: Frauen und Frauenorganisationen in der Schweiz des 19. Jahrhunderts* (Basel & Frankfurt-am-Main: Helbing & Lichtenhahn, 1988), p. 310; transl. KO.

12. Hedwig Dohm, *Der Jesuitismus im Hausstande, ein Beitrag zur Frauenfrage* (Berlin, 1873), reprinted in *Die deutsche Frauenbewegung*, vol. 2, *Quellen: 1843–1889*, ed. Margrit Twellmann (Meisenheim am Glan: Verlag Anton Hain, 1972); transl. SGB, in *WFF*, vol. 1, doc. 139. On Dohm, see *Hedwig Dohm: Erinnerungen und weitere Schriften von und über Hedwig Dohm*, ed. Berta Rahm (Zurich: ALA Verlag, 1980); and Julia Meissner, *Mehr Stolz, Ihr Frauen! Hedwig Dohm, eine Biographie* (Dusseldorf: Schwann, 1987).

13. Hedwig Dohm, *Der Frauen Natur und Recht* (Berlin, 1876), transl. Constance Campbell, in Dohm, *Women's Nature and Privilege* (London: Women's Printing Society, 1896); quotes, here and below, pp. 117, 119–20, 151.

14. See Aletta Jacobs, *Memories: My Life as an International Leader in Health, Suffrage, and Peace*, ed. Harriet Feinberg, transl. Annie Wright (New York: The Feminist Press, 1996; orig. Dutch publ. 1924).

15. "Women's Newspapers," *The Englishwoman's Review* (15 Oct. 1878), 433.

16. Membership card of Matilde Bajer, in the Bajer Collection, Women's History Collection, State and University Library, Aarhus, Denmark.

17. Based on manuscript and printed materials in the Bajer Collection, Aarhus, and in the Gosteli Foundation Archive, Worblaufen, Switzerland.

18. *Congrès international du droit des femmes. Ouvert à Paris, le 25 juillet 1878, clos le 9 août suivant. Actes et Compte-rendu des séances plénières* (Paris: Aug. Ghio, c. 1878), p. 195.

19. "Discours de Madame Venturi," *ibid.*, p. 202.

20. Hubertine Auclert, *Le Droit politique des femmes, question qui n'est pas traitée au Congrès international des femmes* (Paris, 1878), transl.

WFF, vol. 1, doc. 142; quotes, p. 515. On Auclert, see Steven C. Hause, *Hubertine Auclert: The French Suffragette* (New Haven: Yale University Press, 1987). A selection of Auclert's articles from this period have been republished in *Hubertine Auclert: La Citoyenne, articles de 1881 à 1891*, ed. Édith Taïeb (Paris: Syros, 1982).

21. Frances Power Cobbe, "Introduction," to *The Woman Question in Europe: A Series of Original Essays*, ed. Theodore Stanton (New York, London, and Paris: G. P. Putnam's Sons, 1884), xiv.

22. The English version of Auclert's letter was published in May Wright Sewall's book, *Genesis of the International Council of Women (1888–1893)* (Indianapolis: n.p., 1914), p. 5.

23. Among the notable treatises published by members of this group were Yves Guyot's *La Prostitution* (1882), which was translated into several languages, and Charles Secrétan's highly philosophical *Le Droit de la femme* (1886), which was frequently reprinted well into the twentieth century. On the program and politics of the federation, see Anne-Marie Käppeli, *Sublime Croisade: Éthique et politique du féminisme protestant, 1875–1928* (Carouge-Geneva: Éditions Zoé, 1990).

24. In addition to the French studies listed above, see Tito Mammoli's *La Prostituzione considerata nei suoi rapporti con la storia, la famiglia, la società* (1881); John Chapman's "Prostitution at Paris," originally written for the 1878 Paris congress and published in the *Westminster Review*, n.s., 63:1 (April 1883), 494–521; and *La Revue de morale progressive* (1887–92).

25. Mary S. Gibson, *Prostitution and the State in Italy, 1860–1915* (New Brunswick: Rutgers University Press, 1986), p. 49.

26. Judith R. Walkowitz, "Male Vice and Feminist Virtue: Feminism and the Politics of Prostitution in Nineteenth-Century Britain," *History Workshop*, no. 13 (Spring 1982), 86.

27. Bjørnson's pathbreaking lecture was published in a number of languages, following its original appearance as *Engifte og mange gifte* (1888). On the ensuing controversy, see Elias Bredsdorff, "Moralists Versus Immoralists: The Great Battle in Scandinavian Literature in the 1880s," *Scandinavica*, 8 (1960), 91–111.

28. Marie L. Neudorfl, "Masaryk and the Women's Question," in *T. G. Masaryk (1850–1937): Thinker and Politician*, ed. Stanley B. Winters (New York: St. Martin's Press, 1990), vol. 1, pp. 258–82.

29. Elizabeth Cady Stanton, "Closing Address," in *Report of the International Council of Women, Assembled by the National Woman Suffrage Association, Washington, D. C. . . . , March 25 to April 1, 1888* (Washington, D.C.: Rufus H. Darby, 1888), p. 436; emphasis added.

30. Hubertine Auclert, "Le Quatre-vingt-neuf des femmes," *La Citoyenne*, no. 145 (June 1889), reprinted in *Hubertine Auclert: La Citoyenne*, pp. 126–27; transl. KO.

31. Maria Deraismes, "Congrès français et international du droit des femmes," *Nouvelle Revue internationale (matinées espagnoles)*, no. 10 (1

June 1889), 303. For other articles and speeches by Deraismes, see the collection *Maria Deraismes: Ce que veulent les femmes, articles et discours de 1869 à 1894*, ed. Odile Krakovitch (Paris: Syros, 1980).

32. Maria Deraismes, opening address, in *Congrès français et international du droit des femmes* (Paris: E. Dentu, 1889), pp. 2–11 (quotes, pp. 4–5); transl. KO.

33. Richer toast, *ibid.*, p. 265.

34. Léon Richer, *La Femme libre* (Paris: E. Dentu, 1877), p. 90.

35. Anna-Maria Mozzoni, in Rina Macrelli, *Indegna Schiavitù: Anna Maria Mozzoni e la lotta contra la prostituzione di stato* (Rome: Riuniti, 1981); transl. Gibson, *Prostitution*, p. 53.

36. Regina Wecker, "Equality for Men? Factory Laws, Protective Legislation for Women in Switzerland, and the Swiss Effort for International Protection," in *Protecting Women: Labor Legislation in Europe, the United States, and Australia, 1880–1920*, ed. Ulla Wikander, Alice Kessler-Harris, and Jane Lewis (Urbana: University of Illinois Press, 1995), p. 72.

37. Hubertine Auclert, "Femmes! vous allez prendre notre place," *La Citoyenne*, 31 July 1881; transl. in Patricia Hilden, *Working Women and Socialist Politics in France, 1880–1914: A Regional Study* (Oxford: Clarendon Press, 1986), p. 196.

38. Deraismes, opening address, in *Congrès français et international du droit des femmes* (1889), pp. 3–4.

39. Many historians have explored the disagreements between socialists and feminists in the later nineteenth century. For Germany, see in particular, Jean H. Quataert, *Reluctant Feminists in German Social Democracy, 1885–1917* (Princeton: Princeton University Press, 1979); Richard J. Evans, "Bourgeois Feminists and Women Socialists in Germany, 1894–1914: Lost Opportunity or Inevitable Conflict?" *Women's Studies International Quarterly*, 3:4 (1980), 355–76, reprinted in *Comrades and Sisters: Feminism, Socialism, and Pacifism in Europe, 1870–1945* (New York: St. Martin's Press, 1987), pp. 37–65; and the works of Alfred G. Meyer on Lily Braun (see also Chap. 7 notes below). For France see the differing perspectives of Marilyn J. Boxer and Charles Sowerwine, beginning with their articles in *Third Republic/Troisième République*, no. 3–4 (1977); Boxer's "Socialism Faces Feminism: The Failure of Synthesis in France," in *Socialist Women*, ed. Marilyn J. Boxer & Jean H. Quataert (New York: Elsevier, 1978), pp. 75–111; and Sowerwine's *Sisters or Citizens? Women and Socialism in France Since 1876* (Cambridge: Cambridge University Press, 1982). See also Françoise Picq, "'Bourgeois Feminism' in France: A Theory Developed by Socialist Women Before World War I," in *Women in Culture and Politics*, ed. Judith Friedlander et al. (Bloomington: Indiana University Press, 1986), pp. 330–43. I have reexamined the socialist sources of the 1880s and early 1890s to reconstruct the theoretical development of the Marxist-socialists' position from a feminist perspective. See also below, Chapter 7 notes.

40. August Bebel, *Woman in the Past, Present, and Future*, transl. H(arriet) B. Adams Walther (London: Modern Press, 1885); originally: *Die*

Frau in der Vergangenheit, Gegenwart, und Zukunft (1878). The quotations below are from the "Introduction," pp. 1–5, 7.

In the later and far better-known English translation, *Woman Under Socialism* (1904), by Daniel de Leon, based on Bebel's revised and expanded edition, this latter passage (p. 5) is worded far more strongly:

> The goal, accordingly, is not merely the realization of the equal rights of woman with man within present society, as is aimed at by the bourgeois women emancipationists. It lies beyond,—the removal of all impediments that make man dependent upon man; and, consequently one sex upon the other. Accordingly, this solution of the Woman Question coincides completely with the solution of the Social Question.

41. Friedrich Engels, *Der Ursprung der Familie, des Privateigenthums und des Staats* (Hottingen-Zurich: Schweizerische Genossenschaftsbuchdruckerei, 1884); 4th ed. (1891) transl. Alick (Alec) West, *The Origin of the Family, Private Property, and the State, in the Light of the Researches of Lewis H. Morgan* (New York: International Publishers, 1942): excerpted in *WFF*, vol. 2, doc. 13 (quotes, pp. 79–81).

42. Eleanor Marx & Edward Aveling, "The Woman Question: From a Socialist Point of View," *Westminster Review*, 125:1 (Jan. 1886), 207–22; excerpted in *WFF*, vol. 2, doc. 14; quote, p. 83.

43. Clara Zetkin, "Für die Befreiung der Frau! Rede auf dem Internationalen Arbeiterkongress zu Paris, 19 Juli 1889," in *Protokoll des Internationalen Arbeiter-Congresses zu Paris, 14–20 Juli 1889* (Nuremberg, 1890); transl. SGB in *WFF*, vol. 2, doc. 15 (quotes, pp. 90, 91).

44. The SPD program, adopted at the party congress, Erfurt, 21 Oct. 1891, as transl. in Louise Wilhelmine Holborn et al., *German Constitutional Documents Since 1871* (New York: Praeger, 1970), pp. 51–53; quotes, pp. 51, 52.

45. See Richard J. Evans, "Theory and Practice in German Social Democracy 1880–1914: Clara Zetkin and the Socialist Theory of Women's Emancipation," *History of Political Theory*, 3:2 (Summer 1982), 285–304.

46. Hubertine Auclert, *Égalité sociale et politique de la femme et de l'homme, discours prononcé au Congrès ouvrier socialiste de Marseille* (Marseille, 1879), as reproduced in *Romantisme*, no. 13–14 (1976); transl. KO in *WFF*, vol. 1, doc. 143 (quotes, pp. 515–17 *passim*).

47. Léonie Rouzade, *Développement du programme de la Société "L'Union des femmes," par la citoyenne Rouzade* (Paris: Au Siège social de l'Union des femmes, 1880), p. 24; transl. KO. On Rouzade, see the contributions of Boxer and Sowerwine (cited above, n. 39), and Anne Cova, *Maternité et droits des femmes en France (XIXe–Xxe siècles)* (Paris: Anthropos, 1997).

48. See the conflicting interpretations of Marilyn J. Boxer and Charles Sowerwine, cited in n. 39 above.

49. On this debate, see Pil Dahlerup, *Det moderne gennembruds kvinder* (Copenhagen: Gyldendal, 1983); the chapters on Italian, Swedish,

and Russian writers in Donald Meyer's *Sex and Power: The Rise of Women in America, Russia, Sweden, and Italy* (Middletown: Wesleyan University Press, 1987); and for Russia, Laura Engelstein, *The Keys to Happiness: Sex and the Search for Modernity in Fin-de-Siècle Russia* (Ithaca: Cornell University Press, 1992). My understanding of the Scandinavian debates in this period has been greatly enhanced by the insights of Ida Blom, Kathleen Dahl, Ulla Manns, and Verne Moberg.

50. Elizabeth Deis, "Marriage as Crossways: George Meredith's Victorian-Modern Compromise," in *Portraits of Marriage in Literature*, Essays in Literature Series (Macomb: Western Illinois University, 1984), p. 24.

51. Olive Schreiner, *The Story of an African Farm* (London: Chapman and Hall, 1883), p. 217; repr. in *WFF*, vol. 2, doc. 3 (quote, p. 33). On Schreiner, see Ruth First & Ann Scott, *Olive Schreiner: A Biography* (London, 1980; repr. New Brunswick: Rutgers University Press, 1989).

52. Marie Bashkirtseff, *Journal of Marie Bashkirtseff*, 2 vols., transl. A. D. Hall (Chicago & New York: Rand, McNally, 1908), vol. 1, p. 402.

53. George Bernard Shaw, "The Womanly Woman," from *The Quintessence of Ibsenism* (London, 1913; orig. publ. London: Walter Scott, 1891); quote as repr. in *WFF*, vol. 2, doc. 5, p. 45.

54. Judith R. Walkowitz, "Science, Feminism and Romance: The Men and Women's Club 1885–1889," *History Workshop*, no. 21 (Spring 1986), 37.

55. Karl Pearson, "The Woman's Question" (1885), repr. in Pearson, *The Ethic of Freethought and Other Addresses and Essays* (1888); quote, 2d ed. (London: A. & C. Black, 1901), p. 355.

56. Karl Pearson, "Socialism and Sex" (1887), repr. in *The Ethic of Freethought*, 2d ed., p. 422.

57. Mona Caird, "Marriage," *Westminster Review*, 130:2 (Aug. 1888), 196. On Caird, see Ann Heilman, "Mona Caird (1854–1932): Wild Woman, New Woman, and Early Radical Feminist Critic of Marriage and Motherhood," *Women's History Review*, 5:1 (1996), 67–95.

58. Mona Caird, "Ideal Marriage," *Westminster Review*, 130:5 (Nov. 1888), 624.

59. Grant Allen, "Plain Words on the Woman Question," *Fortnightly Review*, 52, n.s. 46 (1 Oct. 1889), 448–58; quotes, pp. 449, 452, 455.

60. Concepción Arenal, speech delivered to and debated at the *Congreso pedagógico hispano-portugués-americano*, 1892; transl. in Mary Nash, "The Rise of the Women's Movement in Spain," unpublished paper, Stuttgart/Birkach, 1995.

61. Judith Jeffrey Howard, "The Feminine Vision of Matilde Serao," *Italian Quarterly*, 18, no. 71 (Winter 1975), 67. See also Wanda De Nunzio Schilardi, "L'antifemminismo di Matilde Serao," in *La parabola della donna nella letteratura italiana dell'Ottocento*, ed. Gigliola De Donato et al. (Bari: Adriatica, 1983), pp. 277–305.

62. Fanny Zampari Salazaro, "Condition of Women in Italy," *Report of the International Council of Women, . . . 1888*, p. 208.

63. Hubertine Auclert, "À Monsieur le Préfet de la Seine," in *La Citoyenne*, no. 64 (4 Sept.–1 Oct. 1882), 1.

64. Hubertine Auclert, petition of the Cercle du Suffrage des Femmes to the National Assembly, published in *La Citoyenne*, no. 88 (Sept. 1884), 1.

65. Virginie Griess-Traut, "Manifeste des femmes contre la guerre," *Le Travailleur*, 16 Nov. 1877, p. 12. (I thank Sandi E. Cooper for providing a photocopy of this document.) The 1883 petition was published in *La Citoyenne*, no. 73 (4 June–1 July 1883), 2. See Sandi E. Cooper, "The Work of Women in Nineteenth Century Continental European Peace Movements," *Peace & Change*, 9:4 (Winter 1984), 11–28; and her book *Patriotic Pacifism: Waging War on War in Europe, 1815–1914* (New York: Oxford University Press, 1991).

66. Friedrich Nietzsche, *Beyond Good and Evil*, in *Basic Writings of Nietzsche*, transl. and ed. Walter Kaufmann (New York: Modern Library, 1968; orig. publ. as *Jenseits von Gut und Böse*, 1886); quoted in *WFF*, vol. 2, doc. 6, p. 47.

67. On Kovalevskaia, see Ann Koblitz, *A Convergence of Lives: Sofia Kovalevskaia: Scientist, Writer, Revolutionary* (Boston & Basel: Birkhäuser, 1983).

68. See Karen Offen, "The Second Sex and the *Baccalauréat* in Republican France, 1880–1924," *French Historical Studies*, 13:2 (Fall 1983), 252–86; and Jo Burr Margadant, *Madame le Professeur: Women Educators in the Third Republic* (Princeton: Princeton University Press, 1990).

69. Eibhlin Breathnach, "Charting New Waters: Women's Experience in Higher Education, 1879–1908," in *Girls Don't Do Honours: Irish Women in Education in the 19th and 20th Centuries*, ed. Mary Cullen (Dublin: Women's Education Bureau, 1987), p. 68.

70. See Michelle Perrot, "Stepping Out," in *Emerging Feminism from Revolution to World War*, ed. Geneviève Fraisse & Michelle Perrot, vol. 4 of *A History of Women*, ed. Georges Duby & Michelle Perrot (Cambridge, Mass.: Harvard University Press, 1993), pp. 449–81.

71. See, e.g., for the Netherlands, Francisca de Haan, *Gender and the Politics of Office Work: The Netherlands, 1860–1940* (Amsterdam: University of Amsterdam Press, 1998); and for Germany, Carole Elisabeth Adams, *Women Clerks in Wilhelmine Germany: Issues of Class and Gender* (Cambridge: Cambridge University Press, 1988).

72. Rosalie Ulrica Olivecrona, "Sweden," in *The Woman Question in Europe*, ed. Stanton, p. 213.

73. For France, see the discussion in *Métiers de femmes*, ed. Michelle Perrot, special issue of *Le Mouvement social*, no. 140 (July–Sept. 1987). For Norway, the work of Kari Melby on teachers' and nurses' organizations should be consulted: see especially *Kall og Kamp: Norsk Sykepleierforbunds historie* (Oslo: Cappelens, 1990).

74. See Ida Blom, "Equality and the Threat of War in Scandinavia, 1884–1905," in *Men, Women and War: Historical Studies XVIII* (Dublin: Lilliput Press, 1993), pp. 100–118. For an overview, see Ida Blom, "The Struggle for

Women's Suffrage in Norway, 1885–1913," *Scandinavian Journal of History*, 5:1 (1980), 3–22; and especially Blom, "The Norwegian Women's Movement from the 1880s to 1914: Continuities and Changes in Gender Relations," unpubl. paper presented at Stuttgart/Birkach, 1995.

75. Quotes from Sophie Adlersparre, "En öfverblick af arbeet på den svenska qvinnans framåtskridande," *Tidskrift för hemmet*, 27 (1885), 17; transl. in Ulla Manns, "The True Emancipation: Gender and Feminism in Sweden," unpubl. paper, Stuttgart/Birkach, 1995.

76. Elisabeth Grundtvig, *Nutidens sedliga jemnlikhetskraf* (Helsinki, 1888); transl. Manns, "True Emancipation," 6.

77. Pearson, "The Woman's Question," in *The Ethic of Freethought*, 2d ed., p. 354.

78. Elizabeth Robins Pennell, "A Century of Women's Emancipation," *Fortnightly Review*, n.s., 48 (1 Sept. 1890), 408–17; quotes, 408.

79. See Karen Offen, "Women's Memory, Women's History, Women's Political Action: The French Revolution in Retrospect, 1789–1889–1989," *Journal of Women's History*, 1:3 (Winter 1990), 211–30; Joyce Senders Pedersen, "The Historiography of the Women's Movement in Victorian and Edwardian England: Varieties of Contemporary Liberal Feminist Interpretation," *The European Legacy*, 1:3 (May 1996), 1052–57.

80. Patrick Geddes & J. Arthur Thomson, *The Evolution of Sex* (New York: Scribner & Welford, 1890; orig. publ. London, 1889), p. 267.

CHAPTER 7: FEMINIST CHALLENGES AND
ANTIFEMINIST RESPONSES

1. See Annelise Maugue, *L'Identité masculine en crise au tournant du siècle, 1871–1914* (Marseille: Rivages, 1987); and Elaine Showalter, *Sexual Anarchy: Gender and Culture at the Fin de Siècle* (New York: Viking, 1990).

Tracts and learned treatises on all aspects of the woman question—few of which were authored by feminist scholars—proliferated in this period. As the knowledge wars continued, the publications seemed to grow increasingly thick, and the scholarly apparatus increasingly bulky. These publications included volumes such as the Finn Edvard Westermarck's *History of Human Marriage* (1891; 2d ed. 1894); *La Femme au point de vue du droit public: Étude d'histoire et de législation comparée* (1892), by the pro-reform Moïse Ostrogorskii, which subsequently appeared in English and German translations; Jeanne Chauvin's doctoral thesis in law, *Des Professions accessibles aux femmes en droit romain et en droit français, et l'évolution historique de la position économique dans la société* (1892); Lina Morgenstern's two-volume inquiry into women's work, *Frauenarbeit in Deutschland* (1893); *La donna delinquente, la prostituta, la donna normale* (1893), by the Italian criminal anthropologists Cesare Lombroso and Guglielmo Ferraro, which was subsequently translated into French, English, and other languages; Havelock Ellis's *Man and Woman: A Study of Human Secondary Sexual Characters* (1894); the Austrian Otto Weininger's idiosyncratic doctoral treatise *Geschlecht und Charakter* (Sex and Character, 1903); Rosa Mayreder's *Zur Kritik der Weiblichkeit* (1905); Jeanne (Oddo-)Deflou's *Le Sexualisme: Critique de la prépondérance et de la mentalité du sexe fort* (1906); Marianne Weber's *Ehefrau und Mutter in der Rechtentwicklung: Eine Einführung* (1907); and Pauline Tarnowski's *Les Femmes homicides* (1908)—to name only a few of the most substantial and significant publications.

2. Review of Lydie Martial, *La Femme et la liberté* (London: privately published, 1901), *The Englishwoman's Review* (15 Oct. 1901), 287. For additional discussion of first usages, see Karen Offen, "Defining Feminism: A Comparative Historical Approach," *Signs*, 14:1 (Fall 1988), 119–57. Many of the examples in this chapter supplement those provided in "Defining Feminism."

3. E. Belfort Bax, "The 'Monstrous Regiment' of Womanhood," in his *Essays in Socialism* (London: E. Grant Richards, 1907), p. 113.

4. On the Dutch distinctions, see Marijke Mossink, "Tweeërlei Strooming? 'Ethisch' en 'rationalistisch' feminisme tijdens de eerste golf in Nederland," in *Socialisties-Feministiese Teksten 9*, ed. Selma Sevenhuisjen et al. (Baarn: Ambo, 1986), pp. 104–20. Pauline Kergomard, "Il y a 'féminisme' et 'féminisme,'" *L'École nouvelle*, suppl. no. 5 (1897), 17. My thanks to Linda L. Clark-Newman for this reference. On Kergomard, see Clark-Newman, "Pauline Kergomard: Promoter of the Secularization of Schools and Advocate of Women's Rights," *Proceedings of the Western Society for French History, 1989*, ed. Gordon C. Bond, 17 (1990), 364–72.

5. On Marguerite Durand and *La Fronde*, see Jean Rabaut, *Marguerite Durand (1864–1936)* (Paris: L'Harmattan, 1996), and Katherine McClintock Felsen, "*La Fronde*: The Voice of French Feminism at the Turn of the Twentieth Century," Honors Thesis, Harvard College, Harvard University, 1988. For a postfeminist reading, Mary Louise Roberts, "Acting Up: The Feminist Theatrics of Marguerite Durand," *French Historical Studies*, 19:4 (Fall 1996), 1103–38, and Roberts, "Copie subversive: Le journalisme féministe en France à la fin du siècle dernier," *Clio: Histoire, femmes, et sociétés*, no. 6 (1997), 230–49.

6. See, for example, Käthe Schirmacher, "Le Féminisme en Allemagne," *Revue de Paris* (1 July 1898), 151–76; Lily Braun-Gizycki, "Le Mouvement féministe en Allemagne," *Revue politique et parlementaire*, 20, no. 58 (April 1899), 21–65. On Schirmacher, see Anke Walzer, *Käthe Schirmacher: Eine deutsche Frauenrechtlerin auf dem Wege vom Liberalismus zum konservativen Nationalismus* (Pfaffenweiler: Centaurus, 1991).

7. Ethel Snowden, *The Feminist Movement* (London: Collins' Clear-Type Press, 1911), pp. 62, 63–64.

8. Ellis Ethelmer, "Feminism," *Westminster Review*, 149 (Jan. 1898), 59.

9. Snowden, *Feminist Movement*, 9.

10. See Claire Goldberg Moses, "Debating the Present, Writing the Past: 'Feminism' in French History and Historiography," *Radical History Review*, no. 52 (1992), 81–82.

11. Nelly Roussel, "Qu'est-ce que le 'féminisme'?" *Le Petit Almanach féministe illustré* (1906; orig. publ. 1904), pp. 4–5. On Roussel, see Anne Cova, "Féminisme et natalité: Nelly Roussel (1878–1922)," *History of European Ideas*, 15:4–6 (Aug. 1992), 663–72; and Elinor Accampo, "Private Life, Public Image: Motherhood and Militancy in the Self-Construction of Nelly Roussel," in *The New Biography: Performing Femininity in Nineteenth-Century France*, ed. Jo Burr Margadant (Berkeley & Los Angeles: University of California Press, forthcoming).

12. Odette Laguerre, *Qu'est-ce que le féminisme?* (Lyon: Société d'éducation et d'action féministes, 1905), pp. 1–3.

13. Mme Avril de Sainte-Croix, *Le Féminisme* (Paris: V. Giard & E. Brière, 1907), p. 6. On Mme Avril de Sainte-Croix (and other French feminists in this period), see Steven C. Hause, with Anne R. Kenney, *Women's Suffrage and Social Politics in the French Third Republic* (Princeton: Princeton University Press, 1984); and Laurence Klejman & Florence Rochefort, *L'Égalité en marche: Le Féminisme sous la Troisième République* (Paris: des femmes, 1989).

14. Ellen Key, *The Woman Movement*, transl. Mamah Bouton Borthwick (New York & London: G. P. Putnam's Sons, 1912; orig. publ. as *Kvinnorörelsen*, 1909), pp. 59–60.

15. See Ellen Jordan, "The Christening of the New Woman: May 1894," *Victorian Newsletter*, no. 63 (Spring 1983), 19–21. The verse from *Punch* is quoted on p. 21.

16. See the "new woman" caricatures reproduced in Paul Ducatel, *Histoire de la IIIe République, vue à travers l'imagerie populaire et la presse satirique*, vol. 2 (Paris: Jean Grassin, 1975); Gustave Kahn, *La Femme dans la caricature française* (Paris: A. Méricourt, 1907); and Eduard Fuchs & Alfred Kind, *Die Weiberherrschaft in der Geschichte der Menschheit*, 3 vols. (Munich: A. Langen, 1913–14).

17. Elizabeth Rachel Chapman, *Marriage Questions in Modern Fiction, and Other Essays on Related Subjects* (London: John Lane, 1897).

18. See, most recently, the studies by Ann L. Ardis, *New Women, New Novels: Feminism and Early Modernism* (New Brunswick: Rutgers University Press, 1990), which includes a listing of "new woman" fiction in English, 1880–1920; and Jane Eldridge Miller, *Rebel Women: Feminism, Modernism and the Edwardian Novel* (Chicago: University of Chicago Press, 1994; London: Virago Press, 1994).

19. On the "new woman" theater, see *New Woman Plays*, ed. Viv Gardner & Linda Fitzsimmons (London: Methuen, 1991); *The New Woman and Her Sisters: Feminism and Theatre 1850–1914*, ed. Viv Gardner & Susan Rutherford (Ann Arbor: University of Michigan Press, 1992); and Gail Finney, *Women in Modern Drama: Freud, Feminism, and European Theater at the Turn of the Century* (Ithaca: Cornell University Press, 1989).

20. See the "veritable iconography of misogyny" discussed by Bram Dijkstra in his *Idols of Perversity: Fantasies of Feminine Evil in Fin-de-Siècle Culture* (New York: Oxford University Press, 1986). The quote is from Dijkstra's preface, viii.

21. Jennifer Waelti-Walters, *Feminist Novelists of the Belle Epoque: Love as a Lifestyle* (Bloomington: Indiana University Press, 1990), p. 178. See also the translations from these French novels in *Feminisms of the Belle Epoque*, ed. Jennifer Waelti-Walters & Steven C. Hause (Lincoln: University of Nebraska Press, 1994).

22. Laura Marholm Hansson, *Six Modern Women: Psychological Sketches*, transl. Hermione Ramsden (Boston: Roberts' Brothers, 1896; orig. publ. as *Das Buch der Frauen*, 1895), p. 33. On Marholm, see Susan Brantly, *The Life and Writings of Laura Marholm* (Basel & Frankfurt-am-Main: Helbing & Lichtenhahn, 1991); and the articles of Marilyn Scott-Jones, including "Laura Marholm (1854–1928): Germany's ambivalent feminist," *Women's Studies*, 7:3 (1980), 87–96; and "Laura Marholm and the Question of Female Nature," in *Beyond the Eternal Feminine: Critical Essays on Women and German Literature*, ed. Susan L. Cocalis & Kay Goodman (Stuttgart: Akademischer Verlag Hans-Dieter Heinz, 1982), pp. 203–23. On the German naturalist writers' circle in which Marholm Hansson's work must be situated, see Linda Schelbitzki Pickle, "Self-Contradictions in the German Naturalists' View of Women's Emancipation," *German Quarterly*, 52:4 (Nov. 1979), 442–56.

23. Laura Marholm, *Studies in the Psychology of Woman*, transl. Georgia A. Etchison (Chicago and New York: Herbert S. Stone, 1899; orig. publ. in German, 1897), p. 222.

24. Zénaïde Wenguerow (Zinaida Vengerova), "La Femme russe," *Revue des revues*, 22, no. 18 (15 Sept. 1897), 489–99; quotes, 496, 499. On Wenguerow (there are various spellings: e.g., Wengeroff in German), see Charlotte Rosenthal, "Zinaida Vengerova: Modernism and Women's Liberation," *Irish Slavonic Studies*, no. 8 (1987), 97–106.

25. Aleksandra Kollontai, "Novaya zhenschchina," *Sovremennyi mir*, 10 (1913); republ. and transl. as "The New Woman," in Kollontai, *Autobiography of a Sexually Emancipated Communist Woman*, transl. Salvator Attanasio (New York: Herder & Herder, 1971), p. 54. For works on Kollontai, see below, n. 69.

26. Kollontai, "New Woman," p. 94. Kollontai may have been alluding to Anton Chekov's famous short story, "The Darling" (1898); see *WFF*, vol. 2, doc. 9.

27. Gisela Brude-Firnau, "A Scientific Image of Woman? The Influence of Otto Weininger's *Sex and Character* on the German Novel," in *Jews and Gender: Responses to Otto Weininger*, ed. Nancy A. Harrowitz and Barbara Hyams (Philadelphia: Temple University Press, 1995), p. 173. See also the other essays in this collection.

28. Otto Weininger, *Sex and Character*, transl. of the 6th ed. (London:

William Heinemann; New York: G. P. Putnam's Sons, 1906); quotes, pp. 64, 65, 66, 68, 70, 75, 332, 345.

29. Rosa Mayreder, *A Survey of the Woman Problem* [*Zur Kritik der Weiblichkeit*. Transl. Herman Scheffauer (New York: George H. Doran, Co., 1913; originally published in Vienna, 1905)], pp. 90, 239–40. The English translation of the title is inaccurate; a better rendering would be "To Critics of Femininity." On Mayreder, see Harriet Anderson, *Utopian Feminism: Women's Movements in Fin-de-Siècle Vienna* (New Haven: Yale University Press, 1992).

30. Havelock Ellis, "The Changing Status of Women," chap. 2 of his *The Task of Social Hygiene* (Boston & New York: Houghton-Mifflin, 1912), p. 63. On Ellis, see Phyllis Grosskuth, *Havelock Ellis: A Biography* (New York: Knopf, 1980).

31. Ellis, "Changing Status," pp. 65–66; see also Havelock Ellis, *Man and Woman: A Study of Human Secondary Sexual Characteristics* (London: Walter Scott, 1894), pp. 17, 385–86.

32. Havelock Ellis, "Sexual Inversion in Women," in *Sexual Inversion* (1897); repr. in *Studies in the Psychology of Sex*, vol. 1 (New York: Random House, 1936), p. 262.

33. See Suzanne Vroman, "Georg Simmel and the Cultural Dilemma of Women," *History of European Ideas*, 8, no. 4–5 (1987), 563–79.

34. Georg Simmel, "Female Culture," in *Georg Simmel: On Women, Sexuality, and Love*, transl., ed., and introd. Guy Oakes (New Haven: Yale University Press, 1984), pp. 65–102 *passim*; orig. publ. as "Weibliche Kultur," *Archiv für Sozialwissenschaft und Sozialpolitik*, 33 (1911), 1–36; repr. in Simmel, *Philosophische Kultur: Gesammelte Essais* (Leipzig: Klinkhardt, 1911).

35. Georg Simmel, "The Relative and the Absolute in the Problem of the Sexes," *ibid.*, pp. 102–32 *passim*.

36. Leo XIII, "Arcanum," 10 Feb. 1880; repr. in *Social Wellsprings*, ed. Joseph Husslein, vol. 1 (Milwaukee: Bruce, 1940), pp. 25–46; excerpted in *WFF*, vol. 2, doc. 44.

37. Leo XIII, "Rerum Novarum," 15 May 1891, in *Social Wellsprings*, vol. 1; excerpted in *WFF*, vol. 2, doc. 16 (quote, p. 95). On the evolution of Catholic teachings, see Adriana Valerio, "Pazienza, vigilanza, ritiratezza: La questione femminile nei documenti ufficiali della chiesa (1848–1914)," *Nuova DWF*, no. 16 (Spring 1981), 60–79; and Richard L. Camp, "From Passive Subordination to Complementary Partnership: The Papal Conception of Women's Place in Church and Society since 1878," *Catholic Historical Review*, 76:3 (July 1990), 506–25.

38. Henry Edward, Cardinal Archbishop Manning, "Leo XIII on 'The Condition of Labour'," *Dublin Review*, 3d ser., 26:1 (July 1891), 165–66.

39. Augustin Rösler, *Die Frauenfrage vom Standpunkte der Natur, der Geschichte und der Offenbarung, auf Veranlassung der Leo-Gesellschaft beantwortet* (Vienna, Freiburg-in-Breisgau, Berlin, etc.: Herdersche Verlag-

shandlung, 1893). A French edition, *La Question féministe examinée au point de vue de la nature, de l'histoire et de la révélation* (Paris: Perrin, 1899), was followed in 1915 by an Italian edition.

40. Marie Maugeret, "Le Féminisme chrétien," *La Fronde* (11 Dec. 1897), 1; transl. KO in *WFF*, vol. 2, doc. 17 (quotes, pp. 96–97). On Maugeret and the politics of Christian feminism in France, see Steven C. Hause & Anne R. Kenney, "The Development of the Catholic Women's Suffrage Movement in France, 1896–1922," *Catholic Historical Review*, 67:1 (Jan. 1981), 11–30; and James F. McMillan, "Wollstonecraft's Daughters, Marianne's Daughters and the Daughters of Joan of Arc: Marie Maugeret and Christian Feminism in the French Belle Epoque," in *Wollstonecraft's Daughters: Womanhood in England and France, 1780–1920*, ed. Clarissa Campbell Orr (Manchester: Manchester University Press, 1996), pp. 186–98.

41. Maugeret, "Féminisme chrétien."

42. See the collection of reprinted primary texts in *Il femminismo cristiano: La questione femminile nella prima democrazia cristiana (1898–1912)*, ed. Francesco Maria Cecchini (Rome: Ed. Reuniti, 1979). See also Michela De Giorgio & Paola Di Cori, "Politica e sentimenti. Le organizzazioni femminili cattoliche dall'età giolittiana al fascismo," *Rivista di Storia contemporanea*, 9:3 (July 1980), 337–71.

43. Pius X, as quoted in translation by Odile Sarti, "The Ligue Patriotique des Françaises (1902–1933): A Feminine Response to the Secularization of French Society," (Ph.D. dissertation, Indiana University, 1984), pp. 243, 238. See also Sarti's book, *The Ligue Patriotique des Françaises, 1902–1933* (New York: Garland, 1992).

44. On this group see Francis M. Mason, "The Newer Eve: The Catholic Women's Suffrage Society in England, 1911–1923," *Catholic Historical Review*, 72:4 (Oct. 1986), 620–38.

45. Margaret Fletcher, *Christian Feminism: A Charter of Rights and Duties* (London: P. S. King & Son, Ltd., 1915), pp. 7, 9–17 *passim*, 74.

46. Benedict XV, letter "Natalis trecentesimi," 27 Dec. 1917, to the Superior General of the Roman Union of Ursulines; repr. in *Papal Teachings: The Woman in the Modern World*, ed. The Monks of Solesmes (Boston: St. Paul Editions, 1959), p. 27. The next quotation is also from this source.

47. Dolors Monserdà de Macia, *Estudi feminista: Orientacions pera la dona catalana*, 2d ed. (Barcelona: Lluis Gili, 1910), p. 14; amended transl. based on that in Mary Nash, *Defying Male Civilization: Women in the Spanish Civil War* (Denver: Arden Press, 1996), p. 12.

48. Millicent Garrett Fawcett, "The Woman Who Did," *Contemporary Review*, 67:5 (May 1895), 630–31. On Fawcett, see David Rubenstein, *A Different World for Women: The Life of Millicent Garrett Fawcett* (Columbus: Ohio State University Press, 1991).

49. On Valette, see Marilyn J. Boxer, "French Socialism, Feminism, and the Family," *Third Republic/Troisième République*, no. 3–4 (1977), 128–67;

and for a broader understanding of Valette's place in the maternity politics in 1890s France, see Anne Cova, *Maternité et droits des femmes en France (XIXe–XXe siècles)* (Paris: Anthropos, 1997), chap. 2.

50. Aline Valette, in "Le Féminisme à la Chambre 1893 à 1898," *La Fronde*, 29 April 1898, p. 2.

51. Valette, "Sténographie et machine à écrire," *La Fronde*, 6 Feb. 1898. This article and a number of Valette's other articles on women's work have been republished in *Aline Valette, Marcelle Capy: Femmes et travail au XIXe siècle: Enquêtes de La Fronde et La Bataille syndicaliste*, ed. Marie-Hélène Zylberberg-Hocquard & Evelyne Diebolt (Paris: Syros, 1984).

52. Ute Gerhard, "A Hidden and Complex Heritage: Reflections on the History of Germany's Women's Movements," *Women's Studies International Forum*, 5:6 (1982), 563.

53. Alys Russell, "The Woman Movement in Germany," *Nineteenth Century*, 40:233 (July 1896), 98.

54. Auguste Schmidt, "Die Parteien in der Frauenbewegung," *Die neue Bahnen*, 33 (15 Nov. 1898), 233–34; as quoted and discussed by Amy Hackett, "The German Women's Movement and Suffrage, 1890–1914: A Study of National Feminism," in *Modern European Social History*, ed. Robert Bezucha (Lexington: D. C. Heath, 1972), pp. 363–64.

55. Clara Zetkin, "Women's Libbers' Stupid Dreams about Harmony," from *Die Gleichheit*, 9 Jan. 1895; as transl. by Alfred G. Meyer from Lily Braun's article, "Left and Right" ["Nach links und rechts," *Die Frauenbewegung*, 1, nos. 5 & 7 (1895)], in his *Lily Braun: Selected Writings on Feminism and Socialism* (Bloomington: Indiana University Press, 1987), p. 48. See also Meyer's biography, *The Feminism and Socialism of Lily Braun* (Bloomington: Indiana University Press, 1985). The disagreement between Zetkin and Braun is also treated in Jean H. Quataert, *Reluctant Feminists in German Social Democracy, 1885–1917* (Princeton: Princeton University Press, 1979); Anna-E. Freier, *"Dem Reich der Freiheit sollst du Kinder gebären": Der Antifeminismus der proletarischen Frauenbewegung im Spiegel der "Gleichheit," 1891–1917* (Frankfurt-am-Main: Haag & Herchen Verlag, 1981); and Ute Gerhard, *Unerhört: Die Geschichte der deutschen Frauenbewegung* (Hamburg: Rowohlt, 1990).

56. Braun, "Left and Right," pp. 52, 48.

57. Zetkin's speech of 16 Oct. 1896 to the SPD congress was published in pamphlet form, *Nur mit der proletarischen Frau wird der Sozialismus siegen!*, and was reprinted in her collected works. An English translation can be consulted in Hal Draper & Anne G. Lipow, "Marxist Women versus Bourgeois Feminism," *The Socialist Register 1976*, ed. John Saville & Ralph Miliband (London: Merlin Press, 1976), pp. 192–201. For an excellent analysis, see Lise Vogel, *Marxism and the Oppression of Women* (New Brunswick: Rutgers University Press, 1983), pp. 107–15.

Similar conflicts can be traced in Italy, where in 1892 Anna-Maria Mozzoni challenged the Russian-born Italian Marxist-socialist party activist and journalist Anna Kuliscioff: "The *Critica Sociale* [which Kuliscioff edited]

believes that the woman question is fundamentally and exclusively an economic question and that it will simply resolve itself along with the latter. I
do not merely doubt this; I believe it is wrong." See Mozzoni, *I socialisti e
l'emancipazione della donna* (Alessandria, 1892), repr. in Mozzoni, *La liberazione della donna*, ed. Franca Pieroni Bortolotti (Milan: Gabriele Maz-
zotta, 1975), p. 212 (transl. KO).

58. For German formulations of these motherhood issues, see Ann Taylor Allen, *Feminism and Motherhood in Germany, 1800–1914* (New Brunswick: Rutgers University Press, 1991).

59. Bund Deutscher Frauenvereine, "Programm" (1907), transl. in
Katharine Anthony, *Feminism in Germany and Scandinavia* (New York:
Henry Holt, 1915), pp. 20–26; originally published in *Centralblatt des Bun-
des deutscher Frauenvereine* (July 1907); repr. in *WFF*, vol. 2, doc. 20.

60. International Socialist Women's Conference, resolution on woman
suffrage, Stuttgart, 1907; from *Dokumente und Materialien zur Geschichte
der deutschen Arbeiterbewegung*, vol. 4 (Berlin, 1967); transl. Alfred G.
Meyer, in *Women in Russia*, ed. Dorothy Atkinson, Alexander Dallin, &
Gail Lapidus (Stanford: Stanford University Press, 1977), pp. 93–94; also in
WFF, vol. 2, doc. 59.

61. Madeleine Pelletier, "Féminisme bourgeois et féminisme socialiste," *Le Socialiste* (5–12 May 1907), 2. See also articles in her monthly publication, *La Suffragiste* (1907–14); and Felicia Gordon, *The Integral Feminist: Madeleine Pelletier, 1874–1939* (Minneapolis: University of Minnesota Press, 1990). See also Charles Sowerwine & Claude Maignien, *Madeleine Pelletier, une féministe dans l'arène politique* (Paris: Éditions ouvrières, 1992); *Madeleine Pelletier (1874–1939): Logique et infortunes d'un
combat pour l'égalité*, ed. Christine Bard (Paris: côté-femmes, 1992); and
Marilyn J. Boxer, "Placing Madeleine Pelletier: Beyond the Dichotomies
Socialism/Feminism and Equality/Difference," *History of European Ideas*,
21:3 (1995), 421–38.

62. Hubertine Auclert, "Socialistes et bourgeoises," *Le Radical* (3 Sept.
1907); transl. in Hause, with Kenney, *Women's Suffrage and Social Politics*,
p. 70.

63. From *Die Gleichheit*, 29 Aug. 1910; transl. in *Clara Zetkin: Selected
Writings*, ed. Philip S. Foner (New York: International Publishers, 1984), p.
108. See also Temma Kaplan, "On the Socialist Origins of International
Women's Day," *Feminist Studies*, 11:1 (Spring 1985), 163–71, and Pam
McAllister, "A Tale of Two Days," in her book, *This River of Courage:
Generations of Women's Resistance and Action* (Philadelphia: New Society
Publishers, 1991), esp. pp. 84–92.

64. See William G. Wagner, "The Trojan Mare: Women's Rights and
Civil Rights in Late Imperial Russia," in *Civil Rights in Imperial Russia*, ed.
Olga Crisp & Linda Edmondson (Oxford: Clarendon Press, 1989), p. 66.

65. Ekaterina Shchepkina, *Zhenskoe dvizhenie v otzyvakh sovremen-
nykh deiatelei* (1905), quoted in translation by Linda Edmondson, "Wom-
en's Rights, Civil Rights and the Debate over Citizenship in the 1905 Revo-

lution," in *Women and Society in Russia and the Soviet Union*, ed. Linda Edmondson (Cambridge: Cambridge University Press), p. 96 n. 3.

66. Program of the All-Russian Union of Equal Rights for Women, Moscow, May 1905; transl. Linda Edmondson in *Sbornik: Study Group on the Russian Revolution*, no. 9 (Leeds, 1983), 125–26. Excerpts also in Edmondson, *Feminism in Russia, 1900–17* (Stanford: Stanford University Press, 1984), pp. 40–41. My thanks to Linda Edmondson for sending a photocopy of her translation.

67. Reported in *Zhenskii vestnik*, no. 5 (1905), 143–44; transl. Edmondson, *Feminism in Russia*, p. 37.

68. Petition cited by N. Mirovich, *Iz istorii zhenskogo dvizheniia v Rossii* (1908); transl. in Rose Glickman, *Russian Factory Women: Workplace and Society, 1880–1914* (Berkeley & Los Angeles: University of California Press, 1984), p. 244.

69. Aleksandra Kollontai, "Towards a History of the Working Women's Movement in Russia," (1920), as reprinted in *Selected Writings of Alexandra Kollontai*, transl. with introduction and commentaries by Alix Holt (New York & London: W. W. Norton, 1980), pp. 50–51. On Kollontai, see Barbara Evans Clements, *Bolshevik Feminist: The Life of Aleksandra Kollontai* (Bloomington: Indiana University Press, 1979), and Beatrice Brod Farnsworth, *Aleksandra Kollontai: Socialism, Feminism, and the Bolshevik Revolution* (Stanford: Stanford University Press, 1980).

70. Kollontai, "Towards a History," in *Selected Writings*, p. 51. On these events, see Linda Edmondson, "The Women's Movement and the State in Russia before 1917," unpublished paper given at IFRWH Bielefeld conference, April 1993, p. 8.

71. Anna Kal'manovich, in *Soiuz Zhenshchin*, no. 9 (1908), 3; as translated by Glickman, *Russian Factory Women*, p. 262.

72. Kal'manovich, from the congress proceedings, *Trudy I vserossiiskogo shenskogo s"ezda* (St. Petersburg, 1908), p. 784; transl. in Glickman, *Russian Factory Women*, p. 257.

73. Aleksandra Kollontai, "Zhenshchina-rabotnitsa v. sovremmenom obshchestve [The Woman Worker in Contemporary Society]," in *Trudy I vserossiiskogo*, pp. 800–801; as transl. in Clements, *Bolshevik Feminist*, p. 63.

74. Glickman, *Russian Factory Women*, p. 272.

75. Alexandra Kollontai, *The Autobiography of a Sexually Emancipated Communist Woman*, transl. Salvator Attanasio (New York: Herder & Herder, 1971), p. 41.

CHAPTER 8: NATIONALIZING FEMINISMS AND

FEMINIZING NATIONALISMS

1. Josefa Humpal Zeman, "The Women of Bohemia," *The Congress of Women Held in the Woman's Building, World's Columbian Exposition,*

Chicago, U.S.A., 1893, ed. Mary Kavanaugh Oldham Eagle (Chicago: W. B. Conkey,1894), vol. 1, p. 129.

2. Amy Hackett, "The German Women's Movement and Suffrage, 1890–1914: A Study of National Feminism," in *Modern European Social History*, ed. Robert Bezucha (Lexington: D.C. Heath, 1972), p. 354. See also Amy Hackett, "The Politics of Feminism in Wilhelmine Germany, 1890–1918," 2 vols. (Ph.D. dissertation, Columbia University, 1976). See also the still valuable work by Richard J. Evans, *The Feminist Movement in Germany, 1894–1933* (London & Beverly Hills, Calif.: Sage, 1976).

3. Paris and Berlin, 1896; Brussels, 1897; London, 1899; Paris, 1900; Berlin, 1904; Toronto, 1909; Brussels, 1912; Paris, 1913; and Rome, 1914. A full listing of the international congresses from 1878 to 1914, with their official titles, is in Ulla Wikander, "International Women's Congresses, 1878–1914: The Controversy over Equality and Special Labour Legislation," in *Rethinking Change: Current Swedish Feminist Research*, ed. Maud L. Eduards et al. (Uppsala: HSFR, distributed by Swedish Science Press, 1992), p. 14.

National congresses began to proliferate as well. The first Swiss women's rights congress took place in 1896; the first Italian congress, in 1908; the first Portuguese congress, in 1909.

4. See Leila J. Rupp, *Worlds of Women: The Making of an International Women's Movement* (Princeton: Princeton University Press, 1998). Thanks to Leila Rupp for allowing me to consult her manuscript before publication.

5. "Finsk Qvinnoforening, The Finnish Women's Association—Address by Baroness Gripenberg of Finland, Read by Meri Toppelius of Finland," *The World's Congress of Representative Women* (15–22 May 1893), ed. May Wright Sewall (Chicago & New York: Rand, McNally, 1894), p. 523.

6. Baroness Aleksandra Gripenberg, as quoted by Irma Sulkunen, "The Mobilisation of Women and the Birth of Civil Society," in *The Lady With the Bow: The Story of Finnish Women*, ed. Merja Manninen and Päivi Setälä, transl. Michael Wynne-Ellis (Helsinki: Otava, 1990), pp. 50–51. Irma Sulkunen has informed me that Gripenberg's speech of January 1897 was quoted in print by Lilli Lilius in the Finnish temperance publication *Kylväjä* (1898, no. 1), 2.

Sulkunen (p. 51) provides insight into this feminist attempt to redefine and revalue femininity with respect to national identity: "Motherhood emerges as the key concept in the new identity, but this characteristic does not relate to any traditional female role—as is often misleadingly thought—but to something quite new in content. Motherhood, that is the ability to care, bring up, understand, is considered woman's highest quality, and this must be freed from the debilitating and allegedly biological bonds of the traditional female role. The new institution of motherhood, energetic and caring in character, started by the women's rights activists themselves and supported by all 'progressive' organisations, began to penetrate the whole fabric of society to become the only acceptable qualification for citizenship for emancipated woman."

7. Alexandra [sic] Gripenberg, "The Great Victory in Finland" (29 June 1906), in *The Englishwoman's Review*, n.s., 38:3 (16 July 1906), 155–57; repr. in *WFF*, vol. 2, doc. 57 (quote, p. 230). English-language scholarship on feminist activism and the 1906 suffrage victory includes: Riitta Jallinoja, "The Women's Liberation Movement in Finland: The Social and Political Mobilisation of Women in Finland, 1880–1910," *Scandinavian Journal of History*, 5:1 (1980), 37–49; and Aura Korppi-Tommola, "Fighting Together for Freedom: Nationalism, Socialism, Feminism, and Women's Suffrage in Finland 1906," *Scandinavian Journal of History*, 15:3 (1990), 181–91. On the socialist women, see Maria Lähteenmäki, "The Foreign Contacts of the Finnish Working Women's Movement (c. 1900–18)," *Scandinavian Journal of History*, 13:1 (1988), 29–37.

8. See Martha Bohachevsky-Chomiak, *Feminists Despite Themselves: Women in Ukrainian Community Life 1884–1939* (Edmonton: Canadian Institute of Ukrainian Studies, University of Alberta, 1988).

9. Natalia Kobryns'ka, in *Nasha dolia*, vol. 2 (L'viv, 1895), p. 10; transl. in Martha Bohachevsky-Chomiak, "Natalia Kobryns'ka: A Formulator of Feminism," in *Nationbuilding and the Politics of Nationalism: Essays on Austrian Galicia*, ed. Andrei S. Markvits and Frank E. Sysyn (Cambridge, Mass.: Harvard University Press, 1982), p. 214.

10. On the Czech feminists' educational initiative, see Karen Johnson Freeze, "Medical Education for Women in Austria: A Study in the Politics of the Czech Women's Movement in the 1890s," in *Women, State, and Party in Eastern Europe*, ed. Sharon L. Wolchik & Alfred G. Meyer (Durham: Duke University Press, 1985), 51–63.

11. Petition to the Reichsrat, April 1890; transl. in Bohachevsky-Chomiak, *Feminists Despite Themselves*, pp. 87–88.

12. Kobrynsk'a, in *Nasha dolia*, vol. 2, p. 99; transl. in Bohachevsky-Chomiak, *ibid.*, p. 217.

13. Eleni Varikas, "The Women's Movement in Greece," unpublished paper presented at the conference on nineteenth-century European women's movements, Stuttgart/Birkach, June 1995, p. 1. See also Varikas,"La Révolte des dames: Génèse d'une conscience féministe dans la Grèce du XIXe siècle (1833–1917)" (Ph.D. dissertation, University of Paris VII, UER Histoire et Civilisation, 1986). A Greek-language version of Varikas's study was published in Athens in 1987; here, however, I have drawn on the French version. A recent article in English by Varikas is "Gender and National Identity in *fin de siècle* Greece," *Gender & History*, 5:2 (Summer 1993), 269–83.

14. "Callirrhoë Parren of Greece, Representing Her Country by the Particular Appointment of Queen Olga," in *World's Congress of Representative Women*, ed. Sewall, p. 28; and "The Solidarity of Human Interests—An Address by Callirrhoë Parren of Athens, Greece," *ibid.*, pp. 639, 640.

15. "The Real Queens," *Efimeris ton Kyrion*, 15 April 1907; transl. KO from the French rendering by Varikas, in "Révolte des dames," p. 402.

16. *Efimeris ton Kyrion*, 21 Feb. 1902; transl. KO from the French rendering by Varikas, *ibid.*, p. 335.

17. Parren, "Subjects and Objects," *Efimeris ton Kyrion*, 25 Oct. 1898; transl. KO from the French rendering by Varikas, *ibid.*, p. 425.

18. On the Belgian feminist movement, see especially the contributions by Denise De Weerdt, *En de Vrouwen? Vrouw, vrouwenbeweging en feminisme in belgie (1830–1960)* (Ghent: Masereelfonds, 1980); Denise Keymolen, Greet Castermans, & Miet Smet, *De Geschiedenis geweld aangedaan: De Strijd voor het vrouwenstemrecht, 1886–1948* (Antwerp: Nederlandische Boekhandel, 1981); the special issue *Féminismes* of *Sextant: Revue du Groupe interdisciplinaire d'études sur les femmes*, ed. Éliane Gubin, no. 1 (Winter 1993); and most recently Éliane Gubin, Valérie Piette, & Catherine Jacques, "Les Féminismes belges et français de 1830 à 1914: Une approche comparée," *Le Mouvement social*, no. 178 (Jan.–March 1997), 36–68, with bibliographical notes indicating earlier articles.

19. Patricia Penn Hilden, *Women, Work, and Politics: Belgium, 1830–1914* (Oxford & New York: Oxford University Press, 1993), p. 238. See also Marinette Bruwier, "Le Socialisme et les femmes," in *1885–1985: Du Parti Ouvrier Belge au Parti Socialiste, Mélanges publiés à l'occasion du centenaire du P.O.B. par l'Institute Émile Vandervelde* (Brussels, 1985), pp. 309–36.

20. See Karen Offen, "Exploring the Sexual Politics of Republican Nationalism," in *Nationhood and Nationalism in France: From Boulangism to the Great War, 1889–1918*, ed. Robert Tombs (London: HarperCollins, 1991), 195–209.

21. Hackett, "Politics of Feminism," vol. 1, iv.

22. See Katherine David, "Czech Feminists and Nationalism in the Late Habsburg Monarchy: 'The First in Austria,'" *Journal of Women's History*, 3:2 (Fall 1991), 26–45.

23. See the essays in *Suffrage and Beyond: International Feminist Perspectives*, ed. Caroline Daley & Melanie Nolan (Auckland: Auckland University Press; London: Pluto Press; New York: New York University Press, 1994). For a comparative analysis of the campaigns for woman suffrage, see Steven C. Hause and Anne R. Kenney, "The Limits of Suffragist Behavior: Legalism and Militancy in France, 1876–1922," *American Historical Review*, 86:4 (Oct. 1981), 781–806.

24. *Female Suffrage, a Letter from the Right Hon. W. E. Gladstone to Samuel Smith, M.P., 11 April 1892*. Originally published in London and reprinted by the American Women Remonstrants to the Extension of Suffrage to Women (n.p., n.d.); in *WFF*, vol. 2, doc. 55 (quote, p. 224).

25. Susan Elizabeth Gay, *A Reply to Mr. Gladstone's Letter on Woman Suffrage* (London, 1892); in *WFF*, vol. 2, doc. 56, p. 227.

26. On the NUWSS and WSPU campaigns, see Leslie Parker Hume, *The National Union of Women's Suffrage Societies* (New York: Garland, 1982); Andrew Rosen, *Rise Up, Women! The Militant Campaign of the Women's*

Social and Political Union, 1903–1914 (London: Routledge & Kegan Paul, 1974); Jill Norris & Jill Liddington, *One Hand Tied Behind Us: The Rise of the Women's Suffrage Movement* (London: Virago, 1978); Les Garner, *Stepping Stones to Women's Liberty: Feminist Ideas in the Women's Suffrage Movement 1900–1918* (London: Heinemann, 1984); and Sandra Stanley Holton, *Feminism and Democracy: Women's Suffrage and Reform Politics in Britain, 1900–1918* (Cambridge: Cambridge University Press, 1986). See also Midge Mackenzie, *Shoulder to Shoulder* (New York: Knopf, 1975); and Lisa Tickner, *Spectacle of Women: Imagery of the Suffrage Campaign* (London: Chatto & Windus, 1987).

27. Emmeline Pankhurst, in *Votes for Women*, no. 34 (29 Oct. 1908), 77–83 (quote, 81); repr. in *WFF*, vol. 2, doc. 61. This speech seems to offer a conclusive answer to Brian Harrison's puzzlement over the WSPU's move to militant tactics: see "The Art of Militancy: Violence and the Suffragettes, 1904–1914," in Brian Harrison, *Peaceable Kingdom: Stability and Change in Modern Britain* (Oxford: Clarendon Press, 1982), pp. 26–81.

28. See Rosemary Cullen Owens, *Smashing Times: A History of the Irish Suffrage Movement* (Dublin: Attic Press, 1984); Cliona Murphy, *The Women's Suffrage Movement and Irish Society in the Early Twentieth Century* (Philadelphia: Temple University Press, 1989); Margaret Ward, *Unmanageable Revolutionaries: Women in Irish Nationalism* (Dingle: Brandon, 1983; and London: Pluto Press); and *In Their Own Voice: Women and Irish Nationalism*, ed. Margaret Ward (Dublin: Attic Press, 1995). See also *Women in Ireland, 1800–1918: A Documentary History*, ed. Maria Luddy (Cork: Cork University Press, 1995). On Hanna Sheehy Skeffington, see Leah Levenson & Jerry H. Natterstad, *Hanna Sheehy Skeffington, Irish Feminist* (Syracuse: Syracuse University Press, 1986); and Maria Luddy, *Hanna Sheehy Skeffington* (Dublin: Dundalgon Press, 1995).

29. Resolution of the Irish Women's Franchise League, published in *Votes for Women*, no. 189 (20 Oct. 1911), 34. Endorsing the IWFL demands in *Votes for Women*, Christabel Pankhurst argued: "It is now too late in the world's history to create parliaments and grant constitutions without giving equal franchise rights to women. This wrong was done for the last time, so far as this Empire is concerned, in South Africa. It cannot be done in Ireland." See her article "Woman Suffragists and Irish Home Rule," in the issue cited above, 41.

30. Mary E. Cousins, Hon. Sec. I.W.F.L., "Letter to the Editor," *Votes for Women*, no. 215 (19 April 1912), 458. Christabel Pankhurst was equally furious with the Irish party's attitude: "Nothing more reactionary could be conceived," she wrote in the same issue, "than to establish a brand-new constitution which gives political rights to men only. . . . We are determined that Irishmen shall wait forever for Home Rule unless women are to have it too." See her "Votes for Irishwomen," *ibid.*, no. 215 (19 April 1912), 456.

31. See Beth McKillen, "Irish Feminism and Nationalist Separatism, 1914–23," *Eire—Ireland*, 17:3 (1982), 52–67; quotes, p. 59; from Mary Mac-

Swiney, writing in *The Irish Citizen*. For references on Constance Markievicz, see the notes to Chapter 9.

32. See, e.g., Pierre Rosenvallon, *Le Sacre du citoyen* (Paris: Gallimard, 1992); and Joan W. Scott, *Only Paradoxes to Offer* (Cambridge, Mass.: Harvard University Press, 1996). For another approach to French suffrage efforts, see the publications of Hause & Kenney, cited in previous chapters; and Karen Offen, "Women, Citizenship and Suffrage with a French Twist, 1789–1993," in *Suffrage and Beyond*, ed. Daley & Nolan, pp. 151–70.

33. René Viviani, as reported in *La Fronde* (10 Sept. 1900). The full speech is also published in the congress proceedings, *Congrès international de la condition et des droits des femmes, tenu les 5, 6, 7, et 8 septembre 1900*... (Paris: Imprimerie des Arts et Manufactures, 1901), p. 201.

34. Carrie Chapman Catt, address of 15 June 1913, in IWSA, *Report of the Seventh Congress, Budapest, Hungary, June 15–21, 1913* (Manchester, 1913), p. 85; repr. in *WFF*, vol. 2, doc. 64.

35. See Angus McLaren, *Sexuality and Social Order: The Debate over the Fertility of Women and Workers in France, 1770–1920* (New York: Holmes & Meier, 1983); Karen Offen, "Depopulation, Nationalism, and Feminism in Fin-de-Siècle France," *American Historical Review*, 89:3 (June 1984), 648–76; Richard Allen Soloway, *Birth Control and the Population Question in England, 1877–1930* (Chapel Hill: University of North Carolina Press, 1982); and Barbara Brooks, *Abortion in England, 1900–1967* (London: Croom Helm, 1988). Most recently, see Anne Cova, "French Feminism and Maternity: Theories and Policies, 1890–1918," in *Maternity and Gender Policies: Women and the Rise of the European Welfare States, 1880s–1950s*, ed. Gisela Bock & Pat Thane (London & New York: Routledge, 1991), pp. 119–37; and Cova's *Maternité et droits des femmes en France*.

36. See especially Anna Davin, "Imperialism and Motherhood," *History Workshop*, no. 5 (Spring 1978), 9–65. Much work remains to be done on these connections for countries other than England.

37. Evelyn Baring, First Earl of Cromer, speech at Manchester, as reported in the *Anti-Suffrage Review* (Nov. 1910), p. 10. Not surprisingly, such sentiments were expressed most vociferously in antisuffrage circles: see Brian Harrison, *Separate Spheres: The Opposition to Women's Suffrage in Britain* (London: Croom Helm; New York: Holmes & Meier, 1978); and Diane Trosino, "Anti-Feminism in Germany, 1912–1920: The German League for the Prevention of Women's Emancipation," Ph.D. dissertation, Claremont Graduate School, 1992. For antifeminism in Austria, see Birgitta Zaar, "Dem Mann die Politik, der Frau die Familie—Die Gegner des politischen Frauenstimmrechts in Österreich (1848–1919)," *Österreichische Zeitschrift für Politikwissenschaft*, 16:4 (1987), 351–61.

38. Figures provided by Louise Compain, in her report to the Tenth International Congress of Women, Paris, 1913. *Le Dixième Congrès international des femmes. Oeuvres et institutions féminines. Droits des femmes.*

Compte rendu des travaux, 1913, ed. Mme Avril de Sainte-Croix (Paris: Brieux & Giraud, 1914), pp. 232–33.

39. Wikander, "International Women's Congresses," p. 13. See also the editors' introduction and various essays in *Protecting Women: Labor Legislation in Europe, the United States, and Australia, 1880–1920,* ed. Ulla Wikander, Alice Kessler-Harris, & Jane Lewis (Urbana: University of Illinois Press, 1995).

40. See Mary Lynn Stewart, *Women, Work and the French State: Labour Protection and Social Patriarchy, 1879–1919* (Montreal: McGill–Queen's University Press, 1989); the pathbreaking essays in *Gender and the Politics of Social Reform in France, 1870–1914,* ed. Elinor A. Accampo, Rachel G. Fuchs, & Mary Lynn Stewart (Baltimore: Johns Hopkins University Press, 1995); and for comparisons with Britain, the essays in *Différence des sexes et protection sociale (XIXe–XXe siècles),* ed. Leora Auslander & Michelle Zancarini-Fournel (St. Denis: Presses Universitaires de Vincennes, 1995).

41. Paul Leroy-Beaulieu, "The Influence of Civilisation upon the Movement of the Population," *Journal of the Royal Statistical Society,* 54 (1891), 372–84.

42. Émile Faguet, in the *Journal des Débats* (12 Dec. 1895), 2; transl. in Susanna Barrows, *Distorting Mirrors: Visions of the Crowd in Late Nineteenth-Century France* (New Haven: Yale University Press), p. 59.

43. Marya Chéliga-Loevy, in *La Justice;* quoted in Clotilde Dissard, "Féminisme et natalité, *La Revue féministe,* 20 Nov. 1895, p. 176.

44. "Women's Work and the Factory Acts," *The Englishwoman's Review,* no. 228 (15 Jan. 1896), 7.

45. On Schreiner, see the references in Chapter 6. See also Joyce Avrech Berkman, *Olive Schreiner: Feminism on the Frontier* (Toronto: Eden Press, 1979); Ruth First & Ann Scott, *Olive Schreiner* (New York: Schocken Press, 1980); *An Olive Schreiner Reader,* ed. Carol Barash (London: Pandora Press, 1987); and Joyce Avrech Berkman, *The Healing Imagination of Olive Schreiner: Beyond South African Colonialism* (Amherst: University of Massachusetts Press, 1989). The Ellis quote is from Mrs. Havelock Ellis, "Political Militancy" (ca. 1913), in *The New Horizon in Love and Life* (London: A. & C. Black, 1921), p. 154.

46. Mrs. Sidney (Beatrice) Webb, in *Women and the Factory Acts,* Fabian Tract no. 67 (London, 1896); repr. in *WFF,* vol. 2, doc. 50 (quotes pp. 207, 211).

47. Alice Salomon, "Protective Legislation in Germany," in *Women in Industrial Life: The Transactions of the Industrial and Legislative Section of The International Congress of Women, London, July 1899,* vol. 6 of the proceedings (London: T. Fisher Unwin, 1900), pp. 38, 39. On Salomon, see Allen, *Feminism and Motherhood;* and Christoph Sachsse, *Mütterlichkeit als Beruf: Sozialarbeit, Sozialreform und Frauenbewegung 1871–1929* (Frankfurt-am-Main: Suhrkamp, 1986).

48. Beatrice Webb, "Special Legislation for Women," in *Women in Industrial Life,* pp. 40, 43.

49. See Marie-Helene Zylberberg-Hocquard, *Féminisme et syndicalisme en France* (Paris: Anthropos, 1978).

50. M. I. Pokrovskaia, in *Zhenskii Vestnik*, no. 5 (1906), 162–63, 148; transl. in Rose Glickman, *Russian Factory Women* (Berkeley & Los Angeles: University of California Press, 1984), p. 251.

51. See Ulla Jansz, "Women or Workers? The 1889 Labor Law and the Debate on Protective Legislation in the Netherlands," in *Protecting Women*, p. 199. See also Mineke Bosch, "Historiography and History of Dutch Feminism, 1860–1919," unpublished paper presented at Stuttgart/Birkach, June 1995.

52. See Marilyn J. Boxer, "Socialism Faces Feminism: The Failure of Synthesis in France, 1879–1914," in *Socialist Women: European Socialist Feminism in the Nineteenth and Early Twentieth Centuries*, ed. Marilyn J. Boxer & Jean H. Quataert (New York: Elsevier, 1978), pp. 75–111; quote, p. 111 n. 77. See also Charles Sowerwine, "Workers and Women in France Before 1914: The Debate over the Couriau Affair," *Journal of Modern History*, 55:3 (Sept. 1983), 411–41; and Jeremy Jennings, "The CGT and the Couriau Affair: Syndicalist Responses to Female Labour in France Before 1914," *European History Quarterly*, 21:3 (July 1991), 321–37.

53. On Denmark and Norway, see Anna-Birte Ravn, "'Lagging Far Behind All Civilized Nations': The Debate over Protective Legislation for Women in Denmark," and Gro Hagemann, "Protection or Equality? Debates on Protective Legislation," both in *Protecting Women*, pp. 210–34, 267–89.

54. Resolution, *Dixième Congrès international*, p. 519; transl. in Wikander, "International Women's Congresses," p. 32.

55. Jane Misme, "Un Congrès féministe à Paris," *La Revue* (1 July 1913), 58; Jeanne Crouzet-Benaben, "Une Assemblée des femmes en 1913: Le Congrès international de Paris (2–7 Juin)," *La Grande Revue* (10 July 1913), 64.

56. "Introduction," *Maternity and Gender Policies: Women and the Rise of the European Welfare States 1880s–1950s*, ed. Gisela Bock & Pat Thane (London & New York: Routledge, 1991), p. 14.

57. Mrs. Henry Fawcett (Millicent Garrett Fawcett), *Home and Politics: An Address Delivered at Toynbee Hall and Elsewhere* (London: Women's Printing Society, n.d.), p. 3.

58. Léonie Rouzade, transl. in Wynona H. Wilkins, "The Paris International Feminist Congress of 1896 and Its French Antecedents," *North Dakota Quarterly*, 43:4 (Autumn 1975), 5–28; quote, p. 23.

59. Ellen Key, *Missbrukad Kvinnokraft och Naturenliga arbetsområden för Kvinnan; Tvenne föedrag* (Stockholm: Albert Bonnier Förlag, 1896); in German, *Missbrauchte Frauenkraft*, transl. Therese Krüger (Leipzig, 1898). See Kay Goodman, "Motherhood and Work: The Concept of the Misuse of Women's Energy, 1895–1905," in *German Women in the Eighteenth and Nineteenth Centuries*, ed. Ruth-Ellen B(oetcher) Joeres & Mary Jo Maynes (Bloomington: Indiana University Press, 1986), pp. 110–27. For two oppos-

ing interpretations of Key's ideas, see Cheri Register, "Motherhood at Center: Ellen Key's Social Vision," *Women's Studies International Forum*, 5:6 (1982), 599–610; and Torborg Lundell, "Ellen Key and Swedish Feminist Views on Motherhood," *Scandinavian Studies*, 56:4 (Autumn 1984), 351–69. See also Ronald de Angelis, "Ellen Key: A Biography of the Swedish Social Reformer" (Ph.D. dissertation, University of Connecticut, 1978); and Ruth Roach Pierson, "Ellen Key: Maternalism and Pacifism," in *Delivering Motherhood: Maternal Ideologies and Practices in the Nineteenth and Twentieth Centuries*, ed. Katherine Arnup, Andrée Lévesque & Ruth Roach Pierson (London & New York: Routledge, 1990), pp. 270–83.

In Swedish, see Beata Losman, *Kamp för ett nytt kvonnoliv: Ellen Keys idéer och deras betydelse för sekelskriftets unga kvinnor* (Helsingborg: Liber, 1980); Ulla Manns, "Kvinnofragörelse och moderskap: En diskussion mellan Fredrika-Bremer-förbundet och Ellen Key" (Women's Freedom or Motherhood . . .), and Ellinor Melander, "Vän eller fiende? Ellen Keys mottagande i sekelskriftets tyska kvinnorörelse" (Friend or Foe: Ellen Key's Reception in the Turn-of-the-Century German Women's Movement), in *Det evigt Kvinnliga: En historia om förändring*, ed. Ulla Wikander (Stockholm: Tidens förlag, 1994), pp. 51–79, 103–32.

60. Ellen Key, *Love and Marriage*, transl. Arthur G. Chater (New York & London: G. P. Putnam's Sons, 1911); repr. in *WFF*, vol. 2, doc. 26 (quote, p. 123).

61. Ellen Key, *The Woman Movement*, transl. Mamah Bouton Borthwick, introd. Havelock Ellis (New York: G. P. Putnam's Sons, 1912; originally *Kvinnorörelsen*, Stockholm: Albert Bonnier, 1909), p. 191.

62. Annarita Buttafuoco, "Motherhood as a Political Strategy: The Role of the Italian Women's Movement in the Creation of the *Cassa Nazionale di Maternità*," in *Maternity and Gender Policies*, p. 180.

63. Manifesto of the League for the Protection of Motherhood, in *Archiv für Rassen- und Gesellschaftsbiologie*, 2 (1905), p. 164; transl. in Ann Taylor Allen, *Feminism and Motherhood in Germany, 1800–1914* (New Brunswick: Rutgers University Press, 1991), pp. 179–80.

64. In addition to Allen, *Feminism and Motherhood in Germany*, chap. 10, see Amy Hackett, "Helene Stöcker: Left-Wing Intellectual and Sex Reformer," in *When Biology Became Destiny: Women in Weimar and Nazi Germany*, ed. Renate Bridenthal, Atina Grossmann, & Marion Kaplan (New York: Monthly Review Press, 1984), pp. 109–30. See also Bernd Nowacki, *Der Bund für Mutterschutz, 1905–1933* (Husum: Matthiesen, 1983); Christl Wickert, *Helene Stöcker, 1869–1943: Frauenrechtlerin, Sexualreformerin und Pazifistin* (Bonn: Dietz, 1991); and Gudrun Hamelmann, *Helene Stöcker, der "Bund für Mutterschutz," und "Die Neue Generation"* (Frankfurt-am-Main: Haag & Herchen, 1992).

65. Helene Stöcker, ed. *Resolutionen des Deutschen Bundes für Mutterschutz, 1905–1916* (Berlin, 1916), transl. in *European Women: A Documentary History, 1789–1945*, ed. Eleanor S. Riemer and John C. Fout (New York:

Schocken Books, 1980), doc. 39, pp. 169–71; quotes (here and below), pp. 170, 171.

66. Bund Deutscher Frauenvereine, "Programm" (1907); transl. in Katharine Anthony, *Feminism in Germany and Scandinavia* (New York: Henry Holt, 1915), pp. 20–26, from the *Centralblatt des Bundes Deutscher Frauenvereine* (Berlin, July 1907); repr. in WFF, vol. 2, doc. 20 (quote, p. 102).

67. Katti Anker Møller, transl. in Ida Blom, "Voluntary Motherhood 1900–1930: Theories and Politics of a Norwegian Feminist in an International Perspective," in *Maternity and Gender Policies*, p. 23. On the inspiration from Møller and labor politics on Elise Ottesen-Jensen's subsequent campaigns for sex education, see Doris H. Linder, *Crusader for Sex Education: Elise Ottesen-Jensen (1886–1973) in Scandinavia and on the International Scene* (Lanham: University Press of America, 1996), chaps. 1 and 2.

68. See Offen, "Depopulation, Nationalism, and Feminism"; and Cova, "French Feminism and Maternity."

69. Nelly Roussel, letter published in *Régénération*, no. 22 (March 1903), 153; transl. KO. For scholarship on Roussel, see Chapter 7 n. 11.

70. Nelly Roussel, speech given at the women's meeting called to protest the centennial of the Civil Code, 29 Oct. 1904; publ. in *La Fronde*, 1 Nov. 1904; transl. KO in WFF, vol. 2, doc. 29 (quote, p. 136).

71. See Nelly Roussel, "L'Éternelle sacrifiée," transl. as "She Who Is Always Sacrificed," in *Feminisms of the Belle Époque*, ed. Jennifer Waelti-Walters & Steven C. Hause (Lincoln: University of Nebraska Press, 1994), pp. 18–41.

72. Lily Braun, "Introduction" to *Die Mutterschaft: Ein Sammelwerk für die Probleme des Weibes als Mutter*, ed. Adele Schreiber (Munich: A. Langen, 1912), pp. 3–4; transl. Alfred G. Meyer, in *Lily Braun: Selected Writings on Feminism and Socialism*, ed. Alfred G. Meyer (Bloomington: Indiana University Press, 1987), pp. 112–13.

73. Friedrich Naumann, *Neudeutsche Wirtschaftspolitik* (Berlin: Schöneberg, 1911), p. 37; transl. from the 1906 edition, pp. 30–31, in Hackett, "Politics of Feminism," vol. 1, pp. 332–34.

74. Kaiser Wilhelm II, speech of 25 Aug. 1910, in *Schulthess' europäischer Geschichtskalender, 1910* (Munich: C. H. Beck), p. 339; rev. transl. after Hackett, "Politics of Feminism," vol. 1, pp. 370–71. See also Heinrich Rosebrock, *Kaiser Wilhelm II und die Frauenfrage* (Berlin, 1910). My thanks to Diane Trosino Guido for assistance with the kaiser's speech.

75. Mona Caird, *Daughters of Danaus* (London: Bliss, Sands & Foster, 1894; repr. New York: Feminist Press, 1989), pp. 341, 343.

76. Sibilla Aleramo (pseud. Rina Faccio), *Una Donna* (1906); in English as *A Woman*, transl. Rosalind Delmar (Berkeley & Los Angeles: University of California Press, 1980), pp. 193–94. Within only a few years of its initial publication, this novel appeared in Spanish, English, Swedish, French, German, and Polish. See *Svelamento: Sibilla Aleramo intellettuale*, ed. Annarita Buttafuoco & Marina Zancan (Milan: Feltrinelli, 1988).

77. On Madeleine Pelletier, see the refs. in Chapter 7, n. 61. Additional translations of Pelletier's texts can be consulted in *Early French Feminisms, 1830–1940*, ed. Felicia Gordon & Máire Cross (Cheltenham: Edward Elgar, 1996), chaps. 5 and 6.

78. Madeleine Pelletier, "Le Droit à l'avortement," chap. 3 of *L'Émancipation sexualle de la femme* (Paris: M. Giard et E. Brière, 1911); transl. Marilyn J. Boxer, "'Feminism and the Family: The Right to Abortion,' by Madeleine Pelletier," *The French-American Review*, 6:1 (Spring 1982), 3–26; quotes, pp. 15, 17.

79. See Allen, *Feminism and Motherhood in Germany*, pp. 188–89. For another comparison, see Elisabeth Elgán, *Genus och politik: En jämförelse mellan svensk och fransk abort- och preventiv-medelspolitik fran sekelskiftet till andra väridskriget* (Gender and Politics: A Comparison of Swedish and French Abortion and Contraceptive Policies from the Turn of the Century to the Second World War), Acta Universitatis Upsaliensis, Studia Historica Upsaliensis, 176 (Uppsala, 1994).

80. S(ebald) R(udolf) Steinmetz, "Feminismus und Rasse," *Zeitschrift für Sozialwissenschaft*, 7 (1904), 752; transl. in Allen, *Feminism and Motherhood*, p. 189. See also his earlier attack *Het feminisme* (Leiden, 1899). I am grateful to Ann Taylor Allen for transmitting the full text of Steinmetz's German article.

81. Allen, *Feminism and Motherhood*, p. 193.

82. E(mma) Pieczynska(-Reichenbach), *L'École de la pureté* (Geneva: Eggimann, 1897). The best work to date on Pieczynska-Reichenbach remains E. Serment, "Emma Pieczynska, née Reichenbach, dans ses oeuvres," *Annuaire des femmes suisses 1926/27*, 10 (1927), pp. 81–111.

83. Dr. Alfred Mjøen, "Legal Certificates of Health Before Marriage: Personal Health-Declaration versus Medical Examination," transl. Dr. Bergen, in *The Eugenics Review*, 4:4 (Jan. 1913), 362; orig. publ. in the Norwegian women's-rights journal *Nyelande* (April 1912); repr. in *WFF*, vol. 2, doc. 53 (quote, p. 217).

84. Christabel Pankhurst, "A Woman's Question," in *Plain Facts About a Great Evil* (London, 1913); originally published in *The Suffragette*, 8 August 1913; as reprinted in *WFF*, vol. 2, doc. 54; quotes, pp. 219–20. On Christabel Pankhurst's feminism, see David J. Mitchell, *Queen Christabel: A Biography of Christabel Pankhurst* (London: Macdonald and Jane's, 1977); and Elizabeth Sarah, "Christabel Pankhurst: Reclaiming Her Power," in *Feminist Theorists: Three Centuries of Key Women Thinkers*, ed. Dale Spender (New York: Pantheon, 1983). For background on her critique of male sexuality, see Sheila Jeffreys, *The Spinster and Her Enemies: Feminism and Sexuality, 1880–1930* (London: Pandora Press, 1985); and for an excellent collection of sources, see *The Sexuality Debates*, ed. Sheila Jeffreys (London & New York: Routledge & Kegan Paul, 1987). A bold argument connecting sexual emancipation and suffrage demands can be found in Susan Kingsley Kent, *Sex and Suffrage in Britain, 1860–1914* (Princeton: Princeton University Press, 1987). Compare also Lucy Bland, *Banishing the*

Beast: English Feminism and Sexual Morality, 1885–1914 (New York: The New Press, 1995); and Laura E. Nym Mayhall, "'Dare to Be Free': The Women's Freedom League, 1907–1918," Ph.D. dissertation, Stanford University, 1993.

For comparable concerns in the Netherlands, see *De eerste feministische golf: 6de Jaarboek voor Vrouwengeschiedenis,* ed. Jeske Reys et al. (Nijmegen: SUN, 1985); Ulla Jansz, *Denken over sekse in de eerste feministische golf* (Amsterdam: Van Gennup, 1990); and Marianne Braun, *De prijs van de liefde: De eerste feministische golf, het hywelijksrecht en de vaderlandse geschiedenis* (Amsterdam: Het Spinhuis, 1992).

85. Christabel Pankhurst, "What Women Think," in *The Great Scourge and How to End It* (1913); repr. in *The Sexuality Debates*: quote, pp. 333–34.

86. Bertha von Suttner, *Das Maschinenzeitalter: Zukunftsvorlesungen über unsere Zeit* (Dresden & Leipzig, 1899; orig. publ. Zurich, 1889), pp. 165–66; transl. SGB in *WFF*, vol. 2, doc. 12 (quote, p. 72). On Suttner, see Brigitte Hamann, *Bertha von Suttner: A Life for Peace,* transl. Ann Dubsky, introd. Irwin Abrams (Syracuse: Syracuse University Press, 1996; orig. publ. Munich, 1987); and Regina Braker, *Weapons of Women Writers: Bertha von Suttner's "Die Waffen nieder!" as Political Literature in the Tradition of Harriet Beecher Stowe's "Uncle Tom's Cabin"* (New York: Peter Lang, 1995).

87. Bertha von Suttner, *Lay Down Your Arms: The Autobiography of Martha von Tilling,* transl. T. Holmes (London: Longmans, 1894; repr. New York: Garland, 1972), p. 255.

88. See the manifesto of the Ligue des Femmes pour le Désarmement International, reproduced in Caïel (pseud. of Alice Pestana), *La Femme et la paix: Appel aux mères portugueses* (Lisbon: Imprensa nacional, 1898), pp. 52–54. For the 1899 effort mounted by Selenka on the occasion of the Hague Peace Conference, see Margarethe Lenore Selenka, *La Manifestation internationale des femmes pour la Conference de la Paix du 15 mai 1899* (Munich: A. Schupp, 1900). This work also appeared with German and English titles, and contained a full set of translations of the various texts and petitions. Selenka's group presented the peace conference with a petition signed by over a million women. On these efforts, see Sandi E. Cooper, "The Work of Women in Nineteenth Century Continental European Peace Movements," *Peace & Change,* 9:4 (Winter 1984), 11–38. For Belgium and Sweden, see Nadine Lubelski-Bernard, "The Participation of Women in the Belgian Peace Movement (1830–1914)," in *Women and Peace: Theoretical, Historical, and Practical Perspectives,* ed. Ruth Roach Pierson (London: Croom Helm; New York: Routledge, Chapman & Hall, 1987), pp. 76–89; and Abby Peterson, *Women as Collective Political Actors: A Case Study of the Swedisn Women's Peace Movement, 1898–1990,* Research Report no. 107 (Gothenburg: Department of Sociology, University of Gothenburg, 1992).

89. Heinrich von Treitschke, "The Family," chap. 7 of *Politics,* transl.

Blanche Dugdale & Torben de Bille (New York: Macmillan, 1916; orig. publ. as *Politik*, 2d ed., Leipzig, 1899–1900), vol. 1, p. 248. See Sybil Oldfield, "The Dubious Legacy of Bismarck and von Treitschke," chap. 1 of *Women Against the Iron Fist: Alternatives to Militarism, 1900–1989* (Oxford: Basil Blackwell, 1989), pp. 3–18.

90. Theodore Joran, *Le Mensonge du féminisme* (Paris: Jouve, 1905), p. 295, and *Autour du féminisme* (Paris: Plon, 1906), pp. 20–21.

91. Filippo Tommaso Marinetti, "The Futurist Manifesto," in *Marinetti: Selected Writings*, ed. R. W. Flint, transl. R. W. Flint & Arthur A. Coppotelli (New York: Farrar, Straus and Giroux, 1972), p. 42.

92. Annelise Mauge, *L'Identité masculine en crise au tournant du siècle* (Marseille: Éditions Rivages, 1987), p. 8.

93. Valentine de Saint-Point, "Manifeste de la femme futuriste: Réponse à F. T. Marinetti" (25 March 1912); repr. in *Futurisme: Manifestes, proclamations, documents*, ed. Giovanni Lista (Lausanne: Éditions d'Age d'homme, 1973), pp. 329–32 (quote, p. 330; transl. KO). This text was read by the author at avant-garde gallery presentations in Brussels and Paris during the late spring and summer of 1912, and published in Italian, French, and German.

94. Oliver Schreiner, "Woman and War," in *Woman and Labour* (1911; repr. London: Virago, 1978); quotes, pp. 169, 178. This text can also be consulted in *An Olive Schreiner Reader*, ed. Carol Barash (London: Pandora Press, 1987), pp. 198–211.

95. Cooper, "Work of Women," 11.

96. Fanny Clar, "Le Mensonge des trois ans," *L'Équité*, 15 March 1913; repr. in *Le Grief des femmes: Anthologie des textes féministes du Second Empire à nos jours*, ed. Maïté Albistur and Daniel Armogathe (Paris: Éditions hier et demain, 1978), p. 202; transl. KO.

97. Concerning Maria Vérone's sensational speech, see *La Française*, 23 May 1914, p. 1, and Mary Sheepshanks, "The Suffrage Meeting in Rome, May 15, 1914," *Jus Suffragii*, 8:11 (1 July 1914), 137–38. I was unable to locate a published text of this speech.

PART III: THE TWENTIETH CENTURY

1. Gisela Kaplan, *Contemporary Western European Feminism* (New York: New York University Press, 1992), p. 283.

2. M(ary) Sargant Florence & C. K. Ogden, "Women's Prerogative," *Jus Suffragii*, 9:4 (1 Jan. 1915), 218–19; see also their brochure *Militarism versus Feminism* (1915), repr. in *Militarism versus Feminism: Writings on Women and War*, ed. Margaret Kamester & Jo Vellacott (London: Virago, 1987).

3. Rosa Mayreder, "Geschlecht und Sozialpolitik," in her *Geschlecht und Kultur* (Jena: Eugen Diederichs, 1923), p. 108; transl. in Harriet Anderson, *Utopian Feminism: Women's Movements in Fin-de-Siècle Vienna* (New Haven: Yale University Press, 1992), p. 172.

4. On women's participation in World War I and its effects on them, see the essays in *Behind the Lines: Gender and the Two World Wars*, ed. Mar-

garet Randolph Higonnet, Jane Jenson, Sonya Michel, & Margaret Collins Weitz (New Haven: Yale University Press, 1987); Diana Condell & Jean Liddiard, *Working for Victory? Images of Women in the First World War 1914–1918* (London: Routledge & Kegan Paul, 1987); and various essays in *The Upheaval of War: Family, Work and Welfare in Europe, 1914–1918*, ed. Richard Wall & Jay Winter (Cambridge: Cambridge University Press, 1989). See especially Françoise Thébaud, *La Femme au temps de la guerre de '14* (Paris: Stock, 1986); and her masterful comparative essay, "The Great War and the Triumph of Sexual Division," in *Toward a Cultural Identity in the Twentieth Century*, ed. Françoise Thébaud, vol. 5 of *A History of Women in the West*, ed. Georges Duby & Michelle Perrot (Cambridge, Mass.: Harvard University Press, 1994), pp. 21–75. On Russia, see Alfred G. Meyer, "The Impact of World War I on Russian Women's Lives," in *Russia's Women: Accommodation, Resistance, Transformation*, ed. Barbara Evans Clements, Barbara Alpern Engel, & Christine D. Worobec (Berkeley & Los Angeles: University of California Press, 1991), pp. 208–24.

5. Recent studies on women's formal participation in national parliaments and other governmental bodies between 1914 and 1950 include:

For England, Beverly Parker Stobaugh, *Women and Parliament, 1918–1970* (Hicksville: Exposition Press, 1978); Melanie Phillips, *The Divided House: Women at Westminster* (London: Sidgwick & Jackson, 1980); Brian Harrison, "Women in a Men's House: The Women MPs, 1919–1945," *The Historical Journal*, 29:3 (Sept. 1986), 623–54; and Patricia Hollis, *Ladies Elect: Women in English Local Government, 1865–1914* (Oxford: Clarendon Press, 1987).

For France, see Siân Reynolds, "Women and the Popular Front in France: The Case of the Three Women Ministers," *French History*, 8:2 (June 1994), 196–224; and Paul Smith, *Feminism and the Third Republic: Women's Political and Civil Rights in France 1918–1945* (Oxford: Clarendon Press, 1996).

For Austria, see Gabriella Hauch, *Vom Frauenstandpunkt aus: Frauen im Parlament, 1919–1933* (Vienna: Verlag für Gesellschaftskritik, 1995); see also Hauch, "Rights at Last? The First Generation of Female Members of Parliament in Austria," *Women in Austria*, special issue of *Contemporary Austrian Studies*, vol. 6, ed. Günther Bishop, Anton Pelinka, & Erika Thurner (New Brunswick & London: Transaction, 1998), 55–82. See also the essays by Birgitta Bader-Zaar, "Women in Austrian Politics, 1890–1934: Goals and Visions," and Gerda Neyer, "Women in the Austrian Parliament: Opportunities and Barriers," both in *Austrian Women in the Nineteenth and Twentieth Centuries*, ed. David F. Good, Margarete Grandner, & Mary Jo Maynes (Providence: Berghahn Books, 1996).

For Germany, see Patricia K. Fessenden, "The Role of Women Deputies in the German National Constituent Assembly and the Reichstag, 1919–1933," Ph.D. dissertation, Ohio State University, 1976; and "More than a Question of Numbers: Women Deputies in the German National Constituent Assembly and the Reichstag, 1919–1933," in *Proceedings of the Second*

Annual Women in German Symposium, ed. Kay Goodman & Ruth H. Sanders (Oxford, Ohio: n.p., 1977), pp. 80–98; Christl Wickert, *Unsere Erwählten: Sozialdemokratische Frauen im deutschen Reichstag und im preussischen Landtag 1919 bis 1933,* 2 vols. (Göttingen: Sovec, 1986). See also Claudia Koonz, "Conflicting Allegiances: Political Ideology and Women Legislators in Weimar Germany," *Signs,* 1:3, pt. 1 (Spring 1976), 663–83.

For Spain, see Judith Keene, "'Into the Clear Air of the Plaza:' Spanish Women Achieve the Vote in 1931," *Constructing Spanish Womanhood: Female Identity in Modern Spain,* ed. Victoria L. Enders & Pamela Ratcliff (Albany: SUNY Press, 1999).

For Denmark, see Drude Dahlerup, *The Women's Sections within the Political Parties of Denmark: Their History, Function and Importance—for the Political Parties, for Women, and for Feminism* (Aarhus: Institute of Political Science, University of Aarhus, 1978).

For Sweden, see Sondra Herman, "Feminists, Socialists, and the Genesis of the Swedish Welfare State 1919–1945," in *Views of Women's Lives in Western Tradition,* ed. F. R. Keller (Lewiston: Edwin Mellen Press, 1990), pp. 472–510; see also *Kvinnors Roest och Raett* (Women's Vote and Rights), ed. Ruth Harmrin-Thorell, Ulla Lindstrom, & Gunborg Stenberg (Stockholm: Allmaennaförlag, 1969).

For Ireland: Maurice Manning, "Women in Irish National and Local Politics, 1922–77," in *Women in Irish Society: The Historical Dimension,* ed. Margaret MacCurtain & Donncha O'Corrain (Dublin: Arlen House, The Women's Press, 1978), pp. 92–102.

For Belgium, see Anna Morelli, "L'Action parlementaire des premières femmes députés belges, 1929–1945," in *Femmes, libertés, laïcité,* ed. Yolande Mendes da Costa & Anne Morelli (Brussels: Éditions de l'Université de Bruxelles, 1989), pp. 59–70.

6. "Die erste Parlementrede einer Frau in Deutschland," *Die Gleichheit,* 14 March 1919; transl. in Karen Hagemann, "Men's Demonstrations and Women's Protest: Gender in Collective Action in the Urban Working-Class Milieu during the Weimar Republic," *Gender & History,* 5:1 (Spring 1993), 101.

7. See the essays by Françoise Thébaud, Anne-Marie Sohn, Victoria De Grazia, Gisela Bock, Danièle Bussy Génevois, Hélène Eck, and Françoise Navailh in *Toward a Cultural Identity,* ed. Thébaud; in a review of this work, I characterized this cluster of otherwise stellar essays as "a gloomy collage": see Karen Offen, "Women in the Western World," *Journal of Women's History,* 7:2 (Summer 1995), 145–51.

8. On women and national population politics, see all the essays in *Maternity and Gender Policies: Women and the Rise of the European Welfare States, 1880s–1950s,* ed. Gisela Bock & Pat Thane (London & New York: Routledge, 1991). Of particular relevance to this study are the essays by Mary Nash, "Pronatalism and Motherhood in Franco's Spain," pp. 160–77; and Karen Offen, "Body Politics: Women, Work, and the Politics of Moth-

erhood in France, 1920–1950," pp. 138–59. See also the following pertinent articles: Denise Destragiache, "Un Aspect de la politique démographique de l'Italie fasciste: La Repression de l'avortement," *Mélanges de l'École française de Rome*, 92:2 (1980), 691–735; Marie-Monique Huss, "Pronatalism in the Inter-War Period in France," *Journal of Contemporary History*, 25:1 (Jan. 1990), 39–68; Cheryl A. Koos, "Gender, Anti-Individualism, and Nationalism: The *Alliance Nationale* and the Pronatalist Backlash Against the *Femme moderne*, 1933–1940," *French Historical Studies*, 19:3 (Spring 1996), 699–723.

On Russia, see Laura Engelstein, "Abortion and the Civic Order: The Legal and Medical Debates," in *Russia's Women: Accommodation, Resistance, Transformation*, ed. Barbara Evans Clements, Barbara Alpern Engel, & Christine D. Worobec (Berkeley & Los Angeles: University of California Press, 1991), pp. 185–207; and in the same volume, Wendy Goldman, "Women, Abortion, and the State, 1917–1936," pp. 243–66. See also Susan Gross Solomon, "The Demographic Argument in Soviet Debates over the Legalization of Abortion in the 1920s," *Cahiers du monde russe et soviétique*, 33:1 (1992), 59–81.

On Germany, see Jill Stephenson, "'Reichsbund der Kinderreichen': The League of Large Families in the Population Policy of Nazi Germany," *European Studies Review*, 9:3 (July 1979), 351–75; Cornelie Usborne, *The Politics of the Body in Weimar Germany: Women's Reproductive Rights and Duties* (London: Routledge, 1992); also her "Abortion in Weimar Germany—The Debate Amongst the Medical Profession," *Continuity and Change*, 5:2 (Aug. 1990), 199–224. See also Gisela Bock, *Zwangssterilisation im Nationalsozialismus: Studien zur Rassenpolitik und Frauenpolitik* (Opladen: Westdeutscher Verlag, 1986); and Bock, "Antinatalism, Maternity and Paternity in National Socialist Racism," in *Maternity and Gender Policies*, 233–55; Atina Grossmann, "Abortion and Economic Crisis: The 1931 Campaign Against Paragraph 218," in *When Biology Became Destiny: Women in Weimar and Nazi Germany*, ed. Renate Bridenthal, Atina Grossmann, & Marion Kaplan (New York: Monthly Review Press, 1984), pp. 66–86; and Fridolf Kudlein, "The German Response to the Birth-Rate Problem During the Third Reich," *Continuity and Change*, 5:2 (Aug. 1990), 225–47.

On Sweden, see Ann-Katrin Hatje, *Bevolkningsfrågan och välfärden: Debatten om familjepolitik och nativitetsökning under 1930- och 1940-talen* (The Population Question and Prosperity: The Debate About Family Policy and the Rise of the Birth Rate in the 1930s and 1940s) (Stockholm: Allmäna Förlaget, 1974); Ann-Sofie Kälvemark (Ohlander), *More Children of Better Quality? Aspects of Swedish Population Policy in the 1930s* (Uppsala: Studia historica Upsaliensia, 115; distrib. by Almqvist & Wiksell, Stockholm, 1980); and Ann-Sofie Ohlander, "The Invisible Child? The Struggle for a Social Democratic Family Policy in Sweden, 1900–1960s," in *Maternity and Gender Policies*, pp. 60–72. See also Ida Blom, "Voluntary Motherhood 1900–1930: Theories and Politics of a Norwegian Feminist in an International Perspective," in *Maternity and Gender Policies*, pp. 21–39; and Doris H. Linder, *Crusader for Sex Education: Elise Ottesen-Jensen (1886–1973) in Scandinavia and on the International Scene* (Lanham: University Press of America, 1996).

A more male-centered perspective is available in the otherwise skillful overview by Michael S. Teitelbaum and Jay M. Winter, *The Fear of Population Decline* (Orlando: Academic Press, 1985). This book speaks in terms of "French obsession" and "British emphasis," without posing the question of "who" specifically feared population decline and why.

9. Efforts to restrict women's access to university education were made in England, Hungary, Nazi Germany, and other countries. I have not yet located any comprehensive studies of these initiatives, which were doubtless tracked by the International Federation of University Women (IFUW), founded in 1920. The work of Alison Mackinnon on the IFUW from an Australian and British perspective may help to shed further light on these issues; research is needed on the parallel continental European developments.

10. With regard to post–World War I developments in women's employment, see, among other works: for France, Annie Fourcaut, *Femmes à l'usine: Ouvrières et surintendantes dans les entreprises françaises de l'entre-deux-guerres* (Paris: Maspero, 1982); for Russia, Melanie Ilič, *Women Workers in the Soviet Inter-War Economy: From "Protection" to "Equality"* (Houndmills: Macmillan; New York, St. Martin's Press,1999); for the Netherlands, Francisca De Haan, *Gender and the Politics of Officework: The Netherlands 1860–1940* (Amsterdam: Amsterdam University Press, 1998); for Greece, Efi Avdela, "Rapports salariaux et division sexuelle du travail: Les Femmes fonctionnaires dans la première moitié du 20e siècle en Grèce," doctoral thesis, University of Paris VII, 1989; and for Italy, the later essays and bibliography in *Il lavoro delle donne*, ed. Angela Groppi (Rome & Bari: Laterza, 1996).

On European women's participation in labor unions after 1918, see the essays in *The World of Women's Trade Unionism: Comparative Historical Essays*, ed. Norbert C. Soldon (Westport: Greenwood Press, 1985), including Theresa McBride, ' French Women and Trade Unionism: The First Hundred Years"; see also *Women and Trade Unions in Eleven Industrialized Countries*, ed. Alice H. Cook, Va. R. Lorwin, and Arlene Kaplan Daniels (Philadelphia: Temple University Press, 1984). For England, see the essays in *Women in the Labour Movement: The British Experience*, ed. Lucy Middleton (London: Croom Helm, 1977); Norbert C. Soldon, *Women in British Trade Unions, 1874–1976* (Dublin: Gill & Macmillan, 1978); and Pamela M. Graves, *Labour Women: Women in British Working-Class Politics, 1918–1939* (Cambridge: Cambridge University Press, 1994). For Ireland, see Mary E. Daly, "Women, Work and Trade Unionism," in *Women in Irish Society*, ed. MacCurtain & O'Corrain, pp. 71–81.

11. Works that discuss efforts to reconfigure gender during the first decade following World War I include Klaus Theweleit, *Male Fantasies*, 2 vols.

(Minneapolis: University of Minnesota Press, 1987–89); Susan Kingsley Kent, *Making Peace: The Reconstruction of Gender in Interwar Britain* (Princeton: Princeton University Press, 1993); and Mary Louise Roberts, *Civilization Without Sexes: Reconstructing Gender in Postwar France, 1917–1927* (Chicago & London: University of Chicago Press, 1994). On the contrasting situation in Russia, see Elizabeth A. Wood, *The Baba and the Comrade: Gender and Politics in Postrevolutionary Russia* (Bloomington: Indiana University Press, 1997).

12. Recent works concerning the cultural and literary productions of women in the period 1920–50 include: *Textual Liberation: European Feminist Writing in the Twentieth Century*, ed. Helena Forsås-Scott (London & New York: Routledge, 1991); and *Women Writers in Russian Modernism: An Anthology*, transl. & ed. Temira Pachmuss (Urbana: University of Illinois Press, 1978). See also the Athlone Press series (London & Atlantic Highlands) including (to date) Janet Garton, *Norwegian Women's Writing, 1850–1990* (1993); Sharon Wood, *Italian Women's Writing, 1860–1994* (1995); Diana Holmes, *French Women's Writing, 1848–1994* (1996); Helena Forsås-Scott, *Swedish Women's Writing, 1850–1995*; and Catherine Davies, *Spanish Women's Writing, 1849–1996* (1998). See also *Scandinavian Women Writers: An Anthology from the 1880s to the 1980s*, ed. Ingrid Claréus (Westport: Greenwood Press, 1989); and *The Longman Anthology of World Literature by Women 1875–1975*, ed. Marian Arkin & Barbara Shollar (New York & London: Longman, 1989). On women's arts and letters in the international cultural capital of Paris, see Whitney Chadwick, *Women Artists and the Surrealist Movement* (London: Thames & Hudson, 1985); Shari Benstock, *Women of the Left Bank: Paris, 1900–1940* (Austin: University of Texas Press, 1987); Gillian Perry, *Women Artists and the Parisian Avant-Garde* (Manchester: Manchester University Press, 1995); and Paula J. Birnbaum, "Femmes Artistes Modernes: Women, Art, and Modern Identity in Interwar France," Ph.D. dissertation, Bryn Mawr College, 1996. For Germany, see *Visions of the "Neue Frau": Women and the Visual Arts in Weimar Germany*, ed. Marsha Meskimmon & Sharon West (Aldershot: Scolar Press; Brookfield: Ashgate, 1995).

13. Recent studies of women in religiously affiliated women's movements after 1914 include:

For France, on the Patriotic League of French Women, Anne-Marie Sohn, "Catholic Women and Political Affairs," in *Women in Culture and Politics: A Century of Change*, ed. Judith Friedlander et al. (Bloomington: Indiana University Press, 1986), pp. 237–55; and Odile Sarti, *The Ligue Patriotique des Françaises, 1902–1933: A Feminine Response to the Secularization of French Society* (New York & London: Garland, 1992); also Sylvie Fayet-Scribe, *Associations féminines et catholicisme, XIXe–XXe siècle* (Paris: Éditions ouvrières, 1990); and, more generally, on organizations of Protestant and Catholic women, Evelyne Diebolt, "Les Associations face aux institutions: Les Femmes dans l'action sanitaire, sociale et culturelle (1900–1965)," doctoral thesis, University of Paris VII, 1993; and, in English, Diebolt, "Women and Philanthropy in France," working paper, Graduate School and University Center, City University of New York, Center for the Study of Philanthropy, 1996.

For the Italian Catholic women's movement, Paola Gaiotti di Biase, *Le origini del movimento cattolica femminile* (Brescia: Marcelliana, 1963); *Il femminismo cristiano: La question femminile nella prima democrazia cristiana (1898–1912)*, ed. Francesco Maria Ceccini (Rome: Riuniti, 1979); Michela De Giorgio & Paola Di Cori, "Politica e sentimento: Le organizzazioni femminili cattoliche dall'età giolittiana al fascismo," *Rivista di storia contemporanea*, 9:3 (July 1980), 337–71; Stefania Portaccio, "La donna nella stampa popolare cattolica: *Famiglia Cristiana*, 1931–1945," *Italia Contemporanea*, no. 143 (April–June 1981), 45–68; and Cecilia Dau Novelli, "'Daremo sei milioni di voti': Il movimento delle donne cattoliche nei primi anni della Repubblica," *Memoria*, no. 21 (1987), 45–55.

For Germany and Austria, Maria Elisabeth Backhaus, *Probleme des Frauenbilds der katholischen Frauenbewegung Deutschlands seit 1900* (Aachen: Paedogogische Hochschule, 1979); Alfred Kall, *Katholische Frauenbewegung in Deutschland: Eine Untersuchung zur Gründung katholischer Frauenvereine im 19. Jahrhundert* (Paderborn: F. Schoningh, 1983); Doris Kaufmann, "Von Vaterland zum Mutterland: Frauen im katholischen Milieu der weimarer Republik," in *Frauen suchen ihre Geschichte*, ed. Karin Hausen (Munich: C. H. Beck, 1983), pp. 250–75; also Kaufmann, *Frauen zwischen Aufbruch und Reaktion: Protestantische Frauenbewegung in der ersten Hälfte des 20. Jahrhunderts* (Munich: Piper, 1988); Friedrich Steinkellner, "Emanzipatorische Tendenzen im christlichen wiener Frauen-Bund und in der katholischen Reichsfrauenorganisation Österreichs," in *Unterdrückung und Emanzipation: Festschrift für Erika Weinzierl*, ed. R. G. Ardelt et al. (Vienna: Geyer-Edition, 1985), pp. 55–67; and Ursula Baumann's and Birgit Sack's articles on confessional women's movements, in Irmtraud Götz von Oleuhusen et al., *Frauen unter dem Patriarchat der Kirchen* (Stuttgart: Kohlhammer, 1995); Laura S. Gellott, "Mobilizing Conservative Women: The Viennese Katholische Frauenorganisation in the 1920s," *Austrian History Yearbook*, 22 (1991), pp. 110–30.

For the Netherlands, Mieke Aerts, "Catholic Constructions of Femininity: Three Dutch Women's Organizations in Search of a Politics of the Personal, 1912–1940," in *Women in Culture and Politics*, ed. Judith Friedlander et al. (Bloomington: Indiana University Press, 1986); and the articles in *Naar natuurlijk bestel: Vrouwenorganisaties in de jaren dertig* (Women's Organizations in the Thirties), ed. Werkgroep Vrouwen en Fascisme (Amsterdam: SUA, 1980).

14. Recent studies on women's participation in secular (nonfeminist) political women's organizations include:

On the noncommunist Labour and Socialist International, Christine Collette, "Gender and Class in the Labour and Socialist International 1923 to 1939," in *Geschlecht-Klasse-Ethnizität*, ed. Gabriella Hauch (Vienna & Zurich: Europa Verlag, 1993), pp. 229–40.

For France, Charles Sowerwine, *Sisters or Citizens? Women and Socialism in France since 1876* (Cambridge: Cambridge University Press, 1982), pt. 3.

For Denmark, Drude Dahlerup, "Kvinders organisering i det danske socialdemokrati, 1908–1969," *Meddelelser om forskning i arbejder-bevaegelsens Historie*, no. 13 (Oct. 1979), 5–35.

On women and the German SPD during the Weimar Republic, Renate Pore, *A Conflict of Interest: Women in German Social Democracy, 1919–1933* (Westport: Greenwood Press, 1981); the essays of Ute Daniel, Ute Frevert, Karen Hagemann, and Alfred G. Meyer on women and social democracy, in *Bernstein to Brandt: A Short History of German Social Democracy*, ed. Roger Fletcher (London: E. Arnold, 1987); also Karen Hagemann's argument that space for women's autonomous protest actions actually narrowed in the 1920s as left political parties (both social-democratic and communist) developed a more militarist and increasingly violent street activity: "Men's Demonstrations and Women's Protest: Gender in Collective Action in the Urban Working-Class Milieu during the Weimar Republic," *Gender & History*, 5:1 (Spring 1993), 101–19.

For Austrian social democracy between war and annexation, Thomas Lewis Hamer, "Beyond Feminism: The Women's Movement in Austrian Social Democracy, 1890–1926," Ph.D. dissertation, Ohio State University, 1973; and Edith Prost, ed. *'Die Partei hat mich nie enttäuscht': Osterreichische Sozialdemokratinnen* (Vienna: Verlag für Gesellschaftskritik, 1989).

On women and the national communist parties and their fascist opponents: for England, Sue Bruley, *Leninism, Stalinism and the Women's Movement in Britain, 1920–1939* (New York: Garland, 1986); Tricia Davis, "'What Kind of Woman Is She?' Women and Communist Party Politics, 1941–55," in *Feminism, Culture and Politics*, ed. Rosalind Brunt & Caroline Rowan (London: Lawrence & Wishart, 1982), 85–107; Martin Durham, "Women in the British Union of Fascists, 1932–1940," in *This Working-Day World: Women's Lives and Culture(s) in Britain, 1914–1945*, ed. Sybil Oldfield (London: Taylor & Francis, 1994). For Weimar Germany, Silvia Kontos, *Die Partei kämpft wie ein Mann: Frauenpolitik der KPD in der weimarer Republik* (Basel: Stroemfeld; Frankfurt-am-Main: Roter Stern, 1979). On France, Jean-Louis Robert, "Le P.C.F. et la question féminine, 1920–1939," *Bulletin du Centre de recherches d'histoire des mouvements sociaux et du syndicalisme* (Paris: University of Paris I, Panthéon-Sorbonne), vol. 3, pp. 56–82; and for the right-wing response, Kevin Passmore, "'Planting the Tricolour in the Citadels of Communism': Women's Social Action in the *Croix de Feu* and *Parti Social Français*," manuscript communicated by the author, 1997 (forthcoming in the *Journal of Modern History*).

15. The question is posed by David Carroll, "Can Fascism Be Assigned a Sexual Identity?" in his *French Literary Fascism: Nationalism, Anti-Semitism, and the Ideology of Culture* (Princeton: Princeton University Press, 1995).

Recent scholarship on both women and fascism in Italy and women and Nazism in Germany is referenced extensively in the notes to Chapter 10. Two basic works on the Nazi period are Jill Stephenson, *The Nazi Organisation of Women* (London: Croom Helm, 1981); and Claudia Koonz, *Mothers in the Fatherland* (New York: St. Martin's Press, 1987). A valuable documentary work on Nazi ideas on the woman question before 1933, which I discovered only after completing the chapter, is *Nationalsozialistische Frauenpolitik vor 1933: Dokumentation*, ed. Hans-Jürgen Arendt, Sabine Hering, & Leonie Wagner (Frankfurt: Dipa, 1995).

For Austria, see Johanna Gehmacher, *Völkische Frauenbewegung: Deutschnationale und national-sozialistische Geschlechterpolitik in Österreich* (Vienna: Döcker, 1998).

For Ukraine, see Martha Bohachevsky-Chomiak, "Feminism in Action: The Ukrainian Women's Union Between the World Wars," *Women's Studies International* (Feminist Press), no. 2 (July 1982), 20–24.

For Yugoslavia, see Jovanka Kecman, *Zene Jugoslavije u radnickom pokretu i zenskim organizacijama 1918–1941* (Women of Yugoslavia in the Workers' Movement and Women's Organizations, 1918–1941) (Belgrade: Narodna Knjiga & Institut za savremenu istoriju, 1978); and Lydia Sklevicky, "Karakteristike organiziranog djelovanja zena u Jugoslaviji u razdoblju do drugog svjetskog rata [Characteristics of Women's Organized Activity in Yugoslavia during the Period up to the Second World War]," *Polja*, no. 308 (Oct. 1984), 415–16; *ibid.*, no. 309 (Nov. 1984), 454–56.

For women's organizational activity in Romania, see the series of articles by Elisabeta Ionita in the *Anale de Istorie* during the 1980s.

16. Concerning the effects of World War II on women in various combatant countries, see the pertinent essays in *Behind the Lines*, ed. Higonnet et al.

On England, see Harold L. Smith, "The Effect of the War on the Status of Women," in *War and Social Change: British Society in the Second World War* (Manchester: Manchester University Press, 1986); and Penny Summerfield, *Reconstructing Women's Wartime Lives: Discourse and Subjectivity in Oral Histories of the Second World War* (Manchester: Manchester University Press, 1998); for France and Spain, the essays in *Identités féminines et violences politiques*, ed. François Rouquet & Danièle Voldman (Paris: Les Cahiers de l'Institut d'Histoire du Temps Présent, no. 31, Oct. 1995); Sarah Fishman, *We Will Wait: Wives of French Prisoners of War, 1940–1945* (New Haven: Yale University Press, 1991).

On Germany, see the remarkable interviews in Alison Owings, *Frauen: German Women Recall the Third Reich* (New Brunswick: Rutgers University Press, 1993); and the essays in *Féminismes et Nazisme*, ed. Liliane Kandel (Paris: CEDREF, University of Paris VII, 1997). On the Holocaust and women, see *Women in the Holocaust*, ed. Delia Ofer & Lenore J. Weitzman (New Haven: Yale University Press, 1998).

For the participation of women in antifascist resistance movements, see Sybil Oldfield, "German Women in the Resistance to Hitler," in *Women, State and Revolution*, ed. Siân Reynolds (Brighton: Wheatsheaf; Amherst: University of Massachusetts Press, 1986), pp. 81–101; and Florence Hervé, "Zwischen Anpassung und Widerstand: Zur Lage der Frauen und zum Widerstand 1933 bis 1945," in *Geschichte der deutschen Frauenbewegung*, ed. Florence Hervé (Cologne: Papy Rossa, 1995), pp. 111–25. For Austria, see Laura Gellott & Michael Phayer, "Dissenting Voices: Catholic Women in Opposition to Fascism," *Journal of Contemporary History*, 22:1 (Jan. 1987), 91–114.

For France and Italy, see *Mémoire et oubli: Women of the French Resistance*, ed. Margaret Collins Weitz, special issue of *Contemporary French Civilization*, 18:1 (Winter/Spring 1994); Margaret Collins Weitz, *Sisters in the Resistance: How Women Fought to Free France, 1940–1945* (New York: Wiley, 1995); the essays in "Resistances et libérations (France 1940–1945)," ed. Françoise Thébaud, special issue of *Clio: Histoire, femmes et sociétés*, no. 1 (1995); Jane Slaughter, *Women and the Italian Resistance, 1943–1945* (Denver: Arden Press, 1997); and Marina Addis Saba, *Partigiane: Le donne nella resistenza italiana* (Mursia: La Casa Editrice, 1998). For Yugoslavia, see Barbara Jancar-Webster, *Women and Revolution in Yugoslavia, 1941–1945* (Denver: Arden Press, 1990); and for Greece, Tasoula Vervenioti, *H gynaika tis antistasis: H eisodos ton gynaikon stin politiki* (The Woman of the Resistance: Women's Entrance into Politics) (Athens: Ekdoseis Odysseas, 1994).

CHAPTER 9: FEMINISM UNDER FIRE

1. Meg Connery, in *The Irish Citizen*, 19 Sept. 1914; repr. in *Women in Ireland, 1800–1918: A Documentary History* (Cork: Cork University Press, 1995), doc. 76, p. 278.

2. Mary Sheepshanks, "Patriotism or Internationalism," *Jus Suffragii*, 9:2 (1 Nov. 1914), 184. On Sheepshanks, see Sybil Oldfield, *Spinsters of This Parish: The Life and Times of F. M. Mayor and Mary Sheepshanks* (London: Virago, 1984). A moving account of efforts by Sheepshanks and other feminists affiliated with the IWSA (including the Hungarian activist Rozika Schwimmer) to save the peace is Anne Wiltsher, *Most Dangerous Women: Feminist Peace Campaigners of the Great War* (London: Pandora, 1985).

On British feminists and the peace issue in this period more generally, see Jo Vellacott, "Feminist Consciousness and the First World War," *History Workshop*, no. 23 (Spring 1987), 81–101; Johanna Alberti, *Beyond Suffrage: Feminists in War and Peace, 1914–28* (Basingstoke: Macmillan, 1989); and, more generally, Susan Kingsley Kent, *Making Peace: The Reconstruction of Gender in Interwar Britain* (Princeton: Princeton University Press, 1993).

On French feminists, patriotism, and the difficulty of antiwar politics under martial law, see Christine Bard, *Les Filles de Marianne: Histoire des féminismes, 1914–1940* (Paris: Fayard, 1995), chaps. 2 and 3. For protests by French feminists, see *Le Grief des femmes: Anthologie de textes féministes*, ed. Maïté Albistur & Daniel Armogathe (Paris: Éditions Hier et Demain, 1978), vol. 2, 202–39; for protests by French socialist women, see the documents reproduced in *L'Opposition des femmes*, vol. 2 of *Le Mouvement ouvrier français contre la guerre, 1914–1918*, ed. Aude Sowerwine & Charles Sowerwine (Paris: EDHIS, 1985).

For German antiwar feminist activism, see the texts in *Frauen gegen den Krieg*, ed. Gisela Brinker-Gabler (Frankfurt-am-Main: Fischer, 1980).

For an overview of the "failure" of both feminist and socialist women's peace efforts, see Richard J. Evans, "Women's Peace, Men's War?" in Evans, *Comrades and Sisters: Feminism, Socialism and Pacifism in Europe, 1870–1945* (Brighton: Wheatsheaf; New York: St. Martin's Press, 1987), pp. 121–56.

3. Clara Zetkin, "To the Socialist Women of All Countries," *Die Gleichheit*, 7 Nov. 1914; repr. in *Clara Zetkin: Selected Writings*, ed. Philip S. Foner (New York: International Publishers, 1984), pp. 114–16; Aleksandra Kollontai, "Till de socialistiska Kvinnorna i alla länder," *Stormklockan*, 15 Nov. 1914; transl. in Barbara Evans Clements, *Bolshevik Feminist: The Life of Aleksandra Kollontai* (Bloomington & London: Indiana University Press, 1979), p. 85.

4. Lida Gustava Heymann, "Women of Europe, When Will Your Call Ring Out?" *Jus Suffragii*, 9:5 (1 Feb. 1915), 232. See also Regina Bracker, "Bertha von Suttner's Spiritual Daughters: The Feminist Pacifism of Anita Augspurg, Lida Gustava Heymann, and Helene Stöcker at the International Congress of Women at the Hague, 1915," *Women's Studies International Forum*, 18:2 (March–April 1995), 103–11.

5. The Ogden-Florence pamphlet of April 1915 is reprinted in *Militarism versus Feminism: Writings on Women and War: Catherine Marshall, C. K. Ogden & Mary Sargant Florence*, ed. Margaret Kamester & Jo Vellacott (London: Virago, 1987). Orig. publ. as Supplement to *Jus Suffragii*, 9:6 (March 1915), i–viii.

6. "The Outlook," *Votes for Women*, 8, no. 354 (18 Dec. 1914), 91. Also discussed in Lucy Bland, "In the Name of Protection: The Policing of Women in the First World War," in *Women-in-Law: Explorations in Law, Family, and Sexuality*, ed. Julia Brophy & Carol Smart (London: Routledge Kegan Paul, 1985), p. 29.

7. See Marie Monique Huss, "Pronatalism and the Popular Ideology of the Child in Wartime France: The Evidence of the Picture Postcard," in *The Upheaval of War: Family, Work and Welfare in Europe, 1914–1918*, ed. Richard Wall & Jay Winter (Cambridge: Cambridge University Press, 1989), pp. 329–67; Ruth Harris, "The 'Child of the Barbarian': Rape, Race and Nationalism in France during the First World War," *Past and Present*, no. 141 (Nov. 1993), 170–206; and Judith Wishnia, "Natalisme et nationalisme

pendant la première guerre mondiale," *Vingtième siècle*, no. 45 (Jan.–March 1995), 30–39.

8. Cornelie Usborne, "'Pregnancy Is the Women's Active Service': Pronatalism in Germany during the First World War," in *Upheaval of War*, p. 390.

9. Dr. Alfred Grotjahn, *Die Wehrbeitrag der deutschen Frau: Zeitgemässe Betrachtungen über Krieg und Geburtenrückgang* (Bonn: Marcus & Weber Verlag, 1915); transl. in Usborne, "'Pregnancy,'" p. 389.

10. Call to congress, *Jus Suffragii*, 9:6 (1 March 1915), 245–46; repr. in *European Women: A Documentary History, 1789–1945*, ed. Eleanor S. Riemer & John C. Fout (New York: Schocken Books, 1980), p. 82.

11. "Manifesto Issued by Envoys of the International Congress of Women at The Hague to the Governments of Europe and the President of the United States," in Jane Addams, Emily G. Balch, and Alice Hamilton, *Women at The Hague: The International Congress of Women and Its Results* (New York: Macmillan, 1915; repr. New York: Garland, 1972); repr. in *WFF*, vol. 2, doc. 69 (quote, p. 267). On the congress, see also Wiltsher, *Most Dangerous Women*.

12. Heymann; transl. in Bracker, "Suttner's Spiritual Daughters," 108.

13. Helena Maria Swanwick, *Women and War*, UDC Pamphlets, no. 11 (London, 1915); repr. in *WFF*, vol. 2, doc. 70 (quotes, pp. 269, 271).

14. F(rancis) Sheehy Skeffington, "War and Feminism," *The Irish Citizen*, 12 Sept. 1914.

15. On Sylvia Pankhurst's activities, see the biographies by Patricia Romero, *E. Sylvia Pankhurst: Portrait of a Radical* (New Haven: Yale University Press, 1987); and Barbara Winslow, *Sylvia Pankhurst* (London: UCL Press, 1995). See also the articles in *Sylvia Pankhurst: From Artist to Anti-Fascist*, ed. Ian Bullock & Richard Pankhurst (Houndmills: Macmillan; New York: St. Martin's Press, 1992); and *A Sylvia Pankhurst Reader*, ed. Kathryn Dodd (Manchester: Manchester University Press; New York: St. Martin's Press, 1993).

16. "L'Affaire Hélène Brion au 1e Conseil de Guerre," *Revue des Causes Célèbres*, no. 15 (2 May 1918); repr. in *WFF*, vol. 2, doc. 71 (quote, p. 274). On Helene Brion, see Huguette Bouchardeau's preface to *Hélène Brion: La Voie féministe* (Paris: Syros, 1978), pp. 7–47.

17. The attribution is by Robin Pickering-Iazzi, in her introduction to the edited volume *Mothers of Invention: Women, Italian Fascism and Culture* (Minneapolis: University of Minnesota Press, 1995), xix.

18. Mary Sheepshanks, "Peace," *Jus Suffragii*, 13:3 (Dec. 1918), 25.

19. Mary Sheepshanks, "What Women Should Demand of the Peace Congress," *Jus Suffragii*, 13:5 (Feb. 1919)), 58–59.

20. The details of the feminists' campaign are reported by Suzanne Grinberg, "Women at the Peace Conference," *Jus Suffragii*, 13:6 (March 1919), 71–73; and "The Inter-Allied Suffrage Conference," *Jus Suffragii*, 13:7 (April 1919), 88–89. I have also drawn on Grinberg's accounts in *La*

Française, issues of 22 Feb. 1919 and 26 April 1919, and her more detailed reports in *La Renaissance*, issues of 29 March and 26 April 1919, as well as Maria Vérone's reports in *Le Droit des femmes*, Feb., March, April 1919. Additional information can be found in dossiers at the Bibliothèque Marguerite Durand, Paris.

21. As cited in the commission proceedings, republ. in *The Origins of the International Labor Organization*, ed. James T. Shotwell, 2 vols. (New York: Columbia University Press, 1934), vol. 2, p. 275.

22. See Grinberg's report in *La Renaissance*, 26 April 1919.

23. For the text of the Treaty of Versailles, see *Major Peace Treaties of Modern History, 1648–1967*, ed. Fred L. Israel, vol. 2 (New York: Chelsea House, 1967).

24. Resolution of the Second International Congress of Women, Zurich, 12–19 May 1919; repr. in Gertrude Bussey & Margaret Tims, *Women's International League for Peace and Freedom, 1915–1965: A Record of Fifty Years' Work* (London: George Allen & Unwin, 1965), p. 31.

25. See Linda Edmondson, *Feminism in Russia, 1900–1917* (Stanford: Stanford University Press, 1984), pp. 165–67 for a fuller account of these developments. All quotations in translation are from Edmondson.

26. Edmondson, *Feminism*, p. 167.

27. See Richard Abraham, "Maria L. Bochkareva and the Russian Amazons in 1917," in *Women and Society in Russia and the Soviet Union*, ed. Linda Edmondson (Cambridge: Cambridge University Press, 1992), pp. 124–44.

28. Edmondson, *Feminism*, p. 170. The details concerning the fate of the Russian feminists are under investigation by Rochelle Ruthschild:; personal communication, May 1999.

29. Wendy Z. Goldman, "Women, the Family, and the New Revolutionary Order in the Soviet Union," in *Promissory Notes: Women in the Transition to Socialism*, ed. Sonia Kruks, Rayna Rapp, & Marilyn B. Young (New York: Monthly Review Press, 1989), p. 62.

30. Richard Stites, *The Women's Liberation Movement in Russia* (Princeton: Princeton University Press, 1978), p. 395.

31. Lenin, speech at the First All-Russian Congress of Women, 19 Nov. 1918; repr. in Lenin, *Women and Society* (New York, 1938); also in *WFF*, vol. 2, doc. 76 (quotes, pp. 287, 288).

32. Armand's remarks, in *Kommunisticheskaia partiia i organizatsiaa rabotnits* (Moscow & Petrograd: Kommunist, 1919), p. 41; transl. in Clements, *Bolshevik Feminist*, p. 155.

33. Aleksandra Kollontai, *Communism and the Family* (1918; repr. San Francisco: The Western Worker, n.d.), p. 2.

34. Lenin, "The Tasks of the Working Women's Movement in the Soviet Republic," speech delivered at the Fourth Moscow City Conference of Non-Party Working Women, 23 Sept. 1919, reported in *Pravda* (25 Sept. 1919); transl. and repr. in *The Emancipation of Women: From the Writings of V. I. Lenin* (New York: International Publishers, 1966), p. 69.

35. Lenin's interview with Clara Zetkin, in *Emancipation of Women*, pp. 109–10.

36. Lenin, in *Emancipation of Women*, p. 111.

37. A fine new study of the Bolshevik reconfigurations of gender and of the rise and demise of the Zhenotdel is Elizabeth A. Wood, *The Baba and the Comrade: Gender and Politics in Postrevolutionary Russia* (Bloomington: Indiana University Press, 1997). In addition, see Wendy Z. Goldman, *Women, the State and Revolution: Soviet Family Policy and Social Life, 1917–1936* (Cambridge: Cambridge University Press, 1993); and Barbara Evans Clements, *Bolshevik Women* (Cambridge: Cambridge University Press, 1997).

38. Madeleine Pelletier, *Mon Voyage aventureux en Russie communiste* (Paris: Giard, 1922; repr. Paris: côté-femmes, 1996); quoted in Charles Sowerwine & Claude Maignien, *Madeleine Pelletier, une féministe dans l'arène politique* (Paris: Éditions ouvrières, 1992), p. 169; transl. KO.

39. Fannina W. Halle, *Woman in Soviet Russia*, transl. Margaret M. Green (London: Routledge, 1934; orig. German publ. *Die Frau im Sowjetrussland* [1932; in English, 1933]), ix–x.

40. Winifred Holtby, *Women and a Changing Civilization* (London: John Lane, 1934; repr. Chicago: Academy Press, 1978), pp. 182, 185, 187–88.

41. For parallel historical approaches to reconfiguring gender in postwar France and England, see Mary Louise Roberts, *Civilization Without Sexes: Reconstructing Gender in Postwar France, 1917–1927* (Chicago & London: University of Chicago Press, 1994); and Kent, *Making Peace* (see n. 2).

42. Georges Clemenceau, in the French senate, 12 Oct. 1919; quoted in Edouard Bonnefous, *Histoire Politique de la IIIe République*, vol. 3 (Paris: Presses Universitaires de France, 1968), p. 58; transl. KO.

43. See Françoise Basch, *Victor Basch: De l'affaire Dreyfus au crime de la Milice* (Paris: Plon, 1994), pp. 186–87; and William D. Irvine, "Women's Rights, Democracy, and the Ligue des Droits de l'Homme," unpublished paper presented to the Society for French Historical Studies, Boston, March 1996.

44. On the advent of Mothers' Day celebrations in postwar Europe, see Karin Hausen, "Mother's Day in the Weimar Republic," in *When Biology Became Destiny: Women in Weimar and Nazi Germany*, ed. Renate Bridenthal, Atina Grossmann, & Marion Kaplan (New York: Monthly Review Press, 1984), pp. 131–52; Anne Cova, *Maternité et droits des femmes en France*, pp. 249–54.

45. Arabella Kenealy, *Feminism and Sex Extinction* (London: T. Fisher Unwin, 1920), vi.

46. Gina Lombroso, *The Soul of Woman* (New York: Dutton, 1923), p. 15. On Gina Lombroso, see Delfina Dolza Carrara, *Essere figlie di Lombroso: Due donne intellettuali tra '800 e '900* (Milan: Franco Angeli, 1990).

47. Karl Abraham, "Manifestations of the Female Castration Complex," *International Journal of Psycho-Analysis*, 3:1 (1922), 1–29. The term "penis envy" first appears on p. 6.

48. Sigmund Freud, "Some Psychological Consequences of the Anatomical Distinction Between the Sexes," transl. James Strachey, *International Journal of Psycho-Analysis*, 8:2 (1927), 133–42; orig. publ. in German, 1925.

49. Helene Deutsch, *The Psychology of Women: A Psychoanalytic Interpretation* (New York: Grune & Stratton, 1944). See also her earlier work, *Psychoanalyse der weiblichen Sexualfunktionen* (Vienna: International Psychoanalytische Verlag, 1925); and Carl Gustav Jung, "Woman in Europe," in *Contributions to Analytical Psychology*, transl. H. G. Baynes and Cary F. Baynes (London, 1928; orig. publ. Oct. 1927 in *Europäische Revue* [Leipzig]).

50. Karen Horney, "The Flight from Womanhood: The Masculinity Complex in Women as Viewed by Men and Women," *International Journal of Psycho-Analysis*, 7, pts. 3–4 (July–Oct. 1926); repr. in Karen Horney, *Feminine Psychology*, ed. Harold Kelman (New York: Norton, 1973), pp. 54–70.

51. Alfred Adler, *Understanding Human Nature*, transl. Walter Beran Wolfe (London: Allen & Unwin; New York: Garden City/Star Books, 1927), p. 135.

52. Pierre Drieu la Rochelle, *La Suite dans les idées* (Paris: Au Sans Pareil, 1927), p. 125; transl. in Roberts, *Civilization Without Sexes*, p. 2; Roberts's comment, p. 4.

53. Wieth-Knudsen's work was published in English under two different titles: for the British market, *Feminism: A Sociological Study of the Woman Question from Ancient Times to the Present Day* (London: Constable, 1928); and for the American edition, the more benign *Understanding Women: A Popular Study of the Question from Ancient Times to the Present Day* (New York: E. Holt, 1929).

54. Robert Teutsch, *Le Féminisme* (Paris: Société française d'éditions littéraires et techniques, 1934), p. 261; transl. in Carolyn J. Dean, *The Self and Its Pleasures: Bataille, Lacan, and the History of the Decentered Subject* (Ithaca: Cornell University Press, 1992), p. 64.

55. Dean, *Self and Its Pleasures*, p. 92.

56. Peter Nathan, *The Psychology of Fascism* (London: Faber & Faber, 1943), pp. 52–53, 57.

CHAPTER 10: FEMINIST DILEMMAS

1. Zeev Sternhell, *Ni Droite ni gauche: L'Idéologie fasciste en France* (Paris: Seuil, 1983); in English as *Neither Right nor Left: Fascist Ideology in France*, transl. David Maisel (Berkeley & Los Angeles: University of California Press, 1986).

2. For the English-language texts of these papal encyclicals, see *Social Wellsprings: Eighteen Encyclicals of Social Reconstruction, by Pius XI*, ed. Joseph Husslein, vol. 2 (Milwaukee: Bruce, 1949).

3. See Barbara Caine, *English Feminism* (Oxford: Oxford University Press, 1997), chap. 5, for a sensitive survey of recent historical writing on

this period. Historians have found it very difficult to be dispassionate, generally taking sides with the views of one or another of the major figures or groups. Among the important treatments of English feminism between 1919 and 1939 are Jane Lewis's pioneering article, "Beyond Suffrage: English Feminism in the 1920s," *Maryland Historian*, 6:1 (Spring 1975), 1–17; Brian Harrison, *Prudent Revolutionaries: Portraits of British Feminists between the Wars* (Oxford: Clarendon Press, 1987); Carol Dyhouse, *Feminism and the Family in England, 1880–1939* (Oxford: Basil Blackwell, 1989); Martin Pugh, *Women and the Women's Movement in Britain, 1914–1959* (Basingstoke: Macmillan, 1992); and Susan Kingsley Kent, *Making Peace* (Princeton: Princeton University Press, 1993). See also recent articles in the *Women's History Review*; and articles by Harold L. Smith, Susan Kingsley Kent, Deborah Gorham, Hilary Land, Pat Thane, and Martin Pugh in *British Feminism in the Twentieth Century*, ed. Harold L. Smith (Amherst: University of Massachusetts Press, 1990).

4. "What Is Feminism," *The Woman's Leader and the Common Cause*, 17 July 1925, p. 195.

5. See Susan Pedersen, *Family, Dependence, and the Origins of the Welfare State: Britain and France, 1914–1945* (Cambridge: Cambridge University Press, 1993).

6. Eleanor Rathbone, "The Old and the New Feminism," *The Woman's Leader and the Common Cause*, 13 March 1925, p. 2; repr. in *WFF*, vol. 2, doc. 91, pp. 326–27. On Rathbone, see Mary D. Stocks, *Eleanor Rathbone: A Biography* (London: Gollancz, 1950); Hilary Land, "Eleanor Rathbone and the Economy of the Family," in *British Feminism*, ed. Smith, pp. 104–23; and the works listed in n. 3 above. For a strongly worded condemnation of Rathbone's relational approach, see Susan Kingsley Kent, "The Politics of Sexual Difference: World War I and the Demise of British Feminism," *Journal of British Studies*, 22:3 (July 1988), 232–53.

7. *Time and Tide*, 6 April 1928; quoted in Shirley M. Eoff, *Viscountess Rhondda: Equalitarian Feminist* (Columbus: Ohio State University Press, 1991), p. 328. On Lady Rhondda, see also *Time and Tide Wait for No Man*, ed. Dale Spender (London: Pandora Press, 1984).

8. Susan Kingsley Kent, "Gender Reconstruction After the First World War," in *British Feminism*, ed. Smith, p. 66.

9. *Our Freedom and Its Results, by Five Women*, ed. Ray Strachey (London: Hogarth Press, 1936), p. 10.

10. Virginia Woolf, *Three Guineas* (London: Hogarth Press, 1938; repr. New York: Harcourt Brace Jovanovich, 1983), p. 101.

11. Victoria De Grazia, *How Fascism Ruled Women: Italy, 1922–1945* (Berkeley & Los Angeles: University of California Press, 1992), p. 1. In addition to other works cited in the notes below, see the indispensable work of Franca Pieroni Bortolotti, *Femminismo e partiti politici in Italia, 1919–1926* (Rome: Editori riuniti, 1978); and Fiorenza Taricone, *L'associazionismo femminile in Italia dall'unità al fascismo* (Milan: Edizioni Unicopli, 1996). On the twentieth-century suffrage campaigns, see Mariapia Bigaran,

"Il voto alle donne in Italia dal 1912 al fascismo," *Rivista di storia contemporanea*, 16:2 (April 1987), 240–65. On the fascist period, see Elisabetta Mondello, *La nuova italiana: La donna nella stampa e nella cultura del ventennio* (Rome: Riuniti, 1987); and the articles in *La corporazione delle donne: ricerche e studi sui modelli femminili nel ventennio fascista*, ed. Marina Addis Saba (Florence: Vallecchi, 1989).

12. De Grazia, *How Fascism Ruled Women*, p. 7.

13. "Educazione morale, civile e fisica delle piccole e delle giovani italiane," *I fasci femminili* (Milan: Libreria d'Italia, 1929); repr. in *Sposa e madre esemplare: Ideologia e politica della donna e della famiglia durante il fascismo*, ed. Piero Meldini (Florence: Guaraldo, 1975), p. 157; transl. in Robin Pickering-Iazzi, *Mothers of Invention: Women, Italian Fascism, and Culture* (Minneapolis: University of Minnesota Press, 1995), xi. See also Pickering-Iazzi, *Politics of the Visible: Writing Women, Culture, and Fascism* (Minneapolis: University of Minnesota Press, 1997).

14. Benito Mussolini, "Al congresso dell'Allianza internazionale pro suffragio femminile," 14 May 1923; reported in *Il Popolo d'Italia*, no. 115 (15 May 1923); and repr. in *Opera omnia di Benito Mussolini*, ed. Eduardo & Duilio Susmel, vol. 19 (Florence: La Fenice, 1956), p. 215; transl. in De Grazia, *How Fascism Ruled Women*, p. 36. A slightly different translation was published at the time in *Jus Suffragii*, 17:9 (July 1923), 149.

15. Matilde Serao, "Ma che fanno le femministe?" *Il Giorno*, 20 June 1925; transl. in Nancy A. Harrowitz, *Antisemitism, Misogyny, and the Logic of Cultural Difference* (Lincoln: University of Nebraska Press, 1994), p. 101; repr. in *Matilde Serao giornalista*, ed. Wanda de Nunzio Schilardi (Lecce: Millela, 1986), p. 223.

16. *Donne e diritto: Due secoli di legislazione*, ed. Agata Alma Cappiello et al., vol. 2 (Rome: Istituto poligrafico dello Stato, 1988), p. 1496; transl. in Sandi E. Cooper, "Can Pacifism Be Above the Fray? French Feminist Pacifists Confront Fascism," paper delivered to the American Historical Association, Atlanta, January 1996, p. 25.

17. "Lisistrata" (pseud.), "La donna, il fascismo, e S. E. Turati," *La Chiosa*, 17 Feb. 1927; transl. in Alexander De Grand, "Women under Italian Fascism," *The Historical Journal*, 19:4 (1976), 956.

18. Ester Lombardo, "Rassegna del movimento femminile italiano," *Almanacco della donna italiana, 1927*; transl. in De Grazia, *How Fascism Ruled Women*, p. 38.

19. "Il doganiere" (identified as Gherardo Casini), "Donne a casa," *Critica fascista*, 19 (1929), 378; repr. in *Sposa e madre esemplare*, ed. Meldini, p. 168; transl. in Robin Pickering-Iazzi, "Introduction" to *Unspeakable Women: Selected Short Stories Written by Italian Women during Fascism* (New York: Feminist Press, 1993), p. 7.

20. Bonnie G. Smith, *Changing Lives: Women in European History Since 1700* (Lexington: D. C. Heath, 1989), p. 461.

21. In Emil Ludwig, *Talks with Mussolini*, transl. from the German by Eden Paul & Cedar Paul (Boston: Little, Brown, 1933), p. 170.

22. Benito Mussolini, "Macchina e donna," in *Il Popolo d'Italia*, no. 206 (31 Aug. 1934); repr. in *Opera omnia di Benito Mussolini*, vol. 26 (1958); transl. Jane Vaden in *WFF*, vol. 2, doc. 103.

23. De Grazia, *How Fascism Ruled Women*, pp. 237–38.

24. Pierre Taittinger, "Les Féministes et la patrie," in *Les Cahiers de la jeune France* (Paris: Éditions du "National," 1926); quotes, pp. 29–30, 31; transl. in Robert Soucy, *French Fascism: The First Wave, 1924–1933* (New Haven: Yale University Press, 1986), pp. 80–81.

25. Oswald Mosley, *The Greater Britain* (London: Greater Britain Publications, 1932), pp. 41–42.

26. On Mosley's movement and its publications, see Martin Durham, "Gender and the British Union of Fascists," *Journal of Contemporary History*, 27:3 (July 1992), 513–19.

27. Woolf, *Three Guineas*, p. 53; repr. in *WFF*, vol. 2, doc. 109 (quote, p. 388). For Woolf's and other feminist responses, see Johanna Alberti, "British Feminists and Anti-Fascism in the 1930s," in *This Working-Day World: Women's Lives and Culture(s) in Britain, 1914–1945*, ed. Sybil Oldfield (London: Taylor & Francis, 1994), pp. 111–22.

28. Klara Mautner, "Die Frau von Morgen," *Arbeiterinnen-Zeitung*, 25 March 1916, p. 8; transl. in Thomas Lewis Hamer, "Beyond Feminism: The Women's Movement in Austrian Social Democracy, 1890–1926" (Ph.D. dissertation, Ohio State University, 1973), pp. 156–57.

29. Adelheid Popp, "Die Frau in neuen Staat," *Der Kampf*, 11 (Nov. 1918), 731–32; transl. in Hamer, "Beyond Feminism," pp. 168–69.

30. Adelheid Popp, *Frauen der Arbeit, schliesst euch an!* (Vienna: Verlag der Wiener Volksbuchhandlung, 1919), p. 2; transl. in Hamer, "Beyond Feminism," p. 177.

31. Johanna Gehmacher, "Le Nationalisme allemand des femmes autrichiennes et l'idéologie de 'communauté ethnique,'" in *Femmes—Nations—Europe*, ed. Marie-Claire Hoock-Demarle (Paris, 1995); quote, p. 102; transl. KO. See also Johanna Gehmacher, *"Völkische Frauenbewegung": Deutschnationale und national-sozialistische Geschlechterpolitik in Österreich* (Vienna: Döcker Verlag, 1998). The SDAP dropped the "Deutsch" after 1921, according to Birgitta Bader-Zaar, Vienna; personal communication, 1999.

32. Adelheid Popp, in *Arbeiter-Zeitung*, 20 March 1911; transl. in Birgitta Bader-Zaar, "Women in Austrian Politics, 1890–1934: Goals and Visions," in *Austrian Women in the Nineteenth and Twentieth Centuries: Cross-Disciplinary Perspectives*, ed. David F. Good, Margarete Grandner, & Mary Jo Maynes (Providence: Berghahn Books, 1996), p. 65. On women in parliament, see also Gabriella Hauch, *Vom Frauenstandpunkt aus: Frauen im Parlament 1919–1933* (Vienna: Verlag für Gesellschaftskritik, 1995).

33. *Frauenarbeit und Bevölkerungspolitik: Verhandlung der sozialdemokratischen Frauenreichskonferenz, 29. und 30. Oktober 1926 in Linz* (Vienna, 1926), transl. Ingrun Lafleur, "Five Socialist Women: Traditionalist Conflicts and Socialist Visions in Austria, 1893–1934," in *Socialist*

Women: European Socialist Feminism in the Nineteenth and Early Twentieth Centuries, ed. Marilyn J. Boxer & Jean H. Quataert (New York: Elsevier, 1978); quotes, pp. 238–39.

34. Hamer, "Beyond Feminism," pp. 232–33.

35. Gisela Urban, in *Das Frauenstimmrecht: Festschrift* (Vienna, 1913); transl. in Bader-Zaar, "Women in Austrian Politics," p. 64.

36. On Maria Schneider, see Gehmacher, *Völkische Frauenbewegung*, pp. 213–21. Thanks to Johanna Gehmacher for forwarding a copy of Schneider's 1931 speech to the BÖF.

37. Helene Granitsch, "Politische Übersicht," *Das Wort der Frau*, 2:9 (1932), 1–2; transl. in Bader-Zaar, "Women in Austrian Politics," p. 83.

38. Tormey quote transl. in Mária M. Kovács, "The Politics of Emancipation in Hungary," *Central European University History Department Working Paper Series*, no. 1 (1994), 84. No date given.

39. Quote from the 1930 Statutes of the National Association of Hungarian Women; transl. in Andrea Petö, "Hungarian Women in Politics," in *Transitions, Environments, Translations: Feminism in International Politics*, ed. Joan W. Scott, Cora Kaplan, & Debra Keates (New York: Routledge, 1997), p. 160 n. 4. Thanks to Andrea Petö for sharing her article prior to publication and for her assistance with Hungarian materials.

40. The bibliography on German women's history in the Weimar and Nazi periods has expanded tremendously since the 1970s, and the history of feminism in Germany has developed apace. For the history of German feminism in wartime and under the Weimar Republic, I have built on the work of Hugh Wiley Puckett, *Germany's Women Go Forward* (New York: Columbia University Press, 1930); Amy Hackett, "The Politics of Feminism in Wilhelmine Germany, 1890–1918," 2 vols. (Ph.D. dissertation, Columbia University, 1976); Richard J. Evans, *The Feminist Movement in Germany, 1894–1933* (London & Beverly Hills: Sage, 1976); Barbara Greven-Aschoff, *Die bürgerliche Frauenbewegung in Deutschland, 1894–1933* (Göttingen: Vandenhoeck & Ruprecht, 1981); Ute Gerhard, *Unerhört: Die Geschichte der deutschen Frauenbewegung* (Reinbeck-bei-Hamburg: Rowohlt, 1990), chap. 9; the essays on the women's press by Marianne Walle and Nicole Gabriel in *La Tentation nationaliste, 1914–1945*, ed. Rita Thalmann (Paris: Deuxtemps Tierce, 1990); and the essays by Florence Hervé in *Geschichte der deutschen Frauenbewegung*, ed. Florence Hervé, new ed. (Cologne: PapyRossa Verlag, 1995). I have relied heavily on the stream of English-language publications by Renate Bridenthal, Claudia Koonz, and Atina Grossmann, many of which are listed in the notes below. See especially the articles in *When Biology Became Destiny: Women in Weimar and Nazi Germany*, ed. Renate Bridenthal, Atina Grossmann, & Marion Kaplan (New York: Monthly Review Press, 1986); and in the first and second editions of *Becoming Visible: Women in European History*, ed. Renate Bridenthal et al. (Boston: Houghton-Mifflin, 1977, 1987). See also Cornelie Usborne, *The Politics of the Body in Weimar Germany: Women's Reproductive Rights and Duties* (London: Macmillan, 1992); Atina Gross-

mann, *Reforming Sex: The German Movement for Birth Control and Abortion Reform, 1920–1950* (New York: Oxford University Press, 1995). Other valuable works include: Christl Wickert, *Unsere Erwählten: Sozialdemokratische Frauen im deutschen Reichstag und im preussischen Landtag, 1919 bis 1933*, 2 vols. (Göttingen: Sovec, 1986); Hiltraud Schmidt-Waldherr, *Emanzipation durch Professionaliserung? Politische Strategien und Konflikte innerhalb der bürgerlichen Frauenbewegung während der weimarer Republik und die Reaktion des bürgerlichen Antifeminismus und des Nationalsozialismus* (Frankfurt-am-Main: Materialis Verlag, 1987). Works on the Nazi period are included in n. 66 below.

41. Agnes von Zahn-Harnack, *Die Frauenbewegung: Geschichte, Probleme, Ziele* (Berlin: Deutsche Buch-Gemeinschaft, 1928), pp. 77–78; transl. in Ute Gerhard, "The German Women's Movement before 1914: Towards Locating It in an International Context," unpublished paper presented at Stuttgart/Birkach, 1995.

42. "Aufruf, Deutscher Bund zur Bekämpfung der Frauenemanzipation," as discussed by Diane Trosino, "Anti-Feminism in Germany 1912–1920: The German League for the Prevention of Women's Emancipation," Ph.D. dissertation, Claremont Graduate School, 1992; quote, p. 33. On the antifeminists, see also Ute Planert, "Antifeminismus im Kaiserreich," *Archiv für Sozialgeschichte*, 38 (1998), 67–92.

43. Quotes: Trosino, "Anti-Feminism," pp. 38–39.

44. Renate Bridenthal & Claudia Koonz, "Beyond *Kinder, Küche, Kirche*: Weimar Women in Politics and Work," in *When Biology Became Destiny*, p. 56.

45. Figures from Helen L. Boak, "'Our Last Hope': Women's Votes for Hitler—A Reappraisal," *German Studies Review*, 12:2 (May 1989), 291.

46. See Karen Hagemann, "La 'Question des femmes' et les rapports masculin-féminin dans la social-démocratie allemande sous la République de Weimar," *Le Mouvement social*, no. 163 (April–June 1993), 25–44; and Hagemann, "Men's Demonstrations and Women's Protest: Gender in Collective Action in the Urban Working-Class Milieu during the Weimar Republic," *Gender & History*, 5:1 (Spring 1993), 101–19.

47. Claudia Koonz, "Conflicting Allegiances: Political Ideology and Women Legislators in Weimar Germany," *Signs*, 1:3, pt. 1 (Spring 1976), 674.

48. Evans, *Feminist Movement*, p. 245.

49. Sybil Oldfield, "German Women in the Resistance to Hitler," in *Women, State and Revolution*, ed. Siân Reynolds (Amherst: University of Massachusetts Press, 1986), p. 82. See also Karin Hausen, "Unemployment Also Hits Women: The New and the Old Woman on the Dark Side of the Golden Twenties in Germany," in *Unemployment and the Great Depression in Weimar Germany*, ed. Peter D. Stachura (London: Macmillan, 1986), pp. 131–52.

50. Bridenthal and Koonz, "Beyond *Kinder, Küche, Kinder*," p. 56.

51. Evans, *Feminist Movement*, p. 235.

52. Marie Diers, *Die deutsche Frauenfrage in ihrem Zusammenhang mit Geschichte, Volkswirtschaft und Politik* (Potsdam, 1920), p. 185; transl. in Puckett, *Germany's Women*, p. 313.

53. Renate Bridenthal, "Professional Housewives: Stepsisters of the Women's Movement," in *When Biology Became Destiny*, p. 154.

54. On the Catholic and Protestant evangelical groups, see Maria Elisabeth Backhaus, *Probleme des Frauenbilds der katholischen Frauenbewegung Deutschlands seit 1900* (Aachen: Paedagogische Hochschule, 1979); Doris Kaufmann, "Von Vaterland zum Mutterland: Frauen im katholischen Milieu der weimarer Republik," in *Frauen suchen ihre Geschichte*, ed. Karin Hausen (Munich: C. H. Beck, 1983); and Kaufmann, *Frauen zwischen Aufbruch und Reaktion: Protestantische Frauenbewegung in der ersten Hälfte des 20. Jahrhunderts* (Munich: Piper, 1988).

55. Hackett, "Politics of Feminism," vol. 1, xiii.

56. See Marion Kaplan in *The Jewish Feminist Movement in Germany: The Campaigns of the Jüdischer Frauenbund, 1904–1938* (Westport: Greenwood Press, 1979).

57. See Edward Bristow, *Prostitution and Prejudice: The Jewish Campaign against White Slavery, 1870–1939* (Oxford: Clarendon Press, 1982).

58. From the *Israelitische Familienblatt* (Hamburg), 20 March 1924, pp. 2–3; transl. in Kaplan, *Jewish Feminist Movement*, p. 159.

59. Kaplan, *Jewish Feminist Movement*: quotes, pp. 76, 81.

60. Usborne, *Politics of the Body*, p. 30.

61. Adele Schreiber, transl. in Usborne, *Politics*, p. 39; from the *Protokolle* of the SPD women's conference (Berlin, 1920), p. 91.

62. Stegmann, maiden speech in the Reichstag, 18 March 1925; transl. in Usborne, *Politics of the Body*, p. 39.

63. Friedrich Wolf, *Cyankali*; transl. in Atina Grossmann, "Abortion and Economic Crisis: The 1931 Campaign Against Paragraph 218," in *When Biology Became Destiny*, p. 73; quote from Grossmann, also p. 73.

64. KPD Second Reichs Congress, Halle, 14–15 March 1931; quoted in Atina Grossmann, "Abortion and Economic Crisis," p. 72.

65. Dr. Else Kienle, *Frauen: Aus dem Tagebuch einer Ärtzin* (Berlin, 1932), p. 309; transl. in Grossmann, "Abortion and Economic Crisis," p. 75.

66. On the NSDAP and the woman question, see Clifford Kirkpatrick, *Nazi Germany: Its Women and Family Life* (Indianapolis: Bobbs-Merrill, 1938); and the many works by George L. Mosse. The bibliography is enormous and growing, but the following works in English and German are invaluable: Jill Stephenson, *Women in Nazi Society* (London: Croom Helm, 1975); Stephenson, *The Nazi Organization of Women* (London: Croom Helm, 1981); Hannelore Kessler, *"Die deutsche Frau": Nationalsozialistische Frauenpropaganda im Völkischen Beobachter* (Cologne: Pahl-Rugenstein, 1981); Gisela Bock, *Zwangssterilisation im Nationalsozialismus: Studien zur Rassenpolitik und Frauenpolitik* (Opladen: Westdeutscher Verlag, 1986); Claudia Koonz, *Mothers in the Fatherland: Women, the Family, and Nazi Politics* (New York: St. Martin's Press, 1987).

In France, the contributions of Rita Thalmann to the study of Nazism and women have been particularly important; see her *Être femme sous le IIIe Reich* (Paris: Laffont, 1982). See also the articles by Thalmann, Liliane Crips, and Marianne Walle in the following collections: *Femmes et fascismes*, ed. Rita Thalmann (Paris: Tierce, 1986); *La Tentation nationaliste, 1914–1945*, ed. Rita Thalmann (Paris: Deuxtemps Tierce, 1990); *Nationalismes, féminismes, exclusions: Mélanges en l'honneur de Rita Thalmann*, ed. Liliane Crips et al. (Frankfurt-am-Main: Peter Lang, 1994); and *Féminismes et nazisme, colloque en hommage à Rita Thalmann*, ed. Liliane Kandel (Paris: CEDREF, University of Paris VII, 1997). See also *Gender, Patriarchy and Fascism in the Third Reich: The Response of Women Writers*, ed. Elaine Martin (Detroit: Wayne State University Press, 1993).

The following documentary volumes in German provide essential sources: Christine Wittrock, *Das Frauenbild in faschistischen Texten und seine Vorläufer in der bürgerlichen Frauenbewegung der zwanziger Jahre* (Frankfurt-am-Main: n.p., 1981); *Frauen im deutschen Faschismus*, ed. Annette Kuhn & Valentine Rothe, 2 vols. (Düsselsorf: Schwann, 1982); and *Nationalsozialistische Frauenpolitik vor 1933: Dokumentation*, ed. Hans-Jürgen Arendt, Sabine Hering, & Leonie Wagner (Frankfurt-am-Main: Dipa-Verlag, 1995).

67. NSDAP proposal no. 1741, 13 March 1930; transl. in Usborne, *Politics of the Body*, app. 3, p. 220.

68. See Gisela Bock, "Equality and Difference in National Socialist Racism," in *Beyond Equality and Difference: Citizenship, Feminist Politics, Female Subjectivity*, ed. Gisela Bock & Susan James (London: Routledge, 1992), p. 106; see also Bock, "Racism and Sexism in Nazi Germany: Motherhood, Compulsory Steriization, and the State," *Signs*, 8:3 (Spring 1983), 400–421.

69. The 1921 Nazi conference ruling: "A woman could not be accepted for a leadership position in the Party"; quoted in Oldfield, "German Women in the Resistance to Hitler," p. 83.

70. Adolf Hitler, *Mein Kampf* (New York: Reynal & Hitchcock, 1939; orig. German publ. 1925); quotes, pp. 342–43.

71. Alfred Rosenberg, *Der Mythos des XX. Jahrhunderts* (Munich: Hoheneichen-Verlag, 1930), p. 512; transl. in *Nazi Culture*, ed. George L. Mosse (New York: Grosset & Dunlap, 1966), p. 40. See the introduction (pp. 22–25) and documents in *Nationalsozialistische Frauenpolitik*, ed. Arendt, Hering, & Wagner.

72. Hitler, April 1932; quoted in Hilda Browning, *Women Under Fascism and Communism* (London: Martin Lawrence, 1934), p. 3.

73. Engelbert Huber, *Das ist Nationalsozialismus* (Stuttgart: Union Deutsche Verlagsgesellschaft, 1933), pp. 121–22; transl. in *Nazi Culture*, ed. Mosse, p. 47.

74. Adolf Hitler, "Die völkische Sendung der Frau," speech to the Nationalsozialistische Frauenschaft, 8 Sept. 1934, Nuremberg; repr. in *Hitler, Reden und Proklamationen*, ed. Max Domarus, vol. 1 (Würzburg, 1962), pp.

449–54; transl. SGB in *WFF*, vol. 2, doc. 105, pp. 375–78. All quotations are from this translation.

75. Josef Goebbels, 12 Feb. 1934; quoted in Leila Rupp, "Mother of the *Volk*: The Image of Women in Nazi Ideology," *Signs*, 3:2 (Winter 1977), 363; also in Browning, *Women Under Fascism and Communism*, p. 8.

76. Gertrud Scholtz-Klink, speech to the Nationalsozialistische Frauen-schaft, 10 Sept. 1935; repr. in *Der Parteitag der Freiheit 1935, officieller Bericht über den Verlauf des Reichsparteitages mit sämtlichen Kongress-reden* (Munich, 1935), p. 172; transl. SGB in *WFF*, vol. 2, doc. 106 (quotes, pp. 378–81).

77. Discussions of the Nazi feminists include: Richard L. Johnson, "Nazi Feminists: A Contradiction in Terms," *Frontiers: A Journal of Women Studies*, 1:3 (Winter 1976), 55–62; Rupp, "Mother of the *Volk*," 362–79; Jost Hermand, "*All Power to the Women*: Nazi Concepts of Matri-archy," *Journal of Contemporary History*, 19:4 (Oct. 1984), 649–67; and Gisela T. Kaplan & Carole E. Adams, "Early Women Supporters of National Socialism," in *The Attraction of Fascism*, ed. John Milfull (Oxford: Berg, 1990), pp. 186–204. See also Liliane Crips, "Une Revue 'national-féministe': *Die deutsche Kämpferin* 1933–1937," in *La Tentation nationaliste 1914–1945*, pp. 167–82.

78. Sophie Rogge-Börner, "Denkschrift an den Kanzler des deutschen Reiches, Herrn Adolf Hitler, und an den Vizekanzler Herrn Franz von Pa-pen," in Irmgard Reichenau, ed., *Deutsche Frauen an Adolf Hitler* (Leipzig: Adolf Klein, 1933), pp. 7–11; transl. in Johnson, "Nazi Feminists," 57; also repr. in *Frauen im deutschen Faschismus*, vol. 1, doc. 23.

79. Sophie Philipps, *ibid.*, p. 49; transl. in Johnson, p. 58.

80. From *Die Deutsche Kämpferin*, July 1934 and Sept. 1934; transl. in Browning, *Women Under Fascism and Communism*, pp. 16, 20.

81. Adolf Hitler, 1935 speech to the NS-Frauenkongress, publ. in *Völkische Beobachter*, 15 Sept. 1935; transl. in *Nazi Culture*, ed. Mosse, pp. 39–40.

82. Adolf Hitler, 1936 speech to the NS-Frauenschaft, publ. in *Völkischer Beobachter*, 13 Sept. 1936; transl. in *Nazi Culture*, ed. Mosse, p. 39.

CHAPTER 11: MORE FEMINISMS IN NATIONAL SETTINGS

1. The 1909 and 1910 statutes of the Liga Republicana are reproduced in João Gomes Esteves, *A Liga Republicana das Mulheres Portuguesas: Uma organização politica e feminista (1909–1919)* (Lisbon: Organizaçoes nã Go-vernamentais do Conselho Consultivo da Comissão para a Igualdade e para as Direitos das Mulheres, 1991), pp. 177–84.

2. Elina Guimarães, *Femmes portugaises hier et aujourd'hui*, 2d ed. (Lisbon: Comissão da Condição Feminina, 1989), p. 18; orig. publ. in Portu-guese, 1987.

3. Anne Cova and Antonio Costa Pinto, "Les Femmes et le sala-zarisme," in *Encyclopédie historique et politique des femmes*, ed. Chris-tine Fauré (Paris: Presses Universitaires de France, 1997), pp. 685–99. I am

grateful to Anne Cova for sending a copy of this article prior to its publication.

4. For a splendid guide to the burgeoning literature on Irish women's history and the history of Irish feminism, see the special issue of the *Journal of Women's History*, 6:4–7:1 (Winter–Spring 1995), *Irish Women's Voices: Past and Present*, ed. Joan Hoff & Moureen Coulter. On women and Irish nationalism, see especially Margaret Ward, *Unmanageable Revolutionaries: Women in Irish Nationalism* (London: Pluto Press, 1983); and Ward, *Maud Gonne: A Life* (London: Pandora Press, 1990). An older work is Lil Conlon, *Cumann na mBan and the Women of Ireland, 1913–1925* (Kilkenny: Kilkenny People, 1969).

5. Constance de Markievicz, *A Call to the Women of Ireland, Being a Lecture Delivered to the Students' National Literary Society, Dublin, under the Title of "Women, Ideals, and the Nation"* (New York: The Irish Industries Depot of the Gaelic League of Ireland, n.d. [ca. 1917–18]); quotes, pp. 6, 4, 16, 12. Since 1985 two biographies of Constance de Markievicz (sometimes called Constance Markievicz) have been published: Diana Norman, *Terrible Beauty: A Life of Constance Markievicz* (London: Hodder & Stoughton, 1987); and Anne Haverty, *Constance Markievicz* (London: Pandora, 1988). Earlier biographies by Jacqueline Van Voris and Anne Marreco should also be consulted.

6. Proclamation of the Irish Republic, Easter Monday 1916; repr. in Rosemary Cullen Owens, *Smashing Times: A History of the Irish Suffrage Movement* (Dublin: Attic Press, 1984), p. 113.

7. *The Present Duty of Irishwomen* (issued by the executive of *Cumann na mBan*, Dublin, ca. 1918); repr. in *Women in Ireland, 1800–1918*, ed. Maria Luddy (Cork: Cork University Press, 1995), p. 319.

8. Hanna Sheehy Skeffington, in *The Irish Citizen*, issue of Sept.–Dec. 1920; quoted by Owens, *Smashing Times*, p. 129; a slightly different version appears in Mary Cullen, "How Radical Was Irish Feminism between 1860 and 1920?" in *Radicals, Rebels, & Establishments*, ed. Patrick J. Corish, *Historical Studies* [Irish Conference of Historians], 15 (1985), p. 195.

On Sheehy Skeffington, see the biographies listed in Chapter 8 n. 28. On the *Irish Citizen*, see also Louise Ryan, "The *Irish Citizen*, 1912–1920," *Saothar*, 17 (1992), 105–11; and Dana Hearne, "The *Irish Citizen* 1914–1916: Nationalism, Feminism, and Militarism," *Canadian Journal of Irish Studies*, 18:1 (1992), 1–14.

9. Owens, *Smashing Times*, p. 130.

10. Mary Clancy, "Aspects of Women's Contribution to the Oireachtas Debate in the Irish Free State, 1922–1937," in *Women Surviving: Studies in Irish Women's History in the 19th & 20th Centuries*, ed. Maria Luddy and Cliona Murphy (Dublin: Poolbeg, 1990), p. 209.

11. See Marie O'Neill, *From Parnell to De Valera: A Biography of Jennie Wyse Power, 1858–1941* (Dublin: Blackwater Press, 1991); and Kathleen Clarke, *Revolutionary Woman: An Autobiography, 1878–1972* (Dublin: O'Brien Press, 1991).

12. Maryann Gialanella Valiulis, "Defining Their Role in the New State: Irishwomen's Protest Against the Juries Act of 1927," *Canadian Journal of Irish Studies*, 18:1 (July 1992), 43.

13. Irish Women's Citizens Association resolution, publ. in *The Irish Times*, 12 March 1924; quoted in Valiulis, "Defining Their Role," 44.

14. *The Irish Times*, 22 Feb. 1927; quoted in Valiulis, "Defining Their Role," 46.

15. *Senate Debates*, 30 March 1927 (vol. 8, cols. 682–83); quoted in Valiulis, "Defining Their Role," 49.

16. Letter to the editor, *The Irish Times*, 17 Feb. 1927; quoted in Valiulis, "Defining Their Role," 51.

17. Edward Cahill, S.J., "Notes on Christian Sociology," *Irish Monthly*, 54 (Jan. 1925); quoted by Maryann Gialannella Valiulis, "Power, Gender, and Identity in the Irish Free State," *Journal of Women's History*, 6:4–7:1 (Winter–Spring 1995), 134 n. 21.

18. See Richard Michael Fox, *Louie Bennett: Her Life and Times* (Dublin: Talbot Press, 1958); and Mary Jones, *These Obstreperous Lassies: A History of the Irish Women Workers' Union* (Dublin: Gill & Macmillan, 1988).

19. All quotations from the 1937 Irish Constitution as repr. in Yvonne Scannell, "The Constitution and the Role of Women," in *De Valera's Constitution and Ours*, ed. Brian Farrell (Dublin: Gill & Macmillan, 1988), p. 124.

20. G(ertrude) G(affney), "A Woman's View of the Constitution," *Irish Independent*, 7 May 1937, 5–6; quotes, 6.

21. Mary S. Kettle, letter to the editor, "Constitutional Status of Women," *Irish Press*, 11 May 1937.

22. Louie Bennett, open letter to De Valera, publ. under the heading "Readers' Views: Women and the Constitution," *Irish Press*, 12 May 1937.

23. Letter from Betty Archdale, LL.B., to Eamon De Valera, 14 June 1937, in the archives, Department of the Taoiseach, National Archives, Dublin. My thanks to Catriona Crowe for forwarding a photocopy of this letter and the following one, as well as the clippings quoted in nn. 18–20 above.

24. Letter from Margery Corbett Ashby, on behalf of the IAWSEC, to De Valera, 7 July 1937, Department of the Taoiseach, National Archives, Dublin.

25. Despite the convocation in 1970 of the Commission on the Status of Women in Ireland, the issuance of several reports—on equal pay (1971), a full report (1973), a progress report (1976)—and litigation testing the constitutional clauses, it has still taken many years for feminists to change even a few of the legal disabilities that constrained Irish women. As Mary Robinson, a feminist attorney, and recently president of the Irish Republic, has also underscored, the pressure placed on Ireland by the European Economic Commission to conform to its equality clauses has provided an important motivation for change. According to the 1976 Progress Report of the Irish Commission on the Status of Women:

While considerable progress has been made in implementing certain areas in the Report [of 1973], particularly the areas of social welfare, equal pay, family law reform and jury service, other major areas of discrimination still remain. For example, penal tax laws are still in operation against married working women; no maternity protection legislation has been enacted and no progress has been made in relation to the provision of child care facilities for working mothers.

From the "Progress Report on the Implementation of the Recommendations in the Report of the Commission on the Status of Women, by Women's Representative Committee to Minister for Labour, December 1976"; quoted in Mary Robinson, "Women and the New Irish State," in *Women in Irish Society: The Historical Dimension*, ed. Margaret MacCurtain & Donncha O'Corrain (Westport: Greenwood Press, 1979; orig. publ. Dublin, 1978), p. 65.

26. For a survey of Spanish feminism and its cultural context, see the introductory chapter in Mary Nash, *Defying Male Civilization: Women in the Spanish Civil War* (Denver: Arden Press, 1996); on its historiography to 1990, see Mary Nash, "Two Decades of Women's History in Spain," in *Writing Women's History: International Perspectives*, ed. Karen Offen, Ruth Roach Pierson, & Jane Rendall (London: Macmillan; Bloomington: Indiana University Press, 1991), pp. 392–93. Indispensable works include: Geraldine M. Scanlon, *La Polémica feminista en la España contemporánea, 1868–1974*, 2d ed. (Madrid: AKAL, 1986; orig. publ. 1976); Concha Fagoaga de Bartoloma, *La Voz y el voto de las mujeres, 1877–1931* (Barcelona: Icaria, 1985); the articles in Pilar Folguera, ed., *El Feminismo en España: Dos siglos de historia* (Madrid: P. Iglesias, 1988); Rosa María Capel Martínez, *El Sufragio femenino en la Segunda República Española*, 2d ed. (Madrid: Horas y horas, 1992); and the documentary volumes *Mujer, familia y trabajo en España, 1875–1936*, ed. Mary Nash (Barcelona: Anthropos, 1983), and *Textos para la historia de las mujeres en España*, ed. Ana María Aguado et al. (Madrid: Cátedra, 1994). In "The Rise of the Women's Movement in Spain," an unpublished paper presented at Stuttgart/Birkach, 1995, Mary Nash contests the emphasis on political rights in the works of Capel Martínez and Folguera; see also Nash, "Experiencia y aprendizaje: La formación histórica de los feminismos en España," *Historia social*, no. 20 (Autumn 1994), 151–72.

On feminism and nationalism in regional contexts, see Mary Nash, "Political Culture, Catalan Nationalism and the Women's Movement in Early Twentieth-Century Spain," *Women's Studies International Forum*, 19:1–2 (1996), 45–54; and Mercedes Ugalde Solano, "The Discourse of Gender and the Basque Nationalist Movement in the First Third of the Twentieth Century," *History of European Ideas*, 15:4–6 (Aug. 1992), 695–700; see also Mercedes Ugalde Solano, "Evolución de la diferenciación de género e identidad feminina: Las Nacionalistas vascas, . . ." in two parts, in *Teoría feminista: Identidad, género y politica*, ed. Arantza Campos & Lourdes Méndez (San Sebastian: Universidad del País Vasco, 1993), pp. 117–31, 133–45.

27. See Gregorio Martínez Sierra, *Feminismo, feminidad, españolismo* (Madrid: Renacimiento, 1917). María Lejárraga's practice of publishing under her husband's name is well known: see Patricia W. O'Connor, *Gregorio & Maria Martinez Sierra* (Boston: Twayne, 1977); see also Antonina Rodrigo, *María Lejárraga: Una mujer en la sombra* (Barcelona: Circulo de Lectores, 1992). She wrote again under Gregorio's name in *Cartas a las mujeres de España* (1930), arguing that the very future of Spain—indeed, of humanity—lay in women's hands. But in 1931 she published her series of lectures *La mujer española ante la República* under her own name, with a dedication to Gregorio.

28. The ANME Program is reprinted in several works mentioned above, including Scanlon, *Polémica feminista*, and in *Textos para la historia*, ed. Aguado.

29. Nash, *Defying Male Civilization*, p. 40.

30. Margarita Nelken, *Por qué hicimos la revolución* (Barcelona: Ediciones sociales internacionales, 1936), p. 78; transl. in Robert Kern, "Margarita Nelken: Women and the Crisis of Spanish Politics," in *European Women on the Left*, ed. Jane Slaughter & Robert Kern (Westport: Greenwood Press, 1981), p. 155.

31. See Danièle Bussy-Genevois, "The Women of Spain from the Republic to Franco," in *Toward a Cultural Identity in the Twentieth Century*, ed. Françoise Thébaud (Cambridge, Mass.: Harvard University Press, 1994), pp. 177–93; Judith Keene, "'Into the Clear Air of the Plaza': Spanish Women Achieve the Vote in 1931," in *Constructing Spanish Womanhood: Female Identity in Modern Spain*, ed. Victoria Lorée Enders & Pamela Beth Radcliff (Albany: SUNY Press, 1999); and Frances Lannon, "Women and Images of Woman in the Spanish Civil War," *Transactions of the Royal Historical Society*, 6th ser., 1 (1991), 213–28.

32. "Les Dones de Catalonia," in *L'Opinio* (Barcelona), 29 June 1931; transl. in Nash, "Political Culture, Catalan Nationalism," 51.

33. On the suffrage debates, see Capel Martínez, *Sufragio feminino*, and Keene, "'Into the Clear Air.'"

34. Victoria Kent, in *Diario de las Sesiones de las Cortes Constituyentes de la República Española*, 1 Oct. 1931, p. 1352; transl. Judith Keene. I am most greatful to Judith Keene for forwarding copies of the *Diario* and for translating the two speeches.

35. Clara Campoamor, in *Diario de las Sesiones*, 1 Oct. 1931, pp. 1352–54; transl. Judith Keene.

36. On Mujeres Libres, see Nash, *Defying Male Civilization*; see also the collection *Mujeres libres: España 1936–1939*, ed. Mary Nash (Barcelona: Tusquets, 1976), which has also appeared in French and German editions. See also Martha A. Ackelsberg, *Free Women of Spain: Anarchism and the Struggle for the Emancipation of Women* (Bloomington: Indiana University Press, 1991).

37. From the statutes, *Estatutos de Mujeres libres: Carnet de afiliación*; transl. in Nash, *Defying Male Civilization*, p. 78.

38. Ilse, "La doble lucha de la mujer," *Mujeres libres,* 8th month of the revolution; transl. in Nash, *Defying Male Civilization,* p. 85.

39. Nash, *Defying Male Civilization,* p. 87.

40. Federica Montseny, "Feminismo y humanismo," *La Revista blanca,* 33 (1 Oct. 1924); transl. in Shirley Fredricks, "Feminism: The Essential Ingredient in Federica Montseny's Anarchist Theory," in *European Women on the Left,* ed. Slaughter & Kern, p. 133. A number of Montseny's important texts from the *Revista blanca* in the 1920s have been reprinted in *Arenal,* 1:2 (July–Dec. 1994), 307–29, with an introduction by Susanna Tavera García.

41. See Mary Nash, "Pronatalism and Motherhood in Franco's Spain," in *Maternity & Gender Policies: Women and the Rise of the European Welfare States 1880s—1950s,* ed. Gisela Bock & Pat Thane (London: Routledge, 1991), pp. 160–77.

42. Nash, *Defying Male Civilization,* p. 73.

43. Astrea Barrios, "Hombres a la vanguardia! Mujeres en la retaguardia!" *Mujeres* (Bilbao ed.), 17 April 1937; transl. in Nash, *Defying Male Civilization,* p. 77.

44. Victoria L. Enders, "Nationalism and Feminism: The Sección Femenina of the Falange," *History of European Ideas,* 15:4–6 (1992), 676. See also Enders, "Problematic Portraits: The Ambiguous Historical Role of the *Sección Femenina* of the Falange," in *Constructing Spanish Womanhood,* pp. 375–97; and María Teresa Gallego Méndez, *Mujer, Falange y Franquismo* (Madrid: Taurus, 1983).

45. Pilar Primo de Rivera, 1938; transl. in Enders, "Nationalism and Feminism," p. 674.

46. Enders, "Nationalism and Feminism," p. 675.

47. *Fuero de los Españoles,* July 1945; repr. in *Textos para la historia,* ed. Aguado, p. 386; transl. KO.

48. Nash, "Pronatalism and Motherhood," p. 175.

49. Lannon, "Women and Images of Woman," p. 215.

50. Swedish scholarship in women's history has only recently begun to address the history of feminism, preferring earlier to focus on women's work, labor unions, and "social" issues; during the decades of Social Democratic government, "women's issues" were appropriated and channeled by the ruling party, and independent "feminism" was not viewed favorably. See Yvonne Hirdman, "The State of Women's History in Sweden," in *Writing Women's History: International Perspectives,* pp. 239–58. This is beginning to change, with the publication of articles and books by Hirdman, Ulla Manns, Lina Eskilsson, Christina Carlsson Wetterberg, Margareta Lindholm, and others. For this case study of the 1930s, I have relied heavily on the publications in English by Sondra Herman, many of which are listed below, and am deeply grateful for her advice and assistance with the Swedish case.

51. See Lena Eskilsson, *Drommen om kamratsamhallet: Kvinnliga medborgarskolan pa Fogelstad* (Female Citizenship: The Women Citizens'

School at Fogelstad, 1925–1935) (Stockholm: Carlsson, 1991); Jarl Torbecke, "Kvinnolisten 1927–1928—Ett kvinnopolitiskt fiasko [The Woman's List: A Woman's Political Fiasco]," *Historisk Tidskrift*, 1969, no. 2, 145–84; Margareta Lindholm, *Talet om det kvinnliga: Studier i feministiskt tankande i Sverige under 1930-talet* (Gothenburg: Dept. of Sociology Monograph no. 44, 1990); and especially Sondra Herman, "Feminists, Socialists, and the Genesis of the Swedish Welfare State," in *Views of Women's Lives in Western Tradition*, ed. Frances Richardson Keller (Lewiston: Edwin Mellen Press, 1990), pp. 472–510.

52. Quote from *Tidevarvet* (1928); transl. in Herman, "Feminists, Socialists," p. 477. Concerning this periodical, see Sarah Death, "*Tidevarvet*: A Radical Weekly Magazine of the Inter-War Years," *Swedish Book Review*, 1 (1986), 38–40.

53. Herman, "Feminists, Socialists," p. 482.

54. Herman, "Feminists, Socialists," p. 481. On Wägner's *Väckarklocka*, see also Helena Forsås-Scott, "The Revolution That Never Was: The Example of Elin Wägner," *The European Legacy*, 1:3 (May 1996), 914–19.

55. For an extensive, less welcoming analysis of the 1933 debates, see Allan Carlson, *The Swedish Experiment in Family Politics: The Myrdals and the Interwar Population Crisis* (New Brunswick: Transaction Publishers, 1988). On the Swedish population crisis, see Ann-Katrin Hatje, *Bevolkningsfrågan och välfärden: Debatten om familjepolitik och nativitetsökning under 1930- och 1940-talen* (Stockholm: Allmäna Förlaget, 1974); Ann-Sofie Kälvemark (Ohlander), *More Children of Better Quality? Aspects on Swedish Population Policy in the 1930s* (Stockholm: Almqvist & Wiksell, 1980); Ann-Sophie Ohlander, "The Invisible Child? The Struggle for a Social Democratic Family Policy in Sweden, 1900–1960s," in *Maternity and Gender Policies*, pp. 60–72; and Elisabeth Elgán, *Genus och politik: En jämförelse mellan svensk och fransk abort- och preventiv-medelspolitik fran sekelskiftet till andra väridskriget*, Acta Universitatis Upsaliensis, Studia Historica Upsaliensia 176 (Uppsala, 1994).

56. *Tidevarvet*, 16 Sept. 1933; this reference courtesy of Sondra Herman.

57. Yvonne Hirdman, "Social Engineering and the Woman Question: Sweden in the Thirties," *Studies in Political Economy*, no. 44 (Summer 1994), 82, 83. See also Hirdman, "Utopia in the Home," *International Journal of Political Economy*, 22:2 (Summer 1992), 5–99.

58. Alva Myrdal, "Swedish Women in Industry and at Home," in *Social Problems and Policies in Sweden*, ed. Bertil Ohlin, Annals of the American Academy of Political and Social Science, vol. 197 (Philadelphia, May 1938) pp. 216–31; quote, pp. 230–31. On Alva Myrdal's campaigns, see Sissela Bok, *Alva Myrdal: A Daughter's Memoir* (Reading: Addison-Wesley, 1991).

59. From the Report Concerning Married Women's Paid Employment (Stockholm: Isaac Marcus Boktryckeri, 1938), pp. 339–49; transl. in Sondra Herman, "Children, Feminism, and Power: Alva Myrdal and Swedish Reform, 1929–1956," *Journal of Women's History*, 4:2 (Fall 1992), 96.

60. Alva Myrdal, *Nation and Family: The Swedish Experiment in Democratic Family and Population Policy* (London: Kegan, Paul, 1945); excerpted in *WFF*, vol. 2, doc. 112, p. 394.

61. Pius XII, "Woman's Dignity: Political and Social Obligations" (*Questa granade vostra adunata*), broadcast from Vatican City, 21 Oct. 1945; repr. in *Vital Speeches*, 12 (1 Nov. 1945), pp. 42–45; and in *WFF*, vol. 2, doc. 118.

62. Pius XII, "Woman's Dignity," in *WFF*, vol. 2, p. 419.

63. W. W. Rutgers-Hoitsema, letter to the editor, *Jus Suffragii*, 12:2 (1 Nov. 1917), 24.

64. See Doris H. Linder, *Crusader for Sex Education: Elise Ottesen-Jensen (1886–1973) in Scandinavia and on the International Scene* (Lanham: University Press of America, 1996); and Ida Blom, *Barnebegrensning—Synd eller sunn fornuft* (Sin or Common Sense? Limiting Family Size in Norway, 1890s–1930s) (Bergen: Universitets Forlaget, 1980).

65. See Ruth Hall, *Marie Stopes: A Biography* (London: André Deutsch, 1977); and June Rose, *Marie Stopes and the Sexual Revolution* (London & New York: Faber & Faber, 1992); Sheila Rowbotham, *A New World for Women: Stella Browne, Socialist Feminist* (London: Pluto Press, 1977); and Barbara Brookes, *Abortion in England, 1900–1967* (London: Croom Helm, 1988). See also Johanna Alberti, "The Turn of the Tide: Sexuality and Politics, 1928–31," *Women's History Review*, 3:2 (1994); and Margaret Jackson, *The Real Facts of Life: Feminism and the Politics of Sexuality, c. 1850–1940* (London: Taylor & Francis, 1994).

66. Anna Löffler-Herzog, quoted in Susanna Woodtli, *Du Féminisme à l'égalité politique: Un Siècle de luttes en Suisse, 1868–1971* (Lausanne: Payot, 1977), pp. 80–81.

67. Madeleine Vernet, "Sur un brochure: L'amour libre," *La Mère éducatrice*, 3:9 (June 1920), 72.

68. Winifred Holtby, "King George V Jubilee Celebrations," *Time and Tide*, 4 May 1935; repr. in *Testament of a Generation: The Journalism of Vera Brittain and Winifred Holtby*, ed. Paul Berry & Alan Bishop (London: Virago, 1985), p. 92.

69. Louise Bodin, in *L'Humanité*, 9 Aug. 1920; quoted in Colette Cosnier, *La Bolshevique aux bijoux: Louise Bodin* (Paris: P. Horay, 1988), p. 121. On the complexities of sexual-maternal politics in 1920s France, see Cova, *Maternité et droits des femmes en France*; and for background, see Jean Elisabeth Pedersen, "Regulating Abortion and Birth Control: Gender, Medicine, and Republican Politics in France, 1870–1920," *French Historical Studies*, 19:3 (Spring 1996), 673–98.

70. See Francis Szipiner, *Une Affaire de femmes, Paris 1943: Exécution d'une avorteuse* (Paris: Bailand, 1986); and the film by Claude Chabrol based on this extraordinary case.

71. Holtby, "King George V Jubilee," pp. 90–92.

72. Bertie Albrecht, "La Femme dans le monde moderne," *Le Problème*

sexuel, no. 4 (1934); quoted in Michèle Blin Sarde, *Regarde sur les fran-çaises* (Paris: Stock, 1983), pp. 578–79.

73. In these chapters it has not been possible to consider the cases of a number of other countries: for example, the new nations of Czechoslovakia, Poland, the Baltic republics of Estonia, Latvia, and Lithuania, and the new Balkan states, not to mention other smaller seaboard nations such as the Netherlands, and the other Scandinavian nations besides Sweden, all of which deserve fuller treatment. For some, substantial scholarly inquiry has been undertaken on the history of feminism, but for others—particularly those states that were under communist rule from the late 1940s to 1989—it is just beginning. Some additional works concerning feminism in these nations are listed in the bibliography at the end of this book.

74. Karen Johnsen, "The General Legal Status of Women," in *Women in the Community*, ed. Kirsten Gloerfelt-Tarp (London and Oxford: Oxford University Press; orig. publ. in Danish, 1937), p. 282.

75. Kirsten Gloerfelt-Tarp, "Status of Women in Social Legislation," in *Women in the Community*, ed. Gloerfelt-Tarp, p. 283.

CHAPTER 12: EUROPEAN FEMINIST INTERNATIONAL

ACTIVITY

I wish particularly to thank Sondra Herman, Doris H. Linder, Shulamit Magnus, and the Scholars' Group at the Institute for Research on Women and Gender, Stanford University, for their many good suggestions for improving this chapter. My thanks also to Leila J. Rupp, for allowing me to consult the manuscript of her *Worlds of Women* prior to its publication; I trust she will find my sources and interpretation complementary to her own. I also wish to acknowledge the magnificent documentary and microfilm holdings of the Stanford University and Hoover Institution libraries, as well as the supportive staff members who have so greatly facilitated my access to these materials. I regret not being able to consult Carol Miller's "Lobbying the League: Women's International Organiations and the League of Nations" (Ph.D. dissertation, St. Hilda's College, University of Oxford, 1992), or her forthcoming book prior to completion of this chapter.

1. Charlotte Perkins Gilman, "The Woman Suffrage Congress in Budapest," *The Forerunner*, 4:8 (Aug. 1913), 204. See above, Chapter 7, for the earlier phases of international feminist organization, and for the broad span, the now indispensable work of Leila J. Rupp, *Worlds of Women: International Women's Organizations, 1888–1945* (Princeton: Princeton University Press, 1998).

2. The Petite Entente des Femmes held at least three conferences in the 1920s. I have located published proceedings for the 1924 meeting and a brief report on the 1925 meeting by Avra Theodoropoulos in *Jus Suffragii*, 20:5 (Feb. 1926), 69. To my knowledge, there has been no scholarly work on this group. Nor is there as yet much scholarship on feminist activity in the member countries during the 1920s and 1930s.

3. See Conseil National des Femmes Françaises, *États-généraux du féminisme, 30–31 Mai 1931* (Paris: CNFF, 1931); and on the subsequent conference in Algeria, see *Jus Suffragii*, 26:6 (March 1932), 55, 65; and contemporary clippings from the Algerian press in Malaterre Sellier's dossier. Both can be consulted at the Bibliothèque Marguerite Durand, Paris. See also Marie Bugéja, "Ce qui fut le Congrès des femmes méditerranéennes," *Bulletin de la Société de Géographie d'Alger et de l'Afrique du Nord*, 37, no. 132 (1932), 544–68.

4. Carol Miller, "'Geneva—The Key to Equality': Inter-War Feminists and the League of Nations," *Women's History Review*, 3:2 (1994), 219–45.

5. Constance Drexel, "Feminism More Effective in Europe than America," *Current History*, 24:2 (May 1926), 211–15.

6. Quoted in Carol Riegelman Lubin & Anne Winslow, *Social Justice for Women: The International Labor Organization and Women* (Durham: Duke University Press, 1990), p. 32.

7. For insights into the IFWW and ICWG from a British perspective, see Pamela M. Graves, *Labour Women: Women in British Working-Class Politics, 1918–1939* (Cambridge: Cambridge University Press, 1994); and the essays in *Women in the Labour Movement: The British Experience*, ed. Lucy Middleton (London: Croom Helm, 1977). See also Naomi Black, "The Mothers' International: The Women's Co-Operative Guild and Feminist Pacifism," *Women's Studies International Forum*, 7:6 (1984), 467–76.

8. See Rupp, *Worlds of Women*; and Rupp, "Constructing Internationalism: The Case of Transnational Women's Organizations, 1888–1945," *American Historical Review*, 99:5 (Dec. 1994), 1571–1600.

9. For discussion of this term, see Jo Vellacott, "'Transnationalism' in the Early Women's International League for Peace and Freedom," in *The Pacifist Impulse in Historical Perspective*, ed. Harvey L. Dyck (Toronto: University of Toronto Press, 1996), pp. 362–83. Francesca Miller also speaks in terms of transnationalism in *Latin American Women and the Search for Social Justice* (Hanover & London: University Press of New England, 1991).

10. See Magdeleine Boy, *Les Associations internationales féminines*, thèse de doctorat, Faculté de Droit, Université de Lyon (Lyon: Imprimerie Paquet, 1936).

11. Willemijn Hendrika Posthumus–van der Goot, *Vrouwen vochten voor de vrede* (Arnhem: Van Loghum Slaterus, 1961), p. 209; transl. in *Politics and Friendship: Letters from the International Woman Suffrage Alliance, 1902–1942*, ed. Mineke Bosch with Annemarie Kloosterman (Columbus: Ohio State University Press, 1990), p. 177.

12. Treaty of Versailles, Article 7, as reprinted in *Major Peace Treaties of Modern History 1648–1967*, ed. Fred L. Israel, 2 vols. (New York: Chelsea House Publishers, 1967), 2:1277.

13. Margery Corbett Ashby, in *Women at Work in the League of Nations*, ed. D(orothea) M(ary) Northcroft (London: Page & Pratt, 1923), p. 1. See also Ki-Tcheng, *La Femme et la Société des Nations*, published thesis, Faculté de Droit, Université de Paris (Paris: Presses Modernes, 1928). In ad-

dition, I have drawn on the excellent reports on international feminist activity in the annual volumes of the *Jahrbuch für Schweizerfrauen/Annuaire des femmes suisses*.

14. Emilie Gourd, "Switzerland," *Jus Suffragii*, 8:7 (1 March 1914), 78.

15. For details, see Sibylle Hardmeier, *Frühe Frauenstimmrechtsbewegung in der Schweiz (1890–1930): Argumente, Strategien, Netzwerk und Gegenbewegung* (Zurich: Chronos, 1997).

16. Siân Reynolds, *France Between the Wars: Gender and Politics* (London: Routledge, 1996), p. 188.

17. These publications included: (1) *Collaboration of Women in the Organisation of Peace: Report by the Secretary-General, 25 August 1932*; (2) *Collaboration of Women in the Work of the League: Report by the Sixth Committee, [Kerstin Hesselgren, rapporteur], 10 October 1932*; (3) *Nationality of Women: Report of the Secretary-General on the Information Obtained in Execution of the Resolutions of the Assembly and the Council* (1934); (4) *Nationality and Status of Women: Statements Presented by International Women's Organisations, 30 August 1935*; (5) *Status of Women: Communications from Governments and Women's International Organisations since September 27th, 1935* (1936); (6) *Status of Women: Report Submitted by the First Committee, 25 September 1937 [rapporteur, Kerstin Hesselgren]*; and (7) *Committee for the Study of the Legal Status of Women: Report on the Progress of the Inquiry (adopted on January 10th, 1939)*.

18. Treaty of Versailles, art. 427 (ILO CHARTER), paragr. 7; repr. in *Major Peace Treaties*, ed. Israel, 2: 1523.

19. International Labour Office, *The International Protection of Women Workers*, Studies and Reports, ser. 1, no. 1 (Geneva, 1921), p. 4.

20. See Mary E. Daly, "'Fanaticism and Excess' or 'the Defence of Just Causes': The International Labour Organisation and Women's Protective Legislation in the Inter-War Years," in *Chattel, Servant or Citizen: Women's Status in Church, State, and Society*, ed. Mary O'Dowd & Sabine Wichert [*Historical Studies, XIX*] (Belfast: The Institute of Irish Studies, The Queen's University of Belfast, 1995), pp. 215–27.

21. See, for the British "equal rights" advocates, Barbara Caine, *English Feminism, 1780–1980* (Oxford: Oxford University Press, 1997), chap. 5, "Feminism and the Woman Citizen in the Interwar Years"; and for their French counterparts Vérone and Lehmann, see Laurence Klejman & Florence Rochefort, *L'Égalité en marche: Le Féminisme sous la Troisième République* (Paris: des femmes, 1989); and Christine Bard, *Les Filles de Marianne: Histoire des féminismes, 1914–1940* (Paris: Fayard, 1995).

22. Dora Russell, *Hypatia, or Woman and Knowledge* (New York: E. P. Dutton, 1925; orig. publ. London: Kegan Paul, 1925), p. 67.

23. *New York World*, 26 May 1926; clipping quoted in Rupp, *Worlds of Women*, ms. p. 263. For discussion of the American disagreements on these issues, see Nancy F. Cott, *The Grounding of Modern Feminism* (New Haven: Yale University Press, 1987).

24. See Karen Offen, "Body Politics: Women, Work and the Politics of

Motherhood in France, 1920–1950," in *Maternity and Gender Policies: Women and the Rise of the European Welfare States, 1880s–1950s,* ed. Gisela Bock & Pat Thane (London: Routledge, 1991), pp. 138–59.

25. Marguerite Thibert, "The Economic Depression and the Employment of Women," *International Labour Review,* 17:4 (April 1933), 443–70, and 17:5 (May 1933), 620–30.

26. Thibert, "Economic Depression" (part 2), 621.

27. Abraham Flexner, *Prostitution in Europe* (New York: Century, 1914).

28. Saiza Nabarawi; quoted in Margot Badran, *Feminists, Islam, and Nation* (Princeton: Princeton University Press, 1995), p. 200.

29. League of Nations, *Report of the Special Body of Experts on Traffic in Women and Children,* pt. 1 (Geneva, 1927), p. 45. In addition, see H(enry) Wilson Harris, *Human Merchandise: A Study of the International Traffic in Women* (London: Ernest Benn, 1928).

30. Miller, "Geneva—The Key to Equality," 238.

31. Rupp, *Worlds of Women,* pp. 210, 215.

32. Communication, dated 21 Sept. 1936, from the Committee of Representatives of Women's International Organisations." *League of Nations. Assembly. Records. 18th Session, 1937,* Annex 3, p. 46.

33. Such questions are addressed by Linda Rennie Forcey, "Women as Peacemakers: Contested Terrain for Feminist Peace Studies," *Peace & Change,* 16:4 (Oct. 1991), 331–54.

34. Black, "The Mothers' International," 468.

35. Sandi E. Cooper, "Women's Participation in European Peace Movements: The Struggle to Prevent World War I," in *Women and Peace: Theoretical, Historical and Practical Perspectives,* ed. Ruth Roach Pierson (London: Croom Helm, 1987), p. 51.

36. Linda Gordon, "The Peaceful Sex? On Feminism and the Peace Movement," *NWSA Journal,* 2:4 (Autumn 1990), 634.

37. "Statement of Aims, 1926," in *Report of the Fifth Congress of the Women's International League for Peace and Freedom, Dublin, July 8 to 15, 1926,* English ed. (Geneva: WILPF [1926]), p. 184; repr. in *Women's International League for Peace and Freedom, 1915–1938: A Venture in Internationalism* (Geneva: WILPF, 1938), p. 20.

38. Mary Sheepshanks, "The Kellogg Peace Pact and After," *Pax International,* 3:9 (Aug. 1928). This publication is unpaginated.

39. "The W. I. L. Deputation on Disarmament to the League of Nations," *Pax International,* 3:11 (Oct. 1928).

40. Maria Vérone, "Les Femmes et la paix," *L'Oeuvre,* 11 Sept. 1929. My understanding of Vérone's contribution has been enhanced by Gisèle Garcia's undergraduate honors thesis, "Maria Vérone and the Feminist Campaign in Inter-war France, 1926–1936," Vassar College, 1991.

41. Miss (Mary A.) Dingman, quoted in Adele Schreiber, "Women at the Disarmament Conference," *Jus Suffragii,* 26:6 (March 1932), 55.

42. Schreiber, "Women at the Disarmament Conference," 55.

43. League of Nations. *Collaboration of Women in the Organisation of Peace. Report by the Secretary-General, 25 August, 1932* (Geneva, 1932. General Publications, 1932, no. 4), p. 1.

44. WILPF, "Statement on Fascism," *Pax International*, 8:6 (May 1933).

45. "Defence of Women Against Fascism,'" *Pax International*, 8:10 (Dec. 1933).

46. "Statement of Aims of the Women's International League for Peace and Freedom, Decided at the Zurich Congress, 1934"; repr. in Gertrude Bussey & Margaret Tims, *Women's International League for Peace and Freedom, 1915–1965: A Record of Fifty Years' Work* (London: George Allen & Unwin, 1965), pp. 122–23.

47. *Report of the Ninth Congress of the W.I.L.P.F., July 27th to 31st, 1937, Luhacovice, Czechoslovakia* (Geneva: The International Headquarters, 1937), p. 104.

48. *Jus Suffragii*, 30:1 (Oct. 1935), 2.

49. Kerstin Hesselgren, in League of Nations, *Official Journal*, special supplement No. 151. *Records of the Sixteenth Ordinary Session of the Assembly. Plenary Meetings (June 30th to July 4th, 1936). Text of the Debates. Part II*, p. 63. Session of 3 July 1936.

50. Eleanor Roosevelt, "La Grève des ventres," *Le Droit des femmes* (May 1938), 78; quoted in Christine Bard, *Les Filles de Marianne*, p. 304; Orig. English version in Eleanor Roosevelt's syndicated column, "My Day," April 1938.

51. Margery Corbett Ashby, "War," *Jus Suffragii*, 34:1 (Oct. 1939), 1.

52. Marthe Boël, in ICW *Bulletin*, 18:7–8 (April–May 1940); quoted in Rupp, "Worlds of Women," from the manuscript version, chapter 2, p. 83. This quotation did not make it into the published book.

53. Margery I. Corbett Ashby, "The History of the Alliance," *Jus Suffragii*, 35:1 (Oct.–Nov. 1940), 5.

54. Winston S. Churchill, "Man-power and Woman-power," address to the House of Commons, 2 Dec. 1941; repr. in *Winston S. Churchill: His Complete Speeches, 1897–1963*, ed. Robert Rhodes James, vol. 6 (New York & London: Chelsea House Publishers, 1974), p. 6520.

55. See "Women in Combat and as Military Leaders: A Survey," prepared by Staff Support Branch, Center of Military History, U.S. Army, 1 March 1978. My thanks to Romana Danysh for sharing this report.

56. Bussey & Tims, *Women's International League*, p. 180.

57. Margery I. Corbett Ashby, "What Is the Alliance?" *Jus Suffragii*, 22:5 (Feb. 1928), 69.

58. Helena Swanwick, "Preface" to *The Future of the Women's Movement* (London: G. Bell & Sons, 1913), vii.

59. Henri Joly, *Le Droit féminin* (Paris: Flammarion, 1922), p. 7.

60. C. Nina Boyle, letter to the editor, 15 Dec. 1927; publ. in *Jus Suffragii*, 22:4 (Jan. 1928), 59–60.

61. Boyle, letter to the editor, 15 March 1928; publ. in *Jus Suffragii*, 22:7 (April 1928), 106.

62. Corbett Ashby, in *Jus Suffragii*, 22:5 (Feb. 1928), 69.

63. Marie Stritt, in *Jus Suffragii*, 22:6 (March 1928), 87.

64. Carrie Chapman Catt, "What Is the Alliance?" *Jus Suffragii*, 22:8 (May 1928), 117–18.

65. Helen A. Archdale, in *Jus Suffragii*, 22:9 (June 1928), 140.

66. Archdale, letter to the editor, 30 Oct. 1928; publ. in *Jus Suffragii*, 23:3 (Dec. 1928), 41–42.

67. See Regine Deutsch, *The International Woman Suffrage Alliance: Its History from 1904 to 1929* (London: Board of the Alliance, 1929).

68. "Statement of Aims . . . , 1934"; repr. in Bussey & Tims, *Women's International League*, p. 122.

69. Corbett Ashby, in *Jus Suffragii*, 31:1 (Oct. 1936), 1.

70. See Pauline Johnson, *Feminism as Radical Humanism* (St. Leonards: Allen & Unwin; Boulder, Colo.: Westview Press, 1994), vii.

71. Corbett Ashby, "The Woman Pilgrim's Progress," *Jus Suffragii*, 33:9 (June 1939), 68.

72. Germaine Malaterre Sellier, "Vers l'avenir," *Jus Suffragii*, 33:9 (June 1939), 68–69.

73. IAW, "Declaration of Principles," *International Women's News* (*Jus Suffragii*), 33:10–11 (Aug.–Sept. 1939), 82; partly repr. in Adele Schreiber & Margaret Mathieson, *Journey Towards Freedom: Written for the Golden Jubilee of the International Alliance of Women* (Copenhagen: IAW, 1955), p. 52; and in Arnold Whittick, *Woman into Citizen* (London: Athenaeum; Santa Barbara: ABC-Clio, 1979), p. 139.

74. *The United Nations and the Advancement of Women, 1945–1996* (New York: United Nations, 1996), doc. 1, p. 103. My understanding of the UN issues has been greatly enhanced by the suggestions and unpublished work of Doris H. Linder, particularly her unpublished paper "Scandinavian Women's Rights Leadership at the Early U.N., 1946–1952" (1995).

75. *Yearbook of the United Nations, 1946–1947* (Lake Success: United Nations, Department of Public Information, 1947), pp. 77–78.

76. *Yearbook, 1946–47*, p. 179.

77. Corbett Ashby, "United Nations' Assembly. Women Out-Numbered Fifty to One by Men," *International Women's News* (*Jus Suffragii*), 40:5 (Feb. 1946), 51.

EPILOGUE

1. "Programme for Amsterdam," *International Women's News* (formerly *Jus Suffragii*), 43:6 (April 1949), 1. All quotations in this paragraph are from this source.

2. See Christine Fauré, *Democracy Without Women: Feminism and the Rise of Liberal Individualism in France* (Bloomington: Indiana University Press, 1991).

3. See Elizabeth Heineman, "The Hour of the Woman: Memories of Germany's 'Crisis Years' and the West German National Identity," *American Historical Review*, 101:2 (April 1996), 354–95. German women also be-

came the objects of male violence by occupying troops: see the special issue of *October* no. 72 (Spring 1995)—"Berlin 1945: War and Rape, 'Liberators Take Liberties,'" and especially Atina Grossmann's essay, "A Question of Silence: The Rape of German Women by Occupation Soldiers," 43–63.

4. Hanna Rydh, "President's Message," *International Women's News*, 43:11 (Sept. 1949), 158. On Rydh's career, see Elisabeth Arwill-Nordbladh, "Archaeology, Gender and Emancipation: The Paradox of Hanna Rydh," in *Excavating Women: A History of Women in European Archaeology*, ed. Margarita Díaz-Andreu & Marie Louise Stig Sørensen (London & New York: Routledge, 1998), 155–74.

5. George N. Serebrennikov, *The Position of Women in the U.S.S.R.* (London: V. Gollancz, 1937), p. 7. Comparable claims can be found in N(adezhda) K. Krupskaya, *Soviet Woman: A Citizen with Equal Rights—A Collection of Articles and Speeches* (Moscow: Co-Operative Publishing Society of Foreign Workers in the USSR, 1937). Krupskaya was Lenin's widow.

6. "The Soviet Family Law of 8 July 1944, Decree of the Praesidium of the Supreme Soviet of the U.S.S.R."; transl. in *The Family in the U.S.S.R.*, ed. Rudolf Schlesinger (London, 1949), pp. 367–72; repr. in *WFF*, vol. 2, doc. 116 (quote, p. 407).

7. For a detailed account of the French woman suffrage battles, and the final decisions of 1944, see Paul Smith, *Feminism and the Third Republic: Women's Political and Civil Rights in France 1918–1945* (Oxford: Clarendon Press, 1996). See also Florence Rochefort, "La Citoyenneté interdite, ou les enjeux du suffragisme," *Vingtième siècle*, no. 42 (Apr.–June 1994), 41–51.

8. Mattei Dogan & Jacques Narbonne, *Les Françaises face à la politique: Comportement politique et condition sociale* (Paris: A. Colin, 1955), p. 189.

9. See Renée Rousseau, *Les Femmes rouges: Chronique des années Vermeersch* (Paris: Albin Michel, 1983); and Jeannette Thorez-Vermeersch, *La Vie en rouge: Mémoires* (Paris: Belfond, 1998).

10. "Les Trois Devoirs de la femme française: Rapport de Madame Claudine Michaut—9er Congrès de l'U.F.F.," *Femmes françaises*, no. 41 (5 July 1945), 3; transl. KO.

11. On the rapidly mutating images of "the communist woman" in Germany, France, and Italy, see Eric D. Weitz, "The Heroic Man and the Ever-Changing Woman: Gender and Politics in European Communism, 1917–1950," in *Gender and Class in Modern Europe*, ed. Laura L. Frader & Sonya O. Rose (Ithaca: Cornell University Press, 1996), pp. 311–52. The Italian case should be compared with the French case; see, for the UDI, Giulietta Ascoli, "L'UDI tra emancipazione e liberazione (1943–1964)," in Giulietta Ascoli et al. *La Questione femminile in Italia* (Milan: Franco Angeli, 1977), pp. 109–59; and for the subsequent period, Judith Adler Hellman, "The Italian Communists, the Women's Question, and the Challenge of Feminism," *Studies in Political Economy*, no. 13 (Spring 1984), 57–82. For the feminist challenge to French communists in the 1970s, see Jane Jenson, "The French Communist Party and Feminism," *The Socialist Register*

1980, ed. Ralph Miliband & John Saville (London: Merlin Press, 1980), pp. 121–47.

12. Mouvement Républicain Populaire, *Femme face à vos responsabilités dans la vie familiale, la vie sociale, la vie économique* (Paris: MRP, 1946); quotes, pp. 1, 34; transl. KO.

13. *Les Femmes dans la nation: Rapport présenté par Jeannette Vermeersch, membre du Comité Central, Député de Paris, Vice-Présidente de la Fédération Démocratique Internationale des Femmes, XIe Congrès National du Parti Communiste Français, Strasbourg, 25, 26, 27, 28 Juin 1947* (Paris: Editions du PCF, 1947), p. 31.

14. Maurice Duverger, *The Political Role of Women* (Paris: UNESCO, 1955); quotes, pp. 125–26.

15. See Claire Duchen, *Women's Rights and Women's Lives in France, 1944–1968* (London: Routledge, 1994).

16. Duchen, *Women's Rights*, p. 44.

17. To date I have been unable to locate any scholarly discussions of the WIDF and its dealings with nationally based communist-front women's organizations—apart from the rather abbreviated account of the French beginnings in Rousseau, *Femmes rouges*. A thorough inquiry into the activities of this umbrella organization and its affiliates would probably require an international team research effort.

18. M[argery] Corbett Ashby, "International Congress of Women, Paris 1945," *International Women's News (Jus Suffragii)*, 40:4 (Jan. 1946), 39–40; quotes here and below, p. 39.

19. (WIDF) *World Congress of Women, Copenhagen, June 5th–10th, 1953: Documents* (pamphlet in the collection of the Hoover Institution).

20. William Henry Beveridge, Baron Beveridge, *Social Insurance and Allied Services: Report by Sir William Beveridge*, American ed. (New York: Macmillan, 1942); quotes, pp. 48–53.

21. Eleanor Rathbone, "Foreword," to Erna Reiss, *Rights and Duties of Englishwomen: A Study in Law and Public Opinion* (Manchester: Sherratt & Hughes, 1934), ix.

22. See Susan Pedersen, *Family, Dependence, and the Origins of the Welfare State: Britain and France, 1914–1945* (Cambridge: Cambridge University Press, 1993).

23. Vera Brittain, *Lady into Woman: A History of Women from Victoria to Elizabeth II* (London: Andrew Dakers, 1953), p. 224.

24. Helge Pross, "Die gesellschaftliche Stellung der Frau in Westdeutschland," *Deutsche Rundschau*, 81 (1958), 26–33; transl. Robert Moeller, *Protecting Motherhood: Women and the Family in the Politics of Postwar West Germany* (Berkeley & Los Angeles: University of California Press, 1992), p. 226.

25. Moeller, *Protecting Motherhood*, p. 228.

26. See Annette Kuhn, "Power and Powerlessness: Women after 1945, or the Continuity of the Ideology of Femininity," *German History*, 7:1 (1989),

35–46; see also Annette Kuhn, with Doris Schubert, eds., *Frauen in der deutschen Nachkriegzeit*, 2 vols. (Düsseldorf: Schwann, 1984–86). For Austria, see Irene Bandhauer-Schöffmann & Ela Hornung, "War and Gender Identity: The Experience of Austrian Women, 1945–1950," in *Austrian Women in the Nineteenth and Twentieth Centuries*, ed. David F. Good, Margarete Grandner, & Mary Jo Maynes (Providence, R.I.: Berghahn Books, 1996), pp. 213–33.

27. There is as yet little published historical scholarship on feminism between 1918 and World War II in the countries that fell under Soviet Russian influence from the 1940s to 1989. The archives of some pre–1945 Hungarian women's (including feminist) organizations have been rediscovered in the Hungarian National Archives, where they slumbered for decades following dissolution of all competing women's organizations and their ultimate merger by 1949 into the official women's organization of the new communist regime; see Andrea Petö, "As the Storm Approached: The Last Years of the Hungarian Women's Societies Before the Stalinist Takeover," *Central European University History Department Yearbook, 1994–95*, ed. Andrea Petö (Budapest: Central European University, 1995), 181–206.

28. Simone de Beauvoir, *The Second Sex*, ed. and transl. H. M. Parshley (New York: Modern Library, 1968 [orig. French publ. 1949; English transl. 1952]). For discussion of the book's context and reception, see (among other works) Deirdre Bair, *Simone de Beauvoir: A Biography*; and *The Condition of Women in France—1945 to the Present*, ed. Claire Laubier (London & New York: Routledge, 1990), chap. 2. See also Eva Lundgren-Gothlin, *Sex and Existence: Simone de Beauvoir's "The Second Sex"* (London: Athlone, 1996 [orig. Swedish publ. 1991]).

29. Beauvoir, *Second Sex*, 267. See Karen Offen, "Before Beauvoir, Before Butler: Genre and Gender in France and the Anglo-American World," unpublished article.

30. Paul Crouzet, *Bachelières ou jeunes filles* (Toulouse: Privat, 1949), p. 101; transl. in Lisa Greenwald, "Not 'Undifferentiated Magma': Refashioning a Female Identity in France, 1944–55," *Historical Reflections/Reflexions Historiques*, 22:2 (Spring 1996), 422. Greenwald's unpublished Ph.D. dissertation, "The Women's Liberation Movement in France and the Origins of Contemporary French Feminism, 1944–1981" (Emory University, 1996), which is now being revised for publication, discusses French feminist contributions during this period. Unfortunately, I did not have an opportunity to consult it before finishing this chapter.

31. See Jane Lewis, "Myrdal, Klein, *Women's Two Roles* and Postwar Feminism 1945–1960," in *British Feminism in the Twentieth Century*, ed. Harold L. Smith (Gloucester: Edward Elgar, 1990), 167–88.

32. Susan Groag Bell & Karen Offen, "General Introduction," in *WFF*, vol. 1, p. 11.

Bibliography

This summary bibliography is intended to provide a readers' guide primarily to recently published volumes concerning European feminist thought and practice. With some important exceptions (including several works that have appeared since the manuscript was completed, or are forthcoming in 1999–2000), it is restricted to works published from 1986 through 1997. It is presented in two sections, (1) English-language publications and (2) publications in other European languages.

Readers should be warned, however, that this listing is far from exhaustive; they should also consult the endnotes to the Part introductions and Chapters, which cite a number of valuable articles, particularly those concerning individuals and organizations, as well as other published collections of sources. For older, still valuable resources, see the bibliographical essay following my article "Liberty, Equality, and Justice for Women: The Theory and Practice of Feminism in Nineteenth-Century Europe," in *Becoming Visible: Women in European History*, 2d ed., ed. Renate Bridenthal, Claudia Koonz, & Susan Mosher Stuard (Boston: Houghton-Mifflin, 1987) and the revised notes in "Contextualizing the Theory and Practice of Feminism in Nineteenth-Century Europe (1789–1914), in *Becoming Visible: Women in European History*, 3d ed., ed. Renate Bridenthal, Merry E. Wiesner, & Susan Mosher Stuard (Boston: Houghton-Mifflin, 1998). The essays in *Writing Women's History: International Perspectives*, ed. Karen Offen, Ruth Roach Pierson, & Jane Rendall (London: Macmillan; Bloomington: Indiana University Press, 1991), contain additional references. See also the following journals for pertinent articles: in English, *Feminist Studies, Journal of Women's History, Gender & History*, and *Women's History Review*; in other European languages, *Arenal: Revista de historia de las mujeres; Clio: Histoire, Femmes et Sociétés; Ariadne: Almanach des Archivs der deutschen Frauenbewegung; Métis: Zeitschrift für historische Frauenforschung und feministische Praxis; Feministische Studien; L'Homme; Nuovadwf: Donnawomanfemme; Mémoria* (now discontinued); *Agenda* (published by the Società Italiana delle Storiche); *Jaarboek voor Vrouwengeschiedenis* (Dutch); *Sextant* (Belgian French); *Nora* (Scandinavian works published in English); and the new *European Journal of Women's Studies*.

I hope that one day the massive full bibliography of books and articles that undergirds this book can be separately published.

I. BOOKS, ARTICLES, ARTICLE COLLECTIONS, AND
DOCUMENTARY COLLECTIONS IN ENGLISH

Akkerman, Tjitske, and Siep Stuurman, eds. *Perspectives on Feminist Political Thought in European History, from the Middle Ages to the Present*. London: Routledge, 1998.

Albisetti, James C. *Schooling German Girls and Women: Secondary and Higher Education in the Nineteenth Century*. Princeton: Princeton University Press, 1988.

Allen, Ann Taylor. *Feminism and Motherhood in Germany, 1800–1914*. New Brunswick: Rutgers University Press, 1991.

Anderson, Bonnie S. *Joyous Greetings! The First International Women's Movement, 1860–1860*. New York: Oxford University Press, 2000.

Anderson, Bonnie S., & Judith P. Zinsser. *A History of Their Own: Women in Europe from Prehistory to the Present*. Vol. 2. New York: Harper & Row, 1988.

Anderson, Harriet. *Utopian Feminism: Women's Movements in Fin-de-Siècle Vienna*. New Haven: Yale University Press, 1992.

Andreasen, Tayo, et al. *Moving On: New Perspectives on the Women's Movement*. Acta Jutlandica 67:1, Humanities Series 66. Aarhus: Aarhus University Press, 1991.

Banks, Olive. *Faces of Feminism: A Study of Feminism as a Social Movement*. New York: St. Martin's Press, 1981.

———. *The Politics of British Feminism, 1918–1970*. Aldershot: Edward Elgar, 1993.

Bauer, Carol, & Lawrence Ritt. *Free and Ennobled: Source Readings in the Development of Victorian Feminism*. Oxford: Pergamon Press, 1979.

Bell, Susan Groag, & Karen M. Offen. *Women, the Family, and Freedom: The Debate in Documents, 1750–1950*. 2 vols. Stanford: Stanford University Press, 1983.

Bidelman, Patrick Kay. *Pariahs Stand Up! The Founding of the Liberal Feminist Movement in France, 1858–1889*. Westport: Greenwood Press, 1982.

Black, Naomi. *Social Feminism*. Ithaca: Cornell University Press, 1989.

Bland, Lucy. *Banishing the Beast: English Feminism and Sexual Morality, 1885–1914*. New York: The New Press, 1995.

Bock, Gisela, & Pat Thane, eds. *Maternity and Gender Policies: Women and the Rise of the European Welfare States, 1880s–1950s*. London & New York: Routledge, 1991.

Boetcher Joeres, Ruth-Ellen, & Mary Jo Maynes, eds. *German Women in the Eighteenth and Nineteenth Centuries*. Bloomington: Indiana University Press, 1985.

Bohachevsky-Chomiak, Martha. *Feminists Despite Themselves: Women in Ukrainian Community Life, 1884–1939*. Edmonton: Canadian Institute of Ukrainian Studies, University of Alberta, 1988.

Bolt, Christine. *The Women's Movements in the United States and Britain from the 1790s to the 1920s*. Amherst: University of Massachusetts Press, 1993.

Bosch, Mineke, ed., with Annemarie Kloosterman. *Politics and Friendship: Letters from the International Woman Suffrage Alliance, 1902–1942*. Columbus: Ohio State University Press, 1990.

Boxer, Marilyn J., & Jean H. Quataert, eds. *Socialist Women: European Socialist Feminism in the Nineteenth and Early Twentieth Centuries*. New York: Elsevier, 1978.

Caine, Barbara. *Victorian Feminists*. Oxford: Oxford University Press, 1992.

———. *English Feminism, 1780–1980*. Oxford: Oxford University Press, 1997.

Coulter, Carol. *The Hidden Tradition: Feminism, Women and Nationalism in Ireland*. Cork: Cork University Press, 1993.

Cross, Máire, & Tim Gray. *The Feminism of Flora Tristan*. Oxford: Berg, 1992.

Cullen, Mary. "How Radical Was Irish Feminism between 1860 and 1920?" *Historical Studies*, 15 (1985), 185–201.

Daley, Caroline, & Melanie Nolan, eds. *Suffrage and Beyond: International Feminist Perspectives*. Auckland: Auckland University Press; New York: New York University Press; London: Pluto Press, 1994.

David, Katherine. "Czech Feminists and Nationalism in the Late Habsburg Monarchy: 'The First in Austria,'" *Journal of Women's History*, 3:2 (Fall 1991), 26–45.

Dooley, Dolores. *Equality in Community: Sexual Equality in the Writings of William Thompson and Anna Doyle Wheeler*. Cork: Cork University Press, 1996.

Drewitz, Ingeborg, ed. *The German Women's Movement: The Social Role of Women in the Nineteenth Century and the Emancipation Movement in Germany*. Transl. Patricia Crampton. Bonn: Hohwacht, 1983.

Dyhouse, Carol. *Feminism and the Family in England, 1880–1939*. Oxford: Basil Blackwell, 1989.

Edmondson, Linda. *Feminism in Russia, 1900–1917*. Stanford: Stanford University Press, 1984.

Evans, Richard J. *The Feminist Movement in Germany 1894–1933*. London & Beverly Hills: Sage Publications, 1976.

———. *The Feminists: Women's Emancipation Movements in Europe, America, and Australasia, 1840–1920*. London: Croom Helm, 1977.

———. *Comrades and Sisters: Feminism, Socialism, and Pacifism in Europe, 1870–1945*. New York: St. Martin's Press, 1987.

Fauré, Christine. *Democracy Without Women: Feminism and the Rise of Liberal Individualism in France*. Bloomington: Indiana University Press, 1991.

Forsås-Scott, Helena. *Textual Liberation: European Feminist Writing in the Twentieth Century*. London & New York: Routledge, 1991.

Fout, John C., ed. *German Women in the Nineteenth Century: A Social History.* New York: Holmes & Meier, 1984.

Fraisse, Geneviève. *Reason's Muse: Sexual Difference and the Birth of Democracy.* Transl. Jane Marie Todd. Chicago: University of Chicago Press, 1994.

Fraisse, Genevieve, & Michelle Perrot, eds. *Emerging Feminism from Revolution to World War.* Vol. 4 of *A History of Women in the West*, ed. Georges Duby & Michelle Perrot. Cambridge, Mass.: The Belknap Press of Harvard University Press, 1993.

Frevert, Ute. *Women in German History: From Bourgeois Emancipation to Sexual Liberation.* Oxford: Berg, 1989.

Friedlander, Judith, et al. *Women in Culture and Politics: A Century of Change.* Bloomington: Indiana University Press, 1986.

Gibson, Mary S. *Prostitution and the State in Italy, 1860–1915.* New Brunswick: Rutgers University Press, 1986.

Gillis, John R., Louise A. Tilly, & David Levine, eds. *The European Experience of Declining Fertility, 1850–1970: The Quiet Revolution.* Oxford: Blackwell, 1992.

Goldberger, Avril H., ed. *Woman as Mediatrix: Essays on Nineteenth-Century European Women Writers.* Westport: Greenwood Press, 1987.

Good, David, Margarete Grandner, & Mary Jo Maynes, eds. *Austrian Women in the Nineteenth and Twentieth Centuries.* Providence: Berghahn Books, 1996.

Gordon, Felicia. *The Integral Feminist: Madeleine Pelletier, 1874–1939.* Minneapolis: University of Minnesota Press, 1990.

Gordon, Felicia, & Máire Cross, eds. *Early French Feminisms, 1830–1940: A Passion for Liberty.* Cheltenham: Edward Elgar, 1996.

Haan, Francisca de. *Gender and the Politics of Office Work: The Netherlands, 1860–1940.* Amsterdam: University of Amsterdam Press, 1998.

Harrison, Brian. *Prudent Revolutionaries: Portraits of British Feminists between the Wars.* Oxford: Clarendon Press, 1987.

Hause, Steven C. *Hubertine Auclert: The French Suffragette.* New Haven: Yale University Press, 1987.

Hause, Steven C., with Anne R. Kenney. *Women's Suffrage and Social Politics in the French Third Republic.* Princeton: Princeton University Press, 1984.

Hellerstein, Erna Olafson, Leslie Parker Hume, & Karen M. Offen, eds. *Victorian Women: A Documentary Account of Women's Lives in Nineteenth-Century England, France, and the United States.* Stanford: Stanford University Press, 1981.

Helsinger, Elizabeth K., Robin Lauterbach Sheets, & William Veeder. *The Woman Question: Society and Literature in Britain and America, 1837–1883.* 3 vols. New York: Garland Press, 1983; Chicago: University of Chicago Press, 1989.

Hollis, Patricia, ed. *Women in Public: The Women's Movement—Docu-*

ments of the Victorian Women's Movement (1850–1900). London: G. Allen & Unwin, 1979.

Holton, Sandra Stanley. *Feminism and Democracy: Women's Suffrage and Reform Politics in Britain, 1900–1918.* Cambridge: Cambridge University Press, 1986.

———. *Suffrage Days: Stories from the Women's Suffrage Movement.* London: Routledge, 1996.

Hume, Leslie Parker. *The National Union of Women's Suffrage Societies, 1897–1914.* New York: Garland Press, 1982.

Hunt, Karen. *Equivocal Feminists: The Social Democratic Federation and the Woman Question 1884–1911.* Cambridge & New York: Cambridge University Press, 1996.

Jackson, Margaret. *The Real Facts of Life: Feminism and the Politics of Sexuality, c. 1850–1940.* London: Taylor & Francis, 1994.

Jeffreys, Sheila. *The Spinster and Her Enemies: Feminism and Sexuality, 1880–1930.* London: Pandora Press, 1985; 2d ed., Melbourne: Spinifex Press, 1997.

———, ed. *The Sexuality Debates.* London: Methuen, 1987.

Kaplan, Marion A. *The Jewish Feminist Movement in Germany: The Campaigns of the Jüdischer Frauenbund, 1904–1938.* Westport: Greenwood Press, 1979.

Käppeli, Anne-Marie. "Feminist Scenes," in Fraisse & Perrot, eds., *Emerging Feminism (q.v.),* pp. 482–514.

Keller, Frances Richardson, ed. *Views of Women's Lives in Western Tradition.* Lewiston: Edwin Mellen Press, 1990.

Kent, Susan Kingsley, *Sex and Suffrage in Britain, 1860–1914.* Princeton: Princeton University Press, 1987.

———. *Making Peace: The Reconstruction of Gender in Interwar Britain.* Princeton: Princeton University Press, 1993.

Koven, Seth, & Sonya Michel, eds. *Mothers of a New World: Maternalist Politics and the Origins of Welfare States.* New York & London: Routledge, 1993.

Lacey, Candida, ed. *Barbara Leigh Smith Bodichon and the Langham Place Group.* London: Methuen, 1987.

LeGates, Marlene. *Making Waves: A History of Feminism in Western Society.* Toronto: Copp Clark/Addison Wesley, 1996.

Lerner, Gerda. *The Creation of Feminist Consciousness: From the Middle Ages to 1870.* New York: Oxford University Press, 1993.

Levine, Philippa. *Victorian Feminism.* London: Hutchinson, 1987.

McFadden, Margaret H. *Golden Cables of Sympathy: The Transatlantic Sources of Nineteenth-Century Feminism.* Lexington: University of Kentucky Press, 1999.

Mackenzie, Midge. *Shoulder to Shoulder: A Documentary.* New York: Random House, 1975, new ed. 1988.

Marcus, Jane, ed. *Suffrage and the Pankhursts.* London: Methuen, 1987.

Mendus, Susan, & Jane Rendall, eds. *Sexuality and Subordination*. London: Routledge, 1989.

Meyer, Alfred G. *The Feminism and Socialism of Lily Braun*. Bloomington: Indiana University Press, 1985.

Meyer, Donald. *Sex and Power: The Rise of Women in America, Russia, Sweden, and Italy*. Middletown: Wesleyan University Press, 1987.

Moses, Claire Goldberg. *French Feminism in the Nineteenth Century*. Albany: SUNY Press, 1984.

Moses, Claire Goldberg, & Leslie Wahl Rabine. *Feminism, Socialism, and French Romanticism*. Bloomington: Indiana University Press, 1993.

Murphy, Cliona. *The Women's Suffrage Movement and Irish Society in the Early Twentieth Century*. Philadelphia: Temple University Press, 1989.

Nash, Mary. *Defying Male Civilization*. Denver: Arden Press, 1995.

Neudorfl, Marie L. "The Development and Activity of the Czech Women's Movement before 1914." Unpublished article, 1997.

Offen, Karen, ed. *Women in European Society and Culture*. Special issue of *History of European Ideas*, 8:4–5 (1987).

Offen, Karen, Ruth Roach Pierson, & Jane Rendall, eds. *Writing Women's History: International Perspectives*. London: Macmillan; Bloomington: Indiana University Press, 1991.

Owens, Rosemary Cullen. *Smashing Times: A History of the Irish Suffrage Movement*. Dublin: Attic Press, 1984.

Paletschek, Sylvia, & Bianka Pietrow-Ennker, eds. *Women's Movements in Europe in the Nineteenth Century: A Comparative Perspective*. Ms. in preparation.

Pietrow-Ennker, Bianka, & Rudolf Jaworski, eds. *Women in Polish Society*. Boulder: East European Monographs (no. 344), 1992.

Prelinger, Catherine M. *Charity, Challenge, and Change: Religious Dimensions of the Mid-Nineteenth Century Women's Movement in Germany*. Westport: Greenwood Press, 1987.

Pugh, Martin. *Women and the Women's Movement in Britain, 1914–1959*. Houndsmill: Macmillan, 1992.

Quataert, Jean H. *Reluctant Feminists in German Social Democracy, 1885–1917*. Princeton: Princeton University Press, 1979.

Rendall, Jane. *The Origins of Modern Feminism: Women in Britain, France, and the United States, 1780–1860*. New York: Schocken Books, 1984.

Rendall, Jane, ed. *Equal or Different: Women's Politics, 1800–1914*. Oxford: Basil Blackwell, 1987.

Reynolds, Siân, ed. *Women, State, and Revolution: Essays on Power and Gender in Europe since 1789*. Amherst: University of Massachusetts Press, 1986.

———. *France Between the Wars: Gender and Politics*. London: Routledge, 1996.

Roberts, Marie Mulvey, & Tamae Mizuta, eds. *Controversies in the History of British Feminism*. 6 vols. London: Routledge/Thoemmes Press, 1995.

Rosen, Andrew. *Rise Up, Women! The Militant Campaign of the Women's Social and Political Union, 1903–1914*. London: Routledge & Kegan Paul, 1974.

Rubenstein, David. *Before the Suffragettes: Women's Emancipation in the 1890s*. Brighton: Wheatsheaf; New York: St. Martin's Press, 1987.

Rupp, Leila J. *Worlds of Women: International Women's Organizations, 1888–1945*. Princeton: Princeton University Press, 1998.

Sarah, Elizabeth, ed. *Reassessments of 'First Wave' Feminism*. Oxford & New York: Pergamon Press, 1982. Originally published as a special issue of *Women's Studies International Forum*, 5:6 (1982).

Scott, Joan Wallach. *Only Paradoxes to Offer: French Feminists and the Rights of Man*. Cambridge, Mass.: Harvard University Press, 1996.

Shanley, Mary Lyndon. *Feminism, Marriage, and the Law in Victorian England, 1850–1895*. Princeton: Princeton University Press, 1989.

Slaughter, Jane, & Robert Kern, eds. *European Women on the Left: Socialism, Feminism, and the Problems Faced by Political Women, 1880 to the Present*. Westport: Greenwood Press, 1981.

Smart, Carol, ed. *Regulating Womanhood*. London: Routledge, 1992.

Smith, Harold L., ed. *British Feminism in the Twentieth Century*. Amherst: University of Massachusetts Press, 1990.

Smith, Paul. *Feminism and the Third Republic: Women's Political and Civil Rights in France, 1918–1945*. Oxford: Clarendon Press, 1996.

Spender, Dale. *Women of Ideas (and What Men Have Done to Them)*. London: Routledge & Kegan Paul, 1982.

———, ed. *Feminist Theorists: Three Centuries of Key Women Thinkers*. New York: Pantheon, 1983.

———, ed. *Time and Tide Wait for No Man*. London: Pandora Press, 1984.

———, ed. *The Education Papers: Women's Quest for Equality in Britain 1850–1912*. London: Methuen, 1987.

Stites, Richard. *The Women's Liberation Movement in Russia: Nihilism, Feminism, and Bolshevism, 1860–1930*. Princeton: Princeton University Press, 1978. New edition, with afterword, 1991.

Stowell, Sheila. *A Stage of Their Own: Feminist Playwrights of the Suffrage Era*. Manchester: Manchester University Press, 1992.

Tax, Meredith. *The Rising of the Women: Feminist Solidarity and Class Conflict, 1880–1917*. New York & London: Monthly Review Press, 1980.

Taylor, Barbara. *Eve and the New Jerusalem: Socialism and Feminism in the Nineteenth Century*. New York: Pantheon, 1983. [Rev. ed., Cambridge, Mass.: Harvard University Press, 1993.]

Thébaud, Françoise, ed. *Toward a Cultural Identity in the Twentieth Century*. Vol. 5 of *A History of Women in the West*, ed. Georges Duby & Michelle Perrot. Cambridge, Mass.: The Belknap Press of Harvard University Press, 1994.

Vicinus, Martha. *Independent Women: Work and Community for Single Women, 1850–1920*. Chicago: University of Chicago Press, 1985.

Waelti-Walters, Jennifer. *Feminist Novelists of the Belle Epoque*. Bloomington: Indiana University Press, 1990.

Waelti-Walters, Jennifer, & Steven C. Hause, eds. *Feminisms of the Belle Epoque*. Lincoln: University of Nebraska Press, 1994.

Walkowitz, Judith R. *Prostitution and Victorian Society: Women, Class, and the State*. Cambridge & New York: Cambridge University Press, 1980.

Wikander, Ulla, Alice Kessler-Harris, & Jane Lewis, eds. *Protecting Women: Labor Legislation in Europe, the United States, and Australia, 1880–1920*. Urbana: University of Illinois Press, 1995.

Yeo, Eileen Janes, ed. *Mary Wollstonecraft and 200 Years of Feminisms*. London & New York: Rivers Oram Press, 1997.

Zucker, Stanley. *Kathinka Zitz-Halein and Female Civil Activism in Mid-Nineteenth-Century Germany*. Carbondale: Southern Illinois University Press, 1991.

2. BOOKS, ARTICLE COLLECTIONS, AND DOCUMENTARY COLLECTIONS IN OTHER EUROPEAN LANGUAGES

Aguado, Ana Maria, et al., eds. *Textos para la historia de las mujeres en España*. Madrid: Cátedra, 1994.

Åkerman, Brita, ed. *Vi Kan, Vi Behovs: Kvinnorna Går Sammen i egna förengar* [We Can, We Are Needed: Women Enter Their Own Associations]. Stockholm: Akademiklitteratur, 1983.

Albistur, Maïté, & Daniel Armogathe, eds. *Le Grief des femmes: Anthologie de textes féministes*. 2 vols. Paris: Éditions Hier et Demain, 1978.

Avdela, Efi, & Angelica Psarra, eds. *Ho Pheminismos sten Hellada tou mesopolemou: Mia anthologia* [Feminism in Interwar Greece: An Anthology]. Athens: Gnosi Publications, 1985.

Bard, Christine. *Les Filles de Marianne: Histoire des féminismes, 1914–1940*. Paris: Fayard, 1995.

Bonacchi, Gabriella, & Angela Groppi, eds. *Il Dilemma della cittadinanza: Diritti e doveri delle donne*. Rome & Bari: Laterza, 1993.

Borkus, Marja, et al. *Vrouwenstemmen: 100 jaar vrouwenbelangen, 75 jaar vrouwenkiesrecht*. Zutphen: Walburg Pers, 1994.

Bosch, Mineke. *Het Geslacht van de Wetenschap: Vrouwen en hoter odernwijs in Nederland 1878–1948*. Amsterdam: SUA, 1994.

Braun, Marianne. *De prijs van de liefte: De eerste feministische golf*. Amsterdam: Het Spinhuis, 1992.

Brinkler-Gabler, Gisela, ed. *Frauenarbeit und Beruf*. Frankfurt-am-Main: Fischer Verlag, 1979.

———. *Frauen gegen den Krieg*. Frankfurt-am-Main: Fischer Verlag, 1980.

Bussemer, Herrad-Ulrike. *Frauenemanzipation und Bildungsbürgertum: Sozialgeschichte der Frauenbewegung in der Reichsgründungszeit*. Weinheim & Basel: Beltz Verlag, 1985.

Buttafuoco, Annarita. *Cronache femminile: Temi e momenti della stampa emancipazionista in Italia dall'unità al fascismo*. Siena: Università degli studi di Siena, 1988.

———. *Questioni di cittadinanza: Donne e diritti sociali nell'Italia liberale*. Siena: Protagon Editori Toscani, 1997.

Buttafuoco, Annarita, Rosanna De Longis, & Maria Pia Bigaran. *La Piccola Fronda politica e cultura nella stampa emancipazionista (1861–1924)*. Special issue of *Nuovadwf: Donnawomanfemme*, no. 21 (1982).

Capel Martínez, Rosa. *El Sufragio femenino en la Segunda República*. Madrid: Comunidad de Madrid, 1992.

Carlsson, Christina. *Kvinnosyn och Kvinnopolitik: En studien av svensk socialdemokrati 1880–1910* [Perceptions of Women and Women's Politics: A Study of Swedish Social Democracy, 1880–1910]. Lund: Lund University Press, 1986.

Clemens, Bärbel. *Menschenrechte haben kein Geschlecht? Zum Politikverständnis der bürgerlichen Frauenbewegung*. Pfaffenweiler: Centarus, 1988.

Cohen, Yolande, & Françoise Thébaud, eds. *Féminismes et identités nationales: Les Processus d'intégration des femmes au politique* Lyon: Centre Jacques Cartier, 1998.

Corbin, Alain, Jacqueline Lalouette, & Michèle Riot-Sarcey, eds. *Les Femmes dans la cité*. Grâne: Créaphis, 1997.

Courtois, Luc, Jean Pirotte, & Françoise Rosart, eds. *Femmes et pouvoirs: Flux et reflux de l'émancipation féminine depuis un siècle*. Louvain-la-Neuve: Collège Érasme; Brussels: Éditions Nauwelaerts, 1992.

Cova, Anne. *Maternité et droits des femmes en France (XIXe–XXe siècles)*. Paris: Anthropos, 1997.

De Giorgio, Michela. *Le italiane dall'unità a oggi: modelli culturali e comportamenti sociali*. Rome: Laterza, 1992.

De Weerdt, Denise. *En de vrouwen? Vrouw, Vrouwenbeweging en feminisme in Belgie (1830–1960)*. Ghent: Masereelfonds, 1980.

Esteves, João Gomes. *A Liga Republicana das Mulheres Portuguesas: Uma organização política e feminista (1909–1919)*. Lisbon: Organizaçoes Não Governamentais do Conselho Consultivo da Comissão para a Igualdade e para as Direitos das Mulheres, 1991.

Fagoaga, Concha. *La Vox y el voto de las mujeres: El sufragismo en España, 1877–1931*. Barcelona: Icaria, 1985.

Fauré, Christine, ed. *Encyclopédie politique et historique des femmes*. Paris: Presses Universitaires de France, 1997.

Folguera, Pilar, ed. *El Feminismo en España: Dos siglos de historia*. Madrid: Editorial Pablo Iglesias, 1988.

Fraisse, Geneviève. *La Raison des femmes: Essai*. Paris: Plon, 1993.

Fraisse, Geneviève, ed. *Opinions de femmes: De la veille au lendemain de la Révolution française*. Paris: côté-femmes, 1989.

Frederiksen, Elke. *Die Frauenfrage in Deutschland, 1865–1915*. Stuttgart: Reclam, 1981.

Fritschy, Wantje, ed. *Fragmenten vrouwengeschiedenis.* 2 vols. The Hague: M. Nijhoff, 1980.

Garrido Gonzáles, Elisa, ed. *Historia de las mujeres en España.* Madrid: Editorial Síntesis, 1997.

Geiger, Ruth-Esther, & Sigrid Weigel, eds. *Sind das noch Damen? Vom gelehrten Frauenzimmer-Journal zum feministischen Journalismus.* Munich: Frauenbuchverlag, 1981.

Gerhard, Ute. *Verhältnisse und Verhinderungen: Frauenarbeit, Familie und Rechte der Frauen im 19. Jahrhundert.* Frankfurt-am-Main: Suhrkamp, 1978.

Gerhard, Ute, with Ulla Wischermann. *Unerhört: Die Geschichte der deutschen Frauenbewegung.* Reinbek bei Hamburg: Rowohlt, 1990.

Gerhard, Ute, ed. *Frauen in der Geschichte des Rechts: Von der frühen Neuzeit bis zur Gegenwart.* Munich: C. H. Beck, 1997.

Greven-Aschoff, Barbara. *Die bürgerliche Frauenbewegung in Deutschland, 1894–1933.* Göttingen: Vandenhoeck & Ruprecht, 1981.

Gubin, Eliane, ed. *Cent ans du féminisme [en Belgique].* Special issue of *Sextant: Revue du Groupe interdisciplinaire d'Études sur les femmes [Belgium]*, no. 1 (Winter 1993).

Hardmeier, Sibylle. *Frühe Frauenstimmrechtsbewegung in der Schweiz (1890–1930): Argumente, Strategien, Netzwerk und Gegenbewegung.* Zurich: Chronos, 1997.

Hervé, Florence, ed. *Geschichte der deutschen Frauenbewegung.* Rev. ed. Cologne: PapyRossa Verlag, 1995.

Hummel-Haasis, Gerlinde, ed. *Schwestern, zerreisst eure Ketten: Zeugnisse zur Geschichte der Frauen in der Revolution von 1848–49.* Munich: Deutscher Taschenbuch Verlag, 1982.

Jansz, Ulla. *Denken over sekse in de eerste feministische golf.* Amsterdam: Van Gennup, 1990.

Joris, Elisabeth, & Heidi Witzig, *Frauengeschichte(n).* Zurich: Limmat, 1986; 3d ed., 1991.

Käppeli, Anne-Marie. *Sublime Croisade: Éthique et politique du féminisme protestant, 1875–1928.* Carouge-Geneva: Éditions Zoé, 1990.

Kandel, Liliane, ed. *Féminismes et nazisme: En hommage à Rita Thalmann.* Paris: CEDREF, University of Paris VII, 1997.

Klejman, Laurence, & Florence Rochefort, *L'Égalité en marche: Le Féminisme sous la Troisième République.* Paris: des femmes & Presses de la Fondation nationale des sciences politiques, 1989.

Manns, Ulla. *Kvinnofrågan 1880–1921: En artikelbibliografi* (with author's introduction). Lund: Arkiv, 1991.

Mendes da Costa, Yolande, & Anne Morelli, eds. *Femmes, libertés, laïcité.* Brussels: Éditions de l'Université de Bruxelles, 1989.

Mesmer, Beatrix. *Ausgeklammert, eingeklammert: Frauen und Frauenorganisationen in der Schweiz des 19. Jahrhunderts.* Basel & Frankfurt-am-Main: Helbing & Lichtenhahn, 1988.

Möhrmann, Renate. *Frauenemanzipation im deutschen Vormärz: Texte und Dokumente*. Stuttgart: Reclam, 1978.

Moksnes, Aslaug. *Likestilling eller Saerstilling? Norsk Kvinnesaksforening 1884–1913*. Oslo: Gyldendal Norsk Forlag, 1984.

Neudorfl, Marie L. České ženy v. 19-stoletti. Úsili a sny, úspěchy i zklameni na cesté k emancipaci [Czech women in the nineteenth century: stirrings and dreams, victories and disappointments on the way to emancipation] (Prague, forthcoming)

Outshoorn, Joyce. *Vrouwenemancipatie en socialisme, een onderzoek naar de houding der SDAP t.o.v. het "vrouwenvraggstuk," 1894–1919*. Nijmegen: SUN, 1973.

Paletschek, Sylvia. *Frauen und Dissens: Frauen im Deutschkatholizismus und in den freien Gemeinden 1841–1852*. Göttingen: Vandenhoeck & Ruprecht, 1990.

Pietrow-Ennker, Bianka. "Russlands 'Neue Menschen': Die Frauenemanzipationsbewegung von den Anfängen um 19. Jahrhundert bis zur Oktoberrevolution." Habilitationsschrift, University of Tübingen, 1994.

Reys, Jeske, et al., eds. *De eerste feministische golf (Zesde jaarboek voor vrouwengeschiedenis)*. Nijmegen: SUN, 1985.

Riot-Sarcey, Michèle. *La Démocratie à l'épreuve des femmes: Trois figures critiques du pouvoir, 1830–1848*. Paris: Albin Michel, 1994.

Rossi-Doria, Anna, ed. *Il primo femminismo (1791–1834)*. Milan: Edizioni Unicopli, 1993.

Sachsse, Christoph. *Mütterlichkeit als Beruf: Sozialarbeit, Sozialreform und Frauenbewegung, 1871–1929*. Frankfurt-am-Main: Suhrkamp, 1986.

Scanlon, Geraldine M. *La Polémica feminista en la España contemporánea, 1868–1974*. 2d ed., Madrid: Ediciones AKAL, 1986.

Schröder, Hannelore, ed. *Die Frau ist frei geboren: Texte zur Frauenemanzipation*. 2 vols. Munich: C. H. Beck, 1979–81.

Sevenhuisjen, Selma L. *De orde van het vaderschap: Politieke debatten over ongehuwd moederschap, afstamming en huwelijk in Nederland, 1870–1900*. Amsterdam: Stichting Beheer IISG, 1987.

Studer, Brigitte, Regina Wecker, & Béatrice Ziegler, eds. *Frauen und Staat/Les Femmes et l'État*. Special issue of *Itinera*, no. 20 (1998).

Taricone, Fiorenza. *L'associazionismo femminile in Italia dall'unità al fascismo*. Milan: Edizioni Unicopli, 1996.

Varikas, Eleni. "La Révolte des dames: Génèse d'une conscience féministe dans la Grèce du XIXe siècle (1833–1908)." Doctorat du Troisième cycle, University of Paris VII, 1986.

Veauvy, Christiane, & Laura Pisano. *Paroles oubliées: Les Femmes et la construction de l'État-nation en France et en Italie, 1789–1860*. Paris: Armand Colin, 1997.

Viennot, Éliane, ed. *La Démocratie à la française, ou les femmes indésirables, 1793–1993*. Paris: CEDREF, University of Paris VII, 1996.

Volet-Jeanneret. *La Femme bourgeoise à Prague 1860–1895: De la philanthropie à l'émancipation*. Geneva: Éditions Slatkine, 1988.

Wischermann, Ulla. *Frauenfrage und Presse: Frauenarbeit und Frauen-bewegung in der illustrierten Presse der 19. Jahrhunderts*. Munich: Saur, 1983.

Zimmermann, Susan. "Wie die Feministennen wurden: Wege in die Frau-enbewegung im Zentraleuropa der Jahrhundertwende," *L'Homme*, 8:2 *(1997)*, 272–306.

————. "Frauenbestrebungen und Frauenbewegung in Ungarn: Zur Organi-sationsgeschichte der Jahre 1848 bis 1918." In Beate Nagy et al., *Szerep és alkotás: Nok a magyar tarsadalomban és muveszetben*. Szeged, 1997.

————. *Die Bessere Hälfte? Frauenbewegung und Frauenbestrebungen im Ungarn der Habsburgermonarchie 1848 bis 1918*. Budapest: Napvilág Kiadó; Vienna: Promedia, 1999.

Index

In this index an "f" after a number indicates a separate reference on the next page, and an "ff" indicates separate references on the next two pages. A continuous discussion over two or more pages is indicated by a span of page numbers, e.g., "57–59." *Passim* is used for a cluster of references in close but not consecutive sequence.